FUNDAMENTALS OF
Social Psychology

This textbook brings social psychology up to date, including material on social networking, gaming and other aspects of modern living, as well as covering established theories, debates and research. The book explores a number of fascinating topics, including:

- Both traditional and contemporary theories of social influence.
- How our personal psychology is shaped by our interactions with other people.
- How social psychological insights have been applied in various aspects of modern life.

Intended as a core social psychology text, and including features such as boxed talking-points, real-world examples and case studies, and self-test questions, the book and associated website will cover all the essential topics of an undergraduate course in social psychology in a concise, fresh and up-to-date way.

A comprehensive and contemporary undergraduate introduction to social psychology, it draws together and integrates insights from different areas of research and schools of thought, and features uniquely strong coverage of the online world and our cyberselves.

Written particularly for degree students of psychology, it will be useful to anyone looking for a comprehensive and readable account of social psychological research and theories.

Nicky Hayes is a well-known social psychologist and author with an academic background in psychological research, teaching and assessment, and extensive experience of teaching and writing about psychology. She was awarded the British Psychological Society's Award for Distinguished Contributions to the Teaching of Psychology, and is a Fellow of the British Psychological Society and an Honorary Life Member of the Association for the Teaching of Psychology.

FUNDAMENTALS OF
Social
Psychology

Nicky Hayes

Routledge
Taylor & Francis Group

LONDON AND NEW YORK

First published 2018
by Routledge
2 Park Square, Milton Park, Abingdon, Oxon OX14 4RN

and by Routledge
711 Third Avenue, New York, NY 10017

Routledge is an imprint of the Taylor & Francis Group, an informa business

British Library Cataloguing in Publication Data
A catalogue record for this book is available from the British Library

Library of Congress Cataloging in Publication Data
Names: Hayes, Nicky, author.
Title: Fundamentals of social psychology / Nicky Hayes.
Description: New York : Routledge, 2017.
Identifiers: LCCN 2017018031| ISBN 9781848721876 (hbk) | ISBN 9781848721883 (pbk) |
    ISBN 9781315157863 (ebk) | ISBN 9781351654876 (Adobe reader) | ISBN 9781351654869
    (epub) | ISBN 9781351654852 (mobipocket)
Subjects: LCSH: Social psychology--Textbooks.
Classification: LCC HM1033 .H39 2017 | DDC 302--dc23
LC record available at https://lccn.loc.gov/2017018031

ISBN: 978-1-84872-187-6 (hbk)
ISBN: 978-1-84872-188-3 (pbk)
ISBN: 978-1-315-15786-3 (ebk)

Typeset in Sabon and Vectora LT by
Servis Filmsetting Ltd, Stockport, Cheshire

Printed and bound in Great Britain by
Bell and Bain Ltd, Glasgow

Visit the companion website: www.routledge.com/cw/hayes

This book is dedicated to my good friend
Taz Mirza

Contents

Figures

Tables

Boxes

Talking points

Introduction

A human being is a social animal

It has become a bit of a cliché to say that humans are social animals, but that doesn't stop it from being true. Being social shapes us in ways that we neither suspect nor expect: it even colours how we understand our own selves. In this book, we will be exploring just what it means to be social, and how our personal psychology has been not just influenced, but even shaped by our interactions with other people.

TWO SOCIAL CHANGES

Estimates vary as to how long human beings have actually existed – anywhere from 250,000 to 4 million years. But even with the most conservative estimate, it is clear that throughout most of our history, human experience took place within what we would today see as smallish social groups. The usual estimate of the typical size of human groups in "normal" times – that is, not times of hardship, famine or conflict – seems to have been about 250 or so individuals, and this has also been found to be roughly the number of individuals with whom we can interact comfortably in depth – people that we can "know personally", to put it more simply.

Historically, human social experience appears to have been marked by two major changes in social organisation. It is unlikely that these changes were consistent enough over time or wide ranging enough across social groups to have produced actual genetic change, particularly since some groups or tribes did not actively participate in those changes yet still remain unquestionably human. But the human being, a primarily social animal with a massive capacity for learning, adapts to the society it finds itself in and adjusts to it. Those adjustments add to the range of our social psychology, complementing our evolutionary heritage and adding new dimensions of social awareness and interaction.

These two social changes brought about profound differences, both to everyday society and to our social psychological development. The first was the change from hunter–gatherer societies to settled agricultural societies – a change which is sometimes identified as having originated around the Nile Delta some 50,000 years ago (although that may be a Euro–centric view, not taking account of social development in China and other parts of the world). However, the change from foraging for plants, roots and berries and following wild game

as it migrated to different feeding grounds, to growing and rearing one's own food was enormous. It generated many new social phenomena, ranging from social stratification, wars and other intergroup conflicts as a result of "ownership" of or competition for land and resources, to the production of food surpluses allowing scope for the development of specialised activities or professions.

The second change was the emergence of large civilisations, bringing smaller communities together into wide-ranging groups. These were generally linked by trade and funded through taxes of one sort or another. They imposed another level of social awareness, generating a common ground which meant that people from one small community were aware that they had something in common with others in their region, and they also provided some means of communicating with people more than one day's travel away. It is thought that these large civilisations began to emerge roughly 7000 years ago, probably as a result of the increased growth of trade which archaeologists have detected around that time.

That was a development which produced many changes in everyday social living. It resulted in an increased awareness of social diversity, a perception of the need for common languages, and some of the very first recordings of language through writing or symbols. These changes probably began in response to the demands of trade, but they also opened the door to the sharing of stories, myths and experiences between different communities. This period also, and not coincidentally, saw the emergence of the first major world religions, seen by some as widely held social representations acting as socio–cognitive "glue" to hold together the diverse groups contained within the larger society.

HUMAN ADAPTATION

Each of these changes left their mark on human social psychology, and humans being the adaptive animals that we are, we were able to adjust to them. So even though our deepest tendencies might be geared towards face-to-face interaction with known others, by the time we enter later childhood we have acquired most of the social skills and knowledge which we need to deal effectively with the broader aspects of life. The primitive arousal response to the presence of a stranger, for example, has become muted to a mild interest, and in some contexts almost suppressed entirely. Our non-verbal communication remains much the same, but our communication has become augmented by a plethora of written language and other symbols. Our tendency to see the world in terms of "us" and "them" has extended to encompass many different kinds of "us" and a much wider awareness of "them". And our social beliefs have become much more sophisticated, applying in some contexts and not in others.

The human societies that we know today tend to take the experiences and requirements of complex societies for granted. But it is important to remember that our genetic inheritance equips us to deal primarily with a group of 250 or so personally known individuals – that is, to deal best with face-to-face interpersonal and social interaction. Although we have adapted to deal with people in much larger numbers, many of our inherent and inherited social tendencies work on the basis that the people we are dealing with are well known, and often related – such as our preference to keep the peace and be conciliatory rather than to confront others or to be hostile. We'll be looking at that in more depth later in this book.

A THIRD SOCIAL CHANGE

It is early days yet, but it can convincingly be argued that we are facing another monumental change in how we interact with one another through the various manifestations of the internet. In the same way that the rise of large civilisations created an awareness of, and the potential for interaction with, people who were far outside the immediate social group, so the opportunities provided by the internet extend the range of possible human contact and interaction right across the globe, and even, as we have seen from astronauts on the International Space Station, into space. As human beings, we may spend our early years nested in the social group of family and friends, and our early school years finding out about our wider culture; but as we participate in the internet we become part of a global community offering a diversity of experience and an immediacy of contact which couldn't have been imagined a couple of generations ago.

It remains to be seen just how much growing up in this extended social world will affect human social psychology in the long run; but we are already becoming aware of some fundamental changes. For example, a modern young person growing up with social networking is rarely alone: friends are always just a click away, and conversations can happen at any time. When the TV star Joey Essex visited Patagonia, facing intense cold and hardships for the first time, he described the most significant aspect of his experience to be not the physical privation, but having been out of internet contact for over a week. He said he had never been out of Wi-Fi contact for so long, and when he was finally reconnected, his first comment was: "This is living; this is reality!" (*Educating Joey Essex*, ITV2, May 2015).

This constant sense of being connected with others is very different from the isolation experienced by 19th- and 20th-century children, whose contact with their peers was mainly direct, through school, neighbours or playmates. The experience itself may not be new, though, in terms of a broader sweep of human history. It has close parallels with an older form of social experience, still apparent in a few cultures such as Native Australian or traditional South American lifestyles. In these cultures, people grew up in close village networks and extended families, and were rarely alone. It could be argued that this aspect of internet living is actually more congruent with our evolutionary history and our fundamental social needs than the artificial isolation produced by the nuclear family.

Other aspects of the internet may have different effects, and we are unlikely to become aware of its full implications until the generations have turned full cycle. Already, the idea of growing up in a household with limited TV channels, one telephone, and with letters as a major form of social interaction seems unreal to younger people; soon it will be a history which seems as distant as the Victorians. In the meantime, though, we are able to identify a number of ways in which the internet has affected social psychology, and how our knowledge of basic social psychological processes has relevance in the digital age. We will be exploring these throughout this book, as we look at the fundamental mechanisms of human social psychology.

Contents

Chapter 1

To be human is to be social

Social psychology is a broad and complex area of study, but it is all about how we interact with other people, and how they affect us. So we will begin our study of human social psychology by looking at what it is to be social: how other people are important to us from the very beginning of our lives, and the many different ways in which we affiliate with other people as we grow older.

SOCIAL FROM BIRTH

As human beings, we spend our lives in social environments. Being social begins at a very early age – in fact, even from before birth. New-born infants respond differently to voices that they have heard before birth. Above all, they respond to their mother's voice, but while in the womb they also hear other sounds, and it has been shown that they also respond differently to familiar music and familiar voices than they do to ones they haven't encountered before. They also learn to respond to the cadences of their own languages, preparing them for life in their own cultures.

The new-born infant also reacts strongly to visual images suggestive of people. As early as the 1950s, Ahrens (1954) found that at just a few days old, infants will look more at oval shapes with dots suggesting eyes, and this interest

in face-like stimuli becomes more sophisticated as the infant's visual acumen develops. And they don't just look – they smile, or at least try to. It does take time for babies to learn to control their muscles, but the evidence shows that they really do react in this way. Their response is stronger when it is a real person rather than a picture, and strongest of all when it is someone familiar.

Interacting with others

We are hard-wired, then, to react to other people. And this has a powerful survival value. For a baby's caregiver, being smiled at is a charming and rewarding experience (that reaction is hard-wired into us as well). Human babies need a lot of looking after, so if interacting with the baby is rewarding for the caregiver, the baby is more likely to get the attention and care that it needs.

One of the first applications of these research findings was to help mothers of blind babies. Sighted mothers often find it difficult to understand blind infants because instead of turning towards them when they hear their voices, as sighted babies would, they turn their heads away. Turning your face away is usually a sign of rejection, so these mothers often felt that they were not connecting with their babies, or even that their babies didn't like them. Once a mother understands that her baby is turning its face away so that it can hear her better, that it is actually a sign of approach rather than rejection, she is much more able to relax with her infant and develop a close bond with it.

This example also shows us how sensitive we are to the kind of signals we now call "body language". Body language is important for all social animals: for example, eye contact is important because it says "I have noticed you", but prolonged eye contact is likely to be taken as an aggressive or hostile message, possibly because it says: "I am noticing you a lot; in fact, my whole attention is focused on you, and perhaps this is because I am going to attack you." The main exception to prolonged eye contact being a hostile message is if it is taken as evidence of an equally powerful emotion, such as being in love. We'll be looking at the whole subject of body language and non-verbal communication in Chapter 3; but when we realise that even tiny infants are able to use and respond to a number of social signals (proximity, quality of touch, tone of voice), we can see just how fundamentally hard-wired we are to be social.

We also form **attachments** with other people from a very early age. That doesn't happen suddenly, although for many years child psychologists thought it did – mainly because animal studies showed that some animals (the ones which were mobile from birth) developed a sudden imprinted bond almost as soon as they were born. What is more important for the human infant, though, is the interaction that it has with other people (Schaffer and Emerson, 1964).

Those interactions begin from day 1 as people talk or play with infants and respond to how those infants react. The attachment builds as the child becomes familiar with the person and their interactions become more sophisticated. Stern (1977) showed how even infants as young as three months would make head and face movements in time with their caregiver's speech – as if they were actually taking part in a conversation, and Jaffe et al (1973) showed how the turn-taking games played between adults and infants share the characteristic timings of the turn-takings in adult conversation. The interaction between the infant and the other people around it forms the foundation for later social skills.

Moreover, human infants don't just attach to their mother or primary caregiver, they can also form multiple attachments – that is, to several people. It

Key Terms

attachments
Very close personal relationships, generally with some degree of dependency.

depends on the nature and quality of the interactions they have. The higher the quality of that interaction, in terms of the transactions and interactions between the infant and the other person, the stronger the attachment that the infant is likely to form with that person, regardless of whether that person is the primary caregiver or not.

Developing social understanding

Those may be the basic mechanisms of social interaction, but we also develop much more sophisticated social understandings quite quickly. Summarising findings from a wide range of observations of toddlers in the home, Dunn (1988) showed how even from 18 months of age, they have a powerful and growing sensitivity to other people, both to the non-verbal signals they give out, and to their emotions and intentions. They will try to comfort others showing emotional distress, may deliberately tease or "wind up" their siblings or caregivers, and even, as Martin and Olson (2013) showed, work out the intentions of others and assess the help they can offer them in terms of how practical it would be (e.g., not cooperating with a request to pass a cup with a hole in the bottom when the experimenter wanted to pour some liquid, but passing a cup with a broken handle instead).

One of the important stages we pass through as young children involves the development of what is known as a **theory of mind**, or TOM (Harris, 1988). This generally develops at around age three and a half. TOM is all about our ability to understand that other people see the world differently from the way we see it ourselves. It's an important milestone in the development of social interaction, and some researchers have identified the failure to develop TOM as one of the symptoms of autism because of the profound way in which it affects how autistic people relate to other people.

In another study, Evans and Lee (2013) showed that even two- and three-year-olds are able to lie. They tested each child individually, asking them not to peek at a toy, then leaving them alone with it, then asking them whether they had peeked. Most of the three-year-olds and about a quarter of the two-year-olds lied, although not particularly well. When they were asked what the toy was, three-quarters of the liars gave themselves away by revealing the answer. By the age of four, however, children have become able to lie and stick to those lies, having developed a theory of mind which predicts what other people are likely to believe.

Talking point 1.1   Is lying natural?

There is considerable debate about the evolutionary advantages of deception. Some biologists have argued that any form of communication automatically leads to the ability to deceive because using deception will inevitably give an organism an evolutionary advantage. Others argue that if deception becomes inevitable and commonplace, then communication itself becomes meaning-less. It is only because most communication is usually truthful that deception can work at all. Deception is an ability which can only be used occasionally, and among social animals, only if social circumstances demand it.

Are we all natural liars? What do you think?

Key Terms

theory of mind (TOM)
The development of the idea that other people have minds of their own, and may hold different beliefs or ideas.

So we are social more or less from birth, and we become more so as we develop through childhood. And being social is how human beings have survived. As individual animals, we don't stack up too well against other species, certainly not enough to justify our role as top predator of the planet. We don't have much in the way of natural weaponry, nor do we have defences such as quills or toxins. By working together, human beings have been able to overcome – or at least avoid – even the most fearsome predators, and have managed to gather enough food to eat and create safe places to live. Being part of a social group, though, allows us to go far beyond basic survival: human beings have produced complex societies and completely transformed the planet (whether for the better or not is quite another story)!

BELONGING

Belonging to social groups, then, is fundamental to us as human beings. But just what do we mean by a social group? The first type of social group that we become aware of is probably the immediate social group represented by our family and its close friends. This is the social group which shapes our earliest social interactions and define acceptable social behaviour, although we generally modify our social learning from that group as we grow older and our social experience widens. Every family has its distinctive patterns of behaviour and its own social mores, so part of growing older and socialising more widely is learning to distinguish between the behaviours or expectations which are unique to that group, and those which are more widely acceptable or expected.

As we grow older, our membership of wider social groups – classes or age cohorts at school, gender categories, possible ethnicity – begins to become integrated into our social identities. Even at a local level, modern societies offer a multiplicity of social groups, ranging from hobby and interest groups to localised street or area communities. The "Who am I?" exercise (see Talking Point 1.2) usually produces more responses defining people in terms of their social group membership than responses which emphasise personality or individual characteristics. This shows how important our social belongings are to how we see ourselves.

> ### Talking point 1.2 The "Who am I?" exercise
>
> Who we say we are depends upon the context of the question that is being asked. It might have a lot of different answers. Try this exercise: complete 20 sentences, each of which begins with the words "I am . . .".
>
> Then look at the kinds of things you have said about yourself. How many are about your personality, how many are about your social roles, and how many are about your emotional reactions? Are there other categories of description that you have included? How does your list compare with a friend's set?

The important aspects of belonging can include indirect groups as well as direct ones. As our awareness of wider society develops, we also adopt membership of what might be called notional groups – groups which are self-defined or informally defined rather than being formally part of general society. Many of the teenage fashion groups – Goths, mods, punks and so on – began in that way, as young people looked for a distinctive social identity which was theirs and not imposed by society. Later on, of course, as these groups became more widely recognised, they joined the range of socially defined lifestyle options. Notional groups may be based on personal interest, appearance, lifestyle choices or aptitudes, but they too contribute to how we see ourselves in relation to others, and what we define as "belonging". They may also (e.g., BMW drivers, caravanners, jobsworths, etc.) define how we categorise other people, and so affect the ways that we interact with them.

Belonging is more important than we realise, and we can see just how important it is when we look at the effects of rejection. DeWall and Bushman (2011) showed how social rejection has negative effects on many different aspects of our selves: it has emotional effects, cognitive effects, behavioural effects and even biological ones, affecting our general sense of well-being and even lowering our resistance to illness. Most television programmes, they pointed out, are about social acceptance and rejection, because it is such a fundamental part of our human experience.

Social support

In 1984, Argyle and Henderson reported a series of investigations into long-term social relationships, and, in particular, friendships. These relationships, they found, produce a number of psychological benefits for the people who are involved. For example, they found that people who had strong and supportive social networks tended to be in better health than those who didn't. Brown and Harris (1978), in their classic study of the social origins of depression, also found that strong social support at home could reduce or ameliorate many of the effects of stressful life events. It seems that having a good support network gives people a buffer against stress.

One of the ways in which having a support network helps may be because it allows people to talk over their problems with someone else, rather than keeping it all "bottled up". However, Wellman (1985) showed that although talking things over is sometimes helpful, sometimes it can make matters worse, having what they called a **negative buffering** effect and sensitising people to additional negative aspects of their situation.

In one study reported by Wellman, research participants were asked to talk to other people for ten minutes about the most depressing thing they had done recently. A control group were asked to think about it for the same period of time. The group who talked to others showed more negative mood change than those who had just been asked to think about it, suggesting that talking in and of itself isn't the most important thing. It is more to do with the quality of advice or support which can be received through talking.

The implication, then, is that much of the positive effect of talking things over depends upon what happens in the conversation itself. Cognitive psychotherapy focuses on this aspect, encouraging people to make positive attributions about their circumstances and helping them to look for ways in which they can reduce the bad effects and maximise their own control over things. This sometimes happens through "talking things over" with friends, as well; and it is those conversations which have positive, stress-reducing effects. It's not just the talking but the interaction between the two people

Key Terms

negative buffering
Over-sensitising someone to a negative experience.

which causes the effect: hearing the friend's point of view helps the person to see things differently. As we've seen, just talking could make things worse if it simply ended up confirming negative viewpoints rather than helping the person to re-evaluate their situation.

That raises the question of whether the talking things over needs to take place in a physical context. The answer seems to be no: one of the very first artificial intelligence programmes was a "counselling" module known as ELIZA. It conducted an on-screen "conversation", using the principles of non-directive therapy and reflecting back to the individual the statements they themselves had made. Although a very simple programme in essence, ELIZA proved enormously popular, with versions of it lasting through the 1990s, and some people insisting that they found it therapeutically useful.

Times have moved on, and so has computing, with the result that online facilities for counselling and therapeutic support are now much more sophisticated. Carlbring and Andersson (2006) explored a number of different internet-based therapeutic approaches, and found that in general they tended to report positive results. The caveat was, of course, that they were mainly effective with those who felt comfortable using online technology. But as a general rule, **online therapy** has been shown to be effective in a number of different contexts.

Counsellors themselves, though, need to be prepared to use online methods. Osborn and Flood (2014) explored this question in the context of online methods of counselling when dealing with issues of substance use. They found that the counsellors were generally positive about the potential. Not surprisingly, though, they expressed a general preference for webcam based methods, which allow face-to-face communication – a preference even expressed by those who rarely used webcams in their day-to-day lives. For those counsellors, the internet was not a replacement for face-to-face talking, but a way of enabling it in distant situations.

Other kinds of relationships, too, provide important sources of social support. Argyle (1990) pointed out that the relationships which we form with people at work may be more significant than we generally assume. According to Argyle, there are a number of characteristics of work friendships which have been shown to be psychologically healthy. These include fooling about

Key Terms

online therapy
Psychotherapy which is conducted or delivered by means of the internet.

and teasing, and cooperation with routine tasks. Unfortunately, there has been relatively little social psychological research into this area, although the long-standing and highly structured nature of working relationships suggests that they may be quite special in many respects.

Pinto et al (2015) conducted a study of online identity development in male internet gamers aged between 15 and 26. These young men, they found, tended to develop and articulate different identities within the games, and they also extrapolated some aspects of those constructed identities into their real lives. Within the gaming process, the researchers identified two different approaches which they used in identity construction: self-extension, which consisted of developing idealised avatars with idealistic qualities; and self-aggregation, which was all about becoming part of groups of players ("guilds", in World of Warcraft) and using these to cooperate and to share virtual possessions. This development of social interaction and recognition of the importance of coop-eration was, the researchers observed, one of the significant aspects of online identity which translated into real-world behaviour.

Tierney and Palmer (2014) explored how collaborative internet use can act both as a support network, and also as continuing professional develop-ment for teachers dealing with dyslexia. They set up a wiki – that is, a shared website which allows a group of people to access, read, edit, reorganise and manage its pages – dealing with various aspects of dyslexia, and found that teachers rated it as helpful and interesting, although not all members of the group participated in it to the same degree. It was noticeable, though, that the aspect of the wiki (which was quite highly structured) which generated most interest and responses was one that dealt with a particular case study, where teachers were really able to bring their own experience to bear on the question. Other features, such as a "true/false" quiz were rated as enjoyable, but not as particularly educational.

So friendship groups, working groups and even virtual groups can be a source of belonging and social support. Belonging to social groups is a fun-damental aspect of our psychology. As we will see throughout this book, it is something which influences many different aspects of our day-to-day interac-tions, and it is ubiquitous in human life. There is a good case for saying it is a significant part of what makes us human. But how does it work, and why is it so important to us?

WHAT IT IS TO BELONG: THE PROCESSES OF SOCIAL IDENTIFICATION

We grow up, as we have seen, nested amongst other people. So an ability which is just as important as interacting socially with one another is the ability to recognise people from our own social group. This too appears to be hard-wired into the human psyche: we naturally see our social worlds in terms of "us" and "them", and it has been shown that we have specific brain areas devoted to the recognition of familiar faces.

But who counts as "us" and who counts as "them" can be variable – even in the least complex of human societies, people grow up with multiple social groups. There are families, age groups such as teenage cohorts or elders, friendship groups, village groups, professional groups such as hunters or child-rearers, and often other groups as well. So we are quite used to "us" being a variable thing, but the process of belonging to social groups is absolutely fundamental to being human.

Belonging, in this context, involves the psychological process known as **social identification**. There have been many different versions of this idea, but the basic processes and their psychological consequences were articulated explicitly by Henri Tajfel back in 1982. Effectively, social identification begins with the human ability to categorise aspects of our experience. Without that cognitive ability, we would simply become overwhelmed by the amount of information we encounter in the course of our day-to-day lives. So it's an essential way of making information manageable.

Categorisation

The social implications of this mechanism lies in the fact that we categorise other people, as well as other aspects of our experience. We all do it: friends, pedestrians, home-owners, politicians, celebrities: our lives are full of categories which express how we organise our social worlds. Some of these categories are idiosyncratic – you might have your own ideas about Volvo drivers, for instance, but that's likely to be personal and based on your own experience rather than being a general category shared by society as a whole.

Some social categories, however, are more widely shared. Social identity theory takes the view that society consists of numerous social categories which relate to one another in terms of their relative power and status – in other words, some groups have more social status or more power than others. Tajfel argued that belonging to a social category is only meaningful if it allows us to distinguish between people who belong to that category and those who do not. That might seem obvious, but it means that social categories really only exist in terms of their contrast with others. And it is this contrast which forms the basis for both social cohesion and social conflict (Tajfel, 1982).

Key Terms

social identification
A theory which emphasises membership of social groups as part of the self-concept, determining some social responses.

Comparison

Not every social category, of course, conflicts with every other one. Many overlap: someone might be both "Swiss" and "Christian", for instance, with no conflict between the two because they relate to different spheres of interaction. But if social categories differ on the same dimension – in other words, if there are direct power or status comparisons to be drawn between them, things become rather different. What happens then, according to Tajfel, is that each group strives to differentiate itself, and to enhance its own status vis-à-vis the others.

Comparison between social groups is a consistent, and probably inevitable psychological phenomenon. And those comparisons can carry serious social messages – for example, about the desirability or otherwise of belonging to your own particular group. Which means that belonging to a social group is not just a factual observation, but has deeper psychological implications.

Self-evaluation

Feeling that we belong to a particular social group isn't just a matter of objective recognition, or of simply satisfying survival needs. A central tenet of social identity theory is that social identification is a fundamental, possibly essential, source of **self-esteem** for the individual (Hogg, 2001). We can see this in the way that we react to insults to our particular group. Bond and Venus (1991) found that people react much more strongly to insults directed at their social group than they do to insults which are directed at them personally. And that wasn't just a matter of defending the group in public: it was equally strong whether they were insulted in private, with members of their own group, or with "outsiders" present.

Social groups don't happen in a vacuum. They occur in the real world, and in the real world, everything is not equal. Groups differ from one another along many dimensions. But two of the most important dimensions in this respect are the dimensions of power and status. Some groups have more access to the resources of society than others. Some groups have more social status than others. Some groups are relatively powerless; others are relatively powerful. If our group doesn't stack up positively in its comparisons with other social groups, we react at an emotional level – we may be ashamed of it, for example, or rebellious, denying that we are really true members of that particular group. Table 1.1 lists the various strategies which people adopt when they find themselves in that type of situation.

Table 1.1 Strategies for esteem

Social mobility: leaving the group for a higher-status one; only possible where the group boundaries are permeable.

Social competition: changing status of the group through direct confrontation in the political, economic or cultural arena.

Social creativity (rationalisation): emphasising the social desirability of group membership.

Social creativity (redefinition): redefining what the group stands for.

Social creativity (re-comparison): emphasising comparison with lower-status groups rather than higher-status ones.

Source: Hayes (1992)

Key Terms

self-esteem
The evaluative dimension of the self-concept, which is to do with how worthwhile and/or confident people feel about themselves.

The purpose of adopting these strategies is essentially to maintain our own self-esteem. We generally adopt ways of thinking which mean that we can avoid threats to our self-esteem – in Chapter 5 we'll be looking at cognitive dissonance, for example, which, like social identification, is another powerful motivator that shapes our social experiences. Each of the strategies in Table 1.1 can be viewed as this type of mechanism: protecting us from having to see ourselves as inferior or degraded by comparison with others.

Alternatively, we may feel proud of belonging to our particular social group, and that too will shape our social behaviour. We may use insignia – uniforms, badges, flags and so on – to communicate our membership of that social group when we are with other people. We may adopt particular forms of language – using technical abbreviations, verbal short-hands or convoluted vocabularies that only the "in-group" will understand. Or we may emphasise positive comparisons between our own group and others in our conversations with other people.

Siddiquee and Kagan (2006) conducted an in-depth case study exploration of the relationship between identity and empowerment in a group of six refugee women, using a combination of direct observation and semi-structured interviews. Becoming a refugee, as you might expect, involves a significant loss of both social and personal identity, and it is often difficult for such people to re-establish their social confidence. The women in the case study were participating in a project which was teaching them internet skills, and the researchers found that these generated significantly positive outcomes, fostering a sense of personal empowerment as well as enhancing identity processes.

 In the normal run of things, group behaviours simply form part of the colour of everyday life. We only really notice them when they are carried to extremes – when someone is constantly boasting about their status, for example, or becoming obsessive about a particular set of symbols and insignia. But even in milder form, they serve to reinforce and maintain our social identifications, and to shape our everyday conversations in those terms. They form the basis of much of the "common ground" of conversations, and form the psychological substrate for social representations, which we will be looking at in Chapter 4.

"We are different but they are all the same"

We have a strong tendency to see members of other groups as more similar to one another than members of our own group. In early versions of social identity theory, it was generally assumed that members of a social group felt they belonged together because the group members were basically similar. But researchers quickly found that we accentuate the similarities between out-group members much more than we do for our own group – we see "them" as being all the same, whereas "we" are individuals, and quite different from one another (Wilder, 1984). Partly, this comes about simply because we have less information about the members of groups that we don't belong to, and a lot more about our own. So we focus on what the "others" have in common, whereas when we are dealing with our own group, we are much more aware of individual differences.

Just how different we judge ourselves to be depends on the size of our group. Simon and Brown (1987) showed that members of smaller groups saw their own people as more similar than "outsiders", whereas people who belonged to large social groups did the opposite. So, for example, someone who belonged to, say, the TV Test Card Appreciation Society, which is relatively small, would be likely to see the other TV test card enthusiasts as quite similar to themselves, whereas someone with a hobby like reading science fiction, which involves millions of people, would see sci-fi fans as much more variable. Simon and Brown also found that people who belonged to smaller groups identified with their groups much more strongly than people belonging to larger ones.

We are also more tolerant of members of our own group than we are of others. Marques and Yzerbyt (1988) showed that people make so many allowances for members of their own group that they will often overrate the performance of in-group members, even when it is quite obvious that they haven't done at all well on things they have been asked to do. But if out-group members act in the same way, they are heavily criticised. Sometimes, too, a group will even tolerate a "black sheep", accepting far more deviance or unusual behaviour from them than they would accept from anyone who wasn't a member. Loyalty to the group is also a factor: Crane and Platow (2010) showed that people who are highly loyal to their group, and identify strongly with it, are much more likely to risk being a "black sheep" and challenge what they feel are misleading assumptions or norms than people who don't have a particularly strong social identification with their group.

It has long been shown that we are more ready to accept opinions or ideas from in-group members. Gallagher et al (2013) demonstrated that this affects us at a very deep level. When they measured physiological stress responses in reaction to a math test that the participants had been told was either challenging or easy, they found that those responses varied according to whether the information about the test had come from an in-group or an out-group member. Physiological stress reactions were higher if an in–group member had told the person that the test was difficult or challenging, but not if the same information came from an out-group member.

Although early research into social identity processes implied that differentiating between social groups would automatically lead to aggression and conflict, later research showed that this is far from being the case. When Tajfel and others allocated people into groups on purely arbitrary criteria, those groups tended to favour themselves and regard others as rivals. But this turned out to result from the way in which the experimental task was framed. When these **minimal group tasks** were reframed in such a way that evenly balanced alternatives were possible, the tendency towards out-group conflict disappeared.

Box 1.1   Minimal group studies

In 1971, Tajfel et al showed how just being a member of a group was enough to produce a bias towards in-group favouritism – no matter how arbitrary that group membership was! One of their studies involved sorting people into two groups just by tossing a coin, or by asking them whether they preferred the painters Kandinsky or Klee. They referred to these as minimal group studies, because the membership of the groups was so superficial: it didn't actually represent real group affiliation of the sort they adopted in their everyday lives.

The participants worked on their own, and were asked to play a game which involved allocating points to other people in the study. The only information they had about them was which group they had been allocated to.

Key Terms

minimal group tasks
Activities or tasks required of groups constructed on the basis of minimal characteristics (e.g., coin-tossing or art preferences).

Tajfel et al found that they would always allocate the points in a way which favoured their own group – even though it was possible to cooperate with other groups and sometimes win the game in that way.

These studies were frequently replicated, and showed very reliable results. Tajfel and others took it as evidence for the profound nature of our tendency towards in-group favouritism. We prefer "us" to "them" in a very basic kind of way, even if "they" are only different because of some obviously random reason.

Slightly more sophisticated studies, though, showed that people generally show far more capacity for intergroup cooperation that people believed at first. Some of this evidence came from real-world studies, and some came from re-casting the minimal group studies to reduce the demand characteristics which seemed to require favouritism. After all, if you're taking part in a study and all you know is that the experimenters have gone to the trouble of forming groups but not told you anything else, it is reasonable to assume that you are expected to act on the basis of the information that you have. When alternatives were made clear, and also when the number of points was unlimited so that there was no competition, the in-group favouritism disappeared.

That hasn't invalidated the minimal group studies completely: it does seem to be clear that where group identity is salient and there is competition for resources, we will favour our own group over others. But it also shows that in-group favouritism isn't inevitable, and that other social factors can override that tendency relatively easily.

So, identifying the mechanisms of social identification is important if we are to understand how our sense of belonging comes about. But belonging is a continual and dynamic process, not a single experience; we are constantly redefining ourselves in light of the different social groups to which we belong. None of us are exempt: even mediaeval anchorites, who shunned human company and went to live in remote places, belonged to (and identified with) their Church and were obedient to their bishops. Other social isolates, from any culture, belong to social groups of one kind or another, whether those groups are centred round religion, political rejection, medical beliefs or just eccentricity. They belong in terms of their social reality, if not in their conscious awareness.

AFFILIATION AND RELATIONSHIPS

Part of our sociability means that we are particularly ready to affiliate with other people. We affiliate with other group members, with work colleagues or with groups of people who we come to regard as friends. Some of our relationships may be relatively superficial, while others have profound significance in our lives. Adams et al (2011) found that the presence of a friend during negative life-events increases feelings of self-worth, and definitely makes people feel better. It works at a physiological level too; having a friend present at such times, the researchers found, directly affects levels of the stress hormone cortisol, so the person's physiological condition is also more resilient.

Forming relationships can be a difficult process for some people, because so much depends on social skills, personal confidence, and the situations in which people find themselves. We will be exploring many of these issues when we look at liking and attraction in Chapter 7. Regardless of these individual differences, though, there has been a significant amount of research into relationships. Studying relationships can be tricky, because they are both nebulous and personal; but Hinde (1987) identified eight dimensions which we can use to begin to describe relationships. These eight dimensions are listed in Table 1.2, but we will look into them in more detail here.

Table 1.2 Dimensions of relationships

Content	The type of activities participants do together.
Diversity	The number and range of different activities that people do together.
Quality	How participants go about their interactions.
Patterning	Distinctive patterns and frequencies in types of interactions.
Reciprocity and complementarity	How far each participant either shares actions (reciprocity); or adopts different roles (complementarity).
Intimacy	How much self-disclosure participants engage in.
Interpersonal perception	How each participant sees and understands the other.
Commitment	Participants' beliefs in their own and partner's commitment, and likely duration of the relationship.

Source: Hinde (1987)

Content is important, because what a mother and infant do together, for example, is quite different from the activities engaged in by the same woman and her husband. If we want to examine different relationships content is an important starting point. Similarly, relationships vary in terms of the range of different things that participants in the relationship do. The relationship which you have with your best friend, for instance, is likely to cover a much wider range of activities than the relationship you have with your course tutor. So diversity matters: some relationships are very restricted and task oriented, while others cover a much wider range of activities.

The quality of a relationship concerns how the people involved go about their relationship, for example, whether a mother is sensitive to her infant's needs, rather than simply attending to the child mechanically; or if a friendship involves a lot of laughing and joking rather than just being together in the same place. That isn't quite the same as patterning, although it is similar, so the frequency and patterning dimension is all about when people do things together and whether there are systematic patterns in what they do. That might include, for instance, how often one person responds to the other's needs, as compared with how often the other would like them to.

Another important dimension in relationships – some would say the most important of all – is **reciprocity** and **complementarity**. These concern whether the relationship involves exchanges such as taking turns at particular roles, or having sets of behaviours which "fit" together. For example, in some relationships one person may like to lead and the other to follow which would be complementarity; in others they may take turns, balance tasks out between

Key Terms

reciprocity
The idea that some relationships work because each member of a couple provides the other with the same qualities.

complementarity
The idea that some relationships work because each member of a couple provides the other with the opposite qualities.

them, or settle on an amicable exchange ("I'll clean out the garage if you'll sort out the spare room"), which would be reciprocity.

Intimacy is all about psychological closeness and **self-disclosure**. We keep some of our relationships superficial, while others involve a considerable amount of sharing of secrets and personal disclosure. Interpersonal perception is another way that relationships can vary. It is all about how the participants in the relationship see one another, and therefore the way that they interpret one another's actions. And the eighth dimension in this particular set is commitment – that is, how strongly each partner feels themselves "contracted" to the relationship, and pledged to the other person.

Talking point 1.3 Appraising relationships

Every relationship is unique and has its own special characteristics. Try using Hinde's dimensions to compare some of your own relationships – for example, comparing the relationship you have with a friend, and your relationship with a family member.

Draw up a chart with a column for each relationship, and a line for each of Hinde's dimensions. Fill in the chart according to how appropriate or strong the dimension is for describing your relationship with that particular person.

Did you find the categories useful?

In your opinion, did they describe the important aspects of your relationships adequately?

Forming relationships

Hinde's dimensions give us a way of comparing the personal relationships we have with other people, ranging from group affiliations to family ties, which allows us to explore the psychological meanings of our affiliation with others. Other psychologists have looked at how relationships are formed and broken, and one of the pioneers in this field was Steve Duck.

Being social, we generally spend a lot of our time with other people. Even when we are alone, our activities may be social in origin in that we do them for, or share their outcomes with, the others in our lives. Our connections with other people run deep, and our relationships with other people are a significant source of social emotions. They begin with our immediate family, extend to the partner or partners whom we take during our lifetimes, and also include many others – usually people in our friendship networks. We also develop less profound but also socially meaningful relationships with many other people – friends, acquaintances and colleagues of one sort or another. Each of these may influence us in some way, and even remote strangers can affect our emotional reactions.

Forming relationships can be a difficult process for some people, while being easy for others. A lot depends on the social skills of the people concerned and the situations in which they find themselves. When we first meet other people, according to Duck (2007), we tend to react to them mostly in terms of the effect that they have on us – in other words, we treat them mainly as stimulus objects (e.g., "She makes me laugh"). But if we get to know them better,

then the relationship changes, and we come to react to them much more as people ("She's a lovely person when you get to know her"). It is this personal attraction, as opposed to the more superficial social attraction of the initial relationship, which Duck identified as the basis of long–term relationships.

Cacioppo et al (2013) conducted a survey of nearly 20,000 individuals who had married between 2005 and 2012. They found that about a third of those people had met their spouses online. And they also found that people who had met their partners online reported higher marital satisfaction, and had lower levels of marital break-up than the couples who had met through more traditional circumstances. The researchers suggested that the use of the internet might be actually changing the dynamics of how relationships develop – possibly by allowing the opportunity for more intimate disclosure in a "safe" context, which means that people get to know one another better before they engage in personal contact.

Various theories about how relationships develop have been put forward by psychologists over the years. The most influential of these are cognitive similarity, social exchange theory and equity theory. The approach known as **cognitive similarity** takes the view that people form relationships – or at least long-term relationships – because they share attitudes and beliefs, or their **personal construct systems** are similar. So we come to like people who think in the same way that we do and are more likely to form lasting friendships with them.

Social exchange theory, on the other hand, sees the development of friendships as if it were an economic transaction, with people looking for or trying to negotiate the "best deal". So relationships such as friendships are weighed up in terms of costs and benefits, with one of the most important "currencies" being social approval. Because we value the esteem of others, we also value people who give us positive reinforcement (Homans, 1974). Our relationships are like a balance sheet, in which we weigh up the advantages we get from the relationship against the costs.

Key Terms

cognitive similarity
Having the same sort of thinking patterns or personal constructs as other people or another person.

personal constructs
Individual ways of making sense of the world, which have been developed on the basis of experience.

social exchange theory
An approach to the understanding of social behaviour that sees social interaction as a "trade", in which the person acts in certain ways in return for some social reward or approval.

Schmitt (2002) carried out a questionnaire survey with 44 dating couples. The questionnaires specifically investigated three perspectives: similarity, complementarity and social exchange. Similarity, Schmitt found, was actually negatively associated with relationship satisfaction – that is, the couples who were least similar actually reported having the most satisfying relationships. Complementarity didn't seem to influence relationship satisfaction, but couples high in complementarity had higher ratings for commitment. Overall, Schmitt found that an exchange perspective seemed to be the most useful in predicting satisfaction in close personal relationships.

The third of these older approaches is known as **equity theory**, which developed from social exchange theory but argued that it isn't about a balance between costs and benefits, but about how "fair" the relationship is perceived to be (Carrell and Dittrich, 1978). For example, someone with very low self-esteem may remain in what looks to outsiders like a very unbalanced relationship because they may perceive what they get back as being "fair" given that they aren't worth as much as the other person. Much of the therapy needed by people emerging from abusive relationships tends to focus on helping them to see that they are not worthless, and are entitled to a positive and helping relationship with someone else.

Not all relationships are as close and personal as others. We might usefully identify a continuum of intimacy in relationships, starting at one end with acquaintances – that is, people we know individually but who are relatively less close to us; through friendships which again might be closer or less close, to personal and intimate relationships which would include family as well as partners.

We need to remember, though that for some people, their relationships with their very closest friends may be more intense, personal and significant than those with other members of their families. Not everyone conforms to the norm, and the most common relationships don't apply to everyone. We vary a great deal in who we count as our "significant others". Recently, psychological interest has tended to focus on more specific aspects of relationships, including the virtual relationships which people are able to develop through the internet.

Internet relationships

When we are first forming a relationship, we tend to use a number of non-verbal signals, particularly eye-contact and smiling, to indicate that we are attracted to someone, rather than saying so directly. This may be because we are trying to keep the message deliberately ambiguous: Kurth (1970) argued that keeping things unclear allows us to avoid risking being rejected, so instead of asking someone "do you like me" and risking the answer "no", we try to signal it by indirect means. Relationships on the internet, however, offer fewer of these indicators, so they tend to happen in slightly different ways.

People have been finding and initiating relationships on the internet for many years now. In a study reported in 2000, Utz found that nearly 77 per cent of multi-users of the internet reported having formed an online relationship which developed into an offline personal one. Opportunities for casual encounters in the real world have decreased with the increasing use of cars and the sophistication of the modern home. In the 1970s, for example, the launderette was cited as the most common place for young couples to meet for the first time: now most rented flats have their own washing machine. But the

Key Terms

equity theory
The idea that social conventions and norms are based around a principle of fair, though not necessarily strictly equal, exchange.

opportunities for getting to know people via internet-based mechanisms have increased dramatically.

The most obvious of these are the social media sites, such as Facebook, Myspace and Twitter. These sites allow people to come across one another based on shared locations, experiences, hobbies and other characteristics, and allow people to develop degrees of intimacy and friendship through internet-based conversations and the sharing of images, experiences or ideas. Others have reported forming relationships through their participation in what are often referred to as **MMORPGs**, or massive multi-player online role-playing games, such as World of Warcraft, Second Life or Minecraft. Still others have used online forums and chatrooms to build up acquaintances through the posting of messages.

Li et al (2016) explored the different patterns of socially-oriented computer use and internet participation in a sample of 253 adolescents. They found three basic patterns – those who were friendship oriented, those who were gaming oriented and those who were most oriented towards the opportunities for creativity offered by their internet participation. The gaming-oriented young people tended to be less socially active than the others, but interestingly, it was the creative participators who tended to have the highest ratings for liking and socialising. They were also generally recognised as being more expert than other members of their peer group.

Other forms of networking using the internet are based directly on everyday life, so that people in similar situations can share knowledge and extend the range of options available to them. Groups such as Mumsnet, for example, don't just provide practical advice and a forum for questions and answers to their members; they also take up issues of general interest, and represent the interests of their members to the wider society. Membership of, and identification with, groups of this type allows people who may be physically quite isolated from others to experience a satisfyingly broad range of social interaction, and to participate in social issues in ways which would have been impossible, or at least very difficult, in previous years.

Box 1.2   Networks on the internet

From the moment of its inception, the internet has generated new social networks. At first, it was networks of "tekkies" playing early computer games, or sharing ideas. Later, it included networks of academics sharing research interests, and artists exploring the possibilities offered by digital representation. And from the moment that it became realistically open to the general public, the networks proliferated to include hobbies, interests, activities, public service groups and just about any other form of social gathering you could name.

In modern times, it would be hard to find any interest which was not represented on the internet by some network or another – even for those who want to withdraw from society and reject other networks (see http://www.wikihow.com/Be-a-Hermit, for example)! The internet offers the opportunity to find like-minded others and to share experiences, even when we feel that we have nothing in common with the people we are surrounded

Key Terms
MMORPG Acronym for massive multiplayer online role-playing game.

with in day-to-day life. People being naturally social, we have embraced the possibilities offered by the internet to come together in this way.

As the internet has become increasingly accepted in everyday living, the nature of networking has also changed. From the activity-focused, semi-serious networking of the early years, internet networking includes trivia, ephemera (sites such as Snapchat, for instance, which share a very temporary image to others on the network, that disappears after it has been seen), jokes, images, silly video clips and many other "lightweight" examples of people's humour. The serious stuff is still there, of course, and immensely useful; but for many people, the internet is a playground rather than a library.

One particularly charming example of this way of using the internet has been the growth of Secret Cake Clubs. Since their inception in 2013, they have become popular worldwide – although they don't seek publicity. In essence, they are networks for people who enjoy baking, and also enjoy eating cake, and who for various reasons would like to share their hobby with others. They have meetings in secret venues, passed on to group members by an anonymous email before the event; everyone who attends brings a cake they have baked, and the members meet and share their cakes. Part of the fun is the secrecy: members don't talk about the club except to one another. But its existence brings a level of humour and lightness to many people's lives – very different from the serious information-laden use of the internet envisaged by its early users, but in many ways even more social!

The nature of friendship

There can be many kinds of friendship, ranging from close, intimate "best friends" to formal, structured professional or networking friendships. As a general rule, identifying someone as a "friend" means quite a close personal relationship in everyday life (although identifying someone as a "friend" on the internet may only mean a slight acquaintance). Personal friendships involve a certain amount of reciprocal obligation, and while close friendships can often survive quite a lot of problems, there are certain expectations which are likely to bring the friendship to an end if they are broken. Argyle and Henderson (1984) identified six "rules" of friendship, which are listed in Table 1.3.

Table 1.3 "Rules" of friendship

1. Stand up for the other person in their absence.
2. Share news of any successes you have with them.
3. Provide emotional support for the other person if they need it.
4. Trust and confide in one another.
5. Volunteer to help the other person if they need it.
6. Strive to make them happy while in your company.

Source: Argyle and Henderson (1984)

We can often develop quite close virtual friendships too: for example, Kowert and Oldmeadow (2015) looked at the relationships developed through shared gaming spaces. These, as they pointed out, are highly social environments, which allow the participants to interact with and learn from one another. While some people have argued that these virtual friendships might interfere with ordinary sociability, others see them as a useful social environment for those who might otherwise avoid face-to-face friendships. Kowert and Oldmeadow's research supported that idea. As they looked at the social gains and losses of continued internet game-playing, they found that they promoted a sense of closeness, belonging and security, particularly for the "insecurely attached", who might otherwise avoid ordinary social relationships.

Relationships vary in the amount of attention and "maintenance" that they need to keep them going. Rose and Serafica, (1986) found, for example, that best friendships tend to be expected to last without the two parties having to put a great deal of effort into their maintenance (maybe because they have already put considerable effort into the earlier stages of the relationship). Close friendships and marriages or other partnerships, on the other hand, need quite a lot more effort, and it also needs to be continuous or at least fairly frequent.

Wright (2004) argued that people use rather different methods of maintaining their relationships on the internet than they do in everyday life. This is partly because the ordinary non-verbal aspects of communication are not present, but also because there is an awareness of the relative anonymity, and perceived safety, of online interactions. This makes people more prepared to risk the degree of self-disclosure that is the basis for more intimate relationships. But it also means that they require ongoing reassurance as to the stability of the relationship. There have been several documented examples of people "spying" on their internet partner's communications with others, and even, in the case of Second Life, employing avatar private detectives. More than one divorce case has arisen as a result of this type of distrust of, or within, virtual relationships.

As our online sophistication develops, so too does the range of possibilities for online social experience; the internet offers wide scope for "belonging". Twitter, Facebook, Myspace and many other sites base themselves on the social group created by their members, which is why they are known as social networking sites. These sites are often structured in such a way as to enhance the individual's sense of belonging and affiliation, regardless of the reality of those people's lives. Other internet groups are explicitly set up to provide social support for their members (Tanis, 2007).

For some people, their internet activities can become a real passion. That isn't necessarily a bad thing. Seguin-Levesque et al (2003) showed that passion for the internet can take different forms: harmonious passion, in which it is a meaningful hobby forming a significant part of daily life but not interfering with the rest, and obsessive passion in which the internet activity becomes all important. Seguin-Levesque demonstrated how the second type of passion was also associated with greater conflict in interpersonal relationships, and lower levels of adjustment in couples. Harmonious passion, on the other hand, connected with greater self-determination, lower levels of conflict and better adjustment in couples. So, having strong passion for internet activities was not in itself damaging to relationships, they concluded, it was the way that the person internalised that passion.

Quinn and Oldmeadow (2012) explored the use of social networking sites among a group of 443 children, using a self-report questionnaire. They found that the older boys who used social networking reported a stronger sense of belonging to their friendship groups, and those who used it most intensely also reported to strongest sense of belonging. As a result, the researchers suggested that social networking was a positive aspect of growing up for modern youngsters. Far from generating the social isolation of the stereotypical "nerd", it actually enhanced social interactions and the development of relationships. Their conclusions have been backed up by other studies: an ongoing longitudinal study conducted in America reported that adults who had grown up with and used social networking demonstrated a healthy balance in their personal and social networks (Miller, 2013).

In another study, Frostling-Henningsson (2009) found that young adults who played World of Warcraft and Counter-Strike at online gaming centres in Stockholm reported the social opportunities provided by the games as one of their main motives for participation. The gamers also said that they felt that online gaming gave them a richer experience than they could get from everyday living, allowing them to develop new skills and encounter new situations. But while some of the gamers were motivated by escapism, most of them reported the opportunities for cooperation and communication as being significant aspects of the experience, and felt that they were more able to develop friendships through this activity than through everyday life.

We can see, then, that although what counts as a relationship can vary a great deal, they do mean a lot to us. Our natural tendency towards sociability means that we are prepared to affiliate with others, whether that is by participating in real-world networks or through the internet. McKenna and Bargh (2000) argued that internet relationships are particularly easy for people to develop, because they are accessible to everyone and don't involve the outlay of additional costs as physical dating does. Also, the fact that internet relationships are anonymous in the early stages provides a degree of perceived safety. Joinson (2001) showed how this can lead to increased levels of self-disclosure: far more than we might reveal in a face-to-face situation.

The anonymity of the internet, however, also means that there is considerable scope for deception and misrepresentation. Online predation, where child abusers and others "groom" unsuspecting young people to reveal personal information leading to their later abuse has become a significant social problem (Mishna et al, 2009). Cyberstalking is another documented phenomenon, where one partner adopts a disguised persona in order to keep track of what their partner is doing online. As with relationships in real life, things can often go wrong, but the internet offers wider scope for retaliation or the expression of severely disturbed behaviour than does everyday living (Finn and Banach, 2000).

Social networks

Networking has always been a crucial part of modern living. As we have seen, in non–technological societies, people tend to live in relatively small communities, typically of about 200 or so individuals. That means that they know pretty well everyone, and strangers are both uncommon and a major source of interest. In the modern world, though, the number of familiar people that we have direct contact with may be very much smaller, but the number of strangers we encounter is huge. But we compensate for that by networking, developing social groups linked together by common interests or activities.

Networking is not unique to the computer age – it has happened ever since human societies became so large that not everyone knew everyone else, and probably even before that. People link together through common interests, and discuss matters which are interesting to them, but have little relevance to those who do not share those interests. Over time, those networks become social groups, of the kind we have just been discussing (Hogg and Abrams, 1988).

Some hobbies and interests are widespread, shared by many people. Following football or rugby, for example, is a popular social pastime, and one where the social identifications which result from that activity become absolutely paramount. Other hobbies may be less popular, but still have their own social groups and networks. It is less common now, but there was a time when every large train station had its huddle of train spotters, usually at the end of platform 5 – separate from the ordinary commuters, but forming a cohesive social group based around a common interest.

Modern living, though, can result in a significant amount of social isolation, at least in terms of direct social contact. In the most extreme cases, people live either alone or in very small groups, travel in cars, which also limits their contact with random strangers, and work alone, sometimes even from home. Unless they actively participate in sport or interest groups, they may have very little direct interaction with other people in the course of an ordinary week. But now we have a range of other forms of interaction. What counts as a social group has become extended in ways which were inconceivable before the widespread acceptance of the internet.

Networking through the internet has become so much a part of everyday life that the ability to communicate through Facebook or Twitter is taken for granted by many organisations, used as marketing research or for other types of feedback or communication. Because of its size, Facebook has frequently been

Key Terms

cyberstalking
Pathological following of individuals through the internet, involving tracking their communications and intervening in their activities, often unpleasantly.

networking
Developing groups of acquaintances or colleagues to achieve personal goals.

a focus for academic research into social networking – for example, Gilbert and Barton (2014) investigated motivation and personality traits involved with Facebook usage, but there are many others. At the time of this writing, social networking sites include Flickr, a site for sharing photographs; LinkedIn, which is a network specifically aimed for professional networking; Instagram, for immediate social impressions and images; Last.fm, which encourages its uses to share and discover music; Foursquare, aimed at bringing together its user's geographical activities; Reddit, a site for sharing interesting items of information; and many more. New sites emerge all the time, and fashions can change rapidly.

Whatever their precise characteristics, though, social networking sites offer the opportunity for people to develop their own friendship networks, and to identify things which they may have in common with other people who are part of that network (Haythornthwaite, 2007). Some social networking sites are broad, offering scope for informal interactions, live chatting, sharing of images and the option of developing quite close interpersonal relationships. Other social networking sites, such as LinkedIn, are more focused, acting as contact vehicles between people with professional interests. Such sites tend to be more formalised in nature and less closely personal.

Wrzus et al (2013) conducted a meta-analysis which brought together 277 studies of how people use social networks at different ages. The studies they examined included those of general networking as well as studies which focused on particular life events such as the transition to parenthood, entry into the world of work or the loss of a spouse. Despite the range of studies, though, they found very consistent findings across the board, showing reliable network changes with age (see Table 1.4). Their conclusion was that changes in networking, whether internet-based or physical, are due primarily to normative age-related life events – as people age, they find different uses for the internet, and it serves different purposes for them.

Table 1.4 How people use social networks

1. Global social networking generally increases until young adulthood and steadily decreases after that.

2. Personal and friendship networks both decrease throughout adulthood.

3. The family network remains stable in size throughout life: from adulthood to old age.

4. Networks with co-workers or neighbours only become important in specific age ranges.

Source: Wrzus et al (2013)

SOCIAL RESPECT

In 1979, the social philosopher and psychologist Rom Harré proposed that human beings have a fundamental need for respect from others, and that this is one of the prime motivations underlying human social behaviour. It begins, he argued, from an early age. Any visitor to a children's playground will have seen how much children like to be noticed – "look at me!" when they are doing things, and primary teachers recognise how important it is to give every child the opportunity to obtain some respect from the others in the class.

From psychology's earliest days, researchers have explored how the presence of other people affects our behaviour. Triplett (1898) showed that children would turn a fishing reel faster if there were other children watching than when they were on their own, and Allport (1920) showed that college students solved multiplication problems faster when working alongside other students. As many athletes have found since, the presence of an audience produces **social facilitation** – it acts as a positive factor to help performance.

Other people, though, experience anxiety when watched – and perform less well. Audiences make a difference, but the nature of that difference can vary. In 1965, Zajonc suggested that it is well-learned habitual tasks which improve with an audience, while those performing tasks which require attention or concentration are more likely to suffer from **audience anxiety**. Zajonc explained this in terms of drive states: that people doing complex tasks were in a high drive state which was easily disturbed, while those doing familiar easy tasks were more relaxed. Baron (1986), however, suggested that the potential distraction provided by an audience meant that people experienced a conflict in how they should divide their attention, and the tension resulting from that conflict meant that they were more likely to make mistakes.

Other researchers argued that it is all about **evaluation anxiety**. When people are watching, we become concerned about how they will evaluate us. This anxiety can interfere with our performance, and if what we are doing is not well learned and rehearsed, or at least very familiar to us, it can interfere with our performance. As Bond (1982) pointed out, we all like to present a favourable image of ourselves to others.

Unconditional respect for persons

Social respect may derive from many different sources. Fortunately, respect based solely on class position or inherited wealth is becoming less widespread as society moves to become more egalitarian. But people also earn respect from others through achievement, prosocial actions (or, in the case of some subcultural groups, anti-social actions) or our personal characteristics such as patience and good humour in adversity. But Lalljee et al (2007) argued that the most fundamental kind of respect is what they described as "unconditional respect for persons" – that is, respect which is due to people simply because they are human beings.

This unconditional respect means that the person is recognised as an autonomous person, and their integrity as a person is acknowledged. This orientation is the basis of most statements of human rights and political constitutions, but Lalljee et al argue that it has been under-recognised in social psychology. They went on to develop a scale to enable researchers to measure individual differences in how much people tend to maintain unconditional social respect towards others. In a further study, Lalljee et al (2009) used this scale to carry out a set of studies which showed how unconditional social respect was closely associated with a tendency for positive action towards other social groups, and a rejection of negative actions, particularly in situations of perceived threat, such as those presented by terrorism or social displacement. Their research implied that unconditional respect should be recognised as an important factor in intergroup relations, and taken into account in developing policies in this area.

Avoiding social disapproval

In most of our adult life we may not (at least overtly) seek to be noticed all the time, as children might; but we do expect to be acknowledged, or at least respected, by the people with whom we interact. For example, Rogelberg et al (2013) showed how a major consequence of people being late for meetings is that the other people attending the meeting feel disrespected. They feel that the late-comer is implying that their own needs, plans and issues are of no concern, and may often become upset or even hostile as a result. Late-coming accompanied by a valid excuse, however, such as snowfall or known transport difficulties, generates no such problems.

Clegg (2012) conducted a study of socially awkward moments. To explore this, Clegg set up deliberately embarrassing situations, with trios of male undergraduates being seated facing one another, with a table carrying a microphone and a plate of five biscuits between them, and knowing that they were being filmed through a two-way mirror. They were given no instruction at all for the first three minutes. Then a stooge came in with a chair and sat down with them for another three minutes before a researcher came into the room, at which point the stooge left. The participants were then asked to begin an ice-breaker activity, and after three minutes of discussion they were asked to introduce each other to the group.

After all this, the participants watched the film of themselves, and were asked to indicate how awkward they were feeling at given moments during the event. The situations which generated most social awkwardness are listed in Table 1.5. But Clegg also found that social awkwardness was reduced at times when people were sharing common interests, helping or supporting one another or using humour. Clegg argued that the source of the awkwardness comes when we feel we are risking our acceptance from others. The unspoken fear of social rejection means that we become more focused on our own behaviour and actions, and try even harder than usual to make sure that we will act in a socially acceptable way.

Table 1.5 Sources of social awkwardness

1. When the person didn't know what they were supposed to do.

2. When someone broke a social norm (e.g., infringing on another's personal space).

3. When things didn't conform to a social standard (e.g., a long silence in a conversation).

4. If a social standard wasn't kept up.

5. If norms around eating were broken (e.g., messy eating).

6. If one person makes negative social judgements about another, either explicitly or implicitly (e.g., by making faces).

7. When people aren't recognised or names are forgotten.

8. When social processes are made explicit (e.g., during ice-breaker tasks).

Source: Clegg, (2012)

Key Terms

sanctions
Social forms of punishment or disapproval.

Our need for social respect also leads us to avoid social disapproval. In another study, Nelissen and Mulder (2013) showed that social disapproval produces more lasting changes in behaviour than physical **sanctions** such as fines. They conducted a study comparing the two types of sanctions, in which participants played a game which offered considerable incentives for cheating behaviour. Members of the groups playing the game responded to cheating either by fines or by social disapproval. Although both types of sanction were effective as ways of encouraging fair play while they were active, when the participants moved on to playing without any sanctions there was noticeably less cheating in the groups which had used social disapproval, while in those in which cheating had been fined, cheating rapidly became re-established. Nelissen and Mulder argued that their findings had implications for social policy, in that simply fining people for socially inappropriate behaviour is not likely to be nearly as effective as communicating social disapproval publicly – "naming and shaming".

Belonging to social groups is part of what makes us human. We are not isolated individuals, with other people just forming an element of the environment in which we live. We are social at the very deepest level, in that belonging to social groups of one sort or another is basic to how we see ourselves and how we feel about ourselves. The three-part process of social identification – categorisation, comparison and self-evaluation – is a fundamental aspect of human psychology, which colours just about all of our social experience. And how we interact with others, and how they act towards us, is an essential aspect of our lives. Both the sense of "belonging" and the quest for social respect are fundamental in our personal motivation, and the source of many of our reactions and responses.

MODERN SOCIAL PSYCHOLOGY

When we look at the various aspects of human sociability described above, we see the outcomes of many different types of social psychological research. Some of it focuses on social behaviour, for example, the studies of infant sociability. Some research focuses on social cognition, the way that we make sense of our social experience, such as the research into how we deal with awkward moments. Some social psychologists are more interested in the way that our social experience is nested in society and our membership of social groups, such as those investigating social identification; and others emphasise understanding the personal meanings of our experience through the qualitative analysis of discourse, such as the research into social support.

Box 1.3   Reductionism and levels of explanation

Any type of research, and especially research in social psychology, has to limit itself to some extent. We can't just study everything – it would be too broad. So we have to define what we are studying, and look for ways to investigate what we think are the most important aspects of it.

This can produce very different approaches. For example: suppose a social psychologist wanted to look at the ways in which other people understand the social aspects of anger – that is, how they realise that someone is angry, so that they can know what to do about it. They might go about it by looking at how we describe anger – comparing, for example, our own use of words such as "furious" or "raging" which describe the state someone is in, with Ifaluk words (Chapter 2) describing anger which indicate what has caused the anger (a sense of injustice, or the narkiness produced by illness, etc.). Another social psychologist might look at how people recognise the non-verbal signals of anger (Chapter 3): flushed face, thinned lips, intense gaze, etc., so that they realise that the person is in an angry state.

But which is right? The answer, of course, is both: we can look at the same problem from lots of different angles, and at lots of different levels. The first example is looking at the topic from the socio-cultural level, showing how language can shape our perceptions. The second is looking at it from the behavioural level, showing how people are sensitive to the small changes in behaviour which signal emotional states.

When we are doing research, we have to choose which level we will use to explore any given topic. But we have to avoid falling into the trap of saying that our particular level of analysis is the only one that matters. Other ways of looking at things give us different insights, and they all contribute to our overall understanding of the topic. Claiming that just one level is the only one that matters is an approach known as reductionism, and it was very popular in the first half of the 20th century, when the modernist movement believed that there would be simple elements or formulae to explain everything, and it was just a matter of finding them.

The implications of this way of thinking are quite serious, since reductionist explanations have often given opportunities to "explain away" issues which are actually reflecting real social problems. One classic example of this is explaining inner-city riots, which typically occur in hot weather, as resulting from the heat. While that may be a factor, using it as if it were the explanation for the behaviour diverts attention away from the perceptions of social injustice which often underlie such riots. There is nothing wrong with recognising contributory factors; it is when we take just one level of analysis as the complete answer that it becomes problematic.

The modern approach, then, recognises that we can adopt many different approaches to investigation, and that different levels of explanation work together, not in opposition. If we are to have any chance of understanding something as complex as the human being, we need to be able to look at things using several different levels of explanation. We will come back to this idea again in Chapter 10.

Modern social psychology draws on all of these approaches. A social psychologist undertaking research will select that approach which most suits their own perspective, and that in turn will direct how they go about studying the topic in which they are interested. Those who believe that the best approach for research is to look objectively at behaviour, without interpreting it, will conduct a very different study to someone who believes that the best approach is to find out what a particular social experience means to the people taking part in it. If they were both concerned with investigating a riot, for instance, the first would be likely to gather information about what happened and which types of people did what, from closed-circuit camera records and other sources such as eyewitnesses, while the second would focus on how the people taking part understood what they were doing, what they felt and why they were doing it. Both types of study would provide us with valuable data to help us to understand the social psychology of the whole event.

The development of social psychology

This range of perspectives didn't come about all at once, though. It arose as a result of different perspectives on science and research, and some quite heated disagreements. To understand it, we need to look back at the origins of social psychology, although psychologists hold different views even about that. Some say, for instance, that social psychology really began with the work of Floyd Allport, in America at the beginning of the 20th century, who worked extensively in the area of social attitudes and prejudice. Others attribute the origins of social psychology to Wilhelm Wundt, now known as one of the founders of the experimental method in psychology, but who was also concerned with the social aspects of experience, and wrote an extensive textbook on social psychology, published in ten volumes between 1900 and 1920. Wundt encouraged a number of his followers to take up social psychology in their research, and was also a significant influence on Emile Durkheim, the "founding father" of sociology.

Wilhelm Wundt.

These two "founding fathers" had a very different focus and generated different types of research. Floyd Allport operated within the American empirical tradition, stimulating the study of attitudes and an "objective" approach to research which emphasised the importance of studying social behaviour in ways which could be subjected to quantitative analysis. His emphasis on objective methods also influenced the development of behaviourist psychology, articulated most strongly by Watson (1913). Wundt, on the other hand, was interested in social meanings, and fostered a European tradition of **hermeneutic** research which looked closely at the way that social experience and the membership of social groups affected the person's social awareness and knowledge. Wundt's pupils included the Gestalt psychologists as well as many of the earliest American psychologists, who emphasised knowledge of the individual's social understanding and experience, as well as the use of the experimental method.

Emigration and international connections meant that many of these ideas were shared in the early years of social psychology. It was the rise of Adolf Hitler in Germany in the first half of the 20th century, however, which led to the relocation of many important intellectuals, including social psychologists, in the US and UK, and resulted in even more mixing of ideas and approaches. After World War II, the behaviourist-oriented social psychology emerging from America was dominant in psychology as a whole, but social psychological research continued in Europe, and in 1970 the *European Journal of Social Psychology* was founded to allow a greater awareness of that work and its findings.

European social psychology differed from much of the American research of the time, mainly in the way that it emphasised how each individual's social experience was embedded in their social group membership and the societal context. The experience of Hitler's rise to power had given the people of Europe first-hand experience of how a major shift in social beliefs could affect

Key Terms

hermeneutic
To do with meanings and interpretations.

the social behaviour and experience of even those who did not share in the beliefs of the dominant group.

This meant that much of the research taking place in European social psychology at the time tended to emphasise the importance of social and group experiences in determining social action. Social psychologists in Europe typically studied phenomena like minority influence and shared social representations, while social psychologists in America tended to investigate topics like interpersonal attraction and attitude. Effectively, American researchers tended to focus on the individual, seeing the group and societal influence as just one out of several factors affecting social behaviour, while European social psychologists saw group and societal influence as an all-encompassing context which could determine the behaviour itself. That's an over-simplification, of course; but the general tendency was towards individualistic approaches in the US as opposed to more group-focused approaches in Europe.

During the 1980s another perspective in social psychology became apparent. Taking their inspiration from the **deconstructionist** approaches of Saussure (1993) and Derrida (1989), supporters of discursive social psychology argued that it was the meanings of social experience which should be the major approach of social psychology, rather than the empirical description or analysis of social behaviour. To this end, they emphasised the study of discourse, and in particular the analysis of what conversations were being used for – their social meanings and functions. Inevitably this involved a move into qualitative analysis and away from quantitative or statistical approaches, which engendered a number of somewhat heated disagreements between those at one extreme who believed that only a quantitative approach could be considered to be truly scientific, and those at the other extreme who argued that social measurement and even empiricism itself was invalid and inappropriate for social psychology. As with most such disagreements, however, the majority of researchers adopted a middle ground, acknowledging the value of discursive and qualitative approaches while recognising that empiricism and measurement are also a fundamental aspect of the discipline.

Ethics in modern psychology

The various perspectives in psychology often draw on "keynote" studies, which illustrate or form the framework for topics in modern psychology, or which stimulated important research in the area. Many of these studies were conducted in the 1960s, or even earlier, and for that reason they are rarely accepted purely at face value nowadays. This is partly because they often worked on fairly simplistic assumptions about human beings, but also, importantly, because they rarely considered the ethical implications of what they were doing. Until the 1970s or so, the dominant zeitgeist was one which held that "science = progress", so scientists felt largely justified in conducting whatever research they believed was necessary to further knowledge. The people who participated in their research were experimental "subjects", and could therefore be subjected to whatever demands the researcher made of them.

It wasn't quite as extreme as that, of course. Most researchers were careful what they did, and deeply concerned about the welfare and well-being of their subjects. But some studies, notably those which relied on prison inmates or "volunteers" whose volunteering enabled them to avoid other consequences (such as those who volunteered for the Minnesota Starvation Study in order

Key Terms

deconstructionist
An approach to social research which involves examining the underlying social assumptions and beliefs of existing theories.

to avoid being conscripted for the war) were more extreme. That Minnesota study, for example, was a year-long project in which people were deliberately starved to lose 25 per cent of their body weight (Keys et al, 1950). Its purpose was to identify appropriate rehabilitation diets for Europeans who had experienced similarly restricted diets during the war years, which was a good aim. But those involved in the study experienced severe emotional distress, depression, social withdrawal, and other psychological and physical consequences including self-mutilation. Although they had volunteered for the project, neither they nor the researchers had foreseen such distressing outcomes.

By and large, studies in social psychology were less extreme. But that didn't mean that they were harmless: some studies certainly had the potential for psychological damage, even when they were conducted carefully. Also, given the prevailing ethos of the time, many social researchers failed to consider that potential at all. Ironically, despite being cited as a classic example of research with ethical concerns, Stanley Milgram, in his 1963 behavioural study of obedience, was not one of those researchers. He took great care to ensure the psychological well-being of his participants, including a long-term follow-up programme to make sure they didn't experience lasting damage. But his study was so dramatic, and its results so counter-intuitive (see Chapter 6) that it attracted attention from the start, and it was a paper discussing the potential harm which might have accrued to his obedience participants which really spearheaded the change of emphasis in social psychology.

That change of emphasis was definitely needed. Zimbardo (2007), looking back on the Stanford Prison Experiment he had reported in 1973, and which we will also be looking at in Chapter 6, described how he and his fellow researchers had become so caught up in the study that they entirely failed to recognise the unacceptability of how their participants were being systematically abused. It was only when it was sharply pointed out by a colleague that they realised what they were doing, and terminated the experiment. Other researchers simply took their rights to manipulate people in the interests of science for granted. A famous study by Felipe and Sommer (1966), for example, involved deliberately

disrupting people working in a library by invading their personal space. At no point did the researchers consider that perhaps the people they were disrupting had the right to work uninterrupted. That may seem a relatively trivial example, but it is symptomatic of the way that much social research was conducted.

Modern social psychology is very different. A project like the Minnesota Starvation Study would not be permitted nowadays, or if it were permitted, would be monitored and stopped at the point where it was apparent that people would be harmed. Modern researchers work within a framework of ethical guidelines and requirements, and any proposal for research with human participants must be approved by an ethical committee. That doesn't mean that researchers are actually prohibited from doing realistic research, but it does mean that any project which might involve harm must involve appropriate precautions, is carefully monitored and will be terminated if harm seems imminent.

We will look into the ethical demands on researchers in more detail in Chapter 10, by which time you will have more information about the different ways that social psychological research has been conducted. Also, throughout this book you will find ethical "flags" in the margins, like the one on this page. These highlight studies or issues which have raised or might raise, ethical concerns. If you check out the "Guidelines for Research with Human Participants" which we have listed in Chapter 10, you will be able to identify for yourself just what those concerns might be. The studies which have flags by them may or may not have been unethical in themselves. It might be that they just raise ethical concerns – either because of their topic, or because of the implications of their findings. So when you see an ethical flag, take a little time to work out what type of ethical concern might be involved.

Social psychology in this book

Social psychology today, then, is a mixture of approaches. Modern social psychology encompasses a range of different perspectives, a complex set of ethical demands, and an even greater range of research methods, which we will explore in more detail in Chapter 10. Before that, though, we will have considered several different topics in social psychology, each of which will involve a range of different approaches to social psychological research.

In the next chapter, we will look at social emotions. We all experience emotions of various kinds, and in many ways, they direct and determine the nature of our social interactions with other people. We take a look at some of our major emotions, including loving, grief and anger, loneliness, happiness and humour. Social psychologists have studied these areas in many ways, and we explore some of the insights their research has given us.

After that we will begin an investigation of what some would see as the very core of social experience – how we go about communicating with other people. The complexity of human experience means that communication can take many forms, and we will begin our exploration by looking at the way we communicate with other people directly, using language and also using ways of communicating meanings or intentions non-verbally. But modern social living involves far more than direct communication; we experience indirect communication in many different ways, through the written word, the mass media, advertising and the internet. Each of these forms of communication has different characteristics, but all of them form part of our experience as social beings.

In Chapter 4, we will be looking at some of the deeper meanings of human communication, particularly those communicated through language and discourse. We begin by looking at discourse analysis, and how it broadens the study of communication from a simple awareness of communicative forms to the inclusion of fundamental social processes such as power and control. We will look, too, at how people attribute intentions to other people, and at the common errors which we often make in the process. And, finally, we will examine the theory of social representations, and see how stories, anecdotes and "common knowledge" all contribute to our shared understandings of why the world is like it is.

The next chapter looks more closely at some of our individual social characteristics. Attitudes have been at the centre of social psychological research since the early years of the 20th century; for many of the early social psychologists, they were the core of the discipline. As a result, we have learned quite a lot about the characteristics of attitudes, and also about ways of changing them. This chapter deals with attitude change, and the role that cognitive dissonance and minority influences can play in the process. We will also look at advertising: an industry which is essentially based on the idea of persuasion.

It has long been known, though, that our attitudes don't always predict how we actually behave towards other people. In Chapter 6, we will look at some of the most famous studies in social psychology – studies of helping behaviour, of obedience to authority and of deindividuation, the social psychological process which enables people to engage in brutality and torture, and which may also underlie both positive and negative aspects of crowd behaviour. We will examine how influential these processes are, and how some people manage to resist social pressures while others do not.

In more ordinary contexts, though, our social behaviour is also affected by apparently simple matters such as whether we like or dislike someone. In Chapter 7 we will explore the process of person perception, and what social psychologists have found out about liking and attraction – what makes us more inclined to like someone or be attracted to them. We'll also look at the opposite side of the coin, through studies of prejudice and aggression.

We talk happily about our "selves", but what do we mean by it – and how much does our sense of self depend on our social experience? In Chapter 8 we will explore these questions, looking at the origins of the self–concept and the theories of the self that psychologists have developed. We will also be looking at aspects of self–awareness, self–image and self-esteem before going on to see how different cultures often maintain very different ideas about the self.

In Chapter 9 we will discuss how insights and knowledge from social psychology have been applied in the non–academic world. We will begin that exploration by looking at group processes and leadership – research which has had particular relevance in management and organisational contexts. But there are many other areas of common experience where social psychological insights can be particularly helpful, including clinical work in addiction, counselling and hypnotherapy, cognitive contexts where we see social factors at work in memory and perception, and of course the various ways social psychology can be applied in learning and education.

The final chapter in this book deals with the process of social psychological research, and the variety of different approaches which have been taken in trying to understand how we function in our social worlds. No discussion of social psychological research can be complete without an exploration of the ethical issues and standards involved in these studies – standards which have changed so much over time that many of the classic studies we learn about would not be permitted today. We will then go on to look at different methods of social psychological research, and at some of the pitfalls and challenges which conducting research with human beings produces.

Social psychology, like all other areas of psychology, is an active discipline, constantly developing and changing as its researchers identify new areas and gain better insights. In a changing world, we need to be able to adapt. But we can also learn from what went before, building up our awareness as the years go on. The social psychology of today is very different from the social psychology of 50 years ago, and in 50 years' time it will be different again. But some of it will still be recognisable, as some of the topics and issues covered in this book would have been recognisable 50 years ago.

Chapter 1: Summary

1. Human beings are social from birth, with innate mechanisms which ensure that we respond preferentially to other people who interact with us.

2. Social understanding develops early and becomes more sophisticated as we grow older. One important milestone is the development of TOM (theory of mind): the ability to understand that others may think differently from ourselves.

3. Belonging to social groups is fundamental in our social experience, and social support is an important mechanism for dealing with the stresses of everyday living.

4. The process of social identification, which is at the core of our sense of belonging to social groups, involves categorisation, social comparison and self-evaluation.

5. Social groups may tolerate diversity within their membership more readily than they tolerate diversity in outsiders.

6. Relationships are significant aspects of our social experience. They can be diverse in nature and include a range of dimensions.

7. Internet relationships can also be significant aspects of our social experience. Social networking can include aspects of sociability which are not apparent or less accessible in real-world contexts.

8. The need for social respect is very important in human motivation; it includes avoiding social disapproval as well as seeking positive respect.

9. Social psychology can be seen as having two origins: the American empirical tradition emphasising individualism, and the European

hermeneutic tradition emphasising the importance of group processes and cultures.

10. Modern social psychology places a great deal of emphasis on the ethical conduct of research. This has become necessary, partly as a reflection of modern concerns, and partly because of the ways in which participants were treated in earlier research.

Chapter 2

Contents

Social emotions

2

Our profound sociability, as we saw in the last chapter, means that our social experiences really matter to us. This also means that we react to social experiences on an emotional level as well as on a cognitive one, and our emotional states can directly influence, or even determine, our social interactions.

WHAT ARE EMOTIONS?

Emotions are an important part of being human. One of the things which makes the Doctor Who Cybermen particularly scary is the fact that, while they were once human, all emotional capacity has been "deleted", making them into inhuman monsters. We recognise implicitly that our capacity for emotion gives colour to our experience, and makes us more than simple information-processing machines – and that this is a positive side of our natures, not just an inconvenience, as the Cybermen might see it.

The ancient Greeks saw emotion, or **affect**, as being one of the two main motivators driving human behaviour; the other one being **conation**, or intention. Their metaphor was of a charioteer driving a two-horse chariot – the cognitive domain was the charioteer, steering the chariot and deciding which route it should take, while the affective and conative domains provided the motive

power which moved the chariot along: emotions and intentions working side by side to energise our actions.

But what exactly are emotions? Emotion has never been a particularly easy concept to pin down, partly because it has so many different aspects. We know that it involves changes in our physiological and mental states which change the way we see and react to events, but it is hard to be more specific than that, because there are so many different ways of feeling. The more dramatic emotions, such as fear and anger, have been studied for over 100 years; but, in keeping with much of the rest of the modern world, relatively little research was devoted to positive emotions such as happiness or gratitude, until the very end of the 20th century. Since then, positive psychology, which explores the more positive dimensions of human emotions and experience, has increased in importance, which has given us a more rounded picture of human nature.

Some of our emotions are more extreme than others, but many of them are ways that we respond to different social experiences. Some social emotions arise directly as a result of how other people's actions impinge upon ourselves, possibly enhanced by our own internal states as well, such as anger, irritation and grief. Other social emotions are more concerned with how other people will react to us – or how we think they will react, such as shame, shyness and performance anxiety. And a third set of social emotions, such as liking, loving or respect, is concerned with how we ourselves feel about other people.

It is well established that emotions affect the body as well as the mind. One of the reasons why fear and anger were so extensively studied in psychology's early years was because they produced such dramatic changes in physiological states: hormonal changes in the bloodstream, heart and pulse rate increases, sweating and so on (Cannon, 1929). More recently, researchers have also been looking at physiological changes associated with happiness or positive cognitions, but these are more subtle and less dramatic. Increasingly, health researchers have found a relationship between physical healing and positive emotion,

Key Terms

affect
A general term for feelings and emotions.

conation
Intentionality: having intentions, plans or strategies.

WHEN FACED WITH ANXIETY, PHYLLIS WOULD ALWAYS ACT PROMPTLY.

which indicates that there are significant physiological changes associated with these emotions too. In a meta-analysis of 83 different studies, Rasmussen et al (2009) showed that optimism and the positive emotion that it generated, was a significant predictor of positive physical health outcomes.

Emotions, then, are well established as being both physiological and cognitive – that is, affecting how we think or analyse situations. But there is a significant social dimension to emotions which is often overlooked. Parkinson (2011) showed how, ever since the 1960s, researchers have identified social factors in emotions. But they have often overlooked their impact, and the way in which the social context shapes the emotions that people experience. Instead, research into emotional experience has tended to see emotions as being a response to private meaning which might be influenced by social factors.

In Parkinson's view, the social dimension in emotions is much more than that. The interaction of group identification and interpersonal processes means that our social life context actually shapes our experiences, both in terms of the emotional appraisals that we make, and in terms of the ways that we interpret our reactions. Moreover, our emotions in their turn affect what happens around us, and the ways that people respond, so emotions are active in our whole social experience.

Totterdell et al (2010) also discussed how our emotions are affected by other people. They explored the impact of the emotions of other people in their participants' social networks, and found that people are often influenced by whether the other people in their social networks generally showed positive emotions or negative ones. This research was part of a more general project exploring emotional regulation – the ways in which we can control or influence our emotions, and the various factors which can influence that. Another part of the research project used diary methods to highlight the way that having, or even witnessing, consistently negative interactions such as quarrels or arguments between colleagues at work is emotionally draining, and leads to higher levels of fatigue, and also long-term stress (Totterdell et al, 2012).

People whose work involves dealing with the public often have to make considerable psychological efforts, both to control their own feelings and to influence other people's emotional reactions. Niven and Totterdell (2012) showed how this type of emotional labour can be physically demanding for people, but also how it makes a significant contribution in the development of high-quality working relationships. Controlling emotions, though, isn't easy. It can be influenced by how we think about things and explain things to ourselves; but feeling emotion is part of being human, and not something that we can suppress altogether – even if we wanted to.

Empathy

People vary, too, in how sensitive they are to other people's emotions, and this sensitivity also affects our everyday interactions. Goleman (1996) argued that **emotional intelligence**, by which he meant sensitivity to other people's emotions and social signals, was just as important as IQ, and should be recognised as a significant aspect of human cognitive functioning.

Some people are clearly more empathic than others (Bierhoff, 2002), but we have all had the experience of being influenced by other people's emotional reactions. As we saw in the last chapter, even two-year-old children will react to other people's emotional distress, often responding by attempting to comfort

Key Terms
emotional intelligence The degree to which an individual is sensitive to other people's reactions or expressions of emotion.

the other person, despite the fact that they don't develop a full theory of mind until they are three or four years old (Dunn, 1988).

Empathy often happens in crowd situations as well as individual ones. Bee and Madrigal (2012) discussed how sports fans can often take pleasure from an event even if their own team or the person they are supporting is unsuccessful. In large events, such as the Olympics or Paralympics, Bee and Madrigal argued, people get caught up in factors such as the story behind the person's competition, or their personality when interviewed, and are happy to celebrate their success, even when it is someone they hadn't heard of before.

We can be remarkably accurate, though, when we are judging other people's emotions. In one study, Pillai et al (2012) asked people to observe videos of people reacting to a real-life scenario, and to say what was likely to have led to the emotional reaction they could see. There were four social scenarios in total: one where the person was listening to a joke, one where they were listening to a story about a series of misfortunes, one where the person they were watching was being paid a compliment, and one while the person they were watching was having to wait for five minutes until the researcher was ready for them.

Pillai et al found that people were surprisingly accurate at telling which emotion they were observing. It wasn't perfect – about 60 per cent accuracy altogether – but it was much better than it would have been by chance, even though the people they were observing had all responded very differently. Even though these were not particularly extreme emotions, people were sensitive to how others were feeling and could interpret them with a reasonable degree of accuracy.

 Other human beings are often the stimulus for changes in our emotional states, and other human beings may be the recipients of our emotions as well. During the course of our everyday lives, we experience a range of what we might call social emotions – that is, emotions which directly affect our social interactions, such as shyness, liking, loving, aggression, anger and grief, and some of these are the subject of this chapter.

LOVING AND RELATIONSHIPS

In the last chapter we saw how relationships form a fundamental part of our lives – so much so, that when we are first meeting other people, we quite often use our relationships to explain why we are there: "I am Sally's friend", or "This is Jason's mum." Affiliation and relationships are a fundamental part of our sociability, and several studies (e.g., Perlman, 2007) have shown how social isolation can be profoundly distressing. We naturally affiliate with others, and sometimes very strongly indeed, so much so that losing a relationship can cause us very deep disturbance.

Love is recognised in modern society as one of the most profound emotions that we experience. But "love" is also a word which is seriously misused. Apart from the obvious everyday exaggerations ("I just love ice-cream!"), we use the word equally to apply to a passionate infatuation with someone, or a comfortable caring relationship between a couple who have been together for many years. The one is a dramatic, all-consuming emotion, while the other may be equally profound but less conscious; it doesn't really affect the person's everyday awareness until it is threatened or lost. Then there is the kind of love felt by parents for their children, or children for their parents or other family members. Again, this can vary considerably, but it is often unspoken, and again only becomes apparent how deep it is until it is lost or threatened in some way.

For the most part, social psychologists have tended to focus on the kind of personal love which occurs between two people rather than on love within families. But even there, we may be talking about a number of different emotions. Sternberg (1987) attempted to identify some of the elements of this by proposing a three-dimensional model of characteristics of the loving experience. He identified three major factors – passion, commitment and intimacy – and proposed that these could be used to differentiate between the various forms of love.

For example: the romantic love experienced by a young couple who are fond of one another but not yet ready to settle down might be high on passion and intimacy, but low on commitment, whereas the type of love between long-term married couples might be high on commitment and intimacy, but low on passion. Using this model, Sternberg identified several different types of love, which are listed in Table 2.1.

Table 2.1 Types of love

Type of Love	Passion	Commitment	Intimacy	Example
Liking	✗	✗	✓	A very close friendship
Companionate love	✗	✓	✓	A long-term marriage
Romantic love	✓	✗	✓	A young uncommitted couple
Infatuation	✓	✗	✗	An obsession with the other person
Fatuous love	✓	✗	✓	A whirlwind affair
Empty love	✗	✓	✗	A "dead" marriage
Consummate love	✓	✓	✓	A deep, fulfilled and lasting relationship

Source: Sternberg (1987)

Over time, Sternberg argued, the dimensions of love change as partnerships continue. He interviewed 80 men and women of average age 31, but ranging from 17 to 69, and found a definite increase in the intimacy and commitment sides of the relationship, with a decline in the passion angle in the longer-term relationships. Other researchers have found similar results (e.g. Ahmetoglu et al, 2010). However, since the passion component is primarily concerned with the satisfaction of unmet needs, this might just mean that initial needs had become satisfied, and were not important any more.

Sternberg identified a number of aspects of relationships which seemed to become more important as time went on. These included sharing values, being willing to change in response to one another, being tolerant of one another's flaws, and having an equal intellectual level. But other characteristics which were seen as important at the beginning of the relationship became less so over time. These included how interesting each partner seemed to be to the other person, how much they paid attention to one another, and how well they handled each other's parents. Some things, too, increased in importance at first, but became less so as the relationship became several years older. These included lovemaking ability and physical attractiveness, knowledge of what each other was like and how they expressed affection towards one another.

Sternberg's study has been criticised because of its relatively limited sample, but other studies too have shown how relationships do change over time, and how what counts as important in a relationship in the long term is not the same as what was considered important at first. Sternberg suggested that one source of failed marriages might be because some couples make decisions based on their short-term needs, rather than looking at longer-term factors. But any individual relationship is complex, and is likely to have several reasons for failure rather than just one.

Some researchers have suggested that personality characteristics may also be connected with these aspects of loving relationships. Over 16,000 people responded to a survey which was conducted over the internet, but advertised through national newspapers and television (Ahmetoglu et al, 2010). The volunteers were asked about the length of their relationships, and the rest of the survey measured Sternberg's three dimensions of love, and the Big Five personality dimensions which are listed in Table 2.2.

Table 2.2 The big five personality dimensions

Openness to experience

Conscientiousness

Extraversion

Agreeableness

Neuroticism

Source: Gosling et al (2003)

The researchers found, perhaps not surprisingly, that the personality factor of "conscientiousness" was positively linked with intimacy and commitment, while "agreeableness" linked positively with all three of Sternberg's dimensions. In common with other researchers in this area, they found a negative association between age and passion, but a positive association between age and intimacy and commitment.

There has been some independent confirmation of Sternberg's theory that the three dimensions of passion, intimacy and commitment are independent of one another, and so justify being seen as separate characteristics (e.g. Aron and Westbay, 1996). Psychoanalysts used to assert that romantic love and sexual desire were strongly linked, and that where romantic love was Platonic, or not apparently sexual, it was only because its sexual dimension had been suppressed by the unconscious mind. For Freud, for example, all positive emotions towards other people were essentially sexual in nature, drawing on the libido, or sexual energy, of the person (Freud, 1901).

Other researchers, however, take a more sophisticated view, and there is some evidence that sexual desire and romantic love are actually quite separate emotions. Diamond (2003) proposed that they actually derive from two separate psychological systems: romantic love being derived from and drawing on the human tendency for attachment, caring and affiliation, while sexual desire derives from the sexual mating system. These two psychological systems, Diamond argued, are entirely separate, involving different parts of the brain as well as different emotional characteristics.

Frost and Forrester (2013) conducted a study of well-being and closeness in the relationships, in a study of partners over a two-year period. They found that it was important that the partners had matching ideas about the ideal and practical degrees of closeness between the two of them – if one partner wanted to be emotionally closer to the other, it was unlikely that the relationship would be satisfying, or that the partners would express a sense of well-being as a result of it. But they also found that the ideal degree of closeness varies considerably: some couples liked to be very close to one another, while others were happy to be more emotionally distant.

Arranged marriages

The way in which relationships change over time, and the idea that love can grow from a positive partnership, is part of the rationale underlying arranged marriages. These have been common in many human societies – in fact, the idea of romantic love as the sole basis for entering into a long-term relationship appears to be a relatively recent phenomenon, historically speaking.

For some young people in cultures where arranged marriages are common, the practical considerations taken into account by parents in arranging marriages are seen as a stronger basis for a long-term relationship than the idea of romantic love – provided the parents also take the young person's personal preferences into account (Umadevi et al, 1992). The young people in their study didn't object to love-matches, but thought it was important that the parents were also happy about them too. They trusted their parents to make sure that the likely future prospects of the partnership were at least practical.

What is important, though, the researchers found, is that the parents arranging the marriage are sensitive to and take account of the young person's preference. There is a big difference between arranged marriage, which happens with the willing consent of both partners, and forced marriage, in which young girls are bullied into accepting partners whom they have not chosen and do not want. Forced marriage is illegal in most countries, but has nonetheless been shown to be a problem for many girls who are taken to another country to be married, and find themselves alone and powerless to do anything about it.

Limerence

In 1954, Maslow suggested that there are two distinct types of love, which he called D-love and B-love. "D" in this model stands for "deficiency". D-love is where the person uses the other person to fulfil themselves, rather than being half of a balanced partnership. "B" stands for balance, and represents a more equitable relationship with mutual passion and intimacy, rewarding for both partners.

Following on from this, Tennov (1979, 1998), argued that love as the powerful all-consuming emotion illustrated in *Romeo and Juliet* isn't really anything like the more lasting emotion that we also call love, and shouldn't go by the same name. Instead, she argued, it was better to call it by a different name: limerence; and to reserve the term "love" for the less dramatic but probably more meaningful long-term emotional and passionate attachment.

Limerence, Tennov argued, is essentially a self-centred emotion in which the person becomes so absorbed in their relationship with the other that it dominates their whole life and thinking. She identified 12 core characteristics of the state of limerence, which are listed in Table 2.3. As a condition, Tennov argued, limerence can last for several years, and could happen to people of any age; but it becomes more intense and lasts longer when it is unfulfilled, because that maintains the fantasy element of the relationship.

Table 2.3 The characteristics of limerence

1. Idealisation of the other person's characteristics.
2. Uncontrollable and intrusive thoughts about the other person.
3. Extreme shyness and confusion around the other person
4. Fear of rejection and despair.
5. Euphoria in response to real or perceived signs of reciprocation.
6. Searching obsessively for signs of reciprocation.
7. Being reminded of the person in everything around.
8. Mentally replaying every encounter with the other person in detail.
9. Maintaining romantic intensity despite problems or challenges.
10. Analysing every word and gesture for possible meaning.
11. Maximising possible encounters with the other person.
12. Having physical symptoms (e.g., trembling or palpitations when around the other person).

Source: Tennov, 1998

Given its intensity, and the way in which it has been known to disrupt people's lives, limerence has been described as an obsessive-compulsive disorder; and there has been some discussion as to whether it should be included in the *Diagnostic and Statistical Manual of Mental Disorders*, the main listing used by psychiatrists and psychologists to indicate the need for clinical intervention. In healthy relationships, it is argued, people may be in love but they are able to sustain their ordinary lives, and do not experience constant obsessive thoughts about the other person.

Other researchers simply see the state of limerence as being one of the early stages of love, much like Sternberg's idea of infatuation, although Tennov insisted that limerence is much stronger than infatuation. One of the means of distinguishing between the two, she argued, is the way in which infatuation may form the base of a rewarding relationship for the other partner as well, while limerence tends to be experienced as "smothering" for the other person. This is because limerence demands emotional reciprocation from the other person, but doesn't actually take account of their own psychological or physical well-being.

The case for regarding limerence as a separate emotion has also been strengthened by neurology. Sack (2014) discussed how recent research suggests that the emotion of limerence may be a distinct biological state, in that it involves a distinctive combination of neurotransmitters which is different from those involved in other types of love and affection.

Talking point   2.1 Is love just cultural?

Tennov's attempt to distinguish limerence from longer-term loving makes it clear that the two emotions have very different characteristics. They also have different histories: romantic love as a concept wasn't really discussed in Western literature until the 12th century or so. Which raises the question: is the concept of romantic love just a product of Western culture? Does it only exist because we believe in it, and so we allow it to?

In Ursula K. Le Guin's classic novel *The Left Hand of Darkness*, romantic "love" is dismissed as a selfish and self-indulgent emotion. And many supporters of arranged marriages say that as long as both partners are happy with the idea (which is the really important thing), having a marriage arranged by older relatives who can be practical about income, prospects and so on is preferable to just jumping into a long-term relationship on the basis of a powerful passion and little else.

What do you think?

Types of love

Not all love is romantic love, of course: there are many different styles of loving. For some people, their relationship may be deep and affectionate, but still quite hard-headed and practical in many ways; while others experience love as an idyllic partnership, overlooking each other's faults and experiencing fulfilment in the other person's company. An early attempt to classify the various styles of love was spelled out by Lee in 1976, and used as the basis of later research by Hendrick and Hendrick (1988).

These styles were named "colours of love" and were: eros, ludus, storge, mania, agape and pragma. They are described in more detail in Table 2.4. Lee argued that any one person could adopt more than one style at different times; but a couple using different styles at the same time would find it easy to slip into misunderstandings.

Hendrick and Hendrick (1988) asked 789 research participants about their attitudes towards being in love. Roughly 63 per cent of them answered "yes" when asked: "Are you in love at the moment?" But the researchers found that these people were more concerned with the erotic and agapic dimensions, and far less with the ludic dimension than those who said they were not in

Table 2.4 Colours of love

Eros	Love in which a physical ideal is sought and the person is looking for someone who fits it.
Ludus	A playful form of relatively uncommitted love where the relationship is perceived as a source of fun and enjoyment.
Storge	Love based initially on friendship which increases gradually in intimacy, affection and companionship.
Mania	Emotionally intensive love, involving possessiveness and jealousy.
Agape	An altruistic, one-sided form of love, in which one person does all the giving without expecting return.
Pragma	A practical and utilitarian style of loving, with material and objective factors being regarded as just as important as emotions.

Source: Lee (1976)

love. They also seemed to have a much more idealised attitude towards their partner, and tended to see things "through rose-coloured spectacles". Those who adopted other styles (or colours) of loving, however, were more realistic and practical, although generally still positive and affectionate.

Internet loving

Internet loving contains many of the same issues as loving in face-to-face contexts. It is not uncommon for internet relationships to have a strong fantasy element, particularly when they involve **avatars**, such as the relationships developed through Second Life or similar shared platforms. People are able to present an idealised version of themselves through their avatars, and they are equally liable to idealise relationships in what they often perceive as a relatively "safe" context. Some of those relationships stay on the internet, while others progress to face-to-face meetings and even marriage.

Other types of intimate internet relationships can be found in the increasingly common phenomenon known as "**sexting**". This involves sharing intimate sexual information and sometimes photographic images of intimate parts of the anatomy with another person. Some of these relationships progress to virtual sex, or even real-time mono-erotic sex while the participants communicate through the internet and fantasise about being with the other person. The widespread nature of this phenomenon means that a surprising number of people engage in it. Studies have shown that the prevalence of sexting appears to increase with age; relatively few minors engage in it, but as many as 50 per cent of adults in one survey admitted to having sent nude or nearly nude pictures of themselves to other via email (Drouin and Landgraff, 2012).

Döring (2014) analysed the content of papers on sexting published between 2009 and 2013 and found evidence of a distinct change of emphasis. While sexting was initially regarded as problematic or deviant behaviour among young people, its prevalence means that it is increasingly being regarded as relatively normal, or at least just another lifestyle choice made by autonomous individuals. There is some evidence that sexting can actually promote harmonious and positive relationships (Parker et al, 2013). However, problems can arise when the relationship breaks down, and the information is disseminated

Key Terms

avatar
A fictional image of a character, used in computer gaming to represent the player.

sexting
Internet messaging which involves transmitting intimate or sexy images of the self to another person.

by one of the partners. Teenage girls have been identified as being particularly vulnerable to this, with some documented cases of girls who have committed suicide after intimate photographs they shared in what they saw as a close personal relationship were disseminated among their peers, producing ridicule and ostracism (Ahern and Mechling, 2013).

Maintaining relationships

Falling in love is one thing – maintaining a long-term relationship may be quite different. Karney and Bradbury (1995) carried out a longitudinal study of satisfaction in married couples, and found that there was no single factor which could be identified as the "key" to a successful marriage. There were, however, factors which made it more likely, such as shared educational levels, employment and shared interests; and there were also some factors which made it less likely, such as unhappy childhoods, negative behaviour towards the other person, and neuroticism. But even these factors could exist in some long-term relationships, with the person concerned learning to cope with their personal history, or other partner simply adjusting to them.

Some researchers have used **equity theory** to assess the likelihood of relationship survival. Clark and Grote (1998) assessed factors which could help a relationship – in other words, the positive factors – as being those in which partners deliberately act to make the other feel good, either intentionally or unintentionally. Negative factors were those which made the other person feel worse – again, either deliberately or intentionally. Overall, they argued, a long-term relationship would need to show a balance (equity) between positive and negative factors; if the negative factors outweighed the positive ones too much, the relationship would be likely to break down.

Reis and Patrick (1996) found that **attachment styles** could be an important factor. People with **insecure attachment** styles, they found, were less likely to provide their partners with comfort and support, and more likely to react strongly to negative events within their relationship. Those with **secure attachment** styles, on the other hand, were more able to resolve differences effectively and together, and less likely to refuse to discuss issues or to react destructively to them. This meant that they were more able to develop lasting intimate relationships.

Intimacy, according to Reis and Patrick is at the core of long-term attachment. They argued that there are three conditions to intimate relationships: caring, understanding and validation. Each of the partners must feel that the other cares about them; that they have an accurate view of who that person is, and what is important to them; and that they accept and support their views and characteristics. Without these three conditions, a relationship would not achieve the level of intimacy required for happy, long-term relationships.

Another factor concerns the investment the couple may have made in their relationship. Rusbult (1983) argued that people become linked to their partners in various ways: for example, through having mutual friends and social lives, through their children, through joint decisions made about their home and through the shared memories they have developed during their time together. All of these, and other factors, combine to reflect a considerable personal investment in the relationship with that person, which in turn may increase their level of commitment to the relationship and their reluctance to end it.

Key Terms

equity theory
The idea that social conventions and norms are based around a principle of fair, though not necessarily strictly equal, exchange.

attachment styles
Distinctive patterns in the ways that attachments are formed and maintained.

insecure attachment
A style of attachment in which the individual is anticipating rejection, and as a result may show excessive dependency.

secure attachment
An attachment style marked by confidence in the lasting nature of the relationship, allowing exploratory and similar behaviours.

Other researchers have focused on the importance of the **attributions** which people in relationships make about themselves and their partners. We will be looking more closely at attributions in Chapter 4, but in essence, attributions are the reasons that we give for why things happen. Fincham (2002) showed how those in positive relationships tend to make relationship-enhancing attributions, seeing their partner's positive actions as being intentional and typical, while their negative actions are judged as being unusual and untypical. This is in contrast with those in more negative close relationships, who often make distress-maintaining attributions which see the other person's negative actions as deliberate and typical, aimed at causing discomfort or distress. When their partner acts positively, they attribute it to temporary or external factors, rather than being typical of the person concerned. As a result, the relationship becomes unhappy, and less likely to be maintained in the long term.

These factors, though, do not make the success or failure of a long-term relationship inevitable. There is also the factor of commitment, as identified by Sternberg (1987). Rusbult and Buunk (1993) argued that whether a couple stay together is partly dependent on the level of satisfaction in their relationship, but also strongly affected by the perceived quality of alternatives. So, people may stay together, even in an unsatisfactory relationship, because the alternatives that they see are worse than the situation that they are in. It is for this reason that external obstacles, such as social or family attitudes, can be such a barrier to the ending of relationships; and also why changes in social attitudes – that is, a weakening of the external pressures – can result in an increasing divorce rate (Attridge and Berscheid, 1994).

Sometimes, pressures from external events can actually lessen the likelihood of divorce. Hansel et al (2011) analysed divorce statistics occurring in New York State between 1991 and 2005, comparing them with other regions of America. They found a significant drop in divorce rates after the attack on the World Trade Centre in 2001, implying that once the immediate impact was over, people turned to one another for support and valued their family interactions more. The decline was particularly apparent in the metropolitan areas around the city, but less so in the city itself, which did show a decline in divorce rates but not until a year or so later. The authors explained this in terms of the immediacy of the trauma for the city-dwellers, who took longer to recover from the shock and distress caused, and so had relatively little mental capacity to devote to relationship issues by comparison with the more distant residents, who recovered from the immediate shock more quickly.

Overall, Fletcher and Simpson (2006) found that people who remain in relationships which are less than satisfying tend to adapt to the situation using a number of cognitive strategies. One of these is to minimise their partner's faults, while exaggerating their good qualities, so convincing themselves that remaining with that person is "worth it". Another is to reduce their general expectations: if you don't expect anyone to be particularly easy to live with anyway, then remaining with a difficult partner becomes less of a personal challenge. And a third is to adjust their ways of perceiving their partner – sometimes even blinding themselves to faults that other people can perceive quite clearly – in order to feel that their partner matches up more closely to their ideal.

Key Terms

attributions
The reasons people give for why things happen.

BREAKDOWN AND BEREAVEMENT

Despite the various strategies which people can use to maintain relationships, many relationships do eventually end, and the end of a close relationship can be one of the most painful experiences in many people's lives. Regardless of the factors which eventually led to the break-up, as a general rule the couple will have shared a good chunk of their lives, and breaking those bonds may involve loneliness, bitterness and betrayal, and many other emotional responses as well as economic and social consequences.

As we have seen, maintaining close relationships requires a certain amount of effort from both parties. Often, though, the maintenance efforts are lacking, or fail, and a relationship breaks down. Naturally, research into this area has tended to focus on "what went wrong", and often concentrated on identifying demographic or social factors in unstable marriages. For example, Bentler and Newcomb (1978) showed that marriages between young partners are less likely to survive than marriages where the partners are older; and Jaffe and Kanter (1979) demonstrated that if people come from very different backgrounds, their marriages are less likely to last than those between people who come from similar backgrounds. Noller (1985) showed how couples in a disintegrating relationship often show disrupted patterns of communication, and other researchers showed how devastating the impact of deception within a relationship can be (e.g., Miller et al, 1986).

As a fairly typical example of research in this area, Baxter (1986) reported a study which identified the essential expectations that people in intimate relationships have about the relationship itself and each other's behaviour. There were eight of these altogether, listed in Table 2.5. Failure to meet these expectations, Baxter argued, was likely to result in dissatisfaction with the relationship, which could easily develop into being seen as a sufficient cause for relationship breakdown.

Table 2.5 Expectations about intimate relationships

1. Each partner should have a certain amount of autonomy.

2. There should be a good basis of similarity between partners.

3. Partners should support each other in terms of their feelings and self-esteem.

4. Partners should be loyal and faithful to one another.

5. Partners should be honest and open.

6. Partners should spend time together.

7. Each partner should devote an equitable share of effort and resources to the relationship.

8. The relationship should retain some "magical quality".

Source: Baxter (1986)

Duck (2007) argued that the breakdown process for a long-term relationship such as a marriage involves four steps. The intra-psychic phase is where at least one of the partnership is making up their mind that it has to end. The dyadic phase is where both parties become aware that their relationship is ending – which can be a traumatic period for one or both, even though they may have been dimly aware of it. Sometimes this shock is sufficient for them to take steps to renegotiate their relationship – perhaps through direct discussion, or with the help of counselling organisations like Relate.

Failing such renegotiation, the third phase is what Duck described as the social phase, where the couple are working out the social implications of what they are about to do, telling friends and family, and so on. Occasionally, the separation is reasonably amicable, but at other times it isn't and other people may become involved – either to try to get the couple to resolve their problems, or to assist one or other of them in the separation process. The fourth phase, according to Duck, is the grave-dressing phase, where the partners concentrate on getting over the partnership, familiarising others with their personal version of what happened, and either establishing a total separation, or establishing the basis for a longer term friendship.

LEAVING WORK

Ending less-involved relationships can also be a challenge at times. One example of this is leaving work, where the move signals an end to the less significant friendships and acquaintances involved in everyday working life. Although this is less intense than the breakdown of a personal partnership, it nonetheless raises a number of social challenges, and has an emotional impact upon the people concerned.

In a study of how people go about leaving work, Klotz and Bolino (2016) surveyed 476 people who had recently left a job, and identified seven different styles of leaving. These are listed in Table 2.6. Some of these styles, such as bridge burning or impulsive quitting, generally reflect quite intense emotional feelings on the part of the person who is leaving. But in another part of the study, the researchers looked at the emotional impact that the leaving style had upon managers and supervisors. They asked nearly 500 managers or supervisors to reflect on their own past experiences, and describe how they would be likely to feel in a scenario where the person resigned according to one of the seven styles.

 Not surprisingly, the managers generally reported more negative emotions than positive ones when people left. But when the leaver had used one of the first three styles in Table 2.6, they reported higher levels of positive emotion and lower negative ones. The final two styles, again not surprisingly, generated a higher level of negative emotions, but so did perfunctory style leavings, which came as more of a surprise. Even though these people had acted perfectly properly according to regulations, the managers found that the fact that they had done so clinically, without interpersonal contact, personally upsetting. Even breaks in less personally significant relationships can be disturbing.

Relationship breakdown on the internet

Internet-based affairs are increasingly featuring in accounts of relationship breakdown, with the development of intimate, often sexual relationships based on internet interaction. While not all such relationships are sexual in nature, sexual aspects of internet use can influence several different types of internet-based relationships (Griffiths, 2001). We have seen how sexting, or sex-based interaction and relationships which have developed through internet communication, has become relatively frequent. Suler (2004) argued that this

Table 2.6 Styles of leaving work

Style	Description	Percentage found
By the book	Initial conversation, then resignation letter, standard notice and openness about reason for leaving.	31
Grateful goodbye	Positivism; willing to make the departure as painless as possible for supervisor and team.	9
In the loop	Open about process of resignation, and reasons for leaving with supervisor as well as management.	8
Perfunctory	Going through standard procedure for leaving but without explanation or discussion.	29
Avoidant	Minimising contact with boss, acting through a third party or sending a message over the weekend to announce leaving.	9
Impulsive quitting	Generally precipitated by an incident or frustrations building to breaking point.	4
Bridge burners	Leaving abruptly and being openly angry with and/or abusive to boss.	10

Source: Klotz and Bolino (2016)

is because of the relative disinhibition which results from the perceived anonymity of the interaction. However, it appears that many people who find that their partner is engaging in internet sex regard it as no different from "real" infidelity – mainly because it still involves a breach of the trust and closeness of the initial relationship (Whitty, 2005).

Relationship breakdown is an intensely emotional event. Davis et al (2003) surveyed over 5000 people through the internet, exploring the ways in which they had responded to the breakdown of close emotional relationships. They found differences in how people had reacted which were closely linked with their attachment styles. Those who had anxious attachments, for example, tended to show much more preoccupation with the loss of their partner, more emotional distress and a greater inclination towards vengeful behaviour than those who generally had secure attachments. They were also more likely to turn to alcohol or drugs as a relief from the emotional strain. People with secure attachment styles, on the other hand, tended to gain support from friends and family, and to cope more effectively with the breakdown of the relationship.

Bereavement

Many of the emotions associated with traumatic breakdown of a marriage or other close relationship are similar to those of bereavement, and this is not a coincidence. Both involve the sudden loss or disruption of a close relationship, and in cases of relationship breakdown where emotions have become extreme and bitter, that personal loss can be as total as it is when someone dies. Of course, most cases of relationship breakdown are not as extreme as this, and many couples achieve amicable relationships despite the separation. But for some, the similarities are quite strong.

The experience of bereavement shows us just how powerful our relationships with other people are. The severing of a close relationship through death results in a complex of emotional reactions, which can swing wildly from one emotion to another, and which creates an experience which is sometimes quite unexpected to the person experiencing it.

There are at least nine significant mental states associated with bereavement and grieving, which all contribute to the complex of emotional experience. One of them is the feeling of numbness or unreality, that it can't be really true. This is particularly common at first, but phases of numbness can continue throughout the grieving process. The experience of denial isn't quite the same, as it is a less passive emotion, sometimes accompanied with an angry element, in which the person actively denies the truth of the death. Grieving generally includes periods of depression, in which the person may feel despairing, or simply desolated and abandoned. Anxiety attacks are also a common feature of grieving which, like the other mood swings, may come on without warning.

One of the things which often surprises modern people, particularly those who see themselves as down to earth and practical, is just how much cognitive disorganisation can accompany the loss of someone close to you. Even when the death has been expected, its actual event can result in an inability to focus on things, such that the person feels unable to get anything done. Funeral arrangers are familiar with this feature of grieving, and their particular social skills are often focused on helping the bereaved person deal with necessary things while in this condition. The prescribed rituals of most funerals are also helpful in this respect, making it possible for the bereaved to go through them in a semi-aware state if their cognitive disorganisation is still persisting.

At times grieving may also include a strong component of guilt. The person feels as though they should have done something, or might have been able to make a difference, and blames themselves for what has happened. While most people experience this to some degree, it is demonstrably strongest in people who had disturbed or disrupted relationships with the person who died. The sense of "unfinished business" or unspoken resentment against the person can amplify their sense of guilt to what outsiders would see as quite an unreasonable level, as well as prolonging their grief for a much longer period than is experienced by most mourners (Parkes and Weiss, 1983).

This guilt may be accompanied by, or alternate with, periods of anger and aggression. Anger, in fact, is a common emotional reaction in grieving, and may be directed against almost any target – nursing or medical staff, care workers, other members of the family or even inward towards the person themselves. The hostility and anger accompanying bereavement can be extremely destructive, but it usually alternates with other emotions and gradually dies down as the person begins to accept what has happened. But anger, too, is often amplified in those who had disturbed relationships with the deceased.

The final phase of grieving, according to Ramsay (1977) comes as the person begins to reintegrate the structure of their lives and regain their emotional balance. Typically, the mood swings become less severe, and the cognitive disorganisation gradually becomes less. There isn't a definite time when this happens, and some people experience it as a kind of "disloyalty", as if recovering from the bereavement implies that their relationship wasn't really important. But for many, the worst period is over within two to three weeks, and while their grief has not vanished, they are able to take up their usual lives again, or begin to create a new life without their partner.

Clinical and counselling psychologists have commonly identified "stages" of bereavement, such as is shown in Table 2.7. Individuals pass through these stages in different ways and at different times. But what clinical findings about bereavement and grieving show us is just how profound the disruption of a close personal relationship can be, and how deeply it can affect our other relationships too. The process of grieving is not just an individual affair, but a social experience, affecting our own interactions with other people, as well as influencing how other people respond to us.

Table 2.7 "Stages" of bereavement

1. **Denial**. The bereaved person expresses disbelief that the death has really happened, refusing to see it as "real".

2. **Pining**. The bereaved person longs for the other, becoming restless and fidgety, and searching unconsciously for a glimpse of the person.

3. **Depression**. Acceptance of the death is accompanied by intense apathy, often including elements of self-blame and sudden waves of anguish. This may re-emerge on anniversaries or visits to special places, even after it has died down.

Source: Parkes (1972)

The effects of counselling

We can see how important social factors are in dealing with our emotions when we look at the impact of counselling. Counselling is a well-developed and highly successful technique, which is used in a variety of contexts, including helping people deal with bereavement. What counsellors do can also vary quite widely, but as a general rule they are teaching the person how to deal with the issues and problems that are besetting them – perhaps through learning new coping skills, or perhaps by re-evaluating those issues cognitively, such that they can perceive better ways of approaching them.

As we saw in the last chapter, counselling is a fundamentally social activity in that it rests strongly on the relationship between the counsellor and the client. As another human being, the counsellor is able to understand the mental and emotional situation of the client, and through their interaction, can propose or develop strategies for dealing with the client's problems or difficulties in living. But counselling doesn't always have to be a face-to-face affair. In online counselling, the client is still dealing with another person, but instead of being in a face-to-face situation, they are interacting without the usual set of non-verbal cues and responses which are characteristic of face-to-face interaction.

For some people, this can be an advantage, particularly in highly charged emotional situations. This is one of the issues which has been investigated by researchers exploring the practicality of online counselling. In that context, Wellman and Haydornthwaite (2002) argued that the relative impersonality of online communication created a feeling – possibly an illusion – of privacy, which some people found preferable to the face-to-face situation. This idea was supported by Haberstroh et al (2007), who found that people who needed counselling for embarrassing topics felt less pressurised and less threatened by online counselling than by direct personal interaction with a counsellor. For bereavement, though, it appears that people tend to prefer the personal approach of face-to-face counselling rather than a more indirect approach.

Box 2.1   Coping with bereavement

Many people who have been recently bereaved feel as though the person they have lost is still around – that they are with them in the house, or as they do familiar things which they used to do together. In Western society, we see these feelings as a natural outcome of sharing one's life with someone else; it takes the mind time to get used to being alone, and these not-quite-hallucinations come from mental habits. So the person experiencing these feelings knows that the person is not "really" there, but they still have to cope with feeling as though they are.

Other cultures deal with these experiences quite differently. In many non-technological societies around the world, the experiences of the recently bereaved are dealt with explicitly. There is a specific place where they can take food or other things, and talk to the person they have lost, telling them what has happened recently, and generally bringing them the news. Early Western anthropologists saw these practices as "ancestor worship", but that was a misunderstanding. It was a recognition and acknowledgement of the ancestors, rather than actual worship. In these cultures, someone who has died remains as a named individual until the last person who knew them alive dies, at which point they join the great mass of that society's ancestors.

So instead of feeling that they are just having hallucinations, someone who has been through a recent bereavement and feels as though that person is still around has a constructive and positive way of dealing with their experience. Their society recognises what they will be feeling, and offers them a way of dealing with it. In the West, we have little such help to give. Which raises the question: which is the psychologically healthier approach?

Anger

Anger, as we've seen, is a frequent component in grieving – or, indeed, in most reactions to losing a relationship. Anger is a common social emotion, but it can take many different forms and arise from several different sources. It can also be strongly influenced by social experience – something which has been well known in psychology for many decades, and in society for even longer: "A soft answer turneth away wrath" (KJB: Proverbs 15). The classic psychological study used to illustrate this was somewhat dubious in its design, and its general acceptance can be seen as an illustration of social representations, or the power of scientific paradigms. But it does make a point.

That classic study – highly controversial and badly controlled, but a classic nonetheless – was reported by Schachter and Singer in 1962, and involved injecting some people (but not others) with adrenaline, a hormone known to enhance the physiological symptoms of anger, and then putting them in different social situations – either with someone who appeared to be becoming increasingly frustrated and angry, or someone who appeared to be happy or even euphoric. Their conclusions, which remain generally supported by more mundane research even if not entirely by their own, were that the social situation influences which emotion people experience, while their physiological state influences to what degree they experience it.

Following on from this, Spielberger et al (1988) described anger as an emotional state which can vary in intensity from mild irritation to intense fury and rage. They regard susceptibility to anger as a demonstrable personality trait, in that some people are more inclined to become annoyed or angry

about things going on around them than others; but even the most phlegmatic of us generally experience anger to some degree or another at some time in their lives.

There appears to be a general consensus that what brings anger on is usually a perceived threat of some kind. In the modern, world such a threat is usually social. Some people may become angry because they feel that others are threatening their personal sense of well-being in some way, such as by not taking that person seriously, or repeatedly doing things which they "know" will be irritating to that person, or because Governmental or social policies seem to be threatening their security or well-being. Others may be unaffected by those types of things, but become angry at perceived social injustice, and still others may only become angry at some perceived threat to their family or close friends.

Clarifying exactly what we mean by anger isn't helped by lack of precision. For example, one of the main problems which psychologists studying anger have to deal with is defining what the term actually means. That becomes clearer if we look at how other communities define experiences which we would identify as anger. The Ifaluk people of Micronesia, for example, have five different words, each of which describes what we would call anger, but each of which identifies a different source of the emotion and so differentiates it more clearly (Lutz, 1990). These words are: *tipmochmoch*, which is the anger or irritability arising from feeling ill or unwell; *nguch*, or anger with relatives or friends who have not done what they should, or as they promised; *tang*, which is the kind of anger which comes from feeling helpless or frustrated in response to personal misfortune or unfairness; *lingeringer*, or the type of anger which builds up slowly as a series of small but annoying or unpleasant events happen; and *song*, which is a sense of "justifiable anger", or righteous indignation.

We recognise all of these emotions, and three out of the five are clearly social in origin. But in English we use the term "anger" to describe all of them, and that failure to discriminate between them can lead to problems. It can lead to social problems; we may, for instance, take someone's irritation with us as a personal thing, when, in fact, it was simply because they were unwell and feeling particularly rotten.

It can also lead to scientific problems, in that a number of researchers may all be investigating "anger", but actually looking at quite different emotions. Rose et al (1984) pointed out that researchers investigating both "anger" and "aggression" are often studying several very different concepts. As a result, different emotions become conflated and therefore confused. Is the study of trait anger, for example, actually the same as the anger felt by an idealistic young person wanting to fight for their country or their beliefs?

 The other problem of failing to clarify exactly what we mean by anger is that we may believe that we are studying one thing when we are actually studying something which is much more limited. Researchers may have investigated just one specific type of anger as a result of operationalising their research, but then may end up generalising their conclusions to "anger" in general.

Studying anger, then, is a bit problematic. It has usually been dealt with as a physiological state, rather than as a social emotion – so much so that despite its important social implications, anger rarely features as a social psychological topic in textbooks. Instead, it tends to be dealt with as a clinical problem in terms of strategies of anger management; or as a physiological condition. Rather than studying anger, social psychologists have tended to focus on aggression, a form of interaction which is often closely linked with anger, and is the most obvious way that anger manifests itself in a social situation. We will be looking at aggression more closely in Chapter 7.

SHYNESS

Most of us feel shy at some point in our lives. We may feel apprehensive or awkward when we are dealing with other people, and not be sure how to talk to them or what the correct way to behave is. This is particularly common when we are in new situations or move out of our "comfort zone". But most of us will get over these feelings as the situation becomes more familiar. For some people, though, their shyness is more extreme and forms a real barrier to making friends and developing relationships. We have seen how important it is for human beings to be sociable, so extreme shyness of this kind can generate a number of problems.

One of the first papers which opened the topic of shyness up to modern research was published by Zimbardo in 1986. This began a series of research programmes which was rapidly taken up by others. In a further study, for example, Henderson and Zimbardo (1998) proposed that shyness manifests itself at four different levels: cognitive, affective, physiological and behavioural. At the cognitive level, shy people experience negative thoughts, worry and self-blame. On the physiological level, they may experience increased heartrate, sweating or shaking, or feelings of faintness and dizziness when in what they perceive to be a difficult social situation. At the affective level, they easily feel embarrassment or shame, are often lonely and may also experience depression and anxiety. And on the behavioural level, shy people tend to avoid eye-contact with others, speak in low voices and show nervous body movements or defensive postures.

These symptom are the extreme forms of shyness, of course. When shyness reaches these levels, it is often regarded as a clinical condition, known as social anxiety disorder, and there are a range of therapies which have been adopted to help people to deal with it. For most people, though, their experience of shyness is less severe, but still limits the amount that they feel able to participate in everyday society.

Carducci (2000) identified a critical aspect of everyday shyness as being that shy people are slower to warm up in social relationships. They take longer to relax and participate in events, and need more time to develop relationships to the point where they want to move into a more intimate closeness with the other person. So everyday encounters may simply move too quickly for them, and they may not have the opportunity to observe people for a while before engaging in friendly discussions with them.

Another aspect of shyness identified by Carducci is the way that shy people tend to make inappropriate social comparisons. Instead of comparing themselves with other more ordinary people, they tend to compare themselves with the most dynamic, popular or socially successful people around. Those negative comparisons then become the passive justification for their shyness: "I wasn't born like that", or "I can't socialise with other people like that."

The third important aspect of shyness emerging from Carducci's work is the way that shy people tend to believe that other people are constantly evaluating them and making judgements. So when they are with other people, they are particularly self-conscious of what they say and of how they must appear, and this means that they feel less likely to be able to relax and contribute to any everyday interaction that is going on.

It affects what we are prepared to say, as well. Wright et al (2010) looked at how social anxiety can influence how we behave with other people. They were particularly interested in conformity in memories: when two people experience the same thing, the second person to report will often imitate what the first person has said. Using a face recognition task, they found that adolescents with high social anxiety were strongly influenced by what the first person had said, while more confident and less socially anxious adolescents would make more independent observations about what they had seen.

 Shyness is quite common. Henderson et al (2001) found that some 48 per cent of people describe themselves as shy. However, their research also showed that for most people, shyness isn't really a problem; shy people might take longer to get into relationships, but they usually manage it in the end. Their main problem, according to these researchers, tends to be starting relationships, and for many, the opportunities offered by the internet or other options for meeting like-minded people means that they can eventually manage to overcome their shyness.

Box 2.2   Shyness and evaluation

Most people feel a certain amount of apprehension when they know that other people will be watching them and judging them in some way. The most common example of this is performance anxiety, which is felt by even some of the most successful performers. Before they go on stage, they feel apprehensive, and even physically sick; but when they are actually there and begin their performance, it all goes away.

In everyday life, too, we may feel apprehensive about the idea of people watching and judging us. For most adults, that occurs in specific social situations like parties or interviews, and much of the advice given by Zimbardo and his colleagues is directed towards helping people to get over that sort of social shyness. For many teenagers, though, that evaluation apprehension applies in a much wider range of social situations. When we first begin to interact in wider society, we often pay a great deal of attention to our appearance, and we feel that people are constantly judging how we look, and measuring it up to some kind of ideal. It takes some years before we realise that in most public situations, people are far too involved in what they themselves are doing to be particularly concerned with how the rest of us look – unless we choose to dress particularly unconventionally, that is.

That doesn't apply, of course, to situations where people really are on show. Matinees, dances and similar events are all about dressing up and being in the spotlight, so it is fairly reasonable to assume that some social judgements are taking place, and it is entirely ordinary to feel a certain amount of apprehension before taking part in them. Many shy people avoid those situations altogether, without anyone particularly noticing. But shyness becomes a real problem when we avoid ordinary all social situations – friends' parties, going out for a drink with work colleagues, joining in a lunchtime excursion. That is when shyness starts to prevent us from meeting new people and making friends, and when it forms its strongest link with loneliness.

Internet interactions are one solution, but the TV series *Catfish*, which seeks out internet "trolls" and faces them with what they are doing, shows how these can often result in deception and even abuse. Seeking interaction without evaluation is another strategy used by many. Joining large audiences and communicating lightly with immediate neighbours about what is being watched reduces the chances of personal evaluation to a level that many find acceptable; as does joining hobby or interest groups where the primary attention is on the subject matter of the group rather than on the people concerned. For many chronically shy people, the priority is in finding ways of dealing with the fear of social judgement as much as in practising social skills.

Dealing with shyness

Shy people, the researchers found, use several different strategies to overcome their shyness. The most common one is to put themselves in contact with other people deliberately, and to try to force themselves to act in a more extraverted fashion. But for most, this is not a very successful strategy, as their supply of "small talk" tends to dry up quite quickly, and they are then left not knowing what to say. The reason for this, Henderson et al argued, is twofold: firstly, because they expect other people to approach them and direct the conversation, and, secondly, because shy people tend to expect themselves to be perfect. Their fear of evaluation means that they feel that everything they say has to be interesting or witty. Less shy people on the other hand, are not troubled by such doubts, they simply say what they want to say without worrying so much about social evaluation.

Another strategy is what the authors referred to as "cognitive modification" – following the advice given in self-help books or trying to use positive self-talk to convince themselves that people like them. But this only works when it is also combined with opportunities for extraversion. Talking to oneself may be useful, but it is not enough – we need to talk to other people too. In those circumstances, the researchers found, self-help books and other strategies could work well.

A third strategy involves the use of alcohol for its disinhibiting effect. But Henderson, Zimbardo and Carducci found that this was a self-limiting strategy; it didn't help the overall problem of shyness, but made people feel that they could only be interesting when under the influence of alcohol – and not when they were just being themselves.

Some shy people, however, deal with their shyness in a positive way. They acknowledge that they are shy, and take steps to deal with it. Instead of being anxious about maintaining conversations, for example, they practice asking questions of the other person, or plan things they might like to say before actually going to the event or social occasion. In this way, they manage to let go of their self-consciousness and social anxiety, and by accepting that they are shy and working around it, they manage to interact with other people, in much the same way that non-shy people do.

The other thing that successfully shy people do is to get more involved with other people – even at a very trivial level such as making eye contact with and chatting to the checkout person at the supermarket. According to one researcher, the most useful thing that shy people can do is volunteering. Becoming more involved in the lives of other people takes their attention away from themselves and on to other people, and through that they experience more and fuller everyday interactions.

In the modern world, shy people have the opportunity for much "safer" types of social interaction. Baker and Oswald (2010) found that social networking sites like Facebook offered shy people the opportunity to interact with other people in ways which they found less threatening than face-to-face interaction. In a study of 207 female students, they found that shy people felt that the friendships which they developed through Facebook gave them better quality and more supportive friendships. Even though they still struggled with face-to-face relationships, Baker and Oswald argued that their growing social confidence was a benefit in itself, and was likely to reduce loneliness over time.

The important aspect of internet communication of this kind, according to Baker and Oswald, is the control it offers over self-disclosure, something which shy people typically find difficult. Zimbardo and Carducci (2001), for example, found that while most people go through a process of gradual self-disclosure in a developing relationship, shy people tend either to disclose too much in the early stages of a relationship, or too little so that the relationship never progresses beyond a superficial level. There is a downside, though, in that it is shy and isolated individuals who appear to be most vulnerable to cyber-bullying, although there are occasional exceptions.

In developing approaches for extremely shy people to tackle their problem, Zimbardo and Carducci argued that the strategies they needed to adopt were essentially those which are already used by highly social people. They identified eight characteristics of highly popular people which are listed in Table 2.8.

Table 2.8 Habits of highly popular people

Scheduling their social life. Practice makes perfect, and social skills improve with practice.

Thinking positively. Recognising that other people will generally respond positively, not critically, when they are approached.

Engaging in social reconnaissance. Directing one's focus outward to others rather than inwards, and being interested rather than interesting.

Entering conversations gracefully. Noticing how the conversation is going and looking for a chance to step in at an appropriate time. The goal is to help the group have a better conversation.

Handling failure. Popular people are resilient to rebuffs, recognising that they usually arise from external causes which are nothing to do with them.

Managing emotions. Well-liked people have a firm handle on their emotions and tend to shift the focus of interactions from negative to positive wherever possible.

Defusing disagreements. People who can defuse tension or resolve conflicts by proposing compromises, apologising or suggesting joint activities tend to be popular.

Using humour. Humour is a fast track to being liked for all people, and even in threatening situations.

Source: Zimbardo and Carducci (2001)

LONELINESS

Shyness, and a lack of socially satisfying relationships, often results in loneliness. Here again, though, we find that people may mean different things when they use the same word. Most people experience feeling lonely at some point in their lives; perhaps if they have just moved to another town, or when they are coming to terms with the ending of a close personal relationship. But for some people, loneliness is more of a problem than for others.

Cutrona (1982) distinguished between **situational loneliness** – loneliness which occurs as a result of a kind of change in our personal situation – and **chronic loneliness**, which seems to be a subjective experience which doesn't really correlate with social isolation. In fact, a study by Jones (1981) showed that in some cases, people who report themselves as lonely may even have more social contacts than people who don't feel particularly lonely. Conversely, Marangoni and Ickes (1989) argued that some people – particularly those with social skills and personal attention skills deficits – may be unaware that they have fewer social contacts than others, and so may be chronically lonely without realising it.

If we view loneliness as an emotion, however, it becomes clear that what is important is what people actually experience. If some people have only a limited amount of social contact yet remain fairly happy, then it would be reasonably safe to say that they do not experience the emotion of loneliness. For many of those experiencing situational loneliness, the emotion appears to be relatively temporary: if their social contacts widen,

Key Terms
situational loneliness Loneliness which happens as a result of the circumstances in which the person finds themselves.
chronic loneliness An ongoing subjective experience of loneliness which may be experienced despite high levels of social interaction.

either through their own efforts or those of others, their emotional experience tends to disappear.

Internet use and loneliness

Some people experiencing situational loneliness of this type have found that the social contacts they can experience through the internet provides them with a rich and satisfying substitute for "real-world" social experience. Internet games such as Second Life, for example, allow the person to create an avatar who makes friends, has a variety of work and social experiences, develops life-skills and can even acquire an education through one of the universities participating in the scheme. It can be, quite literally, a second life.

Just how much that second virtual life can mean depends on the nature of the person experiencing it. There have been several cases where second life experiences have spilled over into the real world. Perhaps the most famous is the Dave Barmy affair, where a couple became engaged and married as a result of their contact through Second Life, and when he later had a virtual affair it resulted in a real-life divorce (*The Guardian*, 13 November 2008). Since then, a number of other divorces based on virtual experiences – not just Second Life, but also Facebook and Twitter – have been reported. Some participants have set their Second Life avatars up as relationship counsellors or divorce lawyers.

In psychological research dealing with real-world experience, it has been shown that chronically lonely people are much less likely to engage in self-disclosure than people who are not lonely (Williams and Solano, 1983). Self-disclosure is a distinctive feature of intimate relationships, and the lack of it generally means that a relationship remains formal or semi-formal. Lonely people also tend to act differently in social situations. In a series of observational studies, Jones et al (1982) found that people who describe themselves as lonely are generally less talkative, give their companions less attention and ask them fewer questions. When they gave these people specific training in conversational and partner attention skills, they found a significantly lowered rate of reported loneliness.

The internet offers differing opportunities to lonely or shy people, and many studies have shown how people are prepared to engage in quite high levels of self-disclosure on the internet – far more than they would do in interpersonal conversation (Whitty and Joinson, 2008). In addition, Joinson et al (2007) found that self-disclosure varies according to how private or anonymous people feel. If their recipient is more immediately present, or their privacy is reduced, people tend to engage in less self-disclosure online. For some, the internet acts as a personal confident. Chesney (2005) reported such high levels of self-disclosure in online diaries that some of the participants claimed that they would never withhold information from their diary – despite the fact that such diaries are often available for access by others. Similarly, many Facebook users show a remarkable level of self-disclosure, often rendering them vulnerable to trolling and other forms of internet bullying.

Avatars, such as those used in Second Life, can offer safer opportunities for self-disclosure, and some psychologists have recommended their use in clinical settings for this reason. Gaggioli et al (2003) suggested that group therapy using avatars could be more effective than face-to-face group therapy because participants would regard the interaction and the self-disclosure itself as less threatening than they would if they were sharing the information directly. Moreover, they argued, the choice of avatars that the patients make can sometimes offer significant insight into the nature of their psychological problems.

Chronically lonely people also seem to make different attributions about social experiences than people who don't see themselves as lonely. In particular, they are more likely to see interpersonal difficulties in terms of stable, dispositional aspects of other people than in terms of temporary situational ones; which means that they don't feel that they can do anything about them. We will be looking at attribution more closely in Chapter 4, but what this amounts to is that lonely people are particularly passive when it comes to dealing with interpersonal problems. In a study by Horowitz et al (1982), people were asked to think up possible solutions to a set of interpersonal problems. It was noticeable that those who saw themselves as lonely generated far fewer solutions than the others – although when they were dealing with problems that didn't involve people, there was no difference between the two groups.

Kahlbaugh et al (2011) carried out an intervention study in which student volunteers visited elderly people, and spent an hour a week for ten weeks either watching television with them or playing simulated bowling games using a Wii console. The idea was that playing with the Wii was a more sociable and active way of spending the time than simply watching TV, although both groups of students were instructed to be sociable and friendly. The researchers found that those who played the Wii games reported less loneliness than they had at the start of the study – although it is difficult to draw clear conclusions because the sample size was small (35) and there was no comparison with other, non-technological forms of activity such as playing cards or dominoes.

Another intervention with elderly people is the V2me project, developed in Austria, which consists of a virtual sitting room, where users meet a personal coach who takes them through a series of friendship lessons. These were developed by psychologists to help them to meet new people through the internet and to become more socially active. The aim of the programme is for the old people concerned to make sustainable friendships, which will prove a lasting remedy for them at least, in dealing with the problem of loneliness in the older generation (Tantinger and Braun, 2011).

We can see, then, that the internet offers chronically lonely people a way of interacting with others which makes fewer demands on their social skills. Stepanikova et al (2010) found a clear positive correlation between loneliness and the amount of time spent internet browsing. However, whether the increased browsing time leads to loneliness, or whether lonely people are just more inclined to spend time on the internet is open to question.

Talking point 2.2   Loneliness and the internet

Loneliness is a growing problem in our increasingly structured society. Living alone, travelling to and from work by car and shopping online are all common aspects of modern living, and each of them reduces the number of everyday social contacts we experience. For those who find it difficult to join active hobby clubs, the internet may have become their only source of human contact. They live a virtual social life rather than a real one. And people who are chronically shy may embrace this option as a way of not dealing with their shyness.

So the question is: can a virtual social life really substitute for physical contact with other people? Is it psychologically healthy, or does society need to establish other ways that people can make contact with one another? And what forms might such initiatives take?

At a more physical level, researchers have shown that subjective feelings of both sociability and loneliness can even be affected by temperature. In a study of 51 undergraduates and 41 ordinary members of the community, Bargh and Shalev (2011) found that those who saw themselves as lonely tended to take longer baths or showers, and to use warmer water. They also asked people to evaluate warm or cold therapeutic packs, and found that those testing the warm packs showed a decrease in reported loneliness after the test, which was not shown by those evaluating the cold packs. They also experienced increased feelings of inclusion and sociability.

These findings are not suggesting that loneliness as an emotion is purely a matter of physical sensation. Rather, they suggest that subjective feelings of comfort can influence how lonely we feel, or perhaps make it easier for the mind to occupy itself with other thoughts and emotions. It has been well established that context influences how likely we are to retrieve memories, and feeling physically comfortable is part of that context, establishing a framework within which some memories come more easily to mind than others. If we feel good, we are more likely to recall positive experiences and less likely to bring to mind negative ones.

Key Terms

positive emotions
Emotions which enhance personal feelings of well-being or promote social harmony.

POSITIVE EMOTIONS

One of the most striking shortcomings in the psychological literature is its coverage of **positive emotions**. For example, a typical list of human emotions in a major psychology textbook published in 2008 comprised anger, fear, disgust, sadness and surprise in a large table dominating a double-page spread. As a side-line, the author mentioned that the original research being cited had included acceptance, anticipation and joy; but these were left off the main table and not discussed in the chapter. Even including those three, though, we can see that the positive emotions are distinctly under-represented.

While humanistic psychologists and therapists have always worked towards developing positive mental outlooks, the implications of their findings have often been under-recognised – or under-valued. For example, the link between happiness and positive self-esteem is frequently documented, but the emphasis has always been on the self-esteem rather than the happiness. Relatively few theories of emotion have concerned themselves directly with positive emotions such as happiness, pleasure or serenity.

Argyle and Crossland (1987) attempted to re-open this area by conducting a survey in which people were asked to describe positive emotional experiences. From this they developed a list of 24 pleasant situations, such as enjoying a social evening with friends, luxuriating in a long hot bath, feeling successful at work or experiencing awe at the beauty of nature. Then they asked research participants to think about each situation one at a time and describe how being in that situation would make them feel. They used these descriptions to identify four dimensions for positive emotions.

The first dimension was **absorption**, and it was all about the amount of attention or concentration which they demanded. It ranged from private, absorbing experiences to more superficial social ones. The second dimension was called **potency**, and was concerned with how active and capable the person felt. Experiences such as success at sport or work were at one end of the dimension, while experiences like enjoying a hot bath or listening to music were at the opposite end. The third was **altruism**, how far the emotion was other-centred. One end of the scale included commitment activity, like volunteer or charity work; the other end involved more self-indulgent situations, such as receiving a valuable present or engaging in a personal hobby. And the fourth dimension they identified was **spiritual**. At one end it was concerned with personally meaningful experience like enjoying nature or solving a challenging puzzle, while the other end was concerned with pleasant but less meaningful activities, like buying a treat for oneself, or watching an exciting film or TV programme.

These dimensions form a valuable attempt to identify and document some of the wide range of positive emotions which we experience. Gradually, the idea of positive psychology has become more widely known. It received a significant boost when one of its major proponents, Martin Seligman, was elected president of the American Psychological Association and actively promoted positive psychology in his presidential address in 1998. Seligman had become well known in psychology in the 1970s as a result of his work into learned helplessness and depression; but his later research led to an interest in the ways that psychology could be used to enhance happiness.

In his discussion of positive psychology, Seligman emphasised its social as well as its individual aspects. Individual aspects of positive psychology include social experience such as the capacity for love, interpersonal skill and forgiveness, while group aspects included responsibility, nurturance, altruism, civility and tolerance. He saw this as bringing back into psychology an emphasis on the promotion of happiness and positive social experience, which had been present in its early years but lost with the outcomes of the World Wars and the emphasis on measurement and behavioural objectivity which had been

Key Terms

absorption
The degree to which an activity demands concentrated attention.

potency
The strength, or powerfulness of a positive emotion.

altruism
Acting in the interests of others and not oneself.

spiritual
A dimension of positive emotion which includes uplifting sensations, and sometimes religious ones.

characteristic of psychology during most of the 20th century.

Seligman and Csikszentmihalyi (2000) identified three significant aspects of positive psychology. The first of these is about the quality of positive experiences – what makes an experience "better", or more rewarding, than another one. The second has to do with the idea of the positive personality: how characteristic patterns of thinking, **resilience** and other qualities can generate more positive life experiences. This is not taking the view that personality is fixed and unchangeable; it is concerned with the ways in which people can adjust their characteristic patterns of responding to life-events in order to experience a more positive life. The third aspect of positive psychology identified by the researchers is the recognition of the social context – the way that positive psychology can help to promote positive communities and institutions, which serve to enhance the general quality of life and to encourage full self-realisation for the individuals participating in them.

Box 2.3　Positive psychology and mindfulness

The idea of mindfulness has recently attracted attention, not just from those studying positive psychology, but also among popular self-help groups. "Mindfulness" is derived from an ancient Buddhist practice, which involves deliberately paying attention to the here and now, in a non-judgemental manner. Effectively, it asks the person to devote their whole mind to the immediate present, to appreciate the sounds, smells and physical sensations of the moment, and to dwell on these without thinking of the future, the past, or making other associations which will form a mental distraction from the here and now.

Mindfulness also has connections with the state of mind which the Gestalt therapists aimed for in the 1930s and subsequently. Their classic example was to use an orange, or a similar object, and to focus exclusively on it without reference to anything else. That meant keeping one's whole mind on its texture, scent, shape and orangeness without distraction. It's not quite the same; mindfulness doesn't involve external objects, for example, but the idea of shutting out the memories, worries, ideas and distractions which we experience most of the time in our day-to-day living is similar.

Both techniques allow the individual to experience a temporary respite from the constant minor stresses brought about by everyday random thoughts and images. As a result, they can promote a sense of calm and personal integrity, which helps to produce a positive mood and a generally positive mental outlook. This in turn promotes positive social interactions and effective coping with minor setbacks, which is why it has become a significant aspect of modern positive psychology.

Key Terms

resilience
The ability to "bounce back" and take positive action again after negative life-experiences.

In 2013, Guadagno et al carried out an investigation into internet videos which had "gone viral" – that is, which had become widely viewed and shared between viewers. They found that it was the videos which elicited positive emotions like joy and humour which were most likely to be forwarded. The next most likely were those eliciting feelings of alertness and attentiveness, and the least, not surprisingly, were boring or dull videos. Videos which elicited anger or disgust were more likely to be forwarded than dull ones, but much less likely than the positive ones.

HAPPINESS

One of the ongoing debates is whether happiness, in general, is a response to circumstances, or a dispositional trait. In 1987, Costa et al argued strongly that it was the latter, showing that some people are consistently happy, and respond to events in a consistently positive way, while others are less so, regardless of what actually happens to them. Some researchers (e.g. Lopez and Snyder, 2009) believe that there is a genetic "set-point" for happiness, citing examples of lottery winners and others who revert to their previous levels of happiness once the initial euphoria is over. Other researchers, though, challenge this idea, arguing that a significant number of people do show dramatic changes in their happiness levels as a result of life-events and changes in cognitive strategy (e.g. Headey, 2008).

Seligman himself explored how people's tendencies towards positive thinking could be enhanced. His early research had shown how consistent negative experience can produce learned helplessness, in which both people and animals fail to make efforts to improve their situations because previous efforts have been unsuccessful. Seligman found, though, that people are also capable of learned optimism, revising their thought processes and outlook towards positive anticipations and positive attributions. This made a great difference to their everyday experiences and ability to cope (Seligman, 1998). Other researchers also found that the types of attributions which people make can strongly influence their tendencies towards positive or negative thinking styles, and Cheng and Furnham (2001) showed how a positive attributional style can be a significant predictor of both happiness and mental health. We will be looking at attributions more closely in Chapter 4.

A number of other concepts have emerged from the study of positive psychology and happiness. One of these is the idea of **flourishing**, or optimal human functioning. Fredrickson and Losada (2005) argued that it consists of four parts: goodness, generativity, growth and resilience (see Table 2.9). Another, as we saw in Box 2.3, is the idea of mindfulness, which includes the ability to focus fully on what is at hand instead of being constantly distracted and worried about other things. Brown et al (2007) demonstrated how learning to practice mindfulness can cause significant reductions in depression, stress, anxiety and even chronic pain – and generally make people more likely to feel happy.

Moods

Enhancing positive emotions, however, doesn't necessarily mean that we want to be happy and jolly all the time. We all experience fluctuations in mood, and having a period of quiet reflection or even sadness isn't always a bad thing; it

Key Terms
flourishing
Living life to the full, utilising one's potential and enjoying it.

Table 2.9 Aspects of flourishing

Goodness: happiness, contentment and effective performance.

Generativity: making life better for future generations.

Growth: the positive use of personal and social assets.

Resilience: survival and growth after enduring hardship.

Source: Fredrickson and Losada (2005)

can mean that we appreciate the other times in our lives more, for example. Often, if we are in a slightly depressed mood, we quite enjoy dwelling on it for a while. The last thing we want is for someone to come along to "jolly us out of it".

Van den Tol and Edwards (2013) conducted a **qualitative** study to explore why people like to listen to sad music when they are feeling depressed or sad. Their participants gave various explanations, which the researchers classified into two groups: strategies and functions. The set of reasons they described as strategies included choosing music to match their current mood, using music to trigger nostalgic memories, choosing it because it gave a helpful or hopeful message, or choosing it just because it was beautiful music. The "functional" reasons included using music to re-experience an emotion so as to be able to move on from it, choosing sad music to remind yourself that you are not alone and that troubles are part of the human experience, and choosing music which acted as a friend, sharing and understanding the mood.

We have all experienced occasions where we feel disinclined to cooperate with other people's requests or demands. Milberg and Clark (2011) showed how people are more likely to comply with requests when they are in a happy mood than if they are feeling neutral. Similarly, if they are in an angry mood they are less likely to cooperate. The importance of the requests didn't seem to matter, it was their general mood which made people more or less inclined to respond.

Moods can also affect our moral judgements. In one study by Pagano and Debono (2011), people were shown film extracts designed to induce either a happy or sad mood. They were then asked to carry out a number of moral reasoning tasks. Not everyone was affected the same way by their moods. Some of their participants were what the researchers classified as high self-monitors – in other words, people who were very aware of their personal states and how it might affect them. Those people's judgements were not affected by mood. But the "low self-monitors" were quite strongly affected, producing more sophisticated and principled moral reasoning if they were in a positive mood than if they were in a negative one.

Humour

One well-known and often used strategy for dealing with negative moods is humour. While sometimes, as we have seen, people prefer to stay with a sad mood, at other times it helps to have something to take our attention away from it and lift our spirits. As with many of the positive emotions (and other emotions too, as we have seen) social factors are a very important facet of the experience. With humour, particularly, social factors are more than important, since humour is by definition a social phenomenon.

Bell et al (1986) explored different personality characteristics associated with humour, and found that those people who were judged to be humorous, and who typically used humour in social situations, also tended to be particularly good at both **self-monitoring** and at identifying the social cues coming from other people. They also found a relationship between assertiveness and humour, and suggested that being more assertive made it easier for people to test out social interaction strategies such as humour, so they were more likely to receive positive feedback and continue to adopt humorous social strategies.

In 1969, Emerson pointed out that humorous remarks and jokes tend to be judged differently from other forms of social interaction. The consensus is that they don't officially "count" as part of a serious exchange, so people can take risks with humour which they wouldn't feel able to take if they felt that the remark was going to be taken seriously. This means that humour can become an important social tool for defusing tense situations and encouraging people to take a fresh look at a problem. It can serve other purposes too: Kahn (1989) identified five primary functions that humour serves for individuals and groups, which are listed in Table 2.10.

Table 2.10 Functions of humour

Coping. Humour helps people to become detached from potentially threatening aspects of their situation, so that they can cope with it better (e.g., workers in emergency services may use what seems like callous humour, but it helps them to cope).

Reframing. Humour allows people to see things in a new light, or to restructure their experience so as to perceive different implications from it.

Communicating. Humour allows people to say things they would otherwise not be able to say, for example in emotionally significant contexts like bereavement, where certain comments would be socially "taboo".

Expressing hostility. Humour is sometimes used to express hostile feelings, such as racist or sexist opinions. It is framed as humour to pre-empt social disapproval, and also to ridicule or derogate members of the disliked group.

Constructing identities. "In-jokes" are often used to maintain group cohesion and show that the speaker is a member of that particular social group.

Source: Kahn (1989)

Whatever its function, it is clear that humour, and the ability to be humorous in a socially acceptable way, is definitely a social asset. Cowan and Little (2013) showed that in a study of social and sexual attraction, those who were seen as witty were definitely favoured as potential candidates for a date, particularly in the case of men. Witty women were also favoured, but to a lesser degree than their male examples.

Exchanging humorous emails has been one of the life enrichments of the information age, but it can sometimes disguise underlying social issues. Kenny and Euchler (2012) looked at daily life in an organisation in which the staff spent an unusually large amount of time sending humorous emails to one another. They found that the humour was used to subvert various forms of control, including the rigid application of managerial authority and gender norms. Effectively, the use of humour relaxed tensions which would otherwise have created difficult and unpleasant situations: it was subversive and uncontrollable, but had a positive effect on the working situation.

Theories of humour

There have been a number of theories put forward to explain humour – and it seems likely that all of them are correct to some extent. Freud (1901) regarded humour as an example of an ego-defence mechanism, in which the use of humour served to cover up or distract attention from deeper conflicts or issues. As most people can testify, this is certainly one of ways that humour can be used, and it can be very effective. But there are other explanations as well.

Talking point 2.3   Different types of humour

Humour is used in many different ways and in many different situations. Thinking about your everyday experiences with friends, family and at work or college, how many examples of humour can you identify?

Do these examples represent different types of humour? Do some people typically use different forms of humour than others? Have you personally (ignoring the stereotypes) found cultural differences in the sorts of humorous comments or jokes that people make?

Try discussing these matters with your friends or family: are your ideas similar to theirs?

One related approach to understanding humour is known as relief theory. Buijzen and Valkenberg (2004) proposed that humour acts as a homeostatic mechanism for reducing built-up nervous tension. Because humour can reveal our unconscious desires and (at least partly) overcome our social inhibitions, it allows us to dissipate and relieve the nervous tension built up in social situations. When we laugh, we release this nervous energy in much the same way as laughing when we are being tickled relieves the tension from the tickling. This is why difficult social situations are often dealt with or defused by humour and jokes.

Other theories have adopted a more cognitive approach. **Incongruity theory** (e.g., Boyd, 2004) sees humour as arising from shifts in perspective, which highlight incongruities or differences between reality and the ideas around that reality. This is similar to the onto-epistemic theory of humour proposed by Marteinson (2006), who argues that it is the clash between our perceptions which produces the reaction of laughter. We use two sets of perceptions in our day-to-day living: one which relates to the real or actual world, and one which is all about social reality and social assumptions. For the most part, they are reasonably congruous – that is, they fit with what we expect, but sometimes they clash. At such times, the awareness that our social world doesn't seem to fit reality produces a cognitive impasse which we react to with humour.

There have been many theories of humour, but then there are also many kinds of humour. Not many of the theories are able to take into account all of its many variations. One theory, known as the **benign violation theory**, sees humour in general as happening when (a) our idea of how the world "should" be is threatened or violated; (b) we perceive that threatening as harmless or

Key Terms

incongruity theory
A theory of humour which states that we are amused by things we find distinctively unusual or disconnected.

benign violation theory
A theory of humour which emphasises challenging assumptions about the world in a non-threatening way.

benign; and (c) we perceive both of these interpretations simultaneously. This generalisation, they argue, applies to a wide range of different types of jokes and humour, but it is questionable whether it can really be regarded as all-inclusive.

Following on from this, Hurley et al (2011) proposed that humour serves an evolutionary function because it strengthens our cognitive ability to detect mistaken or incongruous reasoning, and so helps our problem-solving ability. Again, while this is true of some forms of humour, it doesn't take account of its social-tension defusing functions, or even just the way that it is used casually in everyday life.

Pundt and Herrmann (2014) looked at how humour is used in exchanges between managers and their subordinates. They found that humour from the leader could help to establish high-quality relationships, particularly if it is affiliative humour rather than aggressive humour. They explored the potential of a programme to help sensitise leaders to the use of humour, and particularly to the distinction between aggressive and affiliative humour, and concluded that it was useful to help people to identify habitual ways of behaving, and to improve relationships at work. But they cautioned against too much formal "humour training", as it could lead to emotional exhaustion and lack of spontaneity. It could be useful in some circumstances, they argued, but should be used with care.

Studying humour is always somewhat problematic: what one person finds funny another does not. Some humour is completely situation and time-dependent and has no meaning outside its context; and there are massive cultural variations in humour. Heim in 1936 published an extensive study of humour, presenting people from various cultural backgrounds with different types of jokes, and came to the conclusion that the main outcome of her study was that researchers should be extremely wary of trying to classify types of humour or set up any rules on the subject. She concluded that it would probably just end up as a listing of individual jokes found funny by individual people.

Humour forms part of our everyday social interactions, and as such is a significant aspect of human social behaviour. Its myriad uses can shift awkward social situations into positive ones, augment our meanings, redefine situations, and establish common bonds in adversity. As part of the discourse of everyday living, it is an important aspect of our communication. We will look at other aspects of communication in the next chapter.

Chapter 2: Summary

1. Emotions are a crucial part of human experience, affecting how we interact with other people as well as how affecting our physiology and cognitions. Sensitivity to other people's emotions is important in social interaction.

2. Loving can take many forms, ranging from close companionship to intense passion.

3. Limerence is a name given to an all-consuming and self-centred romantic passion, which may be a separate emotion from other types of love.

4. Relationships need to be maintained through strengthening behaviours. Relationship breakdown often follows distinct stages, dealing with social as well as emotional consequences.

5. Bereavement can produce many different states of mind and wildly different mood swings. Typically, people will pass through several stages, and may be helped by counselling.

6. Anger is a significant aspect of grieving, which can easily become displaced onto other people such as care staff or doctors. As an emotion, anger is generally seen as a reaction to a perceived threat of some kind.

7. Shy people tend to interact with others differently than non-shy people. The internet can be a significant way in which shy people can overcome their social anxieties.

8. Loneliness appears to be a subjective state rather than an observable condition. Subjective feelings of loneliness may be affected by many factors, including levels of activity and internet use.

9. Positive emotions such as happiness can be enhanced by positive cognitive strategies, and by other techniques such as mindfulness. Moods are transient states which can be affected by, and also affect, choices of social interaction or environmental stimuli such as music.

10. No single theory of humour can address all aspects of humour. However, two common observations are that it often involves surprise, and that humour is often exempt from the normal rules of social behaviour.

Chapter 3

Contents

Communicating with others

3

The past couple of chapters have shown how social human beings are. But what does being social actually mean? An important part of being social is interacting with other people, in one way or another. That interaction might take place through language, through signs and indicators, or through symbols of one form or another – and all of these are forms of communication. Communication may be direct or indirect, personal or general; but it exerts a constant influence on how we feel, what we understand, and what we do.

In this chapter we will be looking at the different forms that communication can take. It can be direct, in the form of messages exchanged between specific people, or it can be indirect, in the form of information which is transmitted less consciously through symbols, or through the shared understandings of social meaning. Communication can also be closed or open: closed communication is about conveying very specific, deliberate messages to specific targets; open communication is available to many people, and can take many forms, including variations of language and symbolic conventions.

Communication isn't just about the information which is transmitted. How that information is received depends upon our knowledge of its context and social purpose, what we understand about the people we are communicating with and what they understand about us, and more general forms of social awareness. Social scripts, schemas and social roles all have their part to play in our communication with one another, and we will be looking at these in the later part of this chapter.

Our most immediate form of social communication, however, comes through face-to-face interaction. We tend to take it for granted, and it comes easily to most of us; but it is far from being simple. We talk to one another using words, but that isn't all. We also convey information in all sorts of other ways, like the posture we adopt, the clothes that we wear, the settings that we choose to interact in, and so on. Even when we talk directly to one another, there are different social meanings conveyed by our choice of words, our tones of voice, timings and hesitations, and the social knowledge we already have about the speaker and the situation. Face-to-face communication is direct, but it is far from being simple.

NON-VERBAL COMMUNICATION

What we call **non-verbal communication**, or NVC, is the most basic form of communication, and much of it is shared by other animals. In humans, it can serve several purposes, for instance, the set of functions identified by Argyle in 1984 (Table 3.1). These purposes are achieved using several different types of **non-verbal cues** – that is, signals which we use to convey information without using words. They include facial expression, eye-contact, posture and gesture, proxemics and touch, paralanguage and dress; and each of these is important enough in human communication that they are worth looking at in detail.

Facial expression

This is one of the first forms of non-verbal cues which comes to mind. We smile when pleased, frown when angry or puzzled, scowl when annoyed. People have very mobile faces, which means that we can produce a large range of different expressions. Sometimes, these are idiosyncratic – that is, adopted by just one individual or small group; sometimes they are cultural in origin; but many facial expressions appear to be universal: they are found in all human cultures.

Emoticons – that is, small symbols used in typed language – often take the form of simplified faces, looking happy, sad, quizzical or angry to enhance

Table 3.1 Functions of non-verbal communication

Assisting speech	e.g., stressing important words
Replacing speech	e.g., shrugging the shoulders to signal "I don't know"
Signalling attitudes	e.g., adopting a bored facial expression when not interested
Signalling emotions	e.g., hugging a close friend to express pleasure at seeing them

Source: Adapted from Argyle (1975)

what is being said. Yuki et al (2007) compared Japanese and American students in a study of how they recognised emoticons. They found that all of the students recognised the basic emotions being expressed through the emoticons, but that there were cultural differences in terms of whether they considered the eyes or the mouths to be more important in signifying happiness. Japanese students gave the highest rating to faces with happy eyes, while American students gave the highest ratings to faces with happy mouths.

So there was a shared understanding of the basic aspects of emotional expression (in this case, happiness); but some cultural differences in emphasis and the specific ways that the intensity of the emotion was judged – a difference which Yuki et al concluded was a result of cultural socialisation. We will come back to the use of emoticons when we look at communication through written language, but they show us how important, and how universally recognised, basic facial expressions can be.

These basic expressions may also be shared by some animals. Charles Darwin argued in 1872 that the expressions indicating basic emotions such as hunger or fear are innate, and can be seen in other mammals as well as humans. For example, the fear response in many mammals involves high-pitched whimpers and the pilomotor response, in which the hair stands on end. Since we are relatively hairless, this shows in humans as "goose-pimples". This response is common to dogs, cats, chimpanzees and monkeys, as well as in humans. Similarly, most mammals share the "fear-grin", in which the skin is pulled back from the teeth and the mouth is stretched wide. Dogs, as dog-owners are aware, can smile or look tense, and for Darwin all this was evidence of our common evolutionary origins.

Facial expressions often signal attitudes, and this too may show some connections with other species. For example, Goodall (1974) observed that young chimpanzees show a "play-face", which is very similar to the "play-face" of children. It signals that what they are doing is a game. But human beings also use these signals in more sophisticated ways, such as indicating social approval

Figure 3.1 Emoticons

or sanctions as well as personal feelings. Friedman et al (1980) showed how the facial expressions of television presenters changed to indicate approval or contempt, depending on the topic that they were discussing. In one case – the 1976 American presidential elections – the differences in facial expressions when TV presenters talked about Carter were strikingly different from those used when talking about Ford.

It is possible, too, that the facial expressions that we show can influence the emotions that we actually feel. This is known as the **facial feedback hypothesis**, and one of the main ways it has been investigated is by a task developed by Strack et al (1988), in which people are asked to hold a pen in their mouths while doing various tasks. The pen has to be held either between the lips, producing a pouting expression usually associated with negative emotions, or between the teeth, producing a facial expression similar to smiling. In their study, Strack et al found that participants in the "smiling" condition rated cartoons as more funny than they did if they were in the "pouting" one.

In a second part of the study, Strack et al asked a new set of participants two questions: firstly, was the cartoon itself funny; and, secondly, how amused did it make them feel? While there was little difference between the two conditions for the first question, there was considerable difference for the second. This is an important part of the study, because it was disregarded in a meta-analysis of replications by Wagenmakers and others, who claimed to have shown that Strack's finding didn't hold up to scrutiny. Although their meta-analysis was unpublished, it received quite a lot of publicity, but it is questionable how valid their findings were. For example, over half of the studies in the meta-analysis had found a strong facial feedback effect, and in a commentary, Strack suggested that it would have been more useful to compare the two sets of studies, looking at why the results were so different, rather than averaging them all out to a zero result.

In a different study using the same technique, Bilewicz and Kogan (2014) found that facial feedback could even influence intergroup attitudes. They asked Polish participants to evaluate a story concerning intergroup contact with Romanians, who were selected because they were the third most commonly disliked national group in Poland. Those in the "smiling" condition expressed more positive attitudes towards the group, while those in the "pouting" condition expressed either neutral or negative attitudes. In another investigation, Hennenlotter et al (2009) showed that people who had experienced Botox treatment, paralysing facial muscles which are commonly involved in angry expressions, reacted less emotionally to anger-inducing tasks. The evidence overall, then, suggests that facial expression can be a factor in influencing how we ourselves feel, as well as how others feel in response to what we are communicating.

Osgood (1966) suggested that there are seven main groups of facial expressions which are common to human societies: surprise, fear, happiness, sadness, anger, interest, and disgust or contempt. Some may be shared with other species, but other facial expressions seem to be unique to human beings. Eibl-Eiblesfeldt (1972) showed, for example, that the "eyebrow flash" of recognition which happens when we are greeting a known person seems to be a cultural universal for humans, but is not used by other animals.

Key Terms
facial feedback hypothesis The idea that we infer our own emotions from the expressions on our faces.

Eye-contact

Eye-contact is another powerful signal. Even fleeting eye-contact is something which we often try to avoid, in case it is taken wrongly; and prolonged eye-contact is really powerful. Moreover, it can signal either affection or hostility; with someone you are fond of it signals affection, but with a stranger it can mean either deep interest or an aggressive challenge.

Attraction isn't only signalled by the length of eye-contact – the pupil of the eye dilates when we are looking at something we like (which is why restaurant lighting is usually quite dim). When people were asked to rate photographs for attractiveness, they consistently chose images of people with dilated pupils as more attractive (Hess, 1965), although they were almost always unaware of the basis for their choice.

However, prolonged gaze states that the recipient is the subject of deep interest, and that can be very threatening. Ellsworth and Langer (1976) showed how prolonged gaze is very likely to invoke flight – people will withdraw from such a threatening situation. Others may respond angrily, but not many of us can disregard it altogether. That in itself tells us something about the power of non-verbal communication, and it is interesting, too, that reactions to eye-contact are equally strong in many mammals.

When we are in conversation with other people, we use eye-contact to indi- cate when it is the other person's turn to speak. Kendon (1967) filmed a number of conversations between pairs of students who were asked to "get acquainted" with one another. These showed that we use quite a sophisticated set of social rules of eye-contact to regulate our conversations. For example, the speaker will tend to avoid eye-contact while she or he is speaking, but will look up at the end of an utterance, as if to "hand over" to the other person. The listener, on the other hand, tends to maintain eye-contact, and indeed, if we find that the person we are talking to is looking away from us for any length of time, we often conclude that they are not paying attention to what we are saying.

Eye-contact is also an important signal in regulating social interaction. Argyle et al (1968) showed that when normally sighted people are deprived of this cue because one of the pair is wearing dark glasses, conversations are much more hesitant and include more pauses and interruptions. And a study by Argyle and Dean (1965) showed that there is a relationship between conversational distance and eye-contact. Subjects who were asked to converse for three minutes across a distance of 10 feet made more eye-contact than those talking at a more comfortable distance of about 6 feet. When the subjects were standing so close to one another that they felt uncomfortable, at just 2 feet, they made far less eye-contact than in the other two conditions.

Breaking the conventional pattern can also be used as communication in its own right. Dovidio and Ellyson (1982) showed how one strategy people use to maintain social control over the interaction is to maintain prolonged eye-contact while speaking, and to look away while listening. As such, it can be a signal of power and status in social interaction, and is often used that way by politicians and other public figures.

Box 3.1   The power of gaze

Being stared at is disturbing for apes as well as humans. Zoo animals learn to cope with it because most visitors don't stay for long. Back in the early 1970s, I undertook a research project studying the social behaviour of chimpanzees in Chester Zoo, which had a big social group with a large and diverse living space. From the first day, I found that they had a strong reaction to my observations, which involved my looking – staring – at them for much longer than ordinary zoo visitors. I was generally behind a strong glass screen, but during the first week of my observations the dominant male of the group frequently dug up chunks of mud from the bank of the island, and hurled them at me to signal his displeasure.

Another mature female, Jeannie, didn't try to throw mud while I was behind the screen; but on the first day of my observations, she settled down in a hollow facing my window, and watched me steadily while I observed the troop. From then on she continued with her everyday activities, apparently taking no notice of me. I thought she had simply become accustomed to my presence, but learned differently on the day I was late. Hurrying to the chimpanzee enclosure, I found that they had already been released to the island, so rather than miss observation time, I stood on the pavement at the side of the moat and made my recordings from there.

At one point I saw Jeannie on the other side of the island tearing up a chunk of grass and mud from the bank. She then wandered nonchalantly over towards me with one hand behind her back, and sat down facing me. Being a little suspicious I glanced at my watch and noted the time. Ten full minutes later – a long time for anyone to wait – she suddenly hurled the chunk of mud, quite accurately. I caught the movement and jumped immediately to one side, so that it missed me – but if I hadn't been on the alert, it would have hit. I was impressed by her planning, and also by the message that my staring was still unwelcome, whether the troop seemed to ignore it or not.

A gorilla who I also used to observe didn't like my staring any more than the male chimpanzee did. When he saw me, he would come down to his moat, wait for a while with his hand behind his back, and then suddenly hit the water hard, creating a huge splash and soaking me and any other zoo visitors within reach. What was even more impressive was that when I revisited the zoo some 12 years later, he showed that he remembered me with the same statement!

Gesture and posture

Gestures are specific actions which we make during communication, either amplifying it or as the full communication in itself. They are usually made with the hands and arms during speech, but may involve other parts of the body such as the head. They are often used to amplify and illustrate speech, and there are cultural as well as individual differences in the amount of gesture which is used: people from some cultures have a more expressive conversational style than those in others, and so use more gestures when they are talking.

Gestures can have very precise, culturally specific meanings. For example, most Western cultures have a specific gesture to indicate that someone is "crazy". In some cultures, this is expressed by tapping the side of the forehead, in others by twirling the finger in the air by the side of the head; and there are other signals too. There are also some cases where a gesture with one meaning in one culture can have an entirely opposite meaning in a different culture. Many hitchhikers in Europe, for instance, found that the "thumbs-up" gesture, while OK in Northern Europe and Britain, had an insulting meaning in several of the Mediterranean countries and was therefore rather unsuitable when asking someone for a lift!

Using gestures can also affect the nature of our communication. Parzuchowski and Wojciszke (2014) found that asking people to put their hand on their heart when they were making a potentially negative social comment resulted in far more honesty in the participants' behaviour than they showed without the gesture. Asked to judge whether particularly unattractive women were physically attractive, their normal response was to tell a "white lie". But when they were asked to make the gesture signalling honesty before commenting, they were far more truthful.

Posture involves the whole orientation of the body. Where gestures are often used to signal specific messages, posture is a powerful signal of general attitude – so powerful, indeed, that we generally take a message conveyed by posture as a more reliable indicator of someone's attitude than what they actually say. In fact, the word "attitude" originally meant the physical posture that someone was adopting. The fact that it now refers to our mental orientation shows how powerful an indicator of attitudes posture is. We instantly recognise a casual posture, an aggressive stance or a relaxed, friendly position.

One of the more interesting uses of posture in conversation occurs when we are listening closely or in deep conversation with someone else. At such times, the two people concerned will often adopt the same physical posture – a phenomenon known as **postural echo**. It is thought that this provides an unconscious message that we are interested in what the person is saying, and on the same wavelength as they are.

McGinley et al (1975) showed how the posture which someone adopts affects whether we are likely to like them, and also whether we see them as powerful. An open stance, such as leaning back in a chair with legs extended and knees and feet apart, tends to be interpreted as more likeable and a sign of confidence. More closed postures, such as having the legs or arms crossed, are seen as implying that the person is being less open and more self-protective, so we are less likely to like them. Similarly, Knapp et al (1974) demonstrated that minor self-grooming gestures, like running the fingers through the hair or touching the face, are often interpreted by observers as a sign of deception.

Proxemics and touch

From our earliest years we learn very specific rules about **proxemics** – that is, what we consider to be an acceptable distance between ourselves and other people during social interaction. It varies for different forms of interaction, and for different relationships; for example, people signal their degree of emotional closeness by the physical distance they maintain between themselves and others. Lovers sit much closer together than friends, and they in turn sit closer to one another than two strangers would.

Hall (1968) identified four main interpersonal distances: intimate (up to about 18 inches), personal (up to about 4 feet), social (up to about 12 feet) and public (up to about 18 feet). But these distances were representative of the typical UK and US cultures of the time; in many cultures, particularly Middle Eastern ones, the acceptable social distance for strangers is much less than that, which can make conversations between people from Western and Middle Eastern cultures quite awkward, as each person strives to achieve what they feel to be a comfortable social distance.

These preferences appear to have remained reasonably consistent over time. Beaulieu (2004) explored the personal distances used by Anglo Saxons, Asians, people from Mediterranean cultures and Latin Americans. She found that Anglo Saxons tended to maintain the largest personal distances when interacting, and also preferred to orient themselves to the side of the interviewer, rather than sitting face to face. Asians preferred less personal distance

Key Terms

proxemics
The study of personal space.

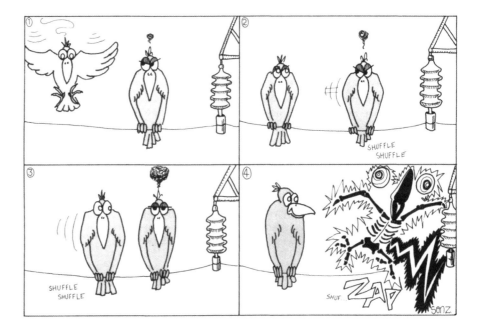

than the Anglo Saxons, but more than the other two groups, who preferred to sit face to face and quite close to the other people.

There are also individual preferences in what we know as our personal space. Some people feel more comfortable with a larger distance between themselves and others, and can find very close contact quite distressing. Others like to be physically close to the people they are with, and even in physical contact with them. When we are in public, we often defend our personal space, such as by using coats or bags to maintain distance between us and other people.

Touch is an even more powerful social signal than distance, as we might expect, given its primeval association with vulnerability and even physical threat. As with personal space, there are conventions about what sort of touch is acceptable in different social situations. Jourard (1966) asked white Western college students to describe which parts of the body could acceptably be touched. In general, they only considered touching the hands or sometimes the shoulders of the other person to be acceptable for family members or same-sex friends. Touch is also used as a signal of power and status. Higher-status individuals, such as senior managers, may often place an arm across the shoulders of a lower-status employee, to signal approval or inclusiveness; but lower-status employees don't make these kinds of contacts with those in higher positions (Henley, 1977).

Touch is a powerful social influence, and we are not always aware of how much it affects us. Seger et al (2014) found that even casual touching could significantly reduce implicit prejudiced attitudes towards other social groups, even though it didn't affect the explicit attitudes which participants expressed. They found that these influences were consistently reliable, even though the people concerned were completely unconscious of them.

In another study, Schirmer et al (2015) found that even watching images of people touching one another can affect how we judge those people. They showed their participants pictures of two people interacting, half of which showed casual, socially acceptable touching and half of which showed people interacting without making any physical contact. They found that the characters being portrayed were judged as being more likeable and more positive if they were touching than when they weren't, even though recordings of the direction of participants' gaze didn't show them paying any particular attention to the touching itself. The effect seems to have been relatively automatic, and also unconscious, which indicates how powerful a part touch can play in our social communication.

Dress

Dress, too, has always been a powerful medium of communication. Uniforms signal occupations, social roles, power and authority. High fashion signals wealth and luxurious living, while much street fashion implies a deliberate rejection of those values. Business people are expected to wear formal, neat clothing, while those in artistic or creative occupations receive different expectations. Sometimes, both religious and social beliefs are indicated by costume; for example, the wearing of the chador by women in some Muslim countries makes a statement about the role of women in those societies, as well as about religious belief.

Much modern fashion in Western societies is concerned with projecting specific images, Moreover, the way we interpret these images is highly sophisticated – after all, we are trained in it from the moment we first become aware of advertisements! These images often contain what we know as **implicit personality theories,** the idea being that they actually make statements about what type of person the wearer is. Someone who wears bright, fashionable clothes would be seen by others as a different type of personality – more outgoing and sociable – than someone who wears muted or neutral colours in old-fashioned or drab styles.

That doesn't mean, of course, that these implicit personality theories are correct. Most of us are aware of what a given style of dress symbolises, and many people deliberately choose to project a specific image for a specific social situation, while dressing completely differently in other circumstances. And users of internet **avatars** may elect to have their avatar dress in wildly different clothing, to express an aspect of their own personality which rarely comes to the fore in their everyday lives.

Paralanguage

Paralanguage is another important non-verbal cue. It is all about how we say things, rather than the words we actually say. When we talk, we use different tones of voice, vocal "fillers" such as "er" or "um", and differences in how rapidly we speak, and these are all non-verbal cues. They augment the words we are using, and so help us to clarify what we mean. And they can also be used to control the conversation. People often use these as strategies to stop other people from interrupting them, as a message that says "I haven't finished what I'm saying yet."

Tones of voice can also be a powerful non-verbal signal about how competent or authoritative we are. For example, speaking with a high-pitched voice is often seen as reducing the credibility of what we are saying (Apple et al, 1979). Advisers to politicians often suggest that they should use a deep authoritative voice for this reason – the classic example being former British Prime Minister Margaret Thatcher, who consciously deepened her voice and slowed down her

---

Key Terms

avatar
A fictional image of a character, used in computer gaming to represent the player.

paralanguage
Non-verbal cues contained in how people say things, such as in tones of voice, pauses or "um" and "er" noises.

rate of speech, as a strategy for enhancing her media credibility before winning her first General Election in 1979.

Okado et al (2012) explored the way we link particular emotions with musical intervals. We experience some of these as dissonant, and interpret them as conveying negative emotions, while other intervals are experienced as consonant, and pleasant to hear, and we associate these with positive emotions and friendliness. They found that in conversations where two people were agreeing with one another, the pitch of the last word by one of the pair was consonantly related to the pitch of the first thing that the other person said in reply. But in conversations where the two people were disagreeing, the pitch of the final utterance was dissonant with the pitch of the first utterance of the next person.

How we say things matters, too. Whether we talk fluently or not is often taken as a sign of competence. Speech errors can increase dramatically if we are nervous or unsure; and these too can be interpreted as non-verbal cues. The use of vocal fillers in conversation, such as "er" and "um", hesitancies in speech, or the use of phrases such as "you know", "kind of" and "I guess" can often reduce credibility, particularly in a formal situation such as in court (Erikson et al, 1978).

USING NON-VERBAL COMMUNICATION

All of these non-verbal cues are important aspects of direct communication. Ekman and Friesen (1969) identified five different types of non-verbal signals, which are listed in Table 3.2.

As you may have noticed, any given type of non-verbal cue can serve several different functions. The most powerful ones, such as tone of voice, eye-contact or facial expression, can serve as illustrators and affect displays or regulators, and we can use them interchangeably. Any social situation involves innumerable complex meanings, and non-verbal signals may be communi-

Table 3.2 Types of non-verbal signals

Name	Function	Examples
Emblems	Signals with a well-defined meaning, standing for a specific idea or concept.	A policeman's uniform, technician's coat, dressing as a "Goth"
Illustrators	Non-verbal actions which accompany speech, and help to show meaning or intention.	A warm tone of voice to indicate approval or sympathy.
Affect displays	Indicators of emotional states or "states of mind".	Body posture to signal depression, tone of voice or smiling to indicate friendliness.
Regulators	Non-verbal signals which help social interactions to take place smoothly.	Eye-contact used to check that a listener has understood or is still listening.
Adaptors	(Usually) involuntary non-verbal signals occurring at times of uncertainty.	Clearing the throat before public speaking, playing with pencils in meetings.

source: Adapted from Ekman and Friesen (1969)

cating messages on a number of different levels simultaneously. We call them direct communication, but really they can be both direct and indirect.

One of the striking aspects of non-verbal communication is the way that we unconsciously copy one another. We have already seen how we often echo the posture of the person we are talking to. The same applies to facial expressions: someone who is smiling generally elicits smiles in return from the other people around them (with the exception of London tube passengers, of course). These responses may even be hard-wired. We have "mirror neurones" in the brain which respond to other people's expressions of emotions by stimulating related areas in our own brains. Other physiological measures suggest similar effects. Spapé et al (2013) examined the brain activity (EEG) and facial muscle reactions of partners in computer games and found that the two players tended to show similar facial expressions of emotion and similar brainwaves at the same times, whether they were playing co-operatively or competitively. The more competitive the gaming got, the more synchronised the players' emotions became.

Non-verbal communication involves much more than just using cues. It is about social meanings, and the importance of the social activities that we are doing. As Harré pointed out in 1979, social interaction isn't just a collection of discrete acts; it takes place in meaningful episodes. So if we really want to understand what is going on, we need to look at those episodes as a whole. That means looking at the whole context, including the people concerned, how they express themselves, the cultural context and history of what is going on, the setting in which events are taking place, and so on.

Ritual

Ritual is a good example of this. It is a deeply meaningful form of communication in any human society, and often non-verbal in its form; but it is about complete episodes, not individual acts or actions. And we can only really understand rituals if we look at the social meaning of what is going on.

For example, every human society has rituals to deal with death and bereavement, although the form of the ritual may vary from one culture to another. These rituals are important for structuring the bereaved person's experience, and giving them a socially acceptable way of expressing their personal grief. By prescribing what should happen and when, these rituals provide a "script" for the event, which draws on any number of different verbal and non-verbal cues to make up a meaningful whole. The ritual is the episode of social experience, in Harré's terms, and provides a framework within which that experience can be understood with the minimal amount of explanation.

A set of studies by Norton and Gino (2014) showed how useful rituals can be, even to people who don't necessarily "believe" in the religion concerned. Their first study was a retrospective one in which they asked their participants, who were recruited online, and had an average age of 33, to describe a recent bereavement. Half of them were also asked to describe a coping ritual they had performed at the time, and they found that those who recalled their ritual also reported feeling less grief about the loss that they had experienced – regardless of whether they subscribed to the religion underpinning the ritual. Norton and Gino suggested that this was because going through the sequences and patterns involved in the ritual had given them a greater sense of control over the experience of bereavement.

Their next study wasn't about bereavement, but concerned responses to financial loss – this being somewhat more amenable to experimental manipulation! Their participants this time were students, organised into groups of between 9 and 15, who they were told that one of their group would win a cash prize of US$200. They were all asked to write about what this money would mean to them, and then one member of the group was randomly awarded the prize, and left the experiment. The others were then sorted into two groups: one group was asked to perform a simple, four-stage ritual to cope with their loss, while the others were just asked to draw their feelings on a piece of paper. When asked later, those who had carried out the ritual reported much less upset or anger than the others. Norton and Gino proposed that this, too, was because carrying out the ritual had given them a greater sense of control in dealing with the loss. They suggested that the act of carrying out a multi-stepped procedure in itself gives people a sense of control which had nothing to do with associated religious or mystical beliefs.

Everyday life can be full of small episodes which have become rituals in themselves. In 1973, Berne wrote a book called *Games People Play*, which identified a number of social "games" which happen in everyday interactions. For example, Berne showed how many of our everyday conversations have a ritual function, rather than a straightforward communicative one. They serve to affirm participation in social life, rather than to communicate information. For example, asking someone "How are you?" is part of a social greeting ritual, and we don't actually expect a literal answer. We expect the usual response, and are often quite disconcerted if the person actually tells us in detail how they are! The ritual has more to do with reaffirming the social relationship than with its literal meaning.

Everyday games and rituals also have time and structure. There are occasions, for example, when you would greet someone and other times when it would be inappropriate. Some greetings involve more exchanges than others the minimum is usually three: "How are you?", "Fine, and you?", "Fine". But sometimes it may extend to exchanging five or more utterances – all equally ritualistic.

Ritual, then, serves an important function in social life because it gives us a clear structure and some shared understandings of what is going on. But it also carries higher-order meanings. As anthropologists know, the nature of the ritual can tell us a lot about power structures and social organisation. The rituals associated with formal exams, for instance, are all about control and distrust, both with regard to those conducting the examination and to the students taking the exams. The actions of all of the participants, invigilators, instructors and students, are strictly prescribed. We only perceive these messages unconsciously, but they are still powerful – sometimes even more so because we don't realise we are absorbing them.

Context and environment

Non-verbal communication is also apparent in the environmental messages conveyed by a particular setting or situation. For example, in an average classroom, one person controls about one third of the space, while all the others sit close together in the remaining two-thirds. In a lecture theatre, the lecturer has a wide open area, while the students sit closely packed in tiers. In both locations the teacher/lecturer is the one who has freedom to move about, whereas the students are expected to stay still, in one place. Moreover, the students sit side by side facing the teacher, which allows convenient eye-contact between teacher and student – a signal of attention – but not between student and student.

The whole environment conveys non-verbal messages about power, authority and the relationships between teachers and students. These environmental signals contribute directly to controlling the social interaction which goes on. This is why a teacher who is interested in group work and social participation between students will often rearrange the layout of the room; arranging chairs in small circles helps people to talk to one another more freely, and tends to lead to better discussion.

Non-verbal messages, then, are not just transmitted by specific cues. We can find non-verbal messages in all sorts of aspects of social living – in the layout of rooms, in what people wear, in how they say things or what they don't say, in the everyday rituals of social living, and in the symbols which are all around us. Non-verbal communication operates on a number of levels, ranging from specific signals to more general messages about social assumptions. It is a major factor in how we perceive and respond to other people, and so is much more important than we think. Argyle et al (1971) showed that if we receive a non-verbal message which contradicts the verbal message that we are hearing, we are five times more likely to believe the non-verbal signal. People often attach more weight to non-verbal cues as indicating the person's "real" attitudes, than they do to what they actually say.

One of the important outcomes of research into non-verbal communication is the way that it has enhanced our understanding of everyday social skills. As a result, it has become possible to help people who might otherwise have become socially isolated to make friends, and to interact with people in a positive and rewarding way. Foxx et al (1987) showed how a social skills training programme established to help severely emotionally disturbed adolescents produced a range of positive outcomes, helping them to communicate effectively with other people, and allowing them to benefit both from therapeutic social support, and also everyday interpersonal interaction.

Internet communication

Barak (2007) identified a number of ways in which internet communication differs from everyday communication. One of these is the fact that the communicants are unable to see one another (apart from those involving webcams). What that means is that the normal everyday judgements about appearances, stereotypes, etc. are not part of the person's awareness, nor are the mitigating aspects of facial expressions or gestures which normally add clarity to the communication. Douglas and McGarty (2001) argued that this makes it easy for aggressive behaviours to become exaggerated, because misunderstandings are so easy and because the messages being transmitted are so stark. The lack of eye-contact links with this idea, because eye-contact is one of the major signals of personal honesty, self-disclosure and openness; and without it, again, it is easy for misunderstandings to occur.

Whatever the differences, interactions through the internet still seem to follow the same rules as they do in the real world. Yee et al (2007) found that the avatars in Second Life obeyed the same rules of non-verbal communication as those we follow in the real world. They recorded details of face-to-face interactions between pairs of avatars in Second Life over a seven-week period, noting particularly aspects of personal space and eye-contact, and found that, as in real life, when people stood closely together they made less eye-contact, that two characters of the same gender tended to stay further apart than opposites, and so on. Their conclusion was that the social interactions in Second Life mirrored very closely the pattern of social interaction we would expect in everyday living.

We will be looking at other aspects of internet communication, such as the "trolling" behaviour made possible by the relative anonymity of contributor sites like Twitter, as they become relevant later in this book. And, of course, much of the communication we do through the internet is still by means of text, which we will discuss later in this chapter.

VERBAL COMMUNICATION

Despite all that, what we actually say is also important. As human beings, we don't just have the richness of non-verbal communication to interact directly with one another. Talking gives us a social advantage which isn't shared by other animals, and language is another social ability that seems to be hard-wired into the human brain.

Language

Children pick up language very quickly, both from hearing it around them and from the interactions they have with older people. In fact, even in the absence of input from adults, children will invent languages to communicate with one another. A pair of severely neglected twins brought up without contact with other people, for example, developed quite a sophisticated sort of language between them (Koluchova 1976), and even ordinary twins often develop a shared "twinspeak", a form of language only used by themselves.

It is only those rare cases of **feral children** who have grown up without any human contact who don't develop language, and even they generally manage to learn something once they begin to have contact with normal people – although if they have not been found until they are 12 or so, they do find it harder than younger children. We do seem to pick language up more readily in childhood than later on, but we can still do it later if we get the right conditions (Curtiss, 1977).

Animals, on the other hand, don't really do it at all. That doesn't mean that they don't communicate; social animals in particular have very sophisticated ways of communicating, which often include "words" as symbols for threats or significant aspects of their lives (Marler, 1982). Experiments in teaching animals language have been successful in terms of day-to-day language use, showing that some animals are able to communicate everyday needs and observations, and may sometimes even make jokes or tell lies (Savage-Rumbaugh et al, 1978)! But that is still a very limited use of language by comparison with how human beings use it. Any of these animals would be hard pressed, for example, to make up stories about imaginary worlds, or to discuss what happened at a different time or what might have happened on another occasion, or

Key Terms

feral children
Children who have apparently grown from infancy to childhood with no contact with human beings.

what might be about to happen. Human language use widens our social world to an extent that no other animals can achieve.

Vocabulary

The words that we choose to use in our conversations also shape their meanings. That might sound obvious, but they can affect them in profound ways. For example, consider whether the ruling body in a foreign country is referred to on the news as a "government" or as a "regime". The first carries connotations of legitimate authority; the second has connotations of despotic abuses of power. Whether a newsreader uses one or the other depends on the country from which they are reporting (is their country in alliance with the other one?), and the way that the government in question is currently perceived. Similarly, militaristic opposition to a government in another country may be described either as the work of terrorists or as the actions of freedom fighters. Both have very different connotations, and give the communication very different meanings.

There are similar examples, though perhaps less dramatic, in everyday life. In fact, we use them all the time. The factual experience may be the same, but the meaning of what you are saying is completely different if you describe a child as "energetic" rather than "fidgety", or if you speak of someone as a "fashion guru" or a "fashion victim". We all choose our words to express what we mean, and in that meaning we put a social slant on the factual reality which we are trying to describe.

Eiser and Ross (1977) asked a set of Canadian students to write essays on capital punishment. Half of them were asked to include words with anti-capital-punishment overtones, such as "callous" or "barbaric". The others were asked to include words implying pro-capital-punishment attitudes, such as "over-sentimental" or "irresponsible". The students' attitudes showed a distinct shift towards the stance suggested by the words they had used. Eiser (1979) explained this by suggesting that language communicates a specific thematic framework, which gives the person guidelines for interpreting information.

Talking point 3.1   Loaded words

Some words are particularly powerful in terms of the emotions they conjure up. We refer to them as emotively loaded terms, and they can shape our perceptions far more than we realise. Try watching a favourite TV programme, either factual or fiction, and list the number of emotively loaded words you hear during a ten-minute sample of the programme.

It would also be interesting to do this with a friend or group of friends, to see if you each identified the same emotively loaded words, or defined the same words as emotive. We sometimes become so used to particular words or phrases that we don't recognise their emotive content.

Pennebaker and King (1999) found that the words people choose to use both in writing and in written communication are often closely related to aspects of their individual personalities, reflecting characteristics such as optimism, openness to experience and social awareness. In another study, Pennebaker and Evans (2014) found that the choice of words in therapeutic contexts could be powerful agents in aiding psychological recovery from trauma, or from chronic anxiety. These might be the words that the therapists used, or words that the clients were encouraged to use when writing about their feelings or experiences. This, and other research in the area, shows just how strongly we respond to the language that we hear and use – even if we are not really aware of it at the time.

Accents and dialect

The way we express our language can also be influential in terms of the messages we convey to other people. Lyons (1981) distinguished three major forms of everyday variation: accent, dialect and idiolect. An **accent** is a regional or social variation in the way that words are pronounced by the speaker – a special kind of inflection or emphasis. A dialect, on the other hand, is a variation of a language, which has its own distinctive grammatical constructions and vocabulary. Dialects can be either regional or social; but it is notable in Britain that social class tends to take precedence over geography. Upper-middle-class people living in Yorkshire or Northumberland, for instance, tend to speak Standard English, while their middle- or working-class compatriots speak the regional dialect.

In previous times this was also associated with a certain amount of snobbery – early tapes from the BBC, for example, reveal how presenters were required to speak "BBC English", which was a very formal speech style with an upper-class accent. Working-class people who sought to be upwardly mobile were obliged to lose or at least modify their regional accents. In more recent decades in the UK, however, accents have become much more democratised Not only is it now ordinary to find presenters and politicians with regional accents, but a regional accent is now more likely to be taken simply as an indicator of where the person lived when they were younger, rather than as an indicator of social status or standing.

Dialects, which are very different from the standard form, are sometimes seen as another language altogether. But Haugen (1966) argued that distinguishing between a dialect and a language is really only a matter of size and prestige – or, to put it another way, politics. If there are a large number of people who speak it, and they have reasonably high social status, it is likely to be considered a language; if not, it will be seen as a dialect. Flemish, for example, is now generally acknowledged as a language in its own right; but for many years, the French-speaking sector of Belgian society insisted that it was merely a dialect of Dutch. The recognition comes from improvements in the social status of Flemish speakers in Belgium; it has nothing to do with any change in the language.

The third form of language variation described by Lyons is **idiolect**. Each one of us has developed a personal style of language use, which includes individual speech patterns and habits, family conventions, and sometimes characteristic grammatical constructions. But since everyone has several alternative styles of language use available to them, and will adopt whichever seems appropriate in any given context, the notion of idiolect isn't much used in the study of the social uses of language, although it can be very helpful in a detailed study of one person or family.

Key Terms

accent
A shared distinctive speech pattern of emphasis and tone.

dialect
A distinctive pattern of language use shared by a regional or socio-economic group, which has its own vocabulary and grammatical forms.

idiolect
The personal or idiosyncratic form of language used by a single individual or family.

Language registers

Language registers are often considered to be a form of paralanguage, but they have to do with the words that we choose as well as the ways in which we use them. Effectively, we use language differently depending on the social situation that we are in. Some of these differences have recognisable social functions – for example, you use language in a different way if you are out with your friends than you would if you had to give a speech on a formal occasion. There are lots of subtle differences in speech use, but we can broadly identify five main language registers: intimate, familiar, consultative, formal and declamatory.

We reserve the intimate register for close friends and family. It tends to involve lots of verbal short-hands, in-jokes and references which only our intimates will understand. As such, it relies on a great deal of shared experience by the participants. In a similar vein, we use the familiar speech register in conversations between more general friends, or people who know each other reasonably well but not intimately. It often involves slang terms, and may use grammatical forms which would seem incomplete or inconsistent if they were written down.

Both of those speech registers are personal ones, used with people that we know. But there are three formal registers which we also employ. The consultative register is for talking to strangers when we want to be polite but not too formal – like asking someone the time of the next train, or where a certain shop is. It can include abbreviations and may also include a little well-accepted slang. The formal register, on the other hand, involves a carefully accurate use of grammar and vocabulary, and is what we tend to employ if we address people in authority. And the most formal of all, the declamatory language register, is the one that we use if we are giving an official speech, or in some kinds of factual writing. In this register, grammar and vocabulary are precise and accurate, even to the point of using phrases or words which are never actually heard in normal conversation – words such as "thus" or "albeit".

Language of this kind has been around as long as human beings have had structured societies. But modern living allows us to communicate in ways that are not face to face. We can use technology to communicate directly with people who are not actually in the same place that we are, and that has meant an adaptation of how we use language in order to deal with how the information is transmitted.

Telephones and video-links

In the modern world, we have several technological means of direct communication. Some of them have been around for quite a long time; for example, there are not many people still living who can remember a time before telephones. Being able to contact people directly even when they are somewhere else in the world has become a feature of life that most of us take entirely for granted. When it was first introduced, it was revolutionary. It was only when the early communications satellites like Telstar were brought into service in the 1960s that intercontinental communication came within reach of ordinary people.

The telephone allows direct contact, but because it only involves one sensory channel it means that users need to adjust how they communicate. So when we are talking on the telephone, we tend to augment the auditory cues

Key Terms

language registers
Patterns of language use which are relevant for different types of social interaction.

that we normally use in communication, such as tones of voice or pauses. Also, most of us manage to suppress or at least ignore our habitual visual cues such as head-nodding or smiling. Being limited to just one form of sensory input also means that we use our imaginations to replace visual input. If we meet someone who we have only previously spoken to on the phone, we are often quite taken aback by their appearance – we have visualised someone quite different! And that in itself shows us how powerful visual input can be. Vision is, after all, our primary sense, and we bring it into play even when it is totally irrelevant.

Ever since the telephone became an everyday form of communication, people have been anticipating the videophone. But it is only with the advent of the internet and the development of applications such as Skype and Facetime that it has become an everyday form of communication. Video-communications of this type allow us to interact with other people in ways that include the visual channel, and so are nearly face to face, no matter where the person actually is in the world. By including so many more non-verbal aspects of conversation, they create an experience which is very different from an auditory telephone call.

Some aspects of non-verbal communication are still missing, of course, such as whole-body posture or touch, so face-to-face conversation still remains richer than video-links. Many business meetings nowadays are held using videoconferencing, which avoids the inconvenience and expense of having to bring people together across large distances and enables reasonably full participation in discussion. How successful the meeting is depends upon the skills of whoever is chairing the meeting, of course, but that is true of all large meetings! However, despite the ability to see facial expressions and actions like head-nodding, there is still a preference for face-to-face meetings whenever possible. A video-link may augment and clarify our spoken communication, but it limits or omits too many other non-verbal channels to be a complete replacement.

At a more personal level, though, video-based communication has become increasingly taken for granted in modern family life. It plays a major role of maintaining contact between people at a distance; and thereby reinforcing emotional attachments such as family relationships or friendships. Families who are separated by distance can communicate with one another in ways which are much richer and more satisfying than letter-writing or telephone calls.

Box 3.2   Contact through the internet

Being able to see a new grandchild make its early attempts at walking, or receiving a smile from a loved partner travelling in another country can enhance social relationships in a powerful way. In one case, for example, it converted an elderly woman who up until then had been completely computer-phobic and refused to have anything more modern than telephone and TV in her house, despite several attempts by her grown children to persuade her. However, on this particular occasion her grandson was visiting and she had a face-to-face video conversation with her great-grand-daughter. She was able to see the girl as well as talk to her, and even to use the iPhone to take a look around their house and garden. This incident changed her mind completely. Within six months she had come to terms with the new technology, and was even calling up her grandson herself to talk with her great-grandchildren! As a result, her social isolation was greatly reduced, and she was able to develop much closer bonds with the children than would otherwise have been practical.

INDIRECT COMMUNICATION

All social animals have some form of direct communication. Human communication may be a bit richer than that of other animals, but direct communication is the glue that holds all social groups together. What really distinguishes human beings from other animals, though, is the way we can also communicate indirectly. Signs and symbols are one way that we do it, and the use of images and pictograms seems to have emerged fairly early in human evolutionary history. But our most powerful form of indirect communication derives from our ability to use language. Language can be represented even when other people are not present at all, through writing. And writing makes any amount of communication possible.

Reading

Writing, of course, involves reading, and there has been a constant debate as to whether the advent of mass media, and in particular television, has had a detrimental effect on the child's developing mind and on society in general. There is some evidence that television can be detrimental to the acquisition of reading skills, since it provides such easy access to information about the wider world, while reading involves considerable effort with little immediate reward. This, of course, is one reason why parental involvement is so helpful in facilitating learning to read. The enjoyment of the social interaction provides the additional motivation for the child to progress through the initial, difficult stages. While children without that type of interaction and unlimited access to TV do usually learn to read in the end, it is less common for them to achieve the same level of reading fluency or to read for pleasure.

Reading for pleasure can also enhance social skills. Reading, particularly of fiction, has long been known to develop imagination and mentally creative skills in ways that are not possible for TV – partly because the reader must contribute so much of their own knowledge to make sense of the information they are receiving. Kidd and Castano (2013) showed that reading literary fiction can also improve social empathy, and **theory of mind** – that is, the ability to see things from the other person's point of view. It was already known that people with increased empathy read more literary fiction, generally speaking, but these researchers adopted an experimental approach, showing that levels of empathy can actually change with more exposure to this type of reading.

Letters and texts

The growth of literacy didn't just open people up to new ideas through reading; it also allowed us to communicate with one another even at a distance. For centuries, this took the form of letters, which continued to dominate even when the emergence of telephones made possible more direct communication at a distance. Letters, being lasting and concrete items, can be read more than once, as most love-letters are, and kept as mementoes. They can be used as evidence in disputes, or as attempts to share experiences, for example of foreign travel. As such, they remain a significant form of interpersonal communication even though they are being increasingly superseded by emails and texts.

What all of these forms of communication depend on is the written word. But the written word is much less sophisticated than the spoken word, because it lacks the **paralinguistic cues** which we use to clarify meaning and reduce ambiguity. As a result, we have to replace some of the paralanguage with punctuation to make our meanings clear – to indicate, for example, whether something is a question or an exclamation; or to describe where, in a complex sentence like this one, a speaker might pause to draw breath and check that their audience is still paying attention.

Language registers have their relevance for written communication, too. We use much more informal language if we are writing a postcard to a friend than we do if we are writing to an official at a bank (Lyons, 1981). It can be argued that choosing the appropriate style of written language is as much of a social skill as using the appropriate language register in face-to-face situations, and many writers and educationalists believe that this is the core of achieving social competence in writing.

Txtspk

Some of the newer forms of communication have developed their own forms of written language. Txtspk, for example – spoken as "textspeak" – is a form of written language used in texts sent by phone or other media where the number of available characters is limited. It is a highly abbreviated version of the written word, which uses few vowels, many acronyms for common phrases (such as "lol" for "laugh out loud") and often includes numerical symbols as words or parts of words (such as "2" for "to", or "h8" for "hate"). For experienced texters, it is a much quicker means of communication than using formal language.

The case has been made for regarding txtspk as a written dialect in its own right. It is certainly widespread and shared by the texting community, but so are a number of different variations of spoken languages, such as those shared by enthusiasts of particular sports or hobbies. Like anything "new", there has been opposition to the use of txtspk, such as fears that it will limit the person's ability to write conventional language. However, although the idea has been supported by some educationalists, the evidence implies that knowledge of txtspk does not detract from the individual's knowledge of formal language – rather, it seems to be stored as a separate and parallel skill, similar to the diglossia shown by people who can speak both in dialect or in formal language (Plester et al, 2009).

Netiquette

Other forms of internet communication have their own conventions. Ever since the first emails, back in the late 1980s, there have been conventions about the proper ways to use this mode of communication. Writing in capital letters, for example, is viewed as shouting and is not really acceptable. Emphasis is more properly expressed using *asterisks* at either end of the word or sentence being stressed. Other information about the emotions or intentions of the writer is provided by means of emoticons, which are symbols expressing emotions, such as punctuation marks arranged to represent faces on their side. like this :), or, more recently, **emojis**, such as those in Figure 3.2, which can convey a range of emotions or common reactions.

Netiquette is another form of paralanguage, which has emerged along with the new form of written communication. Emails are a less formal and more immediate type of writing than conventional letter-writing, and netiquette evolved by consensus among the internet community in its early years. It has been maintained as a convention ever since.

New conventions have emerged as internet users become more sophisticated. Bryant and Marmo (2012) identified a number of unwritten rules observed by Facebook users. They found 36 rules in all, emerging from focus group sessions with students who were regular Facebook users, and then asked

Key Terms
emojis (aka emogees) Small icons shared in text messages and other internet contexts, illustrating emotions.
netiquette "Rules" of acceptable internet behaviour.

Figure 3.2 Emojis showing different emotions

Table 3.3 Facebook's unwritten rules

1. I should expect a response from this person if I post on his/her profile.

2. I should not say anything disrespectful about this person on Facebook.

3. I should consider how a post might negatively affect this person's relationships.

4. If I post something that this person deletes, I should not repost it.

5. I should communicate with this person outside of Facebook.

6. I should present myself positively but honestly to this person.

7. I should not let Facebook use with this person interfere with getting my work done.

8. I should not post information on Facebook that this person could later use against me.

9. I should use common sense while interacting with this person on Facebook.

10. I should consider how a post might negatively impact upon this person's career path.

11. I should wish this person happy birthday in some way other than Facebook.

12. I should protect this person's image when I post on his/her profile.

13. I should not read too much into this person's Facebook motivations.

Source: Bryant and Marmo (2012)

a wider group of nearly 600 individuals (aged 18–52) how relevant these rules were for interaction with particular Facebook friends or acquaintances. The 13 rules which survived the second stage are listed in Table 3.3.

Overall, the researchers found that there seemed to be five distinct types of rules: communication rules, about how or when you should respond; control and deception rules, such as those involving blocking people who showed up as dishonest or manipulative; rules which were concerned with maintaining relationships, such as remembering people's birthdays; rules which protected against personal negative consequences, like not posting information which could be used against themselves; and rules which protected against potential negative consequences for others.

 Bryant and Marmo also found that the "communication" and "protection of other people" rules were considered to be more important for close friends, while the "control and deception" rules and the "relationship maintenance" rules were more important for acquaintances and casual friends. The researchers speculated that perhaps relationship maintenance was less important for close friends because they also interact outside of Facebook, while it forms a more important vehicle of communication for acquaintances and casual friends.

One of the distinctive features of text-based internet communication is the way that it can be saved, copied and re-played to the originators or to other people as well (Barak, 2007). Of course, this has always been possible with letters, but not easily. With internet text, it can be done immediately, on the spur of the moment. As relationships change, this can become a major source of embarrassment or worse for the erstwhile participants; shared inappropriately, or taken out of context, personal interactions can easily become the source of serious social misunderstandings.

The "bluntness" of text-based communication can also mean that information comes across more starkly, and so can be more easily misinterpreted, than would happen with the same communication in a face-to-face context. In modern internet communication, though, it has become very easy to add richness to the message by using images, animations or video-links, which can serve to clarify or amplify meaning. And as we have seen, the text of the message can be augmented by emoticons, which help to clarify the overall emotional tone of the message and replace some of the important emotional information of face-to-face interaction which is lost in the written word.

Open communication

One of the distinctive characteristics of open communication is that it is available to anyone who chooses to take notice of it. In that sense, it is not targeted to any specific individual, and the person issuing the communication has very little control over how it is received. In earlier times, open communications took the form of the printed word, or of broadcast information through radio, TV or recordings, and tended to be only made by select groups or privileged individuals. While the way it was received could not be controlled, there were frequent attempts by social authorities to control its content (see Box 3.3).

Box 3.3 The development of literacy

In early civilisations, reading and writing tended to be restricted skills, maintained by a closed elite. Sometimes this was a priesthood and sometimes it was a professional group such as a guild of scribes. The restriction of such skills was directly political – "knowledge is power" – in the sense that people who could read could learn things which other people didn't know, and could also pass on information or knowledge in ways which were inaccessible by people who didn't share the same skill. By the 11th century in many parts of the world, however, being able to read and write was gradually becoming more widespread.

Much of this growth of literacy had to do with reading the Bible or other religious texts; and in this respect, Islamic cultures had a distinct advantage, with their emphasis on direct knowledge of the Koran. Literacy tended to be quite common in Islamic countries, whereas in China, it was particularly associated with those destined to go into government and administration; and in mediaeval Europe, reading and writing were generally the province of the religious orders, although they did also educate other children who might go on to become reeves or clerks. Gradually, literacy increased in Europe, until by the beginning of the 19th century in England, it was estimated to be about 60 per cent. Most families had at least one member who could read the Bible and write or print a simple letter.

As society became more complex, literacy was increasingly recognised as a significant social tool. Fool for example, it enabled governments to issue their decrees with an expectation that (a) they would last and (b) the public would read them. In China, laws have been written down for the past three millennia; written laws and administrative edicts began in England with Alfred the Great and have continued to accumulate ever since; and a similar process has happened in many other societies.

For centuries, literacy was the means to open people's awareness to the wider society. Until the advent of the electronic mass media, such as TV and radio, it was pretty well the only window to the world, which is why the development of the printing press was such an extremely radical influence in Western society. Ideas could be shared beyond the immediate social group, and the awareness of the wider world enabled the gradual transition from the old feudal systems into the more modern economic structures of today.

This transition was often painful, and accompanied by resistance from the states concerned. Following the way in which the publication of propaganda pamphlets and challenging books inflamed the French Revolution, Western states attempted, with varying degrees of success, to censor the content of the printed media. As each new form of technology emerged, similar attempts at censorship were made. Radio broadcasting was very tightly controlled in its early years, as was the content of movies, while restrictions on the printed word became looser. Controls over radio and films relaxed a little more with the advent of television, which itself was closely censored in its first few decades. As television stations proliferated, however, and with the advent of the internet, tight censorship became more difficult. Nowadays social debate on censorship centres on the desirability (but also the impossibility) of controlling or regulating the content of internet and video games.

The social psychological consequences of these changes has been profound, in that people become far more aware of their wider world, and more likely to become engaged with certain aspects of it. The success of large charity events and the worldwide responses to natural disasters show how the insularity produced by more limited forms of communication has broken down over the past few decades. But it isn't just a matter of people becoming more widely aware of the wider world: there is also the shift in control of that awareness, from establishment-controlled to personal.

Recent technological development has produced direct challenges both to censorship and to the social control of communication. Those challenges centre on how instruments of mass communication have become available to ordinary people. Mobile phones with video and internet capacity mean that eyewitness records of social events such as riots or attacks are readily communicated to other interested parties, which makes public acts which the perpetrators might previously have been able to cover up. Open internet media such as Twitter and Facebook allow ordinary people to communicate publicly about social issues and questions, as well as about their own interpersonal concerns. As a result, social institutions are no longer seen as monolithic and unaccountable, and many people are becoming far more actively engaged with what happens in society as a whole.

The political challenges raised by this are still playing out, and are likely to do so for some time to come, as social structures based on one-way communication and unaccountability become increasingly challenged. At present, attempts to censor such communications or to criminalise those who use them in ways which are considered socially unacceptable are in the ascendant. It will be interesting to see whether this changes as society adapts and becomes more accustomed to open mass debate. To come back to the point at issue, though, it all illustrates the power and diversity of human communication, and the richness which images, language and the written word have to offer us – even when we are not actually in contact with the person who originated them.

INDIRECT SOCIAL COMMUNICATION

We might define indirect social communication as being communication which is not directed towards the individual personally, but has more to do with the general society or social groups to which the person belongs. But as with just about any aspect of human psychology, making a clear distinction between the two – personal and social communication – is not that easy.

Internet gaming

One case in point concerns internet **gaming**. Computer games have been around ever since the first computers; and they account for an amazingly large proportion of our leisure time. While most computer games are engaged in as individual pursuits, since the advent of the internet it has been possible for people to play games with people in real time, but at both social and physical distance. Often, two people playing an online game are not acquainted with one another at all – except through their internet personas – and have no intention of developing any further relationship. But within the game, they may compete or cooperate intensely. In that sense, it can be regarded as a personal, though very limited, relationship; but its anonymity means that it could equally be classified as a social rather than personal form of communication.

Some internet games are less ambiguously social. Avatar-based games such as Second Life or World of Warcraft mean that the person develops their own avatar, or alternative person, deciding everything about them even in terms of what they will wear or what they will look like. Second Life is a virtual social world that was created to represent the real world but without physical limits. In Second Life, the avatar has no specific goal: the person may choose a profession or not, as they choose, and their avatar simply interacts with others playing other roles within the virtual community. World of Warcraft has the same level of personal choice with regard to the avatar itself, but it is a war strategy game where the players have missions, tasks and goals, and can team up with other players or not. In 2012 World of Warcraft was the world's largest

Key Terms

gaming
The playing of computer or video games.

MMORPG (massively multiplayer online role playing game), with 9.1 million monthly subscribers.

The popularity of these games also has implications for our understanding of social identification and self-image. The ability to develop an alter-ego with entirely different social constraints and social memberships may allow people to explore different aspects of themselves in a safe environment. For example, Suler (2004) found that men playing World of Warcraft were more likely to use avatars of a different gender than themselves, than are women. Suler's research findings implied that there were two reasons for this. One was so that they could explore aspects of their personalities which would normally be repressed in their real lives as incompatible with their male social roles. The other was more pragmatic: female avatars tend to receive more help and assistance in game-playing situations than male ones. This was backed up by Wadell and Ivory (2015), who found that people with more attractive avatars tended to be helped more by gifts and aids, and so found it easier to achieve the game's goals.

With regard to the last motivation, the reverse can also hold true. Coghlan and Kirwan (2013) found that some women played World of Warcraft using male avatars because that made the game more demanding and more of a challenge. Other women the researchers interviewed felt uneasy at the thought of "gender-bending" in this way. The researchers found a clear difference between these two groups of women in terms of their Need for Achievement (nAch) scores: the first group were more goal-oriented and motivated to win than those who found the change of gender disturbing.

Debates about the social acceptability of computer gaming have been around as long as the games themselves, and are really the same social debate as that concerning violence on TV and in films. We will examine that more closely in Chapter 7, when we look at social aspects of aggression. But these interactive games bridge the gap between personal and social forms of indirect communication, in that the person interacts as an individual, but within a wider, if virtual, social context.

Talking point 3.2   Social identification in gaming

The social nature of internet gaming sometimes shows up in terms of group affiliations. One case in point is of a young woman who was playing an internet scrabble game. When two of the other game-players entered the game with the greeting "I love Jesus", she, not being particularly religious and of a humorous frame of mind, responded with "I love my son." The bible-belters were not amused, and froze her out of the game, so she was unable to continue playing. Can you think of other examples of social identifications affecting internet gaming?

The mass media

The mass media encompasses several other forms of indirect social communication. Some of them use the written word, such as books, newspapers and magazines. We have looked at the implications of literacy at a wider social level, but they are also a significant vehicle for social messages to reach the individual. Before the advent of TV and radio, books were the main agent of socialisation into the wider culture, which is why the children's books of that time were so very different from modern ones. Books, like computer games, allow the person to enter another world, but require a different level of cognitive involvement and less active decision-making. However, it is the more ephemeral but more widely shared media of newspapers and magazines which play the most active role in interpreting social events and situations, and so shaping social representations.

A similar role is played by the other linguistic media: TV and radio. Both current affairs programmes and TV drama shape how people see the world; for most people, it is their main window into the wider society. But the view they get from that window is not necessarily realistic. It is in the nature of TV to report or discuss only that which is exceptional or particularly dramatic. Back in 1976, Gerbner and Gross showed that people who watch a lot of television saw the world as being a much more dangerous place than it really is, and more recent evidence suggests that the trend has increased rather than diminished since that time.

Radio appears to have taken on a different social role, either as entertainment through music and sport, or as a medium which is predominately discursive and informative, offering a deeper level of social analysis than is the norm for TV. Such programming is just as important in shaping the social representations with which we make sense of society, but it does so in a slightly different and often more verbal way.

Advertising

Perhaps the most influential vehicle for shaping our social experience, however, is advertising. Advertising uses all of the various media, but more importantly it draws on a sophisticated social knowledge to influence the individual. For example, in Chapter 1, we saw how social identification is a fundamental aspect of human awareness. Our membership of social groups can even define how receptive we are to information, and this is used extensively by the advertising industry. Advertisers target their material explicitly towards specific social groups, so that they can maximise the impact that their information will receive. They use the power of social identification to link their products with particular groups or lifestyles, making it appear that ownership of, or participation in, whatever they are selling is a natural part of belonging to such groups.

In doing so, the forms of communication used by advertisers are both verbal and non-verbal. Verbal messages are carefully selected and words are chosen to express exact meanings; but careful selection also goes into the voices chosen to deliver those messages. These are generally the voices of well-known entertainers, whose public images are congruent with either the product being advertised or the target group they are aiming to reach. This again is one of the ways in which advertisers use social identity processes to achieve their goals.

Imagery and semiotics

Advertisers are also well versed in the **semiology** of modern life. Semiology is the study of the way that we use symbols in everyday living. Advertisers use symbols all the time – from the use of blues, whites and greens in toothpaste advertisements to symbolise freshness and clarity, to the use of East London

Key Terms
Semiology The study of symbolism in everyday life.

accents in getting adverts to symbolise working class pragmatism. Memorable advertising has often created entirely new symbols which have become part of the semiotics of everyday life, and in fact this is the explicit goal of many advertising campaigns.

This brings out another major form of communication used by human beings: communication through imagery. From the very first **pictograms**, we have used imagery to express what we mean – sometimes communicating directly through pictures, sometimes using images to enhance and clarify other forms of communication. Magazines and some newspapers draw heavily on images in this way, and some types of internet experience are entirely based on shared imagery. YouTube, Snapchat and Flicker, for example, are open-access sites where people can share their own images. These sites, and others like them, have proved hugely popular and have become a significant vehicle of communication in their own right.

The use of imagery as communication only works because of the shared interpretations we place on those images. For some types of images, like those portraying explicit human suffering, our shared interpretations arise directly from our common knowledge of both everyday reality and non-verbal cues. These images are largely unproblematic, in the sense that we can interpret them directly and most human beings will interpret them the same way.

Other types of images, though, are more culturally specific. Our perception of the Nazi swastika, for instance, is based on shared common knowledge of the associations of that symbolism, and most particularly with the cruelties and genocide of Hitler's Germany. This social awareness is so strong that it has entirely superseded awareness of how the symbol was used before it was taken up by the Nazis, when the reversed version of the image was associated with goodness and light. Even knowing this, modern people seeing the swastika on mediaeval buildings often still view it with distaste because of those negative associations.

The meanings of some images are reasonably constant, while others change over time and as society changes. The symbolic image of a luxurious car, for example, is deliberately manipulated by advertisers to change over time so that people continue to aspire to owning them. Fashions, by definition, are transient; but the picture of the model on the catwalk remains a constant and powerful image.

How we interpret images, then, is based on a common social awareness and cultural knowledge. What shapes those images and gives them the power to express shared experience is the way that society uses its various forms of communication to give meaning to our life events and experiences. In the next chapter we will be looking at some aspects of how this happens – how the processes of explanation and discourse utilise the forms of communication to shape our social experience. In the rest of this chapter, we will look at another aspect of social communication: how our shared understandings structure social life, and the roles which schemas and scripts play in our understanding of everyday living.

Key Terms

pictograms
Signs expressing meaning through pictures or images.

SCRIPTS, ROLES AND SCHEMAS

Our comprehension of social information is wider than just interpreting specific units of information like images or sentences. We also apply a higher-order level of understanding to the information that we receive, knitting it into meaningful wholes, and using the result to direct or predict our social actions. These range from our knowledge of particular scripts, directing our actions in specific situations, to the development of the whole units of understanding which we call schemas, and to the full-scale stories and beliefs which are known as social representations, and which explain why the world is like it is. We will be looking at social representations in the next chapter, but here we will see how social scripts and schemas also form part of our communication.

Social scripts

One fundamental mechanism in everyday social interaction is the **social script**. This idea was most clearly developed by Schank and Abelson (1977), who pointed out that much, if not most, of the social action which we engage in takes the form of planned sequences, where everything is regulated and expected – much like the script of a play. They give the example of eating out at a restaurant. This activity involves several different people, in one way or another – yourself, your companions, the waiter, the bar staff or wine waiter, and possibly others. Regardless of who is actually involved, though, the sequence of who should do what, and when, is familiar, even if the actual people are strangers. You know roughly what to expect at any given moment, and how you should behave, and the whole process generally happens in an orderly sort of way.

Schank and Abelson argued that this is because all of the people involved are acting according to the same, implicitly understood script, and so smoothly regulated social interaction becomes possible. Much of social life is scripted in this way; we know what we are supposed to do or how we are supposed to act because the situation is familiar to us, in the sense that we have encountered similar scenarios in the past and have learned the appropriate ways of acting

Key Terms

social script
A pattern of accepted social action, followed automatically in everyday situations.

from them. We know how we should behave when we are students at school or college, when we are shopping, when we are visiting relatives and even when we are having a regular meal with other members of our family. There are established sequences of behaviour – we know who is likely to do what, in fact, if someone breaks the sequence, it can be a talking point for weeks!

Social scripts play in important part in shaping our social understanding. For example, Zadny and Gerard (1974) asked research participants to watch a videotape of two students wandering around a flat and discussing minor drug and theft offences. One group of research participants was told that the students were planning to burgle the flat, a second group was told that they were looking for drugs and a third group was told that they were waiting for a friend. When the research participants were asked what they remembered later, they remembered information which was relevant to the script that they were applying. So, for instance, those who thought the students were burglars remembered vulnerable items in the flat, such as credit cards, and also more parts of the conversation which related to theft, than those applying different scripts.

Social roles

 If much of everyday life is scripted, like a play, then how do the actors know their lines? The concept of role is a very important one in understanding everyday life, and in many ways it is used in much the same way as we use it when we speak of actors or the theatre. When we are engaging in social life, we take on "roles" which tell us how we should behave towards other people – essentially, we play our parts, and other people play theirs.

During the course of an ordinary day, you probably play a number of different roles, ranging from those which concern family relationships (daughter, son, parent, partner) to brief, passing ones, like that of a bus passenger, to longer-term but still temporary ones, like that of a student. Each of these roles involves very specific kinds of behaviour. Think of how you act as a bus passenger, and imagine doing that at home. They'd think there was something wrong with you! Similarly, the behaviour which you engage in during your role as "student-in-coffee-bar" is likely to be quite different from your role as "student-in-lectures".

Social roles are always reciprocal – they come in pairs, because the role is always held with respect to the other person. So we would play a nurse role, for example, when interacting with someone in another role: as nurse/patient, for example, or nurse/doctor, or junior nurse/senior nurse. If two nurses of equal status were together, their behaviour and conversation would likely be much more individual and personal, because their "nurse"-style role behaviour wouldn't be quite as appropriate in their interaction.

Goffman (1959) argued that the roles that we play as part of everyday social life gradually become internalised, so that they become part of the self – the personality. When we are first called to take on something new – like, say, doing a Saturday job in a shop for the first time – it often feels unreal, as though we are acting the part. But when we have been doing it for a while, it becomes internalised, into the self-concept, so that we play that role automatically, and can adopt that "persona" whenever the social context is appropriate. We will be looking at this idea again in Chapter 8.

Key Terms

Social roles
The parts people play in society.

Imitation and modelling

But we don't just learn our own roles in life. We also learn quite a lot about other people's. Bandura (1977) argued that imitation and modelling are important social-learning processes, by which we are able to pick up whole patterns of social actions and appropriate role behaviour. Children acting out "mummies and daddies" or "shopping" are practising their learning of these roles, and we continue to learn as we get older – mainly by observing others and learning from them. But that learning is vicarious – that is, we don't necessarily use it straight away. Instead, we produce it when it is appropriate.

In one famous study, Haney et al (1973) asked students to participate in a role-playing experiment, in which some of them would play the part of prisoners and others would take the part of guards (we will be looking at other aspects of this study in Chapter 6). Nobody told the students how to behave, and the way they acted out these roles was entirely up to them. The experiment was conducted as realistically as possible, using a mock-up "prison", and was supposed to last for two weeks. In fact, the experimenters had to stop it after six days, because the people who were acting the role of guards had become so strict, and at times so psychologically cruel, that the experiment could not be allowed to continue.

Although they did not use physical punishment directly, the guards developed a number of ways of humiliating the prisoners, like making them stand in rows and say their identification numbers over and over again. One prisoner rebelled, and refused to cooperate, and he was put in a small closet as punishment. Although the other prisoners were given the opportunity to free him, by making a small token sacrifice (giving up a blanket), they refused to do so, as they regarded him as a "troublemaker" and didn't want anything to do with him.

Those who were acting the roles of prisoners rapidly became apathetic and dispirited, and those who were acting the roles of guards became aggressive and bullying – not because of their personalities, but because of the situations that they were in and the roles which they were playing. Many of the guards, who in their ordinary lives were quite gentle people, were shocked at how they had acted, and had not realised that they were capable of such behaviour. But their understanding of the role of guard (gleaned mostly from TV and films) was such that they had in fact been much more brutal than real prison guards – who would have had a riot on their hands if they treated their real prisoners as badly.

Even more disturbingly, the study had become so well known by the 21st century that the actions and attitudes portrayed by the "guards" provided role models for the real-life torturing of prisoners in Abu Ghraib during the Iraqi conflict which began in 2003. In-depth investigations of how these atrocities had come to take place showed the influence of the study at a personal level, as well as the systemic collusion and subtle encouragement of these actions by the higher authorities (Zimbardo, 2007).

By showing us so clearly how our latent knowledge of other social roles can be brought to the fore when needed, this study tells us quite a lot about the importance of role knowledge in human social behaviour. It also tells us something about the way that power and control are portrayed and understood in modern society – like the idea that this type of authority is automatically coupled with cruelty or bullying. But most of the roles which we play in society are much more ordinary, and less controversial.

Social schemas

The idea of the mental **schema**, bringing together chunks of information and memories into a usable form, was first developed by Bartlett (1932), in his work on meaningful memory. It became particularly popular through the work of Piaget (1952), who saw schema development as the core of mental development in children.

Social scripts are often regarded as a type of **social schema** – a way in which we organise and use the knowledge that we have gained through our experience. Scripts are concerned with the immediate directing of social actions, which is why they are sometimes referred to as **event schemas**. The restaurant example we looked at earlier is an example of that. If the script were to be broken – if, say, the waiter brought coffee at the beginning of the meal – we would find it very disorientating. In reality, of course, social scripts are almost never broken, and so social interaction is able to proceed smoothly on the basis of the shared understanding of the script that all the participants have.

Talking point 3.3　Social scripts in everyday living

We follow social scripts just about every day of our lives. Try taking an ordinary day, and noting down every time you find yourself following an established social script – for example, responding to someone's greeting in a particular way, or doing certain things in a particular order. If you're not sure whether a set of actions are actually a social script or not, imagine what would happen if you acted completely differently from the way that people expect you to act. Would anyone notice, and if so, how seriously would they take it?

There are other types of schema which are common in social interaction, as well. For example, **role schemas** (or schemata) are concerned with the frameworks we use when we are dealing with others in particular, pre-specified social relationships. So, for instance, a role schema might include how we think about the likely behaviour and personality of a gardener, or another one might be what we think about teachers. Role schemas also allow us to draw out general principles concerning broad social groups or categories of people in society. Hamilton (1981) described them as the basic cognitive processes which underlie stereotypes and prejudice, although they can also be much more open than that. Research into implicit personality theories also often taps into our underlying role schemata. We will be looking at this more closely in Chapter 6.

The **person schema** is another type of schema which we use in social living. As we get to know somebody, we develop an increasingly clear idea about them, which allows us to make predictions. We then use those predictions to guide our behaviour towards that person. For example, if you want to buy someone a birthday present, you will draw on the person schema you have developed about that person, and use it to predict (or at least make a reasonable guess at) what they are likely to appreciate. The more we interact with people, the more sophisticated our understanding of them becomes, as a general rule. The person schema which we have of them accumulates more

Key Terms

schema
A mental framework or structure which encompasses memories, ideas, concepts and programmes for action which are pertinent to a particular topic.

social schema
The collection of cognitions which we use to guide social action.

event schema
The implicit social script which we use to guide our actions in response to specific circumstances or events.

role schema
The total set of memories, actions and intentions associated with a particular social role: the understanding of that role.

person schema
The set of memories, knowledge and intentions which someone holds about a particular person.

information and becomes richer the more we interact with them. Unless, of course, we have developed a rigid and fixed idea about them and have become closed to any new information!

Our person schemas don't have to be about individuals; they can be more general. We may for example, have a person schema about "a typical career woman". If we then meet someone who we think fits that schema, then that will determine what we notice about them. We will tend to focus on the particular traits which we believe such people are likely to have, and may not even notice aspects of their behaviour which are different. So a person schema can concern itself with the uniqueness of a particular individual, or it can involve a form of stereotyping as we generalise about likely traits or characteristics of that person.

A fourth group of schemas are those which relate to ourselves – our **self-schemas**. Some people experience themselves as having a stable, inner self-concept, whereas others find it more elusive to identify; but all of us can infer what we are like from our observations of our own behaviour. From this, we can build up a range of self-schemata which we use to predict what we are likely to do. For example, the process of choosing a holiday involves predicting what sort of things we are likely to enjoy; some people like to have very active holidays, whereas others like the type of holiday in which they lie about in the sun all day. We are usually fairly good at predicting which kind we ourselves will like – although those predictions may become narrower as we grow older, and we can sometimes surprise ourselves by getting "out of our comfort zones" and trying something completely different!

Social schemas give us a way of drawing together a vast range of information, and extracting general rules for directing action from it. As a result, they allow us to deal with many more different situations than we could manage if we were to treat each situation separately. Moreover, since the schema itself is continually being modified and adjusted as our social experience grows, it helps us to adapt our behaviour to complex and changing social demands.

Some researchers have argued that the idea of the schema is too vague, and doesn't provide clear predictions. But Fiske and Taylor (1983) pointed out that the schema is a concept, not a full theory in itself. They argued that, in order to be useful, the concept of schema needs to be developed as part of a wider theoretical understanding of social processes. For example, they argue, the schema is to do with the knowledge that someone holds, whereas attributions are concerned with how people go about applying that knowledge. In this way, the idea of the schema and the idea of attribution can complement, rather than compete with, each other. In the next chapter, we will go on to look at attributions and explanations, and how they, too, can help us to understand social interaction.

Summary: Chapter 3

1. Communication can take many forms. It may be direct – that is, between particular individuals and usually face to face or indirect, affecting people who are not personally known to the communicator.

2. Non-verbal communication is a significant aspect of direct communication. It involves a wide range of cues and signals.

Key Terms

self-schema
The total set of memories, representations, ideas and intentions which one holds about oneself.

3. Different types of non-verbal communication can serve a range of functions: for example, rituals often help people to deal with the details of everyday life.

4. Verbal communication involves language, which can carry different messages through choice of vocabulary, accents and dialect, and language registers.

5. Open communication results from mass media, literacy and the availability of vehicles of communication through the internet. It allows communication with large numbers of people, often unknown to the communicator.

6. There are many conventions of open communication, and it can take many forms. Apart from simple language, modern open communication includes txtspk, netiquette and the use of emoticons and emotes.

7. Forms of indirect social communication include gaming, advertising and the mass media.

8. Much of the detail of everyday life is directed through social scripts, which contain shared expectations about the way in which everyday interactions should be conducted.

9. A significant part of social living involves the playing of social roles, which are often learned through imitation and modelling.

10. Our social understanding and awareness of types of social interaction may be stored as social schemas. These include social scripts, role schemas, person schemas and self-schemas.

Chapter 4

Contents

Explaining ourselves

4

Communication lies at the heart of social interaction. Everyday life is full of communication, of one sort or another. We communicate with other people, or receive communications from them, all the time, by talking to one another and through written language. We also signal to one another, using a whole range of cues, and we respond to the more general forms of communication used by society, which apply to everyone, and don't just originate from any single person. As we saw in the last chapter, communication can take many forms. But what is really important is how people actually use communication – the function it serves, as opposed to its form.

DISCOURSE ANALYSIS
Language is perhaps the most important vehicle for human communication. Language allows us to express concepts and ideas which don't have any

"GO ON... ADMIT IT...I'VE AROUSED YOUR PROFESSIONAL CURIOSITY HAVEN'T I?"

immediate, concrete reality – it lets us talk about things which "might be" or "will be" or "used to be", as well as what actually exists in the present. Language also offers us the opportunity for subtle communication: we can communicate nuances of emotions or attitudes by selecting our words carefully; we can use language to lie, to tell half-truths or to tell literal truths.

In 1962, Austin proposed that communication using language should be analysed, not just in terms of the words chosen or the structure of the sentences, but in terms of the way that language is bound up with doing things. Austin argued that when we say something, we are performing a **speech act**, which has a social dimension. So, for instance, if someone says something which appears to be a simple factual statement, like "the earth is round", it isn't enough just to look at what was said, and whether it was true or false. We also need to look at the context in which they said it, and how the action of saying it fits in with the social and interpersonal context. Saying "the earth is round" to a small child represents an entirely different kind of speech act from saying it to another adult within a conversation. The full meaning of what has been said can only really be grasped when we look at language as a way of doing things, as opposed to just analysing the utterance itself.

Austin's work represented a new way of analysing language, and has been described as a significant development for opening up the area of study known as **discourse analysis**. Discourse analysis, according to Lalljee and Widdicombe (1989), is concerned with looking not just at how language occurs, within its social context, but also at what it is being used for. So research into discourse analysis is concerned with talking and conversation as a subject of study in its own right.

In 1974, Sacks argued that the study of talk should differ from traditional approaches by concentrating much more on naturally occurring data, and on analysing what emerges from such data. This was quite a challenge to the traditional ways of conducting psychological research, in two ways. Firstly, it challenged the idea of obtaining data under controlled laboratory conditions, requiring researchers to obtain samples of talk from the "real world", as it were. The other challenge concerned the standard hypothetico-deductive research approach, in which hypotheses are generated first, and then research is conducted to see whether they are supported. By contrast, modern discourse analysis has been much more concerned with obtaining samples of real-world talk first, and then going on to analyse what emerged from them. This approach to research is known as the inductive approach. We will look at these two approaches in more detail in Chapter 10.

Taking this approach has proven to be extremely useful in revealing the underlying assumptions which people hold, and the strategies which they use in conversations. For example, Gilbert and Mulkay (1984) performed a series of interview studies with 34 scientists, in which they compared what the scientists had said in their formal publications and what they said when they were being interviewed. One very apparent difference was that the language used in the papers was much more tentative than that used in face-to-face conversation; someone might be quite definite about the implications of some findings when talking to an interviewer, but would only say that "results suggest that . . ." when writing formally.

Another observation was how the scientists explained the different beliefs held by other scientists, who had opposing views. While they always explained

their own theories by referring to direct physical evidence, they generally explained the views of their opponents in terms of personality characteristics, or other such social factors. This links with research into the fundamental attribution error, which we will be looking at later in this chapter.

Discourse and social power

Discourse analysis involves more than simply conducting interview studies. Rather, it examines how talk involves and reinforces underlying social issues such as power and control. In a discussion on the website Discourse Analysis Online, four of the most significant modern researchers into discourse analysis – came together to clarify what is and what is not discourse analysis (Antaki et al., 2003). They identified five ways of treating language-based data which, in their words, "fall short" of discourse analysis, and these are listed in Table 4.1.

Instead, discourse analysis operates at a deeper level, showing how particular repertoires or ideologies are actually being used within the conversation – for example, whether they are being used to enhance the speaker's credibility and dismiss that of the other, or whether they are being used to reinforce social power or authority structures. So, forms of analysis which simply describe the data, or merely group it together, while they may have their own uses, do not penetrate deeply enough to count as discourse analysis. Without bringing in wider evidence or social awareness, it is little more than an interesting observation.

Social discourse has tremendous power, in that it can actually determine how we see reality. Middleton and Edwards (1990) explored discourse within families and social groups. Analysing a series of tape-recorded but naturally occurring conversations, they showed how the exchanges and explanations which occurred during everyday discourse served to negotiate a commonly-accepted version of what had occurred and what it meant. As the discourse proceeded,

Table 4.1 What discourse analysis is not

1. Under-analysis through summary (e.g., limiting the analysis to identifying themes or groups of opinions without further investigation).

2. Under-analysis through taking sides (e.g., supporting a specific point of view and thereby omitting to examine the issue in detail).

3. Under-analysis through over-quotation or isolated quotation (e.g., using quotations as sufficient indication of the issues, rather than engaging in independent and deeper analysis).

4. The circular identification of discourses and mental constructs (e.g., identifying shared ideas, repertoires or discourses and treating that identification as if identifying the commonality was sufficient analysis).

5. Under-analysis through false survey (e.g., treating the insights gained from a specific sample as if they were typical of the population in general).

6. Analysis which consists of simply "spotting" interesting things (e.g., noticing and labelling particular features of the communication).

Source: Antaki et al (2003)

it settled around a consensus of an acceptable shared memory for, and interpretation of, the events which were being discussed – in one case, for example, a Royal Wedding. The shared version of events was what those people remembered when they were asked about it individually at a later date.

This ability of discourse to mediate our social experience is one of the reasons why people are so concerned about the ideologies which are being reflected or transmitted. For example, Van Dijk (1987) looked at how highly prejudiced attitudes are transmitted through discourse. By interviewing white Dutch racists, Van Dijk showed that much of their discourse involved expressing their negative attitudes while simultaneously avoiding the possibility of being charged with racism. They adopted a number of discursive strategies to achieve this, which made it difficult for the listener to accuse them directly of racism. Instead, they defined the context of social interaction in a way which implied that these unpleasant attitudes were socially acceptable.

One of these ways, for instance, was to use credibility enhancing moves, which were designed to indicate that the person had specialist or expert knowledge, or in other ways "knew" what they were talking about. Another was positive self-presentation, in which the person denied being racist, but claimed to have "good" reasons (e.g., unfair competition) for disliking the particular minority group in question. And the third was negative other-presentation, in which the minority group in question was singled out as engaging in negative or illegal behaviour.

Talking point 4.1   Racist strategies in conversation

In modern society, we pride ourselves on challenging racism, with legislation to make it illegal and social condemnation of outright racists. But how successful are we? Try taking Van Dijk's three strategies and seeing if you can find examples of each of them in the modern media.

Conversation analysis

Antaki (2004) described a form of discourse analysis which looks in detail at both how language is used in conversations, and also at other aspects of the conversation, such as timing and paralanguage. **Conversation analysis** is usually performed on recordings of conversations, which might be audio recordings but are ideally videos, so that facial expressions and other aspects of the conversation can also be identified. The conversations are carefully transcribed, using very specific symbols to describe things like timed pauses, rises or falling of pitch, stretched-out sounds, faster or slower speech, and even a symbol to imply that the word has been expressed in a laughing sort of way.

This level of detail allows researchers to identify nuances which would be missed if the researcher was simply looking at vocabulary or tones of voice. Peräkylä (2004) demonstrated how the use of conversation analysis could be invaluable in revealing how emotional aspects of interactions influence, and in some cases even determine, the nature of discussion or other types of inter-action between patients and medical staff. Peräkylä argued that the detailed picture of revealed emotions and emotional nuances which emerges from con-versation analysis highlights several new dimensions concerning the human meanings of what was going on, which could not be identified using more traditional forms of interaction analysis.

In a broader context, Antaki (2011) discussed six different ways of doing conversation analysis, and showed how this approach to analysing discourse could be applied across a range of different areas. The relevant form would depend upon what was appropriate for the topic being investigated. Antaki argued that the fine attention to the forms of language used in conversational interactions can give insights which significantly enrich our understanding of social interaction.

Forms of social discourse

Many studies of discourse have dealt with face-to-face conversations between people; but discourse analysis itself actually spans more than that. As we saw in the last chapter, communication using language can take many forms, from written signs to open discussions. It is the way that language is used and the social purposes it serves which is the main focus of discourse analysis.

That doesn't mean that all verbal communication is necessarily appropriate subject matter for discourse analysis. If we take, for example, hazard warning messages placed on roadside boards in the Highlands of Scotland, one very common one is "High risk of deer on road", which is relatively unproblematic and a simple factual statement. But another is "Don't take drugs and drive", which, while still being a hazard warning, is a manifestation of a social cam-paign concerning the consumption of illegal drugs, and as such might be con-sidered to be part of a wider social discourse. It is the social uses to which the verbal communication is being put which is the focus of interest in discourse analysis.

Much research into discourse analysis has focused on everyday conver-sation, looking at such aspects as the social construction of memories (e.g., Billig, 1990), discrepancies in power relationships between staff and residents in care homes (Antaki et al, 2007), and even the use of apparently silly ques-tions in police interviews (Stokoe and Edwards, 2008). But discourse can take forms other than face-to-face conversation. The social network Twitter, for example, invites brief exchanges between individuals on any number of topics, and has become a significant social influence, highlighting views and reactions to social events and influencing the way in which people deal with social issues.

Internet-based discourse

Other social networks have had similarly widespread influences on social issues. Facebook, for example, has become a major vehicle for market research, in terms of the ways that it allows individuals to express their responses to ideas or events offered through Facebook pages. At a micro-level, whether something is "liked" or not is hardly discourse; but on a wider social level, the patterns of responses and the ways that ideas are spread can be regarded in that way.

The internet in general is host to a large number of different campaigns every year, as concerns about social issues become widely shared through social media or through the "snowballing" effect of emails passed on to their personal contacts by concerned individuals. In 2009, for example, an informal "campaign" took place through the internet in the UK, in which people deliberately downloaded a particular music track ("Killing in the Name Of" by Rage against the Machine), not because they wanted it, but because they wanted to stop the TV programme *The X Factor* having five Christmas no. 1 singles in five consecutive years. The campaign was successful, and the track became the first Christmas no. 1 to come entirely from downloads.

Other campaigns may have been less successful. The Invisible Children campaign, which attempted to bring the person responsible for recruiting child armies in Uganda to justice, is still going on at the time of writing, but appears to have had little effect so far. On the other hand, an email campaign about fuel pricing in the UK attracted widespread support, and made politicians aware

"COME ON', YOU SAID....'WHERE'S THE HARM', YOU SAID....'IT'S ONLY MARKET RESEARCH'.....YOU SAID."

that this was a significant issue for voters which shouldn't be ignored. In fact, the influence of cyber-petitions can be seen in the way that they have become an accepted part of governmental strategy. In the UK, there is an official government site for cyber-petitions, with the undertaking that any issue raised in this form which obtains a specific minimum number of signatories will be debated explicitly by the government.

Internet campaigns that go viral have their effects partly through their immediacy, but mainly as a result of the way that they can crystallise responses from thousands of people around a single issue. As such, they offer a major route for minority communication in the political arena, and are significant vehicles for social discourse. While analysis of this discourse is of necessity at a more abstract level than the specifics of conversation analysis might offer, it can also contribute to our understanding of the importance of particular social explanations and ideas in social living.

Talking point 4.2   Viral campaigns

Most internet posts are read or viewed by just a handful of people. But some, suddenly, achieve thousands or even millions of "hits", as people share the reference to it with their friends, and information about it circulates. The "Gangnam Style" dance video, for example, achieved millions of hits on YouTube, and generated hundreds of versions and imitative references to it in other posts. So what does it take for an internet post to "go viral"?

Nobody really knows, and advertisers would love to find out! While some topics, notably kittens and other cuddly animals, are fairly common in the most-looked-at charts, there have also been some very surprising contributions. It's all a question of what appeals to people at the time. But the openness of YouTube and other sites means that people can post what appeals to them, and just see how other people take it. It's an open window into the creativity of the human mind. Or, from other viewpoints, just an enticement for people to become increasingly silly.

What do you think?

Other forms of discourse

There are many ways that discourse can occur. For some researchers, just about any exchange of meaningful information can be regarded as a form of discourse. The use of colour in advertising, for example, contains its own symbolism. Advertisements which are to do with health or cleaning products, for instance, are likely to have blues, greens or white predominating because these colours are generally accepted as symbolising cleanliness. Advertisements promoting cars, or fashion choices, are more likely to use reds, oranges or other "stimulating" colours, either as backgrounds or in the product itself. The use of symbolism in popular culture is a study in its own right, known as semiotics, but it can also be regarded as a form of discourse when it is conveying social messages about power or desirability, or implicit social explanations.

We often use symbols in everyday living. As we saw in the last chapters, it is now common in texts and messaging to use emojis – small images which

Key Terms

semiotics
The use of symbols to express meaning in everyday life.

emojis (aka emogees)
Small icons shared in text messages and other internet contexts, illustrating emotions.

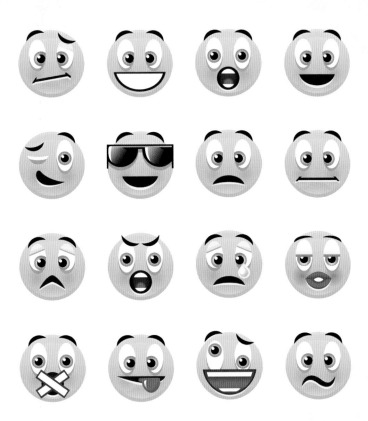

convey emotional responses and attitudes. The use of specific fonts in written discourse, which draw on implicit knowledge of social contexts or history is another example. Some fonts evoke Old English scripts, others adopt the type of lettering used in ancient Roman inscriptions, while others adopt lettering reminiscent of Arabic scripts, even though they are using the conventional alphabet. Each of these conveys social meanings, and can be regarded as tools for of discourse when they are used to communicate social meanings or information with explicit social implications.

More explicit, and perhaps a more common form of discourse, comes in the form of social directives. The road signs discussed above are one example, but there have also been a number of studies of work memos, and of other types of official communication. Te Molder (1999) analysed the discourse used by communication planners as they developed strategies to make sense of government initiatives, in order to convert them into plans which could really be put into action. The planners' discourse showed how important consensus and discussion were in achieving these tasks.

Media reports, too, are a rich source of discourse for researchers. Caillaud et al (2012) compared French and German media reports of the Bali United

Nations Climate Change conference. They found that the two sets of reporters used very different metaphors to communicate what was happening to their audiences. The French media tended to use "war" metaphors, describing the "battle" against climate change, and using other military explanations. The German media, on the other hand, tended to anchor their explanations in human and political terms, drawing on ideas of local and global visions, and even using religious metaphors to emphasise the importance of the issue to people at a personal level. These accounts were closely embedded in the dominant social representations of the two countries, reflecting their different histories regarding climate change, and the different social attitudes towards it. We will look at social representations later in this chapter.

Explanations and attitudes

Wetherell and Potter (1988) showed how discourse analysis provides a much richer source of information about attitudes than can be obtained by just assessing whether the attitude expressed is positive or negative. In an analysis of a set of interviews about the teaching of Maori culture in schools, they showed how white New Zealanders made a number of different types of responses. They classified these into three broad **repertoires**, or general themes which emerged from the interviews. These were: culture fostering – the idea that Maori culture should be encouraged; pragmatic realism – the idea that it was necessary to keep up with the modern world (implying that therefore teaching Maori culture would not be appropriate); and togetherness – the idea that everyone should "work together" for the good of the country (which really meant that everyone else should conform to white New Zealander culture).

Using these three repertoires meant that the speakers could claim to support cultural fostering while at the same time claiming that it was impractical or undesirable. As in the Van Dijk study, these interviews show how racist talk often includes a "positive" view, but then goes on to "discredit" it by bringing

Key Terms
repertoires Patterns of speech or behaviour which, taken together, constitute a fully meaningful action.

in other types of argument; thus making it seem as though the speaker is not really being racist at all, but simply "practical".

Explanations also depend on the social purpose of what we are saying. If you were explaining to your parents why you went to the swimming baths instead of staying in bed one morning, you might just say "I felt like a change"; but explaining the same event to an athletically-minded friend might involve a different explanation, like "I want to get fitter", because they would be more interested in that. And the interpersonal or social consequences of the explanation also affect what we choose to say. If you knew that telling your tutor "I just felt like going out instead of finishing it" would get you into trouble for not handing your assignment in on time, you might look for another explanation, like describing how overloaded with other work you had been.

Antaki and Fielding (1981) argued that much of the explanation which we use in everyday life is actually contained in the way that we describe things. As we saw in the last chapter, the words we use can condense a great deal of meaning into just a single phrase. Imagine visiting a friend and remarking that there seemed to be quite a few people calling on houses in her street. She replies: "They're Jehovah's Witnesses", and that simple description is quite enough to convey an explanation of what is going on, because it draws on shared common knowledge of how Jehovah's Witnesses behave. If she had said that they were, for example, school teachers, then a further explanation would have been needed. Many of the words which are used in reporting news broadcasts on television contain hidden explanations in this way.

Purposes of explanations

Explanations in everyday life can serve a number of purposes in addition to giving causes for events. For example: a study by Antaki and Naji (1987) involved tape-recording and then analysing conversations which took place at tea-time or at dinner parties. The conversations often tended to describe some long-standing social situation (like, say, the relatively small number of women dentists), and then to seek some explanation for it. The reason why a longstanding topic was chosen, Antaki and Naji argued, was because that would ensure that there was some mutual understanding or common ground between the participants, and the explanations which people offered reflected how they wished to appear sensible and intelligent in the eyes of the others.

Scott and Lyman (1968) made an important distinction between "justifications" and "excuses". A justification is the type of explanation which admits that the person concerned was responsible, but argues that performing the action was really an acceptable thing to do. ("I climbed on the fence because I was trying to rescue the cat from the tree"). Excuses, on the other hand, are explanations which deny that the person concerned was really responsible ("the fence was so rotten that it would have broken anyway"). You may find it interesting to apply this distinction to the reasons and excuses you hear around you.

Box 4.1   Superstition as coping

Shared experience is the basis for all our social interaction, but that shared experience may take the form of stories and myths, as well as real-world events. Some of those stories have long-standing roots, having been passed from person to person. The belief that it is lucky to throw coins into water – for example, wells and fountains – can be traced right back to pre-Christian times in the UK and Europe, when precious items were thrown into pools as offerings to the water gods and spirits.

Superstitions, at heart, come from our deep-seated need to exercise some control over our lives. They were particularly common in earlier times, when people's lives were entirely dependent on the vagaries of wind, weather and climate. Although they have much less relevance in modern technological societies, we often turn to them at times when we feel that events are not wholly under our control. Sporting mascots and rituals, lucky charms and astrological predictions are all superstitions which help us to cope by feeling that we can exert just a little control over what happens to us. And of course, they provide explanations for why things happen.

New superstitions develop, as well, although in modern society they are more likely to be personal rather than shared. Someone might have a pair of "lucky pants" for example, having once been successful when they were wearing them, or a lucky charm that they carry around. B. F. Skinner showed that even animals can develop superstitions if something that they do is immediately followed by a food reward, even if it is completely unrelated. The animal will often repeat the unrelated act, such as turning round or scratching an ear, before doing the action which will be rewarded. It's a bit like the way that people "touch wood" for luck – although that particular one, again, traces back to the days when people believed in the spirits of trees.

Animism is a form of superstition which is so common that some people regard it is "hard-wired" into the human brain. We are always ready to attribute intention or emotion to things, even sometimes to simple shapes. Every human culture has included some kind of animism, ranging from acknowledging tree spirits or the spiritual properties of particular stones, to giving names and personalities to boats or ships, or to attributing malevolent intention to a printer or photocopier which fails to perform at times of urgency. It's a very powerful tendency which almost all human beings do to some extent.

Animism seems to happen without much external influence; it's how we think. But most superstitions have been passed on and shared between other people – so much so that a superstitious person will even tell somebody off if they see them acting in a way that they believe to be particularly unlucky. Much of what we learn from other people consists of beliefs about how the world works, and what causes what, and that includes the superstitious beliefs which form part of popular culture. In modern living, where we can exert so much more control over our lives, superstitions are becoming less common, and less widely shared. But they haven't died out altogether, and it's unlikely that they ever will.

Explanations and scripts

There's an interesting question, though, about how much we really expect people to explain their actions. As we saw in the last chapter, a lot of social life takes place using familiar scripts, which means that we know roughly what to expect in a given situation. A study by Langer et al (1978) showed how, in a familiar situation, people don't seem to think very much about what's

Key Terms
script A well-known pattern of social action and interaction which has been socially established and accepted, and is implicitly and automatically followed by people in the relevant situation.

happening. Instead, they seem to take it for granted that what has been said is what they would expect.

In their study, a researcher would interrupt people who were using a photocopier to copy several different things. In one condition, the researcher explained why they wanted to interrupt, by saying: "Excuse me, I have five pages. May I use the Xerox machine, because I'm in a rush?" Over 80 per cent of those asked in this way agreed. Interestingly, though, the same number of people agreed when the researcher said: "Excuse me, I have five pages. May I use the Xerox machine because I have to make copies?", which didn't really give any explanation at all. However, the extra bit added on the end clearly mattered, because when the researcher asked: "Excuse me, I have five pages. May I use the Xerox machine?", without adding anything on the end, only just over 50 per cent of subjects acceded to the request. So it seems that, as long as the request had the expected form – as long as it conformed to the script – people didn't really think much about what was actually said.

However, Langer et al did find that people listened to the content when the request was more serious. When they repeated the study, but this time with the researcher asking to copy twenty pages instead of five, they found a different result. Overall, as you might anticipate, the number of people who agreed to let the researcher interrupt their work was much lower: fewer than 25 per cent of subjects acceded to the requests when no reason was given, regardless of how they were structured. Roughly 40 per cent agreed when the researcher said that they were in a rush.

Sometimes, then, we need to provide explanations for what we are doing, and sometimes we don't. Manis (1977) argued that, most of the time, we don't bother providing reasons for why we do things: we just take it for granted that they don't need any explanation. But at other times, we find that people can go to great lengths to explain the reason for something. Hastie (1984) asked subjects to perform a sentence completion task, and found that when the first part of the sentence was something ordinary and expected, the subjects didn't tend to bother explaining them; but when it was incongruent, and didn't fit with what would normally be expected, people provided explanations or reasons for it. So it seems to be incongruent or unexpected acts which need explaining, not things which are just part of the regular "scripts" of day-to-day living.

When we're looking at the types of explanations which people give, we need to look also at the whole social context in which they occur. Lalljee (1981) argued that we have to consider four dimensions of this social context: assumptions, relationships, social purpose and interpersonal consequences. The assumptions which the speaker can make about what their listener already knows affects just how much they need to explain; saying "I'm going on holiday tomorrow" as a reason for not going out with your friends assumes that they realise that you need to get ready, possibly by packing your things or by going to bed early. Similarly, the relationship that we have with the person that we are giving the explanation to will affect what we say. You might explain cooking something elaborate for dinner to your family by saying "I thought I'd try something a bit special"; but if you were explaining the same thing to a visitor who had come to dinner, and who you had wanted to treat, you might give a different explanation, such as: "I enjoy cookery."

ATTRIBUTION THEORY

Looking at the explanations which people give also involves looking at their underlying theories about why things happen. Both attribution theory and social representations theory are concerned with these theories, exploring how people explain their own and other people's actions. Attribution theory analyses explanations at the individual cognitive level, whereas social representation theory looks at the overall social and societal level of explanation. So, they can both contribute to our understanding of what we are actually using explanations for.

In 1958, Heider proposed that we are always striving to understand our social worlds, and that we do this by forming ideas and theories about what is going on. Some of the most important of these ideas concern the causes which we attribute to actions or events – how we explain why something happened, or why someone acted. Heider (1958) proposed that there are five major **levels of responsibility**, which are all about how much the person actually intended the outcome to happen (see Table 4.2).

Table 4.2 Levels of responsibility

1. **Association:** Where the person is present at the time of the event, but has no direct connection with it (e.g., the cafetière fell off the worktop and broke when John was in the kitchen but had not touched it).

2. **Causality:** Where the person indirectly caused the event to happen, perhaps as a result of an accident (e.g., John dropped a mug which fell on the cafetière and broke).

3. **Justifiability:** Where the person caused the event but had good reasons for doing so (e.g., John broke the cafetière after reading evidence that drinking real coffee was damaging to the health).

4. **Foreseeability:** Where the person could reasonably have predicted the consequences of their actions (e.g., John placed the cafetière right at the edge of the worktop, where it would be easily knocked over).

5. **Intentionality:** Where the person's actions were deliberate and planned (e.g., John broke the cafetière to be spiteful and cause inconvenience).

Source: Heider (1958)

Together they make up different types of **attributions** or causal beliefs. Effectively, Heider argued that we act as "naive scientists", gathering factual information and using it to form theories about the possible causes of what is going on around us. The way we identify these causes is the process of attribution.

Correspondent inference theory

There have been a number of developments to attribution theory since Heider's first discussions. **Correspondent inference theory** explores the different factors which contribute to the inferences which we make about social responsibility. Whether we see someone as responsible for their actions or not depends on a number of factors, including whether we think they are capable or not, and how important the situation is to what they are doing.

Correspondent inference theory rests on three basic concepts. The first is our tendency to look for stable causes for why things happen, so we can predict what is likely to occur next time. Unstable causes, by definition, don't give us any guidance for the future. The second is judging intentionality – whether or not the person performed the act or action deliberately. And the third is

Key Terms
attributions The reasons people give for why things happen.
correspondent inference theory An attribution theory which uses stability and intentionality to attribute causes.

the distinction between dispositional attributions, when we conclude that the source or responsibility for the action lies within the person themselves, and situational attributions, when we conclude that the person acted the way they did because of the constraints they were under in that situation.

Linking these three concepts, Jones and Davis (1965) proposed that we have a powerful inclination to make **dispositional** attributions as opposed to **situational** ones, and the most important factor in this is how we judge intentionality. When we are attributing intentions, we make inferences about the person's knowledge of the likely outcome of what they were doing, and about their ability to undertake the action. By and large, we tend to assume that people have acted deliberately rather than accidentally, unless we have some reason to judge the person as being incapable – for example, because they are too young, or mentally inadequate. Once we have judged an act to be intentional, we look for a personal trait or characteristic which could have produced that intention. This is the correspondent inference for which the theory has been named.

For instance, suppose that your friend Sheila failed her geography exam. If you thought that Sheila had failed her geography exam deliberately, you would be likely to make an internal attribution about it: (e.g., that she doesn't like geography and wants to give it up). But if you thought it was not deliberate, you would be more likely to make a situational attribution (e.g., the room was too noisy which was irritating and interfered with her concentration). The attributions you would make would correspond with the inference you had made about her disposition.

Dispositions and intentions, though, aren't necessarily the same thing. We might make the dispositional attribution that someone was careless; but that might be a way of saying that the consequences were not actually deliberate, rather than that they were. Eiser (1983) suggested that Jones and Davies's idea of correspondent inferences can only be considered to apply when there is some element of choice or control in the situation, not when the outcome is accidental.

Jones and Davies identified several influencing factors in correspondent inference theory. These include **hedonic relevance**, **personalism**, social desirability and the principle of **non-common effects** (see Table 4.3). Each of these factors, in their model, can influence whether we make a dispositional attribution or a situational one in any given situation.

Key Terms

dispositional
To do with the person's character or personality.

situational
To do with the circumstances and environmental pressures active at the time.

hedonic relevance
The tendency to be more likely to make a dispositional attribution about something if it has either pleasant or unpleasant consequences for the person making the attribution.

personalism
The tendency that people have to be more likely to make a dispositional attribution if the target affects them personally.

non-common effects
Effects which only apply in particular situations and not most of the time.

Table 4.3 Principles of correspondent inference

Hedonic relevance: whether an act produces a pleasurable or unpleasant outcome.

Personalism: whether an act directly affects the individual who is making the attribution.

Social desirability: whether an act is likely to be approved by others or not.

Non-common effects: whether an act has a wide range of consequences or is limited in its effect.

Source: Jones and Davis (1965)

Attributional errors

In most everyday situations, we have well-developed beliefs about what we might expect people to do. In 1967, Jones and Harris investigated how people explain the beliefs of someone if they have seen them acting in an unexpected fashion. They asked American research participants to read a short written speech, and to say what they believed the speaker's true attitude was. The speeches were all about support for or opposition to the Castro government in Cuba, which was a "hot" political subject at the time. Since Americans in general were extremely hostile to that government, speeches supporting Castro were unusual. Jones and Harris found that, even when the participants were told that the speaker had been allocated their topic, with no choice which side to support, they attached very little importance to the speaker's situation. About 45 per cent of them still rated the speakers as believing what they had said, and used this as evidence to support their views about the disposition of the speaker.

The effect, though, was much smaller when subjects were judging a speech which was more conventional – in this instance, anti-Castro. Jones and McGillis (1976) suggested that it is only unusual behaviour, which challenges our expectations, that we really find informative. If people just do what we expect them to do, that doesn't tell us much about them. But if they do something which is unusual, we begin to speculate about why they have done it. We feel we have to explain things which deviate from the normal scripts of everyday living, but we don't feel much need to explain the things we are used to.

What Jones and Harris had also shown was that we have a strong tendency to make dispositional attributions and to ignore situational information. This is a recurrent finding, so much so that it has become known as the fundamental attribution error. It has been demonstrated in a number of different ways. For example, in one study, Ross et al (1977) set up a quiz game, in which participants were randomly given the role of questioner or contestant. Although both the observers and the participants knew that the roles had been randomly assigned, the participants nonetheless consistently rated the questioner as being more knowledgeable than the contestant was. They effectively ignored all sorts of situational variables, including the fact that the questioner had free choice of subject and so could choose questions from their own knowledge, whereas the contestant had no such choice.

Gilbert and Malone (1995) argued that people may underestimate situational influences partly because of the way that they are often quite subtle and difficult for an observer to detect, partly because the general expectation is that people will act according to their dispositions, and partly because of the complexities of social information processing. **Situational attributions** are more complex to process than dispositional ones because by definition they make us look at the features of the social situation within which the event is taking place. **Dispositional attributions** are much simpler. So in an everyday situation, where there are usually quite a few demands on our cognitive processing, we tend to opt for the dispositional attribution because it saves time and mental energy.

A matter of perspective

The **fundamental attribution** error is particularly marked when we are comparing our own behaviour with that of other people. When we are looking at our own behaviour, we tend to make situational attributions – we look at the situation that we are in and how it has constrained our actions. But when we look at other people's behaviour, we make dispositional attributions, even when we are trying to explain the very same thing! For example, Nisbett et al (1973) asked male students to explain, in a written paragraph, why they liked their girlfriends, and why they had chosen to study their subject at college. Then they were asked to write an equivalent paragraph about their best friend. When the reasons given in the paragraphs were analysed, the researchers found that the students had made situational attributions about themselves (e.g., "My course will help me to get a good job"), but dispositional attributions about their friends (e.g., "He's good at maths").

It may be, though, that it is simply a matter of perspective. In 1973, Storms made a series of videotapes of conversations in which both sides of the conversation were taped separately. The participants who had taken part in the conversations were then asked to look at the tapes, and to explain why the person was saying what they did. Storms found that their viewpoint seemed to make a difference; when people saw their own behaviour as if from the outside, they made more dispositional attributions about their own behaviour, and more situational ones about the other person's.

Prior knowledge comes into play, too. Kulik (1983) showed that if we are asked to judge someone else's behaviour, who we know, and that behaviour is different from our expectations about that person, then we will tend to make situational attributions. So, for example, if I know that Sheila is a hardworking student and usually passes exams, I'd be likely to make a situational attribution about why she failed, rather than a dispositional one. As Lalljee (1981) reminds us, we have to bear in mind the social context and prior social knowledge which people are applying to the situation.

There may be cultural differences too. In an attributional study undertaken with Hindu children and white American children of the same ages, Miller (1984) found that the Hindu children made fewer dispositional and more situational attributions than the American children did. Moreover, this difference increased systematically with age. While there was a slight difference with children aged 8, the difference was more apparent with children who were 11, and even more so with 15-year-olds. So it appears that **causal attributions** do not simply depend upon the individual's personal history, but also result from socialisation in a particular culture.

Taking this idea further, Choi et al (1999) found that those cultural differences seemed to do with whether the person making the attribution came from a **collectivist** culture, which emphasises the common good above individual needs, or an **individualistic** one. They argued that belonging to a collectivist culture makes, people more sensitive to the power of situations, so their attributions tend to take that into account.

Key Terms

collectivist
A type of culture which emphasises membership of the community over individualism.

individualistic
A cultural approach which emphasises the individual over the group.

Talking point　4.3 Attributions in the media

Attributions are explanations for why things happen. Try watching an everyday news programme and noting down all the attributions which are made – both by newsreaders and also by people who are interviewed during the programme. Do they have a particular pattern (e.g., blaming individuals rather than situations?).

Are the attributions you have identified part of a social discourse, reflecting an attempt to persuade the viewer to see things in a particular way? If so, what alternative attributions might have been possible?

The self-serving bias

A slightly different aspect of how we make attributions, which is related to the fundamental attribution error but not quite the same thing, is known as the **self-serving bias**. It has to do with our tendency to make attributions which will help us to see ourselves in a favourable way, particularly if we are trying to explain our personal success or failure. Miller and Ross (1975) showed how many studies indicate that we tend to attribute success to dispositional causes, and failure to situational ones ("I passed my biology exam because I'm good at biology, but I failed French because my Aunt Millie visited us that week and I didn't get any time to revise").

There have been a number of explanations for the self-serving bias. One of them is that we like to "save face" – to present a favourable impression to others and avoid social shame. If we explain our failure as something that we couldn't help, it means we can avoid looking stupid or incapable. Similarly, explaining success as coming from our own personal qualities makes us look good. As an example, Jones and Berglas (1978) suggested that alcoholics may drink too much partly in order to avoid making personal attributions for failure. By attributing their poor performance to alcohol, they avoid having to attribute it to lack of ability. They described this as a self-handicapping strategy, providing the person with a ready-made excuse for potential failure.

The self-serving bias also allows us to protect our self-esteem. McFarland and Ross (1982) gave research participants false feedback about how well they had done at a fairly difficult task, asking them to explain why they had done well or badly. They found that their participants might make either dispositional or situational attributions about their performance, but those who attributed failure to lack of ability also tended to have very low levels of self-esteem, while those who attributed it to situational causes did not. But, of course, this study shows only that self-esteem and the type of attribution we make might be correlated – it doesn't imply that we change our attributions in order to protect our self-esteem.

We don't always apply the self-serving bias, though. Campbell et al (2000) found that people would take individual credit for success but blame their partner for failure if they were paired with strangers, but not if they were paired with their friends. Friendship, they argued, places barriers on self-enhancement – for example, and may be because we feel less need to protect our self-esteem with friends than we would with people we don't feel know us particularly well.

Covariance

It is apparent, then, that we don't always go for dispositional attributions, even if there does seem to be a bias in that direction. We also apply our knowledge about the usual state of affairs. If I knew that you were usually on time, I would be more likely to think that you had been held up by something external if you were late on one occasion, than to conclude that it was because of your disposition. Kelley (1973) argued that we use **covariance** – looking at when and how often things happen – to judge what type of attribution we should make.

Covariance has three dimensions: consistency, consensus and distinctiveness. The **consistency** of an event is to do with how the person has acted on previous occasions, as in the example above. If you are always late calling for people, that would be high consistency; if you are usually on time, your lateness would have low consistency. **Consensus** is to do with how other people act: if people are always late when they call for me (high consensus), I'd be less likely to attribute your lateness to your own nature. Instead, I might look for something in the situation; perhaps my house is difficult to find, or there isn't a convenient bus. And **distinctiveness** is concerned with the target of the act – it would make a difference to the attribution that I made if you were late each time you called for me, but not when you called for anyone else.

Kelley argued that the pattern of covariance, or the way that each of these dimensions vary, determines the attributions that we are likely to make. Table 4.4 shows the three major patterns of covariance, and the type of attributions that they would be likely to lead to.

Table 4.4 Patterns of covariance

Event: "Jane is laughing at a comedian"

Consistency	Distinctiveness	Consensus	Type of attribution
High	*Low*	*Low*	*Person*
Jane always laughs at this comedian	Jane laughs at most comedians	Other people don't find this comedian funny	It's because of Jane's personal sense of humour
High	*High*	*High*	*Entity*
Jane always laughs at this comedian	Jane doesn't usually laugh at comedians	Other people laugh at this comedian too	It's because the comedian is funny
Low	*High*	*Low*	*Circumstance*
Jane hasn't laughed at this comedian before	Jane doesn't usually laugh at comedians	Other people don't find this comedian funny	It's because there's something special about this occasion

Key Terms

consistency
A factor in the covariance approach to attribution, which is to do with whether the person always, or usually, acts in that way.

consensus
A factor in the covariance approach to attribution, which is to do with whether other people also act in the same sort of way.

distinctiveness
Whether the person acts in the same way in similar situations to the one being considered, or not.

Covariance theory has been sharply criticised for two main reasons. One of the main criticisms concerns its assumption that all people do is analyse the information about that particular situation, without taking into account their prior experience. This information-processing approach assumes that people simply come across an event, and process the information about distinctiveness, consensus and consistency to come to an explanation of it. But people don't act so naïvely. Each of us draws on a huge range of experience and knowledge of different social situations, and we use this past experience to help us to explain what happens. If we treated everything as if we were coming to it completely fresh, as Kelley's theory implies, we would be completely overwhelmed with data.

The other criticism of covariance theory is related, and concerns the social nature of the attributional process. Covariance theory doesn't just ignore people's personal knowledge, it also overlooks what is going on socially. Lalljee (1981) argued that when we are developing explanations, we are drawing on a highly developed set of social knowledge, in terms of experience, scripts, schemas and expectations, and applying that knowledge to the explanation.

This means that while we might accept covariance for something ordinary, if an act was socially uncommon, or socially deviant, we wouldn't just accept the covariance principle mechanically. We might accept a consensus explanation "everyone does it" as a reason for wearing fashionable clothes, for example, but we wouldn't accept it as a causal attribution for why someone stole a car, even if car-stealing was quite common in their neighbourhood. Nor would we accept a consistency attribution for behaviour that was eccentric; saying "He always dresses like that" wouldn't be enough to explain why someone was going around in an old-fashioned frock-coat and top hat. Covariance in itself is not the full explanation for why we form the attributions that we do; it may play some part but we need to take account of other forms of social knowledge, too.

Following Lalljee, other researchers supported the argument that traditional research into attribution is too concerned with the mechanics of information-processing, and doesn't take account of personal interests and motivation. Kruglanski (1980) argued that we need to explore how people gather knowledge and change or don't change their ideas when faced with new information. Kruglanski referred to this as lay epistemology. Epistemology is the study of what counts as knowledge and how knowledge is formed, and the "lay" part means "laypeople" as opposed to experts. In other words, how ordinary people seek and use knowledge.

Several psychologists – for instance, Kelly (1955), Heider (1958) and Neisser (1976) – have shown how people explore the world by generating hypotheses to explain their experience. Kruglanski argued that most people don't really generate new hypotheses all the time. In practice, we take a lot of information for granted. There are, for instance, any number of possible hypotheses to explain why water is falling from the sky – rain, wet birds, someone spraying upwards with a high-powered hosepipe, a film studio special effects team on location, etc. But, in reality, we would just assume it was raining unless we had any reason to think otherwise. Most of our thinking, Kruglanski argued, is fairly routine and doesn't cause us to challenge our conventional assumptions with new hypotheses.

Kruglanski argued that even when we meet new situations, we generally only explore two or three hypotheses and then freeze on to one of them as the explanation. Once that explanation or attribution has become frozen, we ignore alternatives. In one study, Ross et al (1975) asked people to assess whether a series of suicide notes were genuine or not, and gave them false feedback about their level of accuracy. Later on, the researchers admitted that the feedback had been untrue, and showed how the feedback had actually depended on random allocation. But even when they showed the participants the experimenter's random allocation list, they still believed what they had originally been told and ignored the new information.

In a follow-up study, Kruglanski et al (1983) replicated these findings, but then told one of the groups that accurate self-perception was important; their evaluations would be publicly compared with their real scores, so other people could see whether they had changed their ideas. Unlike the others, these people managed to "unfreeze" their beliefs. Kruglanski suggested that whether beliefs become frozen or not depends on two factors: the person's capacity to generate alternative explanations, and their motivation, that is, whether they have a personal reason to change what they believe. Some examples of capacity and motivation are given in Table 4.5.

So motivation, too, is important in the attributions that we make. Kruglanski et al (1983) shows how motivation is not just an optional extra – it's a

Table 4.5 Factors influencing capacity and motivation

Capacity	Prior knowledge
	Availability
	Recency
	Relevance
Motivation	The need for clear structure
	What we wish to believe
	The need for validity

Source: Kruglanski et al (1983)

fundamental part of how we go about making attributions. Rather than being the strictly rational process implied by covariance theory, attributions are simultaneously rational and motivational:; rational in that they have to be cognitively consistent and logically deduced, as shown by Heider and others; and motivational, because they reflect people's personal and cognitive needs.

Attributional styles

The distinction between internal or dispositional attributions, and external, situational ones led to other ideas. In 1978, Abramson et al argued that it is important to distinguish between causes which apply to only one or two situations and causes which apply generally to several different settings. So, for example, you might attribute failing to solve a maths problem correctly to not being particularly good at maths, which would be a specific attribution that would be likely to apply only to maths problems; or you might attribute it to low intelligence, a global attribution that would be likely to be relevant in a number of other situations as well.

In 1966, Rotter had proposed that people could be broadly classified into internal and external attributors in terms of the attributions which they generally make, and that this was important because it determined whether they saw causes as controllable, or not. This led to the idea of locus of control, which became very useful in therapeutic practice. However, it gradually became clear that internal attributions are not always controllable, and that controllability needed to be seen as a separate dimension.

In 1976, Weiner et al proposed that there was a need for an additional dimension of causality, which would distinguish between causes which were temporary and fluctuating (such as mood or weather) and causes which were stable and enduring (such as aptitude or ability). They asked research participants to make copies of patterns using building blocks. After each trial, they were asked to explain why they had succeeded, and they were also asked to guess how well they would do on the next trial (the trials had been set up so that the participant would always be successful). Weiner et al found that people made different types of attributions about their success, and that these attributions correlated with their confidence about the future. People who made stable attributions such as "I'm good at this sort of thing" were also more confident about their likely success in the future, than people who made unstable attributions such as "I succeeded because I was having a good day."

Pasahow (1980) manipulated whether research participants were likely to make global or specific attributions for failing to solve laboratory problems, and found that those research participants who were induced to make global

attributions performed worse on later tasks than did the people who made specific attributions. Similarly, Mikulincer (1986) showed that manipulating the
attributions which people made about failing at a task only seemed to produce
helplessness when the research participants made global attributions, and not
if they made specific ones. However, this was also influenced by how much the
research participants expected to be able to control their situation.

Bringing all this together, in 1986, Stratton et al described a system for
coding attributions which are made in the course of everyday conversation.
They had developed this model from work in family therapy, which had provided them with a considerable amount of material in the form of conversations (all the families who were involved in the research had given permission
beforehand for their data to be used for research, of course). Stratton et al had
found that analysing the attributions which people made had been very valuable in helping the therapists to identify useful areas to emphasise. From this
material, they developed the Leeds Attributional Coding System (Stratton et al,
1988). This lists five attributional dimensions (see Table 4.6). Since its development, this system has been used in a number of different contexts, including
organisational and marketing research as well as family therapy.

Table 4.6 Attributional dimensions

1. Stable / Unstable	Whether the identified cause is regarded as likely to happen again or not.
2. Global / Specific	How wide the range of outcomes is.
3. Internal / External	Whether the cause is judged to come from dispositional or situational factors.
4. Personal / Universal	Whether the outcome is likely to affect the speaker directly.
5. Controllable / Uncontrollable	Whether the identified cause is seen as open to influence, or not amenable to any influence or direction.

Source: Leeds Attributional Coding System, Stratton et al (1988)

Beese and Stratton (2014) used the Leeds Attributional Coding System to
explore delusional beliefs in people who were receiving psychiatric help. They
used a qualitative approach, interviewing the patients and then analysing the
content of the interviews to identify the relevant causal beliefs. They found that
the patterns of attributions which the patients made highlighted several issues
about their delusions which were not identified by standard diagnostic techniques. When patients talked about having outcomes, or purposes, for their delusions, for example, their attributional styles indicated a level of potential control,
while those who saw their delusions as the cause of their problems tended to see
them as stable and uncontrollable, and so felt unable to change them. Moreover,
the researchers found, attributional patterns which were global, personal and
uncontrollable were associated with considerable personal distress. Beese and
Stratton suggested that therapy aimed at changing these patterns would be beneficial, at the least in helping to minimise the chances of relapse.

In 1975, Dweck set up a training course which deliberately aimed to change
the "uncontrollable" attributions which some school pupils made about their
lack of success. The course consisted of a series of small tasks, which were

constructed so that the child experienced both successes and failures. After each failure, the child was told explicitly that they failed because they hadn't tried hard enough. Dweck reported that this strategy had resulted in the children learning to be much more persistent in their efforts, and feeling that such things were much more under their control than they had previously believed.

Stanley and Standen (2000) looked at the attributions about the origins of challenging behaviour made by carers at a day centre. They found that the more outwardly directed the challenging behaviour was (e.g., aggression or verbal aggression towards staff), the more the carers made attributions of control and negative affect, which in turn made them less inclined to help. Where they saw the person's behaviour as uncontrollable and as not particularly negative emotionally, and also as self-directed or dependent, they were far more ready to assist. The nature of the attributions they made about the behaviour directly affected the way that the carers responded.

Fincham et al (2002) found that the type of attributions we make are also linked with the quality of our personal relationships. People in unhappy close relationships tended to make attributions about their partner's behaviour which were internal, stable and global – that is, which were about their dispositions, were unlikely to change, and would be likely to apply to a range of other situations. At least, that was how they interpreted negative events. When their partner acted positively, they attributed that to external, unstable and specific causes – that is, it was for reasons other than that person's disposition, it wouldn't last, and it was only because of the situation. People who had happy long-term relationships, though, showed exactly the opposite pattern of attribution.

Social attribution

Attributions also serve social purposes, and many attribution theorists are less concerned with individualistic information-processing and more concerned with how people develop shared, or collective patterns of attribution. Munton and Antaki (1988) showed how attributions can work at the group level. They looked at families undergoing family therapy, and found that the shared attributions made by family members for why things happen exerted a considerable influence on the outcome of the therapy. Families with shared attributions which focused on stable causes were much less likely to benefit from the family therapy than those with unstable and controllable attributions.

Attributions may be shared by larger groups, too. Some research uses attributions to identify in-group and out-group beliefs developing from social identity processes (see Chapter 1). For example, in one study (Bond et al, 1985), the researchers asked undergraduates in Hong Kong and in America to produce explanations about gender-appropriate behaviour. The American undergraduates showed a much stronger tendency to favour their own group than did those from undergraduates from Hong Kong. Hong Kong culture has a strong emphasis on avoiding social conflict, and American culture has a stronger women's liberation movement. It seems that these differences in attributions were also revealing underlying cultural differences between the two societies.

In a different study, Bond and Hewstone (1988) asked 256 British and Hong Kong undergraduates to complete a questionnaire which asked them to provide explanations for what was happening in Hong Kong – a society undergoing considerable political transformations at the time. The attributions showed a number of differences between the two groups in terms of political factors like resistance to change, and satisfaction with the status quo.

SOCIAL REPRESENTATIONS

Attributions can also reveal shared underlying beliefs, or social representations. As we saw in the last chapter, our rich world of language and symbols allows us to communicate with one another indirectly, and sometimes in ways that have very little to do with spoken language. As human beings, we are particularly sensitive to symbols and signs, and we are very ready to construe meaning in all sorts of things that we encounter as part of our lives. Some aspects of human life make deliberate use of that readiness; organised religion, for example, has always recognised the power of symbolism, and so do many of society's control mechanisms, such as traffic control or medical practice.

Society also exerts control over us through our internalised awareness of regulations and sanctions. A large part of child-rearing involves teaching a child what is and what is not acceptable behaviour. As any mother knows, the ages of two and three can be particularly difficult, as the child has become independently mobile and vocal, but has not yet internalised all of the social rules needed to participate in society. Some traditional societies, such as the Shona people in Africa, deal with this by having the grandparents, as the more experienced child-rearers, take over the main care of the child during these years, which to many harassed mothers might seem to be a very practical solution!

As we grow older, though, those rules and regulations become internalised and we don't need other people there to tell us how we should act. Instead, we have our own internal regulators, which tell us to modify our emotional reactions to act in a civilised way, or to take certain actions in certain situations. This process of internalisation is an essential part of being social; it means that all members of the society have a shared understanding of how they should act, and so it facilitates social co-operation and smooth everyday interactions. Without this social regulation, we would be entirely at sea every time we met someone new, we wouldn't know how to act ourselves, or what to expect from them.

Social representations and culture

Social representations are the shared beliefs held by societies or groups within societies, and they are used to explain why things are as they are. They are called representations because they represent reality at a socio-cognitive level. They may seem like personal beliefs, and nothing much to do with our social psychology, but actually, they help to shape our social experience, just as body language or discourse does. Social representations are part of the vast range of assumptions and shared understandings that we take for granted in our social lives, and they exert a much larger influence over our behaviour than we realise. They can form the basis of friendships or social networks, affect whether we like or dislike someone, or even determine what we do on a particular day.

Every society has its shared assumptions and beliefs – about how things are, about how they have to be, and about why they have come about in that particular way. Often, we only become aware of them if we travel to another country where the social representations are different; otherwise we just take the social representations we have grown up with for granted, and assume that they are self-evident. Social representations colour many of our day-to-day interactions; and they also have a powerful influence on our thinking. Indeed, some social psychologists have been known to argue that they are basically what thinking is all about. We reorganise and reshape our social representations through conversation and what we learn through other sources – mainly the media or internet, and then we apply those social representations to make sense of the day-to-day world that we live in.

> ## Box 4.2   Social representations and science
>
> Many of the social representations which are in common currency consist of traditional knowledge, which has been passed on through the family or through social institutions. But social representations may also emerge from more recent, "scientific" theories. Many psychoanalytic ideas, for example, have become integrated into general knowledge, and form part of everyday thinking; but this was not the case a century ago. It is through this process that common knowledge – also known as lay epistemology – comes to reflect the ideas and assumptions of the society in which it is based.
>
> So, for instance, theories about intelligence as something which can be acquired or learned with the right kind of training were more common in America and Russia, both of which have traditions about equality, than they were in Britain with its historical class tradition, where the belief that intelligence was an inherited "gift" used to be much more common, although it is less so nowadays. As society changes, though, social representations change too, and that contrast between social representations in the different cultures has become much less pronounced in recent years. Over the past 100 years, there have been any number of theories about intelligence developed in the scientific world. As with other scientific ideas, each society tends to adopt or emphasise those which fit the general assumptions of the time, and to ignore or minimise the research which doesn't.

Key Terms

social representations
The shared beliefs which develop and are transmitted in social groups and in society as a whole, and explain why things are as they are.

Social representations tell us a lot about just why language and other forms of communication exert such a powerful influence on our psychology. It has to do with the way that we construe meaning. Moscovici (1984), who developed the theory of social representations, observed that some social representations seem to be shared by large groups of people, and can come to form a dominant theory in that society, while others may be shared by smaller groups of people. Moscovici had developed his theory after extensive research into minority influence – the way in which the beliefs held by small groups of people could gradually come to be accepted more widely, provided that they presented them clearly and consistently over time. We will look at that work more closely in Chapter 6.

If we examine social representations in terms of generally accepted cultural beliefs, we find significant differences between what they would lead us to expect, and the individualistic predictions of attribution theory. For example, in 1989, Guimond et al found that the fundamental attribution error was reversed in a study which compared the attributions about poverty made by social science students and by poor and unemployed people of the same age. Although you might think that unemployed people, being directly in touch with the social realities of being unemployed, would attribute their unemployment to the situation, they tended to make dispositional attributions. The students, on the other hand, made situational ones.

Classic attribution theory would predict a different outcome. But the explanations we choose don't just come out of thin air, and some types of explanation are more generally accepted by society than others. Guimond et al's study shows how the theory of social representations is relevant to the understanding of causal attributions. As they progress into their educational disciplines, students can be seen as progressively acquiring a representation of reality defined by the discipline and distinct from that defined within other disciplines. The social science students in the study had acquired social representations regarding poverty and its causes which were different from those held by members of the general public, and it is our social representations which determined the attributions which we make.

The dynamic nature of social representations

It is important to remember, though, that social representations are not passed on as absolute fact, even though the people holding them may see them as such. Instead, they are negotiated – through conversation, through the application of different knowledge and experience, and above all through social discourse. That discourse may be interpersonal, but it also operates at the societal level, as we take on board the various interpretations of events provided by the mass media and other sources of information.

New social representations can sometimes emerge quite quickly. In 1987, Galli and Nigro explored how children's social representations of radioactivity changed as a result of the Chernobyl explosion. Just after the event, they asked children to produce drawings and definitions of radioactivity, and also to comment on what was produced. Within just a few days, the children's drawings and explanations showed that they had developed a shared representation of radioactivity, and of the Chernobyl explosion itself. A major event like Chernobyl can produce a social consensus very quickly, because it generates so much conversation and discussion.

We use social representations to explain issues as diverse as why someone has moved away from a neighbourhood, why our politicians seem to be acting particularly incompetently, why the spring seems particularly hot/cold or why there are people begging on the street. But we don't swallow social representations wholesale. We negotiate acceptable social representations as we discuss ideas, observations and events with other people, until we have a version which fits acceptably into our own personal belief system. We also incorporate ideas and opinions obtained through the mass media, and through internet sources. So any one person's repertoire of social representations is a combination of **consensual beliefs**, acquired through conversation and discourse, and individual ones acquired through personal experience. Which means that social representations are continuously changing, as they are passed on through society.

Every person is an individual, with their own schemas based on their personal experience, and their own ways of construing the world. So when we are presented with social explanations, or social representations, we weigh them up against our own knowledge, and may entirely reject them if they are too contradictory to what we already know. Alternatively, we may accept them as "partly true", negotiating them through conversation or selective information-gathering until they are congruent with our own beliefs and ideas.

This raises the question of how social representations can be so consistent across cultures and groups, if everyone is negotiating their own version. The answer lies in how they are structured. Any given social representation has a central core which is (relatively) fixed and unchanging – although it may change slowly over time. That central core is known as the **figurative nucleus**, and it is the part of the social representation which is most firmly based in ideology and culture. It remains pretty consistent, although it may change very gradually over time. But it is the part of the social representation which just about everyone in that group or culture shares.

However, as Flament (1989) showed, that central core can manifest itself in many different ways, because each social representation also has a number of **peripheral elements**. These are applications or amplifications of the representation which can change quite quickly over time. They protect the central core, but they can also be selectively shared – that is, not everyone holding the representation needs to accept all of the peripheral elements.

The peripheral elements are what gives the social representation its flexibility in terms of how it integrates with other social beliefs. So when people are negotiating social representations, through conversation and discourse, what they are doing is adjusting the peripheral elements so that they can fit the social representation more effectively into their own belief system. But the central core of the social representation does not change.

Box 4.3   Thinking about food

Fischler (1980) showed how changes in social representations of what constitutes an acceptable diet reflect the social and economic changes which have taken place in Western society over the past half-century. Some of those changes were developments in the production, distribution and consumption of food, while others were new, consumer-based lifestyles which involve different modes of eating – such as the change to fast food and snacks replacing formal meals.

Since that time, there have been even more changes in our beliefs, and also in our eating practices. While not everyone may achieve it, most people accept the "five-a-day" principle for fruit and veg and make some attempt to follow what is believed to be a healthy diet (although controversies about what that actually is become ever stronger!). Convenience foods have also changed; ready meals have become more elaborate and sophisticated, healthy options like salads are prepared beforehand and available in the shops, and supermarkets offer whole-meal combination packages at budget prices. It has even been argued that cooking and food preparation has become a middle-class hobby rather than a basic necessity!

There is also increasing recognition of both personal lifestyle choice and the way in which different individuals may react to different foodstuffs. Vegetarianism is now regarded as a normal everyday choice, where once it was regarded as a "crank" option and rarely catered for; and even veganism is gaining increased acceptance. And labelling regulations insist that ingredients known to be implicated in common allergies, such as soya and peanuts must be highlighted so that they can easily be identified.

It is rare, then, to find a single universally held social representation about what constitutes a healthy diet. Even the views expressed by health councils and other bodies are frequently challenged, and the fact that they change over time and sometimes contradict their own previous recommendations has limited their authority. Like other social representations, different representations are held by different groups, and as people become more curious and better informed, the controversies about what a healthy diet actually is become ever stronger.

How social representations are formed

Social representations are formed as we integrate new social knowledge into our existing knowledge frameworks. That new information may come to us directly, through conversation with others or indirectly through the mass media or through the internet. Edwards (1997) showed how people often try out different metaphors and images in conversation, until they finally settle on one which appears to contain an appropriate meaning satisfactory to all of the participants. This example illustrates how social representations can be negotiated through conversational exchanges.

Conversation isn't the only way in which we acquire or pass on social representations, though. The mass media has always been a significant influence in the acquisition of social representations. Social representations can be expressed through metaphors, images or stories, as well as through everyday explanations, and are often implicit in the ways that news stories, social events or dramas are presented. As we saw in Chapter 3, subtle choices of words such as calling a group "freedom fighters" or "terrorists" can indicate the existence of an underlying social representation, and so make all the difference to our social understanding.

In recent years, the internet has become another major vector in the transmission and presentation of social representations. Open-access sites such as YouTube and Twitter allow the open expression of alternative explanations and points of view (which is why they present a problem for repressive governments). As groups of people interact collectively through these and other sites, new social representations are formed which offer alternative types of explanations for social phenomena, and may eventually become so widespread that they enter the official public debates presented by the mass media.

Anchoring and objectification

New social representations can spread through society very quickly. They are formed, according to Moscovici (1984), by two processes: anchoring and objectification. **Anchoring** involves setting the ideas in a familiar context, so that people can grasp them more easily. **Objectification** involves finding a way of making the idea easier to grasp by making it more concrete and tangible. The two processes are similar, but not precisely identical, so it is worth considering them separately.

The process of anchoring a social representation might involve connecting its core ideas with a well-known social event or process, like construing a problem as an example of "mid-life crisis" or "teenage angst". Or it might mean classifying things in a particular way, like describing ecological protestors as "eco-freaks" or "rent-a-mob". Representing the holders of the ideas like this changes how we regard the ideas themselves. So, the social representation – in this case a dismissal of ecological activism – becomes established by being anchored in familiar aspects of our social experience.

Devine-Wright and Devine-Wright (2009) explored how visual images are often used in anchoring social representations about complex issues. They were investigating social representations concerning the use of renewable technologies for electricity generation, which is a topic which is a common part of everyday life but not necessarily a common part of everyday conversation. Perhaps for that reason, they found that the visual images of pylons, wind turbines, solar panels, etc. were a common way that the social issues concerned had become anchored into social representations.

In another study of social representations, Hungarian and Danish research participants each read the same short story, which told of two peasants being abused by two armed men but engaging in passive resistance. This story related

Key Terms

anchoring
Setting ideas in a familiar context.

objectification
Expressing an idea or belief by representing it as an object of some kind.

directly to Hungarian culture and its existing social representations, but not to Denmark, which has a strong tradition of independence and autonomy among its people. Understandably, then, Larsen and Laszlo (1980) observed that the Hungarians found far more personal relevance in the story than did the Danes, and as a consequence remembered far more of its details.

Objectification is similar to anchoring in that it deliberately connects with accepted social knowledge, but in this case it is people or things rather than established ideas which form the links. There are two common forms of objectification: **personification** and **figuration**. Personification is, as its name suggests, linking the idea with a well-known person. Expert knowledge tends to be fairly obscure for most people, but linking it with someone who is well known in that field can simplify it, so it can be more easily accepted by the general public. Whenever we refer to Newtonian physics, or Blairite policies, we are using personification.

In figuration, images and metaphors are used to represent the concept. The idea of the "killer tomato" is a good example. Wagner and Kronberger (2001) showed how the social representations which grew up around genetically modified food focused specifically on the tomato ("killer tomatoes" as they were described in some press reports). These reports were sometimes accompanied by images of scientists injecting tomatoes with a large syringe, as if in the act of injecting the genetic material into the tomato, and the result was a striking image which was much more powerful in the public consciousness than the original scientific arguments had been.

Many of the metaphors expressing social representations are less dramatic, although they can be even more widely accepted. For example, popular concepts of medicine often represent the body as a "machine" or describe a specific astronomical problem as "dark matter". If an image is convincing enough, we don't even see it as a metaphor. Non-scientists, for example, often believe that

Key Terms

personification
Expressing a social representation in terms of a specific person who might be considered to embody it.

figuration
The use of images and metaphors to represent ideas.

dark matter is a real tangible substance, whereas astronomers and physicists know that the term was only coined to express as yet unexplained aspects of the universe.

The process of familiarisation which happens through anchoring and identification often means that the idea becomes distorted and inaccurate as a result. Wagner and Kronberger (2001) conducted focus groups to listen to people's ideas about genetically engineered foods, and listed three ways that beliefs about how genetic engineering worked differed from the scientific perception of what was actually going on. These beliefs are listed in Table 4.7.

Table 4.7 Beliefs about GM foods

1. The belief that "genes" are things that are introduced by scientists and don't happen in "natural" foods.

2. The belief that introduced genes from genetic modification can "infect" someone who eats the food.

3. The belief that introducing genes into living beings makes them bigger or monstrous.

Source: Wagner and Kronberger (2001)

As we have seen, social representations are often expressed through metaphors, images or stories, which give us a way of understanding our own experience. Researchers into social representations have often found that one of the most useful ways of identifying the social representations which people use is through the anecdotes they express. As organisational researchers have found as well (Hayes, 1991), anecdotes are a favourite way that people being interviewed about the less tangible aspects of everyday life can express what they are saying. For example, people being interviewed about their workplace will often provide anecdotes to make more general points, such as describing an event with a particular manager to illustrate the pervasive managerial style. The example they give is chosen because, to that person at least, it encapsulates and expresses the social representation they are attempting to communicate.

The metaphor may not even be expressed verbally. Jodelet (1991) described a study of social representations of mental illness in a village in France. The policy of the area was to board out mentally ill patients among families, as a kind of "care in the community" system. The families concerned expressed the clear belief that it was better for these people to be with families, and that they were just like anyone else verbally. But when their behaviour was observed, it was found that they acted as though mental illness was contagious; the patients' eating utensils were washed up separately and kept apart from those of the family, they had separate sheets and towels, and so on. The social representation implicit in this behaviour was not expressed in words, but it was quite widely shared in the village.

The scope of social representations

Social representations, then, are what we believe to be acceptable explanations for social phenomena or events. They guide our social action, and link individual cognition and social ideology. And they are often closely linked to group membership. For example, Gervais and Jovchelovitch (1998c) reported a study of social representations among Chinese communities living in Britain. Normally, traditional beliefs tend to be held less strongly by the second generation of a

migrant community. But, interestingly, Gervais and Jovchelovitch found that virtually all members of these communities – even when they had been born and socialised in Britain – shared the Chinese social representations of health and illness. They saw these beliefs as complementary to Western ones, but with more power to identify the root causes of illness or disease.

As the researchers looked more deeply at this question, they found that acceptance of Chinese health and illness beliefs acted as a powerful statement of identification with their parents' community. Like many others born of immigrant parents, they felt torn between their acceptance of Western life-styles, and the cultural inheritance of their parents. So integrating the traditional understanding of health and illness with modern beliefs was also an assertion that they did, somehow, remain Chinese. The social representation was used as an affirmation of their group identification.

The process of social representation can work on a smaller scale, and it is here that the link between social identification and social identity can become particularly evident. For example, Howarth (2002) explored issues of social identification and self-esteem among black teenagers living in Brixton, south London, and found that the issues didn't really make sense without an understanding of the social representations that the teenagers were using to understand the meanings of their own ages, ethnicity and socio-economic situations in the context of the wider society.

One of the clearest places that we can see social representations in action is when we compare the beliefs and explanations given by people working in different large organisations. Often, people working in what seem to be quite similar organisations will hold very different social representations about their industry and how things work in general. Schein (1990) defined organisational culture as being the pattern of underlying assumptions held by the various groups within the organisation. Hayes (1998c) showed how these groups form the basis for social identification with the organisation, and also how organisational culture forms an overriding social representation which acts as a kind of "cognitive glue", linking together the disparate departments and groups within the organisation so that even people playing very different roles share the same fundamental beliefs and assumptions. The processes of anchoring and objectification through metaphors, heroes and organisational stories apply just as much in the nature and transmission of organisational cultures as they do when we are looking at social representations of other groups in society.

Social representations and social identification

Moscovici (1976) argued that the shared social representations held by a group or society are what allow people to communicate effectively, and to come to an agreed view about reality. They create a base of shared knowledge which allows us to communicate effectively with one another. But as we have seen, they are also closely linked to membership of social groups, and society itself consists of many different groups, cultures and subcultures. As a result, there can be many different social representations in any given society (Jodelet, 1984).

One of the characteristics of identifying as a member of a social group is that we are likely to share the social representations held by the group members. This is partly because we are more likely to accept the view of people "like us" as being more valid than those of people who are "different"; but also because we are likely to spend more time discussing events with people with whom we identify, or at least listening to what they have to say.

Festinger (1954) proposed that we are continually evaluating ourselves and trying to present ourselves socially in the best way possible. Because of this, other people's beliefs – particularly those of people close to us – become very important, and we use them as criteria for making social judgements. We make a distinction between physical and social reality, Festinger argued, because one is testable and the other is not. We can test the belief that glass is fragile by hitting it with a hammer, but testing the belief that socialism represents a positive and necessary step forward for society is rather more problematic. So we look to other people to check our beliefs about social reality.

It is questionable, though, whether there is really a clear distinction between physical and social reality. Turner (1991) argued that all knowledge is social really, because most of our physical knowledge has been established by social consensus too. Most of us, he pointed out, accept that glass is fragile without feeling the need to resort to the hammer.

In either case, though, social consensus is important to whether we accept ideas or knowledge as truthful or not, and that produces a direct tendency to accept in-group beliefs. Because we use them as references for social reality, we tend to see them as more "true" than the beliefs held by out-groups. And it also makes us strongly motivated to develop coherent, shared views as part of the process of social identification – in other words, to develop social representations. For many researchers in this area, the two approaches are so closely linked as to become distinct but intertwined facets of social reality.

This also means that different groups can come to share widely different social representations. For example, Di Giacomo (1980) looked at social representations held by student leaders leading a protest movement about the level of the student grant, and compared them with the social representations held by the majority of students. The social representations were obtained by asking members of each group to explain how they saw what was going to, and also by asking them to free-associate to key words. Di Giacomo found that the two groups had widely different social representations – so much so that the two groups ended up almost talking a different language. The student workers, for instance, used phrases such as "student-worker solidarity" to express how they saw the matter, but the majority of students couldn't see any connection between students and workers on the issue. So the student leaders' attempts to mobilise the rest of the students failed, because the two groups held entirely different social representations.

The link between social identification and social representations also means that belonging to a social group means that we "sign up" to the core beliefs central to that group. In one study, Carugati (1990) examined the beliefs about intelligence held by teachers, parents and teachers who were also parents, and found that the teachers who were also parents were most likely to hold to the theory that intelligence was a "gift" because that view allowed them to come to terms more readily with what they were actually doing. Teachers also held that view, but not as strongly, whereas parents who were not teachers, on the other hand, were more likely to see intelligence as something to be enhanced and/or developed by the school. Carugati suggested that the contrast between the two group beliefs made the parent-teachers more defensive about their professional beliefs, and so hold them even more strongly.

Group identification doesn't have to be limited to the groups we belong to in our everyday lives. The networking and affiliation possibilities offered by the internet also open up a broader range of social representations, making alternative explanations and ideologies available to people who are interested in them, or who affiliate with others holding them. By following links or seeking further information about chance remarks made by other people, we can become aware of different ways of looking at or making sense of the world; or we can find that what we believed to be purely idiosyncratic beliefs are validated by the fact that they are more widely accepted than we realised. Many shared internet "jokes" originate in this way.

The way in which social representations can reflect the beliefs of an in-group has a darker side too. If the beliefs of one group are particularly hostile to another group – as Nazis were towards the Jews, for instance – then members of the first group are likely to adopt social representations which foster prejudice and discrimination. And when different social representations come into direct conflict, links with issues of power and control in society become particularly apparent. Wagner and Hayes (2005) give an illustration of how six South American peasants were burned at the stake in 1496 by the Spanish governor for burying religious images in the soil. The Spaniards saw this as an impious act, implying contempt for the images of the Virgin Mary and other saints through the association with soil, which they perceived as dirty. The peasants, on the other hand, were expressing their own positive social representation of the ground as the source of harvest and fruitfulness, and felt that their action were an expression of respect rather than contempt. It was a clash of social representations with tragic consequences.

Evaluating social representation theory

Potter (2012) argued that one of the weaknesses of social representation theory is that the relationship between social representations and social groups is circular. On the one hand, a given social group produces a social representation, while at the same time that social representation may be seen as defining the group. Welsh Nationalists, for example, all subscribe to the social representation of Welsh Nationalism; but holding that representation may be considered to define what it is to be a Welsh Nationalist.

Other researchers, however (e.g., Wagner and Hayes, 2005), see the interconnection between social groups and social representations not as a weakness, but as a strength. The connection between the social group and the social representation is a manifestation of the way that different levels of psychological explanation interact and link together. Group identification operates at the emotional and behavioural level, while social representations are manifestations of the same or a similar phenomenon at a social-cognitive level.

There is a case, too, for arguing that this type of apparent circularity is a positive attribute rather than a weakness. While they are often popular among theoreticians, scientific experience shows that linear relationships are actually very rare. What is more common in the natural world is a reciprocal influence – one thing tends to influence another and in turn is itself influenced by the other. In evolution, for example, animals evolve as a result of the demands of their environments; but even the simplest animals also modify and adjust those environments, which in turn affects their evolution (Rose, 1983). The relationship may seem circular, but when we are dealing with the real world, the question of whether the egg or the chicken came first is pretty meaningless. Both exist, have different attributes, and can be used in different ways.

A similar set of relationships applies when we look at the connections between social experience and brain chemistry; our reactions to experience induce changes in the actions of neurotransmitters in the brain, while the action of those neurotransmitters in turn makes certain reactions more likely. Stress, happiness, depression and many other emotional responses show this type of circular reaction; and most researchers have learned not to make simplistic assumptions about linear causality when it comes to the relationship between brain chemistry and experience.

Another of the particular strengths of social representation theory is the way in which it is not a static "snapshot" theory; it can allow us to analyse how social views and opinions change, and can illustrate the processes by which that happens. Society changes all the time, sometimes gradually and sometimes very quickly. The events of 9/11, for example, produced radical changes in how people understood a number of social issues, ranging from everyday safety to international relationships with the Middle East. Other changes are more gradual. Our views of the ageing process have changed completely over the past thirty years or so as a result of a gradual accumulation of scientific and lifestyle findings and their incorporation into everyday knowledge, not as the outcome of a single dramatic event.

What social representation theory does is to show us how our social knowledge and social awareness is shaped and modified through social interaction and social contacts. As our social contacts are enhanced and developed through the internet, this process becomes more dispersed; but if we are to understand the difference between a social representation and an attitude or belief, what we really need to look at is its underlying ideological implications and social functions. If a belief is widely shared, and serves a social purpose of articulating and legitimising social action, we can accept it as a social representation. If not, it is more likely to be what we would normally regard as an attitude or a personal construct, and we will be looking at these in the next chapter.

Summary: Chapter 4

1. The content of our communication is more sophisticated than the forms it takes. Discourse analysis is about how communicating is in itself a social act, with social implications and consequences.

2. Discourse can take many forms, and studies of discourse include written exchanges, internet communications, symbolism and semiotics, media reports and social directives as well as conversations.

3. One important function of discourse is communicating social attitudes and developing or establishing social explanations.

4. Attributions are the reasons we give for why things happen. Some attribution theories explain differences in attributions through information-processing, inferring responsibility according to situations and beliefs.

5. Common attributional errors include the fundamental attribution error and the self-serving bias. These reflect a tendency to see our own actions as determined by situations and other people's actions as determined by their personalities. These errors may be culturally specific.

6. Covariance theory adopts an information-processing approach to attributions, but other researchers have argued that social contexts and everyday knowledge play an important part in the attributions that we form.

7. Differing attributional styles may lead to characteristic differences, such as a tendency to optimism or to depression. Some therapies have been based on this observation.

8. Social representations are the shared beliefs held by societies of social groups. They change over time, but usually have a consistent core and peripheral elements which adjust to new information.

9. Changes in social representations occur through the processes of anchoring and objectification. Objectification includes the processes of personification and figuration, which connect known people or ideas with the concept being represented.

10. Social representations are closely linked with cultural identity, and also with social identification. These connections have been criticised as circular, but most see them as differing levels of explanation exploring the same social phenomena.

Chapter 5

Contents

Attitudes and persuasion

5

We all know what we mean when we use the word, but what is an attitude? The word itself is in everyday use, and it got there because it used to be a pretty ordinary description of non-verbal behaviour. In the 18th century an "attitude" was a physical pose or positioning of the body. But it was more than that: it was a way of standing or sitting which conveyed some kind of social message – friendliness, disdain, attentiveness, dislike or some other social emotion or reaction. When we talk of someone "striking an attitude" that is exactly what we mean – it's a way of standing or sitting which is acting out a pose which carries a social message of some kind (see Figure 5.1). The word is still used this way in the theatre – actors understand how body language indicates states of mind very well!

With the rise of interest in how the mind works, the word **attitude** came to have a more cognitive meaning – as a generalised state of mind, or if used as a general term, as a way of approaching social understanding. Attitude research began in the early part of the 20th century, and remains a significant interest for some social psychologists. Like many areas of psychology, interest in attitudes has taken different approaches at different times, reflecting the dominating **zeitgeist**, and the social concerns of scientists in general and psychologists in particular. During the 1930s, for instance, there was a particular interest in measuring attitudes, partly as a manifestation of the belief that any scientific approach must of necessity involve numerical measurement, and partly because other aspects of the human mind, such as intelligence, were also being measured, and human measurement was becoming an economic as well as a scientific enterprise.

In later years, particularly in the decades after World War II, psychologists became concerned with the question of attitude change, and attitude research tended to focus on how and how far that could be achieved. This tied in with the growth of social change, particularly the social challenges to established racism and sexism, and also with the explosive growth of advertising, which was all about persuading people that they needed to take a different approach to aspects of life they had previously taken for granted or ignored.

In the latter part of the 20th century, attitude researchers began to emphasise theoretical models of how attitudes worked: their cognitive and social structures. This was partly a response to the increased influence of cognitive

Figure 5.1 Stick figures showing different attitudes

psychology, which brought with it a concomitant interest in how memory, attention and other cognitive processes affected social structures such as attitudes. It was also stimulated by the efforts of computer scientists and others to create artificial systems which would mimic human mental processes, which placed a premium on having a firm understanding of how those processes worked.

Although definitions vary, all of them agree that attitudes are much more than just whether we like or dislike something. In the first part of this chapter, we will look at five questions: what are attitudes, how do we acquire them, what are they for, can they be measured and if so, how, and how do they work? Then in the second part of the chapter we will look more closely at how attitudes can be changed.

Key Terms

zeitgeist
The "spirit of the time", including the established assumptions and general knowledge of that period.

THE NARURE OF ATTITUDES

What are attitudes?

We have already seen how difficult it is to define an attitude exactly. But researchers have also developed or adopted models describing what they believe to be the structure of attitudes, and it is useful to explore some of these.

One of the earliest approaches in attitude research borrowed the concept of domains of the psyche from the ancient Greeks, taking the view that there were three significant domains of an attitude: the **cognitive domain**, to do with beliefs; the **affective domain**, to do with feelings; and the behavioural domain, to do with action. So your attitude to keeping fit, for example, would include a cognitive attitude which was to do with your beliefs about health and the body; an affective domain to do with whether you enjoyed taking exercise or not; and a **behavioural domain** to do with how often you exercise or take other action to keep yourself fit.

This is known as the three-component model of attitudes, because it sees them as having three parts. Rosenberg and Hovland (1960) argued that these dimensions of an attitude can be inferred from different signals. For instance, the cognitive dimension of an attitude can be inferred from what people say. The affective dimension can be assessed from people's physiological reactions like facial expressions or the way that our pupils tend to dilate when we look at something or someone that we like, as well as from their own descriptions of feelings. And the behavioural dimension can be assessed by observing how people actually act towards the particular object.

The problem with the three-component theory, though, is that it had adjusted the original Greek model by converting the third dimension from the conative to the behavioural (see Box 5.1). The **conative domain** originally described by the Greeks involved intention and purpose. But the strongly behaviourist ethos of the time maintained that idea like intentionality were woolly and unscientific, and should be replaced by the more scientific and objective behaviour. Unlike the psychologists of those times, though, modern psychologists recognise that people actually do have intentions and aims. At the same time, there is value in looking at behaviour as well, so modern social psychologists are more likely to use a four domain model than the original three.

Box 5.1 Three components or four?

The three-component model of attitudes has always been claimed to have been derived from the ancient Greeks. That is only partly true. In actual fact, what was borrowed from the Greeks (Galen, to be precise, in the second century BC) was adjusted to fit with the dominant beliefs in the psychology of that time. The original Greek formulation was that the three domains consisted of the cognitive, the affective and the conative domains. The cognitive and affective were to do with thinking and feeling, as in the attitude models; but the conative domain was to do with intention. The Greeks visualised the psyche as being like a chariot pulled by two horses. The conative and affective domains were the horses, providing the "pulling power", while the cognitive domain was the charioteer, steering the horses.

At the time the model was adopted, though, the emphasis was very much on observable behaviour and scientific measurement. Intentions were woolly ephemeral things which might not even happen, and certainly not the sort of things that a scientific approach could deal with. On the other hand, behaviour could be observed directly and was therefore believed to be more scientific, so the model was adjusted accordingly.

During more recent times, psychologists have become more able to recognise the value of intentions, and the conative domain has been, as it were, resurrected. But since there is still value in looking at what people actually do, it has been argued that we need to use a four-part model, of cognitive, conative, affective and behavioural domains, if we want to evaluate what people do effectively.

There were other models, though. Thurstone (1928) argued that there was really only one important aspect of an attitude, which was the fact that it expressed whether you liked or disliked an object. This one-component model summed up the important thing about attitudes for many people, and did help to stimulate some later models, although most researchers at the time considered it a bit too simplistic to be of much use.

Instead, they preferred to adopt the two-component model advocated by one of the most influential of American social psychologists, Gordon Allport, in 1935. Allport believed that attitudes were an absolutely fundamental part of social psychology because, as he said: "Attitudes determine for each individual what he will see and hear, what he will think, and what he will do" (Allport, 1935, p806). The two components in this case were the affective component that Thurstone had identified, and a second component which was to do with predisposition to action, or how far the attitude engendered a state of readiness to act. So an attitude consisted of a preference – that is, a liking or disliking, together with a state of mental readiness. This would also mean that it would guide how we evaluated experience or objects. More about values later.

More recently, researchers have been looking at the distinction between implicit and explicit attitudes. Wilson et al (2000) argued that people often hold contradictory attitudes towards the same object, but that in such cases one of the attitudes is often buried, and implicit rather than explicit. Because they are implicit, people may not even be aware that any contradiction exists, but these dual attitudes can be revealed in their behavioural responses, the words they choose to describe the object, how they respond on subtle measurement tests like how long they take to react to certain stimuli, and by other such indicators.

Other apparent contradictions can arise from the difference between specific and general attitudes. One of the classic studies in psychology is the investigation of prejudice carried out by Lapière in 1934 (see Box 5.2 later in this chapter). Some psychologists have argued that the reason for the difference between the expressed attitudes of the hotel and restaurant managers, and their actual behaviour, was because their expressed attitudes were about Chinese people in general, while their actual behaviour was to do with a specific instance – one particular couple who were actually present at the time.

You may have concluded from all this that we don't actually have a very clear idea of what attitudes are. Well, most of us do have a pretty clear idea in everyday life, but psychological models need to be exact, and there is no single clear agreement about the exact structure of attitudes within psychology. As with so many other psychological phenomena, though, we can still learn a lot by looking at attitudes from several different angles, even if we can't agree on one single precise definition.

Talking point   5.1 Defining attitudes

One difficulty with academic definitions is that they have to try to take account of all possible examples of the thing that they are defining, which sometimes makes them a bit obscure. Allport (1935) defined an attitude as "a mental and neural state of readiness, organised through experience, exerting a directive or dynamic influence upon the individual's response to all objects and situations with which it is related", while Rokeach (1948) said it was: "A learned orientation or disposition . . . which provides a tendency to respond favourably or unfavourably to the object or situation."

Thurstone (1928) defined an attitude as "The affect for or against a psychological object", while the behaviourists, who didn't approve of any reference to mental activities, defined it as "a predisposition to act in certain ways" (Watson, 1927). Some researchers have linked values with attitudes, as well, but these too have proved to be tricky to define.

Can you do better?

How are attitudes formed?

Exposure

One of the accepted characteristics of attitudes is that they involve either positive or negative affect – that is, feelings of either liking or disliking. Bearing that in mind, some psychologists have shown that simply being exposed more to one kind of thing than another is enough for us to like it more – that is, to develop a positive attitude towards it. In a classic study, Zajonc (1968) showed that this even applied to Chinese ideograms – American students who had been shown particular ideograms on previous occasions rated them as being more positive when asked to guess their meanings, by comparison with ideograms they had not been shown before.

Similarly, other researchers showed that we can develop negative attitudes towards objects or people simply because they have been associated with unpleasant or painful experiences. This was particularly highlighted in Sargent's (1957) examination of the various brainwashing techniques used by military forces during and after the World War II, in which he showed how producing negative associations with familiar objects was an important part of the process of dissociation and alienation used by brainwashers.

It is possible that we tend to like familiar things more because they are safer, in that we have come across them several times without coming to any harm. That could be a possible explanation for why such a tendency might have

evolved, as human beings developed and learned to live in a dangerous natural world. Another possibility, which doesn't necessarily contradict the first, is that familiar things present us with fewer cognitive challenges: we don't have to work as hard mentally to identify them or process what they imply, which might result in us feeling more favourable towards them. Whatever the reason, it is clear that simple exposure can produce positive or negative affect.

Learning

Liking or more particularly disliking something because it has been associated with something pleasant or unpleasant might also be a subtle example of classical conditioning. Classical conditioning happens when a neutral stimulus is repeatedly paired with a reaction-provoking one – for example, as when Pavlov repeatedly paired a bell with food for hungry dogs. In humans this type of learning happens most often when something is paired with a painful or emotionally disturbing experience, but it can also occur with relatively mild examples of the same type. Some researchers argued that many, even though not all, attitudes were actually derived from classical conditioning in one way or another (e.g., Zanna et al, 1970).

Certainly attitudes can be generated in this way. Cacioppo et al (1992) tried pairing unfamiliar nonsense words and ordinary words with electric shocks. The participants in the study reacted in a negative manner to both types of words, but more strongly to the artificial ones, like "tasmer", than to the familiar ones, like "finger". The researchers took this to imply that classical conditioning is stronger in determining attitudes when the object of the attitude is unfamiliar than when it is familiar.

It is questionable, however, whether experimental findings of this kind are really the same as attitudes. When we talk about attitude in everyday life we usually mean something much deeper and more socially meaningful than simply positive or negative reactions. Studies of how people respond to isolated words or photographs of strangers may not really be getting near to how we form attitudes in everyday life. As Petty et al (2001) pointed out, at best they may tell us something about the affective component of an attitude (and at worst nothing at all), but they tell us nothing about the other domains.

Other researchers in the post-war period explored the possible role of instrumental, or **operant conditioning** in attitude formation. Insko (1965), for example, showed how students' answers in an attitude survey could be affected by their previous experience of having a particular view encouraged. The participants had taken part in a telephone survey about a week beforehand, in which certain answers received the comment "good" from the researcher. They were more likely to produce those particular attitudes when taking part in a paper-and-pencil attitude survey later.

Key Terms

operant conditioning
The process of learning in which learning occurs as a result of positive or negative reinforcement of an animal or human being's action.

Whether this type of artificial situation mirrors real life or not is still questionable, but it certainly seems to be the case that attitudes can be shaped through **reinforcement** in a social situation like family life. This may be a combination of direct reinforcement through approval, and indirect observational learning from observing other people's experiences or attitudes. Rogoff (2003) discussed how important observational learning in families can be, not just for children but also for adults, in picking up the attitudes people use in their everyday lives.

Heritability

Heritability is another factor which has been suggested as a source of attitudes. Evidence from twin studies (e.g., Tesser, 1993) suggests that some attitudes, especially political ones, are to some extent heritable; that is, they have a genetic component which predisposes the individual to hold certain types of attitude rather than others. The idea emerged from a number of large-scale twin studies, and has been replicated by many researchers into behavioural genetics. Olson et al (2001) surveyed 336 pairs of adult Canadian twins, both fraternal and identical, and found that the attitudes which appeared to show a genetic component ranged from thrill-seeking, such as whether they enjoyed rollercoaster rides, to political attitudes regarding abortion. The identical twins showed much closer connections in their attitudes than fraternal twins did – although the environmental influences on the twins were still dominant, and more powerful than the heritability estimates.

Not surprisingly, this is an idea which has generated considerable conflict. Many of the criticisms which have been made apply generally to the whole question of heritability and twin studies, such as whether the researchers have really ensured that the environments and social expectations experienced by fraternal twins were identical, or at least as similar as those experienced by identical twins. Richardson and Norgate (2005) challenged the **equal environments assumption** of classical twin studies, showing how a number

Key Terms
reinforcement
The strengthening of learning in some way, usually through reward.
heritability
A statistical concept designed to indicate how much of a given trait can be deemed to have come about as a result of genetic influences.
equal environments assumption
The assumption that twins in the same or similar families experience identical environmental influences as they are growing up.

of other circumstances could make the environments of identical twins more similar than those of fraternal twins.

There is also the question of family cultures, and whether researchers have fully taken into account the way that ideas are transmitted through families. It can be argued, for instance, that the similarity in the identical twins' attitudes arose because of a similarity in their readiness to be influenced by family arguments, which in turn would have been affected by greater similarity in how adults interacted with them.

Despite these criticisms, the idea of heritability in attitudes has remained popular among behavioural geneticists. However, they also maintain that a genetic predisposition should not be regarded as a form of genetic determinism. It may incline people towards certain approaches or attitudes, but that doesn't mean that they will always act in similar ways when faced with issues in the real world. Alford et al (2008) explored the data from two large samples of twins: one in Australia and the other in the United States. While their results did indicate that genetic influences played a role in shaping political attitudes and ideologies, they also found that this did not translate into following or identifying with specific political parties. They argued that there were more subtle factors in play when considering the overall question of why a given person holds the attitudes that they do, and that although political scientists might take genetic influences into account, they shouldn't regard them as being the whole explanation.

Need satisfaction

The functional approach to attitude formation takes the view that we develop attitudes in order to satisfy particular needs. Sometimes, these needs derive from unconscious motives, such as the need to avoid facing up to childhood trauma or unconscious conflicts. The classic explanation for homophobia, for example, is that it is a **reaction-formation** deriving from latent or unconscious homosexual desires. These are repressed so strongly by the individual that they turn into their opposite, and become manifest in hatred or other negative attitudes towards homosexuality. In milder form, people may adopt certain attitudes in order to avoid taking personal responsibility for consequences or situations – for example, blaming the government for their being unable to find a job when in fact the person has made relatively little effort to do so.

Other researchers have proposed a **utilitarian** function to attitude acquisition, in which the attitude satisfies a basic need of self-interest, helping the person to gain rewards or avoid sanctions from the social environment in which they live. So someone may express a positive attitude towards a political movement, for example, in order to "keep in" with friends, or to avoid unpleasant social confrontations by expressing contrary opinions.

Another idea is that we have a need to evaluate things in our lives, and that we form attitudes as a consequence of that need. Not everyone shares this need to the same extent. Jarvis and Petty (1996) argued that this need is an individual difference, which can be assessed using a **psychometric scale**, and which makes us more or less likely to evaluate aspects of our everyday lives. People with a high need to evaluate tend to hold very strong opinions, not just about particular issues but about almost everything they encounter, and they don't like being neutral about social issues. Those with a low need to evaluate might

| Key Terms |

reaction-formation
A defence mechanism in which a repressed impulse turns into its opposite (e.g., repressed homosexuality turning into aggressive homophobia).

utilitarian
Having a useful value, emphasising functional purpose.

psychometric scale
One of (usually) several factors measured by a psychometric test, which will have been carefully constructed and standardised.

hold some strong opinions, but they tend to remain neutral on most things and reserve their attitudes for specific issues which really matter to them.

Federico (2004) found that people who have a high need to evaluate tended to hold more extreme attitudes than people who scored lower on the Need to Evaluate scale (NTE). High scorers were also able to bring their attitudes to mind much more readily than the more laid-back individuals. Those following this approach have also argued that these individual differences may affect people's reactions to significant life-events, such as job loss or divorce. According to this model, people who have a high NTE score are more likely to become depressed or suffer severe loss of self-esteem as a result of such events than people with a lower need to evaluate.

Other researchers have identified different needs which may explain why we form attitudes; but there is a sense in which such arguments may become circular, and not particularly helpful in explaining what is going on. It might be more useful to look more closely at the actual mechanisms which are involved when we form attitudes – at what attitudes are for and how they work.

What are attitudes for?

We have already looked at one idea which has been put forward to explain what attitudes are for: the idea that attitudes are formed to satisfy particular needs. The principle behind **need-fulfilment theories** is that the need is some kind of absence or lack which produces tensions and disturbs the normal functioning of the mind, in much the same way as the lack of water disturbs the fluid balance of the body. Providing the wherewithal to satisfy that lack (in this case, attitudes) restores balanced functioning, and reduces tension. The problem with these models is that they tend to be purely theoretical, with little actual evidence to support them; and also circular in that if an attitude exists, it is held to be satisfying the need, while if it doesn't, the need is considered to be satisfied already. Heads I win, tails you lose – there is no way of refuting or challenging the idea.

Table 5.1 Functions of attitudes

A knowledge function	Attitudes can give meaning to our experiences.
An adjustive, or utilitarian, function	Holding certain attitudes may make us more socially acceptable and so help our social interaction.
A value-expressive function	Attitudes allow us to express what we experience as the more positive aspects of our own "inner selves".
An ego-defensive function	Attitudes allow us to defend and protect our unconscious motives and ideas.

Source: Katz (1960)

Knowledge

Katz (1960) suggested that there are four basic functions that are served by attitudes (see Table 5.1). One of them is knowledge, in that attitudes provide us with a frame of reference for the information which we acquire about the world, giving it meaning and structure. Anderson (1981) suggested that attitudes are important factors in how we process new information. We perform

Key Terms

need-fulfilment theories
Theories which propose that a given process occurs because it satisfies an internal need or drive.

what Anderson described as **cognitive algebra**, identifying the salience of each new item of information for the knowledge and attitudes we already hold, and either strengthening or re-evaluating our existing attitudes accordingly. So learning about, say, the importance of rehydration during exercise might add to an overall positive attitude towards taking a systematic approach to exercise and fitness. Alternatively, learning about risks of joint or spinal damage caused by inadequate footwear while running might cause either a re-evaluation of one's attitude towards running as a contribution to overall health, or of one's attitude towards footwear.

Instrumentality

Another attitude function identified by Katz is **instrumentality**. This is the idea that holding a particular attitude may provide us with a way of achieving or moving towards a goal or ambition. So, for example, you might maintain a positive attitude towards engaging in regular sport not for the activity itself, but because that would look good on a CV, and therefore enhance your future job applications and desirability.

Some attitudes are more socially desirable than others, and there is a strong tendency for people to want to be accepted by their own social groups. The instrumental function of attitudes may become important in this context, in that it is more difficult to become accepted if the views and opinions you express are radically different from the people you are associating with. In that context, too adopting or changing certain attitudes may serve an instrumental function, of social desirability or acceptability.

Eagly and Chaiken (1998) argued that in some situations, the question of instrumentality in attitudes has more to do with beliefs than with other forms of motivation. If our motivation for buying perfume is to enhance social interactions, then our attitude towards a given perfume will be mainly to do with whether we believe that this particular perfume will actually do the job. Some attitudes, they argue, place more emphasis on knowledge and beliefs than others, and this affects how we perceive their instrumental function.

Ego-defence

A third function of attitudes is **ego-defence** – that is, protecting one's self-esteem. In this function, we use our attitudes to protect us from facing up to knowledge or information which might make us have to think badly of ourselves. We have already seen how the more extreme versions of this may tap into deeply buried unconscious conflicts or motives, and become so powerful that they become reaction-formations and turn into their opposites. But ego-defence mechanisms can operate at more superficial levels as well – for example, by using an excuse such as "the examiner was in a bad mood" to explain why we failed a driving test.

An ego-defensive attitude is, almost by definition, not grounded in reality; but because of its unconscious nature, the person holding the attitude is usually unaware of how unrealistic it is. This means that these attitudes are very difficult to change, because the process of bringing their unrealistic nature to consciousness will be resisted, psychologically, by the person holding the attitudes, usually through additional excuses and justifications for their attitude.

Key Terms

cognitive algebra
A mental calculation, weighing up costs, benefits and other aspects of an experience.

instrumentality
How useful an attitude is to an individual in terms of achieving goals or ambitions.

ego-defence
Protecting the mind against information which would form negative challenges or unwelcome truths.

Expressing values

The fourth function of attitudes which Katz identified was that attitudes allow us to express our **values**. Values are the personal and emotively-loaded assumptions which we use as guiding principles in our lives. They are different from attitudes, but in many ways closely related. As a general rule, we tend to regard attitudes as broader than values, and sometimes less personal – an attitude is like a combination of beliefs and values together. A considerable amount of research was devoted to exploring the differences between values and attitudes, but in a later evaluation of the concept of value-expression, Maio and Olson (2000) showed how it can often involve several different motivations, so treating value-expression as a single factor can be misleading. As we saw in Talking point 5.1, it can be as difficult to produce a clear definition of a value as it is to define an attitude.

Rokeach argued that values serve two important functions: serving as standards to allow us to weigh up our behaviour and decide what is praiseworthy or blameworthy; and motivating our behaviour in that we try to live up to our values as far as we can. That means that values have a direct influence on attitudes, because we like to believe that our attitudes relate to the values that we hold. Whether that holds true in everyday life or not is another story, which we will explore later in this chapter.

Object appraisal

Another set of functions of attitudes were identified by Smith et al (1956). They saw attitudes as having three major functions: object appraisal, social adjustment and externalisation.

Object appraisal relates to the knowledge function of attitudes which we looked at earlier, but it also links our evaluations of objects with our knowledge about how they affect us. This helps us to assess the features of our environment, so that we know how to act towards them. Because we develop a positive attitude to things we have found beneficial in the past, or a negative one towards things which we have found harmful, we use our attitudes to appraise the objects we encounter in these terms, which lets us recognise immediately whether we should approach or avoid it. Fazio (2000) argued that object appraisal has survival value by allowing our past experience to guide our reactions, so that we don't have to go through the process of learning how we should react each time. Effectively, it's a rapid appraisal of assistance or threat. However, these appraisals can also become a problem when we apply inappropriate appraisals to situations which have changed or are different.

The **social adjustment** function is because, as we have seen, holding certain attitudes rather than others can help us to identify with, or affiliate to, particular social groups. One of the assumptions of social identification, as we saw in Chapter 1, is that we expect others in our social group to share our beliefs (to some extent, at least). So holding the same attitudes as other members of a particular social group is a way of stressing how similar you are to them, and therefore also of defining your own place in society. This means that holding particular attitudes can help the processes of social identification and affiliation.

Smith et al identified a third function of attitudes, which they called **externalisation**. This is to do with how we match up our inner, unconscious motives with what is going on around us. Attitudes, they argued, allow us to externalise our inner fears or anxieties. For example, if we have an inner fear of becoming

Key Terms

values
Personal beliefs of worth or importance.

object appraisal
Weighing up or evaluating things to judge their worth or usefulness.

social adjustment
An attitude function concerned with getting on with other people.

externalisation
The extent to which a person channels innermost motives and emotions into their actions.

too personally involved with someone, we might manifest that fear in a cynical attitude towards close relationships in general. In other words, we treat external objects as if they were relevant to an internal problem – although Smith et al emphasised that this is an unconscious process, not a conscious one.

The three functions identified by Smith et al are not considered to be mutually exclusive: on the contrary, the researchers argued that any given attitude is often serving more than one of these functions, which has implications for attitude change, because some attitudes will be more central than others, serving more personal functions for the individual. The researchers suggested that it is therefore more effective to try to achieve attitude change by starting with peripheral attitudes, rather than central ones, and aiming to change just a little bit at a time, so that the person doesn't have to cope with too much disruption all at once, and doesn't become defensive about it or be very tense or anxious. We will be looking at attitude change later in this chapter.

The function–structure model of attitudes

Maio and Olson (2000) argued that the key to understanding the functions of attitude lies in the question of motivations, and how these influence experiences, beliefs and feelings. Taking into account the work of Katz et al, and bringing in more recent findings which emphasised how motivations could influence different aspects of attitudes, their model proposed that the strongest attitudes are those which show a balance between experience, beliefs and feelings.

Some attitudes reflect a stronger motivation towards feelings, such as the motivation to perform **hedonically relevant** activities – enjoying good food, taking exercise because of the enjoyment of the physicality of the actions, and so on. Other attitudes may reflect stronger motivations towards beliefs: eating a certain kind of diet because of a belief that it promotes health or weight loss; taking exercise because of the belief that it will make one healthier or live longer. And some attitudes reflect motivations based on experience: liking to eat "proper" Sunday dinners because that is a family tradition, or taking exercise because it has become a habit and changing the routine leaves an empty period of time, or makes the person feel guilty.

Each of these areas, then, can be affected by different motives, and some motivations are stronger than others. Which motives are strongest for any individual at any one time depends on weightings such as personal importance, either immediate or long term; negative weightings such as anxiety or potential discomfort, social consequences such as approval or inclusion, and so on. People differ, too, in the balance they give to different types of motives. If someone is particularly anxious to avoid social disapproval, that factor will have a stronger negative weighting for them than it does for someone who is more cavalier about it. So personal motivations affect the weights given to past experiences, beliefs and attitudes, and they in turn affect the strength of the attitude (see Figure 5.2).

Maio and Olson (2000) also argued that when experience, beliefs and attitudes are equally balanced, we find strong attitudes which are particularly resistant to change. Nevertheless, people often show inconsistencies in their attitudes, and if their emotional weightings are unevenly balanced, attitude change may become easier. This is particularly the case when there is relatively little motivational weighting assigned to the minor or inconsistent aspects of

Key Terms

hedonic relevance
Something which has either pleasant or unpleasant consequences or implications for the person making the attribution.

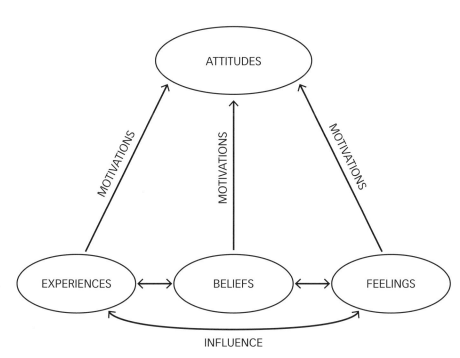

Figure 5.2 The function–structure model of attitudes (based on Maio and Olson, 2000)

the attitude, which don't show strong internal conflicts or dissonance. We will be looking at cognitive dissonance and attitude change later in this chapter.

Can attitudes be measured?

When the concept of attitude first became significant to psychology, it was accompanied by an equal concern with measurement. The first half of the 20th century was a time when there was a belief that everything would be ultimately susceptible to scientific measurement, including all aspects of the human psyche. This belief is still held by some today, but we are no longer dominated by the influence of modernism, and its psychological manifestation behaviourism, so we are able to go about research and measurement in a somewhat more sophisticated manner. We will look at some of the specifics of attitude measurement in more detail later in this book, but in this section we will look at some of the general approaches that researchers have taken to attitude measurement.

Attitude scales

The first approach to attitude measurement was the use of the attitude scale, such as the very popular **Likert scale** which is still used extensively today, and uses an ordinal scale such as strongly agree–agree–neither agree nor disagree–disagree–strongly disagree (see Figure 5.3). These are assessments of attitudes which make three basic assumptions: (1) that attitudes can be expressed by verbal statements; (2) that the same statement has the same meaning for all participants; and (3) that attitudes, when expressed in the form of verbal statements, can be measured and quantified.

These statements are more controversial than they may seem at first sight. One reason is that what people say may not correspond with what they actually do, which we will be looking at later in this chapter. Also, as we saw in

Key Terms

Likert scale
A five- or seven-point ordinal measuring scale, commonly used to assess attitude strength.

Figure 5.3 A typical Likert response scale

earlier chapters, people may interpret the same words or statements entirely differently, depending on their own personal constructs or beliefs. And whether personal beliefs or opinions can be reduced to numerical scores is also a manner of debate – for example, Sherrard (1997) argued that the only realistic way of capturing meaning in attitudes is to look at them qualitatively, not quantitatively, since quantitative analysis loses so much of the subtlety and personal meaning of the attitude.

Other approaches were developed with the aim of bringing to the analysis more of the subtleties of real-life attitudes. One classic example was the semantic differential, developed by Osgood (1966), which used a series of paired adjectives so that the respondent could express some of the nuances of how they felt towards the attitude object. Other methods, such as sociometry, developed by Moreno (1953), explored positive and negative evaluations of other people between different members of "natural" groups. This was as much a measure of relationships as of attitudes, but can also be seen as an attempt to introduce more subtlety into what was essentially a quantitative measurement. Similarly, the Bogardus (1947) social distance scale was developed around the same time as an evaluation of racial and other forms of ethnic prejudice, and comprised a series of statements describing the perceived social distance between the person expressing the attitude and various social groups, by asking what level of contact they would find tolerable.

Problems of attitude measurement

While each of these methods of measuring attitudes attempted to capture the significant aspects of the attitude, they were still limited. Measuring attitudes, or even identifying what they are in the first place, presents a number of problems. Some of these problems are to do with the way in which answers are likely to be biased towards a particular outcome. For example: people do not like to feel that they are expressing attitudes which will be disapproved of, so they often tend to tell researchers what they think they ought to say, rather than, perhaps, revealing what their true attitudes really are. This **social desirability** is one set of problems.

Another set of problems arises from **response bias** from the participants in the research. Attitudes and opinions are wide-ranging things, and people may not even be fully aware or the complexities of their attitudes when they are asked. Instead, they may search for the response which seems appropriate for the situation, or for which the previous questions or situation have prepared them. There is also a consistent response bias which favours "yes" and "agree" answers over "no" and "disagree" ones.

A third set of difficulties arise when we try to interpret attitude statements which people have made. Often, attitude research makes the assumption that a verbal statement of an attitude has a clear and unambiguous meaning. But as we saw in Chapter 4, people view their worlds in very different ways, and may use the same words to describe quite different concepts. We cannot assume that attitude statements have universal meaning.

Key Terms

social desirability
The tendency to adjust one's image or self-report to seem more socially acceptable (e.g., concealing racist attitudes).

response bias
The tendency which people have to respond in ways which will make them appear more socially acceptable than they are.

A fourth problem is that of **quantifiability**. A great deal of attitude research has been dependent on the idea that the strength, or degree, of attitudes can be accurately assessed. But in reality, this is very difficult indeed to achieve. Many attitude measurements involve rating scales, such as the Likert scale, in which people measure how much they agree or disagree with a particular statement. Even though some measures have been systematised and converted into psychometrically valid scales, they are still only able to give us ordinal data – that is, they can tell us whether one person's measured attitude is more extreme than another's, but they can't quantify how much, which limits how firmly we can draw our conclusions.

Talking point 5.2   Measuring attitudes

Researchers have devoted a lot of time to the problem of how to measure attitudes. This implies that there has also been research funding devoted to the problem. That funding has come from a variety of sources.

Why do you think this is? Try developing a list of (a) types of people or organisations who might want to measure attitudes, and (b) reasons why they might want to do this.

Take a look at your list. On the whole, do you believe that either a perfect attitude measurement, or attitude measurement as it exists in the real world, makes a positive contribution to society, or not?

In essence, whether a particular attitude measure is appropriate for use or not depends on the theory of attitudes which is being held. Modern theories are more likely to emphasise intentions, for example, and some researchers regard intentions as being just as important as actions. For those researchers, statements of intentions would be regarded as valid measures of attitudes, while; those emphasising more behavioural approaches might consider them invalid. Which brings us to the question of attitude theories – what researchers have proposed as explanations for how attitudes work.

How do attitudes work?

Since the first half of the 20th century, psychologists have looked at how attitudes work, just exactly how the mind develops and uses particular attitudes.

Balance theory

One idea is that attitudes work by keeping our cognitions nicely balanced – that is, by making sure that our thoughts and ideas are consistent with one another, at least as far as we perceive them. This idea derives from the observations made by Festinger in 1957, which showed how people who became aware that they held contradictory ideas or cognitions found that knowledge to be extremely disturbing; so much so, they would change their opinions or thoughts to bring back some apparent consistency. From this, Festinger developed cognitive dissonance theory, which we will be looking at in detail in the later part of this chapter, when we look at persuasion and attitude change. But the observation that cognitive dissonance produces tension which the

Key Terms

quantifiability
Being able to be measured in terms of numbers and quantities.

individual seeks to reduce led to a number of theories arguing that attitudes work by establishing or reinforcing cognitive consistency.

The first of these theories actually predates Festinger and derives from Gestalt theory; but it was one which Festinger was aware of and used to develop his own thinking in the area. This is Heider's theory of cognitive balance (Heider, 1958). Essentially, Heider argued that we look for balance in our attitudes towards connected objects, or people. So, for example, if you like Sheila and you also like Jim, it is cognitively comfortable if Sheila also likes Jim. If she dislikes Jim, that creates an imbalance in our cognitions around these people – what Heider referred to as the cognitive field – and we find that unpleasant, and have to deal with it in some way.

Balances and imbalances like this, Heider argued, are the source of particular attitudes. If both Sheila and Jim like each other, we maintain a positive attitude towards those people. If they don't, we can deal with it in many ways – by liking one of them less, by believing that they would like each other if they got to know one another better, or by making excuses such as "well, she always did have difficulty getting on with some people" or "Jim can be difficult until you get to know him".

Researchers into **balance theory** looked at the different ways that triads could affect one another, in terms of positives and negatives, and the types of likely results from different combinations. These triads apply to things as well as people – for example, we often assume that what we like is going to be similar to what our friends will like, so if one of our friends doesn't like something that we do like, we rationalise that by developing an attitude which allows us to deal with the imbalance. Heider saw the need for cognitive balance as being the root source of many of our attitudes.

In 1968, Newcomb suggested a modification of Heider's balance theory, which was all about whether we regard other people as suitable sources of information in the triads. According to this model, an imbalance will only produce tension in a **triad** if it is highly relevant. If Sally and I disagree regarding unemployment, and I believe that Sally is an authoritative source of information on social affairs, or influential in deciding government policy, then I may find our lack of agreement disturbing. But if I believe that Sally doesn't know much about such things, her attitude is not likely to trouble me much.

Using this model, Zajonc and Burnstein (1965) argued that balance isn't everything – we also have a **positivity bias**, in that we prefer positive to negative attitudes. That preference affects other cognitive processes too, in that we find triads involving a positive relationship between a person and an attitude object much easier to learn and remember. The researchers found that this applies even if we are comparing an unbalanced positive relationship with a balanced negative one – the positive one is easier to grasp. An unbalanced positive relationship might be one in which one negative cognition challenges two positive ones, for instance: if I approve of Greenpeace and respect Janet's opinions (both positive), but Janet disapproves of Greenpeace (negative). A balanced triad with negative relationships might be, for instance, Sarah and I both agreeing that we disapprove (negative) of blood sports.

Self-perception

Another approach to how attitudes work comes from the idea that we infer our attitudes from our own behaviour – that is, from the way that we act. Bem

Key Terms

balance theory
The idea that incongruent or unbalanced cognitions causes tension which we try to reduce.

triad
A set of three.

positivity bias
Our tendency to prefer positive cognitive connections or interactions.

(1972) argued that we are often unaware of what our attitudes actually are, until something happens that means that we need to know. At that point, we observe our usual behaviour, and conclude that it demonstrates what our attitudes actually are. So basically, we function as observers, making attributions about where our behaviour comes from. If the attribution is external, we infer that it comes from the situation; if it is internal, we infer that it derives from an attitude that we hold (we looked at attributions in the last chapter).

A number of studies have supported this idea, although not for all attitudes. Schnall and Laird (2003) found that asking research participants to maintain a smiling, happy expression resulted in much more positive attitudes if the person had only vaguely defined attitudes towards it beforehand, or if they were unfamiliar with it. But their approach didn't make much difference when they were dealing with topics where people already held strong opinions.

This approach ties in with the **facial feedback hypothesis**, which argues that our facial muscle movements have a direct influence on the emotions that we experience (see Chapter 2). Strack et al (1988) asked people to hold a pen in their mouths while they rated how funny a set of cartoons were. Some of the participants were asked to hold the pen with their lips, producing a pursed mouth expression, while others were asked to hold it between their teeth, producing an open-mouthed "smile". Those holding the pen between their teeth rated the cartoons as funnier than the other participants, which Strack et al attributed to inferring their emotions from the expressions on their faces – the way they were holding their facial muscles.

Although the evidence that altering facial expression can alter mood is pretty clear, there is debate as to whether self-perception is really the mechanism. Zajonc (1994) argued that smiling actually sets off physiological responses which increase the blood supply to the brain. This lowers the blood temperature, producing a pleasant mood. Frowning, on the other hand, decreases the blood flow to the brain, raising its blood temperature and generating unpleasant moods. When Zajonc compared people's moods after asking them to repeat certain vowel sounds twenty times – sounds like "eee" which simulated smiling or "u" which simulated frowning – they found the same effect. But in this case, the participants were not actually aware that they were smiling or frowning, which the researchers interpreted as implying that we don't need conscious self-perception for facial feedback.

> **Key Terms**
>
> **facial feedback hypothesis**
> The idea that we infer our emotions from the expressions on our faces.

Accentuation theory

Eiser (1975) emphasised the importance of social context and evaluative language in attitudes. Eiser's accentuation theory emphasised the importance of the evaluative judgements implied in how people express their attitudes.

As we saw earlier, the words which people use often reveal their underlying attitude: describing someone who takes a lot of risks as "foolhardy" implies quite a different attitude from describing them as "adventurous".

In 1974, Eiser and Mower-White reported a study which began by using an attitude scale to assess teenagers' attitudes towards authority. They were then each given another, similar attitude scale to complete, but they were first sorted into three groups. The control group was told that the second task was a check on the first one, to make sure it was consistent. The second group was told that it would assess "how polite, obedient, helpful and cooperative you are"; and the third group was told that it was to assess "how bold, adventurous, creative and with-it you are". The second group's scores shifted towards a more pro-authority stance, by comparison with the controls, while the third group shifted towards a more anti-authority stance. So their answers had been directly influenced by the descriptions they had been given.

In a similar vein, Eiser (1971) found that where a statement was believed to have originated affected people's responses to statements about recreational drugs. When the statements were labelled as coming from newspapers which took particular approaches towards the idea of recreational drugs and unconventional behaviour, the views tended to reflect the source, either being favourable or unfavourable towards the topic. Participants also produced more extreme views than a control group who received the statements unlabelled.

Labels are another important aspect of **accentuation theory**. As Tajfel and colleagues (1971) showed in their minimal group studies of social identification, people often react surprisingly strongly to quite arbitrary classifications. Eiser found that categorising statements, for example as pro- or anti-authority, or right- or left-wing, made a lot of difference to how they were evaluated. People would decide whether or not they were prepared to see their own ideas as fitting into that category, and judge the statements they were given according to that decision. So Eiser's theory proposed that attitudes often work through description. The words we choose and the labels we give to sources of particular attitudes are highly influential in how far we are prepared to adopt or reflect those attitudes ourselves. As we saw in Chapter 4, this can be particularly significant in media communication; the choice of words used in documentaries or news reports, for instance, can be seen as clear attempts to shape or manipulate public opinion.

Social judgement theories of attitudes

Another set of theories about how attitudes work sees them as social judgements, which do not necessarily imply personal belief or commitment. Thurstone (1928) argued that people can assess how favourable or unfavourable a statement is towards its target object without being particularly affected by their own personal views. So, for instance, if they are given a statement about the Church and its relationship to religion, people can say whether the statement is favourable or unfavourable towards the Church, and how favourable or unfavourable it is, regardless of their own personal views. So attitudes didn't have to operate through a personal motivational process, they could be independent and impartial.

Other researchers, though, argued that people do usually use their own personal views to evaluate beliefs and statements they encounter. Sherif and Hovland (1961) argued that people will rate a statement which they find personally acceptable as more favourable than if they were assessing an equivalent statement on a more general, impersonal scale. This is known as the assimilation effect. For instance, if I hold an attitude of concern about the state of the environment (which I do), and I read that phosphate-free detergents are increasingly popular, I am likely to rate that statement as being a favourable one. On the other hand, someone who regarded the environmental issue as unimportant might rate it differently (e.g. as evidence of the gullibility of the detergent-buying public).

Sherif and Hovland also predicted that there would be a contrast effect, whereby statements are seen as more extreme if they are very different from someone's own personal views. This contrast can be made stronger by the amount of personal involvement which that person has with the area. If they feel very personally involved, they will be inclined to react very definitely when indicating whether they agree or disagree with the statement. So, for example, somebody who felt very strongly about environmental issues would have a larger range of statements that they either agreed with or disagreed with, and would give more extreme ratings. But somebody who didn't care much one way or the other would see a small range of statements as relevant, and respond less strongly.

We all have our own range of statements with which we will agree, and those with which we will reject. Sherif and Hovland called this range the latitude of acceptance and latitude of rejection, and argued that these make all the difference to how readily the person will change their attitudes. Statements which fall within someone's latitude of acceptance can be quite effective in producing attitude change, because people will tend to rate them as being similar to their own views, so they don't need much cognitive adjustment.

Take, for example, someone who is sort of against the death penalty but doesn't hold particularly strong attitudes about it. If they hear a strong statement about the number of cases in which people are wrongfully judged guilty when in fact they are innocent, and that statement falls within their latitude of acceptance, then the statement is likely to be quite influential. Their view would probably shift towards being strongly against capital punishment. But that type of information would have no effect on someone who was rigidly in favour of the death penalty, because it would fall within their latitude of rejection and they wouldn't really take any notice of it.

Sometimes, statements which are really extreme can produce what Sherif and Hovland called a **boomerang effect**, in that the contrast of values is so strong that the person reacts against it, and it produces the opposite attitude change to the one that was intended. But this is uncommon – mostly, we are influenced by statements which fall into our latitude of acceptance, because we can assimilate them more readily. This brings us into the whole area of attitude change, and this is the concern of the second part of this chapter.

CHANGING ATTITUDES

It's easy to assume that the attitudes we hold will determine what we do. But is that really true? Most of us, for example, have full respect for the law. Yet many people will turn a blind eye to what we see as minor crimes, like downloading a music track without permission, or driving over the speed limit on a quiet road. Does that mean that our attitudes towards the law are disrespectful? Not necessarily. What it suggests is that attitudes are only one factor in how we are

| Key Terms |

boomerang effect
When an attempt at persuasion is so extreme that it produces the opposite effect in the recipient.

likely to behave; our motives, beliefs and social knowledge are just as influential. More recent theories of attitudes are more complex than the early ones because they try to incorporate some of these other factors.

Box 5.2   Attitudes and behaviour: The classic study

During the early years of attitude research, one study became a classic. It showed how much people's behaviour could differ from what they actually did. In the 1930s, America was very racist, and there was quite a considerable amount of overt anti-Chinese feeling and open prejudice towards other ethnic groups as well as active discrimination against Afro-Caribbeans. In 1934, LaPière travelled around America with a middle-class Chinese couple, visiting 250 hotels and restaurants. Despite the common prejudice, they were only refused service once, and for the most part the service they received was courteous and considerate. But when LaPière sent out a questionnaire to the same establishments asking their views, and whether they were prepared to accept Chinese people, 92 per cent of those same restaurants and hotels said that they would refuse to serve Chinese guests. Clearly there was a discrepancy between the attitudes they were expressing, and the way that they actually behaved.

Explaining these, and similar research findings, has occupied attitude theorists in one way or another ever since.

LaPière's classic study which is described in Box 5.2, shows how the attitudes which we profess to hold and the way we actually behave are not necessarily always the same. Although this finding was repeated by many researchers, Eiser (1979) argued that for the most part, our attitudes and behaviour are fairly similar, but that the discrepancy was accentuated by the way the researchers studied the area. Typically, a study comparing attitudes and behaviour would assess attitudes in general. But those attitudes would be compared with how the person acted in a very specific situation. For example, the Chinese couple in the study were middle class, well dressed and accompanied by a non-Chinese American companion; so they were untypical of the Chinese stereotype which would have been at the front of people's minds when they were completing the original attitude survey.

Ajzen and Fishbein (1977) performed a meta-analysis of 109 studies of attitudes and behaviour. Fifty-four of those studies had assessed general attitudes and then used them (unsuccessfully) to predict specifically how research participants would behave. That does, of course, still leave 55 studies which did find a discrepancy between attitudes and behaviour, but it does show that maybe we are not always as inconsistent as some of the research might have suggested.

THE THEORY OF REASONED ACTION

In 1963, Fishbein proposed that it was **intentions**, rather than attitudes, which determine how people are likely to act. Attitudes contribute towards intentions of course, but they are also affected by two other factors: beliefs about other people's expectations – for example, about what is the socially acceptable way to behave; and how strongly motivated that person is to comply with relevant social norms or expectations. So behaviour comes from a combination of attitudes, expectations and motivation, not just attitudes alone.

For example, if you didn't like cats, and were visiting a neighbour who had friendly cats, you probably wouldn't stroke them. But if your neighbour clearly expected you to stroke them you might stroke one simply to avoid offending your neighbour, and because it didn't matter that much to you. If it did matter a lot, though, you might explain to your neighbour that you did not want to have the cats near you. So your attitude towards cats alone wouldn't predict your behaviour, it would depend on the social expectations on you in the situation, and on your personal motivation as to how far you were prepared to conform to those social expectations.

This approach effectively argues that on the whole, people usually behave in a sensible manner, taking account of information and considering the implications of their actions. It became the basis for the **theory of reasoned action**, developed by Ajzen and Fishbein in 1980. This theory proposes that we can learn more about what people are likely to do from their statements of intention, than from their attitudes.

In this model, intentions are formed by a combination of two basic factors: the person's attitude towards the behaviour (not, please note, their attitude towards the object or idea); and the person's perception of any social pressures on them as to whether they should to perform or not. The attitudes which we develop towards a behaviour come mostly from our own beliefs, based on what we think is likely to happen if we perform that behaviour. It's an estimate of probability based mainly on our own past experiences. Our perception of social pressure – known as the **subjective norm** – is all about whether we believe that it is socially a good thing that we should perform the action. Subjective norms develop from our personal beliefs about how social judgements work, in a particular group of people.

The theory of reasoned action has been put to work in several instances of attempts to change attitudes. One classic example is in attempts to change people's attitudes towards smoking. As can be seen from old films and TV programmes, smoking used to be very widely accepted. Nowadays, of course, the social view of smoking is completely the opposite; it is regarded as a socially unacceptable habit, both in public and in many private homes. Attempts to change people's attitudes towards smoking on their own had relatively little effect; but when they were combined with attempts to change the subjective norms related to smoking, together with information designed to encourage the intention to stop, the results were demonstrably more successful.

The theory of planned behaviour

In a modification of the theory, Ajzen (1991) proposed the **theory of planned behaviour**, which discussed how self-perception influenced both intentions and actions. In some cases, Ajzen argued, the person did not perceive themselves as having control over their actions, and in such situations merely focusing on intentions would not be sufficient to achieve behavioural change. Instead, Ajzen introduced a further factor to the model – that of perceived behavioural control. Achieving attitude change, Ajzen argued, would depend both on the person's motivation – that is, their intentions, and on whether they saw themselves as capable of achieving that change – their perceived behavioural control.

Key Terms

theory of reasoned action
The idea that people normally behave in a reasonable manner, and will change their attitudes if it seems appropriate in their circumstances.

subjective norm
Our individual perception of what is acceptable in a given situation.

theory of planned behaviour
The idea that attitude change depends on the person's perception that they are in control of their ideas and actions.

This modification to the theory of reasoned action was widely accepted, although it did attract a number of criticisms. One of these was that the researchers did not distinguish between perceived behavioural control and actual behavioural control (Terry et al, 1993). Terry argued that perceived behavioural control contained two different ideas: self-efficacy beliefs ("I believe that I can achieve this"), and beliefs about actual control ("I believe that I can control this"). In studies where the two were separated, Terry showed that the **self-efficacy belief** was essential. If the person did not hold the relevant self-efficacy beliefs, but did believe that the behaviour was controllable, there was little effect on the outcome. So perceived behavioural control was not as important as Ajzen had claimed.

Another criticism was that the theory was too specific, limiting itself to the prediction of specific behaviours rather than acting as a general model for attitude change. However, for many professionals, and particularly those working in health promotion, a model which allowed them to address specific behaviours effectively was distinctly useful, and it is in this applied area that the theory of planned behaviour has been mainly employed.

COGNITIVE DISSONANCE

Some other aspects of attitude change are inherent in some of the theories of attitudes that we have already explored. For example, one implication of the model put forward by Smith et al (1956) regarding the functions of attitudes, is that people are more likely to change their attitudes when they are feeling relaxed and secure, not when they are feeling under threat or attacked. When feeling under threat – either to themselves personally or to a group that they identify with – people are more likely to hold strongly onto their existing attitudes.

That tendency can apply even when we are unaware of it, as we find in the case of **cognitive dissonance**. This is another important mechanism which affects far more of our lives than we sometimes realise. It is connected with balance theory, in the sense that becoming aware that we hold contradictory cognitions is uncomfortable, and motivates us to do something about it. In

THE SALVATION OF DOWNSVILLE '56

fact, Festinger took balance theory as his starting point when developing the theory (Festinger, 1957). But rather than just dealing with triads and dyads, cognitive dissonance is much broader in scope, and it can be a powerful motivator in human action.

Cognitive dissonance theory states that if one of our cognitions – an attitude or a belief, for example – is in direct conflict with another one, and if the two are related in some way, then we will experience cognitive tension. We deal with this tension in one of two ways: either we change one of the cognitions, or we add an extra one to "explain" the apparent discrepancy.

For example, you may know someone as generally very kind and thoughtful towards others. If you then come across them expressing what seem to be very callous attitudes towards someone else, you will experience a cognitive conflict; that experience is in direct contradiction to your existing belief about that person. That is cognitive dissonance, which you then have to deal with. You might do it by changing one of the cognitions – for example, deciding that maybe your friend isn't really a kind person after all. Or you may add another cognition – for example, that their behaviour only seems to be callous but is actually them being "cruel to be kind" because of their previous experience with that person – that they are acting this way because it will help that person in the long run.

Box 5.3   Mrs Keech and the end of the world

Predictions of the end of the world seem to come up fairly regularly, every couple of decades or so. In 1956, Festinger et al reported a natural experiment on cognitive dissonance which they had been able to observe. Mrs Keech, a well-known medium of the time, reported that she had received a "message": the whole of a large US city was about to be destroyed by a great flood. Nobody in the city would be saved, but she and anyone who followed her would be rescued by a flying saucer, as long as they renounced their material goods and spent the night in prayer on a hill overlooking the city. She and her followers then sold all their possessions and went up to the hill to be ready for the fateful date. Festinger and his research team went along as well, being interested to see what would happen when the prediction failed to come true.

When the city failed to be flooded, the researchers asked the believers what had happened and why: was the original prediction wrong? No, replied the followers, the original prediction had been correct but the city had been saved by their actions and prayers. In other words, rather than admitting that the original prediction was wrong, which would have produced dissonance, particularly in view of the fact that they had sold their earthly possessions, they added a new idea: that these actions had saved the city. Instead of facing up to the cognitive dissonance which would have been produced by sticking to their original beliefs, the cult members changed their beliefs, seeing their actions as effective in changing what actually happened, so that without them the flood would certainly have taken place.

Box 5.3 describes a powerful "natural experiment" on cognitive dissonance reported by Festinger et al (1956), which shows how powerful a mechanism it can be in changing people's beliefs and attitudes. Festinger and his research team followed that study up with a number of more controlled laboratory based studies. Typically, these involved a **forced compliance** method, in which the experimental situation deliberately generated contradictory cognitions in the participants. For example, Festinger and Carlsmith (1959) asked participants to engage in extremely tedious tasks, such as giving a quarter-turn to each of a large set of wooden pegs in a board. They had to do this for half an hour at a time. When they had finished, they were asked to return to the waiting room and tell the next participants that the task was very interesting. Then they were asked to report, privately, their own personal attitude towards the task.

The research participants were paid either US$1 or $20. When their reported attitudes were examined later, those paid $20 rated the task, quite accurately, as mind-numbingly boring. But those who had been paid $1 showed a different result. While not saying it was absolutely fascinating, some of them rated the task as moderately interesting, while others saw it as not too dull. Festinger and Carlsmith argued that this was a direct result of the cognitive dissonance they had experienced. For the first group, receiving $20 was enough to justifying lying to the other participants. But $1 was much too trivial a sum to justify anything, so those participants had reduced their cognitive dissonance by adjusting their own beliefs.

In a later variant of the study, Collins and Hoyt (1972) found that what was important was whether the people in the waiting room had seemed to be convinced by the participants' lies. When they seemed unconvinced, the participants showed no attitude change; but if they seemed to have been convinced by the participants words, then the participants showed attitude change; they experienced dissonance if it mattered what they said, but not if it didn't. Similarly, the same researchers found that students who were asked to write an essay arguing for something they didn't believe in showed attitude change towards that something – unless they were allowed to sign a disclaimer beforehand. In that case, they didn't show any attitude change towards the subject at all.

MINORITY INFLUENCE

Cognitive dissonance, then, can be a powerful factor in attitude change. But why would we want to change people's attitudes in the first place? The events in Europe before and during World War II showed how extreme what had been taken for granted as widely shared social prejudices could become, and how important it was for such attitudes to be challenged. During the 50 years since then, many attitudes which were widespread and largely accepted in society have been so successfully challenged that they are now considered socially unacceptable – for example, racial prejudice, homophobia and overt sexual discrimination. Although there are still a few individuals holding these views, they are now in the minority, and the bulk of social opinion and often the law goes against expressing them openly. Originally, though, they were majority views, and it was the influence of the minority which led to the change.

This raises an interesting distinction – the difference between attitude change on an individual scale, and changes in social attitudes. While some researchers focused their efforts on personal attitude change, others, particularly social psychologists based in or originating from Europe, saw it as a problem needing to be tackled on a social level. For them, the experiences before and during World War II had highlighted the importance of social pressures in attitude change, and how the extreme attitudes initially held by a minority could come to dominate a society even when many disagreed with them.

This interest linked with other research by European social psychologists. In Chapter 1 we saw how powerful social identification can be, and how people are more ready to accept the beliefs of their own social groups. In the last chapter we looked at social representations and how they come to be shared and disseminated across social groups and society in general. These too had arisen as a result of social psychological interest in group attitudes and behaviours. Moscovici, the eventual founder of social representation theory, began his work as a result of extensive research into how minorities can produce social change.

In the next chapter we will be looking at people's powerful tendency to conform. As a general rule, we prefer to go along with the majority, rather than confront others and disagree with them openly. But if we always did that, nothing would ever change in society – what the majority wanted would always win out. But change does happen, often quite dramatically, and it usually starts with a much smaller group which manages to influence the majority.

Moscovici et al (1969) set up a study to investigate how **minority influence** works. They used groups of six, like the classic studies of conformity, and showed their participants blue slides, which were always the same blue but not always the same brightness. Each member of the group called out the colour in turn, but sometimes one or two of the participants (primed by the experimenters) would name the colour "green" rather than "blue" – an obviously wrong answer.

In the control condition, there were six real research participants, while the others had four real research participants, and two confederates. In some groups, the confederates were inconsistent, calling the slides green only two-thirds of the time. In the third condition, the confederates called out "green" all of the time. They found that the six real research participants always named the colour correctly, and so did the participants in the group with the inconsistent minority. But in the third group, even though the task was obvious, the participants identified the colour as "green" on nearly 10 per cent of occasions.

The consistent minority seemed to have an effect at an unconscious level, making the participants more prepared to accept the idea of the other colour. Moscovici et al had tested the colour thresholds of their participants – the point at which they judged that a colour had changed – before the study. When they tested them again after the study they found that the thresholds for those in the consistent minority condition had shifted, so that they had a lower threshold for green than they had before, and were more ready to judge a stimulus as that colour. In another study, Moscovici and Personnaz (1980) found that the same effects on judgements happened when they used negative after-images for the test, showing how this type of minority pressure influenced the participants even though they were largely unconscious of it.

Similar effects were found in studies of social judgements. When Maass and Clark (1983) set up discussion groups with majorities arguing either for or against gay rights and minorities taking the opposite view, they found that although their participants tended to respond with the majority in terms of their overt responses, when they were asked in private afterwards, their views had often changed to become closer to the minority's arguments. That topic of study wouldn't work now since gay rights, like anti-racism, is another area where we can clearly see the influence of minorities in social change over the past few decades. But in 1983, the topic was newer as a subject of general social debate, and there was less social consensus.

Several other studies showed how important consistency is in minority influence. Hogg and Vaughan (1995) argued that this is partly because hearing a particular viewpoint consistently challenges the comfortable consensus, and creates a degree of uncertainty. It also gives an alternative to the accepted point of view which may be new to some people; and it attracts attention, being noticeably different. A consistent viewpoint also implies that those holding it are not likely to change their minds easily or without very good reason, and that therefore their viewpoint needs to be taken seriously if conflict is to be resolved. So simply by being consistent, Hogg and Vaughan argued, a minority viewpoint encourages people to explore alternatives and to re-evaluate their own beliefs.

Being consistent, though, doesn't necessarily mean being dogmatic and inflexible. Nemeth and Brilmayer (1987) showed that the most influential minorities were those which showed a flexible approach to the topic. In a small group study, people were asked to decide on compensation for a ski accident. The confederate of the experimenters began by arguing for a very low amount, and in one condition they stuck to that view throughout the session. In the other conditions, the confederate shifted towards the majority view, and these were much more influential as minorities than those who took a more rigid approach.

Other researchers have found similar results: although effective minorities need to be consistent in the position and approaches which they take, they also need to be prepared to negotiate with the majority. Mugny (1982) argued that this is because rigid minorities become labelled as dogmatic, unrealistic and extreme. Friends of the Earth, for example, became more effective in changing industrial attitudes towards pollution when it began to work with industrialists to minimise industrial damage to the environment, instead of insisting that industrial activity was a bad thing and shouldn't happen at all. Their environmental values remained consistent, but being prepared to negotiate how those values could be expressed made them much more influential.

According to Moscovici (1980), majorities and minorities affect us differently. Majority views are accepted passively, without much thought. But minority views demand thought, and even if we don't accept them, they produce a certain amount of cognitive restructuring purely by making us think about what they mean. This sometimes means that we may eventually come round to a point of view that we initially rejected, or it may mean that we continue to reject it but in a more informed manner. But it also suggests that minority influence may be less visible, and take longer, than accepting the majority view. So attitude change may be happening even though it doesn't immediately show up in our behaviour.

PERSUASION

Some attempts at attitude change are completely deliberate – we try to change people's attitudes or ideas towards a topic or a product, in order to persuade them to behave differently in some way. This might be political persuasion – attempting to get people to vote for a particular politician or party or to back a campaign; or commercial persuasion, attempting to persuade people to favour a particular model of car, hair product, washing powder or other consumer artefact.

This, of course, is a whole basis of advertising. Advertising is all about persuasion, and advertisers have drawn on psychological insight and theories since the beginning of the 20th century. When J. B. Watson, the founder of behaviourism, was disgraced in the late 1920s after an affair with his secretary, he left academic psychology and went straight into advertising, applying his insights into learning theory to sales and marketing. Since much of his work had to do with the effectiveness of repetition for learning, this partly accounts for the early "hard sell" approach adopted by American salesman between the wars.

Later, however, following the growth of research into computers and computer models of the mind, the focus of attitude change research emphasised how people process information. In terms of persuasion, the basic assumption was that it is all about conveying information clearly enough to the other person. Researchers argued about what type of information processing was involved – whether, for example, it would be more effective if the person needed to give their whole attention to the message, in which case the message needed to be striking and noticeable, or whether it would be more effective if the information was conveyed in a more subtle manner so that the person was less conscious of it. Petty and Cacioppo (1979) described these two types of information as **central route processing** or **peripheral route processing**.

Chaiken (1980) compared these two types of processing. Research participants received messages containing between four and six arguments, all supporting particular points of view. Half of them were told that questions about the message would be asked later while the others were told that they would be asked about a different topic. The idea was that those who knew they would be asked about the topic would pay full attention to it, while the others would be more likely to use peripheral processing.

The information they were given produced some attitude change in both groups. But it appeared that the change resulted from different factors in the two cases. The central route group appeared to be mostly influenced by the number of arguments being put forward – the messages containing the most arguments showed the strongest attitude change. But the peripheral processing group were more influenced by whether they liked the person delivering the messages or not – not a factor in the case of the central processing group. In a follow-up two weeks later, the attitude changes for the peripheral processing group were almost gone, but the central processing group still showed the attitude change, implying that central processing has a more lasting effect than peripheral processing.

The four-factor approach

The information-processing approach led to a four-factor approach which is still popular among marketing professionals today, and summarised in Table 5.2. Each of these factors was backed up, to some extent, by psychological research, but whether they have been judged relevant for advertising or marketing has been essentially about whether they seemed to make a difference

> ## Key Terms
>
> **central route processing**
> The direct approach to attitude change, (e.g., directly instructing someone to buy something or change their attitude towards something).
>
> **peripheral route processing**
> The indirect approach to attitude change, in which attention is not focused directly on the information being transmitted, but is elsewhere.

Table 5.2 The four-factor approach to communication

Source	Factors concerning from where or whom the message originates.
Message	Factors relating to the actual content of the message.
Receiver	Factors relating to the person or people at whom the message is aimed.
Context	Factors concerning the overall setting of the communication.

to sales, and that has been mainly inferred from case studies of specific campaigns.

For example, in a campaign designed to promote California wine in Britain in the early 1980s (Butterfield, 1989), the advertisers deliberately produced a humorous advertisement which contrasted a very "English" description "It's really jolly good" with American slang "A red that knows where it's coming from." Those areas of the UK which received the adverts showed a dramatic increase of market share for the product, which was not paralleled in the areas without the advert. So the market share was taken as evidence for the effectiveness of the persuasion.

This example highlights several aspects of the four-factor model. Its creators drew on both the source of the communication and the characteristics of the receivers of the message by using the national stereotypes to stimulate a sense of social identification and in-group membership in the receiver. They also used humour in the message itself, and the visuals of the advert reinforced the context of wine consumption.

Psychological research into the source of the message has looked at several variables. One of these is the **credibility** of the communicator. Friedman and Friedman (1979) found that celebrities were much more effective as endorsers of products than professionals or typical consumers. They asked people to watch advertisements for 360 different household products and rate them by assessing the relevance of adjectives such as honest, likeable, informative or powerful. They were also asked about whether they found the advert plausible and whether they were likely to buy the product, and telephoned 48 hours later to see if they still remembered the products.

There may be a difference, though, when it comes to social attitudes, where professional expertise might be more important. In another study, Hovland and Weiss (1951) compared reactions to reports about drug-taking from a prestigious medical journal with those from a mass circulation newspaper. The reports were the same, but the medical journal was the more expert publication. In this case, the difference was dramatic – those who believed that their information came from the medical journal showed a 22 per cent attitude change, while the others showed only 8 per cent.

We don't know, however, whether these were lasting changes. Kelman and Hovland (1953) asked people to listen to a message which advocated lenient treatment of young offenders. In one condition, they were told that the communicator was a high-status court judge, while in the other condition they were told it was a suspected drug-dealer. Not surprisingly, they were more strongly influenced by the more credible message, from the judge – but only at first. When their views were reassessed three weeks later, the differences had largely disappeared. Those who had been swayed by the "judge" were less convinced, while those who had been in the "drug-dealer" condition showed

Key Terms

credibility
Having an air of authoritativeness or expertise, such that their opinion is readily believed.

a shift towards the idea. These changes disappeared when they were reminded of the source of their communication; but until that point they had forgotten it. So it seems there may be a **sleeper effect** – even information from a low-credibility source can produce attitude change over time.

The credibility of the source is also affected by what we perceive as that person or organisation's motivation. Walster et al (1966) showed that we are more influenced by people who we believe are arguing against their own interests, then if they seem to be self-serving. In one of their studies, teenagers assessed arguments purporting to come from either a criminal serving a prison sentence or a successful prosecutor. The arguments in the messages were about whether the courts should have more or less power, and the apparent motives of the "communicators" directly affected how strongly the teenagers were influenced.

Similarly, Walster and Festinger (1962) found that people who had "overheard" a message were more likely to be influenced by it than people who were told it directly. But that only applied if the information had relevance for the person concerned – for example, single women who "overheard" the argument that husbands should spend more time at home were unaffected, but married women were much more persuaded by it.

The other significant characteristic of the source demonstrated by researchers was that people tend to be more influenced by an attractive communicator than by an unattractive one. But although this seems to be mostly true, it isn't always the case. Zimbardo (1960) showed that it applies to information which people just come across – for example, in TV or magazine adverts; but when people have voluntarily committed themselves to listen to a message, an unattractive source can sometimes be more influential than an attractive one. It is possible that there is a degree of cognitive dissonance involved in committing yourself to pay attention to someone you don't particularly find attractive, so you adjust your evaluations of the message to make it seem more worthwhile.

Talking point 5.3   Celebrity endorsements

TV advertisers have an unshakeable belief in the power of the source in advertising – so much so, that having an advertising contract from a large corporation can be worth millions in income to a famous sports or music star. But those stars also have to retain an impeccable lifestyle; any hint of controversies or wrong-doing can mean that those high-level advertisers will pull out their sponsorship.

Devoting time to advertising for their sponsors has become an important part of the working life of many high-level sportspeople. Formula 1 drivers, top level athletes and football stars are all expected to spend some of their time promoting their sponsors' products, and the income which they or their teams receive is an important part of the training and development budget. Some sports – Formula 1 is a good example – simply wouldn't be able to function without sponsorship, and what those sponsors gain is advertising exposure, and above all celebrity endorsement if the teams are successful.

Key Terms

sleeper effect
An effect or result which does not show up immediately, but takes some time to manifest itself.

Taking a typical day, try making a note every time you see a celebrity endorsement of a product or service. Include roadside and transport advertising as well as magazines, TV and radio. I suspect that you'll be amazed at just how many you have collected by the end of the day!

The message itself

While early researchers argued that advertising messages needed to be very clear and unambiguous, other researchers found that it was generally more effective if participants had to do some cognitive work themselves. Heller (1956) gave participants complete or incomplete advertising slogans, and found they remembered the incomplete ones much better. The idea was that the cognitive processing they had to do helped the information to become embedded in their memories, while the other condition was too cognitively passive to be memorable.

In 1963, Janis and Feshbach investigated how whether the emotionality of a message was influential in changing attitudes. High-school students were shown one of three different films about dental health, with a control group getting a film about the eye. One film – the "strong fear" condition – emphasised heavily the pain and distress which could result from neglecting dental hygiene. Another, the "mild fear condition", emphasised the positive benefits which would result from good dental hygiene. A third film was halfway in between, mentioning pain and toothache but not very much.

Interestingly, the results were the opposite of what might have been expected. A couple of weeks later, the researchers asked the students whether they had made any changes to their normal tooth-brushing and dentist-visiting habits. All three groups indicated that they had changed their attitudes because of the films, but only the "low fear" group had changed their habits to any significant degree. In fact, those students receiving a "high fear" talk changed their behaviour much less even than those in the "medium fear" condition, while they in turn were less influenced than those in the "low fear" condition (see Table 5.3). It seems that a small degree of emotionality is better than deliberately trying to exaggerate it; some messages might be too powerful to achieve their purpose. Similar findings have been found for some of the more gruesome anti-smoking messages.

 It is possible that whether a high or low fear message produces different outcomes depending on the topic. Leventhal et al (1965) showed people films about tetanus, varying in terms of how scary they were about the illness. They found that people in the "high fear" condition showed a stronger attitude change than

Table 5.3 Emotionality in attitude change messages

Condition	Number of references to unpleasant consequences of neglecting dental hygiene	Percentage of people changing their behaviour
Low fear	18	37
Medium fear	49	22
High fear	71	8

Source: Janis and Feshbach (1963)

those in the low fear condition immediately after seeing the films, although neither group were more likely to have tetanus inoculations.

One problem with trying to induce attitude change is that people don't take much notice of issues which they think are irrelevant to them. In a public safety campaign trying to reduce chip pan fires, the initial approach warning against the fires was largely ineffective, because people didn't think they would act stupidly in the first place. But chip pan fires were substantially reduced after a campaign which detailed how such fires happened and how to deal with them, ending with the comment: "Of course, if you don't overfill your chip pan in the first place, you won't have to do any of this" (Cowpe, 1989).

It wasn't possible to tell whether people were having fewer such fires, or whether they were simply putting them out more effectively so that they didn't need to call the fire brigade; but there was a 25 per cent lower callout in some areas, and no increase in the seriousness of the fires which were reported (suggesting that it wasn't just that the fire brigade were only being called to the ones which had got out of hand). So, in this case it was making the message directly relevant to the receivers which seemed to make the difference.

The receiver of the message

Not everyone responds to the same information in the same way. For example, Hovland et al (1949) found that people responded differently to propaganda posters and publicity which showed either one or two sides of an issue, depending on their level of education. Those with low levels of education tended to be more persuaded if they were just given a single side of an argument, while those with higher levels of education were more likely to be persuaded if they were given both sides, with one expressed more convincingly than the other. However, this only applied if they didn't already have clearly formed opinions on the issue; if they did, then both groups found single arguments more effective.

Sherif and Hovland (1961) investigated why the attitude that people already hold should influence their susceptibility to further persuasion. They suggested that it might be because when we come across a message similar to our own views, we tend to accentuate its similarity, so that the two seem to be even closer and we can easily assimilate it into our worldview. But if an argument is very different from our own viewpoint, those differences become exaggerated to create an even larger contrast between the two. Our own viewpoint acts as the anchor point or baseline for evaluation, with a surrounding latitude of acceptance determining whether another viewpoint is close enough to be assimilated. Contrasting messages fall outside of that latitude of acceptance and instead fall within our latitude of rejection.

According to Sherif and Hovland people's latitude of acceptance or rejection will vary for any given topic. This variability is affected by how extreme the subject's initial position is, in that people holding very extreme positions have a much smaller latitude of acceptance than people with more moderate views. The latitude of acceptance or rejection will also be influenced by how much the person identifies with the topic. If we have a high level of ego-involvement with a particular approach, we will have a very small latitude of acceptance and find it hard to tolerate much variation. If it doesn't matter to us all that much, we have a wider latitude of acceptance and can tolerate quite a lot of deviation from our personal viewpoint. This ties in with the findings by Himmelfarb and Eagly (1974), who saw the degree of ego-involvement as a major factor in how likely people were to be persuaded. This with a high level of ego-involvement would be very resistant to changing their attitudes, whereas people seeing the issue as relatively unimportant would be able to select arguments much more freely, and so could be persuaded more easily.

The context of the message

A great deal of research by the advertising industry has been devoted to looking at how the context may affect the persuasiveness of a message. In one study, Gorn (1982) showed how musical backgrounds can directly influence consumer choice. Research participants were shown images of coloured pens while either pleasant or unpleasant music (previously rated by other participants) was playing in the background. Later, when given a free choice, the participants showed a strong tendency to choose the colour of pen associated with the pleasant music.

However, although it was widely accepted, the study was not designed particularly well. Kellaris and Cox (1989) replicated Gorn's study, but more carefully and avoiding some of the weaknesses of the previous design. Where Gorn had told the research participants that the study was to "evaluate music for a pen commercial", their research participants were told that it was to "assess perceptions of various products". They also matched the music more carefully than Gorn had done, using pieces with the same instruments, tempo and modality, but which had been rated by independent judges as pleasant or unpleasant (the "pleasant" piece was by Mozart; the "unpleasant" one by Milhaud).

Perhaps most importantly, they set up a different method of pen selection. In Gorn's study, the task had been a bit obvious, as the research participants had been asked to go to separate sides of the room to choose their pen. Kellaris and Cox arranged that both the pens would be available, but that the pens would contain either blue or black ink. So they could identify the choice of pen by the questionnaire they filled in at the end of the experiment. Tidying up the study in this produced research findings in which the music didn't seem to make any difference.

But there is still evidence that the context of a message may be effective. Research into the different responses elicited by different background colours in magazine adverts, for example, has shown fairly robust effects, as have other types of context or setting. In 1979, Murphy et al compared how effective humorous advertisements were when they were shown in different television "environments" – that is, when they appeared during the advertising breaks of different types of programmes. If a humorous advertisement was shown in the middle of an action-adventure programme, they found that it was far more effective than the same advert shown in the middle of a sitcom, where there was already a high level of humour in the content. It appears that context does have some influence, but perhaps one which acts in more subtle ways than the early research suggested.

Involvement

Other research into persuasion has looked at the personal investments which people have in rationalising or protecting their attitudes, or in changing them. Johnson and Eagly (1989) distinguished between three different types of involvement: value-relevant involvement, impression-relevant involvement and outcome-relevant involvement.

Value-relevant involvement links with the research we looked at earlier into the value-expressive functions of attitudes. Rokeach (1973) showed how some attitudes were closely linked with the self-concept as well as with the person's values. In that sort of situation, when a particular attitude is closely linked with someone's values, it can serve an important function in either expressing or defending those values. Because of that deep level of personal involvement, such attitudes can be very resistant to persuasion.

Impression-relevant involvement, on the other hand, has to do with people's self-presentational strategies – in other words, how they like to appear to other people. Drawing on research which looked at how people would adjust their expressed attitudes in terms of how they would be perceived socially (e.g., Zimbardo, 1960) they showed how, for many people, this is not a superficial question. Social acceptability is an important motivator: we tend to evaluate the interpersonal consequences of attitudes that we hold, and, all other things being equal, to adjust our attitudes to make them more socially acceptable. In such cases, persuasion may be more effective when it addresses issues of social acceptability than if it addresses other types of issues.

The third type of involvement described by Johnson and Eagly is **outcome-relevant involvement**, in which a particular attitude or attitude change is linked with outcomes which the person would consider desirable or towards which they are aiming. In these situations, attitudes serve an instrumental function, which helps the person to achieve goals or outcomes which will give them the most benefits. That doesn't have to be a personal benefit, of course; someone who aims to achieve, say, an environmentally-friendly lifestyle will tend to adopt those attitudes most likely to benefit those aims, regardless of personal costs in terms of time and trouble.

These three types of involvement produce very different outcomes when it comes to persuasion. Value-relevant involvement produced a high resistance to persuasion, or at least to persuasion where the result would run counter to the values being held. People with high value-relevant involvement

Key Terms

value-relevant involvement
The role of an attitude in protecting or defending someone's personal values.

impression-relevant involvement
When an attitude is concerned with how someone likes to present themselves to other people.

outcome-relevant involvement
An attitude which helps a person achieve a personal goal or ambition.

seemed to be very receptive to persuasion which was congruent with their values. Outcome-relevant involvement meant that the person was more likely to be persuaded by relevant arguments and ideas than any other way of approaching the issues – as long as those arguments were of high quality. Impression-relevant involvement, on the other hand, was more responsive to persuasion when arguments were focused on social acceptability and desirable self-presentation.

Of course, in real life things are rarely that simple. Levin et al (2000) pointed out that most people hold multiple motives at the same time, so simply addressing one type of motivation without taking any notice of the others was unlikely to be a universal solution to persuasion. However, they argued that taking the different types of involvement into account would enrich persuasion attempts, and make them more effective overall. In the next chapter, we will look at some other types of social influence, and how that can affect how we behave towards other people.

Summary: Chapter 5

1. Attitudes are tendencies to prefer or to respond favourably or unfavourably to people, objects or social events. They incorporate cognitive, conative, behavioural and affective domains.

2. Attitudes may be formed through social exposure, social learning or in order to satisfy unmet social or personal needs. Behavioural geneticists have also argued that there is a genetic component to attitudes, but this is more controversial.

3. Theories of attitude function have included knowledge functions, instrumentality, ego-defence, value-expression and object appraisal. The function–structure model of attitudes links motivation with experience, beliefs and feelings.

4. Psychologists have developed numbers of techniques for measuring attitudes, but challenges in this area include forms of bias, problems of quantifiability and the interpretation of meaning.

5. Balance theory emphasises cognitive balance, while self-perception theory proposes that we infer our attitudes from our own behaviour. Accentuation and social judgement theories of attitudes emphasise the social contexts within which attitudes are formed and used.

6. The theory of reasoned action emphasises the importance of intention in analysing discrepancies between attitudes and behaviour. It was later modified into the theory of planned behaviour.

7. Cognitive dissonance occurs when two of our cognitions directly contradict or conflict with one another. It can be a powerful motivator for attitude or behavioural change.

8. Moscovici showed how small minorities could produce changes in social attitudes, especially if their arguments were presented credibly and consistently.

9. The four-factor approach to persuasion deals with the source of the message, the content of the message, the receiver of the message and the content in which the message is given.

10. Persuasion is also dependent on involvement, which may be of three types: value-relevant involvement, impression-relevant involvement and outcome-relevant involvement.

Chapter 6

Contents

Social influence

6

From the beginning of this book I have talked about people as being social animals, and I hope I have shown just how fundamental this fact is to how we interact with other people. But being a social human isn't only about belonging to social groups; we are strongly influenced just by the presence of others, whether they are in the same group as us or not. Indeed, in some situations, other people can exert quite a lot of control over how we act – even though we don't know them, or are just hearing from them through the internet. In this chapter, we will be looking at some of the ways that other people directly affect our behaviour.

PRESENCE OF OTHERS

One of the early discoveries made by social psychologists was that people can influence our behaviour just by being there when we are doing something. Sometimes, other people's presence can mean that we do things better – a phenomenon known as **social facilitation**. Triplett (1898) demonstrated social facilitation by asking children to turn a fishing reel as fast as they could for a set period of time. The children turned it faster and more energetically if there were other children in the room doing the same thing.

Coaction and audience effects

The reason, Triplett believed, was because they felt they were competing with one another. But Allport (1920) found that even if people were directly instructed not to compete, the same results would happen. In Allport's study, the participants were college students solving multiplication problems; and Allport found that they even worked better if they could just see other people working, even if it wasn't on the same task. Simply being active while others are active nearby – coaction – seems to be a reliable social effect.

It is possible, though, that Allport's students might have been competing in their own ways. In his study, the students were just told not to compete; but when Dashiell (1930) set up a similar study but adjusted the situation so that they couldn't compete, and knew that they couldn't, the coaction effect seemed to disappear. What did seem to emerge, though, in another part of Dashiell's study, were **audience effects**. The students completed a higher number of multiplication problems if there were other people watching what they were doing – but they also made more errors than when they worked alone.

These audience effects were also found by other researchers, and they seemed to be fairly robust. But not all audiences were the same. The size and status of the audience mattered. Porter (1939) found that stutterers were more affected by larger audiences than smaller ones, and Latané and Harkins (1976) found that people rated their feelings of nervousness higher if their audiences were larger or of higher status. They were also affected by whether they were performing alone or with others. Jackson and Latané (1981) demonstrated that people who were about to perform solo rated themselves as much more nervous than people who were about to perform in a group. They explained this in terms of diffusion of impact, the overall impact for the group performers was shared, and so reduced. We will be looking at diffusion of impact later in this chapter.

Audience effects are not always negative. Sometimes the presence of others actually makes us do better – it facilitates our behaviour rather than inhibiting it. Zajonc (1965) explained this in terms of drive theory, arguing that the presence of other people puts us into an energised state – and the more so if those people are of high status or there are more of them – which affects how we act. That energised state means that we will tend to produce whatever behaviour is most habitual. If we are good at something, we will produce a good performance; if we are less good at it we may produce a worse one.

Other psychologists (e.g., Cotterell, 1972) argued that it wasn't necessarily about drives or internal energised states; instead, it was all about whether the person felt that they were being evaluated. If the audience was blindfolded so that they couldn't actually see what the person was doing, the effects disappeared (Cotterell et al, 1968), and when Paulus and Murdock (1971) compared the effects of "expert" observers with the effects produced by audiences consisting of other psychology students, they found that the audience effects were much stronger when the participants felt that their audiences were experts in what they were trying to do.

In another study, Baxter et al (1990) examined the effects of having a passenger on drivers' behaviour. They found that speeding was decreased by having a passenger, but so was signalling. They also found that there were individual differences affecting both speeding and close following, suggesting that the social norms for specific categories of road users were also relevant in

this type of context. Their findings, they suggested, gave more support to the idea that audience effects influence personal control, and challenged the idea of audience effects occurring through the increased arousal predicted by drive-based theories.

Schmitt et al (1986) gave people an easy and difficult task to complete, and asked them to do it under one of three conditions: alone, with a blindfolded companion in the same room (the companion also wore a headset and the participant was told that they were doing a sensory deprivation task), or with someone who carefully scrutinised everything they did. Schmitt et al found that just having someone else present improved the performance of the easy task but slowed performance of the difficult one. The close scrutiny condition gave similar results, not significantly different from the simple presence of others condition.

Baron (1986) proposed that these findings came from the fact that the presence of another person is a constant source of distraction. This produces a division of attention, so people are comfortable with well-known or easy tasks but perform less well on tasks which require them to pay close attention to what they are doing. This is known as the distraction–conflict model, the idea that audience effects are produced by the person concerned being divided between attending to the people in the audience or to the task that they are doing.

But Bond (1982) argued that audience effects actually arise from **self-presentation** issues. Audience effects happen because people want to present a favourable image to those who are watching. That's no problem for easy tasks, because the person can concentrate on the task and be aware that they are doing it well. More complex tasks involve both the demands of the task itself and the awareness that other people can see any errors or mistaken strategies. That awareness can produce embarrassment, anxiety or even a tendency towards defence mechanisms like withdrawal; and those reactions make it even harder for the person to concentrate on what they are doing.

| Key Terms

self-presentation
The image or impression of self that we like to show to others.

Table 6.1 Theories of audience effects

Name	Key proponent	Description
Drive theory	Zajonc (1965)	The simple presence of others creates a high-drive state – energised through arousal. This enhances performance on simple tasks but not complex ones.
Distraction–conflict theory	Baron et al (1978)	The presence of other people distracts the person from paying full attention to the task. Easy tasks are unaffected but complex ones are impaired.
Evaluation apprehension	Weiss and Miller (1971)	Awareness that others are evaluating performance leads to arousal and errors.
Self-presentation theory	Bond (1982)	People want to present a favourable image to those watching, and may become embarrassed or anxious, increasing errors.

There have been a number of theories put forward to explain audience effects, and these are summarised in Table 6.1. In 2006, Feinberg and Aiello set up a large-scale study to assess the two main theories to have withstood the test of time: distraction–conflict theory and evaluation–apprehension. They used word-association tasks because these had been used extensively in other studies of social facilitation studies, and would indicate the effects very clearly, and gave them to 166 undergraduate psychology students, who were assigned randomly either to the six experimental groups or to a control group.

The word-pairs were organised as either complex or simple tasks, and the instructions given to the students were designed to induce either evaluation–apprehension (that the experimenter was a university professor, the task would be evaluated at the end of the session, and it could indicate higher grade averages and intelligence) or a sense of control (instructions were task-focused and would not be evaluated for several weeks). Once they had been given their instructions, the students were either left alone to complete the task, or the experimenter sat on a chair to the left and slightly behind them. In some conditions, also, they were asked to do a less important number comparison task which appeared randomly five times during their word-pair task. This was the distraction condition.

Feinberg and Aiello found that the simple presence of the experimenter didn't produce any social-facilitation effects, but the experimental conditions did. The evaluation–apprehension condition showed significant improvements in performance on the simple task, and significant impairment on the complex task. The distraction–conflict condition did not show any effects on the simple task, but produced significant performance impairment on the complex task.

When the two conditions were combined, performance on the complex task was also impaired. The researchers suggested that these results implied that the two different theories could usefully be consolidated, rather than being seen as completing explanations. It all depends on the type of task; if we're doing something relatively simple, then we can cope with distractions; but evaluation–apprehension may affect us, if we're performing a complex task, both of those will influence how well we do.

Talking point 6.1   Audiences

Some people enjoy being in front of audiences. The attention energises them, and stimulates their performance so that they do really well. Other people hate it. They become nervous and make mistakes which they wouldn't make in a more private situation. It seems on the surface as though there are just two types of people: those who enjoy having an audience and those who don't.

But it isn't really as simple as that. Many actors and comedians who actually enjoy being on stage describe how they feel terrible beforehand – they feel nervous and stressed, and want to run away. All those feelings, though, disappear when they are actually onstage and performing. For some, the hardest part is performing as part of a team – they don't want to let the others down. For others, going on stage alone would be worst, they feel exposed and vulnerable. And even established professionals can feel particularly anxious in front of certain types of audiences. It can be harder to perform, lecture or act in front of your peers – that is, other people in the same profession – than in front of a general audience or a group of students.

So where do you fit it? Do you feel OK reading an essay in front of a study group? Or going on stage as part of a play? And do the nerves disappear when you actually do it? Do some people really not feel it, or are they just good at covering up? What do you think?

Social loafing

Being with others doesn't always mean having an audience, though. People may be paying attention to what they are doing, and not to anyone else. Latané et al (1979) found that when people are conducting a group task, and in particular when everyone's contribution is indistinguishable from the others, some individuals would put less effort into the task, rather than more. Latané et al called this **social loafing**, and demonstrated it in a number of studies. In one of them, college students were tested individually and asked to generate as much noise as they could. They were asked to do the same thing in a group. They found that the students each produced far less noise when they were acting with other people than when they were on their own. A group of six people, for example, would only make 2.4 times the amount of noise that the same people had made on their own – nothing like six times as much. So they were obviously not trying as hard.

Following this, the researchers set up "pseudogroups", or false groups, where the students believed that they were shouting with others but were actually shouting alone. Their results backed up the group findings; they just didn't make as much noise as they did when they believed they were alone. A single student would produce only 82 per cent of the noise that they produced alone, if they believed they were with one other person. If they believed that they were with five other people, they would produce only 74 per cent of the noise.

In some ways, social loafing is the opposite of the normal coaction effect. But they are not interchangeable. **Coaction** effects happen when the person feels personally responsible for the end results. At such times, they try harder to make a positive contribution. Social loafing, on the other hand, seems to be a by-product of anonymity. Williams et al (1981) undertook a noise-generating activity similar to that used by Latané et al, but this time they told the students that their own share would be recorded. There was no social loafing in that situation.

In a more recent study of social loafing, Chidambaram and Tung (2005) found that the group size could make quite a difference to how people performed. They set up a situation in which groups of students worked together to solve a problem, either sitting around a table or individually, and communicating by computer. The groups were of either four or eight students, and in both situations, people worked harder in the groups of four than they did in the groups of eight. But the people who were sitting round a table together worked harder than those co-operating at a distance, and later said they had felt more pressure to look busy.

This, and other studies, have shown that both social expectations and the diffusion of responsibility are factors in social loafing, as is the motivation of the individuals concerned. As we saw earlier, anonymity, too, has been shown to be a major factor in social loafing, and this has been explained in terms of evaluation from others. If you are anonymous, then nobody can say you are being lazy.

These findings also connect with the very different forms of internet behaviour we find when people are able to act anonymously. Personal comments on Facebook and other social media can sometimes be hurtful to the receiver, but rarely achieve the lengths of abuse and vitriol which can be manifest on media which allow anonymous contributions, such as Twitter. It seems that being anonymous allows people to act in ways which they know are socially unacceptable, and which they would not do if they knew they would be personally identified doing it.

Bystander intervention

Being anonymous doesn't inevitably bring out the negative side of people – although for some time researchers believed that might be the case. Research into this area was stimulated as a result of a dramatic news case in the late 1960s, which reported how a young woman, Kitty Genovese, had been dramatically stabbed to death in New York while people in overlooking apartments ignored her cries for help and did not even called the police. A 2004 article in the *New York Times* argued that the original description, which had hit the newspapers as a picture of a prolonged, violent attack ignored by 38 witnesses, had been seriously exaggerated, and that the attack was less visible than had been portrayed and less prolonged. Nonetheless, the girl had been brutally murdered, people had heard her screams and the police had not taken action, and the impact of the news reports was dramatic.

 ## Altruism and helping

The report of the murder prompted a series of psychological investigations into the behaviour of bystanders. Spearheaded by Latané and Darley (1968), researchers produced a number of experimental situations in which people obviously needed help, and investigated various hypotheses about why people acted or didn't act.

As their research progressed, however, they found that people are more ready to help others than they are to ignore them. Detailed investigations of bystander behaviour showed that, contrary to the impression given by the reports of the Kitty Genovese case, **bystander intervention** is more common than bystander apathy. For example, a study carried out in the New York subway and reported by Piliavin et al (1969) showed that most people were prepared to help someone who collapsed and seemed to need help. In that study, an actor seeming to be an ordinary traveller would appear to collapse. In some cases, he carried a cane and seemed weak and ill; in others he smelled of alcohol and seemed drunk. People would help the seemingly weak person some 95 per cent of the time, and even helped the drunk 50 per cent of the time. Moreover, it made no difference whether the victim was black or white, despite the prevailingly racist culture of those times.

Of course, those situations were completely unambiguous; it was obvious that the person needed help. And they also didn't involve the bystanders risking personal harm to themselves, unlike the possibilities involved in helping someone who is experiencing physical violence. Those types of situations are not easily researched; but as psychologists set up more controlled situations they were able to tease out a number of factors affecting whether people were likely to react or not.

Another "real-world" study (Darley and Latané, 1970) involved an actor going up to a passer-by in the street, and asking to be loaned ten cents. If the

Key Terms

bystander intervention
The question of when bystanders will or will not intervene in an event where a person apparently is in need of help.

reason given was a strong one (e.g. that his wallet had been stolen), 70 per cent of the people asked would help out. If it was less strong but still relevant, such as needing the money to make a telephone call (this was before the days of mobile phones), 64 per cent of the people asked would give him the money. And even if he didn't give any reason at all, 34 per cent of people asked would give him the money.

As part of the same investigation, people went into coin dealers asking to sell a set of coins, previously valued at US$12. Sometimes, dealers were told that the coins had been inherited, sometimes that the seller was an impoverished student who wanted the money to buy textbooks. In such cases, the dealers' average offer was $13.63, while if they thought they were inherited, the average offer made was only $8.72. The results, therefore, suggested that we are more prepared to be helpful if we believe a cause is "worthy" of our help.

Helpfulness isn't just about whether we are prepared to part with money, either. Lerner and Lichtman (1968) told research participants that they were investigating the effects of electric shocks on learning. They were given a choice whether they joined the experimental condition, which involved receiving the shocks, or the control condition which did not. They would be paired with someone else, and that other research participant would get the condition they didn't choose.

Not surprisingly, most people (91 per cent) given a free choice opted for the non-shock condition. But in another version of the study, the people being given the choice were also told that their partner had asked if they would take the experimental condition, because they were really scared of the shocks. In that condition, 72 per cent of the participants opted for the shocks. And an even higher percentage (88 per cent) chose to take the shocks if they were told that the other person had been offered the choice first but had decided to stand back and let them choose instead. So it's clear that people don't always act in their own interests; even the simplest request from the other person would make people more likely to take the more painful option.

The Law of Social Impact

What the research suggested, then, was that people are quite often prepared to help others out, even at some cost to themselves. But at other times we act in our own self-interest. As the research evidence accumulated Latané began to develop a theory which later became known as the **Law of Social Impact**. This work was based on a number of studies carried out by Latané and his research group. For example, in one study (Latané and Darley, 1968), male college students waited either alone or in groups of three for an interview. While they waited, a small ventilation grille in the wall began to pour out smoke. When the students were alone, 75 per cent of them reported the smoke within two minutes. But if they were with other people, less than 13 per cent of the students reported the smoke at all, even though it filled the room. They had, it emerged, redefined the situation by working out a possible harmless explanation for the smoke; and then used that redefinition to justify their lack of action.

It was possible, though, that there was some bravado involved, with none of the students not wanting to seem timid in front of other men. Latané and

Figure 6.1 The "light bulb" metaphor of social impact

Rodin (1969) set up a similar situation, but this time they heard a female person seem to fall over and cry out for help, in the next room. There was some improvement, in that 40 per cent of those tested in a group offered help; but it was still lower than the results if they were tested alone, when 70 per cent offered help. Debriefings showed **redefinition of the situation** again, and also suggested that they had been influenced by one another's calmness – each of them waiting for the others to react, and when they didn't, believing that offering help was not really necessary. The researchers defined this as their cultivating a state of **pluralistic ignorance**.

The third factor which emerged from this study was the idea of **diffusion of responsibility**. If there were several other people around, each individual could feel that the others shared the responsibility for action. But if they were on their own, they felt completely responsible for taking any necessary action; nobody was sharing that responsibility with them. In a situation where people were in individual booths but taking part in a group discussion, 85 per cent were prepared to leave their booths to help when they heard someone having a seizure, as long as they believed they were the only ones who could hear it. However, if they thought that two other people could hear it, that figure fell to 62 per cent, and if they thought they were in a group of six, all of whom could hear, the response rate fell to 31 per cent.

Latané (1981) proposed a model which sees the person within a kind of social force-field, with several different social forces acting on them. The metaphor Latané used was like a set of light bulbs all shining on the same object; how brightly it is lit depends on the wattage of the bulbs, how many bulbs there are and how close they are to the object (see Figure 6.1). The social forces involved can be seen in much the same way, varying in strength, number and immediacy.

Other people vary in their "strength" as a social force. It can depend upon a number of factors. People of high status, people with a prior relationship with us or our "significant others" will have a stronger impact than people we

Key Terms

redefinition of the situation
A process used to justify bystander apathy by deciding that the situation is not as serious as it appears.

pluralistic ignorance
When a group of people defines a situation as a non-emergency to justify lack of action.

diffusion of responsibility
The idea that people are less likely to intervene to help someone who seems to need it if there are others present because they perceive responsibility as being shared between all present, and therefore see themselves as being less responsible personally.

don't know and haven't heard of. For instance, you might feel more anxious in an anti-racist argument if you had some militant black friends looking on than you might in the company of less militant white friends; but the same group of friends might have less impact if you were in a discussion about, say, Spanish holiday resorts.

The total number of people observing what you do also adds to the overall social impact. Up to a point, the more people there are, the more powerful the social force is, but there is a law of diminishing returns. An increase from 3 observers to 5 makes much more difference than an increase from 32 observers to 34.

The third variable which Latané identified is **immediacy**, which is usually about how close the other people are to the person doing the actions. People who are a long way away are less likely to affect our behaviour than people who are close by. But there can be psychological closeness too, so it isn't quite that simple. If, for example, you are very close to your mother even though she lives some distance away, you have regular contact, and it matters to you what she thinks of your behaviour, you might experience her impact as immediate even though she is not actually physically nearby. Another person, having less contact with their distant mother, might feel that their mother's opinion was not relevant to what they did, and so would be far less affected.

In many ways, the question of immediacy carries a different meaning in the internet age than it did when Latané first formulated his theory. People can be physically distant but still immediately present through the uses of video-links such as Skype, or the immediate sharing of images and experiences through smartphones and Wi-Fi. The idea of psychological closeness is still valid, in that some people are more important to us than others; but clarifying exactly how that works and what difference it makes for our behaviour at any moment in time is more complex. In addition, most of us have become used to the idea that being in a public place also means that we are likely to be observed through CCTV systems. How far a modern city-dweller regards themselves as unobserved in everyday living is another question which needs some clarification before we can make definite predictions about the social forces impacting on us.

The Law of Social Impact didn't just apply to bystander behaviour. Latané proposed that it could also be used to explain findings in conformity and obedience – topics which we will be looking at later in this chapter. But there are some problems with this form of theory in general. The main one is that it is inherently **reductionist**, assuming that social behaviour arises purely from the sum of the influences on the individual. As we have seen, there are other aspects of social living too, not least of which are the processes of social identification and the social representations people hold. If someone identifies, for example, with a prosocial or helping group; either informally or formally such as being member of the Salvation Army, then they will be much more likely to help other people. That's a matter of how they see themselves in relation to others, not of how other people impact on them. Similarly, as we saw earlier, the social representations people hold about what is likely in social living affect how likely they are to help out. So while the Law of Social Impact may contribute to our understanding of social life, it isn't a full explanation on its own.

Key Terms

immediacy
Exerting influence as a result of being physically in the same place.

reductionist
Focusing on one single level of explanation and ignoring others. The opposite of interactionist.

Box 6.1   A reductionist theory

Social impact theory has been described as a clear example of reductionism in psychology. According to this theory, the origins of social behaviour are in the way that the person combines and unconsciously processes the social forces impinging on them. For Latané, aspects of social living like culture, social identification and discourse are factors which contribute to the strength of the social force, but it is the individual's processing which actually determines how they will act.

It's a plausible argument, but one which is challenged by other social psychologists, who believe that culture and social identities and discourse play a far more active role in determining social action. For example, they shape the range of alternatives available to the individual. We may respond in our own individual ways, but by and large those ways are congruent with the social expectations and social scripts of our cultures. The social identification which is particularly salient for us at any particular moment can also determine how we act. If we see ourselves as devoted members of a team, or as part of an organisation known for its helpfulness and involvement, we would respond completely differently from the way we would respond at a time when our social identification is primarily as an official with responsibilities. Or if the dominant social discourse in our social group is that members of particular groups should not be helped for some reason, we may respond to members of that group differently from someone else in a similar situation.

Those are just three examples, but there are many more. Many social psychologists believe that lumping them all together into a single factor of "strength" means that we lose the ability to differentiate between them, and thereby miss out of some of the most significant aspects which are determining social action. By limiting the theory to the individual level of explanation, so much is lost that the explanation becomes virtually meaningless.

Milgram (1970) proposed that **bystander apathy** can also arise from the anonymity and alienation of living in cities, which means that people tend to withdraw from one another and ignore problems. This alienation comes from a number of factors which don't apply in small communities: the fact that strangers are more likely to be encountered than familiar faces; the way that the pace of life in cities tends to be faster, leaving people feeling pressured for time and less likely to interrupt their journey; and the relative lack of day-to-day superficial interaction with other people. As a result, Milgram argued, people are less likely to respond to strangers if they live in cities than if they live in small towns.

While some of Milgram's arguments have been recently challenged – perhaps as city-dwellers become more sophisticated and aware of their immediate neighbourhoods – other research suggests that the separation from everyday trivial interactions might indeed have some relevance. It appears that coming into contact with other people on a day-to-day basis helps to make sure that we maintain realistic perceptions of the outside world. Being isolated from such contacts – for example, by not going out much and only travelling by car – means that most of our images of the everyday world in the street comes from what we see reported in television or newspapers. Both of these sources always exaggerate dangers, emphasising dramatic events and

Key Terms

bystander apathy
The refusal of bystanders to intervene in an event where a person apparently is in need of help.

anti-social behaviour, so people come to believe that the world is much more dangerous than it really is.

A study of heavy television viewing, conducted by Gerbner and Gross in 1976 but replicated by many more recent findings, showed that people who watch large amounts of TV or violent films estimate the likelihood of rapes, murders or muggings as being much higher than reality. As a result, they may also become much less likely to help other people, because their imagination conjures up dreadful scenarios which might happen if they get involved.

THE EFFECTS OF GROUPS

A certain amount of wariness of strangers appears to be an ordinary part of life, and there is some physiological evidence that our nervous systems do respond to the presence of strangers by increasing arousal levels slightly. But social living would hardly be social at all if it wasn't for the fact that most of the time, we tend to go along with other people and to co-operate with them. That tendency can have devastating consequences, though, when it is consciously manipulated by politicians, as happened in Germany in the 1930s and Rwanda in the 1990s. As a result, it has been a significant focus of interest for psychologists.

Group norms

Interest in the topic had been raised by a series of studies by Sherif (1935), who showed how people's answers to an estimating task tended to converge when they were studied in groups as opposed to individually. Sherif was investigating the **autokinetic effect** – a phenomenon in which a stable point of light in an otherwise totally dark environment appears to move around. People's estimates of how much it moved varied considerably when they were tested alone,

Key Terms
autokinetic effect A visual illusion in which a stationary dot of light in a dark room seems to move around.

"AFTER YOU...NO, NO, YOU FIRST...PLEASE, I INSIST...THIS WAY...ALLOW ME...NO RUSH"

but became very similar if they were tested in groups. Moreover, when Sherif studied people in groups of three, with one person making quite different estimates from the other two, he found that the final group judgement was very similar to that made by the pair. The person with the minority view tended to shift their estimate to agree with the others. Sherif also found that those who were new to the task tended to conform to a group estimate faster than more experienced individuals.

Sherif (1936) argued that this was all about how the group established a norm to which people tended to conform. Their conformity, he argued, is related to the degree of uncertainty which people feel, in that the more uncertain we are, the more we tend to conform to **group norms**. Following the norm is reassuring, it appears, letting us believe we are not alone, and more likely to be right.

Group polarisation

We might imagine that following the norm means that we are always adopting the safe "middle way". But in fact, that doesn't seem to be the case. In 1961, James Stoner, a management student, decided to investigate that idea empirically, and found some surprising results. He began by asking people to consider a series of management-style problems which all involved an element of risk, and indicate what level of risk would be acceptable in each case. Then he asked the same people to form groups and discuss the problems, coming to a group consensus as to what levels of risk would be acceptable for each situation. Interestingly, Stoner found that the group results tended to be riskier than its members' individual decisions had been. Also, when people were tested individually after those group discussions, their own evaluations had shifted to become more risky, in line with the group consensus.

In other words, people tended to make more risky decisions after a group discussion than they had done before – a finding which directly contradicted the assumption that groups or committees would always follow the safe, secure way. Stoner's findings were replicated by a number of social psychologists (e.g., Kogan and Wallach, 1967), and the effect became known as the **risky-shift phenomenon**. Different explanations were put forward: Wallach et al (1962) argued that it arose from diffusion of responsibility, in that the shared nature of the decision meant that the individual group members weren't carrying all the responsibility for the outcome themselves, and so felt free to make riskier decisions.

This explanation was challenged by a new finding from Moscovici and Zavalloni (1969), who discovered that in certain situations, groups can make more conservative decisions rather than riskier ones. Discussing things in groups certainly tended to polarise the outcomes; but whether the final decision moved towards the risky pole or the conservative pole depended on the original evaluations made by the group members. If they were generally in favour of approaching decisions cautiously, the group would shift towards caution. If they were generally in favour of taking a somewhat daring approach, the group would shift towards risk. So the phenomenon became known as **group polarisation** rather than risky-shift.

Lamm and Myers (1978) suggested that group polarisation might happen because the opportunity for discussion offered to the group meant that the members became better informed about the issues, and so felt that they were able to evaluate the risks more clearly. If the group members tended to favour a cautious approach, then reasons for cautiousness would be likely to dominate the discussion, and therefore the outcome; but if most of the group members favoured risk, then there would be a predominance of reasons for taking risks in the discussion, resulting in a more risky final outcome.

That couldn't be the whole explanation, though, because further studies showed that group polarisation happened even when the group members had no opportunity to discuss the issues – they were just informed about one another's evaluations. So an alternative explanation arose, based on Festinger's (1954) **social comparison theory**, which we came across in Chapter 4. Festinger argued that much of social experience derives from the way that we continually evaluate ourselves, and use those evaluations to present ourselves socially in the best possible way. In group discussions, people will want their views to appear socially desirable, so they will tend to adopt the general trend and take it a little bit further – cautious decisions becoming more cautious, and risky decisions becoming more risky.

That idea was supported by research by Jellison and Davis (1973), who showed that research participants tended to evaluate those who took extreme positions more favourably than those who adopted a middle position. They suggested that what was happening was that, once the socially desirable trend had been established, those who expressed that trend in a clear and definite way was likely to be approved of by the group as a whole.

We don't need to look very hard in the modern world to find examples of group polarisation, and in particular groups taking riskier decisions than individuals might have done on their own. The banking crisis of 2008 is generally perceived to have arisen as a result of a culture of risk developing among the echelons of high finance, together with a sense of immunity which also served to reduce the impact of more practical assessments. That sense of immunity was a reflection of one of the more powerful social factors in group decision-making, which goes hand in hand with group polarisation: the phenomenon of groupthink.

Groupthink

Groupthink was first identified by Janis in 1972 as a result of detailed examinations of how groups of powerful decision-makers can become divorced from reality, and end up making disastrous decisions. As we have seen, groups tend to develop their own norms, to which they expect their members to conform. But those norms can sometimes become so strong as to restrict any contradictory information coming into the group. So the group becomes closed to essential information which would keep its decisions realistic.

Janis analysed a number of American foreign policy decisions which had been made between 1940 and 1970, and showed how these decisions had been seriously affected by groupthink. One notable example was the Bay of Pigs fiasco, in which American troops had tried unsuccessfully to invade Cuba – a decision which could have been seen as impractical by any of the group members if they had taken notice of the actual information which was available. However, they had become so complacent in the idea that they were right that they went ahead, with disastrous consequences.

Later examples of groupthink were the *Challenger* space-shuttle disaster in 1986, in which the management group was so taken with the romantic idea of

Key Terms

social comparison
The process of comparing one's own social group with others, in terms of their relative social status and prestige.

groupthink
The way in which a group of people may become divorced from reality as a result of their own social consensus and make decisions which are dangerous or stupid.

putting the first US civilian in space that they ignored the engineer's reports that the weather situation was inappropriate and that the fuel feed system needed checking for a suspected malfunction (Moorhead et al, 1991). As a result, the *Challenger* exploded shortly after take-off, setting the US space programme back by at least two decades. But groupthink isn't just something that happened in the past. The 21st century has seen plenty of examples of complacent decision-making ignoring external information: the US/UK invasion of Iraq in 2003, the international banking crisis of 2008 (and subsequently) and many others.

There are a number of factors involved in groupthink. One of them is how a cohesive group subtly pressurises its members to conform to its dominant view. That pressure may be obvious and explicit, but more commonly it is implicit in the group interactions and non-verbal communication. Group members may worry about challenging the consensus, fearing to be dismissed as maverick, or impractical, or "not one of us", so they keep their doubts to themselves. As a result, the group seems to be unanimous, producing an illusion that it is in the right; moreover, because nobody disagrees openly with that view, there is no attempt to look for any alternative viewpoint.

Often, too, the presentation of an alternative viewpoint is seen as challenging the group's correctness or credibility, leading to negative stereotyping of out-groups. This is a very common effect – for example, a foreign policy group planning an invasion and believing it is the right thing to do will often denigrate people who oppose it as "bleeding-heart liberals" or something similar. It helps to convince them that they are in the right, and at the same time makes sure that the alternative view is not taken seriously.

Table 6.2 Symptoms of groupthink

Invulnerability	The group operates as if it were invulnerable and that disasters are simply not possible.
Rationalisation	The group rationalises away unpopular solutions – it finds excuses and justifications for any negative decisions it wants to make.
Stereotyping	The group or its members stereotype and deride opponents rather than arguing logically against their viewpoints.
Conformity	The group presses any doubters among its membership to conform to the majority view, instead of looking seriously at their doubts.
Self-censorship	Members of the group with doubts about the wisdom of a decision keep quiet rather than speaking up.
Illusion of unanimity	This may be the most important symptom: if every group member seems to agree with all decisions, something is wrong. Either some are hiding their true opinions, or the group needs some new members with a different point of view!
Mind-guarding	Some group members take on the role of "mind-guards": censoring undesirable opinions either directly or through gentle hints to members with differing opinions.
Illusion of morality	The group operates under the illusion that all its decisions and actions are intrinsically moral and correct.

Source: Janis (1983)

Table 6.2 summarises the symptoms of groupthink, according to Janis (1972). Janis also argued that groupthink can happen wherever the following conditions are met: if the group making the decision is very cohesive and if it is insulated from outside sources of information from the outside; if it doesn't appraise all the options systematically when making decisions; if it is dominated by a very directive or charismatic leader; and if the group is under stress because it needs to make a decision urgently.

However, Baron (2005) argued that while Janis's symptoms of groupthink are well backed up by research, the preconditions he identified are not necessarily causal. Groupthink can happen even if not all of the conditions are met, and some of those conditions are less important than others. Baron surveyed a number of studies of groupthink, and concluded that the really important issues are social factors such as social identification, salient norms (which can be social norms as well as specific group norms), and perceptions of low self-efficacy on the part of group members.

It is very easy for any influential and reasonably stable group to slip into groupthink; and the only real way to avoid it is to encourage conscious discussion and debate of alternatives and problems. Janis described how President Kennedy learned from the Bay of Pigs fiasco, and adopted a very different decision-making strategy when the Cuban Missile Crisis came along, encouraging open and free debate and getting his brother, Robert Kennedy, to adopt the role of "devil's advocate", criticising other people's ideas. He also made sure he was absent from meetings from time to time, so that his own views were not too influential. By doing this, his process of decision-making was as far removed from the groupthink problem as he could get it, which many people believe saved the world from nuclear disaster.

One of the aspects of human social interaction which makes phenomena like group polarisation and groupthink so likely to happen is the way that we much prefer to agree with one another, rather than challenge and confront. That's not necessarily a bad thing, in that it helps to keep us social – a species whose main reaction to others was confrontational would not remain social for any length of time! But there are some situations where conformity to others isn't always the appropriate way to behave.

CONFORMITY AND ACQUIESCENCE

In 1951, Asch undertook a series of studies into how people will sometimes conform to others even when they know they are wrong. He recruited people for what was described as an experiment in visual perception, and in the baseline study, organised them so that each of the volunteers was tested in a group of six other people. Unknown to them, the other five were "stooges" – that is, people who were acting as volunteers but really were assistants to the experimenter. The group was asked to undertake a simple line-judging task, stating which of three lines was the shortest. The test was deliberately straightforward, and the correct answer was obvious.

 For the first few trials, all went as expected. Each member of the group gave their answer in turn – the volunteer was second to last of a group of six. But then the confederates began to give wrong answers, and all of them would give the same wrong answer. The question, therefore, was whether the participant would give the same wrong answer as the rest of the group, or whether they would give the correct answer even though that was, in terms of the group, socially deviant.

What surprised the psychologists of the time was that Asch found that only 24 per cent of the participants did not conform to the group they were in at all. A total of 76 per cent conformed on at least one occasion. But when Asch carried out a control version in which people were asked to write down their answers rather than give them out loud, virtually all the participants gave the correct answers.

As we saw earlier, Sherif (1935, 1936) demonstrated that people would conform in uncertain situations, but there was no uncertainty about the correct answers in the Asch studies. Interviews with the participants after the experiments showed that they had felt uncomfortable about having to disagree openly with the others, and in fact a study by Bodganoff (1961) which measured the autonomic arousal levels of people in Asch studies backed this up with physiological support. But they were also highly motivated to avoid conflict, and rationalised their actions in a number of ways – some expressed doubt about their own judgements, or, more often, arguing that it was more important to retain social harmony than to make "correct" assessments in such a trivial task.

Box 6.2   The physiology of disagreeing

Asch's (1951) report contains detailed information about how people responded when it was apparent that they disagreed with the others, and in some ways it is that information which is even more interesting than the overall research findings. Regardless of how they actually answered, the respondents showed every sign of stress – acting nervously, showing increased muscular tension and vocal expression, and often fidgeting. Bogdanoff's study confirmed this, showing high autonomic arousal in virtually all participants as they realised that they either had to lie or to confront the group with open disagreement.

This fits with what we know about social interactions in general. We find confrontation and opposition much more stressful than going along with people and agreeing with them – so much so, that people often describe being with a group or other person who agree with them as being a singularly positive experience in itself. The tendency towards positive social interaction is all part of our evolutionary history as social animals. If we didn't want to be with others, and enjoy it, then we wouldn't have stayed social for very long, and in terms of our evolutionary history, wouldn't have been likely to survive.

The fact that we find confrontation uncomfortable is also one of the reasons why we find it memorable. Everyday life is full of examples where we get on with other people, but it is the disagreements and spats which we notice. One single example of someone else being nasty can spoil our whole day. People working on helplines and customer service jobs need to have special training to deal with the stress of confrontation, partly, in how to deal with the customers themselves, and partly, in dealing with the personal stress and agitation caused by negative interactions. And it's also why the phenomenon of internet bullying can be so powerful – even though it may be a separate, unreal part of everyday living, it is still a matter of knowing that someone is acting nastily to you, which itself produces physiological stress.

The effects of disagreement

What was immediately apparent from the Asch studies, though, was that the pressure exerted by the group had to be unanimous. If even one person disagreed – even if they too didn't give the correct answer – then the research participant wouldn't conform. And Allen and Levine (1971) found that was even true if the dissenter wore thick pebble-lens glasses and admitted to very bad eyesight! It seemed that the credibility of the dissenter was unimportant – it was the fact that someone else disagreed with the majority which mattered.

However, it emerged that this only applied when the task involved physical judgements, with a correct answer. If the same set-up involved a political or social judgement, then the views of the dissenter mattered; the research participant would disagree openly if the dissenter had similar views to the research participant, but would tend to conform to the majority opinion (even if they didn't share it) if the lone dissenter also disagreed with the participant's own social opinions (Allen and Levine, 1968).

Allen and Levine argued that this difference comes about because of our different expectations between physical and social judgements. We expect physical judgements to be straightforward, but we expect social opinions to vary. So one person with dissenting views on a social topic did not significantly relieve the pressure on the research participant from the majority group. How early in the proceedings the dissent happened did make a difference, though. If the dissenter gave their views before the majority of the group had responded, only about 23 per cent of participants conformed to the majority; but if the dissenter came last, then 46 per cent of participants would conform at least once (Morris and Miller, 1975).

Following Asch's findings, other researchers began to explore different aspects of **conformity**. Stang (1973) found that people with high self-esteem generally conformed less than those with low self-esteem. A further study suggested that if we see ourselves as skilled at judgement tasks, we tend to conform less than people who don't see themselves in this way (Wiesenthal et al, 1976). The suggestion, therefore, is that confidence in one's own judgement makes a difference, which has been related back to Sherif's early findings, which showed how uncertainty can increase conformity.

The question also arose as to how important the actual physical presence of other people is. A study set up by Crutchfield in 1955, used military personnel on a management training course. The experimental set-up involved booths with light displays which purported to show the responses of other people in the study, as well as the person's own response. The problems were again straightforward perceptual judgements, such as deciding which of two shapes (e.g., a circle and a triangle) had the largest area, and the answers were generally obvious.

On most trials, the information given fitted with the correct answer. But sometimes, the lights indicating other people's responses implied that everyone else had made the same wrong judgement. On these occasions, Crutchfield found a surprisingly high degree of conformity – roughly 50 per cent of the participants gave a conforming but wrong answer at some point in the study. So even though they were alone and not confronting others, there was still pressure to conform. Since it involved military personnel, who may have placed a higher emphasis on conformity than others, Crutchfield's study may have given more extreme results; but it does imply that there is more to social

Key Terms

conformity
The process of going along with other people and acting in the same way that they do.

conformity than simply avoiding having open disagreements with other people in a face-to-face situation.

Compliance and social influence

Kelman (1958) discussed how going along with others, or social conformity, might reflect any of three different processes: **compliance**, or going along with others but retaining one's differing private beliefs; **internalisation**, or agreeing that the other view is more valid; and **identification**, or actually changing one's own mind and agreeing with the other person, usually because the other person is someone they respect or admire.

Asch's participants, Kelman argued, were clearly showing compliance to the group. However, later interviews showed that they had not internalised the other people's views. Sherif's original participants, on the other hand, did seem to have internalised their group's norms, because they stuck with the group judgement even when they were tested alone later. Kelman proposed that it was the ambiguity of the Sherif situation which led to that internalisation.

In 1976, Moscovici argued that the Asch experiments were seriously inadequate as a way of exploring social influence, because they were too limited. Essentially, the research participant could either conform to the majority or not, and they were not able to influence others, as would have been the case in real life. When Moscovici and Faucheux (1972) re-analysed Asch's data, they concluded that the consistency of the judgements made by the stooges was what mostly influenced the research participants. As we saw in the last chapter, Moscovici had already shown how minorities as well as majorities can influence groups – particularly if they put over their ideas in a consistent fashion.

In their appraisal of Asch's research, Moscovici and Faucheux argued that the researchers had failed to take account of the social context within which the studies were carried out. In fact, they argued, Asch's studies actually demonstrate the influence of the *minority*, not of the majority. What the researchers had not recognised was that people do not suddenly abandon the rest of their lives when they agree to take part in a psychology experiment, so Asch's lone research participants should more accurately be seen as representing a much larger majority. They could see the correct answer to the line-judging task very clearly, and knew that other people would too. So the majority view would therefore be to judge the lines accurately. But because of the social pressures in Asch's study, they gave in and conformed to the minority rather than confronting them directly.

There is a difference, Moscovici (1980) argued, between compliance and conversion. Compliance is what happens when a majority influences a minority. The minority goes along with the majority, partly because the majority has power on its side which it can exercise through rewards and sanctions. But compliance is not **conversion** – someone may go along with the majority, but still not really believe that they are right. Conversion, Moscovici argued, is how a minority will influence a majority. Being in the minority, and therefore not the dominant or accepted view, they need to convince others that their view is valid, and as we saw in Chapter 5, his previous research into minority influence had shown that consistency is the most important factor in this process.

"A child of its time?"

A series of conformity studies reported in 1980 appeared to suggest that the Asch effect was "a child of its time" (Perrin and Spencer, 1981). The research-

Key Terms

compliance
The process of going along with other people without really accepting their views.

internalisation
Absorbing ideas, beliefs or attitudes as one's own.

identification
Feeling oneself to be the same as, or very similar to, another person and basing one's interactions on that comparison.

conversion
Being persuaded that a different point of view is correct, and coming to believe it yourself.

ers argued that the 1950s and 1960s, when the Asch studies had been carried out, were times when society placed a high emphasis on conformity, and deviance was frowned upon. More recently, they argued, society had become much more open to diversity, and this was reflected in their findings when they had replicated the Asch studies. Although the participants became just as anxious when faced with a majority giving a clearly wrong answer, they resisted the social pressure and did not conform. People in general, the researchers suggested, had just become more autonomous and resistant to mindless social pressure.

The idea was attractive, but unfortunately other replications challenged their findings. Doms and Avermaet (1981) argued that they had arisen because of the student sample which Perrin and Spencer had used. In an attempt to find students who would not already have heard of the Asch findings, they had used engineering and medical students. But these students, Doms and Avermaet argued, by nature of their disciplines placed a high value on accurate measurement and judgements and so were less likely to conform in Asch-type tasks. When they used a sample of students from less mathematical disciplines, Doms and Avermaet found conformity rates almost the same as the original Asch findings.

Some other researchers found lower rates of conformity, but still higher than Perrin and Spencer. For example, in a comparison of British and American students, Nicolson et al (1985) found clearly detectable conformity, with little difference between the two samples. In general, the phenomenon of conformity identified by Asch does seem to be quite robust, showing how difficult it can become when we are expected to disagree openly with others in a face-to-face situation.

OBEDIENCE, POWER AND CONTROL

Disagreeing becomes even more difficult when we feel that the person we are disagreeing with is in a position of power or authority. From a very young age we are trained to obey authority, in the form of teachers, police and

other representatives of society as a whole. But as the experiences of pre-war Germany showed, simply going along with authority can have horrific consequences. As Arendt (1963) demonstrated, most of the atrocities performed by the Nazi party in Germany before and during World War II were actually carried out by people who were "just doing their job", even though they found it distasteful. In her book *The Banality of Evil*, Arendt showed how even major figures like Eichmann were not actually malevolent, or even particularly hostile towards Jewish people; he personally argued for a separate Jewish homeland and had helped his Jewish half-cousin to get out of the country. Nonetheless, by "doing his job", he made possible the annihilation of six million Jews and uncounted numbers of Gypsies and other "undesirables". The most common defence of Nazi war criminals at the post-war Nuremberg trials was "I was only obeying orders".

Obedience

Obedience to authority, then, is something that we need to be very aware of. In 1963, Milgram reported a series of studies exploring just how far ordinary people would go in obeying orders. He obtained volunteers through a newspaper advertisement, and asked them to take part in a study of the effects of electric shocks on memory. They were introduced to another person, supposedly another volunteer but really an actor, and drew lots to see who would be the "learner" and who would be the "teacher". The lots were rigged so that the real volunteer would always be the "teacher". Then the "learner" went into an adjacent room, was strapped into a chair (with the volunteer watching), and the learner was given a small test shock to see what it felt like.

From then on the "teacher" and "victim" communicated with one another by sound. The process was overseen by an experimenter wearing a brown lab coat, who instructed the "teacher" to increase the shock by 15 volts each time the "learner" gave the wrong answer. They did this by pressing a series of keys on a board, where the different levels of shock were clearly labelled, and also general descriptions of "slight shock", "moderate shock", "danger: severe shock", and finally "XXX" were marked.

In reality, the sample shock given to the "teacher" was the only real one in the study, but as the study progressed, the volunteer heard different responses (actually pre-recorded, but again the research participants didn't know). At 75 volts there was a slight grunt, and those carried on until 120 volts. At that point the "learner" called out that the shocks were becoming painful. At 150 volts the "learner" yelled to the experimenter to get him out; at 180 volts there were cries of "I can't stand the pain"; and from 270 volts there were increasingly severe screams. At 300 volts the "learner" refused to answer any more questions, but the research participants were told to treat silence as a wrong answer, and continue with the shocks. From 330 volts, the "learner" fell ominously silent.

Whenever the volunteer hesitated or asked to stop the study because of the pain being administered to the victim, the experimenter responded that they had no choice but to continue. He insisted on this no matter how much the "learner" argued with them. All of the "teachers" became very distressed at what they could hear, and tried to minimise the effect – for example, by heavily stressing the right answer, or pressing the keys as lightly as they could. But nonetheless, all of them continued to the 300 volt mark, and 63 per cent of the research participants carried on to the end – even though they felt that they might have killed the person in the next room.

This was an astounding finding. Prior to the study, Milgram had conducted a survey of ordinary people, psychiatrists and psychologists, asking how they thought people would react in this type of situation. The general consensus was that only about 3 per cent of people would actually give shocks to an apparently lethal level. So Milgram's figure of 63 per cent sent shock waves through the professional community. Moreover, Milgram found, the results were remarkably consistent no matter whether the participants were male or female.

Table 6.3 Some of the conditions in Milgram's study

	Percentage of people going to the highest level of shock
No sound from victim throughout	100
Victim pounds on wall at 300 volts	65
Reversed personalities: (friendly experimenter, impersonal "learner")	50
Study conducted in town office block	48
Victim in same room	40
"Teacher" forces victim's hand onto electrode plate	30
Experimenter gives directions by telephone	20.5
Experimenter apparently just a member of the public	20
Others sharing "teacher" role disobey	10
No orders from experimenter (teacher given free choice of shock level)	2.5

Variations on Milgram's study

Milgram performed 21 different variations of the study to tease out different factors. Some of the main findings are illustrated in Table 6.3. Other researchers explored other variations. There was some cultural variance: participants in Amman, Jordan, showed a baseline level of obedience as high as 80 per cent (Shanab and Yahya, 1977) while an Australian sample produced results slightly lower than Milgram's 63 per cent (Kilham and Mann, 1974). In a particularly unpleasant variation, Sheridan and King (1972) asked research participants to give a small puppy real electric shocks of increasing severity. They too found extremely high levels of obedience, even though the research participants could see the puppy howling and yelping as it received the shocks. They also found that women obeyed even more than men; every one of their female research participants shocked the puppy to the maximum possible level.

These studies, of course, would no longer get past any ethical board. The level of deception of the research participants was too high, and would nowadays be considered to place participants' mental health at risk, even though Milgram himself was careful to follow up all the volunteers and make sure that they had not suffered psychologically as a result of finding out what they were capable of. And maltreating animals in this way would never be excusable in modern research.

In fact, Milgram's studies and their follow-ups opened up a powerful lobby objecting to the lack of ethics underlying the treatment of research participants. Following the publication of Milgram's 1963 paper, Baumrind (1964) wrote a paper highlighting these issues, which gave voice to the growing concerns about the social responsibility of science and just how human beings should be treated. Professional psychology organisations began to develop **ethical guidelines** which are now mandatory for all researchers, and the justification of causing harm to people or animals in the name of science became unacceptable. Haslam et al (2014) outlined four ways in which Milgram's study was ethically unacceptable by modern standards, which are listed in Table 6.4.

Table 6.4 Ethical problems with Milgram's experiments

Informed consent: The participants thought they were taking part in a learning study, and that the other person was genuinely being harmed – an unacceptable level of deception.

Short-term harm: Modern ethical standards state that the person should not be exposed to undue physical or mental distress during the course of a study.

Long-term harm: Although Milgram was diligent in following up his participants, and most of them said that they were happy to have participated, it is no longer acceptable to take that kind of risk with people.

Social harm: Studies should not endorse or perpetuate beliefs which make discriminatory or harmful acts towards others seem legitimate, like telling people that they are helping to advance scientific understanding by causing pain.

Source: Haslam and Reicher (2014)

Milgram described the tension shown by his participants as the study progressed as "moral strain". Some research participants coped with this moral strain by using psychological **defence mechanisms**, which are listed in Table 6.5. Milgram also argued that most situations which induce obedience in everyday life have buffers which reduce the level of moral strain – like the distance created by technology, for example; or physical distance, like the pilot of a bomber being unable to see the people who are killed or maimed by the bombs. Social distance acts as a buffer, too; Eichmann took care to have as little direct contact as possible with the concentration camps, or those who worked in them, despite having overall responsibility for them.

Table 6.5 Defence mechanisms

Denial	Some people minimised what was going on, denying that the shocks were really painful or serious.
Avoidance	Many people tried not to look directly at the "learner" or the experimenter.
Degree of involvement	Some people tried to distance themselves by flipping the switches very lightly, as if to minimise the shock.
Helping the learner	Many people tried to help the learner, for example by stressing the correct answer as they read it out.

Source: Milgram (1973)

Key Terms

ethical guidelines
Documents developed by professional bodies which provide guidance and principles concerning ethical aspects of research.

defence mechanisms
Protective strategies that the mind uses to defend itself against unwelcome or disturbing information.

Power and agency

In 1973, Milgram proposed a theory based on the idea that human beings had evolved within hierarchical social systems – a model of evolution which was generally accepted to be universal in social animals at that time, before biologists had become aware of the great variety in social organisation found in the natural world. Within a hierarchical system, Milgram argued, members must be prepared to accept control from superiors in the hierarchy, while still be able to act independently when circumstances warranted it.

As a result, Milgram argued, we have two "states" of social being: the **autonomous state**, where we act as individuals, and the agentic state, in which we act as the agent of a superior or superiors. The **agentic state** involves suppressing conscience, individual control and autonomous decision-making, and means that higher-level control from other people operates more effectively. The suspension of individual conscience allows the person to act in ways which they simply wouldn't do if they were acting autonomously.

Milgram argued that we are all trained into the agentic state from a very early age. Telling a child not to hit a smaller child encourages the idea of moral principles, but it also establishes the idea of obedience to authority. At school the child learns to suppress its individual wants and needs for the "general good" of the class, and to respect the authority of the teacher. This and its reflections in other social institutions, Milgram argued, becomes internalised, so imperatives about the rightness of obeying authority become part of the child's thinking. Because of the way they are linked with social responsibility, they also become firmly associated with "belonging" to the social group, an issue which we will be discussing later in this section.

Table 6.6 Mechanisms of the agentic state

Tuning: The person particularly notices instructions received from superiors, and largely disregards information from those seen as lower down in the hierarchy or not in authority.

Redefinition: The person redefines their situation to accept the explanations or excuses offered by the authority under which they are working.

Lack of responsibility: People no longer feel responsible for their actions, but see it as the responsibility of the authority under whom they are working.

Milgram suggests that the agentic state manifests itself through three main mechanisms, described in Table 6.6. Once the agentic state is established, it is maintained through what Milgram called a "social bond": a kind of unspoken agreement between the controller and the person acting as agent. In Milgram's own studies, the "social bond" was maintained through three mechanisms. The first was the sequential nature of the action (at any one time, the participant was only being asked to do a little more than he or she had already done). The second was the implicit social contract produced by the person volunteering for the study and therefore feeling that it was incumbent on them to act in the "right" way for the researcher. The third was the anxiety felt by the participants at the idea of disobeying the experimenter. Almost everyone tried to rebel more than once, usually by arguing with the experimenter. But in the end, their anxiety about rebelling overcame their desire to stop, and they continued giving the shocks.

Key Terms

autonomous state
A personal condition of independence and self-control.

agentic state
A condition of mind in which the person sees themselves as the agent of others and not able to act independently.

RE-EVALUATING OBEDIENCE AND AGENCY

Milgram's findings were accepted as completely valid for many years, backed up by the way in which he had carried out so many variations of his study, and the replications and related studies carried out by other people at the time. But recently, psychologists have challenged Milgram's conclusions – in particular, the idea that anyone could, and probably would, act in the same way simply by responding to instructions from authority.

Milgram believed that his participants knew that what they were doing was wrong, but that they felt unable to disobey the authority of the experimenter. But Reicher et al (2014) argued that it wasn't a question of blind obedience – it was a question of social identification. In particular, it was a question of whether the participant identified more with the demands of science (which at that time was considered to be a justification for actions we would consider unacceptable nowadays), or whether the participant identified more with the situation of the ordinary person in the next room.

Nowadays, we do not consider that scientists have the right to do almost anything to further knowledge. But it was a common belief at the time of Milgram's experiments. Reicher et al argued that the people who continued to shock the "victim" in Milgram's experiments were doing so because they knew what they were doing, but believed that they were doing it for a worthy cause. This belief was reinforced by the verbal "prods" used by the experimenter – "the experiment requires that you continue" etc. Haslam et al (2014) argued that the researchers had deliberately encouraged and promoted beliefs in the value of progress and science. Rather than simply being in an agentic state, the participants were acting as "engaged followers" – consciously going along with the study in order to promote the aims of the programme.

Not all the verbal prods were effective, either. Haslam et al discussed how many of Milgram's participants stopped cooperating at the point where the experimenter gave them a direct order: "you have no other choice, you must go on", and Burger et al (2011) found, in a replication of the study, that their participants stopped every time this prompt was used. Perhaps they objected to being given a direct order, or perhaps the nature of the order reminded them that they did, actually, have a choice; but whatever the reason, it also challenges the idea that they were in a blindly obedient agentic state.

Packer (2008) discussed how Milgram's evidence also shows that the participants were more likely to break out from the study at the points where the "learner" voices protests most strongly (i.e., 150 volts and 315 volts). Clearly they were listening to the voice of the victim, and not simply acting as blind agents of the experimenter. It wasn't a matter of an agentic state, Reicher and Haslam (2006) argued, but a matter of social identification. The participants who continued identified with the importance of revealing knowledge through scientific enquiry, and saw themselves as being part of that. So although they knew what they were doing, they believed that it was for a good reason.

Those who disobeyed Milgram's experimenter at an early point in the experiment were generally those who had experienced the dangers of compromising personal values for the "higher good". Gretchen Brandt, who turned to the experimenter when the level reached 210 volts, and quite calmly refused to go any further, had grown up in Nazi Germany. Jan Rensaleer, who also refused quite calmly, had been in Holland during World War II. These people made disobedience appear a simple and rational act. Both of them refused to take the view that the experimenter was responsible for the shocks, arguing that they were personally responsible for what they did, no matter what anybody else said.

Their calmness was striking, and contrasted with several others who disobeyed. More typically, people showed increasing anxiety and tension until the point where they actually refused to go any further. But once they had made that firm decision, their tension dissipated, and they too became calm. It was the thought of disobeying which produced the anxiety, rather than the act itself.

Talking point 6.2   Power, agency and power abuse

We consider the rebels in Milgram's study to be heroes, refusing the demands of authority and standing by their own principles. But as we have seen, most of them had experienced directly the consequences of unthinking obedience in Europe during the Nazi years.

Yet in modern society, we are trained into obedience almost from our earliest days – at school, while in work training and in everyday life. We are expected to respect authority and to obey without question people who are significant members of society such as policemen or government officials. Some of this, of course, is necessary to enable society to run smoothly; but sometimes there are occasions when it becomes appropriate to question what we are being told, and to stand up for what is right.

Can you think of any examples of this?

Replications of Milgram's studies

For many years it was assumed that it was impossible to replicate Milgram's work, because of the ethical problems it raised. But modern developments, and in particular the opportunities offered by the internet and social media raised the possibility of revisiting these matters, and seeing how people behave some 50 years later.

Slater et al (2006) used virtual reality techniques to replicate the Milgram experience. They found two things: firstly, that people respond to those situations as if they were real, which justifies their use in replications of this nature; and secondly, that they obtained overall results which were similar to those obtained by Milgram. However, the researchers paid particular attention to the way that the participants related to the victim and to the experimenter – something which they felt Milgram had not really paid enough attention to. They observed how the participants tried to reduce the harm to the "learner", for example, by stressing the right answer. Milgram had dismissed this as another example of "moral strain", but Slater et al pointed out that it showed they were not acting in a blind "agentic state"; rather, they knew what they were doing and didn't like it, but were continuing for other reasons.

 Another alternative was to use different tasks which also induced feelings of dislike and distaste in the participants, in a gradually increasing way. Haslam et al (2014) explored the effects of the verbal "prods" used by Milgram, using a task in which people thought they were investigating the connections between words and mental images. Their participants were shown a series of pictures of groups, and asked to choose from a limited set of five negative statements to describe each picture. The pictures themselves started off as pretty unpleasant, such as images of the Ku Klux Klan, but gradually they became more and more innocuous, until by the end the people were being asked to make very unpleasant statements about a happy, innocent images of a family walking in a park.

The researchers observed that their participants became increasingly distressed as the study continued, and took particular note of the verbal "prod" that they were given (listed in Table 6.7). They found that those prods which emphasised scientific goals were the most effective, while very few participants obeyed prod 4, which was a direct order. In Milgram's study, too, the use of prod 4 was often the key point at which they person disobeyed; being told that they had no choice and must continue was enough to remind them that actually, they did have a choice and could exercise it.

Table 6.7 Verbal "prods"

Prod 1	"Please continue."
Prod 2	"The experiment requires that you continue."
Prod 3	"It is absolutely essential that you continue."
Prod 4	"You have no other choice; you must go on."

Source: Milgram (1963)

Another aid to replication came as a result of a detailed analysis of Milgram's findings by Packer (2008), who showed how nearly 80 per cent of the people who gave a shock as high as 150 volts continued to the end of the study. Burger (2009) argued that this implied that replications which only go as far as 150v, which are much more ethically acceptable, can be used to give meaningful information about how people obey authority. Using these and other forms of **replication**, researchers found repeatedly that the more the person identified with the scientific ideal, the more likely they were to persist at tasks which they found personally distasteful – and the higher the status they placed on scientific achievement, the longer they were likely to carry on. Their relationship, or identification with the social goals of the study overcame their relationship with the learner as another human being.

The challenges to Milgram's explanations which resulted from these re-examinations and replications were not particularly questioning his findings, which seemed remarkably consistent. Rather, they challenged his idea of an agentic state, producing blind obedience. The participants, Reicher et al (2014) argued, were far from blind to what they were doing; they were doing it because of what the researchers called "engaged followership". They knew what was going on but carried on because they identified with the scientific goals of the study.

Similarly, the way that ordinary people can be drawn into committing atrocities such as the Rwandan genocide, those in Nazi Germany or other horrifying social acts, Reicher argued, has more to do with group identity processes (and their conscious manipulation by politicians) than with blind obedience, or because the people concerned are evil beings. The acts themselves are evil, but if they are to be challenged, we need to know how it is that ordinary people are drawn into them. Reicher et al showed how this research demonstrates that we

Key Terms
replication
Repeating a study or research project in such a way as to make sure that all of the important elements are identical, or at least very similar.

need to understand more clearly how the belief systems which allow people to justify, and even celebrate murder, come about.

Real-world contexts

Most people's lives are far more mundane, but that doesn't mean that obedience isn't problematic in those contexts, too. In a now classic study, Hofling et al (1966) conducted a study in a hospital, in which staff nurses on night duty would receive a telephone call from a (fake) doctor. The "doctor" claimed to be treating a particular patient, and asked the nurse to ensure that the locked medicine cabinet contained a particular drug. The drug was clearly labelled as dangerous, stating that 10 milligrams was the absolute maximum dose. When the nurse returned to the telephone and confirmed that the drug was there, the doctor asked her to administer 20 mg to the patient straight away. Being secretly observed, the nurses were stopped from actually giving the medicine to the patient, but 95 per cent of them actually measured out the large dose and were about to administer it when they were stopped.

This, of course, broke all the standard hospital procedures, and according to the rules, the nurses should not have obeyed the doctor. But in real life, they were working in a particularly hierarchical setting, and any nurse who openly disobeyed a doctor would be risking her job, and likely her future career. The nurses also pointed out after the study that many doctors were in the habit of giving orders by telephone, even though it was against hospital regulations, and that they became extremely annoyed if they were not obeyed. So Hofling's study highlighted how social pressures resulting from an imbalance of power could lead to real risks for patients: obeying orders was not always the best thing to do.

In more recent years, the combination of increased professionalisation of nursing and increased bureaucratisation in the health service has meant that individual doctors have less power, and nurses are more able to act according to their own training. But any hierarchical organisation carries the risk of its members acting as mindless agents – operating in what Milgram would have called an agentic state – unless steps are taken to ensure otherwise. In theory, "whistle-blowers" who expose unethical or unacceptable practices are protected by law from victimisation. In reality, though, these laws are rarely effective, and whistle-blowers find themselves all too often ostracised and isolated as the organisation reacts to their actions.

Rebellion

The findings by Reicher and Haslam (2014), then, suggest that the obedience studies illustrate the power of social identification rather than a blind agentic state. Obedience to a different set of social identifications in turn produced different expectations and behaviours. That also seems to be the case in a study reported by Gamson et al (1982), which directly invited rebellion from groups of participants.

They assembled groups of nine research participants at a time, and began by asking them to complete a set of attitude questionnaires. Then they were told that the research was being conducted by a human relations consultancy, which was interested in how legal cases were affected by community standards. They were told that they would be asked to discuss particular cases while being videotaped, and asked to sign a disclaimer making it clear that the tape was the property of the company, to use as it liked.

The case the group was given to discuss was of a manager of a gas station who was living with someone to whom he was not married. The evidence for this had been collected by a private detective working for his employer, who argued that it broke a clause in his contract. The actual cause said that the franchise could be revoked in the event of "arrest, drug addiction, insanity or similar condition", and the company was arguing that living with someone without being married to them was immoral and should be viewed as a "similar condition". The manager had responded by suing the company for invasion of privacy and breach of contract.

As the discussion proceeded, the groups were interrupted by the experimenter. The first time, he turned the videotape off, asked three members of the group to argue as if they were offended by the manager's conduct, then turned the tape back on. There were several more interruptions of this nature, all geared to encourage recordings which would imply that members of the group were deeply offended by the manager's behaviour. In addition, each member of the group was asked to do a personal piece to camera stating that they would not want to do business with someone so immoral and remarking that they thought he should lose his franchise. Finally, each member of the group was asked to sign an affidavit allowing the research company to edit the videotape as they saw fit and use it as evidence in court.

In other words, it was blatantly apparent that the purpose of the video was to gather and falsify evidence against the manager, which would support the oil company's case for revoking his franchise; and that the group members were being asked to collude in this process. As what they were being asked to do became apparent, the groups eventually rebelled. But this was not easy for them. In some groups people became distressed, and in others they became so angry that the researchers became worried about personal distress being caused to the participants, and ended the study early, only running 33 groups instead of the 81 they had originally intended.

The researchers had used the attitude test data obtained at the beginning of the study to arrange some of the groups, and this showed a correlation between anti-authority attitudes and rebellion. Groups with anti-authority attitudes tended see what was happening and to rebel earlier. But all groups except one rebelled in the end. In the pro-authority groups, though, there was generally quite heated argument; whereas in less extreme groups, rebellion quickly became accepted as a group norm.

As we might expect from what we have already learned of minority influence, the fact that other members of the group took a similar position was one which encouraged the group to rebel early. In most of the groups, people expressed open indignation about what they were being asked to do, and that indignation quickly spread through the discussion, leading to corresponding action. But it wasn't just about modelling, because even pro-authority groups rebelled eventually. Milgram's explanation would be that the group members had shifted from the agentic state to the autonomous state as a result of the clearly dishonest nature of what was being asked; it directly challenged their personal integrity. And as with Milgram's studies, personal experience may have contributed to this.

There were several important differences between this study and the earlier obedience ones. One was the way in which people were tested in large groups rather than alone, so they could support each other. It also took place at a later time. Since Milgram's studies, the Watergate investigations in America had shown the importance of challenging established authority, and one member of Gamson et al's groups even cited Milgram's studies as a warning against unthinking obedience.

In the modern world, we can find many examples of everyday rebellion. People very rarely do exactly what they are told to do; they will go about things in their own way, which may or may not produce the same results. Rebellious but harmless actions can spread rapidly through social media. In 2009, for example, a campaign began which aimed to challenge the dominance of a TV talent show in determining the prime Christmas no.1 spot in the British Charts. Thousands of people who didn't even know the song or the band downloaded "Killing in the Name Of" by the band Rage against the Machine in a concerted effort to make that track the Christmas number 1 instead of the latest winner of the TV show *The X Factor*. Their efforts were successful and demonstrated how powerful small rebellions could be once they "went viral".

More seriously, we find that the internet provides opportunities for other kinds of rebellion, including political activism. Reports of young people being seduced into political extremism though social media, even to the extent of leaving their homes and families and travelling abroad to fight for political causes, have become relatively commonplace. In itself, that is not a new phenomenon; several well-known artists and writers went abroad to fight in the Spanish Civil War in the first half of the 20th century, believing that the cause was just and that their support would count. But social media means that it can happen on a much larger scale, and without any direct face-to-face contact, and the public atrocities committed by some terrorist groups produce a very different social response.

In several instances, social media has alerted the world to social rebellions which aim to promote increased freedom from tyrannical regimes. But social media has also resulted in young people being cynically used and

manipulated into committing atrocities or becoming suicide bombers, promoting the aims of those who want to restrict and limit human freedoms. Conning idealistic young people in this way is again not a new phenomenon. The Jonestown massacre, for example, forced suicide on many who had followed a new "religious" leader, and a number of religious cults have preyed on gullible young people in similar ways in the past. But it is the prevalence and accessibility of social media which increases the numbers of people who can be drawn into these situations, in a way which is both anonymous and distant.

INDIVIDUALITY AND DE-INDIVIDUATION

So how is it that ordinary people come to commit atrocities against others? Milgram (or at least the recent re-evaluations of his work) show us how identification with a cause can 'justify' doing what we are told to quite a high degree. But sometimes, people are not directly told what to do and commit atrocities nonetheless. The acts of degradation which the guards in Abu Ghraib prison forced prisoners to commit, and even shared on video, were not the result of direct orders. But they may nonetheless have been the outcome of implicit, though never clearly stated, expectations.

The Stanford Prison Experiment

A study reported by Haney et al in 1973 showed how this can happen. The researchers set up an experimental situation, converting a basement at Stanford University into a simulated prison, with ordinary cells, a very small confinement cell (really a converted broom cupboard) and an observation room for the "guards". They chose 21 volunteers, all male and all of whom had been previously assessed as emotionally stable. Nine of them were assigned to act as "prisoners", and the rest as "guards". To make it seem realistic, the "prisoners" were arrested at their homes by the local police, brought to the prison, stripped, showered and dressed in prison uniforms. The guards wore suitable uniforms, and mirror sunglasses which helped to hide their expressions. They carried batons and whistles, but were instructed not to use physical violence.

Although the study had originally been planned to last two weeks, it was called off after five days. The guards had entered into their roles with gusto, and developed increasingly severe ways of humiliating the prisoners and making their lives difficult. Their increasing psychological brutality meant that the prisoners became increasingly depressed and disturbed. Five of them had to be "released" from the study early because they were showing such acute symptoms of depression and anxiety. Interestingly, Zimbardo (2007) described how the researchers also became caught up in the study, and only realised how serious the whole process had become when they were forcibly told so by a psychologist visiting the experiment for the first time.

Zimbardo identified a number of social mechanisms which were operating in this study. One of the strongest was the matter of **role expectations**. Although they had not been directly told what to do, those acting out the prison guards knew about the social role of "prison guard" from film and TV, and acted accordingly. They knew little, however, about the real-life constraints on prison guards, and so exaggerated their behaviour. Zimbardo also attributed this to

Key Terms
role expectations The behaviour which is expected as a result of a social part that one plays in society.

Key Terms

de-individuation
A condition in which the anonymity produced by the lack of individual identifiers causes people to abandon such aspects of individuality as conscience, consideration, etc.

trolling
A form of internet aggression in which the person directs anonymous spiteful or aggressive hate messages towards another person.

the way that the guards acted in groups so no single individual was responsible, and the way that the use of mirrored sunglasses made the person concerned anonymous: the process of **de-individuation**.

De-individuation occurs when someone has become anonymised, so that they cannot be identified as a particular individual. Their uniform, costume or situation means that their own individual characteristics, facial features, body structure, etc., are not apparent to those who are interacting with them. As a result, Zimbardo argued, they feel able to act in ways which are entirely different from the ways that they would act if they were simply being themselves. They might, for example, act more cruelly, or ignore the cruelty of others. Traditionally, torturers and executioners have always been de-individualised, and many terrorist organisations have adopted costumes which have prevented individuals from being identifiable.

In 1969, Zimbardo asked college women to deliver electric shocks to others. When dressed in ways which hid their identity, the women gave shocks which were twice as strong as those given by women who were normally dressed. Zimbardo (2007) argued that de-individuation is an important factor, not just in experimental findings of this type but also in cases of torture and atrocities. The facelessness of kidnappers and torturers in itself allows them to act in ways which are more extreme than they might do otherwise.

Whether the experimental factors actually show de-individuation is open to question. The costumes of the women in Zimbardo's study were in themselves suggestive of aggression, in that they were similar to the costume of the extreme racist organisation, the Ku Klux Klan. A follow-up by Johnson and Downing (1979) comparing Ku Klux Klan-type costumes, ordinary clothes and nurses' uniforms showed that those wearing nurses' uniforms gave fewer and less severe shocks – suggesting that participants were responding to the role suggested by the uniform rather than de-individuation itself.

Nonetheless, de-individuation is recognised as a factor in anti-social behaviour – particularly in the internet activity known as **trolling**, in which people use the anonymity provided by social media such as Twitter to deliver vicious and hurtful messages to other people – messages which they would not consider saying in a more personal context. This has always existed as a social problem, in the form of poison-pen letters; but the effort involved in producing such letters kept them more limited than the open and instant access provided by social media. Although trolling is by definition an anonymous and impersonal activity, that doesn't stop it from being an extremely hurtful and in some cases devastating experience for the recipient, and there has been more than one instance of suicide as a result.

Box 6.3 De-individuation and bureaucracy

Modern society has become increasingly bureaucratic, and the advent of the computer age meant that bureaucratic activities could extend in scope, and organisations could grow to immense sizes. As a result, policy decisions are often made at levels of the organisation which have little contact with the everyday work of most employees, or with their points of contact with the public. Most people living in the modern world have experienced at least one situation where those policy decisions have been inappropriate, but the employees who were affected felt helpless to change them, because what they could do was so circumscribed by restrictions and rules.

Effectively, those people have become de-individuated – they are unable to exert individual judgement or make real decisions, but are obliged to act in the way that has been prescribed by their management. In the case of public or essential services within the UK, the government has set up a number of Ombudsmen, who are expected to take up the individual's cases, and deal with the organisation on their behalf. Because they are able to deal with the higher levels of the organisation, they can often be far more effective than an individual working alone.

For most people, though, the Ombudsmens' offices (Ofgen, Ofcom, etc.) is too distant, and they feel helpless in dealing with the machine, which builds up resentment. For the de-individualised employee, too, the situation is stressful and often distressing, and the situation is often made worse by their having to work with complex software which denies options for compromise or alternatives. In the worst cases, the decisions made may be life-threatening; but even with legislation supporting "whistleblowing", those who actually make public serious problems are at serious risk of losing their jobs. So whistleblowing rarely happens, and clauses against it are written into many employment contracts.

Top-level managers increasingly recognise this as an unhealthy situation, preferring to have a situation where employees are "on board" with the company and able to exercise their judgement. They realise that de-individuation can too easily generate real problems for the organisation, and that those problems may have escalated to sizeable levels by the time anyone becomes aware of it. Some organisations have implemented empowerment policies, which allow employees much more scope to make decisions and exercise judgement; but these are often resisted by middle managers who feel their jobs might be at risk. Other organisations have gone the other way, implementing inhumane staff systems, where people are monitored automatically and expected to work at a rapid rate for the whole day, without having personal contact with a human manager. It's been an ongoing problem in organisational management for over 100 years, but the computer age has made it even more common, and the de-individuation in many ways more extreme.

De-individuation wasn't the only factor in the guards' behaviour. Zimbardo (2007) observed that many of the guards' actions in the original Stanford Prison experiment were directly copied by the abusers in Abu Ghraib. He argued that these people were responding to implicit expectations, rather than direct orders, Their superiors systematically turned a blind eye to acts of brutality, and a culture emerged in which such acts became regarded as commonplace or even entertainment rather than as the disgusting abuse of other human beings. This did not justify what they had done, of course, but it meant that the responsibility for what had gone on rested at higher levels in the US army as well.

Reicher and Haslam replicated the Stanford Prison Experiment for the BBC in 2002, and found a much lower level of brutality emerging from those playing the guards. They argued that this was not simply because of groups, but because the original experimenters had unconsciously "cued" the guards with the expectation that they would act in a brutal manner. Those acting the role of guards in the original study had picked this up and acted accordingly (Reicher and Haslam, 2006).

Initially, Zimbardo had argued that de-individuation itself was sufficient to produce abusive behaviour. However, this idea has been challenged, on the grounds that the experimenters' behaviour, like those in the Reicher and Haslam experiment, had generated expectations for the guards as to how they should behave. Zimbardo himself admitted that he had become so caught up in the experiment that he was actually thinking like a prison superintendent, and it took specific challenges from another psychologist before he recognised what he was doing.

Other psychologists suggested that there might be some self-selection in the types of volunteers he had obtained for the study in the first place. Carnahan and McFarland (2007) published two advertisements asking for volunteers to join a simulated experiment. One asked for them to join a "psychological study", while the other asked for people to join a "study of prison life". Those who volunteered for the prison study scored noticeably higher in measures of authoritarianism, aggression, social dominance and Machiavellianism, while the other group scored higher on measures of empathy and altruism. It is possible, therefore, that there may have been personality factors involved from the beginning, in that even though the participants were allocated randomly to the two groups, their personality characteristics might have generated role-appropriate behaviours.

Zimbardo (2007) argued that in order to identify the relevant factors, and also to protect from further examples of this kind of abuse, it is necessary to analyse what was going on at three levels. Only the first two were really explored by the original researchers: the individual level where personal factors such as understanding of role expectations come into play, and the situational level, dealing with what it was about the actual situation which encouraged that type of behaviour – bearing in mind that the situation they were in generated expectations and also group pressures.

In Zimbardo's later analysis, derived from a systematic study of torturers and genocide, however, he came to recognise the importance of a third level of analysis, the systemic level. In situations where the system itself is uncaring, provides little overseeing or support, and places people in difficult or unpleasant circumstances, extreme behaviour is more likely to happen. The response of those at higher levels of authority to complaints or suggestions is also important. Zimbardo argued strongly that the **systemic level**, too, needs to be included in any understanding of extreme inhumanity (Zimbardo, 2007).

Systemic analysis explores how the system in general can generate such behaviours – for example, how the structure of the army and the specific nature

Key Terms

systemic level analysis
Analysing social phenomena in terms of the social systems and structures which have made them possible.

of that particular conflict affected the Abu Ghraib abusers, or how the nature of the prison system and associated power relationships affected the Stanford Prison Experiment. Often, Zimbardo argued, the system itself subtly encourages or maintains abusive behaviour of this nature. So while particularly conscientious individuals are sometimes able to resist the pressure, most people find it difficult to avoid getting drawn in, or at the very least turning a blind eye to what others are doing. This is because they are faced with an overwhelming combination of ridicule from their peers, group exclusion, demanding or exhausting situations, and unhelpful support from the system within which they are operating. They are still responsible for their actions, of course; but so are those who create the situations in the first place, and maintain the system which permits these things to happen.

De-individuation can occur in more mundane situations too. The TV programme *Catfish*, which tracks down internet bullies and faces them with their actions, shows how the de-individuation offered by social media can produce a sense of unreality which means that people act in much more unpleasant ways than they would do in face-to-face interactions. When those people are faced with the real individuals who have been affected by their actions, they often feel real regret at what they have done.

Terrorism

Other forms of extreme and inhumane behaviour occur in what are generally referred to as terrorist activities. De-individuation is a common feature of terrorism – indeed, the whole-face balaclava has come to be a symbol of the terrorist in the public mind. But again it only provides part of the story. If we are to understand the psychological aspects of terrorism, we need to look at it at the group and systemic levels as well as at the individual level.

The first thing to remember is the old saying: "one man's terrorist is another man's freedom fighter" – which is to say that terrorism often arises from a social perception of unfairness or restriction within a particular social group, and their attempts to bring attention to, or redress, this perceived imbalance. The label of "terrorist" tends to be applied by the dominant group which is resisting change, and which uses that label to manipulate social perceptions of what is going on (Folomeeva, 2014). The use of discourse as its associated power implications, then, is an important feature in understanding terrorism and the way that it is perceived socially.

Religious terrorism is slightly different, in that it occurs where one group believes that it has the only answer and that it is entitled to impose those beliefs on the rest of society. While extremist fundamentalism of this kind is generally rejected even by others sharing the same religion, it has been responsible for some of the worst and bloodiest confrontations in history. It is estimated that over 8 million people died in Europe in pursuit of religious freedom during the fourteenth and fifteenth centuries, as the Roman Catholic Church fought against the perceived "threat" of Protestantism, and before religious tolerance became accepted as an important social value.

In modern times, religious fundamentalists have also engaged in terrorist activities, some of which appear remarkably similar to the barbarism of the Middle Ages. These extreme activities alienate many who originally saw some validity in their political cause, but see their violent and intolerant activities as contradicting the teachings of their religion. In several cases, this has resulted in the extremists becoming alienated from their "home" communities, rather than acting as spokespeople for them. However, Finlay (2014) showed how the extremist groups supporting violence portray those who disagree with them as cowardly or weak, and use the fear of exclusion to keep the young people they are influencing involved. Those proposing peaceful discussion, even when they are family members, are portrayed as traitors to Islam, or similar. So it remains to be seen how the conflicts with those extremist groups will be resolved in the long run.

Social psychological understanding of terrorism has addressed it in more than one way. Zimbardo's insights into de-individuation has shown how it becomes possible for "ordinary" people to ignore the humanity of their victims, and see them as nothing but enemies. The anonymising "uniforms" often adopted by terrorists are external manifestations of this de-individuation, and the way that they see themselves as distinct from, and not part of the population at large (Zimbardo, 2007).

Zimbardo himself describes terrorism as being the psychology of fear (Zimbardo, 2005). The aim of the terrorist, he argues, is to generate as much fear in the target population as possible, so being faceless, nameless and placeless is all part of the strategy because it makes people feel helpless to target them for counter-attack. In the case of religious terrorists, they will identify their religious cause but not individuals or locations; which is why counter-terrorist operations often like to identify the individuals concerned and make their identities widely known. It challenges the anonymity and de-individuation which they have been using to induce fear.

Other approaches to challenging terrorism have focused on three main areas. The first is reducing intergroup conflict, by addressing real political disadvantages and so removing the sources of perceived social injustice, while also encouraging members of different groups to work together. The second is to create incentives for the reduction of terror, to ensure that there are positive benefits to peaceful strategies, such as health care, education and domestic security. Some supposedly terrorist groups – particularly political ones – have their origins in the need for social care within their communities. And the third is to socialise young people into rejecting violence as a means of solving social problems, by clarifying the political, social and religious arguments which shape their ideas, and establishing ways that they can exert real influence in non-violent ways (Plous and Zimbardo, 2004).

This also involves examining the group identifications and social representations which are prevalent in the terrorist group, by comparison with the "mainstream" social representations and identifications in society (Wagner and Hayes, 2005). Social identifications with minority groups combine with social representations of political injustice to generate a belief that non-violent solutions will not work; and personal experiences within families serve to perpetuate hostility between groups, which are only broken down as a result of explicit reconciliation strategies. In many historical cases of groups labelled as "terrorists" by political opponents, they have spoken up for perceived injustice and often offered social support to members of their community – as a result of which they have been perceived as "freedom fighters" by their own people. In such cases, the use of the "terrorist" discourse by the dominant group is aimed to limit support and prevent the issue escalating into a mass movement.

CROWDS AND MOBS

Ever since the French revolution, politicians and social bureaucrats have feared the power of the mob. In 1895, Le Bon proposed a theory which became known as "mob psychology", in which he proposed that people in angry crowds revert to a kind of animal psychology, lacking in rationality and acting according to primitive impulses. Participation in such crowds, Le Bon argued, led people to abandon individual consciousness, and adopt what he called a "law of mental unity", so the crowd itself operated as one vicious animal.

Le Bon's evidence was not systematic, but largely drawn from anecdotal accounts. But it reflected the zeitgeist, as an increasingly industrial society had brought together large numbers of poor and working class people in urban surroundings, worrying those who led more privileged lives. The theory instantly took on political overtones, and was used as a justification for heavy-handed police action against political demonstrations. It still remains a powerful social influence, and is still believed in many sectors of society.

Zimbardo's early research into de-individuation adopted the general Le Bon perspective, in that he was trying to find out why people act so much more cruelly when anonymous than when they are individually identifiable. A number of explanations were proposed for this. Diener (1979) suggested that when people's attention is focused on something else, they become less self-aware, and therefore more impulsive and less socially inhibited. This leads to five outcomes: the weakening of normal restraints against impulsive behaviour; heightened sensitivity to emotional states and situational cues; an inability to monitor or regulate one's own behaviour; lower concern with social approval of actions; and less capacity for rational planning.

Prentice-Dunn and Rogers (1982) argued that Diener had failed to distinguish between private and public self-awareness. It is decreasing **private self-awareness**, they argued, which leads to de-individuation, and not **public self-awareness**, or our concern with how we look to other people. Private self-awareness decreases:

* * if our attention is centred elsewhere, such as on a football match or public speaker;
* * when there is a high level of group cohesiveness, like that brought about by supporting the same sports team;
* * if people are highly aroused (e.g., the excitement of a match or intense feelings of social injustice); or
* * in situations of anonymity for group members.

Any of these, they argued, can lead to de-individuation.

However, although de-individuation is recognised as a significant process, its early assumptions that people in crowds are not able to think rationally make it a highly controversial theory. It seems likely that de-individuation may have a role to play in understanding why people act as they do, but at the same time more intensive research into crowds, involving individual accounts as well as detailed observation, produces a very different picture which suggests that "mob psychology" isn't nearly as powerful as Le Bon described.

Peaceful crowds

One of the biggest problems with the **mob psychology** approach is how selective it is when it talks about crowds. Crowds form a frequent part of modern living,

Key Terms

private self-awareness
The individual sense of self which we retain, even when participating in crowds.

public self-awareness
The open, participating sense of self involved in events with others.

mob psychology
The idea that a crowd is likely to behave in an irrational and unpredictable manner, even because its members have descended into a conscience-less and impulsive state.

almost everywhere in the world, and the proportion of crowds which actually become disorderly is miniscule when compared with the overall number of crowds we experience. As a general rule, people in crowds recognise the behaviour which is expected of them and perform it. Skilled performers recognise the power of de-individuation and collective action, not as a negative experience but as a positive one, bringing a crowd together in a shared experience of music and entertainment. Many people attend football matches for the exhilarating experience of being part of a crowd, sharing the emotional experience and making noise for their team in common with many other people.

One of the founders of social psychology, the sociologist Emile Durkheim, claimed that large public gatherings serve a valuable social function in promoting social cohesion, or solidarity. We have seen some of that with the Royal Jubilee celebrations in Britain in 2012, which evidenced a powerful social cohesiveness and support for royalty which took many media people by surprise. Similarly, the massive crowds attending and supporting both the London 2012 Olympics and the Glasgow 2014 Commonwealth Games were experienced as a uniformly positive experience for those involved, and also for those participating indirectly through mass and social media.

An interview study reported by Benewick and Holton in 1987 explored the experiences of participants in a massive crowd attending an open-air Mass during the Pope's visit to Britain in 1982. Their interviews showed that it was the sense of unity which people obtained from participating in that crowd which was the most powerful experience of the people who participated. Abandonment of the sense of self, rather than producing an uncontrollable mob, produced an uplifting and spiritual experience for huge numbers of participants.

Unfortunately, although peaceful crowds of one kind or another are much more common, relatively few researchers have considered it worthwhile to investigate them. Aspects of psychology which do not present some kind of immediate problem are much more likely to go unnoticed than those which are more problematic; but we need to bear in mind that this does not mean that they are unimportant. Certainly, for many people in Benewick and Holton's study, their participation in that peaceful crowd was one of the most significant events which they had ever experienced.

Football aggression

Even in crowds which are often regarded as violent, de-individuation may be far less of a factor than it appears to be on the surface. Football hooliganism is often portrayed as a major social problem, but a study by Marsh et al (1978) identified a strong social structure and patterning of behaviour occurring between people who were regarded by the general public as "hooligans", even in terms of their relationships with the opposing groups. They concluded that, far from being unbridled and impulsive behaviour, the fans' behaviour was very clearly established according to established patterns and social convention, Indeed, this was maintained also by a long-term "career" structure, by which fans achieved "promotion" into different groups within their crowd, through proving their skill in performing the ritualised aggression and following the internal rules.

Although the fans used violent language, the ritualised nature of the activity meant that actual free-for-all conflicts between different groups of supporters were extremely rare. But the crowd had its pattern of accepted behaviour, such as seeing the others off by chasing rival fans to the railway station after the match, which they regarded as legitimate activities. They clearly felt aggrieved when these were interfered with by police action. But when the chase was permitted, it was apparent that, although it was pursued energetically, the group was careful not to catch the others – to do so might have produced an embarrassing situation where neither side wanted to engage in any actual acts of violence.

This is not, of course, to claim that nobody has ever been hurt while attending a football match. But the researchers showed that it was more appropriate to attribute these instances to the acts of particular individuals, rather than to any kind of "mob psychology". Even football hooligans, they showed, were far from being the uncontrollable mob that is so often described in the media, having their own self-regulation and behavioural norms. In fact, Marsh et al suggest that outbreaks of uncontrolled violence are actually more likely when the crowd's self-regulating behaviour is interfered with through over-control by the authorities, a view supported by other interview studies with "football hooligans".

Flashpoints

There are, though, instances in which crowds have changed and public demonstrations have suddenly erupted into violence. But contrary to mob psychology, that doesn't just happen randomly. Waddington et al (1987) identified a number of **flashpoints** in political demonstrations, which, they argued, mainly have their effect by being "typical" of their more general sources of grievance. As a result, they provide an open route for the expression of frustration and aggression which erupts into violence.

As with Zimbardo's findings about torture, these researchers found that it is necessary to investigate how these things happen at different levels, rather than simply looking for a single "cause". The levels they identified are listed in

Key Terms
flashpoints Actions or events which generate spontaneous changes in crowd behaviour.

Table 6.8. No single level is going to be sufficient to generate public disorder, but taken together they can make a flashpoint more likely to happen, which in turn can lead to rioting or open conflict. The researchers argued that public disorder is not the result of mob psychology, but is actually predictable and avoidable if the appropriate factors and levels at work in the situation are taken into account. Even when all the factors would seem to indicate that violence is likely, appropriate action on the international or spatial levels can still mean that it is avoided.

Table 6.8 Levels of analysis for crowd behaviour

Structural: For instance, when people are systematically disadvantaged by existing social structures, producing high levels of frustration.

Political / ideological: Sources of political grievance.

Cultural: Social representations and cultural practices.

Contextual: The sequence of events or situations which has led up to the event.

Spatial: For instance, areas of special significance, or the layouts of buildings and spaces.

Interactional: The nature and quality of the interactions between the people involved in the dispute.

Source: Waddington et al (1987)

Waddington et al identified five major sources of grievance which made a crowd more likely to turn, and these findings were summarised in a number of recommendations for successful crowd control, including that the crowd should be permitted to be self-policing wherever possible; that police and organisers should liaise effectively; that police should use a policy of "minimum force" in order to avoid being perceived by crowd members as provoking trouble; that crowd management officials should be trained in effective interpersonal communication; and that police and enforcement agencies should be perceived as accountable for their actions to the community. By removing these sources of grievance, eruptions of violence become less likely; but it is only in recent years, with the advent of phone recording which provide evidence of actions, that they have become policy.

The problem with the whole "mob psychology" perspective is that it can in itself produce disastrous social effects. Banyard (1989) described how the "mob psychology" theories held by the police on duty at the Hillsborough stadium during the tragic occasion in which nearly a hundred football supporters were crushed to death, meant that they failed to take action which could have alleviated the situation – such as explaining what was going on to the public. The belief that the crowd were a "mob", and therefore unable to listen to reason, resulted in the situation becoming very much worse than it need have been. It was not until many years later, in 2015, with the consistent demands by the families for social justice being amplified by social media, that the culpability of the police in the disaster was officially admitted.

In a more recent study, Drury et al (2013) explored the myths about crowd behaviour held by police personnel, emergency planners and football match stewards, as well as members of the public. They found that a disturbingly large proportion of their respondents believed in the myths about crowds: that rumours exaggerate threats and bring about blind mob reactions;

that disasters bring out the worst in people by encouraging criminal behaviour; or that crowds descend into a mindless state of mass panic in disaster situations.

While many of the professional groups also maintained that disasters could sometimes bring positive behaviours from crowds, such as examples of heroism and mutual support, the predominant view was that crowds were inherently dangerous and needed to be controlled in disaster situations. However, the professionals and police did recognise that people often become less selfish and more concerned with others in emergencies; and the professionals in particular strongly rejected the idea that limiting information was helpful. Rather, they argued that it was important to give people as much information as possible, in order to prevent the spread of unhelpful rumours. So although there were some positive findings of this kind, the researchers expressed concern about how strongly the "mindless mob" myths about crowd behaviour were held.

Online collective action

Social media has made it much easier for perceived injustices to become rapidly and widely shared. As a result, the 2011 riots in the UK, sparked off by the perceived injustice of police behaviour in a specific instance, spread rapidly across several districts of London and many other cities in the UK without observable warning. They began with a gathering outside one particular police station, but the heavy-handed response the crowd received was widely and rapidly shared with others through social media, as was the rioting which resulted. This again underlines the importance of perceived justice, rather than injustice, in social control, a finding which acknowledges the characteristics of the crowd as thinking individuals, rather than a mindless mob.

Collective action online is not inevitably negative, though. It can also be influential in generating the will for social change, or in providing the mass basis for alleviating negative situations. Spears et al (2002) showed how computer-mediated communication can help mobilise resistance to powerful out-groups; and other researchers, such as Postmes et al (2005), have highlighted how the increased levels of discussion about political topics can help online groups to clarify their objectives and come together to act effectively.

Spears and Lea (1992) proposed the social identity model of de-individuation effects (SIDE). This model predicted that the anonymity offered by online interactions would enhance the salience of the social group in discussions, and increase conformity to group norms. If people can't see one another, they have fewer cues to work with, so those aspects of group identification become more important. In a later study, Spears et al (2007) showed how online anonymity can increase a range of group-related effects such as stereotyping and group attraction.

Alberici and Milesi (2013) studied a political movement which had originated in Italy when a well-known comedian was banned from national television for criticising political corruption. The participants in their study were activists who had not normally been politically active, but had become so because of this cause. Alberici and Milesi found that participating frequently in online discussions had increased their sense of political identity and encouraged the development of group norms. Interestingly, though, the level of intense discussion had reduced, rather than strengthened, the personal anger felt by the activists. Instead, that anger had become converted into a sense of resolve and determination. The group eventually converted successfully from an online discussion group to a real-world political party.

This finding showed how important and influential online political discussion can be. Van Zomeren et al (2008) proposed three explanations for politically-based collective action through the internet, which are listed in Table 6.9. However, there is also another level of political, or at least societal, action which doesn't seem to involve specific group membership. The example of internet rebellion which brought Rage against the Machine to the top of the music charts which we looked at earlier in this chapter, didn't involve significant discussion or membership of political groups. Instead, it arose as direct individual action from people perceiving a common cause, happened, and then was over.

Table 6.9 Factors in online collective action

Collective identity: identification with a particular political group.

Perceived injustice: group-based anger about illegitimate or unfair treatment.

Group efficacy: beliefs that joint effort will enable the group to respond effectively to events.

Source: Adapted from Van Zomeren et al (2008)

Crowd altruism

Social media also makes possible the enormous amount of online altruism which also forms a kind of indirect mass action. One of the most dramatic examples of this was the teenager Stephen Sutton who, knowing he had only a few months to live, set out to raise UK£50,000 for the Teenage Cancer Trust. His unfailing cheerfulness and positive approach, transmitted through social media and shared by millions, resulted in his eventually raising over £5 million. Another case, where a young woman, Katie Cutler, set up an online giving fund to help a disabled pensioner who had been mugged resulted in a massive response, not only re-homing the pensioner but allowing them to set up a fund to help others in similar situations.

In another remarkable case, a simple mock-up of an Olympic torch circulated on eBay during the months leading up to the 2012 Olympics. It raised thousands of pounds, as people bought it and then re-sold it online and donated all the money to charity. Online altruism can be as powerful a force as online negativism, and as with other forms of positive social interaction, it is important to retain awareness of this.

Altruism of this kind is far more frequent in everyday life than psychologists used to acknowledge. We call an act altruistic when it appears that the act benefits others, but not the person who performs it. In other words, an altruistic act is one which helps someone else, but doesn't get you anything in return. Some explanations for altruism (e.g., Dawkins, 1976) suggest that it is a biological drive, evolved to allow organisms to perpetuate their genes through the survival of close kin. Others have suggested that it is all about reciprocity – we act in an altruistic fashion towards others in order to receive altruistic behaviour ourselves.

Talking point 6.3   Everyday altruism

The internet has made it possible to communicate and share information quickly and effectively. As a result, there are many quite dramatic examples of altruism and generosity which have occurred because of crowd funding or other initiatives. But altruism isn't just about donating to specific causes. Every time you set a little bit of time aside to talk to someone who needs it rather than getting on with what you were doing, you are carrying out an altruistic act. Helping someone with a domestic problem, even if it's only changing a light bulb for them, is an altruistic act. Doing something which makes someone else's day a little more cheerful or brighter, is an altruistic act. Altruistic actions can be tiny, but they are still part of what holds society together.

Select a particular day, and go through that day making a note of any altruistic act or action you have come across. It might be something you see directly, or something you have heard about, or something somebody did for you, and it doesn't have to be significant; it could be a tiny thing.

How many did you come across?

But while these explanations may be adequate for the behaviour of ants and other insects, human behaviour is cognitively more complex. We have already seen how it can be shaped by social representations, identifications, attitudes and many other factors; and there are numerous examples of altruism directed towards non-related others. The massive fundraising achievements of Comic Relief, for example, which has raised over a billion pounds in total, are all dependent on altruistic behaviour towards non-relatives.

What is more likely is that **altruism**, whether reciprocated or not, is one of the important elements in the social bonding which governs our behaviour. Even Milgram (1973), who is widely considered to have exposed some of the "darker side" in human nature, pointed out that our first response when faced with a difficult situation is to co-operate, not to confront. Our capacity for getting along with one another has been seriously under-rated by researchers. It is, of course, important to understand the roots of social conflict; but it is equally important to understand the roots of social harmony.

Summary: Chapter 6

1. The presence of other people can affect our behaviour in many ways. In some circumstances it may lead us to make more effort, while in others it can lead to social loafing.

2. Studies of bystander intervention have identified altruistic behaviour as well as bystander apathy. Latané explained these findings by the Law of Social Impact, which emphasised number, immediacy and relevance (strength) of others, but the theory has been criticised as individualistic and reductionist.

Key Terms

altruism
Acting in the interests of others and not oneself.

3. People's behaviour in groups is often different to their behaviour as individuals. Conformity to group norms is common, and decisions may become polarised. Long-term or powerful groups are particularly vulnerable to groupthink, which can lead to disastrously bad decisions.

4. Asch showed how people prefer to conform to others rather than challenge consensus. Several replications of his studies showed that this tendency applied across cultures and time. However, Asch's studies were criticised as failing to take account of the wider social contexts.

5. Milgram's studies of obedience revealed how people could obey authority to an extreme degree. He explained his findings using the idea of an agentic state, in which people surrender their own autonomy and conscience, and act as agents of authority.

6. Milgram's studies have been replicated, but also challenged on ethical grounds. His idea of the agentic state has also been criticised as failing to take account subtle forms of rebellion and agency.

7. Studies of rebellion have shown that familiarity with Milgram's findings may act as an influence, as well as modern expectations about responsibility and ethics. Many examples of social rebellion can be found through the internet.

8. Zimbardo's Stanford Prison Experiment demonstrated the power of social roles and also the phenomenon of de-individuation. However, modern replications challenged Zimbardo's explanations, and researchers have argued that the study was strongly influenced by experimenter expectations.

9. Studies have shown that the processes of conformity, obedience and de-individuation are significant factors in maintaining and controlling terrorism and torture.

10. Crowd behaviour is often peaceful and non-aggressive, and crowd aggression has been shown to result from significant flashpoints. Crowds may also be altruistic, and the opportunities for communication offered by the internet have led to several examples of this.

Contents

Chapter 7

Reacting to others

In the last chapter, we saw how our social natures mean that we tend, on the whole, to be cooperative and compliant with other people, although that isn't always the case. We respond differently to different people, and sometimes to the same people but in different situations. Sometimes, circumstances mean that we react defensively or aggressively towards others, and sometimes, too, we find that we just don't like someone. In this chapter, we will be exploring how we react to other people. We will begin by looking at some of the processes involved in person perception, and then move on to what psychologists have discovered about liking and attraction.

Liking and attraction, though, are to do with our personal reactions to individuals. Sometimes we don't even get as far as seeing the individual, because of prejudice towards their social group. So in this chapter, we will also explore some of the different types of social prejudice, and how they may be challenged in modern society. Prejudice isn't the same as aggression, of course, but in its extreme form it can certainly produce aggressive behaviour towards other people. There have been many theories developed to explain aggression, and we will look at some of these, and at some of the most common ways that aggression manifests itself in modern society. But we'll begin our investigations by looking at how we perceive other people.

PERSON PERCEPTION

Understanding how we see other people is an important part of understanding our social nature. But we don't see people directly – as the Tardis said when she took on a human incarnation in the TV series *Doctor Who*: "Are all people like this? So much bigger on the inside?" (BBC, 2011)

We don't see directly into people's minds. What we actually see of other people is the outside, and what it communicates to us. As we saw in Chapter 3, people communicate in many different ways, both consciously and unconsciously, and the contexts in which they are interacting with us also varies. Which means that the process of perceiving other people brings together a lot of different factors, some of which come from the person themselves, and some of which come from our own ideas, assumptions, and personal constructs.

The study of **person perception** developed in the 20th century, and social psychologists identified a number of different mechanisms involved in how we

"WELL! I DON'T REALLY NEED TO ASK WHO'S RESPONSIBLE FOR THIS DO I?"

form impressions of other people. We will look briefly at six of these mechanisms: implicit personality theory, stereotyping, the self-fulfilling prophecy, personal constructs, primacy effects and halo effects.

Implicit personality theory

A considerable amount of psychological research has been devoted to teasing out the implicit knowledge and principles which we use in forming impressions of other people. In 1946, Asch showed how we tend to go far beyond the data available, applying our own implicit theories of personality to what we see of the other person. These theories, although unique to each person, have some characteristics in common; for example, we tend to expect people who show one or two of them to show related traits as well. And we regard some personality traits as more central, or important, than others.

Bower (1998) discussed the efforts medical practitioners make to deal with the "whole person" rather than adopting the traditional symptom-focused approach. The relative lack of simple scientific models they could use to understand people meant that most medical practitioners tended to fall back on implicit personality theories, applying these to the patients who presented in their practice. Those theories in themselves determine how we judge people, and how we act towards them.

Implicit personality theories can be triggered off by quite small items of information. Maier (1955) showed that simply describing someone as a trade union official or a company manager was enough to generate theories about their personality and judgements about their likely behaviour. Similar studies have found the same thing. We develop whole theories about people's likely personality based on extremely flimsy information – what car they drive, the colour of their hair, where they live, in fact, just about anything.

When Rosenberg et al (1968) conducted a meta-analysis of the various studies of **implicit personality theory**, they found two main dimensions: one concerned with mental ability and the other with sociability. Each dimension carried both positive and negative evaluative weightings, such as "bright" or "crafty" for the intellectual dimension and "helpful" or "irritable" for the social one. These two dimensions, they argued, represent the core of the criteria which we use to evaluate people, and just about all of our judgements are concerned with one or the other of these dimensions.

There may be another core criterion, though. Being able to make a judgement about whether people are "safe" or "risky" to interact with is also important for social interaction. Oosterhof and Todorov (2009) used the "trustworthiness" of faces to make judgements about how happy or angry people were. In an earlier study by the same team of researchers, Engel et al (2007) showed how making a judgement about whether someone was "trustworthy" or not appears to be hard-wired into our nervous systems. These judgements directly involve the amygdala, a part of the limbic system of the brain which deals with emotional reactions rather than cognitive analysis.

Using magnetic resonance imaging (MRI), the researchers found that the amygdala reacts more strongly to faces it judges as untrustworthy than to those it judges as trustworthy. Moreover, the researchers found, this reaction had more to do with consensual – that is, shared – perceptions of a face as untrustworthy, than to do with the person's own idiosyncratic judgements. So it seems that part of the brain is directly concerned with how we perceive other people's personality – at least in respect to whether we feel we should be wary of them or not.

Stereotyping

Another aspect of person perception which may be hard-wired into our cognitive structures is **stereotyping**. The brain automatically sorts its experiences into categories, so that we can use our experience to deal with the new information coming in. It does this with our perceptions of people as well as of objects or experiences, and that categorisation can easily lead to stereotyping.

When we stereotype, we classify people according to a particular characteristic – often a very superficial one, such as skin colour or the type of car that they drive. Our perceptions of that person are then derived from our assumptions about that category, regardless of what the person is actually like. Some stereotypes are powerful social and political mechanisms, such as race or gender; but, like implicit personality theory, stereotyping can arise from just about any characteristic.

For example, in 1973, Harari and McDavid showed how teachers stereotyped children on the basis of first names. They expected different achievements from a Karen or a David (considered to be positive names at the time) than from an Adele or a Hubert (which were considered to be unattractive names). More to the point, they conformed to these stereotypes in their marking, with a strong tendency to give the children with "positive" names higher marks. Although their stereotyping was quite unconscious, it exerted a significant effect on their work – and on the children.

Stereotypes affect our memory, too. Gahagan (1984) showed how people remembered different information from a passage read to them a week earlier if they had been told that the person was in a homosexual relationship. For example, they forgot that the passage stated that she had dated boys during

Key Terms
stereotyping Classifying members of a social group as if they were all the same and treating individuals belonging to that group as if no other characteristics were salient.

adolescence; in fact, they forgot anything which didn't conform to their stereotype of lesbians.

Stereotyping has often been explained simply in terms of cognitive economy. Stereotypes reduce the amount of mental effort we need to invest in our judgements. But that isn't all that they do. Snyder and Miene (1994) showed how the stereotyping of elderly people actually served three different functions, as shown in Table 7.1. These different functions, the authors argued, need to be taken into account when designing interventions to help to reduce stereotyping of the elderly; but they also show how any stereotype may serve a social function as well as an information-processing one.

Table 7.1 Functions of stereotyping

Cognitive economy function: relieving the cognitive load on people so that new information can be processed more rapidly, such as seeing all old people as likely to respond in similar ways.

Ego-protective function: defending the unconscious mind against perceived threats, such as providing an unconscious justification for not spending much time with the elderly person.

Social function: to do with social identification – for example, regarding elderly people as the out-group and therefore different.

Source: Adapted from Snyder and Miene (1994)

The self-fulfilling prophecy

The classic study of the **self-fulfilling prophecy** – which has been hotly debated by educationalists – was reported by Rosenthal and Jacobsen in 1968. They gave children in an ordinary American city an IQ test, and collected information about how they were doing in school. Nothing was said to the children, but the teachers were told that it was a new form of test which could identify late developers. The researchers set up a situation where teachers "overheard" the researchers discussing the results. In that discussion, they named several children who, they said, might be expected to show unusual improvement in the coming year. In fact, the children had been randomly selected.

When they returned a year later, they found that those children had shown dramatic improvements in their school work, and had also improved their IQ scores. Without realising it, the teachers had responded to the predictions of the researchers. They expected those children to do well, and so had unconsciously acted in a friendlier manner with them, using gentler tones of voice, and always noticing what they were saying. The researchers argued that the results showed the power of the self-fulfilling prophecy; their prediction had come true simply because it had been made. In an even later follow-up study, improvements were still detectable, particularly among the older children concerned.

The self-fulfilling prophecy has been called the **Pygmalion Effect**, after the Greek myth, and has been demonstrated in many different settings, including medical, educational and organisational contexts. Managers with positive beliefs about their staff, for instance, have consistently been shown to generate more productive work in their departments, and to have higher staff retention. Kierein and Gold (2000) carried out a meta-analysis of studies of this effect in organisational contexts, and showed that there was a consistently positive finding – generating positive expectations could be self-fulfilling. The effect, they found, was even stronger if the initial level of performance or achievement in the organisation was low. It was also particularly strong in military or similarly highly-structured contexts.

Box 7.1   The self-fulfilling prophecy

The self-fulfilling prophecy is one of the most controversial, but also one of the most powerful, concepts in social psychology. What it effectively means is that we tend to act in the ways that people expect us to. If we are expected to do badly at something, we tend to do badly; if we are expected to do well, we tend to rise to those expectations and do well.

There isn't anything particularly mysterious about this; it is simply a question of the myriad subtle ways that people communicate. We pick up information from other people all the time, and if someone doesn't expect us to achieve particularly much at a specific task, they usually convey that message somehow – by subtle tones of voice, by becoming more irritable if we show difficulty or by simply not putting much time or encouragement into helping us to do it. It's not deliberate on their part – they may feel that they are being as fair as they can be, and these cues are unconscious. But it is in our nature as social animals to pick up on very subtle cues, and we too may not be aware that we are doing it.

Psychologists, in general, and social psychologists, in particular, accept the self-fulfilling prophecy as an ordinary part of life. We have precautions in experimental research to ensure that it doesn't affect experimental research – and these precautions have the status of law when it comes to research into new therapeutic drugs. We recognise that it can be an important aspect of therapy – people will pick up on the therapist's expectations, so it is important that they retain a positive outlook (fortunately, therapy helps so many people that this is not really difficult). We know it can be a factor in

Key Terms

Pygmalion Effect
The way in which we may come to live up to an image of our own creation.

young people's aspirations and ambitions, so we regard the presence of positive role models as really important.

So where is the controversy? It isn't so much with the phenomenon itself, as with the way that Rosenthal and Jacobsen's study seemed to imply that children's low achievements were entirely the teachers' faults. This criticism appears to have cut deeply (even though a number of other studies found similar results), so there were a number of attempts to devalue and challenge their findings. The phenomenon itself, though, remains pretty well accepted – not just in psychology, but in society as a whole.

Personal constructs

In 1955, Kelly developed the theory of personal constructs, which outlines how we make sense of other people's behaviour by using our own distinctive set of theories, generated through personal experience and social learning. These theories take the form of bipolar constructs, such as "kind–cruel" or "energetic–lazy", but the constructs which one person uses may be quite different from the constructs used by the next person. We build up our personal profile of what people are like by classifying the impressions other people make on us, using our existing constructs, and applying the resulting theory in our interactions with them.

We will be looking at personal constructs more closely in the next chapter, but this idiographic approach to person perception has proved useful in a number of clinical contexts, due to its ability to give valuable insights into why someone is experiencing problems, and it has also been widely used in consumer research, although mainly for analysing reactions to consumer products, such as cars or perfumes, rather than evaluating people's perceptions of other people.

Duck (2011) carried out a study of friendship among young adults, and found that there was a strong tendency for friendships to develop between those with similar personal construct systems. People who looked at the world in similar ways tended to find it easier to communicate with one another, and so would get along better and develop stronger friendships than they did with people whose personal construct systems were very different.

Duck also found that even when there was a basic similarity in personal constructs, people showed a distinct tendency to overestimate the amount of similarity between their own attitudes and thoughts and those of their friends. This, and several other studies, confirmed the idea that we are more likely to like people who see the world in a way that is similar to our own, which is the main prediction of personal construct theory when it is used in person perception.

Primacy effects

We are all familiar with the idea that other people's first impressions can influence how they react towards us, and how they judge us. Most of us will take pains to dress neatly if we are going for an interview, for instance. It has long been shown that the first information which we receive is much more significant in our judgements than information we receive later. This is known as the **primacy effect**. It was first identified through research into memory, where studies dating back to the 19th century showed how our recall is much better for the first information we receive in lists or other types of information

Key Terms

primacy effect
Experimental outcomes which have occurred because this is the first time that the participant has encountered the phenomenon. Or: the way that the first things you encounter make more of an impression than later ones do.

(e.g. Ebbinghaus, 1885). But the mechanism works just as strongly in person perception too. Pennington (1982) carried out a series of mock courtroom studies, and showed that participants' verdicts on a rape trial were powerfully affected by which evidence was given first – whether it was evidence for the prosecution or that for the defence.

The other thing about first impressions is that they can be very difficult to change. Hodges (1974) found that we tend to "fix" on our first impressions, and resist changing them – even more so if the first impressions are negative ones. One possibility is that this is because negative impressions are likely to have come from socially undesirable characteristics, which are more memorable because they are generally less common in the population. As a result, they seem more distinctive. That in itself makes them more memorable than a more ordinary, positive impression would be, so it becomes more resistant to change, even when we are given information which directly contradicts it.

Halo effects

It's not just first impressions which can distort our perceptions, though. Sometimes, we perceive people more positively than the information would really merit because those people have become associated with other positive aspects of our experience. That might be other people that we like or respect, other circumstances which we particularly like, or events which have been particularly pleasant and meaningful for us. Whatever the pleasant thing is, a person associated with it can also take on an air of pleasantness just because of that connection. So they make a positive impression on us, regardless of what they are actually like. This is known as a **halo effect**.

The halo effect means that we can see people as better or more likeable than they really are. We like to believe that our experiences of the world are reasonably consistent, so finding something pleasurable generates a set of expectations that experiences associated with it will also be pleasurable, and we generalise those expectations to any people concerned. So we sometimes find ourselves

> ### Key Terms
>
> **halo effect**
> The attribution of a range of positive qualities to someone on the basis that they already have one liked characteristic.

excusing or overlooking shortcomings of irritating habits in someone which we wouldn't ignore or excuse in anyone else; or we might judge something they have done more positively than it really deserves.

Bagozzi (1998) found that the halo effect can be influenced by the amount of arousal people are experiencing at the time. Bagozzi used attitudes towards blood donation as the context for the study, since it is a subject where most people have mixed attitudes, varying from "it might hurt" to "I am doing something positive for society". Groups of participants received stimuli which were either designed to introduce arousal, such as seeing detailed images of the various stages of blood donation, or to reduce it, such as seeing peaceful images of trees, woods, etc. They were connected to electronic arousal monitors during this process to ensure that the stimuli were actually having the effect the researchers wanted. Then participants were asked to respond to a number of questionnaire items, presented by computer, which asked about a range of topics but crucially asked them to evaluate positive and negative statements about blood donation.

Bagozzi found that an increased **arousal level** was likely to produce an enhanced halo effect for positive beliefs about blood donation, while reducing any halo effect for negative beliefs. This, he argued, was because we tend to draw on the negative beliefs as the "default mode" if we haven't really been thinking about the topic, because they are more immediate and personal, while the positive beliefs are more complex in origin. But if you are aroused, you think more about the topic at hand, so the complex reasons come to mind more easily. It is possible, too, that cognitive dissonance or some other cognitive defence mechanism may become activated, so people actively look for their positive beliefs as a defence against the negative thoughts. Bagozzi's study shows us how halo effects may be quite unconscious, but can nonetheless be powerful influences on social judgements.

DIMENSIONAL MODELS OF PERSON PERCEPTION

Some approaches to understanding person perception have focused on the ways that we generally use more than one set of criteria at a time, so that perceiving people is multidimensional rather than just involving a single criterion. Cuddy et al (2008) developed a dimensional model they referred to as the **BIAS map** – BIAS standing for behaviour from intergroup affect and stereotypes. Their model proposed that person perception involves two fundamental dimensions: warmth and competence. Each of these dimensions involves separate associations and can generate different types of emotions.

The dimension of warmth according to these researchers, was closely linked with the idea of competition. People who were seen as competitors were perceived as colder, while those seen as allies were seen as warm. This dimension, they argued, was therefore also linked with the idea of communion or sharing, and positive regard was directed towards other members of the same social group.

Their second dimension, competence, was closely linked to social status, and also whether the person was perceived as being able to act as an independent agent. These aspects of the competence dimension, agency and social status were all about whether the person appeared to have control over their own decisions and actions, and whether they were perceived to be able to take independent action in their own right. People able to act autonomously were judged as being of higher status, and as competent, while those less able to determine their own actions were seen as being of lower status, and therefore less competent.

On the basis of a number of research studies, Cuddy et al (2008) proposed that the two dimensions of warmth and competence generate a number of emotional reactions to the other person, such as admiration, contempt, envy or pity, which in turn have social consequences, for both individuals and groups. They argued that awareness of how these dimensions worked together or separately could lead to a better understanding of prejudice towards other social groups, as well as of interpersonal liking or perception.

This dimensional model of person perception was supported by a number of studies, but it has been criticised too. One reason is the way that almost all of their research was conducted using students as the main participants. Banyard and Hunt (2000) discussed how this particular type of sample may produce results which are unlike studies using working adult participants, in that those types of studies have to be more grounded in "real-world" experience. Students, too, may be particularly inclined to show response bias in the minimalised contexts of laboratory studies. And another criticism of this study is that it may be ethnocentric, reflecting distinctly American perceptions of interpersonal competition and social status which have less relevance in other parts of the world.

We can see, then, how the processes of person perception draw on our existing knowledge and beliefs, but often seem to have relatively little to do with the actual person that we are perceiving. As we get to know the other person more closely, we begin to build up a store of knowledge about them. If we are motivated to do so, we will gradually revise our ideas to develop a more realistic picture of what they are like. In many cases, though, our initial perceptions mean that we simply don't take the trouble to get to know that particular person, so we continue to apply superficial impressions or negative stereotypes to them. One of the factors which can make the difference between whether we take the trouble to know someone better or not is whether we find them attractive, so we will go on in this chapter to look at the psychology of attraction.

ATTRACTION

Being social inevitably involves interacting with other people, but in our everyday experience, we like some people and don't like others. Sometimes, too, we find ourselves particularly attracted to someone. **Attraction** isn't just about our close or intimate relationships; it affects our working relationships and friendships too. We prefer to spend our time with people that we like, and to avoid people who we find unattractive for one reason or another. We like working with some people and not others. We will take problems or things we want to discuss to certain people, but not to others.

It makes a difference to how we judge people, too. Alicke and Zell (2009) found that social attractiveness had a significant influence on our attributions of blame. They asked participants to consider a legal scenario about a trial of a man who had tried to intervene in what he believed to be an aggressive argument between a man and a woman, and had accidentally punched the woman while trying to restrain the man, resulting in significant harm. The information

Key Terms

attraction
The experience of feeling drawn towards another person, as a positive aspect of interpersonal experience.

they were given about the man either presented him as socially attractive or as unattractive; and this information significantly affected how much the participants judged the man as being to blame for the incident.

Their study dealt with **social attraction** – whether the man seemed to be a nice person or not (e.g., cleaning up his friend's flat while he was still asleep and volunteering at a homeless shelter, or helping himself to his friend's beer while he was asleep, and skiving off work). Attraction isn't just about physical appearance – it is about how we perceive people and whether we feel drawn towards them or would rather keep them at a distance. Some people we find more likeable than others; some we just don't see as particularly likeable. These reactions affect how we act towards those people, so attraction is a significant factor in our social lives.

Physical appearance can count, though. As we'll see later in this section, judgements of physical attractiveness do make a difference to how we perceive people. But before we look at the factors influencing attraction, it might be a good idea to consider what the idea of attraction can include.

ATTRACTION AND ATTRACTIVENESS

It may sound obvious to say that we are attracted to people that we find attractive. But attractiveness is not an easy thing to pin down. Many people find long-term partners who would not be considered to be particularly attractive by standard social judgements, but they have found other aspects of them – their ideas and the way they think, their attitudes to life, or some other personal characteristics – attractive personally.

Nonetheless, in society as a whole, some people are regarded as being more physically attractive than others – and being considered attractive can make a great deal of difference to an individual. Langlois et al (2000) performed a meta-analysis on over 100 studies which looked at whether physical attractiveness was associated with other traits, and found that there was clear evidence that physically attractive people tend to be more extraverted, to have better social skills and to be more self-confident. Given the ways in which modern society promotes ideal images across the media, this may not seem very surprising, and it is not a new finding.

Face-to-face attraction

Back in 1938, in a discussion of how conditioning can affect human behaviour, Guthrie recounted how a group of male students decided to play a joke on an unattractive, shy female member of their class. One by one they asked her for a date, took her out, and acted as though she was interesting and attractive. The joke backfired, in that the girl became more sociable and entertaining and even more physically attractive as she responded to this treatment. By the end, the boys were competing to ask her for a date – what had seemed a chore now became a pleasure.

What this story illustrates is the way that we respond to the ways that other people react to us. It is unlikely that attractive people are simply more sociable from birth; what is more likely is that they become more self-confident, sociable and extravert as a result of the **feedback** they receive from interacting with other people. And, of course, we tend to respond positively to sociable, confident people, so being attractive becomes a self-fulfilling prophecy.

But how do we know whether other people like us or not? In Chapter 3, we looked at how we communicate unconsciously with one another, using what are generally known as non-verbal signals. These can be important indicators of attraction. Eye-contact, facial expression, prolonged gaze and posture have all be shown to signal that we find someone else attractive. Pupil dilation, too, is a reliable indicator; so much so that it is often used in marketing research to indicate whether people like or dislike products, as well as people. In a classic study, Hess (1965) asked men to rate the attractiveness of photos of women. All of them saw the same set of photos, but in one group certain of the pictures had been subtly touched up, by enlarging the pupils of the eyes. These images were consistently rated as being more attractive, although the explanations for their choices given by the participants showed that they had no idea why they had chosen them.

Postural echo, as we also saw in Chapter 3, also indicates interest and liking. If we are paying close attention to someone, we will often unconsciously adopt the same posture. And, of course, people who are attracted to one another require less personal space – they will stand or sit closer together than they would with strangers. It does need to be borne in mind, however, that most of these signals are also indicators of interest. A person someone may be particularly interested in what someone is saying, rather than signalling that they find them particularly attractive. The two often go together, but there may be some social situations in which mistaking them could lead to misunderstandings.

Other kinds of feedback may influence whether we judge someone as attractive in the first place. Dutton and Aron (1974) asked male students to cross a shaky suspension bridge over a river. At the end of the bridge, a female researcher greeted them, asked them to fill out a **projective test** designed to measure anxiety (the Thematic Apperception Test, or TAT), and gave them her phone number so that they could phone her if they had any question about the study. The researchers included controls where men crossed a much safer bridge, and also conditions where the experimenter was male. They found that those who had experienced the scarier crossing (and were therefore more physically aroused) were more likely than any of the other groups to call the experimenter, and to give sexy interpretations of the images in the TAT. It seemed that the men had construed their internal feedback – their feelings of arousal – as a result of the experimenter being attractive, rather than from the scary task they had just carried out.

Internet attraction

Both of these studies are concerned with face-to-face attraction, that is, being attracted to real people, on the basis of having personal contact with them. But in the modern world, many people form relationships and friendships as a result of common interests and social interactions discovered through the internet. Weisbuch et al (2009) looked at how first impressions are made through Facebook pages, and what makes people come across as being attractive. They conducted a study in which participants had a four-minute conversation with another person. The participants thought this other person was also waiting to take part in an experiment, as they were; but in reality, the other person was a confederate of the experimenters, who (after the conversation) rated the likeability of the participant. The participants also agreed to open their

Key Terms
projective test Psychometric tests which involve providing the person with ambiguous stimuli, and seeing what meanings they read into them. The idea is that this will illustrate the concerns of the unconscious mind.

Facebook pages to the researchers, and an independent group of raters judged their likeability on the basis of their pages.

The researchers found a lot of similarity between the personal interview and the Facebook page in their assessment of likeability. People judged as likeable in person also tended to have Facebook pages which led to raters seeing them as likeable. The ratings seemed mainly to depend on **expressivity** – some people were more expressive in non-verbal terms while having conversations, and they also tended to have Facebook pages which were judged as more expressive, with more photos and other information. The researchers concluded that it was probably valid to draw analogies between the two sources of social information, and that perhaps Facebook pages really do provide some information about people in real life.

Walther et al (2001) argued that internet-based attraction often has a strong fantasy element. For some people, interaction with another person through the internet may involve intimacy and affection at a level which they would not feel in face-to-face contact with others. In one of their studies, these researchers showed that ratings of the attractiveness of virtual partners often dropped considerably when the internet information was accompanied by a photograph – even if the photograph itself was reasonably attractive. The researchers' explanation was that bringing the experience more into the real world served to reduce the level of attraction by reducing the element of fantasy involved. Of course, this finding really relates to relationships formed through gaming or chatrooms; modern social media such as Facebook or Instagram are much more image-based.

Bearing this in mind, Whitty and Carr (2006) cautioned against making too many generalisations about the nature of attraction on the internet. As in real life, contact between people can be made in many different ways and take many different forms, and people may respond differently to one another depending on the context. People participating in online dating sites, for example, tend to be more strategic and conscious of their presentations than those interacting through gaming platforms, and they are also very concerned that the impression they give should be at least reasonably truthful, perhaps because they are aware that at some time, the online relationship may involve face-to-face meeting.

In general, then, it seems that internet attraction and face-to-face attraction have a great deal in common. But as with real life, different contexts offer different opportunities. Some, like the friendships made through shared experiences, may develop through greater knowledge of the other person and how they are likely to act; while some are based on more superficial characteristics. But the internet also offers opportunities for considerable deception, so generalising about attraction on the internet is unlikely to cover all contingencies. It doesn't in real life, either.

FACTORS INFLUENCING ATTRACTION

Most of us do our best to get on with the people that we work or study with, because having strong dislikes can make the interactions in our everyday life quite difficult. But we meet strangers all the time, and we can't always predict which of them we will find attractive and which we will regard more neutrally. Since the 1960s, researchers have been investigating how attraction happens, and teasing out some of the factors which might make us more or less likely to like someone else. Table 7.2 summarises the major factors which have been investigated, each of which can influence attraction.

There are four main theories which have been put forward to explain attraction, based on these factors. Berscheid (1985) proposed the idea that attraction arises from **evaluation**. The idea here is that our evolution as social animals gives us a biological predisposition to evaluate other people, to judge who is

Table 7.2 Factors influencing attraction

Factor	Concept	Illustrative studies	Description
Physical attractiveness	We are more likely to like people who are physically attractive.	Sigall and Ostrove (1975)	People recommended harsher penalties for alleged burglars if their picture showed them as unattractive, but more severe penalties for attractive criminals involved in confidence trickery or fraud.
		Commisso and Finkelstein (2012)	In a work situation, participants were more willing to terminate someone's employment if records were accompanied by an unattractive picture.
Similarity	We are more likely to like people who are similar to ourselves.	Walster et al (1966)	Used photos to demonstrate that people were attracted to those with roughly equal levels of attractiveness as themselves (the matching hypothesis).
		Montoya and Horton (2004)	Used rating scales to show that perceptions of attitude similarity were important in attraction. Participants who were aware of ratings of cognitive similarity judged people as more attractive than they did if unaware of the cognitive similarity ratings.
		Gibson (2005)	Studied an international student dormitory facility, with 500 residents from 38 different countries, found that similarity of culture and of gender were the important factors in attraction and friendship.
Complementarity	We are more likely to like people whose attributes complement ours.	Winch (1958)	Interview studies with married couples indicated that having complementary needs in dominance-submission and nurturance-receptivity was a significant factor in attraction.
Familiarity and propinquity	We are more likely to like people if we spend more of our time with them.	Newcomb (1961)	Shared college accommodation resulted in longer-term friendships than other sources of contact.
		Segal (1974)	Students at a police academy tended to form friendships with those whose surnames were close alphabetically – because that was the way that they had been allocated dormitory and classroom places.
Cognitive familiarity	We are more likely to like people who think in familiar ways.	Banikiotes and Niemeyer (1981)	People who rated their personal constructs in similar ways were more likely to find one another attractive than those with dissimilar ratings.

Table 7.2 Continued

Factor	Concept	Illustrative studies	Description
Reciprocity	We are more likely to like people who like us.	Aronson and Linder (1965)	Used stooges and "accidental overhearing" to set up experimental conditions in which people judged how attractive someone was. They found a strong tendency to like those who were positive towards the participant, and particularly those who began as neutral or negative, but changed to become positive.
		Westphal and Shani (2016)	Top managers use cognitive rehearsal to increase their personal liking for those they want to influence, so that their liking comes across as genuine in interpersonal non-verbal behaviour. Those who rehearse most positively generally have more successful outcomes.
Competence versus fallibility	We are more likely to like people who sometimes make mistakes.	Aronson et al (1966)	Liking for a high-achieving quiz-show contestant who spilled coffee was increased, but not for a low-achieving contestant who did the same. Researchers suggested that the blunder made the contestant come across as less of a "know-it-all" and therefore more likeable.
		Helmreich et al (1970)	If people had either very high or very low self-esteem, they generally disliked people who made blunders. The likeable effect of mistake-making only applied to people with moderate, or ordinary, levels of self-esteem.
		Rosenfield et al (1981)	Group membership affects fallibility judgements. Incompetent people were more disliked if working with participants in cooperative groups than when working with them in competitive ones.

safe and who might not be. Our mechanisms of attraction and dislike summarise our responses to other people, based on these unconscious evaluations.

Another idea, proposed by Lott and Lott (1968) is that attraction comes from the **reinforcement** we get from other people. Learning theory proposes that behaviour is strengthened, or reinforced, if it produces a pleasant outcome (positive reinforcement), or allows us to escape or avoid an unpleasant one (negative reinforcement). According to this theory, we like people if we find their company rewarding, and dislike them if it isn't. Being associated with pleasant effects is also rewarding, and this generalises to the people that we meet. So we are also predisposed to like people whom we encounter in pleasant situations, or when we are happy.

A third explanation for attraction was put forward by Byrne (1971), who said that we find people attractive if they think in similar ways to ourselves. The **cognitive similarity** model proposes that the more similar two people's attitudes or thinking styles are, the more they will find one another attractive.

Key Terms

reinforcement
The strengthening of learning in some way, usually through reward.

cognitive similarity
Having the same sort of thinking patterns or personal constructs as other people or another person.

Contradictory attitudes are likely to lead to arguments or disagreements, which are unpleasant and so will tend to generate dislike. Rubin (1973) suggested that the reason we find cognitive similarity attractive is because it validates our own ideas, and so both increases our self-confidence and flatters our vanity. It also provides grounds for common understanding, and so makes it easier for us to communicate with other people.

The fourth explanation is **reciprocity**. In general, we like people who like us. Aronson (1976) argued that we work on a reward-cost principle, which sees liking people who don't reciprocate by liking us as possibly involving costs, such as interactions becoming hurtful or unpleasant. The most rewarding relationships are those in which someone starts off as neutral or negative, but then becomes positive. The next are relationships which have been positive from the start; while we see people who are either negative towards us from the start or become so, as people to avoid as much as we can. A related but slightly different explanation is that we feel a strong inclination for balance in our relationships, so if someone is positive towards us, we feel more or less obliged to reciprocate and be positive towards them (Freeman, 1977).

There is likely to be some validity in each of these explanations, but like most human experiences, attraction can be affected by, and derives from, multiple factors working on many different levels. Social experiences, culture and personal backgrounds as well as the immediate situation all have their effects. So although they may appear limited in scope, these theories may also be relevant to understanding attraction, even if they are not complete explanations in themselves.

A different approach to understanding attraction comes from **evolutionary psychology**, which proposes we find some people more attractive than others because we have evolved those preferences. Buss (1995) argued that we are attracted to specific features in our mates which are positively associated with health and potential reproductive success. So far so good. Certainly, people do tend to think that healthy people are attractive, and also, as Kalick et al (1998) found, that attractive people are healthy. However, other researchers went on to specify the ideal shape, Streater and McBurney (2003) conducted studies on body shape preference, and found that men generally preferred women with "hourglass-shaped" waist-to-hip ratios of 0.7. Previously, Zaadstra et al (1993) had shown that this ratio has a correlation with fertility, so Streater and McBurney argued that it was an example of human evolution shaping ideas of attractiveness.

The problem, though, is that in many non-technological societies, and particularly those in harsh environments, perceptions of female beauty are quite different. There, a woman considered beautiful has a plumper, more rounded figure. That may still be about survival – someone who is large and plump will have reserves of fat which will carry them through the lean times and make them more likely to survive and be able to nurture children. In those societies, therefore, there is more to survival than simply fertility; one also needs to be able to stay alive to bring up the children. Even within modern lifetimes, the ideal figure has changed. Marilyn Monroe, for example, would be considered "fat" by modern standards. So it is unlikely that attraction to "hourglass" figures has actually been inherited through evolutionary pressures. Given that even the non-Western populations in these studies would have been aware of idealised images in the media, particularly advertising, it is more likely that social learning is an appropriate explanation.

Key Terms

reciprocity
The idea that some relationships work because each member of a couple provides the other with the same qualities.

evolutionary psychology
An approach to psychology which looks at how certain types of behaviour may have evolved for survival reasons in the primaeval past.

Evaluating attraction studies

Table 7.2 summarised many years of investigations into the factors which can influence attraction. But these studies have also been criticised, for a number of reasons. One of them is that they have tended to involve mostly student samples, and there is some question how far those findings will generalise to the population at large. The experience of students is a little different from most, in that a large number of young people tend to be interacting with one another, both socially and educationally, with many opportunities for contact and to make relationships with other young people like themselves, and relatively less contact with other members of society. The processes of attraction may therefore be a little different in student samples than in samples of, say, young workers in industry.

Another criticism is that in some studies, attractiveness has been measured by using ratings of photographs. These are almost by definition fairly superficial judgements, and assessing static images may involve very different judgements from our interactions with people in everyday life, where the information available is so much richer. Factors like facial expression and movement contribute significantly to person perception, and so might also be considered likely to influence attraction. And judging whether someone's image is attractive might be quite a different thing from actually being attracted to that person.

There is also the question of how we are measuring attraction, and whether it is the same as liking and friendship. Many of these studies tend to assume that this is the same thing, but that might not be the case. For example, Olk and Gibbons (2010) studied friendships in a cohort of MBA students (i.e., mature students who were experienced professionals) over a period of 30 months. They found that we may like other people who are popular, even if they don't particularly like us; and we may generally like other people if we are gregarious, social people ourselves. Liking and friendship are not always reciprocal, so we need to be careful before we assume that research results for one provide evidence for the other.

 A number of ethical challenges have been made concerning the high levels of deception involved in many of these studies. The deceptions were introduced to combat another methodological problem, which is the way that respondents often attempt to give the responses which they believe the researchers are looking for (Orne, 1962), or ones which they feel are socially desirable. But in modern days, using deception to combat this problem is only considered to be acceptable if the people concerned have given full and informed consent. During the 1970s, researchers paid relatively little attention to such matters, which meant that their research often involved a degree of deception which would be unacceptable in modern times.

Talking point 7.1   What is attractive?

We all vary in what we find attractive in other people. Often, when we ask people about what they initially liked about their partners or friends, for example, we find that they focus on quite trivial events or characteristics. But do we vary quite as much in our ideal views? Try collecting the ideas of several different people on what they find attractive in other people. Ask them what they would be most likely to find attractive in people in different situations, for example:

- in a friend;
- in a short-term partner for a specific activity (e.g., a day trip or a sport);
- in a long-term partner;
- in a work colleague.

Did the same qualities get mentioned by several people? Or did everyone say something different? And do the reports you have obtained differ from people's accounts of their real-world experiences?

Most studies of attraction, as we have seen, have dealt with short-term attraction, and not really with what happens over the long term. But Duck (1977) argued that these are often different types of attraction in the first place. Most of these studies, he asserted, were actually about social attraction – a short-term phenomenon strongly influenced by factors such as similarity, proximity and our membership of social groups.

On the other hand, the kind of attraction which forms the basis for longer-term relationships is based on a much deeper knowledge of the other person's characteristics, such as their opinions and their personality. It is not uncommon, Duck pointed out, for people to change their minds about someone, and to become attracted to them more as we get to know them better. This is because when we first meet people we react to them mainly in terms of the effect that they have on us; but as we get to know them better, we see them more as people and less as social stimuli. Confusing the two types of attraction, Duck argued, can lead to considerable confusion and misleading findings.

PREJUDICE

From attraction to its opposite: **prejudice**. Or at least, that's how we generally think about prejudice – as a fixed, negative attitude which we apply to someone or something regardless of whether they actually deserve it. In fact, prejudiced simply means "pre-judged", and we can be prejudiced in favour of something rather than against it. But for the most part, talk about prejudice and research into the subject tends to deal only with negative prejudice.

If we are prejudiced, we have, quite literally, prejudged things. We don't bother weighing up alternative explanations for actions, or accept the possibility that perhaps an individual is not actually how we have judged them to be. Instead, we apply rigid evaluations which we have made in advance, usually on the basis of stereotyping or some other arbitrary attribute which we believe the other person possesses.

The relationship between prejudice and liking, however, is more problematic. A number of early studies showed that there was very little link between people's expressed prejudicial attitudes, and their behaviour when it came to interacting with real individuals. In one very famous study, LaPière (1934) and two Chinese friends travelled across America, staying at hotels and eating in restaurants. At the time, there was a significant level of anti-Chinese prejudice in American society, but over 90 per cent of the institutions accepted the customers without demur. Six months later, LaPière contacted those same hotels

Key Terms
prejudice A fixed, pre-set attitude, usually negative and hostile, and usually applied to members of a particular social category.

and restaurants to ask whether they accepted Chinese guests, and almost all of them said they did not.

 A number of explanations were put forward for this. Ajzen (1988) argued that this study confused global and specific attitudes; the hoteliers were being asked a very general question which revealed their prejudiced attitudes; but when the three researchers actually turned up on the doorstep, they were faced with a very specific situation, leading to the apparent discrepancy between attitudes and behaviour. Also, turning down paying guests might have conflicted with the hotelier's other attitudes – particularly those relating to operating a profitable business. Other theorists also tried to explain discrepancies between attitudes and behaviour, but more recent research, as we will see later in this chapter, suggests that seeing prejudice as "not-liking" at an individual level is a serious distortion of the actual phenomenon.

Prejudice can take many different forms. We can, in fact, be prejudiced against just about any group of people, for almost no reason. In a well-known study conducted by an American schoolteacher in 1970, not long after Martin Luther King's murder, white children agreed to try an exercise to see what it felt like to be black. The teacher, Jane Elliott, divided the class into two on the basis of the colour of their eyes. The first week, the blue-eyed children were deemed to be the superior group. Brown-eyed children wore distinguishing fabric collars, were given less favourable treatment and no privileges. The following week she reversed the procedure, making the brown-eyed children the "superior" group, and giving them the privileges and favoured treatment.

Each time the "superior" group began to behave in an arrogant and unpleasant way towards their classmates. They also did better at schoolwork, often achieving success in tests they had not managed before. The "inferior" group, by contrast, gradually became timid and subservient, did worse than before on their schoolwork, and isolated themselves as a group from the other children. This study, aimed at demonstrating what the experience of discrimination felt like to the children, became widely publicised, and formed the basis for many diversity training exercises aimed at raising awareness and so reducing prejudice (Peters, 1987).

Elliott's study demonstrates that prejudice can be based on almost any characteristic. However, some types of prejudice are more common than others. Three of the most common types of prejudice that we encounter in society are racism, sexism and homophobia. We will look briefly at each of these before looking more closely at theories of prejudice, where these issues will come back again.

Racism

Psychological research into racism, or **ethnic prejudice**, began with studies of racist attitudes between the wars, and became an area of particular concern in the aftermath of World War II, when the evidence provided by the concentration camps showed graphically how what began as social prejudice could become vicious and systematic cruelty, and ultimately genocide. Allport (1954) identified five stages in this development, beginning with anti-locution, or hostile talk and racist propaganda. The second stage is avoidance, where the ethnic group is segregated from the dominant group, and the third, active discrimination, when the group is excluded from civil rights, employment or housing. The fourth stage is when the group suffers physical attacks, violence towards themselves or their property; and the fifth is extermination, where the attempt is made to annihilate the whole group of people.

Talking point 7.2   Stages of ethnic prejudice

Sadly, examples of ethnic prejudice of one form or another are all too common in the modern world. Society has come a long way in challenging it, though, and for the most part in modern industrial societies, ethnic prejudice is a minority belief rather than the commonly-accepted social representation which it was, for example, in Nazi Germany.

Allport's (1954) stages of ethnic prejudice were drawn from the experiences of Nazi Germany, and how the persecution of Jews, Gypsies and other minority groups became so extreme as to result in attempts at genocide. But this was not the only example of extreme ethnic prejudice, and the less extreme stages can be found in many places. Can you identify real world examples, either current or historical, for each of Allport's stages of ethnic prejudice:

1. anti-locution
2. avoidance
3. discrimination
4. physical attack
5. extermination

Key Terms

ethnic prejudice
Prejudice against a particular social group based on ethnicity, usually translated as skin colour or nation of origin.

There is some question as to how far these examples are really stages, in the sense that some may overlap with others; but Allport was really concerned

Table 7.3 Principles of ethnic prejudice

1. Prejudice may arise from two interacting sources: one based on misinformation and the need to minimise cognitive processing, and the other to do with personality.

2. If two groups are in competition or conflict, discrimination in favour of the in-group and against the out-group will become a social norm.

3. The less information we have about somebody, the more likely we are to fall back on stereotypes.

4. Socially accepted attitudes and stereotypes are widely known and have widespread effects on people's behaviour.

5. Prejudices can generate their own "evidence", and therefore become self-fulfilling.

6. Groups can vary according to the exact category of people towards whom prejudice is directed.

7. Prejudice only changes if social norms change; if they remain stable, prejudice will also remain stable.

8. There is a negative correlation between prejudice and intelligence, education and social class.

9. Children acquire attitudes and prejudices from their families.

10. Children can distinguish between ethnic groups from an early age, but their attitudes and preferences do not stabilise until they are older.

Source: Bethlehem (1985)

with describing how serious ethnic prejudice can build up in a society, as it had done in Nazi Germany and did more recently in Rwanda. Other researchers have explored many different aspects of how ethnic prejudice manifests itself. Bethlehem (1985) explored the outcomes of this research, and distilled the findings into ten "principles of ethnic prejudice". Each principle summarises the findings of research in that particular area. The principles are listed in Table 7.3.

Sexism

Sexism, or discrimination on the basis of gender, is another common form of prejudice. Unlike most occurrences of ethnic prejudice (with a few notable exceptions), discrimination on the basis of gender was enshrined in law for many centuries in the Western world. In Britain, it became seriously challenged by the suffragette movement at the beginning of the 20th century, such that the official laws restricting women's rights to vote had gone by the post-war period. However, sexism in terms of attitudes and workplace discrimination was, if anything, stronger than ever at that time, and discrimination on the basis of gender did not become illegal for many decades. The continuous challenges of an active feminist movement beginning in the 1970s eventually produced a series of laws enshrining women's entitlement to equal treatment.

That did not remove sexism from society, of course, but it shifted the ground to challenging individual and institutional attitudes rather than pressing for new legislation. Sexism has been shown to be different from other common sources of prejudice, partly because it generally involves deep-seated beliefs and assumptions, about the nature of the world as well as about people in general, and partly also because it is often closely bound up with power relationships in society. There are many similarities between sexism and other forms of prejudice, but also many differences.

Homophobia

Although some regard prejudice against homosexuals as a form of sexism, it is probably worthwhile to consider **homophobia** as a separate form of prejudice – it tends to have different origins, and to manifest itself in different ways. Like sexism, though, homophobia was deeply ingrained in Western society until relatively recently, with tragic consequences for a number of important contributors to society in the early part of the 20th century. It was not until the Gay Pride movement became active in the 1970s that any real momentum for change began to build up.

As a result of intensive campaigning and determined efforts to change social norms, changes in legislation in Europe, Britain and America meant that being homosexual was no longer illegal. In most Western countries, homosexuals now have the same rights in terms of their relationships as heterosexuals. There are some noticeable exceptions, of course, such as in Russia, which at the time of writing has a repressive and somewhat 19th century attitude to homosexuality; but even there it is hoped that the combination of external example and internal campaigning will eventually result in a more enlightened approach.

EXPLAINING PREJUDICE

A number of explanations have been put forward for prejudice over the years. These have varied from individualistic explanations which focus on the person holding prejudiced views, to theories which stress the culture within which the individual is operating, and theories which challenge the whole connection between individual attitudes and social discrimination. None of these explanations are sufficient in themselves, but as with other aspects of human behaviour, each approach can contribute something to our understanding of the whole process.

The authoritarian personality

Psychological interest in prejudice, like so many other aspects of social psychology, became much stronger after World War II. This is largely because the experience of Nazi Germany showed so clearly how extreme consequences could become when people were systematically perceived as "things" rather than as whole human beings. Psychology had been a developing field of study in Germany, and many social psychologists had either escaped Nazi Germany themselves, or worked with those who had.

One of the significant theories developed in this area was the idea that prejudice arises from an internal trait or set of traits; that some people are more prejudiced towards others because of their personality. Deriving their ideas from the psychoanalytic concepts of repression and reaction-formation, Adorno et al (1950) proposed that a certain type of rigid, highly disciplined upbringing generated a particular personality type, which he described as the **authoritarian personality**. This personality type included a very rigid sense of what was "right" and what was "wrong" in social behaviour, an inability to accept or tolerate ambiguities, and a strong tendency to be prejudiced towards

Key Terms
homophobia An irrational negative emotional response to homosexuality.

minority groups or other sets of people who appeared to deviate from the social norm.

This personality syndrome, Adorno et al believed, had arisen as a result of the anger and frustration generated by experiencing harsh discipline during childhood. Because those aggressive feelings could not be openly expressed, they had become internalised, and manifested themselves against other targets. The rigid approach to what was socially acceptable meant that the most logical target was those minority groups who were in some way different: ethnic groups were the most visible, but such people also tended to be prejudiced against homosexuals, women, young people (who they saw as "juvenile delinquents") and many other social groups.

This idea was substantiated by the findings of a personality scale designed to measure authoritarianism – the F test – which showed that people who scored highly on authoritarianism as a personality trait also tended to be highly prejudiced. Taking it a bit further, Rokeach (1960) showed that it wasn't just people who held to the Fascist ideology who fitted this model; authoritarianism could be found just as much in extreme left-wingers as in members of the political extreme right.

While it is still possible nowadays to find people who score quite highly in authoritarianism, they tend to be fewer, possibly as a result of more liberal approaches to child-rearing. And there have also been many examples of people who were not particularly authoritarian who still participated in prejudiced social activities. It is not practical, for example, to explain the genocides of Germany or Rwanda simply as resulting from a whole population of authoritarian individuals. So, while recognising that authoritarianism may be a factor for some people, we need to look for other explanations for prejudice.

The scapegoat explanation

One of the most striking findings about social prejudice is that it tends to be at its highest level, or at least most visible, at times of economic hardship. The observation was first made by Hovland and Sears (1940), who compared the number of racist lynchings in the southern United States each year with the price of cotton. They found a strong negative correlation between the two: the lower the price of cotton, the more lynchings. What was happening, they argued, was that the economic frustration being experienced by the white farmers was being taken out onto the black population – they had become the scapegoats, blamed for the farmers' economic problems.

The scapegoat explanation has been proposed as the explanation for prejudice in several different periods of economic hardship and recession, in that it tends to be at those times that prejudice against minority groups is openly expressed – the group is blamed for "taking all our jobs" or similar problems. However, Bagley and Verma (1979) demonstrated that it all depends on whether there is an existing culture which tolerates the open expression of racism. In cultures where there is strong social disapproval of racism, such as the Netherlands in the 1970s, scapegoating was less apparent.

There is also the question of manipulation by politicians. Biro (1995) discussed how some governments in the Balkan states had deliberately encouraged ethnic divisiveness as a way of diverting attention from the serious economic problems resulting from the break-up of the former Yugoslavia. The result was extreme examples of prejudice, with neighbour turning against neighbour and

| Key Terms

F test
A measuring scale for authoritarian attitudes (F for fascism).

"ethnic cleansing" (a euphemism for attempted genocide) becoming accepted social policy, until eventually UN peacekeeping forces were obliged to intervene. This was deliberately manipulated scapegoating, initiated by politicians and taken to extremes by others.

Cultural explanations

Prejudice can only thrive in a social culture which tolerates it. In fact, the culture within which someone is embedded can be a major factor in how prejudiced they are. In 1976, Middleton compared southern and northern Americans, and found that those from the southern states showed more extreme prejudice towards black people than those from the northern states. The participants were also given the F-test, to ensure that it wasn't simply a matter of personality structure, but they found the more extreme attitude from the southerners even when F scores were the same as the northerners.

Culture can change the extent of prejudice too, as has been demonstrated in Europe. Back in 1979, Bagley and Verma found that the levels of racial discrimination were far less in the Netherlands than they were in Britain at the time, despite their being approximately the same proportion of black and white members of the population. The difference was that the Netherlands of the time had an explicitly anti-racist culture. Since then, British cultural attitudes towards racism, both official and unofficial, have changed considerably. Ethnic prejudice, while still in existence, is regarded as being socially unacceptable, and as a result, the overall levels of racism in British society have dropped considerably from that time, although sadly, some examples do still exist.

Intergroup conflict

Other researchers have seen prejudices as arising from **intergroup conflict**. In a classic study, Sherif et al (1961) divided a set of 22 boys attending a summer camp at Robber's Cave into two competing teams. They were unaware of the other team at first, because their huts were out of sight of one another, so initially their time was spent developing relationships within the group. Then Sherif et al arranged a major competition between them. Very rapidly, the boys developed an "in-group" and "out-group" mentality, denigrating the others and maximising their own admirable qualities. Their own team members were described as "brave" and "tough", while the others were "unpleasant" and "underhanded". This rivalry was quite extreme, and was only broken down when the organisers staged a number of situations where they all had to co-operate in order to resolve the situation.

These findings, and others, led Sherif to develop what he referred to as his **realistic conflict theory** – that if two groups are in competition for privileges, those who have them will be defensive and those who haven't will feel frustrated and envious. These findings and others all contributed to Tajfel's theory of social identification.

As we saw in Chapter 1, Tajfel proposed that our membership of social groups is a powerful part of our sense of who we are. In 1970, he showed how just belonging to one identifiable group rather than another seemed to be enough for group members to discriminate in favour of members of their own group and against those of the out-group. This happened in **minimal group studies** – that is, even if membership of the group had been decided in a completely arbitrary way, such as by tossing a coin. Although later researchers showed that these studies only worked this way when the groups had to make forced choices, the general principle of competition for resources being likely to generate intergroup hostility remains valid.

There were three cognitive mechanisms operating in prejudice, Tajfel believed. The first is our tendency to categorise our experience, which can lead to stereotyping. The second is the way that we apply value-judgements to our categories and stereotypes – using evaluations such as good, bad, like and dislike as if they were factual and valid. And the third is what Tajfel referred to as a **search for coherence** – that is, our cognitive need to make sense of our experience and to justify and explain our ideas (Tajfel, 1969). All of these, he believed, are active in generating prejudice, and need to be addressed if we are trying to change it.

In chapter one, we saw how groups apply different standards to their own members than they do to those in the out-group (Marques and Yzerbyt, 1988), and also how we respond differently to feedback from in-group and out-group members (Gallagher et al, 2013). The tendency to see the world in terms of "us" and "them" is so deep-rooted that it can very easily become distorted into active prejudice and discrimination. The interaction of in-group and out-group mechanisms within prejudiced cultures, and also perhaps with scapegoating processes, provides a more rounded general explanation for widespread forms of prejudice.

Ambivalent social prejudice

That is still not the whole story, though. Jackman (1994) argued that there is a difference between the kind of prejudice found in Sherif's classic study, and most of the forms of entrenched prejudice encountered in social living. She argued that Sherif's findings of intergroup hostility and conflict, while valid for their situation and context, could not apply in situations where social relations were protracted over time, with one group of boys being consistently dominant over the other, and their dominance being dependent on systematically gaining benefits from the other group's efforts. In that situation, continued hostility between the two groups would make the whole situation unstable.

Instead, Jackman argued, a paternalistic system emerges, in which those in the dominant group define what are desirable characteristics in the other group, and reward those who show those characteristics with positive feeling, admiration and even love. This makes the exploitation harder for members of the "inferior" group to recognise, and even harder to resist. It also makes it more difficult for members of the dominant group to recognise what they are actually doing. This system can be seen in the history of the slave economy in America, where many slave owners showed real affection and respect for their "dutiful" slaves, and many slaves accepted the system without challenge. It was only those who refused to accept their inferior status, or to act in "acceptable" ways who received the full impact of social condemnation by the dominant group, often in the most extreme and cruel manner.

According to Jackman, sexism is another example of this. Glicke and Fiske (2001) argued that sexism comes in two forms: **hostile sexism**, marked by attitudes of overt dislike and hostility towards women, and **benevolent sexism**, which is marked by attitudes which appear supportive on the surface but really contain an assumption of women as inferior. Comments such as "women are

Key Terms

search for coherence
The way in which we seek to make our cognitions make sense.

hostile sexism
A form of sexism which involves active denigration of the other sex.

benevolent sexism
A form of sexism in which apparently supportive statements contain an implicit message of helplessness or inferiority.

wonderful creatures who must be protected and looked after" would illustrate the benevolent sexism approach, containing as they do an assumption that women are too weak to look after themselves, and are therefore inferior.

The distinction put forward by Glicke and Fiske is known as **ambivalent sexism**, and it shows how social discrimination doesn't have to involve active dislike or hostility. It can be disguised in positive forms, appearing to be supportive and friendly, while still being associated with discriminatory actions and beliefs, and attributions of inferiority. These attitudes may be held by members of the inferior group as well as by those in the dominant one. And, importantly, the individuals holding these attitudes will not be experiencing negative emotions or personal dislike – until they encounter those who refuse to conform to the expected behaviour of their gender and challenge the idea of female dependency. And at that point, prejudice may come from either group. Sibley et al (2007) found that women who scored highly on benevolent sexism were much more likely to support female behaviour which reinforced the idealised role of women (cosmetics, fashion, etc.), and they would judge women who challenged those roles particularly harshly.

Cuddy et al (2008) demonstrated how this mixture of positive and negative elements in social discrimination can apply with other groups as well. Prejudiced attitudes towards Jews, they found, included some elements of admiration, for example for their intellectual abilities, while also including negative elements, such as regarding them as emotionally cold. In the same study, the researchers found that attitudes towards elderly people combined negative evaluations such as their being intellectually incompetent, with positive emotional warmth. This combination of positive and negative attitudes towards "inferior" social groups appears to be much more typical of real-world social discrimination than the extreme attitudes identified by Sherif.

Social neuroscience and prejudice

During recent years, the advent of brain-scanning techniques has allowed researchers to discover far more about how the brain works than was previously possible. Studies have shown how the functional neuroanatomy of the brain allows it to deal with many psychological processes, including learning, attention, cognitive control and action monitoring (Gazzaniga, 2004). Other aspects of how the brain works become manifest in neural pathways, and the connection and activation of sets of nuclei in the brain. In some places, for example the amygdala, researchers have discovered that early ideas (in this case, that the amygdala controlled fear reactions) were too simplistic. Scanning studies showed that it also becomes activated in response to positive stimuli, and in situations where the person is anticipating either reward or punishment (Paton et al, 2006). Our ability to monitor the working brain, as opposed to simply researching through lesions, shows us that this part of the brain is involved in vigilance, arousal and learning, as well as being active in the control of fear responses.

What does this have to do with social psychology? A number of findings have shown how social processes are reflected in brain activity. Some brain cells, for example, have been shown to respond to social signals, such as smiling, and we have mirror neurones in the brain which activate similar responses in ourselves when we receive positive social signals like this from other people. Some research shows that the amygdala also becomes activated in response to

Key Terms

ambivalent sexism
A form of sexism in which the attitudes expressed may be either positive or negative.

stimuli showing people of different races, which has been taken as implying that there is an implicit race bias, even among those who have positive social attitudes towards other racial groups. But the early idea that this implicit race bias derives from fear is now being rethought (Amodio and Devine, 2006), because it might equally well result from an association with reward or other positive outcome.

In other words, we can't tell exactly what is happening in social terms from the activation of brain cells. But we can identify that the brain responds to certain significant social stimuli. Among American subjects, race is certainly one of these, although it is less certain that this finding holds in societies or subcultures where skin colour is a less significant social construct.

Box 7.2   Brain activity and experience

It would be unwise to jump to the conclusion that because a social phenomenon is known to activate parts of the brain, that these are hard-wired. We know from studies of the angular gyrus that nuclei in the brain develop as a result of receiving the appropriate kind of stimulation through life. The angular gyrus is a part of the brain known to be associated with reading. It grows and develops as reading skills are acquired. But reading skills are not inherited. For most of human history, humans didn't read, and even when reading became established it was restricted to a minority of the population for centuries. What we did inherit is a group of neurones – a set of nuclei in the brain – with a propensity to respond to basic symbols (e.g. red for danger), which develop and become more sophisticated as the child learns to read. Other evidence for this process comes in the studies of London taxi-drivers, who show increasing development of those areas of the hippocampus to do with mapping and memory as they learn about London (Woollett and Maguire, 2011).

So there is a constant interaction between the brain and our personal and social experience. Showing that the brain responds to people of different ethnic origin, and that these are entirely unconscious processes does not automatically indicate an implicit racial hostility – although the use of the term "implicit race bias" has sometimes been taken in that way. What the "implicit race bias" finding indicates is that the people being studied pay attention to such differences, but that is a world away from indicating, as some researchers imply, that prejudice is an instinctive or automatic human reaction.

Amodio (2008) showed that there is relatively little connection between this "implicit race bias" and how people behave, and suggested that this may be because there is more than one social process involved. How people act is mediated by a number of other factors, including past experiences and culture, rather than just being about the activation of racial categorisation in the brain in non-prejudiced individuals. By separating implicit stereotyping from implicit evaluative bias – that is, feelings of anxiety or threat – using an experimental procedure which asked participants to judge whether same-race pairs of faces would be more likely to be, for example, a friend or a successful athlete, they showed that implicit evaluative bias was linked with amygdala activation, while implicit stereotyping was not. They also found that implicit evaluations were more likely to be involved in interpersonal interaction, while implicit stereotypes tended to be more involved with decisions about out-group members which didn't involve personal contact. In other words, distinguishing between one group and another wasn't automatically negative or racist; in non-prejudiced individuals, it sometimes appeared to be simply about cognitive categorisation.

In view of all this, Dixon et al (2012) challenged the idea that prejudice is all about whether we like or dislike a person or group. They argued that seeing prejudice as the result of a negative evaluation of other people, made on the basis of their group membership, gives us a very limited view of the whole area of prejudice and social discrimination. As a result, attempts to reduce prejudice simply by getting people to like one another more are not likely to result in significant social change. It may even, they argue, strengthen social discrimination by disguising the very real inequalities between two social groups.

The collective action model

There is another approach to challenging prejudice, which focusses on the outcome of **collective action** rather than **prejudice reduction**. Dixon and Levine (2012) argued that a collective action model of social change is not only more effective, but also in many ways contradicts the conventional individualistic models of prejudice and prejudice reduction. Real world experience, such in Rwanda or the Balkans, shows that extreme social prejudice can arise between neighbours who have been friends for years, as a result of the political manipulation of social representations; and individualistic models of prejudice have no explanations for this. Ironically, Dixon and Levine argue, attempts to reduce prejudice on an individual level may actually have the effect of perpetuating social inequalities, by masking their effects and presenting the problem as one of individual personalities or emotions, rather than of inequalities in social structures.

Table 7.4 illustrates the difference between these two approaches. In the collective action approach, what is important is the way that the disadvantaged group challenges the ideology being perpetuated by the dominant group, and takes action to establish or achieve its equality. The reduction of prejudice and social discrimination occurs as a result of the direct social and political efforts of the disadvantaged group, rather than as a result of attempts to tackle discriminatory attitudes held by the dominant group members.

Key Terms

collective action
Action which is take by a large number of people together towards a common goal.

prejudice reduction
Approaches to challenging prejudice which aim to reduce or eliminate prejudice from the individual.

Table 7.4 Two models of social change

	Prejudice reduction model	Collective action model
Main change agents	Members of historically advantaged groups	Members of disadvantaged groups
Typical interventions	Intergroup contact, re-education, cooperative interdependence	Consciousness-raising, empowerment, building coalitions
Psychological processes	Re-education in stereotype, more positive affect, reduction in salience or importance of group identity	Perceptions of injustice, collective anger, collective efficacy, increased salience of group identity
Outcomes	Fewer individual acts of discrimination, reduction of intergroup conflict	Collective action to change the status quo

Source: Dixon et al (2012)

This approach can be seen in the history of feminism in the UK, ranging from the early consciousness-raising of female intellectuals such as Mary Wollstonecraft's *Vindication of the Rights of Women* (1792), through the political achievements of the suffragette movement in the early 20th century and the consciousness-raising groups of the feminist movement of the 1970s to the challenges to discriminatory working practices and the "glass ceiling" of today. It can also be seen in the challenges to the ideologies of colonial exploitation (Fanon, 1965, 1966), apartheid (Biko, 1978), and in the many subsequent campaigns which involve members of disadvantaged communities as agents of change, rather than simply recipients of it. Howarth et al (2012) discussed how this approach is fundamental to challenging social prejudice, and quite different from attempts to reduce prejudice on a personal level, which are simply concerned with "smoothing daily social encounters" (Howarth et al, 2012, p27), rather than with challenging the social structures which perpetuate prejudice.

This approach to understanding prejudice focuses on prejudice as social discrimination, and rejects the idea that prejudice can meaningfully be understood on an individual level. While it is clear that challenging social discrimination does require a different approach, we do need to be clear what we are talking about when we use the term prejudice, because individual differences in negative attitudes towards out-groups do also exist, and require challenging. To equate prejudice simply with social discrimination is to over-simplify just as much as it is to equate prejudice with "not-liking". Both areas are valid, and as with so many aspects of human psychology, we need to understand the problem using several levels of analysis, rather than just one.

CHALLENGING PREJUDICE

Understanding prejudice is all very well, but what is important is that our understanding should help us to change it. In 1978, Cook summarised the findings of earlier researchers into the area, and identified five conditions which could produce a reduction in prejudice in even severely prejudiced individuals. These five conditions are summarised in Table 7.5.

Table 7.5 Conditions for changing prejudice

1. The participants need to have equal status.
2. There must be the potential for personal acquaintance.
3. There needs to be contact with non-stereotypical individuals.
4. There must be social support for contact between groups.
5. There should be some occasion for cooperative effort.

Source: Cook (1978)

The first of these principles, that of equal status, has been the basis for a considerable amount of social effort in challenging prejudice. The establishment of equality in law, now largely achieved in the Western nations at least, was a significant part of that, but not all of it. It was also necessary for members of the minority group to be openly treated as equal, in such a way that other members of society could see it. The encouragement of role models in TV and the professions meant that young people could grow up with ambition, and an awareness that the negative stereotypes of their group were not universally accepted.

We can see the success of this policy in the fact that it became possible for a black man to become president of the United States – something which the early campaigners hardly dared imagine! It didn't mean that all racial prejudice has disappeared from the US, of course, but it did mean that the society as a whole had become visibly less prejudiced, and that members of other ethnic groups were recognised as having equal status with white people. Open racism is no longer as tolerated, and as a result covert racism has also become less influential, even in the US.

These principles are also apparent when we look at how campaigns against sexism and prejudice against those with disability have operated in modern societies. As a general rule, they have begun with a period of consciousness-raising: the Gay Pride and Women's Lib campaigns which began in the 1970s in America, Britain and Europe aimed to raise people's awareness of the issues, and to establish the importance of challenging these forms of prejudice. More recent campaigns to raise awareness of the need to provide for and accept people with disability as full members of society have also served the same purpose.

Social awareness of the issue also helps to generate opportunities for role models to emerge, ensuring that members of the out-group can become perceived as individuals rather than as simply stereotypes. The increasing visibility of people with disability in the media provides role models for others overcoming similar problems. And events such as the Paralympics have now achieved international recognition, such that countries which don't participate are now more under scrutiny than those who do. Other competitions, such as the Invictus Games or the full participation of disabled athletes in the Commonwealth Games each contribute to breaking down the stereotypical barriers and establishing a culture in which prejudice becomes diminished.

As we have seen, though, prejudice occurs on more than one level, and while changing the culture contributes, challenging individual prejudice may also require some level of individual intervention. It has been shown to be important that people have contact with members of other groups, and so become able to regard them as individuals, but it has also been shown that contact in itself is not enough. It may contribute, but if prejudice is to be seriously reduced, there need to be opportunities for co-operative effort which brings the groups together with a common goal. In Britain, one positive example of this was the street parties which were organised to celebrate the Queens Jubilee and other important social events. By bringing diverse members of the community together, they produced a demonstrable increase in community spirit with a concomitant decrease in racism at the neighbourhood level (Stevenson and Abell, 2011).

Tackling other forms of social prejudice can be more difficult. While the "official" battles against sexism in law, for example, may have been won, the existence of sexist attitudes at an interpersonal level is still a problem for many. And many of the approaches which have been successful in challenging ethnic prejudice simply don't have any effect on sexism – for example, it is not uncommon for men and women to work together on joint projects, but this in itself doesn't challenge sexism.

Major et al (2002) showed how recipients of sexist behaviour adopt a number of cognitive coping strategies to deal with it; but these too do not really address the problem of this type of prejudice in the first place. Some of the most effective challenges appear to be from confrontation at a personal level. But Becker et al (2014) discussed how confrontational approaches remain interpersonally difficult for many people. They argued that organisations should introduce explicit interventions to challenge sexism in the workplace. In this way, any confrontation would be sanctioned through the intervention, rather than being risked by the individual. As we saw earlier, Dixon et al (2012) argued that addressing prejudice from an individualistic point of view is not only insufficient, but may also be counter-productive.

Challenging prejudice, then, can be achieved, but is not without its difficulties. And while it remains all too easy for political groups or leaders to stir up ethnic or other conflicts by manipulating social identity processes, reconciliation between the groups concerned is a more complex process. Biro and Milin discussed how individual factors such as having personal friends or positive experiences with members of the opposing group was a significant factor in encouraging readiness for reconciliation after the traumatic conflicts occurring as a result of the break-up of the former Yugoslavia, but it was not sufficient in itself. Again, we find that such issues need to be addressed on more than one level of analysis. Another significant factor, for example, was a belief in the validity of war crime trials and a willingness to accept that there had been crimes on both sides.

So while there is little room for complacency, insights from social psychologists as well as other social campaigners may also contribute to reducing prejudice in the real world. And the breadth of information, as well as opinions, available to people through the internet and social media make it much less easy for any one single group to dominate social thinking within a society than it was in the days when virtually all the mass media could be controlled by the state, as it was in Nazi Germany.

Talking point 7.3   Challenging prejudice

One consistent finding about social prejudice is that, left to itself and unchallenged, it will tend to grow. This is partly because those who are prejudiced tend to assume that other people share their views; and our natural inclination to avoid confrontation means that unless people are determined to make a stand, they assume that silence means assent. So extremely prejudiced individuals begin to feel able to express their views openly, and may exert far more influence than they would have if those who disagreed with them said so openly.

But there are many different ways of challenging prejudice, and the internet offers a range of possibilities which were not available to earlier generations.

To explore this, identify three different examples of prejudice which you have come across in your real world experience, and for each one, find a strategy using social media or some other aspect of the digital world, which you believe could challenge it effectively.

AGGRESSION

We all understand intuitively what we mean by aggression, but attempts to pin it down have shown that there is often quite a wide difference between what different people understand as aggression. Would you, for instance, regard becoming involved in an intense sporting competition as aggressive? Or standing up assertively against someone's ideas in a group of friends or a committee? Or wilfully damaging someone's property? These are all instances of behaviour which some people would define as aggressive while others would not.

Some social constructionist approaches to aggression propose that much of what we call aggression is actually in the mind of the beholder, in that the same behaviour could be construed quite differently by someone with a different view of the situation. The cultural background, personal constructs, and social representations of the people concerned all affect how the behaviour is perceived, and whether it is seen as aggressive or not.

In one study, for example, Reicher (1984) compared various accounts from people witnessing or participating in the St Paul's riots in Bristol in 1981. He showed how the various social identifications of the people interviewed had a direct effect on how they interpreted what had been happening. While the rioters' actions were portrayed unequivocally by the media as aggressive, those concerned saw them very differently, and often not as aggressive at all, but as making a justified social point.

Hewstone (1989) showed how almost any type of behaviour can be construed either as aggressive, or as its opposite, depending on the social construction which people place on the event. Something described by some as an aggressive attack by "terrorists" may equally be described as justifiable action from "freedom fighters". A fight in a pub might be seen as mindless aggression or a justified response to insult. How people see such behaviour will depend on their own social experience and views. Potter and Reicher (1987) showed how evaluating behaviour as aggressive or anti-social is a social construction deriving from the person's own ideas about social categories, and their personal attributions.

We can see, then, that defining aggression is not easy, and nor is establishing the boundaries between neighbouring concepts such as competition or assertiveness. Carlson et al (1989) argued that intentionality is the real key to aggression, and produced possibly the most useful way of defining it in terms of research: they define aggression as "the intent to harm". Other psychologists have used more explicit definitions, focussing on the social (or rather, anti-social) nature of aggression. Probably the best example of this is the definition adopted by Krahé, who defined aggression as: "A social problem in interactions between individuals and between groups, resulting from the joint influence of the personal characteristics of the actors and the situational and societal conditions in which the behaviour takes place" (Krahé, 2013, Introduction).

It is clear that there are many different ways in which aggression can manifest itself, but not so clear whether these are actually different types of aggression or not. Archer and Coyne (2005) investigated **indirect social aggression**, such as malicious gossip, spreading rumours or manipulating social exclusion – the types of aggression commonly found in school or workplace bullying, and particularly by girls. These forms of aggression have been described as indirect aggression, **relational aggression** and social aggression, and have generally been regarded as distinct from direct aggression. Archer and Coyne, however, concluded that they were essentially the same, in that their main aim is to socially exclude or harm the social standing of a victim. Indirect aggression, the researchers found, is used as an alternative to direct aggression mainly in situations where direct aggression is proscribed or would cause negative effects for the instigator.

 ## Studying aggression

The specific definition adopted by any individual psychologist, however, is probably less important than how they operationalise what they are looking at. In recent years, there has been an increasing number of investigations into

real-world aggression, like the study by Archer and Coyne quoted above. But before that, social psychology – or rather, psychology in general – went through a period where only laboratory evidence was regarded as properly "scientific".

Since it is also unethical to engage in real aggression in the laboratory, researchers often had to fall back on operational definitions of aggression, which often seem a bit unrealistic to modern eyes. Hogg and Vaughan (2011) listed five different examples of "operationalised" aggression used in psychological studies, as given in Table 7.6. The list makes it clear that in many cases, what was taken as an example of aggression for the purposes of research is very different from what we might regard as aggression in everyday life.

Table 7.6 Examples of operationalised aggression

Punching an inflated plastic doll (e.g., Bandura et al, 1963).

Pushing a button supposed to deliver an electric shock to someone else (e.g., Buss, 1966).

Pencil and paper ratings by teachers and classmates of a child's level of aggression (e.g., Eron et al, 1972).

Written self-report by institutionalised teenage boys about their prior aggressive behaviour (e.g., Leyens et al, 1975).

Verbal expression of willingness to use violence in an experimental laboratory setting (e.g., Geen, 1978).

Source: Hogg and Vaughan (2011)

THEORIES OF AGGRESSION

There have been a number of theories attempting to explain the origins of aggression. Some of these are biological in nature, some look to social sources for the origins of aggressive behaviour, and some approaches attempt to integrate both biological and social factors.

Biological theories of aggression

Aggression has sometimes been described as a **biological imperative** – something which is in all of our natures, and stems from our evolutionary origins. The most significant perpetrator of this theory was the ethologist Lorenz (1950), who argued that animals will fight to defend their territory or other natural resources, and that for the most part, that fighting was ritualised, consisting of aggressive displays of natural weaponry and appeasement gestures. The power of the appeasement gestures was such that aggressive conflicts rarely resulted in actual physical harm. In humans, however, lacking natural weaponry such as horns or tusks also meant that we lacked the relevant appeasement gestures, so aggression was easily able to get out of hand and result in real physical harm or even death.

Lorenz (1966) saw aggression as a kind of internal energy which builds up within the individual and has to be released. If it is not released safely, in ritualised aggression such as sport, then, Lorenz argued, it will spill out in anti-social aggression. This is the idea of **catharsis** – the idea that negative emotions such as anger or aggression can be safely dissipated by healthy exercise and competition. This concept has been popular through the centuries – it was proposed

| Key Terms

biological imperative
A behaviour which occurs as a result of inherited biological demands, and is therefore unavoidable.

catharsis
The "draining off" of negative emotions or energies through other activities (e.g., sport).

by Plato, and shared by Freud and many others. But unfortunately, it isn't supported by the evidence. Studies investigating the reality of catharsis have repeatedly shown that allowing people the opportunity to divert aggression into other areas can actually make them more aggressive rather than less (e.g., Buss, 1966; Loew, 1967).

Lorenz's views were very popular in the middle of the 20th century, and his approach became the basis for several other theories put forward to explain human behaviour. They were also, not coincidentally, the foundation for the approach to games, competition and aggression adopted by the Nazi party in Germany in the 1930s, and Lorenz himself was a known Nazi sympathiser. But quite apart from that, his ideas were also methodologically weak, and as researchers gained a better understanding of both human and animal behaviour, they became less influential.

Another "biological" explanation for aggression was proposed by Sigmund Freud, the father of psychoanalysis, who believed that the different aspects of the unconscious mind in his theory (id, ego and superego) had a clear biological base, which would eventually be discovered. He also believed that all human activity was energised by two life-forces: **libido** and **thanatos**, an idea that was even more popular in its day than Lorenz's model.

Libido, according to Freud, was the life-force, creative and sexual in nature, while thanatos was the dark energy, responsible for aggression and other aspects of the darker side of human nature. The apparent contradictions of human nature – how we can be affectionate and caring to some yet vicious and cruel to others – were produced, in Freud's theory, by the conflicts between these two energies. Freud's idea of the two energies in human beings influenced a great deal of creative and imaginative writing. We can recognise them, for example, in the idea of the "Dark Side" and the "Force" portrayed in the science fiction *Star Wars* epics. But fiction aside, finding any biological or neurological basis for these ideas looks increasingly unlikely.

Trait aggression

More orthodox forms of biological explanation suggested that aggression may be a **genetic trait**. Jacobs et al (1965) found a higher percentage of men with an extra Y chromosome among the prison population than among ordinary people, and suggested that this might make them more aggressive and therefore more likely to commit crimes. The theory received widespread publicity, but in a major study by Witkin et al (1976), over four and a half thousand men were tested, and the researchers found no evidence at all that XYY individuals were more aggressive than others. The same was found by a number of other studies.

There is some evidence, though, that some aspects of aggression can be identified as a measurable trait, although whether that trait is inherited or the result of social learning or other experiences in childhood is very much open to question. Nonetheless, it does seem to be the case that some people are consistently more inclined to react aggressively in particular situations than others. Krahé and Fenske (2002) investigated factors contributing to "road rage", and found that **trait aggression**, while not the only factor, was a distinct contributor to whether someone was likely to act aggressively towards another driver or not.

Research indicates that psychological traits tend to combine with specific social situations to produce aggressive behaviour. For example, Twenge and

Campbell (2003) investigated whether some people react more strongly to social exclusion than others, and found a strong influence from the trait of narcissism. In a set of four studies, they found that **narcissists** are more likely to feel anger towards others rather than to experience internal emotions such as shame or depression after social rejection. They also, the researchers found, are more likely to act aggressively towards an innocent third party.

This interaction between personality and social factors is typical of human emotional behaviour. There is rarely one single cause for how we act. Our behaviour has multiple causes which come together to produce a specific response to what is going on. Someone may tolerate, if not particularly like, other family members leaving the top off the tube of toothpaste for many months, and then finally explode and shout about it. What triggered the explosion may be the cumulative history, but also their physiological state on the day, how social relationships have been in the family in general, stress at work and a myriad other contributing factors. Human behaviour is always multi-layered and rarely simple.

Social learning

But that doesn't mean that it is pointless to try to tease out the various factors involved. In 1977, Bandura suggested that people act aggressively because they have learned from other people both how to act aggressively, and also that sometimes, aggression may be an appropriate or acceptable way of reacting. While the study which Bandura, Ross and Ross (1963) used to illustrate this observation was distinctly naïve, involving adults modelling aggressive behaviour towards an inflatable punch-doll (a "Bobo doll") and observations of whether children imitated the behaviour, the finding itself has been reasonably consistent over time.

It is this, and similar findings, which lie at the root of the concern about the extremely violent picture of society which is generally portrayed through the television screen and many video games. While some researchers have failed

Key Terms

narcissists
People who are significantly absorbed in their own selves and the image they project.

to find significant differences when exploring the behaviour of those with prolonged exposure to violent programmes, others have become convinced that it makes a great deal of difference. Anderson (2004) conducted a meta-analysis of studies exploring the effects of playing violent video games, and found that exposure to violent video games is significantly and causally linked to increases in aggressive behaviour and cognition in the real world. It also increases aggressive feelings, and decreases the likelihood of helping behaviour. We will come back to this discussion later in this chapter.

Social identification

In several places in this book we have seen how social identity theory explores our tendency to see the social world in terms of "them and us" groupings. This powerful human trend has been used (and abused) by politicians all over the world, and resulted in some of the worst human atrocities. As a result of systematic propaganda against the "out-group", even friends and neighbours can turn on one another, resulting in violence, murder and even genocide. The examples of Rwanda, Serbia and of course Germany in the mid-20th century show how powerful this type of social pressure can become, with even ordinary people becoming killers or participating in violent attacks towards members of the "out-group". Sadly, there are many more examples as well.

Social identification has to be included as a factor in human aggression. But what is it that stimulates this aggression? In the early days of research into social identification, some researchers argued that aggression was a straightforward result of the processes of social comparison and identification. So aggression, in the form of intergroup conflict was pretty well inevitable if groups were differentiated (Billig and Tajfel, 1973). This view resulted from a set of studies which used the minimal group paradigm – a method which explored what happened when belonging to a group was the only factor in social decision-making which we looked at earlier in this chapter.

Fortunately, however, subsequent research challenged these conclusions. Researchers found that even in minimal group studies, personality differences affected how people respond. Platow et al (1990) demonstrated that research participants who are cooperative and prosocial tend to prefer fair distributions of resources and unbiased group evaluations, while competitive participants generally showed a bias towards their particular in-group.

Mummendey and Schreiber (1983) suggested that the in-group bias shown in minimal group studies was actually a methodological problem, to do with how they were carried out. The early studies had all used forced-choice tasks: if one group received more, then others would receive less. This suggested to the research participants (who, like all human beings taking part in psychological experiments, were trying to work out how the researcher wanted them to behave) that they were expected to favour their own group. When they were able to make entirely separate assessments of the other groups, so that they could be judged as "equally good", in-group bias virtually disappeared.

This is quite an important finding. It shows us, for instance, that making people compete for limited resources is likely to produce intergroup hostility – a message for office managers everywhere. It shows us why highly prejudiced groups always make it appear that the disliked group is in direct competition ("taking our jobs", etc.), even when it is obvious that nothing of the kind is really happening. And it shows us why knowing more about the other group helps to reduce prejudice; we become aware of more dimensions for evaluating that group, and are less likely to see the group in simplistic, competitive terms.

Researchers also found that it is possible for a clear group identity to generate social harmony rather than social conflict. What seems to be important in this, though, is that the groups concerned are clear and distinct. Rabbie and Horwitz (1988) showed that as long as it is apparent who belongs to which group, even groups which are very similar and have comparable social roles can get along perfectly well. Although early studies implied that intergroup aggression was inevitable, we saw in Chapter 1 that it is not inevitable – it is only the case if there is perceived competition for resources.

It appears, then, that there are many factors which can reduce intergroup aggression significantly. Intergroup conflict has often been manipulated by politicians and the mass media, sometimes resulting in horrific outcomes. But it is not an inevitable part of our human nature. It is human to see the world as consisting of "them" and "us"; but that doesn't mean that we automatically see "them" as enemies.

Environmental factors

Some research has focused on how the environment, and particularly environmental stressors, can affect people. There is a clear correlation, for example, between hot weather and inner-city riots, in that riots don't tend to happen when the weather is cold. For some (e.g., Baron and Bell, 1975) this suggested that the heat itself triggered aggressive behaviour as feelings of discomfort spilled into anger against the establishment. Other researchers however, have explored the political and social dimensions of such riots, and as Reicher (1984) showed, the social representations of those involved inevitably include some sense of perceived social injustice.

Some psychologists regard reductionist explanations as political, being used by the media to distract attention away from the underlying social issues and present an image of the rioters as mindlessly aggressive vandals. An alternative explanation for the correlation with hot weather may simply be that people in inner-city areas are more likely to be out on the streets at such times, so rumours spread more quickly and perceived injustices are more rapidly shared. The many occasions of prolonged hot weather without a riot shows that the correlation is not inevitable.

The environment may still have an influence, though. It has been shown that working in a noisy environment is more likely to mean that people are more irritable and likely to react aggressively towards others than if they were working in a quiet place (e.g., Donnerstein and Wilson, 1979). This research also shows that the irritation and aggression is significantly less if people feel that they have some control over how much noise they are experiencing. A road digger outside the window might be extremely annoying, but the equally loud noise produced by your own drill while you are doing some DIY at home is much less so.

Crowding, too, may increase irritability. Aiello et al (1979) showed that if people are crowded together in a confined space, they are more likely to be competitive and aggressive. Zillman (1979) suggested that this happens because of the increased physiological arousal generated by these situations, which makes people more responsive to irritating events. But how much these situations annoy us is also dependent on the social construction we put on them. Crowds generated at music events or festivals rarely show this type of aggression, and nor does the intensive crowding experienced by many commuters.

The frustration–aggression hypothesis

One early but long-lasting theory of aggression is the idea that aggression is often a reaction to being frustrated in our attempts to achieve personal goals – either short-term explicit goals like being able to get home in the face of serious delays; or longer-term implicit ones such as the desire to get on with our lives without interference from others. The idea was first put forwards by Dollard et al in 1939. They suggested that people are fundamentally non-aggressive, but their motivational energies are displaced by frustration, and that energy then diverts into aggression. The displacement explanation was fairly thoroughly discredited; but the observation that frustration can frequently produce aggression has been robust, and has often been used in the psychological laboratory as a way of producing measurable aggressive reactions.

The criticisms of the original formulation of the theory centred around three arguments: that people sometimes respond to frustration in other ways, not inevitably by becoming more aggressive (Bandura, 1977); that the outcome of extreme frustration can often be passivity and helplessness rather than aggression (Seligman, 1975); and that a lot of aggressive behaviour has nothing to do with frustration, such as the aggression shown by a professional boxer or a street gangster (Berkowitz, 1978).

The observation that frustration can lead to aggression is reasonably sound, however, even if it is not acceptable as the explanation of all forms of aggressive behaviour. One case in which it is particularly relevant is when we look at driving aggression, or in its extreme form, "road rage". Driving aggression is generally taken as actions which indicate aggression towards others, like sounding the horn impatiently, or pushing into small gaps in traffic regardless of other drivers who might have a better "claim" to the opportunity (Ellison-Potter et al, 2001).

In the case of road rage, a relatively minor driving event can generate anger in the individual to the point where they may even abandon their original purpose and pursue the "offending" individual, offering verbal and sometimes physical abuse. Frustration in driving situations is the triggering event and in the case of ordinary driving aggression, it has often been taken as a sufficient explanation (given a culture in which these expressions of aggression are considered acceptable). Road rage, however, is more extreme, and although frustration may be a triggering factor, those who engage in actual road rage are almost always experiencing a high level of tension or stress quite apart from their driving experiences. Some researchers have gone so far as to argue that it should be seen as a psychological disorder (e.g., Ayar, 2006).

What is clear from all of these explanations for aggression is that no single explanation is sufficient to account for all human behaviour. Many of the ideas proposed make some contribution to our understanding, but as ever, we find that human behaviour is multi-layered and complex. We need to be able to look at it from several different levels if we are to understand what is going on.

AGGRESSION IN EVERYDAY LIFE

Krahé (2013) identified a number of different areas of aggression which people may encounter in the course of their lives. Some of these concern direct aggression between individuals, such as aggression in the family, such as child or partner abuse, elder abuse, sexual aggression and bullying. We can refer to these as interpersonal aggression. Other forms of aggression are more widely-based, such as media aggression which we have already explored, intergroup aggression and terrorism.

Family aggression

Aggression which happens within the family context is still social in nature, but it is different from most of the other forms of aggression which psychologists have studied, partly because it is largely invisible to the outside world, and partly because it concerns close and personal relationships. The three most common forms of family aggression are child abuse of one form or another, domestic violence between partners, and elder abuse.

The World Health Organisation (2006) identified four major types of child abuse: physical abuse, sexual abuse, psychological abuse and **neglect**. Physical abuse can take many forms: what is important, according to the WHO, is that it results in, or is likely to result in, harm to the child's health, survival, development or dignity. The definition of sexual abuse is wider, including acts which violate the laws or taboos of society as well as those to which the child is unable to give informed consent. Psychological abuse includes acts or general behaviours which have a high probability of damaging the child's mental, spiritual, moral or social development. Neglect involves failing to provide for the development or well-being of the child in terms of its health, education, emotional development, nutrition and the provision of shelter or safe living conditions.

There is considerable psychological evidence for the long-term consequences of these forms of abuse. It includes evidence for the idea that experience of prolonged physical abuse can result in more aggressive interactions in adult life; that early sexual abuse has serious consequences for later attachments and trust as well as for general emotional well-being; that psychological abuse can result in disruptive behaviour in other contexts for the children as well as difficulties in making and retaining friendships; and that neglect may result in both physical and cognitive underdevelopment, as well as producing social difficulties with everyday interactions.

Domestic violence may be invisible, but the evidence implies that it is far more common than is generally recognised. The British Crime Survey for 2010/2011, for example, found that 16.1 per cent of women and 6.9 per cent of men had experienced physical aggression within an intimate partnership at some point since the age of 16. Kelly and Johnson (2008) distinguished between three types of intimate partner violence: **coercive controlling violence**, which involves emotionally abusive intimidation as well as physical violence; **violent resistance** which occurs in response to a coercive controlling partner; and what they described as **situational couple violence**, arising from domestic conflicts.

Partner violence has been shown to produce physical, emotional and social consequences, resulting in trauma, long-term psychological distress which may only be ameliorated by empowerment, often produced by leaving the

Key Terms

neglect
A form of child abuse which involves failing to supply the child's physical and social needs.

coercive controlling violence
Violence which combines emotional with physical abuse.

violent resistance
Domestic violence which happens as one person resists the controlling coercion of the other.

situational couple violence
Violent interactions in domestic disputes resulting from stressful circumstances.

relationship altogether; and low self-esteem resulting in impaired social interaction and confidence.

In recent years, there has been a growing recognition of **elder abuse** – aggression directed towards older members of the family who have become dependent on younger family members. This may be any of the four types of abuse experience by children: physical abuse, sexual abuse, psychological or emotional abuse and neglect; but a fifth type, financial abuse, has also been identified as younger people exploit the helplessness of older relatives.

While enough incidents of elder abuse have been identified for it to be recognised as a growing problem in society, it is particularly difficult to investigate because it occurs in private contexts, and also because those being abused often collude in keeping it hidden from other people – through shame or embarrassment, or even through guilt at having brought up family members capable of acting in this way. The psychological consequences are social as well as emotional, often resulting in increased withdrawal and sometimes expressions of anger, as well as feelings of helplessness and impaired social and physical coping with everyday life situations.

Sexual aggression

Sexual aggression is another common form of interpersonal aggression, which, like much partner violence, is generally recognised to centre around issues of power and control. There are wide individual differences in the ways that people interact sexually, and for the most part, sexual encounters are consensual and affectionate in nature. Sexual aggression, however, is a very different type of interaction, and has little to do with sex as an expression of love or affection. While sexual aggression from women is not unknown, by far the majority of these instances originate from men. Hall and Hirschman (1991) identified four characteristics of sexually aggressive men, which distinguished them from men who were more normal in respect to their sexual behaviour. These characteristics are listed in Table 7.7.

Table 7.7 Characteristics of sexually aggressive men

Physiological response: A higher than normal level of physiological response to sexual stimuli.

Perceptions: A tendency to perceive and process stimuli as sexual in nature and as potentially leading to sexual aggression (e.g., regarding a form of dress as "provocative").

Control: A significantly lower ability to control their emotional reactions.

Socialisation and personality: Having been socialised in or participating in a subculture which "normalises" sexually aggressive behaviour.

Source: Hall and Hirschman (1991)

What actually constitutes sexual aggression is difficult to define, since acts which may be perceived by some individuals as "affectionate" may be seen by others as intrusive and aggressive. Rape – that is, non-consensual sex – is clearly an aggressive act, as are any other instances of non-consensual physical intimacy. But it is a moot point where the line is drawn between inappropriate or aggressive touching and an act which is intended as a physical expression of friendliness. Some forms of touch can be used as expressions of power or

Key Terms

elder abuse
Abuse directed at old people.

control, for example. Research into sexual aggression has tended to emphasise the more extreme forms of sexual aggression such as rape or sexual assault; but some social debates (usually with political overtones) have focused around much more ambiguous actions.

Pornography has been closely linked with issues around sexual aggression. A number of experimental studies have shown that people exposed to violent pornography and then asked to evaluate a rape scenario rated the impact on the victim as significantly less severe. The participants also expressed more permissive attitudes about sexual violence than those who had not previously been exposed to the pornographic material (Mullin and Linz, 1995).

This appears to be quite a consistent finding. Hald et al (2010) conducted a meta-analysis of nine studies, and found a strong effect size indicating that the use of pornography depicting violence links strongly with attitudes condoning violence against women. Reviewing the evidence around pornography, Krahé identified five general conclusions which can be drawn from studies of the effects of pornography, which are summarised in Table 7.8.

Table 7.8 Effects of pornography

1. Pornography containing depictions of violence against women which appear to be enjoyed by the targets is widely used from adolescence onwards.

2. There is evidence for links between explicit depictions of sexual acts and aggression, but no evidence of such an effect for nudity.

3. Pornographic material which contains depictions of violence is more likely to elicit aggressive behaviour than non-violent pornography.

4. Research with sex offenders shows a stronger association between pornography and aggression in those with other risk factors of aggression.

5. Many studies have shown that pornography can increase rape-supportive attitudes, which also link with increased sexual aggression.

Source: Krahé (2013)

During recent years, too, society has become sensitised to other, non-criminal, forms of sexual aggression, such as verbal behaviour which aims to belittle or humiliate a person sexually. These types of sexual aggression are generally perceived as a form of bullying, akin to the other types of bullying which occur in everyday life in the school or workplace, and which we will be looking at more closely in the next section. Bullying is all about power rela-tionships, with the intention being to intimidate the other person physically, verbally or socially, in order to promote or maintain the perpetrator's sense of power and ego. Sexual bullying is no different, and has its main impact from both from the perceived powerlessness of women in contrast to men in some sub-cultures; and in the way that it can open to ridicule deeply personal feelings and anxieties. Similar activities directed towards highly confident or "hardened" individuals have much less power to intimidate: bullies are known to prey on the vulnerable, and sexual bullying is no exception.

The consequences of sexual aggression can be profound. People who expe-rience rape or serious sexual assault frequently experience post-traumatic stress disorder (PTSD), a collection of outcomes including anxiety attacks and disturbed sleep which can last for years. Some people can even become

suicidal. Culbertson and Dehle (2001) showed that the most extreme consequences appear to be when the perpetrator is known and close to the victim.
Those experiencing sexual aggression also often blame themselves, which in
turn increases their distress and coping problems (Littleton et al, 2007).

One problem which victims of sexual aggression may experience, which
is different from other forms of aggression, is the way that sometimes social
reactions can attribute blame to them, rather than to the perpetrators of the
aggression – because of their clothing, attitude or even their presence in a dangerous area at the time. Although victim-blaming is being challenged in society
as a whole, people may still experience it from members of their immediate
social network. Temkin and Krahé (2008) reviewed a number of studies of this
phenomenon, and showed how it can result in what more or less amounts to a
second experience of victimisation.

Bullying

Perhaps the most common form of aggression which we encounter in our
everyday lives is bullying. Bullying is an abuse of power and control directed
towards particular individuals in various ways. It may be verbal or physical,
or even take the form of the use of power, status and non-verbal actions in a
way which forces one particular line of action upon people who would prefer
to act in quite different ways. Whatever form they take, the acts of the bully
are directed towards, and have the effect of, intimidating and disempowering
the other person.

Bullying does not have to be immediate and direct; one of the most common
forms of bullying in modern society is the activity known as **trolling** – the use
of social media to send abusive, aggressive or threatening messages to people
who have attracted the bully's attention. Even though this is happening at a
distance and coming from unknown people, the effects can be profound, and
there are several instances where internet bullying of this kind has driven the
recipient to suicide.

Key Terms
trolling A form of internet aggression in which the person directs anonymous spiteful or aggressive hate messages towards another person.

Just about all societies produce the occasional vicious individual, who talks or acts in spiteful or malicious ways. In previous times, they might have sent hate letters or other nasty messages, but their activities were more limited. What the internet offers is the opportunity for those people to express their vitriol towards people with whom they might otherwise have no contact, and to single out particular individuals for abuse and aggression. Fortunately, society is beginning to act against these activities, and there have been several recent cases of "trolls" being punished by the courts for their antisocial actions.

Although it may help to reduce the phenomenon in the long run, this punishment doesn't really help the victims. Bullying is a social phenomenon, which can bring about profound emotional consequences for the person who is being bullied, ranging from a loss of personal agency or sense of efficacy, to profound emotional disturbance. Table 7.9 outlines some of the major results of the experience of being bullied, in both adults and children.

Table 7.9 The effects of bullying

Depression and anxiety

Sleep disturbance

Health complaints

Headaches and panic attacks

Impaired achievement

Withdrawal

Problems with relationships

Long-term stress disorders

Source: Krahé (2013)

Although counselling has been shown to be of considerable value in helping the victims of bullying come to terms with their damaging experiences, challenging bullying itself requires an approach at a more social level. Nesdale et al (2008) showed that **group norms** have a significant effect on whether children are likely to bully others or not. Some successful interventions in tacking school bullying have focused on social identity processes, aiming to challenge a school culture in which bullies were admired or respected, replacing it with one in which they were despised or treated with contempt. Such interventions involve a "whole-school" approach, in which all children are given guidelines and the aim is to generate an anti-bullying culture in the school as a whole (e.g., Olweus, 1993). Although research implies that these types of interventions may vary in their effectiveness (e.g., Sharp and Smith, 1995), it does appear to be an improvement over the individual approach, and has become widespread in secondary schools in recent years.

Studies of workplace bullying often highlight lack of respect being awarded to employees by insensitive or vindictive managers. Workplace bullying is nothing like as physical as school bullying, usually being verbal in nature, but it nonetheless involves repeated belittling of the efforts or abilities of a particular employee or employees, or repeatedly unfair or unreasonable allocation

Key Terms

group norms
Standards of expected behaviour which are applied to group members.

of duties. And it has been shown to have a variety of damaging effects for the victims (Hershcovis and Barling, 2010). Like all bullying, it involves the abuse of power and the belittling and disempowerment of the victim, and it can have dramatic effects on the individual's self-esteem and sense of self-efficacy.

Tackling the cyber-bullying which has emerged in more recent years is more problematic, because of the opportunities for anonymity which the internet offers. At present the main interventions seem to be in terms of the establishment of state sanctions (prison sentences and the like) for those found to engage in this activity, and most modern schools have programmes aimed at raising awareness of the dangers of cyber-bullying among the pupils. However, all too often their activities are not discovered until they have had tragic consequences.

On-screen aggression

We don't just live our lives directly, we also come across many portrayals of different ways of behaving through various types of screens – through television, films, DVDs and video games, YouTube and many other sources. They illustrate a range of aggressive behaviours and interactions, and have generated ongoing social debates about their influence since the 1970s. The debates initially focused on the content of television and films, and has later moved to encompass video gaming and the various portrayals of human behaviour on the internet.

The debate about violence and aggressive behaviour on TV led to a significant amount of research about its impact, particularly on children. Researchers argued that their evidence showed that television aggression could lead children to believe that such behaviour is a justifiable option for everyday interaction (Eron et al, 1972). Other researchers showed how it desensitises people to violence (Thomas et al, 1977), and can also lead those who watch a great deal of TV to believe that the world is more dangerous than it really is (Gerbner and Gross, 1976). Police officers have frequently expressed the fear that the content of violent TV produces "copycat" crime.

Box 7.3   Market research and social scripts

One of the major problems with the dominance of market research on TV scripting has been how it has distorted our perceptions of what people are actually like, and the acceptable social scripts of everyday living. We can see this in the way that soap operas have changed over the years. In their early days, soap operas such as *Coronation Street* or *Neighbours* emphasised everyday positive interactions, such as people helping one another out, sympathising with problems or celebrating positive events. In doing so, they generated huge audiences.

Although they also dealt with negative events, these were more realistic in proportion, being less common in everyday experience than the positive ones, as they are in real life. What this meant, though, was that, in the same way as in everyday life, these negative events assumed a greater importance and were memorable – the human response of becoming distressed at events which destroy social harmony. As a result, when market researchers asked people about the memorable instances they recalled, almost all of them were dramatic and negative.

Using these findings, it was assumed that drama and negativity was primarily what the audience wanted. The fact they stood out in people's memories precisely because they were uncommon, and different from the rest of the scripting was overlooked. As competition for ratings grew, scriptwriters were encouraged to include more and more of these distressing or dramatic events, and to make them even more extreme. So where a single instance like a budgerigar's death had been a major event in one soap opera's early years – an event that people had noticed and discussed for the quality of the script and the realism of the acting – more dramatic events like murders and other tragedies came to dominate the programmes. Ordinary, pleasant everyday events came to be regarded as unimportant and not the kind of thing the viewers wanted to watch. In some cases, characters were even written out of programmes because their lives were finally going well.

From being a classic example of prosocial values expressed in TV, soap operas became the opposite, portraying almost continual examples of negative events and quarrelsome interactions. But even more worryingly, the patterns of behaviour they portrayed became accepted as valid social scripts for behaviour in real life.

In more recent years, the focus has shifted from the mass media to digital gaming, but it doesn't seem to matter whether the violence is depicted on TV or in video games. Silvern and Williamson (1987) explicitly compared the effects of TV and video games and found no difference between them. But they also found that young children significantly increased their repertoire of aggressive behaviour after playing violent video games. In a similar context, Calvert and Tan (1994) looked at the short-term effects of playing a violent virtual reality game. They found that young people playing these games showed a definite increase in arousal and aggressive thoughts, although interestingly, not with feelings of hostility. The researchers concluded that the emotional dimension of anger or aggression wasn't stimulated by such games; just behaviour and physiological stimulation.

The effects are not limited to children and young people. Bartholow and Anderson (2002) looked for gender differences between adults playing violent and non-violent video games. They found that both groups showed noticeable increase in aggression after playing a violent game (*Mortal Kombat*) as opposed to after a non-violent game (*PGA Tournament Golf*); but that increase was higher for men than for women.

In the Anderson (2004) meta-analysis of studies exploring the effects of playing violent video games which was mentioned earlier in this chapter, 32 different studies were investigated, involving over 5,000 participants. Anderson came to three main conclusions: that the more studies which were being undertaken in the area, the clearer and more consistent the relationships between gaming and aggression-related variables became; that despite the claims of some critics, those studies with better methodology produced stronger results, not weaker ones; and that the better the video game, in terms of the methods it used and the realism of what it portrayed, the stronger the effect was. As a result, Anderson argued that prolonged use of violent video games should be a cause for real social concern.

In a further meta-analysis incorporating studies from both Western and Japanese cultures, Anderson et al (2010) found that there was strong evidence for their assertion that prolonged exposure to violent video games should be regarded as a causal risk factor for increased aggressive behaviour, aggressive cognition and aggressive affect, as well as for decreased empathy and prosocial behaviour. The researchers were careful to ensure that only studies with high-quality methodologies were included, and they also included longitudinal analyses. Interestingly, they also found that these effects seemed unaffected by either cultural or sex differences.

The link between the prolonged playing of violent video games and aggressive behaviour in the real world, Anderson (2004) commented, was stronger than the links found between, for example, passive smoking and cancer, or the effects of condom use on HIV rates. As a result, he argued, society should be making a stand about them. However, social representations, market forces and political ideologies are powerful influences on social action, and despite the consistent psychological evidence for the influence that this type of violence can have, there is little political will – or perhaps an inability – to limit the violent content of either television or computer games.

Positive effects of gaming

That doesn't mean, though, that all video games are anti-social in nature. There is a considerable body of research which explores the positive influence of computer gaming. Computer games, or digital games in general, can take many different forms. Some are all about puzzles or problem-solving, some involve personal skill challenges, some are information-based; and these may have positive effects, but the games which attract the most attention and social comment are those which involve virtual aggression such as shooting people or engaging in hugely destructive warfare.

However, Durkin and Barber (2002) compared 16-year-olds who engaged in gaming with a comparable sample who had never played computer games, and found that the game players scored more favourably on a number of dimensions, including family closeness, school engagement, positive mental health, self-concept and friendship networks. Gee (2003) highlighted the way that many computer games encourage consistent effort on the part of the gamers, with overall content which rewards persistence and learning, helping to build a sense of mastery and self-efficacy, and often also encouraging the development of literacy.

A number of other studies have shown similar effects, and gaming has become acknowledged as a way of carrying out a number of educational or assessment tasks, from the teaching of maths (Kebritchi et al, 2010) to the gamification of psychometric tests (Montefiori, 2016). In a review of nearly 30 years of studies into the effects of computer games, Le and Peng (2006) found that despite the bulk of research being focused on negative effects, non-violent entertainment games had been shown to improve spatial skills, cognitive abilities, academic performance, sociability and training in general. Sublette and Mullan (2012), in an analysis of 16 MMOGs (massive multiplayer online games) studies, found that most gamers reported positive effects to online gaming, including feelings of achievement, friendship and a sense of community.

Most of this chapter has been concerned with the more negative aspects of human social behaviour. But does that mean that we are all at each other's throats the whole time? Not really, but like media news reporters, psychological researchers have tended to focus more on the darker side of human nature than on the more pleasant side. As we saw in Chapter 2, Argyle and Crossland (1987), in their research into positive emotions, pointed out that researchers had investigated the emotions of anger and fear intensively, but there had been relatively little research into happiness or contentment, although there have been a number of modern efforts to redress that balance. Similarly, de Waal (1989), describing primate research, pointed out that there had been considerable research into aggression and dominance, yet little into the rich and varied strategies of reconciliation which are so important in cementing the social bonds of chimpanzees and other primates, including human beings.

Psychologists have devoted considerably research efforts to understanding aggression and prejudice, but it is important to remember that this is partly because it is less common and more problematic than our normal everyday interactions. Being social inevitably involves co-operation, and in Chapter 1 we explored the importance of belonging and relationships for people. In Chapter 6, we also saw how our natural tendency seems to be to help other people out rather than to behave aggressively towards them. As the movement known as positive psychology continues to develop, we can expect research into the more positive aspects of human nature, including how we can become happier in ourselves. In the next chapter, we will explore just what we mean by the "self", and the different ways it has been investigated by psychologists.

Summary: Chapter 7

1. How we perceive other people can be influenced by primacy and halo effects, our implicit personality theories, stereotyping and personal constructs. We often use more than one set of criteria at a time.

2. Attraction can take several forms and may develop through indirect contact such as via the internet, as well as through direct interaction.

3. Early research into attraction identified a number of contributing factors, and theories have suggested that it may develop through evaluation, from social or personal reinforcement or from cognitive similarity.

4. Prejudice is a major problem in modern society, and can take many forms. Three of the most common forms of prejudice are racism, sexism and homophobia.

5. Traditional theories of prejudice range from individual explanations, such as the authoritarian personality, to social and cultural explanations, such as scapegoating or intergroup conflict.

6. More recent approaches to understanding prejudice include the ambivalence model, and approaches which emphasise the importance of collective awareness and action.

7. Research into challenging prejudice has shown that equal status, personal contact and co-operative effort can significantly reduce prejudice. Changes in social representations may also be an important factor in prejudice reduction.

8. Early theories of aggression tended to emphasise individual factors such as biological processes, personal traits, or reactions to individual frustration, while more recent explanations tend to emphasise social learning and social identity processes.

9. In everyday life, aggression can take many forms. Some aggression, such as child abuse or elder abuse, may occur within families, and sexual aggression and bullying also represent significant social problems.

10. Media and online representations of aggression, such as are found in computer games, have repeatedly been shown to increase the likelihood of aggression in real-world behaviour. However, computer games can also have positive effects on the individual and their social development.

Contents

Chapter 8

The social self 8

When we think about the self, we often use the idea of the "self-concept". The self-concept is the idea or mental model that we have about ourselves as individual people. American and European thinking tends to take the idea of a self-concept for granted. But it is interesting to note that the idea only began to emerge in the 17th century, with the work of Descartes, Locke and Hume, who all emphasised the idea of a "self" as the central part of consciousness. As European society moved out of mediaeval feudalism and into merchant-based economies, the idea became increasingly popular, until the concept of the independent individual rather than the individual-within-community became dominant in society. In early psychology, it was further developed by William James (1890), whose work largely established the assumptions about the self which psychologists used for most of the following century.

Towards the end of the 20th century, those ideas were gradually challenged as researchers became more aware of ethnocentricity in psychological theorising, and began to develop theories which had broader relevance than mainstream Western society. As we will see later in this chapter, the idea of a central sense of self has been reasonably consistent across cultures, but the way in which that manifests itself, and how deeply it is located in its social context, have differed considerably from one theoretical model to another. It may be best, therefore, to begin our exploration of the self by looking at its psychological underpinnings, in terms of how the infant, and then the child, develop the basic psychological processes which contribute to the mature sense of self.

HOW DOES THE SELF BEGIN?

Me and not-me

The very beginnings of the self-concept come as the young infant begins to make the distinction that some parts of its world are "me", while others are "not-me". This isn't the same as having perception and memory – even infants in the womb have been shown to respond to sounds and movement. It has even been known for a young child to remember tunes it heard in the womb, when it hasn't heard them at all since birth. But differentiating between "me" and "the outside world" is more than just memory. It takes longer to develop, as the child's experience of different situations and circumstances grows.

That differentiation isn't likely to happen before birth, because the experiences of the foetus in the womb are so closely bound up with its environmental context. But after birth, things become radically different. Some important parts of the child's experience are only there sometimes, and some of those experiences are significantly different from others. It has been shown, for example, that **neonates** respond differently to their mother's voice than to those of other people – probably because of the familiarity it has acquired in the womb.

Gradually, that differentiation results in the child's development of a self-schema: a sense of self which contains the memories and action plans which the child has acquired from the "me" part of their experience. That self-schema continues to grow throughout life. It begins as a body-schema, encompassing physical sensations as well as awareness of the body and what it can and can't do. As we continue to grow and develop, though, the self schema acquires other dimensions such as our beliefs about our mental skills and capabilities, and the impressions we have about ourselves from social and physical feedback.

Piaget (1952) believed that cognitive development in the young child happens through the process of **decentration**, as the child gradually learns that its own experience of the universe is not the be-all and end-all of everything, and that objects and experiences have an independent existence. This begins with recognising that objects can continue to exist even if they are not in direct view, and later broadens to allow the gradual development of abstract thought and formal logic. But although many of Piaget's insights do seem to hold well for purely cognitive problem-solving, it is now believed that he seriously underestimated the importance of social influences – both in the child's cognitive development and in its growing sense of self. Social abilities, and the capacity to receive social feedback, develop at a much earlier age than Piaget suspected, and much of the basic learning that children do also appears to be more complex.

Key Terms

neonate
A new-born infant.

decentration
The process of gradually learning that the world is not centred entirely upon oneself.

Agency and efficacy

One of the most important things that infants learn is that what they do produces effects. Stratton (1983) showed how strongly young infants respond to the **contingencies** and **transactions** which occur in their environment. If an infant performs a simple action and that produces a noticeable result – like reaching out and hitting a rattle – the infant will perform that action again. The sound of the rattle is contingent on the child's action – what it does – and this seems to motivate the infant to do it again – and again. Even very young infants are strongly predisposed to react to the contingencies in their environment, and many of the games and activities designed for infants and young children build on exactly this motivation.

One of the earliest infant-oriented computer games was one originally developed for Apple Macs back in the 1980s, then known as *Babysmash* and evolving into programmes such as *Alphababy* and *Babysmash*, depending upon the operating system. It is a programme which locks out all other functions but produces sounds, letters and coloured shapes when the child hits the keyboard. Even very young babies find these contingencies fascinating, and will bash away at a keyboard for what seems like hours at a time. It might seem a long way away from the self-concept; but like other actions which produce a repeatable effect, it gives the child the beginning of a sense of agency – a sense that the child has an ability to do things which will produce results. In other words, the child is starting to learn how to take effective action in its world. Our sense of agency is an important part of how we see ourselves.

The transactions which the young infant experiences are equally important. Transactions are social exchanges in which one person does something, then the other person does something in return. They are the basis of the social interactions and games which take place between caretaking adults and infants. They have been studied in detail by many researchers into infant development, and as we saw in Chapter 1, they set some of the patterns of future social interaction, like conversational timings, even at a very young age.

The child's growing sense of agency and efficacy is one of the most important aspects of a psychological healthy childhood. It begins with transactions and contingencies, and continues as the child acquires both physical and mental skills, through play and everyday learning. The child learns that it can be an active agent in its world, making things happen as a result of what it does. It also begins to acquire its personal set of **self-efficacy beliefs** – that is, beliefs about the ways that it can act effectively and make a difference to its situation.

Collins (1982) looked at children who had varying mathematical abilities, and either high or low levels of self-efficacy beliefs. Children with high self-efficacy beliefs solved more problems more quickly than those who had low self-efficacy beliefs – regardless of how good they actually were at sums. The children with high self-efficacy beliefs were more prepared to go over problems which they had done wrong, and more likely to correct themselves a second time. Because they believed they could be competent, they put more effort into the problems, whereas the children with low self-efficacy beliefs gave up quickly and did not regard making more effort as being of any use.

Gunderson et al (2013) found that children's self-efficacy beliefs seem to correlate with whether parents praise their young children for their efforts, rather than their actual achievements. They conducted a study in which they observed children and parents interacting, in their homes, at ages 14, 26 and

> ### Key Terms
>
> **contingencies**
> Outcomes which result from specific circumstances or actions.
>
> **transactions**
> A form of behavioural exchange or interchange between two individuals.
>
> **self-efficacy belief**
> The belief that one is capable of acting effectively.

38 months. Then they revisited those children five years later. Even after they had controlled for as many social and psychological variables as they could, they found that the children who had received praise which emphasised their efforts, actions and strategies generally had more positive self-efficacy beliefs when they were seven or eight years old. While it isn't possible to be sure of a causal connection in such a long-range study, their findings do fit with many other studies which suggest that how parents and children interact can make quite a difference to a child's developing sense of agency.

SOCIAL AWARENESS

The child's sense of **agency** can manifest itself in other ways, too. Dunn (1988) showed how even quite young toddlers are able to manipulate other people – particularly their siblings – deliberately. They can actively choose to do things which produce upset or annoyance; they can try to comfort and cheer up someone who is upset; and they can initiate games and activities. Dunn's conclusions came as a result of an extensive series of observations of children in their own homes, with particular reference to how they interacted with their siblings and parents or caretakers.

Even children as young as two years old were able to "wind up" their older siblings; they knew what to do to produce a reaction, even if they didn't have a full understanding of what the person was actually thinking or feeling. The overall implication of these observations is that the ability to interact in meaningful and emotional ways with other people are part of our earliest development, and become important just about as soon as we become able to act independently in the world. These social skills are the beginnings of the sense of personal agency – the self as an active agent in the world, which is an important part of the self-concept.

This, incidentally, is one of the reasons why child abuse is so profoundly damaging. A psychologically healthy childhood can be seen as the incremental development of skills and competencies, with the child becoming increasingly

confident in its ability to deal with its world, and gradually acquiring an internal locus of control, a growing confidence that it can deal with the demands made by its life. But what abuse does is to strip away that sense of agency, rendering the child entirely helpless and unable to take effective action. In the case of sexual and physical abuse, it teaches the child that it doesn't even have the say in what happens to its own body; in the case of psychological abuse, that it has no control over its social and emotional world.

The growing sense of competence and efficacy is suddenly stamped out, and the result is, among other things, a sense of self-worthlessness which can last through adult life as well as distorting the experiences of childhood. That's why therapy – either in childhood or adulthood – is so important. It allows the person to go back and see those experiences more clearly, and become angry about what was done to them rather than feeling guilty or blaming themselves. It also helps people to challenge feelings of self-worthlessness and to develop the more positive levels of self-esteem which would have been the result of a more psychologically healthy childhood.

The development of TOM

Another important milestone in the development of the self-concept comes at the point where the child begins to realise that other people have minds of their own, and that someone else may not be thinking the same thing as the child is thinking. This development usually happens around about the age of three and a half, and is generally referred to as the development of a **theory of mind**, or TOM (Harris, 1988).

The classic experiment used to demonstrate the existence or otherwise of a TOM goes roughly as follows: two children are shown a specific object or event – for example, that a particular box contains pencils. One of the children then leaves the room, and while they are away, the contents of the box is changed – for instance, the pencils are removed and the box is filled with sweets instead. This happens in full view of the other child. That child is then asked what the first child will expect to find in the box when he or she comes back.

Up until about three and a half years of age, the usual reply is that they will expect to find sweets in the box. The child assumes that what it knows, the other child will know as well. Beyond that age, as a general rule, the child will say that the other child will expect to find pencils. It has developed an awareness that other people may think differently – that they have minds of their own. These findings about the age at which the theory of mind usually develops have been supported by other observations, too, such as the ecological observations carried out by Dunn and her team. This change in thinking is fundamental to the development of more sophisticated social understanding. It is also becoming increasingly accepted that autistic children, who are unable to relate fully to the other people around them, have generally failed to develop a theory of mind, and that this may be the root cause of their condition (Baron-Cohen et al, 1986).

Social roles

Childhood is also a time for the gradual acquisition of **social roles**. Some researchers have suggested that training in social roles begins in infancy. In one classic study (Seavey et al, 1975), a baby was dressed either in blue, pink or yellow clothes, and unrelated adults were allowed to cuddle it and choose

Key Terms

theory of mind (TOM)
The development of the idea that other people have minds of their own, and may hold different beliefs or ideas.

social roles
The parts people play in society.

toys for it. If the baby was dressed in blue, it was typically given a toy football, if it was dressed in pink it would be given a doll, and if in yellow it was usually given a teething ring. The adults also attributed different qualities to the infant – "strong and sturdy" to the "boy" and "soft and pretty" if it was thought to be a girl. The study was successfully replicated in 1980, using three different babies as opposed to just one, with even stronger effects (Sidorowicz and Lunney, 1980).

Families, then, are important agents in teaching children appropriate social role behaviour. In a review of influences on the socialisation of gender roles, Witt (1997) examined a range of factors, including school experience, television viewing, and the influence of peers. Parental influence emerged as being by far the most important of these factors. Parents pass on their own beliefs about gender, both overtly in direct advice or sanctions, and covertly in the ways that they react to other social events or other people. Looking at studies of how gender roles impact on the child, Witt concluded that an **androgynous** gender role orientation, which drew from both stereotypes, was more beneficial to children than a strict adherence to traditional gender roles, a conclusion which mirrored earlier work in this area by Bem (1976).

Families may establish the beginnings of the child's understanding of social roles, but when it first goes to school or kindergarten, the child encounters a completely different set of behaviours. From simply acting as it feels, or in accordance with established domestic conventions, the child is now discovering that different situations require different types of actions, and may also elicit different social **sanctions** (Dunn 1988). This experience continues to develop and become more refined as a child grows older. The way that a child is expected to act when in the classroom at school also changes over time; and so does the way it acts in out-of-school leisure activities and when interacting with people who are not part of the immediate family circle.

Children's games often involve rehearsing different social roles. Young children may play at mummies and daddies, or at doctors, dentists, teachers or any other professional adults they have come across. Older children, girls particularly, may have dolls or models which also allow them to practise their understanding of various professions or roles. These games help children to develop their social understanding, and also allow them to explore what it might be like to play that role in society. The child's virtual world, too, offers scope for acting out different social roles and engaging in different types of social interaction. While many of the young child's experiences online or with games consoles are primarily concerned with skill acquisition or adventure, a number of games involve adopting social roles of one form or another, such as farmer, detective, soldier or nurse.

The real explosion in social roles, however, comes when a child is teenage, and begins to interact more extensively with the wider world and particularly with the its peer group. Erikson (1968) argued that the main psychosocial conflict which a teenager needs to resolve is that of maintaining a consistent identity or sense of self in the face of the confusing plethora of different roles which they are expected to perform. School, part-time work, sport and leisure activities and social contacts with friends all involve different roles, and the teenager needs to be able to deal with them without becoming confused as to who they "really" are. But as we shall see, the range of social roles that we play is an important aspect of our self-concept.

Key Terms

androgynous
Having both masculine and feminine characteristics.

sanctions
Social forms of punishment or disapproval.

Personal constructs

As we grow older, our knowledge of the world widens, and we begin to develop our own ideas about it. But since we are all individual, and our experiences are all different, we all develop our ideas differently. The distinctive mini-theories about the world which we form as we bring together our diverse experiences are known as **personal constructs**. These are the ways that we, personally, construe (that is, make sense of) our experience. We looked at personal constructs briefly in the last chapter, but since they form such an important part of our self-development, we will take a more detailed look at them here.

Although each individual's personal constructs are different, Kelly (1955) argued that they tend to adopt a specific form, which is bipolar in nature. For example, one of the constructs we use to evaluate other people might be as "kind", but that would also have its opposite, possibly "cruel". (Possibly not, too, because everyone understands these words in their own ways too!) Kelly developed a way of identifying the personal constructs which people use. As a clinical psychologist, it helped him to understand the people he was dealing with. The technique is known as the **repertory grid**. Talking point 8.1 outlines how it works in an exercise which you can do to identify some of your own personal constructs.

Talking point 8.1   Identifying personal constructs

You can find out about your own personal constructs using a simple exercise. It begins by naming a set of people who are important in your life, in some way – they might be relatives, friends or even people you particularly dislike, but what matters is that they are important to you.

Once you have got your eight people, take a group of three and fit them into the sentence:

"X and Y are . . . while Z is . . . ."

What you are looking for is to find a way that two of your people are similar to each other but different from the third. Once you have done that, take another group of three and repeat the exercise. Keep doing this – the best way is to give each person a letter, and use a chart to tell you which letter combination to use. The full set of possible combinations is below. There are 26 altogether, but you should be able to get a reasonable result from just ten or so, as long as everyone on your list has been included at least twice:

ABC   CDE   ABD   CDF   ABE   CDG   ABF   CDH   ABG   DEF

ABH   DEG   ACD   DEH   ACE   EFG   ACF   EFH   ACG   FGH

ACH   BCD   BCE   BCF   BCG   BCH

Key Terms

personal constructs
Individual ways of making sense of the world, which have been developed on the basis of experience.

repertory grid
A technique for identifying and representing data about personal constructs.

When you have completed your sentences, take a look at the adjectives or phrases you have used to describe each combination. These will be a sample of your own individual set of personal constructs. They will be bipolar – that is, they will have two opposite ends – and you will probably find that you can apply them to other people as well.

Try comparing your own constructs with a friend's. They are unlikely to be the same; your set is your own and unique to you, and you may find it surprising how much other people's differ from yours.

Our repertoire of personal constructs grows and develops with our experience, and never stops developing. It also provides a set of criteria by which we evaluate and either adopt or reject the social representations we looked at in Chapter 4. At an individual level, we are more likely to accept or reject a given set of social representations if they can mesh with our own existing personal constructs. They will make more sense to us and can be integrated into our habitual ways of thinking more easily (Sammut and Howarth, 2014).

Personal constructs are not just about other people, of course. We also develop our own mini-theories about the environment around us, about consumer goods and many other aspects of day-to-day living. Market researchers have found the idea of personal constructs to be useful in consumer research, and they are often used in this way. As we saw in the last chapter, social psychologists have also used it to help our understanding of attraction and the development of personal relationships (e.g., Duck, 2007).

THEORIES OF THE SELF

Traditional theories of the self have tended to emphasise the idea of the independent individual, separate from its wider society. But psychological research into the self quickly dispelled any idea that social influences were unimportant. Even from the earliest days, psychological theories of the self have always acknowledged how important other people are in influencing the development of the self-concept. For example, James (1890) argued that the **social comparisons** that we make are vital in how our self-concept develops, particularly those social comparisons which we make with our "significant others". We don't bother to make comparisons with people who we see as quite different from us. Rather, we compare ourselves with people who we see as being important to us, such as being like us in some way or representing goals which we are striving for.

Social feedback

Cooley, in 1902, argued that the feedback which we receive from other people is essential to the self-concept. According to Cooley, the self-concept is like a mirror – or "looking glass" as he put it – reflecting what we believe other people think of us. This **looking-glass self** includes both evaluative and illustrative dimensions; evaluative dimensions being the judgements that we believe other people are making about us, and illustrative dimensions being what we believe they see when they look at us.

Key Terms

social comparison
The process of comparing one's own social group with others, in terms of their relative social status and prestige.

looking-glass self
The idea that self-concept depends on feedback from others.

So it isn't just a question of the feedback we get from other people responding to what we do, although that matters as well. When we are in an unfamiliar social situation, we are often as much concerned with what other people will be thinking of us, as we are with what we are actually doing. In other words, our opinion of ourselves is formed on the basis of what we think other people think.

Discussing views on appearance as an example, Cooley argued that the self-idea which is produced by the looking-glass self seems to have three separate components: how we imagine our appearance looks to the other person, how we imagine they are judging that appearance and a self-feeling resulting from those two imaginations, like pride or embarrassment. Cooley argued that social emotions like pride, embarrassment and even anger arise directly from how we think other people are perceiving us.

The problem, of course, is that how we think other people are perceiving us may not actually be accurate. Kenny and DePaulo (1993) discussed how people often have ideas about themselves which they wrongly believe other people hold as well, and this colours their interpretation of how other people are acting towards them. If we think of ourselves as emotional and easily upset, for example, we may assume that others think of us that way as well; whereas the way that we try to deal with this aspect of ourselves may mean that actually, the social impression we give other people is of someone who is emotionally quite calm, or quite tough. Overall, though, research does suggest that people are fairly good at knowing how other people in general see them, even though they may be wrong when it comes to particular individuals.

Box 8.1   The looking glass study

One of the most-quoted studies of social influence on the self, possibly because it was one of the earliest, was an informal class experiment reported by Cooley in 1902. Cooley described how a group of boys in a mixed class had decided to play a trick on a particularly plain and unattractive girl. They would take it in turns to ask her for a date, and in the meantime all of them would treat her as if she were interesting and attractive. They didn't expect anything much to come of this, but as they carried out their plan, they found that the girl actually became more interesting and attractive. By the time of the third date, she was really fun to be with, and he enjoyed his time with her very much. In a sense, the joke had backfired, but in a way which was to everyone's benefit.

From these observations and others, Cooley went on to develop his theory of the "looking-glass self". The importance of feedback from other people in the development of our own self-image was established as a recognised social psychological mechanism. But the study was informal and not particularly controlled, which was acceptable at the time. It is questionable, though, whether this type of observation would be regarded as adequate evidence in modern psychology. So what changes would have been needed if it were to be replicated as an acceptable sort of study for modern times? What design principles and ethical concerns would arise if someone proposed an action research study of this kind? Given the level of deception involved, would it be ethical to do it at all? And if not, how else might we gain evidence for this psychological mechanism?

Symbolic interactionism

Cooley's work particularly emphasised how our self-image draws on the feedback we receive from other people. But where Cooley largely saw social influences as impacting on the individual and modifying the person's own independent sense of self, other theorists saw them as running far deeper. Like Cooley, Mead (1934) saw the self-concept as being formed directly through social experience. But social experience in Mead's terms was much broader than simply the reactions of individual people, or even our beliefs about them. It was the entire social structure experienced by the person, controlled by the community's norms, values and cultural patterns.

According to Mead, these dimensions of social interaction become internalised as we develop psychologically. Once internalised, we use them as standards for evaluating our own behaviour, regardless of whether there are other people present or not. Mead also believed that language plays a key part in self-development, since it is through language that people communicate meanings, both social and personal, and we internalise these meanings as well. So the self-concept, as Mead saw it, is almost entirely the outcome of these social dimensions and the shared symbolism which gives all social life its meaning.

Goffman (1959) took a similar view of social dimensions forging the sense of self; but he emphasised how people interact with one another rather than internalised norms or expectations. Social living, Goffman argued, occurs through role play. We interact with one another almost entirely by means of the social roles that we are playing at any given time. That also involves an understanding of how the other person will see or understand the role that we ourselves are playing. So, in a sense, we interact with the symbolic behaviour required by the social role, rather than with the direct personality of the person playing that role, and we understand our own actions in the same way. For that reason, this way of looking at the self is known as **symbolic interactionism**.

In this model, then, the self-concept reflects the collection of social roles played by the individual. We all play a large number of social roles as we go about our daily lives, and we have all learned how we should go about playing them. This learning has two parts: initially we feel as though we are just "acting out" a new role, like playing a game; but after a while, the role becomes internalised – we see it as just part of what we do. Goffman suggested that all social life is actually a succession of roles, adopted by each person in order to interact with other people, and that when we talk about the "self" we actually mean the sum of all of those roles. As each individual takes their place in society, Goffman argued, the range of roles which are available to them develops, so the different aspects of their "self" which they present in everyday living become more highly developed and more sophisticated.

In Goffman's view, the self has several different aspects, each of which comes to the fore during different social "episodes". So the role that you act when you are playing the part of "student-in-lectures" is, in Goffman's view, as much as part of your self as the role that you adopt when you are playing the part of "passenger" on the bus, or "young person socialising with friends". For Goffman, then, the self-concept is a bit like a many-sided dice: each facet represents a side of the personality, but the facet which is uppermost is the one which is appropriate to the "episode" which is being lived at the moment.

Key Terms

symbolic interactionism
The approach to social understanding which looks at how people perceive and respond to one another as social symbols, such as roles, rather than as individuals.

The many-sided dice model can be useful in understanding how we can act so differently in different situations, while still remaining "ourselves", but few psychologists would take the view that the roles apparent in our actions are all there is. Instead, most would argue that there is a central core to the personality which, even when the person is playing an established social role, may manifest itself through more subtle aspects, like distinctive styles or values characteristic of that individual, or of their social group or culture.

Talking point 8.2   The many-sided dice

How well does the idea of the self as a many-sided dice fit with your own impressions of yourself? Can you identify different "selves" which you show in different situations? Think of how you are on the following occasions:

At a party with friends / In a lecture or class.

At a job interview / Working or doing a special job for other people.

At home with your family / At a festival or concert.

Shopping for clothes / Participating in a sport or a hobby.

We would all act differently on these occasions. But do the different ways that you act reflect different aspects of your "self", or are they just put on and nothing to do with the "real" you? Are some of the ways that you act completely different from others, as if they come from the opposite side of the dice? And is there a central core, or style, which you think of as being distinctively "you", and which shows up across a number of situations?

Self-perception

Bem (1967) suggested that how we perceive ourselves is an important part of the self-concept. **Self-perception theory** argues that we observe how we are acting, and draw conclusions from this about what we are like. In one study which illustrated this, Valins and Ray (1967) showed snake-phobic research participants pictures of snakes. As they watched, they sometimes saw the word "shock", which was followed by a mild electric shock. All the research participants experienced this, but the experimental group were also played a recording of a heartbeat, and informed that it was their own heart being monitored. The heartbeat beat faster at the shock slides, but not at pictures of snakes – inferring that the shock was more disturbing.

At the end of the study, Valins and Ray asked the research participants to approach a tame boa constrictor, and found that the people who had been in the experimental group could get much closer to the snake than those people who had been in the control group. During the study, they had looked at the snake but heard what they believed to be their heartbeat remain undisturbed. From this, the research participants had inferred that they were not being particularly upset by the snake.

Bem's self-perception theory proposes that we perceive ourselves in much the same way that we perceive other people. We make similar inferences and attributions about our behaviour, and may adjust those inferences if we find that we

Key Terms

self-perception theory
The idea that we develop an impression of our own personality by inferring what we are like from the way that we act.

are acting in ways which are not what we might have predicted (e.g., "This is my fourth sandwich; I must have been hungrier than I thought."). The attributions and inferences that we make are the basis of the idea about ourselves that we construct.

Other researchers have used self-perception theory to explore the link between personal beliefs or impressions and self-concept. For example, van Gyn et al (1990) showed how imagining training like a professional athlete during a period on exercise bikes produced faster results than a similar group of people not engaging in this mental imagery. They argued that the professional comparison fed into the person's self-perception, and that in turn motivated them to work harder and ride faster than they would have done otherwise. Their perceptions of themselves had directly affected their behaviour.

Self-efficacy

We saw earlier how important self-efficacy is in the development of the self. Bandura (1989) argued that self-efficacy is one of the most important features in self-perception. Self-efficacy beliefs are beliefs about our own perceived competences – what we believe we can do well, or at least adequately. They are instrumental in determining how we interact with our environment and other people (see Table 8.1), but they differ considerably from one person to another; some people see themselves as competent in a wide range of activities or tasks, while others do not perceive themselves to be particularly efficacious at all.

Table 8.1 Psychological processes affected by self-efficacy beliefs

Cognitive processes	Self-efficacy beliefs affect our thought patterns, which in turn affects our behaviour. Weighing up a situation in terms of what we are capable of influences what we are then prepared to attempt.
Motivational processes	Our self-efficacy beliefs directly influence how long we will keep trying at something in the face of initial failure.
Affective processes	Our self-efficacy beliefs can directly affect feelings such as stress or anxiety. For example, people experience lower levels of stress when they feel they are in control of a situation. Having high self-efficacy beliefs is directly linked to feeling capable, and in control.
Selection processes	People tend to choose those activities and situations which they can manage but will present them with challenges. Our beliefs about our personal efficacy will directly affect what we choose.

Source: Bandura (1989)

In a study of physical endurance, Weinberg et al (1979) raised research participants' self-efficacy beliefs by giving them false feedback on how well they had performed in competitive tasks. The feedback was designed to raise or lower their self-efficacy beliefs with respect to those particular tasks. The researchers found that people with raised efficacy beliefs performed better at the endurance tasks, and they also tried harder to recover if they failed. Those with lowered self-efficacy beliefs, on the other hand, tended to be put off by failing, and didn't do as well overall.

In an interesting second part of the experiment, the experimenters deliberately manipulated self-efficacy beliefs and gender, such that female research participants' self-efficacy beliefs were raised while those of male research participants were lowered. When they did this, they found that the normal gender differences in physical endurance tasks disappeared almost entirely. Bandura (1989) pointed out that this raises the question of how far traditional sex differences are a product of lowered self-efficacy beliefs, since most societies traditionally raise girls to believe that they are not as good at doing things as boys are. He also suggested that it may be a good thing if our self-efficacy beliefs are slightly higher than our achievements would suggest, because that means we will put in extra effort and go for new challenges, which in turn helps to develop our abilities and competencies. Overconfidence may be good for you!

Research into self-efficacy in children also formed the basis of Dweck's (2006) model of fixed and growth mind-sets. A **growth mindset** includes the ideas that something like intelligence is can be developed or increased, and that learning happens mainly from the effort we put into it. People with a **fixed mindset**, on the other hand, would see intelligence as an unchangeable quality, and believe that some people are naturally good at learning while others are simply not. The mindset we hold effectively determines how motivated we will be to take on challenges or learn new things – whether we think it will be worth making the effort. But Dweck observed that people can change from a fixed mindset to adopting a growth one, given appropriate training or practice. This profound change in how we perceive ourselves can have life-changing effects on both children and adults, and Dweck's model is proving increasingly useful in education, training and management.

COMPARISON, CATEGORISATION AND EVALUATION

Festinger's social comparison theory (1954) proposed that we learn about ourselves through the comparisons that we make with other people. His social comparison theory built on the work by Cooley and others, but emphasised the way that we need to validate our own impressions. So we may have ideas about what we are like, but we feel the need to validate those ideas, and we do so by making comparisons with other people. For example, we may see ourselves as being "sporty" because we play more sport than the other people around us. If we then move to an area where everyone, or at least most people, engage in quite a lot of sport, we may stop thinking of ourselves as being "sporty" and just see our sporting participation as normal. We use comparisons with the people around us to determine how we see ourselves.

The implications of Festinger's theory is that our self-concept is quite closely linked with the groups that we belong to. But as Tajfel and Turner (1979) pointed out, social groups are not all the same. They differ considerably in terms of their access to power and resources, and membership of different social groups commands different levels of respect from others.

Following on from this, Turner (1991) proposed that we develop our sense of self through a process of **self-categorisation**, in which we draw on our knowledge of social groups and categories to compare ourselves with them. Self-categorisation theory links closely with the processes of social identification which we have explored in earlier chapters. It draws on the way that we compare and evaluate social groups, and then internalise those value-judgements into the ideas we have about ourselves. By internalising these value-judgements, we are internalising information which can have a significant effect on our sense of self-worth.

However, we don't just compare ourselves with any of the possible groups available to us. Wills (1981) showed how we tend to make comparisons which will reflect positively on our **self-esteem**, by choosing social groups which have lower social status or respect to compare ourselves with. However, if we don't actually have a choice in our comparisons, then we may need to adopt different strategies to maintain self-esteem. For example, we may discount the comparison, or provide reasons why the comparison may look negative but is really positive. We might justify consistently lower academic achievement, for instance, by arguing that our peers with consistently higher achievement get more home support. In other words, people try to distance themselves from the group or downplay the importance of their membership of it. Tesser (1988) described this process as **self-evaluation maintenance**, and it links closely with self-categorisation theory and the social creativity strategies described as part of the processes of social identification (see Chapter 1).

The relational self

Andersen and Chen (2002) argued that the self-concept also incorporates the important relationships that we have – how we interact with the significant others in our lives. We tend to regard those aspects of ourselves that we show to our significant others as some of the more central or important aspects of how we see ourselves. Andersen and Chen showed how these aspects of the self-concept could be easily brought to the surface by encouraging people just to think about that significant other, and they are particularly powerful when we are interacting with them. This aspect of the self-concept is known as the **relational self**, and it seems to be all to do with the mental representations we have about the other person, rather than the other person as such.

The relational self is not one single thing, but the way that different people bring out different aspects of ourselves. Fitzsimons and Bargh (2003) found that we have different self-goals and motivations associated with our different relationships, which we are not necessarily conscious of, but which become activated when we are interacting with that other person. We don't need to be interacting face to face for this. They also found that online interaction with the person would brings out the same self-qualities, goals and motivations as they did when they were directly in touch. But their research participants were often unaware that this was happening.

Self-awareness

Human beings have a distinctive capacity for self-awareness – that is, for being aware of ourselves in the same way as we are aware of external objects like a table to a cup. We are not the only animals which have this ability, but the number that do is relatively small. A dog seeing its reflection in a mirror will generally respond as if it was another dog, as will a fish or most birds. Lone budgerigars, for example, are often provided with mirrors in their cages, and will chirp happily away to their "companion" in the mirror, without showing any indication that they recognise that reflection as being of themselves. Siamese fighting fish will attack their reflections, and similar reactions have been obtained from other territorial fish.

Key Terms

self-esteem
The evaluative dimension of the self-concept, which is to do with how worthwhile and/ or confident people feel about themselves.

self-evaluation maintenance
Strategies used to maintain self-esteem.

relational self
The idea that our self-concept includes our significant relationships as well as personal ideas and experience.

Chimpanzees, on the other hand, have a very different reaction. If they are marked with, say a dot of colour on their foreheads and then look at themselves in a mirror, they will attempt to rub the colour off – showing that they recognise themselves in the image, rather than another individual. Studies with dolphins, elephants and other great apes have produced similar results (Plotnik et al, 2006; Patterson and Gordon, 1993; Marten and Psarakos, 1995). When the same test is applied to human children, typically those up to the age of about 12 months react to the person in the mirror as if it were another playmate, but after that time they begin to indicate that they recognise the image as being of themselves, and by the age of two, their self-recognition is well established (Rochat, 2003).

Self-awareness theory proposes that, for some of the time at least, we are actively aware of ourselves, rather than just taking ourselves for granted as we might do at other times. At these times, we compare ourselves with some ideal self or goal that we would like to reach. Since none of us are perfect, this leaves us with a sense of shortcoming which we mostly try to address by self-improvement.

Which is fine as long as the ideals that we have set are reachable. Rogers (1957) argued that, while most people have a reasonably realistic idea of both their selves and their ideal-selves, people who had been brought up by demanding parents who only offered **conditional positive regard** (i.e., love or affection only when the child was being "good" or doing something "right") developed unrealistically high **conditions of worth**, leading to excessively perfect ideal selves. Because of their early experiences, they felt that if they didn't meet those impractical standards they were utterly worthless. This, Rogers argued, was the source of much of the adult neuroticism which he encountered as a clinical psychologist, and his therapy was based on providing the person with the experience they should have had when they were children – **unconditional positive regard**, so that they could be sure they were liked or loved regardless of what they actually did or how much they achieve.

Talking point 8.3   The ideal self

Most of us have an idea of what our ideal selves might be like. Usually, they are fairly similar to our real selves, but just perfect, rather than mixed; for example, my ideal self would never get irritated with other people, but my real self does sometimes.

Try drawing up a chart with two columns: one for your real self and one for your ideal self. Be realistic – there's no point expecting your ideal self to be tall, blonde and slim if your real self is short, brown-haired and chubby. But list the ways that you would like you, yourself, to be ideally.

Key Terms

self-awareness theory
The idea that we are aware of our shortcomings as well as achievements, which motivates self-improvement activities.

conditional positive regard
Love, affection or other positive emotion which is dependent on the person acting in certain ways.

conditions of worth
Internalised ideas about the personal qualities or achievements which will make someone a worthwhile person.

unconditional positive regard
Love, affection or respect which does not depend on the person's having to act in particular ways.

Once you have made your chart, have a look at it. Generally, people don't have perfect agreement between how they see themselves and their ideal self – if someone did, we'd probably find them unbearably smug. So it's OK to find some differences. But equally, most of us do have some ways in which we are a bit similar to what we'd ideally like to be. So are there practical things you could do, or work on, to increase that similarity?

Self-consciousness can be seen as an extreme form of self-awareness, in which the person has a heightened awareness of their own actions. In the case of private self-consciousness, this may simply involve very close monitoring of their own thoughts and feelings. Public self-consciousness, though, can influence people to the point where they feel that they are being constantly judged or evaluated by others, and it is often the source of shyness or embarrassment when dealing with strangers.

Multiple selves

What we are actually aware of when we are self-aware is not always the same. We may, for example, catch a fleeting glimpse of ourselves in a window or mirror and become aware of our personal appearance; or we may be about to speak in a social situation and worried about how we will come across. Researchers have often taken the view that we have more than one version of the "self". In fact, as early as 1890, James argued that we have as many social selves as there are people who recognise us – in other words, that we act differently with everyone we know, and that each of those ways of acting encompasses another of our social selves.

Carver and Sheier (1981) distinguished between the private self and the public self. The **private self** is your personal feelings, thoughts and opinions, while your **public self** is your public image, or the way that other people see you. Markus and Nurius (1986) suggested that in addition to the selves that we know about ourselves, we also have a range of possible selves – versions of the self that we would like to become, and also versions of the self which we would like to avoid turning into. These possible selves help to guide our behaviour and the choices that we make.

Self-regulation

Another variant on this approach was put forward by Higgins, in 1987, who proposed that in addition to our perceptions of our actual selves and our ideal selves, we also have a self-schema of the **"ought" self** – the self that we think we should be. Higgins argued that the ideal and ought selves are motivators which guide and direct our behaviour. As a general rule, the ought self provides us with immediate goals, whereas the ideal self motivates our further-reaching ambitions.

The way this motivation happens because of the discrepancy between the perceived actual self and the other two – the ought self and the **ideal self**. We are motivated to reduce that discrepancy because of the negative emotions which are generated if the gulf between them becomes too extreme. Too large a discrepancy between the ideal-self and the actual self, Higgins argued, can produce depressive emotional responses such as dejection and sadness; too large a discrepancy between the ought self and the actual

Key Terms

private self
Those aspects of the self-concept which are kept hidden from other people.

public self
Those parts of the self-concept which are apparent to other people.

"ought" self
The part of the sense of self which describes how the person should be if they conformed fully to expectations.

ideal self
An internal impression of the perfect person one would like to be.

self, on the other hand, produces threat reaction emotions such as anxiety or fear.

Higgins also proposed that we have two separate psychological systems for **self-regulation**, by which he meant the way that we try to balance our self-concept and minimise these negative emotions. One of these is all about achieving ideas, hopes or aspirations, and is known as promotion. The other is prevention, which is using avoiding strategies to minimise negative outcomes – for example, by taking action to carry out duties or obligations. People who are more focused towards promotion, Higgins argued, will tend to look for ways of achieving their ambitions – learning new skills or improving how they do things. People who are more focused towards prevention will tend to concentrate more on avoiding failure, and so will often tend to avoid new people or situations, concentrating instead on what they already know.

The "true self"

Back in 1951, Rogers argued that while much of our self-concept can be expressed through our interactions and relationships with others, we also have an inner, "true self", which can involve aspects of our selves which we don't easily manage to express to anyone else. He argued that therapy which puts people in touch with their "true selves" and allows them to express it in their behaviour is experienced as deeply satisfying by that person.

We are not always aware of our true selves, or at least not fully; but we are often aware that there are things we know about ourselves that other people don't know. McKenna (2008) discussed how people often find it difficult to express aspects of their "true" selves to their closest others; in fact, this inexpressibility is more or less the way that the true self as defined by Rogers and others.

Sometimes, though, we are able to discuss aspects of our "true" selves to people we don't know personally. McKenna described this as being like the Rubin (1975) "strangers on a train" scenario – **self-disclosure** to someone who you know you are only meeting fleetingly can feel much safer than self-disclosure to people you know you will see again, like your partner or family members. The combination of expectations, constraints and anxieties about possible consequences means that we normally keep some things in reserve; but these don't apply if we know we won't see that person again. So, according to McKenna, people will often tell perfect strangers things about themselves which they would never tell their significant others.

McKenna also found that the internet can also elicit intimate and personal self-expression – often to a greater degree than would happen in a real-world relationship. There are several unique features of the internet which allow this to happen, which are listed in Table 8.2. A number of laboratory studies (e.g., Bargh et al, 2002) have shown that people tend to like one another more when they first become acquainted through the internet, than if they first meet face to face; and they also become intimate more quickly. The researchers suggested that this probably results from the way that people tend to disclose aspects of their "true self" more easily through the internet, and that having disclosed it, they felt closer to the person who had received the information.

This idea was supported by a study conducted by McKenna et al (2002) of 600 internet newsgroup users. They looked at how far their participants felt able to express their "true self" online, which varied from one person to

| Key Terms

self-regulation
Balancing the self-concept and minimising any sense of failure through promotion of successes and trying to avoid negative outcomes.

self-disclosure
Revealing aspects of the private self which would normally not be disclosed.

another. But they also found that the degree to which they felt able to do this correlated, perhaps not surprisingly, with their likelihood of forming close online relationships – even to the extent of having affairs with or becoming engaged to them.

However, we are not necessarily always so open with strangers. McKenna et al found that the degree of self-disclosure which people would make on the internet varied depending on whether they had a friend present in the room or not (even if the friend had no idea what they were saying). But their online interactions with strangers didn't necessarily exaggerate their personal qualities – in fact, quite the opposite. McKenna et al found that people tended to be very modest when they were interacting in private online with a stranger – much more so, than when they met a stranger anonymously but in a face-to-face situation.

Table 8.2 Aspects of internet communication which facilitate self-expression

Anonymity	The ability to interact anonymously frees the person from expectations, constraints and possible sanctions from known acquaintances.
Shared interests	The internet can connect people with others who have shared interests or other important aspects of identity (e.g., sexual preferences, political views), who may not be easily identifiable in their everyday life.
Concealment of physical problems	Socially anxious people such as those with physical problems which affect other people's perceptions of them (e.g., stuttering, obesity) can develop relationships with other people based on less superficial aspects of themselves.
Control over self-presentation	People have more control over how they come across, partly through having more time, and partly because of the lack of unintentional NVC "leakage".

Source: McKenna (2008)

THE SELF-IMAGE

How we perceive ourselves is also closely linked with modern concerns about personal image projection, and what we generally refer to as the self-image. The self-image is sometimes described as the **self-schema**, that is, the set of ideas, impressions, action plans and memories which we hold about ourselves; but it can be more externally focused as well. Also, it isn't always accurate. It has been described as having three sources: how we see ourselves directly, the feedback we receive from others about how they see us, and what we believe others think of us.

In many ways, this links back to Cooley's "looking-glass self", in the sense that we draw on the feedback we receive from others to form our self-image; but we also use other sources of information. In the modern world, for example, consumerism contributes a great deal to the self-image. People choose to dress in certain ways because it projects a particular image; we make lifestyle choices regarding cars, domestic items and forms of transport partly in order to project, socially, a particular image; and we are constantly exhorted by advertisers to make consumer choices based on our ideal version of ourselves.

Not only that, our sources of feedback are very different than in the society of previous eras. Teenagers nowadays still have the previous social influences from family, school and immediate friendship networks which teenagers from all generations have experienced. They are also surrounded by the consumer pressures, advertising and diversity of images presented by "youth culture", as teenagers have been since the middle of the last century. But they also have other, more immediate sources of feedback through social networks and other options offered by the internet. While these are broad-based and may involve feedback from total strangers, they also operate at a level which can be very much more personal than the impact of advertisers, and can affect the person's levels of self-esteem much more deeply than general advertising.

Image projection

The self-image has traditionally been seen as the descriptive part of the self-concept, as opposed to its evaluative aspects which are usually referred to as self-esteem. But the distinction is not completely cut and dried, especially in the modern world where the images we have of ourselves, and in particular the image we project to other people, have become deeply significant aspects of social interaction. The emergence of celebrity culture in the mass media, for example, has focused a great deal of attention on personal image projection – the ways in which people project themselves and come across in the public eye.

Projecting a particular image to others became an essential part of youth culture in the second half of the 20th century, as various social groups began to adopt characteristic styles of dress and hairstyling. For many young people, the social group to which they belonged determined not just the physical image which they projected to others, but also their consumer behaviour: the music they chose and the places they would shop. The idea of image projection and selection through consumer choice became an established part of social living at that time, and has remained so ever since.

In the 21st century, another route for image projection emerged through the social media offered by sites such as Facebook, Myspace and LinkedIn. These allow members to post not just personal details, but also interests, activities, pictures and other aspects of their lives, so that friends and others can see what is important to them. Facebook pages are often constructed as communication with friends, but they also allow wider access from the general public. That means that a Facebook image can conflict with the careful way that people try to control their public images – for example, when drawing up a CV or attending an interview for a job.

In 2013, Stoughton et al published a study of how prospective employers often look at young people's Facebook pages to make judgements about their suitability for certain jobs. The problem the researchers identified was that these pages were often misleading in that context, because they gave false impressions of what those people were like, or would be like at work. For example, the young people concerned tended to highlight social activities, but employers were typically put off by pictures of their prospective candidates drinking or enjoying themselves at parties. The image they were projecting was suitable for their friends, but entirely unsuitable in the context of a job application.

Avatars and cyberselves

Some internet sites are immediate; sites like Snapchat, for example, simply involve the transitory sharing of images between friends. Cooley's work predates the popularity of the "selfie" by over a century; but the practice of collecting (and distributing) immediate images of oneself, made possible by the smartphone and tablet, continues and reinforces the idea of the self, or part of it anyway, as a "looking-glass" reflecting how we and others see ourselves.

Other forms of internet interaction, though, go far deeper into the realms of the self-concept than others. A number of internet or gaming sites invite or require the person using them to develop an **avatar**: an alternate self, whose characteristics are directly relevant to the situation presented in the site or game. Avatars may start off as relatively simple, but through the game will tend to acquire skills and expertise which means that they change and develop as their user gains more experience. Since the user also brings their own prior knowledge to the avatar's role, this means that they can eventually become an alternate self.

The degree to which this happens depends on the context. Some games – the type of games known as massive multi-player online role playing games (**MMORPGs**) such as *World of Warcraft* – bring together avatars from many different individuals, each of whom is making their own choices and decisions in a "theatre" determined partly by the game itself and partly by the previous decisions that those avatars and the others they have interacted with have made. These types of games are generally regarded as similar to participating in hobbies or recreational sport, in that the person concerned is involved, but their overall self-image or true self is not necessarily deeply affected.

The type of avatar used does seem to make a difference to how we behave. Christou and Michael (2014) used an immersive, first-person game in which the player had to block incoming projectiles with their bare hands. The avatars used were either normal-looking humanoids, or tough-looking bipedal aliens. The researchers used body-tracking technology as well as game scores, and found that when people were using the alien avatars, they scored fewer body hits than when they were playing with humanoid avatars. Each participant played with both types of avatars, which ruled out individual differences.

The question is: does the choice of avatar also influence how we represent ourselves? Yee and Balienson (2007) found that people using attractive avatars became more intimate and friendly with strangers. In their study, they set up a situation where the person was allocated an avatar, and told that they would have a conversation with another person in a virtual environment. The avatars were of varying degrees of attractiveness. After a number of introductory exercises, the person was asked to introduce themselves and encouraged to continue doing so for as long as possible. Yee and Balienson found that people with attractive avatars moved closer to the other person, and revealed significantly more pieces of personal information than those with unattractive avatars. This, Lee and Balienson argued, provided support for the idea of the **Proteus Effect**: our self-representations in turn shape our own behaviour.

In a second part of the study, the researchers varied the avatars by size, and found that those with taller avatars would act in a more self-confident manner in a money-sharing game. Players with taller avatars felt more able to reject unfair share offers, while those with shorter avatars were more likely to accept them. The researchers argued that the Proteus Effect could make a difference, not just in online environments, but also in how people interact in other circumstances.

Researchers have also found that men are more likely to choose a female avatar than women are to choose a male one; but some researchers have found that this is often only temporary, and that most people who "gender-bend" in this way tend to return to an avatar of their own gender in the end (Kafai et al, 2008). It is possible, too, that men choose a female avatar for instrumental reasons. Wadell and Ivory (2012) found that attractive avatars tended to be offered more help, support and gifts from other players, and so they progress faster in the game. Women who gender-bend, on the other hand, have been shown to believe that they will be taken more seriously as a male character (Hussain and Griffiths, 2008). This is supported by research by Coghlan and Kirwan (2013) who found that, in a goal-oriented situation, men who gender-bend have a measurably lower **need for achievement (nAch)** than those who do not, but that there was no such difference with people who gender-bend in internet environments which were not goal oriented. Overall, the research indicates that people do use avatars to express aspects of themselves, but equally often, the choice of avatar is instrumental, and doesn't appear to have a profound impact on the self-concept.

The extent of self-involvement in online environments such as *Second Life*, though, can be quite different. Unlike *World of Warcraft*, *Second Life* is not a goal-oriented game. It involves creating an avatar who lives in the society portrayed in the game. The player chooses their avatar's personal characteristics and clothing and then moves them around in the game, acquiring skills, professions and interacting with others. It has its own currency, and many aspects of its environment mirror the real world. Many of the large corporations, including IBM and General Motors and even universities, have their own "Islands" in the *Second Life* world, where avatars can visit, purchase commodities, enrol in courses or engage in paid work.

In other words, *Second Life* provides a virtual environment for just that – a second life, where the individual can make different choices and take up different opportunities. How clearly the alternative selves offered by this platform are differentiated from the person's own self is extremely variable. In a course run by the Baylor College of Medicine in Texas, *Second Life* is being used as a vehicle to help people with disabilities raise their levels of self-esteem. Since their disability is irrelevant to their choice of, and the choices made by, their avatar, participants in the seven-session workshop are able to explore aspects of themselves and interact with people in a more everyday manner. The course organisers argue that this can significantly raise their levels of self-esteem.

It is well known that people use avatars in *Second Life* to present a more attractive version of themselves. Thomas and Johansen (2012) explored the

Key Terms

Proteus Effect
The idea that remodelling images of the self can also change the personal self.

need for achievement (nAch)
An internal motivation to succeed in life, or in attaining particular goals.

ways that avatars can be viewed as "ideal selves" by asking women to develop two avatars: one that looked like themselves, and one which could look like anything they wanted it to be. The researchers suggested that this was a useful way of identifying differences between ideal and real self-image. Interestingly, there was just as much variation in the "ideal" avatars taken as a whole, as there was in the "self" ones: women who regarded themselves as too thin constructed avatars who were larger, while those regarding themselves as too fat constructed slimmer ones. So it wasn't just a question of conforming to a general idealised social image, it was a personal ideal self which the women were constructing.

Box 8.2   Avatars, gaming and the real world

The use of avatars in applications like *Second Life* is sometimes regarded as controversial. Those who dislike the idea of "virtual living" argue that web-sites of this kind distract people from the real world, and that they "ought" to be concentrating on their real-life experiences instead. Other people argue that the experiences obtained from the virtual world can help people to make more positive choices in the real world as well; someone who studies at a university in *Second Life* may be motivated to explore what that university has to offer them in the real world as well, and there are anecdotal examples of people who have been inspired in this way to go on to study as mature students, and successfully achieve degrees.

Another argument is that of dependency, a common fear of parents of teenagers who spend a lot of time gaming. The fear is that they may become so absorbed by the virtual world offered by computer games or experiences that they become unable to cope with reality. However, computer gaming has now been with us for over 30 years, and there are any number of people who appeared to be "addicted" as teenagers who have grown out of it, and got on with their own education and lives. In the case of adults who have become dependent, it can also be argued that society always has problems and people who find it hard to cope. Perhaps using the computer to escape from life's problems is a healthier option than turning to alcohol or other drugs? It's an open-ended question, with no single right answer; but whatever the opinions in society, the virtual world is with us, and people are using it more rather than less as time goes on.

Key Terms

self-image
The factual or descriptive picture which people hold of themselves, without the evaluative component implicit in the concept of self-esteem.

self-esteem
The evaluative dimension of the self-concept, which is to do with how worthwhile and/ or confident people feel about themselves.

Self-esteem

Many researchers draw a distinction between the **self-image**, which is the factual picture which people have of themselves, their likes and dislikes, etc.; and **self-esteem**, which is the evaluative part of the self-concept, containing the social judgements which people have internalised. Having a reasonably high level of self-esteem has been shown to be an important aspect of psychological health. People with low self-esteem are more vulnerable to both psychological and some physical disorders (possibly as a result of a degree of self-neglect), experience more stress and also under-achieve consistently by comparison with similar people with higher levels of self-esteem.

So how do we develop higher or lower levels of self-esteem? In 1968, Coopersmith published an extensive study of self-esteem conducted with "normal", middle-class American boys aged between 10 and 12, sorted into three groups, of high, middle and low self-esteem. Self-esteem was rated using the boys' own self-evaluations, teachers' behaviour reports and psychological tests. (The three measures agreed with each other in more than 80 per cent of the cases.)

The boys with a high level of self-esteem were active, expressive and generally more likely to be successful. They set themselves higher targets than boys with lower self-esteem, and they were more successful in achieving these targets. They also tended to have parents who were not permissive, but reasonably strict and very clear about the limits which they had set. Those parents were very interested in their children, knowing all of their friends by name; and they clearly expected their children to reach high standards.

All of which contrasted sharply with the low self-esteem group, whose parents tended to have lower aspirations and to be much less involved. Low self-esteem boys set themselves lower targets and were also more likely to suffer from ailments like insomnia, headaches and stomach upsets. The middling self-esteem group were generally optimistic and able to cope with criticism, like the higher self-esteem boys; but they also tended to be the most conventional and were extremely dependent on others' opinions.

Coopersmith argued that an important part of parenting is the fostering of positive self-esteem. He regarded it as fundamental to psychological health, and saw both parental styles and personal goals as important factors in its development. Treating children with respect and providing them with well-defined standards and values, demands for competence and guidance towards solutions of problems were, he argued, major factors in fostering personal self-esteem; so an environment which was well-structured and demanding was more helpful in developing independence and self-reliance than a permissive one.

Our levels of self-esteem can fluctuate according to what we are doing and how we feel. There is also some evidence that self-esteem may be more of a social process than simply the outcome of parenting styles. Neff and Germer (2012) carried out a series of five-day studies which involved assessing levels of self-esteem in working couples at the end of the work day, and also at bedtime. They found that people's self-esteem at bedtime was positively correlated with how their partners had felt when they came back from work – if they came back feeling good and with positive self-esteem, their partners had higher self-esteem by the end of the evening. If they came back dejected and with lower self-esteem, their partner would have a lower level of self-esteem by bedtime than they had earlier in the evening.

Neff and Germer argued that this can set up a positive feedback loop – if the partner goes to bed feeling good, that may also result in a positive start to the next day. Positive self-esteem at work has been shown to be closely connected with job satisfaction and good job performance, so that in turn would render a positive outcome at the end of the next day more likely. Similarly, lower levels of self-esteem resulting from difficult or stressful working days could have a continuing effect, carrying across to the next day.

The type of self-esteem being discussed by Neff and Germer is much more variable than the type of self-esteem being discussed by Coopersmith. For Neff and Germer, the assumption is of a fairly positive baseline level of self-esteem which is then affected by day-to-day experience. Coopersmith and others, on the other hand, were concerned with differences in that baseline level, arguing that some individuals can be shown to have consistently lower or higher levels of self-esteem than others.

Self-actualisation and positive regard

Rogers (1961) regarded early experience as being important in the development of baseline level of self-esteem, but also believed that these experiences could be challenged and overcome at any age. Rogers saw people as having two basic psychological needs: to receive **positive regard** of some sort from other people, and to develop their own potentials and abilities (a need which he referred to as the need for **self-actualisation**). The two needs interact with one another, and in a normal, psychologically healthy individual, they are both satisfied. But people who have not had their need for positive regard satisfied would find that need conflicting with their need for self-actualisation.

Most people, Rogers believed, have had at least one person in their lives (usually, but not always, a parent) who provided them with unconditional positive regard – love, affection or respect which remained no matter what they did. This meant that they felt secure and free to develop their own talents or abilities. But people who had not had that experience were in a different position, because for them, positive regard was always conditional on their acting in approved ways. That meant they did not feel able to explore their own potential or self-development, for fear that it should lead to disapproval or lose them positive regard in some way; and the comparisons they made with their unrealistically high ideal-self resulted in very low self-esteem.

Rogers suggested that the low self-esteem resulting from conditional positive regard could be repaired by therapy aimed at providing that unconditional positive regard for other people. This would work by giving them the security to explore themselves and to express their need for self-actualisation. Studies evaluating this approach to therapy gave some positive results. In one, Butler and Haigh (1954) showed that clients who had experienced client-centred therapy showed a substantial increase in the correlation between their self-concept and their ideal self-concept, resulting in an overall increase in their self-esteem.

Rogers's theory shows how our sense of identity can change over time, and depending on the life-situations we find ourselves in. However, we rarely remember exactly how we felt and what we were like in earlier times; we tend to go through a process of **self-reconstruction**, which means that we adjust our memories of how we were to be congruent with how we are now. Lowenthal et al (1975) interpreted this as a motivational process, allowing us to maintain or gain self-esteem by assuming that their current lives are all for the best, and so adjusting their autobiographical memories to support that idea.

Smith (1997) conducted a longitudinal, in-depth study of four women during the course of pregnancy. Pregnancy is a life-changing event but not a negative one, and during the lengthy nine-month period Smith found the women went through a number of changes, both in their memories of how they had felt at different times, and in terms of their general sense of identity. The process of self-reconstruction meant that their memories had become adjusted in accordance with their current experiences. By the end of their pregnancies, and after the birth, difficult times were barely remembered, and the positive aspects of their pregnancies were in the ascendant.

Key Terms

positive regard
Liking, affection, love or respect for someone else.

self-actualisation
The making real of one's abilities and talents: using them to the full.

self-reconstruction
Adjusting memories of the self at earlier times so that they fit the current self-image.

Table 8.3 Theories of self

Theory	Major protagonists	Main mechanism
Social feedback	James, Cooley	Feedback from other's reactions
Symbolic interactionism	Mead, Goffman	Social roles
Self-perception	Bem	Interpretation of one's own actions
Self-efficacy	Bandura	Feedback from others and one's own experience
Social comparison	Festinger	Comparison with other people
Self-awareness	Scheier & Carver	Introspective reflection
Multiple selves	Markus & Nurius	Adjustment to others
Self-regulation	Higgins	Internal moral imperatives
The "true self"	McKenna	Limitations of self-disclosure
Self-esteem	Rogers	Ideal and real self-comparison
Self-categorisation	Tajfel & Turner	Comparison with other social groups
Self-evaluation	Wills, Tesser	Selective comparison with other groups
Relational self	Andersen & Chen	Important relationships and significant others

CULTURAL CONTEXTS OF SELF

Each of the theories of self that we have looked at contributes something to our understanding, as we can see from Table 8.3. It is apparent, too, that our ideas about ourselves don't exist in a vacuum. They bring together the social feedback we have from others, our knowledge of the different aspects of our selves and how they compare, comparisons with social groups and internalisations drawn from the social groups that we belong to, and even the relationships we have with other people.

Social factors, therefore, have always been an important part of the ways that we see ourselves. But do these theories really sum up who we are? Psychological research on the self has been sharply criticised because it has tended to assume that what is true for middle-class Anglo/American culture is true of the whole world; but if we take a global perspective, we find some very different ideas about what constitutes the "self".

The individual or the group

Concepts of self vary in different cultures, in all sorts of ways. But one consistent dimension is the extent to which the individual is seen as separate from the social group, or as a part of it. The dominant perspective in psychology has reflected the American influence on the discipline as it grew, and tends to see the individual as paramount, with group membership being a kind of optional extra. But this is not a view of the self shared by many other cultures – indeed, it could be argued that it is this individualism which makes American culture unique.

In most cultures, the self is seen as embedded in its social matrix. Family, friends and social group are seen as a significant and fundamental part of who the person is, and the general expectation is that social action will recognise that, and act in accordance with the needs of the social group. That doesn't mean that the individual is not recognised; people are seen as being distinct, with their own independent thoughts, talents and personalities. But those have been partly shaped by their social context, and continue to be expressed with it.

For example, when the Native Australian rock band Yothu Yindi began to release records and gain some chart success, their progress and opportunities were all discussed with the tribe's elders, and the decisions which were made took account of the context and their role as representing their Native Australian culture, in their music and in their public appearances. Their success was as an individual rock band, but the band members' experiences were not separated from, or independent of their social group.

The idea of self as embedded in the social group appears to be the dominant model of self in societies across the world. As psychology becomes increasingly internationalised, the difference between this approach and the American model has also become increasingly recognised, and the challenge to modern researchers is to integrate existing theories with ideas about the embeddedness of self in its social context, or, failing that, to acknowledge that many of the theories – including some that we have looked at in this chapter – are culture-specific, rather than universally applicable.

The nature of individuality

If we look at models of the self in different cultures, we find that the nature of individuality itself can vary considerably from one human society to another. The idea of the self as independent of the social context is one which is not shared by all human societies; in fact, most human cultures have traditionally seen people not as isolated individuals, but as firmly embedded in their cultural, social and family contexts. The idea that the self is largely independent and only "influenced" by social factors is one which seems to be unique to Western societies. Marsella et al (1985) argued that this means that most of the theories of the self are completely irrelevant to most of the world.

An African approach

For example: Mbiti (1970) describes how the African philosophical tradition sees the individual self as firmly located within the collective self of the tribe or the people. It is the ongoing life of the people, linked firmly to the rhythms of the natural world, which provides the context for "self" and "being", and the idea that these can exist somehow independently of that context is regarded as simply unrealistic. Moreover, the individuals who make up the tribe or people are regarded as indivisible from it. Mbiti points out that, in many African tribes, counting people was traditionally forbidden, because people are regarded as corporate members of society, and society operates as a whole and therefore cannot be divided into its constituent parts.

It may be worth noting a couple of points here. First, stating that the individual is part of the collective self, as Mbiti does, does not involve denying that people have their own special thoughts and ideas. Every human being is unique, and recognised as such. It is the idea that the self can exist independently of its social context which is being challenged. People need to be understood in the context of their families, their social groups, their friends and their culture if that understanding is to make any sense. Take those away, and the "individual" would be quite different, and not a fully independent entity at all.

This brings us to the second point, which is that while Western philosophy and psychology has often regarded the self as if it were independent, the reality of Western social life is that social contexts – families, religious groups, friend-ship groups – are actually crucially important in how we see ourselves too. We have seen this as we have looked at some of the more practical research in the field. It is simply that this is formally recognised in African traditional thought, whereas traditional Western assumptions don't acknowledge its importance.

As Hayes (1983) pointed out, the social embeddedness of the self is not just assumed in traditional social practices, it is also a fundamental part of traditional African education systems – systems which were designed explicitly to train both men and women to participate as fully developed individuals in the life of the community. In these cultures, Hayes argued, individualism is seen as being irresponsible and virtually uncivilised. The individual is not simply responsible to him or herself, but as an interdependent member of the commu-nity. Hayes went on to emphasise that there is nothing "primitive" or "tribal" about this approach; rather, it represents a highly developed and coherent system of social and moral education.

A Hindu approach

Bharati (1985) described how the Hindu concept of self is quite different again. Rather than emphasising the community and social context of self, Hindu thinking emphasises selfhood – but not in the Western way. At the centre of this thinking, according to Bharati, is the indivisibility of the "true self" with the one-ness of God – the unity of the atman, or "innermost self" with all-being, or Godhood. This innermost self, however, needs to be reached through internal meditation and self-discipline. Although everyone contains it, everyone does not have equal access to it. According to Bharati (1985), other aspects of self in Hindu thinking tend to be concerned with fallibilities and obstructions to the realisation of the atman. For example, *jiva* is the term used to describe the unconscious parts of the self which contain the negative qualities of lust, avarice, egotism and the like.

There is also a layer within the self which Hsu (1985) described as the "unexpressible consciousness". This consists of thoughts and ideas which the individual doesn't communicate to other people, either because of the fear of social rejection, or because other people wouldn't understand even if they tried to. According to Bharati (1985), this corresponds exactly with the Hindu concept of *maya*. A further aspect of Hindu self-awareness concerns conscious interaction with other people and is described as *samsara*. Bharati emphasises, though, that it is almost impossible to translate the precise meanings of these terms, partly because they are meant to be experienced rather than discussed, and partly because linguistic differences between languages distort the meaning of the concept once it has been translated.

A Japanese approach

DeVos (1985) discussed the experience of self in Japanese culture, where it is intimately linked with social interaction and social relationships. According to Azuma et al (1981), Japanese children are disciplined from a very early age into an ongoing awareness of the effect that their actions will have on others.

Rather than confronting the child, and engaging in the kind of "battle of wills" which is so common between Western children and their mothers, the Japanese mother, according to Azuma et al, "suffers" her child, and the child is thus trained to realise that its behaviour has consequences on other people, and may cause them grief and distress. In this way, Japanese people become highly sensitive to interpersonal guilt, and also to social shame, although DeVos feels that the latter is less important than the internalised guilt which an individual feels about the effects that their actions have on others.

The internalised guilt and awareness of interpersonal consequences of behaviour forms an important underpinning to the Japanese perception of self. According to DeVos, Japanese people find ultimate satisfaction in "belonging", and in being aware that they belong. Belonging means that they can avoid the painful self-awareness which is associated with existing as a separate individual, and instead find a location within a group identity. That doesn't mean, of course, that Japanese people are not individuals, with their own thoughts and ideas – every human being is that. But it does mean that many of these thoughts are kept very private, in case they should somehow disturb the social balance, and that the individual's personal sense of identity is rooted much more strongly in social relationships and appropriate social behaviour.

Box 8.3 Cyber-bullying

One of the most frequently found sources of low self-esteem comes from those who experienced bullying as children. We looked at bullying in general in the last chapter. As a form of aggression, it can have profound effects on the self-concept as well as on our confidence and the ways that we interact with other people. Many young people – and older ones for that matter – experience bullying at some point in their lives. Given that research also suggests that it is those with vulnerable self-esteem who are most likely to be picked out for bullying in the first place, it can be a traumatic experience for the person concerned.

Conventional bullying is damaging enough, but cyber-bullying – that is, bullying through the internet or text messaging – introduces other dimensions which are not present with physical bullying. Perhaps the most important of these is the way that cyber-bullies can be more or less anonymous, using pseudonyms, internet messaging, texting and even temporary email accounts to hide their identity. It has been argued that this deindividuation frees the bully from any sense of social constraint, and means that they can be particularly vicious, issuing rape and death threats or other extreme comments. Those who lack the confidence to disengage from the source of such comments, or who for other reasons find it impossible to do so often experience shame and self-hatred as a result, and in more than one instance it has led to suicide.

Unfortunately, because of the anonymity of the bullies, it is not so easy to attempt to tackle cyber-bullying through group approaches, as can be done in schools and workplaces. It remains to be seen whether attempts to control this behaviour at more general social levels such as through the law, will be effective; but the international nature of the internet suggests that there may be some problems establishing general procedures against cyber-bullying.

In the meantime, attempts are being made to establish online and personal counselling for the victims of cyber-bullying, which may help them to challenge the damaging effects on their self-esteem.

The multi-layered self

Hsu (1985) describes a multi-layered model of the self (see Figure 8.1) in which the self is seen as embedded within the different layers of its personal, social and cultural context. Hsu argues that people will resist most strongly any changes to the third layer – that represented by the person's intimate society and culture, because it is the part of the external world to which the individual experiences the strongest feelings of attachment (a view which can also be linked with Tajfel's theory of social identity). This third layer doesn't just comprise important other people, but it may also include cultural features which are perceived as an essential part of self-identity, like the American male's aversion to physical contact with another male, or the Hindu sense of caste pollution.

Hsu's model in many ways provides a more useful model for conceptualising and understanding the various different aspects of the self. The traditional Western view of the independent "self" being affected by social "influences" may give us some insights; but it is really only a small part of what is actually going on. The inner self and the "true" self give us another dimension for understanding the state of being ourselves; while social and community based approaches allow us to see the human being within their own social context – which, as we have seen, shapes so many different aspects of our selves.

Identity in the 21st century

We can see, then, that there are several ways of conceptualising the self. Who we are, and who we regard ourselves as being, is intimately linked with the culture in which we were brought up, and also the social environment in which

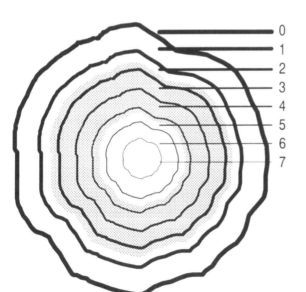

0
1
2
3
4
5
6
7

Hsu's model
of the self in cultural context:
0 = outer world;
1 = wider society and culture;
2 = operative society and culture;
3 = intimate society and culture;
4 = expressible conscious;
5 = unexpressible conscious;
6 = pre-conscious (Freudian);
7 = unconscious (Freudian).
Adapted from Hsu, 1985.

Figure 8.1 Hsu's multi-layered self

we find ourselves. The latter part of the 20th century saw a significant growth in cult membership and religious revivalism in Western societies, which may have been a recognition of the powerful human need for belonging and social identification.

The 21st century, however, offers different opportunities. The internet society provides broader scope for networking, constant social contact and far more opportunities to express public aspects of the self and personal diversity than ever before. It even offers the opportunity for us to develop increasingly complex alternative versions of ourselves, and to "live" those virtual lives as part of our own everyday experience.

Oddly enough, the experiences of young people growing up in the digital age mirrors the ways that human beings grew up for most of their evolutionary history. While the industrial revolution established the nuclear family of parents and children, largely isolated from other relatives and generations, before that people tended to live in much larger family groups and villages – that is, in close-knit communities where everyone knew each other and the idea of the individual being alone, psychologically, was quite a strange one. People, as we have seen, grew up embedded in their cultures, with other people always at hand.

The modern teenager may not be in the same physical situation, but their growing up takes place in the context of social networking and continuous contact with peers, relatives and others. Facetime, Skype and various forms of social networking means that for many, they are rarely actually alone. Instead, they grow up embedded in their communities, in a way which is quite different from the ways that children grew up in the 20th century; and which has some striking similarities with older types of village communities. It has differences, too, of course, and it remains to be see how strongly all this will impact on the ways that we see ourselves.

Whatever the differences, they are not such as to make us less social. Rather, we remain as social beings, and our sense of self is strongly determined by that reality. It is just the ways that we interact with other people have changed over time, as the range of possible interactions has extended through technology. Our fundamental social processes remain much the same, but our forms of communication and the media through which we interact have broadened with modern life. In the next chapter, we will look at some of the applied aspects of social psychology, and how it can help us to understand other aspects of modern living.

Summary: Chapter 8

1. The beginnings of self occur as the infant learns that part of the world is separate, and starts to develop a sense of agency and efficacy.

2. Social awareness begins from birth, but a full recognition of others as independent thinkers takes several years. Social roles and personal constructs also develop the self-concept and make it more sophisticated.

3. Early theories of self included the importance of social feedback, and the idea that self was largely determined by our social roles – an idea known as symbolic interactionism.

4. Self-perception theory examines the way we draw inferences about our-selves from our own behaviour. Our self-efficacy beliefs are also a signifi-cant part of that process.

5. Social comparison theory describes how the self-concept is influenced by our ideas of how we measure up to others. Other researchers have emphasised the importance of our relationships, and how our self-aware-ness relates to our ideal selves.

6. People have multiple "selves" which come into play in different social sit-uations. We are motivated by what we feel we ought to do as well as our own ideas and self-perceptions, and sometimes find personal disclosure of the "true" self easier with strangers than with close friends or family.

7. The self-image includes how we project ourselves to others as well as the ways that we see ourselves. Avatars and cyberselves are means to explore different self-images or project different aspects of ourselves on the internet.

8. Our need for self-actualisation is equally as important as our need for positive regard from others, and we suffer damage to our self-esteem if it is neglected. Bullying, both in real life and through the internet, is also damaging to self-esteem.

9. The idea of the self varies greatly in different cultures. In many societies the self is seen as embedded in the wonder social matrix. In some cul-tures, the public expression of self is carefully controlled, and the "inner" emotional self is kept private.

10. The self can be seen as multi-layered, ranging from an inner personal "core" to the aspects of self manifest in culture and society. The oppor-tunities provided by the internet in modern life can mean that people are more closely linked to others in society than was possible in the pre-in-ternet industrial age.

Contents

Chapter 9

Applying social psychology

9

In this chapter, we will look at some of the ways in which social psychology has contributed to our understanding of how people interact in real-world contexts. Many of the important theories and insights in social psychology have arisen from the work of psychologists operating in industry, in the health professions and in the community. Equally, many of the theories developed by academic researchers in social psychology are tried and tested in "real-world" situations before they are fully accepted. So the applications of social psychology form an important part of our understanding of the discipline.

GROUPS AT WORK

One of the most important interactions between social psychology and applied psychology has been in our understanding of groups. For many years, the study of group processes was maintained and amplified by organisational research. For example, in Chapter 6 we looked in some detail at the phenomenon of **groupthink** – the distortion in decision-making which occurs when groups become too complacent and disregard information which challenges their assumptions. Groupthink became apparent through work on organisational decision-making, although many of its classic examples are drawn from politics; in fact, it can happen in any established group.

But what exactly do we mean by a "group". It is generally agreed that a group should have the five distinct features which are listed in Table 9.1. Gatherings of people which are more transient, or more limited in their interactions, wouldn't really be relevant to the kinds of group processes which have been the subject of psychological research.

Table 9.1 Characteristics of a group

1. People interact over a sustained period of time – not just for a few minutes.

2. The people concerned perceive the group as a group, and themselves as members of it.

3. The group develops its own norms, roles and expectations as to how its members should behave; and sanctions for those who don't conform.

4. The group develops a sense of shared goals or purpose.

5. Relationships of one kind or another develop between the different members of the group.

Research into how groups work has a long history, and much of it stems from applying social psychology in the workplace. An influential series of studies conducted between 1924 and 1927 at the Hawthorne Electric Plant in Chicago opened people's eyes to the idea that motivation at work is not simply about the need to earn money, but involves social factors as well.

The studies involved changing aspects of the working conditions in particular sections of the factory, to see whether they had an effect on production (Mayo, 1933). In one classic example, the researchers increased the lighting levels for a group of workers, and their production increased. Then they lowered the lighting levels to below what they had been originally – and production increased. Finally, they brought the lighting back to what it had been before, and production increased again! This puzzling result told the researchers one thing – that what was happening evidently had nothing to do with the lighting. Further investigations showed that it really boiled down to social factors. The involvement of the researchers left the workforce feeling that management were interested in what they did, and that it mattered.

Group norms

It wasn't all that simple, though. In another part of the factory, neither physical changes to conditions nor social interventions from the researchers had any effect on production levels. The fourteen men working in the area had formed a close group, with everyone expected to conform to the group's norms. From direct observation, and from interviews with each of the men, Mayo identified four distinctive features of those norms:

1   Group members should not turn out too much work.
2   They shouldn't "slack" either.
3   They shouldn't tell anyone in authority anything which might get a colleague into trouble.
4   No group member had the right to act officiously over other group members.

These four principles set the standards for the whole group, and meant that the men kept up a steady rate of production and strongly resisted any external attempts to manipulate their productivity levels. Mayo argued that this is actually typical of most working groups if they work together for long enough. The group establishes its own norms and values, and uses these to regulate its behaviour.

Norms develop in just about any group if they stay together for any length of time. Postmes et al (2000) looked at how **group norms** formed rapidly in computer-mediated communication (CMC) between students on a university course. As the course progressed, conformity to those norms in the students' course-related emails increased, while their communications with those outside of the course showed no such adherence to the norms. The researchers argued that this was another example of the way that increasing social identification with the group led to increased conformity with the group's norms.

Norms make it clear what group members can expect from one another, and how they can avoid embarrassing situations or challenges which might lead to confrontations. Feldman (1984) identified four functions of group norms, which are listed in Table 9.2.

Table 9.2 Functions of group norms

1. Group norms express the central, most important values of the group.

2. Group norms establish common ground and predictability among group members.

3. Group norms define appropriate social behaviour.

4. Group norms maintain the group's distinctiveness.

Source: Feldman (1984)

Norms help group members to have a strong sense of what the group is all about, and what is and isn't acceptable to the group – for example, in a riot simulation held at the Dutch Riot Police Academy, Kroon et al (1991) showed that when non-violent group norms were made particularly salient, the chances of an escalation of conflict between police and rioters became much less.

Schein (1988) argued that working groups tend to have two types of norms: **pivotal norms**, which are central to the group and express its core assumptions; and **peripheral norms**, which are less crucial and deal with minor issues like how to find things out, or where people usually sit at lunchtimes. Schein's observations of working life showed that groups will tolerate much more deviation from the peripheral norms than from its pivotal norms; those were the ones which group members were expected to maintain most seriously.

Sometimes, though, there is a conflict between the group's norms, and some other standard of behaviour. At such times, social identification with the group becomes particularly salient. Packer (2008) put forward the **normative conflict** model, which argued that the relationship between the individual's social identification with the group and their conformity to group norms depends on how the norms of the group agree with other standards of behaviour. If they are very different – for example, if the group is recommending a course of action which some of its members see as irresponsible or morally questionably – then whether a group member will challenge what the group is doing depends on how strongly they identify with the group. Those who only identify weakly with the group are generally unlikely to express public concerns about the group's behaviour, especially if they think their opinion will be unpopular with group members (Packer, 2009), while according to Crane and Platow (2010), people who identify strongly with the group are more likely to challenge deviant behaviour, even if it is shown by the majority of the group's members – not an easy thing to do, as we saw in Chapter 6.

It isn't always that simple, though. People who belong to groups often try hard to conform to their group's norms because the price of failure may be exclusion from the group, or even ridicule – both powerful motivators for human beings. If the stakes are high – for example, if group members see them as involving their immortal souls – then challenging norms is a different matter. Finlay (2014) showed how Al-Qaeda-supporting groups who advocate violent conflict use this fear of exclusion to draw in young idealists and convert them to promoting violence. Effectively, they define cooperation or even association with non-Muslims as working counter to their "true" religion, and use a variety of verbal strategies to describe such cooperation, such as portraying them as ignorant, cowardly, mentally weak or selfish. In this way, they construct prescriptive norms which ensure that any members of the group know

Key Terms
pivotal norms Expectations and assumptions which are considered fundamental and unchangeable.
peripheral norms Expectations and assumptions which are felt as less important than others.
normative conflict Disagreement or conflict concerning what represents the norm or is acceptable.

that they will face judgements from others of being deviant and unworthy if they challenge what the group is promoting. Self-protective strategies such as **cognitive dissonance** (see Chapter 5) then act to strengthen the individual's belief in what they are being told.

Social norms can be implicit as well as explicit. The social norms of internet use, for example, are rarely stated explicitly, yet many people are aware that such norms do exist. Utz and Kramer (2009) studied the privacy practices of social media users, and showed how perceived social norms – that is, what the users understood to be social norms – have a direct influence on the strategies people adopted to protect their privacy. Using two popular European social media sites, the Dutch site Hyves and the German site StudiVZ, both similar to Facebook, the researchers found that over 80 per cent of the users in each sample had adjusted their privacy settings in some way, even if it was only to protect their email addresses. This contrasted considerably with an earlier study (Utz, 2008) in which only 30 per cent had protected their profile, and fitted with a developing social norm regarding the protection of privacy. They also found that the overall level of privacy established by users was directly related to how far they perceived impression management as being the main purpose of their pages – those seeing impression management as its most important function being least concerned with retaining the privacy of their other personal information.

Group roles

Among friends, it isn't uncommon for someone to be regarded as the organiser, someone else as the joker, and so on – even though these roles can be flexible and change around. Much the same applies in other types of groups, like working groups and committees. Belbin (1981) observed the behaviours of managers participating in a series of decision-making exercises, and from that data, outlined eight different team roles which were often adopted by people in a working team (see Table 9.3). It is important to remember, though, that Belbin was identifying the social roles which people might adopt in a team or group situation, rather than personalities.

Table 9.3 Belbin's team roles

Role	Task
The co-ordinator	To clarify the team's goals, allocate tasks and express the team's conclusions.
The shaper	To push team discussions towards agreement.
The monitor/evaluator	To analyse problems and assess everyone's contributions.
The team worker	To give support and help to others.
The implementer	To emphasise getting on with the task, transforming talk into practical suggestions or activities.
The plant	To put forward proposals and make suggestions.
The resource investigator	To locate resources of information, negotiating with outsiders where necessary.
The completer	To push the team to meet its schedules and targets.

Key Terms

cognitive dissonance
The state of cognitive tension produced by holding contradictory beliefs.

At first, Belbin stressed that any one person might adopt more than one of these roles depending on the situation and the way that discussions proceeded. However in later work, Belbin (1993) linked these roles with a set of personality characteristics, for example, describing a typical shaper as highly strung, impatient and dynamic, while a typical co-ordinator would be calm, self-disciplined and a positive thinker. As a result, there was an increasing tendency to treat Belbin's roles as if they were personality types, implying that a single person would tend to adopt just one single role; but this was a distortion of the original observations.

Rather than specifying roles, some researchers have emphasised the interpersonal processes which can happen within a working group. In 1950, Bales developed a set of eight categories which enabled researchers and trainers to describe observations of group interactions in a systematic way (see Table 9.4). The Bales Interaction Process model has been widely used for observing group processes, and is particularly useful when it comes to identifying different types

Table 9.4 Bales's interaction processes

Giving support

Giving suggestions

Giving opinions

Giving information

Asking for information

Asking for opinions

Asking for suggestions

Showing disagreement

Source: Bales (1950)

of verbal strategies. What it can tell us is whether someone is habitually using one particular type of interaction, and whether a group's typical discussions are missing a particular kind of contribution.

This model, though, has been criticised as over-emphasising consensual activities and minimising the importance of dissent. As we saw when we looked at groupthink in Chapter 6, there are times when challenges and disagreements are actually constructive. A disagreement to prevent the group taking a course which might prove misleading has quite a different implication than a challenge made to further the attacker's prestige or ego.

Peräkylä (2004) compared the use of Bales's Interaction Process Analysis (IPA) with Conversational Analysis (see Chapter 4) in investigating group interactions. Although the two appear quite different (IPA is quantitative, theory-oriented and normative, while CA is qualitative, inductive and idiographic), Peräkylä argued that the ways in which Conversational Analysis has developed means that it is now able to fulfil the original aims of interaction analysis in a more effective way. Peräkylä identified those aims as being all about control, solidarity and the allocation of resources, and argued that looking at them in terms of the rules and structures of how people talk with one another is more effective than looking at them by differentiating group participants.

 Other researchers have explored different aspects of communication in organisations. Hayes and Lemon (1990) discussed how developing effective communication is one of the main challenges facing small companies as they grow. In an action research project with a small-but-growing computer company, they interviewed all the staff and found that communication was one of the main problems which they experienced. Following their intervention, improvements encouraged by the management made a great deal of difference to the company, which helped it to maintain positive staff morale as its growth continued.

In a study of communication patterns in working groups, Leavitt (1951) looked at how effective the various communication networks – that is, who speaks to whom – can be. Networks which restricted who could speak to whom, like the hierarchical systems of communication found in many organisations, were shown to be much less effective than open communication patterns in which any member of an organisation could speak to any other. Consequently, many organisational "gurus" of the 1980s advocated better and more open communication for a successful organisation (e.g., Kanter, 1983; Peters and Waterman, 1982).

At that time, establishing open communication was quite a challenge, but this is one of the striking differences which the internet has made to working life. Most large organisations have an intranet, which allows open-access email communication between members. One of the ways that organisational intranets differ from the general use of the internet is that they can be shaped to fit with the requirements and use of the organisation – so one company intranet may be quite different from that of another apparently similar company. Most intranets are designed to be shielded from the "outside", working as complete virtual environments without direct contact with the wider internet, but the connections within those "walls", the accesses offered to different users and the ways that information can be uploaded and shared can vary considerably. Moreover, as people use the intranet, new uses (and interpretations) arise, bringing unexpected consequences for management as well as for the information technology (IT) specialists involved in establishing the structure (Newell et al, 2000).

The official benefits of the internet are considered to be improved communication between members of the organisation, and the ability to disseminate information clearly and rapidly. However, a study of intranet use in a medium-sized high-tech company showed that the consequences of introducing an intranet were much more complex. It did give the employees much greater awareness of how the company functioned, and allowed senior management to promote the company's achievements and identity, and it also allowed more flexibility among those who had creative or innovative jobs. Those whose jobs were more rigid and proscribed, on the other hand, did not perceive themselves as gaining any particular benefit from the intranet (Clarke and Preece, 2005). Effectively, as the researchers put it, the intranet in this company represented different things to different people. Like other researchers, Clarke and Preece also found that as people became more used to their intranet, they developed new ways of using it, and these acted reciprocally, helping to change and shape its nature.

Box 9.1   An early social psychologist?

Interest in the social psychology of leadership goes back far earlier than social psychology itself. One example can be found in the writings of the Florentine politician Niccolo Machiavelli (1513). In his book *The Prince*, he described various strategies and policies which would ensure success at ruling a kingdom – useful advice in a competitive and potentially hostile world. Although Machiavelli's advice was highly manipulative, and much of it seems quite brutal to modern readers, he identified a number of issues which are still valid today.

One of these, for example, concerned the problem of how a ruler could make sure that the information he was getting was true, in a context where he (Machiavelli assumed it was a male) needed to be well informed but was surrounded by flatterers and people saying what they thought would please the ruler rather than what was actually true. Getting accurate information is still a problem for leaders in all walks of life, and the more powerful that leader is, the more difficult the problem becomes. Machiavelli's advice was that the prince should maintain a group of "wise men" who were not afraid of openly disagreeing, listen to them and base his policy on what they had to say, ignoring the flatterers entirely. That idea is just as valid for people at the top of large organisations, surrounded by organisational "yes men", as it was for mediaeval princes.

Organisational cultures

Every workplace is different, and each organisation has its own way of doing things. Many larger organisations are so distinctive in their approach that they are considered to have their own culture, and social psychology has contributed a great deal to the study of how **organisational cultures** operate, and gain their distinctive natures. Early studies of organisational cultures (e.g. Harrison 1972) were fairly simplistic, listing different "typical" cultures (see Table 9.5). But the problem of typologies is that they never really fit the real world (Hayes, 2003). Although they are popular, and often used in management training, they don't really allow people to find out what makes a culture distinctive.

Key Terms

organisational cultures
The distinctive patterns of beliefs, traditions and practices of an established organisation.

Table 9.5 A common typology of organisational cultures

Power cultures: Dominated by concerns about centralised control and rapid action.

Role cultures: Dominated by concerns with strictly defined administrative procedures.

Task cultures: Dominated by concerns with getting the job done.

Person cultures: Dominated by concerns for employee welfare and progress.

Source: Harrison (1972)

One of the most influential people to get to grips with the uniqueness of cultures was Schein (1990), who pointed out that in the real world, organisations are not just large homogenous entities, but consist of numbers of smaller groups linked together by the shared beliefs of the people working in them. According to Schein, organisational culture is the pattern of underlying assumptions within a given organisation, which has developed over time as people make sense of their organisation's experience and as the organisation copes with the problems and challenges of its societal context.

Schein (1996) argued that organisational cultures operate on three levels. At the deepest and most fundamental layer are basic assumptions about the nature of reality, human nature and how people relate to one another. These influence the next layer, which expresses the common values of the organisation, and these in turn are reflected in the content of the surface layer, which consists of slogans and catchphrases, images, and organisational stories and legends (see Figure 9.1). Hayes (1998a) proposed that this structure shows how organisational cultures are actually **social representations**, which as we saw in Chapter 4, use everyday actions, stories and images to reflect deeper assumptions about the nature of reality.

For large modern organisations, the question of a single unifying organisational culture is more challenging. Martin (2015) argued that organisational researchers need to adopt pluralistic approaches to understanding organisational cultures in their research since the cultures within and between organisations are so diverse. As globalisation and the size of multinational organisations have increased, Inkpen (1998) argued that those in charge of such organisations need to accept the existence of multiple and diverse organisational

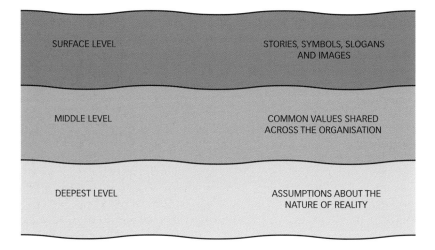

SURFACE LEVEL — STORIES, SYMBOLS, SLOGANS AND IMAGES

MIDDLE LEVEL — COMMON VALUES SHARED ACROSS THE ORGANISATION

DEEPEST LEVEL — ASSUMPTIONS ABOUT THE NATURE OF REALITY

Figure 9.1 Schein's levels of culture

cultures, rather than trying to impose one single approach on all parts of the organisation.

However, it is possible for an organisation to be diverse while still having a unifying underlying culture. Like social representations, organisational cultures are shared at the group level, which is where social identity processes also come into play (Hayes, 1998b). In organisations with a strong organisational culture, people feel proud of belonging to their organisation and derive positive self-esteem from that fact. It encourages an "us-and-them" approach in which all members of the organisation feel bound by the common bond of membership, and different from outsiders. Not everyone sees the culture in exactly the same way, of course – members of an IT department will see it differently from those in the accounts department, who in turn are likely to see it differently from the sales staff. But there is nonetheless overlap, and the degree of the overlap indicates how strongly the underlying social representation of the culture is shared. Hayes (1998b) illustrated the difference between organisations with "strong" cultures, shared by most of the workforce, and those with "weak" organisational cultures, using Venn diagrams, as illustrated in Figure 9.2.

Ogbonna and Harris (2006), in a discussion of the way that the internet has influenced organisational cultures, supported the idea that an organisation's culture can be seen as a mosaic of diverse social groups, each with different ideas and assumptions, and sharing the general practices of the organisation to a greater or lesser extent. In a study of a large financial services organisation which included interviews, grounded theory analysis and **triangulation** (see Chapter 10), they found that the various sectors of the organisation held multi-layered views of its culture, which incorporated both deep and shallow levels. The internet, they argued, impacts all three of Schein's levels of culture.

Organisational cultures, then, can be seen as social representations, maintained and expressed through the social identifications in the organisation. This way of looking at organisational culture challenged many of the "top-down" approaches to culture change, which assumed that simply making changes to the surface artefacts, like introducing a new logo and company slogan, would result in a change of culture. Instead, implementing organisational change requires a deeper change, requiring positive experience and also consistency, which doesn't necessarily take pace all at once. New logos or slogans are only effective in so far as they anchor or objectify the social representation which is the underlying culture of the organisation.

Key Terms
triangulation An approach to research which uses several different methods to "home in" on the target.

Talking point 9.1   Sources of authority

Weber (1921) argued that a leader's authority would derive from one of three sources: rational, traditional or charismatic. Can you find a modern real-world example of each of these? The authority doesn't need to be absolute; you might include, for example, the authority wielded by a particular celebrity talking about fashion, if they are someone who is generally recognised to be a fashion guru.

Try listing a dozen modern authority figures – particular people relevant for particular roles – and for each one, say which type of source their authority comes from.

Figure 9.2 Venn diagrams of "strong" and "weak" organisational cultures

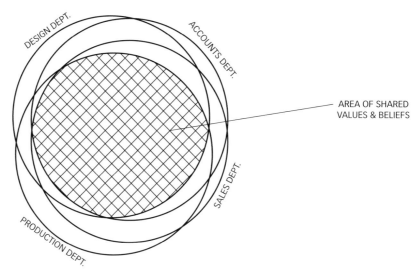

A "STRONG" ORGANISATIONAL CULTURE

DESIGN DEPT.

ACCOUNTS DEPT.

AREA OF SHARED
VALUES & BELIEFS

SALES DEPT.

PRODUCTION DEPT.

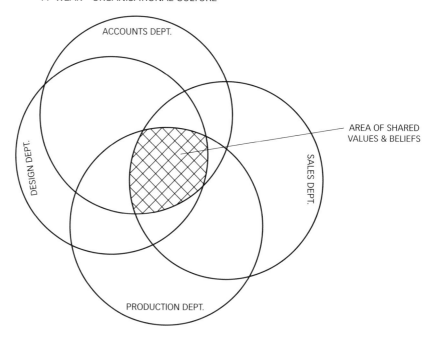

A "WEAK" ORGANISATIONAL CULTURE

ACCOUNTS DEPT.

AREA OF SHARED
VALUES & BELIEFS

DESIGN DEPT.

SALES DEPT.

PRODUCTION DEPT.

LEADERSHIP

Another way in which social psychology has been applied is in the study of leadership. The characteristics of leaders, and the style of leadership that they adopt, can make a considerable difference to how groups and teams act, and to the quality of what they achieve. Leadership can occur in many contexts; political leaders, community leaders, managers and supervisors, and concepts of leadership have changed considerably in the past hundred years or so. Table 9.6 illustrates some of these changing ideas.

Table 9.6 Leadership in the 20th century

	Model of the leader	Ideas	Typical source
Victorian period	Leader as father figure	Leader looks after workforce and directs their activities. Is sole person in charge and has total authority.	Taylor (1911)
1920s	Leader as holder of authority	Leader's authority based on (i) rational (representing norms) grounds, (ii) traditional grounds or (iii) charismatic personality.	Weber (1921)
1950s	Leader as holder of expectations	Theory X: people are naturally lazy and must be made to work; theory Y: people like to work and managers should foster this.	McGregor (1960)
1960s (based on 1930s research)	Leader as social focus for group	Leader should maintain harmonious relationships in the team, and guide work rather than dictate.	Hollander and Julian (1969) (based on Lewin et al, 1939)
1980s	Leader as manager of values and culture	Leader should exemplify and articulate company values to encourage and inspire workforce.	Smith and Peterson (1988)

For most of the past century, though, social factors have been recognised as important in leadership. As early as 1939, in their studies of the Hawthorne Electric Plant in Chicago, Roethlisberger and Dickson showed how some supervisors were entirely task-oriented, concentrating purely on production rates, while others were more socially focused, making sure that people got on well together and resolving interpersonal problems as they arose. They found, consistently, that it was the more socially focussed supervisors who had the most productive departments, rather than the task-oriented ones.

In the same year, Lewin et al (1939) published a study of how leaders interact with their subordinates. They did so by varying the style of leadership in an after-school boys hobbies club, and seeing how the boys acted. The task the boys were engaged in was making model aeroplanes, and they were put into three groups: one with an **authoritarian** leader, who kept close control over what the boys were doing and dictated to them how they should go about each section of the task; one with a democratic leader, who advised the boys on what to do but did so after discussing it with them and taking their ideas into account; and the third with a **laissez-faire** leader, who more or less left the boys to their own devices, without giving them any guidance or personal support.

Each group experienced the same leader for seven weeks, and then the leaders were rotated, to ensure that any differences in the group's behaviour was due to the leadership style rather than the personalities of the boys themselves. The researchers found that the boys in the group with the authoritarian leader tended to work individualistically and competitively, with little cooperation or helping. They also only worked hard if the leader was actually there; when he left the room, work stopped. By contrast, the boys with the democratic leader tended to help one another out, and worked steadily and consistently –

Key Terms

authoritarian
A style of leadership which is commanding, directive and unconcerned with the views of subordinates.

laissez-faire
Uninvolved leadership in which subordinates are left to themselves and can act as they like.

although not as quickly as those in the authoritarian group if the leader was there. They were also cheerful, interested in what they were doing and cooperative rather than competitive.

Those in the group with the *laissez faire* leader showed little interest in the task as the weeks went on. They did very little work on their models, and tended to be quarrelsome and restless. Lewin et al concluded that democratic leaders were demonstrably more effective, and their conclusions have been generally accepted throughout both social and organisational psychology.

There have been some caveats, of course. Smith and Peterson (1988) argued that what the study actually showed is that if all that was needed was high productivity, then an authoritarian leader who was constantly supervising was actually more effective. The democratic style was only better if the aim was to achieve a self-motivated workforce with high morale. However, most organisational leaders would tend to see a self-motivated workforce as the more desirable aim.

Other studies, though, have offered support to these ideas. Harold and Holtz (2015) discussed how passive leaders unwittingly encouraged an atmosphere of workplace incivility, with a direct relationship between the passivity of the leader, and the amount of incivility or rudeness that employees experienced, which in turn led to employees being more likely to be uncivil to one another.

Transactional and transformational leaders

During more recent times, interest has focused on the distinction between transactional and transformational leaders. Bass (1985) described **transformational leadership** as leadership where the leaders instil confidence in their workforce, behaving in ways that encourage employees to follow their examples, and promoting optimism and enthusiasm in the pursuit of their goals. **Transactional leaders**, on the other hand, are more focused on the work situation than the social context, emphasising role and task requirements for their workforce, clarifying goals and encouraging employee confidence in their ability to do what is needed.

Each of these leadership styles has its merits, and may be appropriate for different contexts or different tasks. Clarke (2013) conducted a meta-analysis of studies of safety leadership, in the context of these two styles, and found that active transformational leadership emerged as being most effective in encouraging employee participation, and the generating of a safety-aware climate among employees; while active transactional leadership was more effective in ensuring high rates of compliance with safety-related rules and regulations. Both types of leadership, therefore, had their part to play in establishing good safety at work practices.

We can see, then, that research into leadership has often drawn on social psychological processes to analyse leadership roles and how leaders can influence the people they are leading. For example, Sinclair (2009) suggested that seduction might be a useful metaphor for looking at how some leaders influence their followers – for example, by fostering the idea of the leader as "guru", by sweeping followers off their feet through personal influence or new ideas, and by forestalling criticisms. In a different context, Smith (1983) argued that social psychology has even more to contribute to work psychology than it already has, giving one example as the way that research on group leadership might benefit from adopting some of the ideas which have emerged from the studies of minority influence which we looked at in Chapter 5. After all, a leader is by definition in a minority!

Leadership can also be a temporary affair, rather than a steady role. Back in 1975, Firestone et al suggested that groups tend to choose those people who have qualities appropriate to the task at hand as temporary "leaders", rather than just allocating that role to one person. So a group might have several different leaders at different times, depending on which aspect of the task was important. As this idea gradually took hold, the concept of **team-working** came to replace the earlier interest in management styles and working groups, and at the beginning of the current century, the team rather than the working group had become very much the focus of interest in management research (Hayes, 2002).

TEAM-WORKING

Team-building and team-working are just as important in sport psychology as they are in management. Team sports are all about the contribution of the team's various members to the success of the team as a whole. As such, while individual members of the team strive to perfect their skills, their awareness of the commonly shared goals and the importance of working together is an essential part of their training.

Hayes (2002) argued that social identification is the central factor in team-building. Using social identity processes to build teams in the working environment involves three aspects. The first is creating a sense of unity through clear definition of the team and an awareness of the contribution to the whole organisation which it made. The second involves ensuring that there are good communications, both between team members and with other parts of their organisation, so that people are aware of what is happening both within the team and elsewhere. And the third is generating pride in belonging to the team by enhancing the team members' sense of professionalism, and promoting the achievements of both the team itself and the organisation as a whole.

Key Terms
team-working Organising working practices so that they are carried out by teams, with collective responsibility for the outcomes.

These factors apply to management teams, but they apply just as well to sport teams. Athletes often comment on the importance of their team identification, and even those in individual sports take pride in belonging to their national teams in events such as the Olympic Games. Mach et al (2010) found that team cohesion and trust play a significant role in team performance. In a study of over 600 professional elite footballers, belonging to over 59 clubs, the researchers demonstrated that high-achieving teams are characterised by the players feeling that they are part of a united, cohesive team, and by the trust that they have, both in their team-mates and in their coach.

Effective communication is also important, in any team. Sullivan and Feltz (2003) developed a scale to measure effective team communication. Their initial study used data from a series of studies of 681 team athletes who produced observations which were then subjected to factor analysis. Their scale identified four factors in effective team communication, which are listed in Table 9.7. The first three factors were all aspects of positive communication, while the fourth, negative conflict, indicated a failure of effective communication, or forms of communication which were felt to damage the team's effectiveness.

 In a further study by Sullivan and Short (2011), the researchers interviewed over 400 athletes and found that their factors appeared to be measures

Table 9.7 Factors in team communication

Factor	Characteristic behaviour or quality
Acceptance	Feelings of support and togetherness, appreciation of team members' contributions, consideration for others.
Distinctiveness	Aspects of a shared, inclusive identity with the team.
Positive conflict	Being able to express it when unhappy about some aspect of team behaviour, getting problems out in the open.
Negative conflict	Shouting when upset, angry body language, confronting aggressively when disagreeing.

Source: Sullivan and Feltz (2003)

of effective communication. The strongest of all of these factors was positive conflict, which showed a robust relationship with team cohesions, while, perhaps not surprisingly, negative conflict showed a strong negative relationship with it. This showed, the authors suggested, that how team members deal with differences of opinion can be a key element in how effectively their team functioned. Disagreements were healthy, but needed to be discussed in a positive way; if they became emotional and included personal attacks, the team would become disunited which would affect how well they played together.

Prestwich and Lalljee (2009) explored the relationships between liking, respect and pride in belonging to the team. While many team-building exercises have focused on promoting team pride as a vehicle for achieving success, their study of high-level rowing teams showed that the process is the other way round – pride in, and respect for, the team developed as an outcome

of successful performance. Liking between team members, on the other hand, was not as strongly influenced by success, but was linked with friendliness, fun and helpfulness. Consequently, the researchers argued, it might be more appropriate for trainers to focus primarily on the development of professional skills than on promoting team pride as an end in itself.

It's not just teams where social identification plays a part. Sport in general is increasingly recognised as a way of fostering social identification with the community as a whole. Warner et al (2012) explored the views of participants in both formal and informal sporting activities, and showed that they made a significant difference to community spirit. But it also needed to have support from administrative officials as well as from the community itself. Their studies showed that there were seven factors which emerged as being influential in promoting a positive sense of community. The seven factors are listed in Table 9.8, and show that it is not enough for communities to act alone, a positive attitude from officials can make all the difference.

Table 9.8 Factors in promoting community spirit

Administrative consideration

Common interest

Competition

Equity in administrative decisions

Leadership

Social spaces

Voluntary action

Source: Warner et al (2012)

MEDICAL COMMUNICATION

In Chapters 3 and 4 we looked at various aspects of communication. This part of social psychology has been a major factor in health psychology. One of the early concerns, for example, is the effectiveness of doctor–patient communication. In 1972, Korsch and Negrete published a paper in *Scientific American* which showed how patients often don't really take in what their doctors are telling them, and therefore fail to follow the doctor's instructions for correct doses of medicine or other aspects of their treatment. They discussed how doctors often used medical jargon, and also exercised a high level of control over the conversation, so patients did not feel able to express their uncertainties or lack of understanding. Many subsequent studies affirmed these findings, and a number of medical schools began to include training in non-verbal and other aspects of communication in their programmes of study (Roter and Hall, 1991).

Different aspects of the social psychology of communication have been applied to this problem. In 2003, Edwards proposed that analogies could be useful to aid medical communication. Although a larger study (Edwards et al, 2006) of diabetic patients didn't find the use of analogies particularly effective, Galesic and Garcia-Retamero (2013) argued that this was possibly because they had used a highly-educated sample who were already familiar with their illness and well informed about it, so the analogies didn't mean much to them.

In a deeper study of the use of analogies for helping people to understand the probabilities and risks involved in making decisions about cancer treatments, Galesic and Garcia-Retamero found that the level of education patients have interacts with the challenge of the task. People with high levels of numeracy, for example, found analogies helpful in understanding difficult medical problems, but not for understanding easy ones. Those with low levels of numeracy or education, on the other hand, found the reverse – they found analogies helpful for understanding of easy medical problems, but not with difficult ones.

Other areas of health psychology have looked at how people manage mild or chronic medical conditions, and here, too, communication has its part to play. Morrison et al (2014) explored how effective internet-based health care interventions were in an evaluation of an internet-based programme designed to support the self-care of mild bowel problems. They began by conducting a qualitative study designed to identify salient issues, and followed it up with a larger quantitative study. They found that in situations where there was no specifically tailored feedback, the dropout rate from the programme was significantly higher. When interviewed, it emerged that participants saw the intervention without feedback as being of little value because there was no personalised advice as to future action that they should take.

There are some situations, though, in which internet-based delivery may be directly helpful to clients. Strid et al (2016) compared the effectiveness of internet-based **cognitive behaviour therapy** – mainly text-based but including some images and sound clips – with the usual kind of direct interpersonal delivery of the same type of therapy. In a sample of 879 clients, randomly allocated to three conditions, they found that the clients receiving internet-based therapy had more improvement in psychological functioning, and reduced sleep disturbances, than those receiving TAU (treatment-as-usual), but no improvement for perceived stress.

If they had been allocated to the third condition of the study, clients received a programme of physical exercise conducted at a fitness centre, in which they randomly received one of three levels of intensity: low intensity (e.g., yoga or Pilates), medium intensity (e.g., aerobics) or high intensity (which included spinning and aerobics). They were asked to exercise for three hours a week for 12 weeks, and met with the fitness trainer once a week. This condition, like the internet-based therapy, produced improved psychological functioning and better sleep patterns, but no improvement in perceived stress. The researchers concluded that either internet or physical exercise-based treatment might be helpful for clients with mild to moderate anxiety or depression, but that the more usual forms of therapy were more likely to be effective in more severe cases.

The observation that physical exercise can have beneficial psychological effects is not new, but it is consistent. Clinical and community psychologists studying addiction have also found that the social interaction involved may help to "inoculate" young people who are at risk of addiction. Hallingberg et al (2015) looked at alcoholism vulnerability and participation in organised activities between young offenders and non-offenders. They found that there was a significant negative correlation between the playing of team sports and vulnerability to alcoholism. Young offenders who participated in a team sport engaged in less hazardous drinking, but the researchers also found that these young people were also significantly less likely to play team sports than a matched group of non-offenders. Vulnerable youths who might benefit most from team sports were actually those who accessed them least, and the researchers concluded that more social programmes to include them in this sport would be beneficial, not just to the individuals concerned, but to society as a whole.

> **Key Terms**
>
> **cognitive behaviour therapy**
> A form of therapy which encourages adjustments in cognitions as well as the learning of new habits.

ADDICTION

Addiction of various kinds, including alcohol, is a major problem of society, and social psychology has also made a significant contribution to understanding it. One aspect of addiction research has focused on the attributions which addicts make for their behaviour. Morojele and Stephenson (1992) discussed the Minnesota Model of addictive treatment, which is a residential programme designed to change the ways that people think about their addiction. In particular, the researchers found, the attributions of responsibility control changed their focus as people moved through the programme. From believing that they were responsible for their addiction but were unable to exercise control over it, clients came to perceive their personal responsibility as focused on their recovery, and their attributions of control over the recovery process increased significantly.

The Minnesota Model is a residential treatment in which the people concerned are in a total environment designed to support them as they change their views. But for most addicts, this type of opportunity is not available, and recovery must be done in the context of everyday living. Social interactions, social cognition and personal motivation are as important in those contexts as the cognitive restructuring of attributions; and even after the problem has been recognised and the addict wants to change, the actual process of recovery from addiction is rarely simple.

Prochaska et al (1992) examined a range of personal, clinical and research reports on recovery from addictive behaviours, and found that recovery generally proceeds through five stages (see Table 9.9). More to the point, though, it was unusual for an addict simply to go through these stages in sequence. The usual experience was that an addict would cycle through these stages several times, before eventually completely terminating their addiction (see Figure 9.3). The process of giving up – drinking, smoking, drugs – is not simple and linear, but cyclic, often involving several attempts before achieving final success, which is an important message for those who are struggling to gain control over their addictive behaviours.

Table 9.9 Stages in recovery from addiction

Stage 1 **Pre-contemplation**: The person becomes aware of some disadvantages to their addiction.

Stage 2 **Contemplation**: The person considers the possibility of doing something about giving up.

Stage 3 **Preparation**: The person has decided that they will give up at some time, and is beginning to get ready to take that step.

Stage 4 **Action**: The person takes decisive action to deal with their addiction.

Stage 5 **Maintenance**: The person develops new daily habits and techniques which enables them to continue life without their addiction.

Source: Prochaska et al (1992)

Getting addicts to acknowledge that they have a problem at all is often the first, and most difficult step. Pickard (2016) studied how simply making addicts aware of the negative consequences of their addiction is rarely enough to encourage them to change their behaviour. Pickard concluded that one of the main factors in this is the psychological process of denial. While addicts might acknowledge that their addiction could produce harmful consequences, they denied – to themselves as well as to others – that it affected them personally. Some went even further, and denied that the harmful consequences existed at all. So although to outsiders it appeared that the addict was well aware of what they were doing and simply chose to continue their addictive behaviour, to the addict, that knowledge was blocked, which meant that their behaviour wasn't actually the result of conscious choice. For that reason, Pickard suggested, it might be more helpful to regard continued addictive behaviour as a cognitive deficit, rather than as a motivational problem.

Internet addiction

The phrase internet addiction has existed since the 1990s, as concern about the amount of time some people spent on internet-related activities grew. One of the first publications in this area was Griffiths (1995), who produced a paper on **technological addiction** opening up discussion of the area, which was soon followed by a paper by Young (1996). Young focused specifically on the internet, particularly in the US, while Griffiths had included other aspects of technology use, such as computer gaming, and drew from European sources. These two papers opened up the area, and since then studies of **internet addiction** have been numerous and varied. A summary of research by Kuss et al (2014) analysed 68 epidemiological studies, which were not the full number of studies available. Instead, these were studies which had a minimum of 1,000 participants, were published after the year 2000, and included quantitative data.

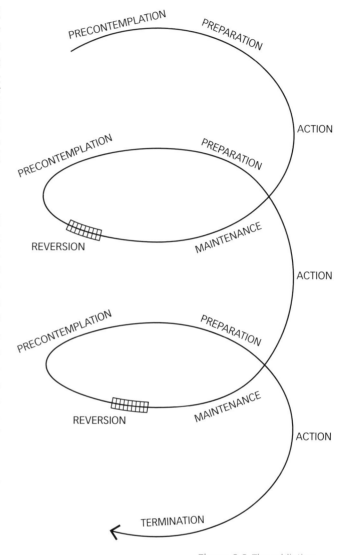

Figure 9.3 The addiction cycle

What Kuss et al found was that there was no single definition of internet addiction. Some 21 different assessment instruments had been used in these studies, each of which defined internet addiction in its own way. Despite the variation, though, there did seem to be a few core symptoms which are also recognised in the diagnosis of other types of addiction. These were compulsive use of the internet, negative outcomes resulting from the time spent on it, and salience – that is, the personal significance and rewarding nature of that particular internet activity to the individual concerned.

Another issue brought out by their research, which had been highlighted earlier by Griffiths (2000), is the question of whether the whole concept of internet addiction is useful. Most people who are identified as having an internet-related addiction, Griffiths argued, are really addicted to something else, and simply using the internet as a means to access their addiction. In this context, the various types of internet addiction which had been identified by Young (1999), such as cyber-sexual addictions, cyber-relationship addictions,

Key Terms

technological addiction
A form of obsessive behaviour in which the person engages in some form of technology-related activity to the extent that it disrupts their ability to live normal lives.

internet addiction
Excessive use of the internet, to the extent that it interferes with normal living.

gaming addictions and information overload (compulsively seeking more and more information on a topic) are not specifically internet addictions. Instead, they are examples of people using the internet to fuel another addiction.

Cases of people being addicted to the internet itself, Griffiths argued, are rare – although there do seem to be some, such as people addicted to the use of internet chat rooms. Griffiths found that the internet, for these people, can sometimes lead to a degree of immersion which produces a psychological and physiological rewarding state of consciousness, and suggested that this could be a psychological compensation for a lack of social rewards in those people's "real-world" lives. However, this type of state is also similar to that experienced by creative writers and artists when deeply involved in their work, so alternative explanations are also possible.

Davis (2001) argued that there are two kinds of pathological internet use: specific and general. Specific pathological internet use is where people engage specifically in a particular function of the internet, such as gambling, gaming or shopping, while general pathological internet use is a more multidimensional dependency on using the internet, involving several different types of activity, but generating obsessive thoughts about the internet, feelings that engagement in the internet is the only way to feel good, and increasing social isolation. This general disorder, Davis suggested, arises from a combination of external factors such as social anxiety or depression, and factors to do with the internet itself, such as the way that it offers new experiences, and the various types of reward cues involved in internet activity. This suggests that dysfunctional internet use should be seen as a **compensatory strategy** for perceived social or personal problems, rather than as a genuine addiction, and also that social therapies such as group support or family therapy might be useful in helping the individual to come to terms with it.

Talking point 9.2   Anti-addiction campaigns

Psychologists have repeatedly found that appealing to fear does little to change negative habits (see Chapter 5). Yet, anti-smoking campaigners continue to try to frighten smokers into giving up. Promoting the positive aspects of life without smoking is a much more effective strategy.

The same might be said for other attempts to challenge common addictions, and also public health campaigns in general. How might applying our understanding of social psychology processes and mechanisms improve public campaigns? For example, how could someone go about developing a campaign promoting "healthy" use of the internet, rather than obsessive or addictive use?

Key Terms

compensatory strategy
A cognitive or behavioural approach designed to adjust for an imbalance or inequality of some sort.

COUNSELLING AND THERAPY

The value of counselling as a social activity has come up on several occasions throughout this book. In Chapter 1 we saw how counselling can provide general social support for people experiencing stress, in Chapter 2 we looked at its value in maintaining relationships and coping with bereavement, and in Chapter 7 we saw how counselling can help the victims of bullying. Counselling is a predominantly social activity, which draws together the mechanisms of social communication with social emotions such as empathy and feelings of belonging or community. As such, there are many aspects of social psychology which have relevance to counselling psychology.

Counselling has often been linked with forms of psychological therapy, such as family therapy, or specific approaches to dealing with problems such as cognitive behaviour therapy (CBT). One issue which has arisen in many different contexts is the relevance of attributional styles in cognitive restructuring. In Chapter 4 we looked at the strong connection between the attributional styles that people make, and different types of beliefs. Therapy which has aimed to change those attributional styles has often been successful in helping people to come to terms with delusional states, or with other types of mental challenges. It is worth noting, though, that this is specifically targeted therapy – it is more complex than simply telling the person to look on the bright side of things!

Attributional style and depression

Interest in the relationship between attributional style and depression began in 1978, when Abramson et al argued that there is a distinctive pattern of attributions which depressed people make, which is related to the apathetic condition known as learned helplessness. In particular, the "depressive" attributional style includes the belief that causes are internal, that they are "global" in their effects rather than just applying to one or two things, and that they are stable rather than transient. This suggests that a key task in helping people to recover from depression is to challenge the attributional style which the person uses.

Stratton et al (1986) showed how this can be applied in family therapy. Using an attributional coding system (the LACS) which classified attributions into the five dimensions of stable, global, internal, personal and controllable, they analysed the statements which participants made during the course of family therapy. Their analysis helped the therapists to know how they should direct the therapy, in order to help people to change their attributional style.

For example, in one study (Stratton and Swaffer, 1988), the attributions made by mothers as they watched their children play were analysed. The mothers watched their children and talked about them while the children played with a special toy, known as a "contingency house", designed to provide a puzzle for the children to solve. This let the researchers see how persistent the children were, and also gave the mothers something that would encourage them to talk about their child.

Some of the mothers in the study were participating in family therapy because they had expressed, or were frightened of addressing, physical violence towards their children. The researchers found that those mothers tended to make different types of attributions from other mothers. In particular, they tended to see their child's behaviour as "uncontrollable", and the researchers felt that this might account for their feelings of frustration and anger when the child misbehaved. In order to ensure that it wasn't just the stress of looking after the child, Stratton and Swaffer compared these mothers with mothers of physically handicapped children (who were thought to have an equal amount of stress in dealing with their child), and mothers of ordinary children of the same age. All of the mothers came from the same socio-economic background.

Stratton and Swaffer suggested that the beliefs which mothers hold about their children could be significant causal factors in child abuse; if you see your child's behaviour as uncontrollable, you may be more likely to become frustrated and angry. The form of family therapy that these mothers received, therefore, focussed on showing them how to influence their children's behaviour, so that they would feel more in control and less frustrated. The family therapists found that this approach did a great deal to solve the problem.

Group therapy

Group therapy involving social contact with similar others has long been a part of clinical psychology. It is generally considered to have begun in the 1950s with the pioneering work of Carl Rogers – the "father of counselling" – who advocated that affirmation of positive regard from another non-judgemental person could in itself help to provide the conditions for personal growth which were often being stifled in people with neurotic disorders (Rogers, 1961). Rogers went on from there to develop the idea of the encounter group (Rogers, 1970), in which groups of people could provide the social environment of positive regard and support.

Rogers was not the first to propose **group therapy**, of course. A similar group-based approach had been adopted by the organisation Alcoholics Anonymous, founded in 1935 to provide support for those struggling to deal with alcoholism, and Taylor (1955) discussed some of the principles of group therapy in the journal *Psychology and Psychotherapy*. What was significant about Rogers's vision was partly the focus on the processes within the group itself – AA had mainly focused on the importance of anonymity – and of opening the group method into the idea of group therapy. At the time, many psychiatric procedures were fairly brutal, and group therapy was quickly adopted by the clinical psychology profession, proving a useful support, and sometimes even a complete therapeutic alternative.

Rogers emphasised the importance of unconditional positive regard, arguing that it freed the person from the need to seek approval and allowed them to devote their personal energies to **self-actualisation,** the process of developing their personal talents and abilities to the full. But there are other social processes involved in group therapy too. For example, Kaës (1984) discussed how group therapy sessions resulted in the development of consensual social representations; shared explanations of social reality which were accepted by the group as the framework within which explanations would be sought. Also, we have seen throughout this book how powerful social identification processes can be, in small groups as well as larger ones.

In more recent times, group therapies have tended to become more focused, with a range of different approaches being developed, and researchers exploring their relevance for specific target groups. For example, Carr et al (2012) found the application of group music therapy to be helpful for people suffering persistent post-traumatic behaviour disorder, while research by Calvert et al (2015) indicated that survivors of childhood sexual abuse could benefit from group-based cognitive analytic therapy. The plethora of different forms

---

Key Terms

group therapy
A form of psychotherapy in which several patients interact with one another and the therapist, as opposed to the one-to-one situation of individual therapy.

self-actualisation
The making real of one's abilities and talents: using them to the full.

of group therapies shows how effective bringing people together in groups can be, but as our understanding of social processes has developed, group therapy has become very different from the direct personal encounter groups proposed by Rogers.

HYPNOSIS AND HYPNOTHERAPY

Hypnotherapy is the application of hypnosis to clinical problems. Some clinical psychologists use **hypnotherapy** as a method for allowing their clients to develop a positive frame of mind about, and sometimes control over, distressing symptoms. Sometimes, this involves the therapist conducting the hypnotherapy sessions, but more frequently it involves teaching the individual concerned how to generate the kind of trance-like state offered by hypnosis by themselves, so they can take control of their own treatment.

While the efficacy of hypnotherapy as a treatment approach has been demonstrated on many occasions, particularly for neuroses or behavioural disorders, debates still rage over what hypnotism actually is. Some see it as a special form of consciousness, in which the person adopts an agentic state and surrenders their personal will-power. Others dispute the special state theory, and see hypnosis as a combination of social psychological processes, operating in a very specific social context to produce often quite dramatic effects.

The "special state" theory was particularly championed by Hilgard (1977), who argued that hypnosis is a special form of consciousness which gives access to hidden parts of the mind. Hilgard saw consciousness as being organised into vertical sections, or columns, which channel our awareness and also our memories. Normally, he argued, we have amnesiac barriers between the columns, causing us to forget what is in the others. So being in one column of awareness means that we are unaware of the memories associated with the other – much like the way in which contexts affect our ordinary memory, only more extreme.

Entering a state of hypnosis, Hilgard argued, allows the person to tap into more than one of these columns of awareness, and even to move between them if they are instructed to do so by the hypnotist. He also believed that it was possible even to contact the "hidden observer" – that part of the mind which observes and comments on what the person is doing while they are hypnotised – at such times. In one study, for example, people were asked to hold their hands in ice-cold water. They all agreed that it was a very painful experience. Then they were hypnotised, told they would not feel any pain, and asked to do it again, while simultaneously writing or doodling on a pad with the other hand. When the hypnotist asked them if they were in pain, they said no. But their writing reported that the experience was very painful indeed. Hilgard's explanation was that writing came from the "hidden observer", which was in a different column of consciousness from the person's hypnotised awareness, but able to express itself by writing.

The real problem is that it is almost impossible to investigate the special state theory directly. Specific studies of hypnosis are open to both kinds of interpretation, and the mind's ability to generate its own trance-like states means that evidence from brain scans is also equivocal. Sarbin and Slagle (1972) gathered the data from a range of extensive physiological tests and found no evidence for any special physiological state associated with hypnosis.

Which raises the question of whether hypnosis really is a special state. Some researchers see hypnosis as more the product of social psychological mechanisms than as a special state of consciousness. In a halfway model, Hunt (1979) argued that the hypnotised condition is similar to Milgram's "agentic state" (see Chapter 6). Milgram had found that seeing other people disobey the experimenter meant that his participants, too, were much more likely to refuse to obey, and Hunt also found that the presence of a "disobedient" participant in a hypnosis situation would lower the susceptibility of other people to being hypnotised. She suggested that hypnosis was an example of an agentic state, with the person giving up their personal autonomy and assigning responsibility for their actions to the hypnotists.

Stage hypnotists are very skilful at selecting people from their audiences who are likely to be suggestible. And once someone has agreed to be hypnotised, there is a kind of informal social contract between them and the hypnotised, which means that they are particularly prepared to be helpful. We have seen elsewhere in this book how people are more inclined to be cooperative than confrontational, and this is another social psychological mechanism which comes into play during hypnosis. People are unwilling to challenge the hypnotist directly, so they "go along" with what is suggested rather than break the implicit social contract.

This explanation also brings into play ideas about appropriate social roles and the expectations associated with them, which can result in people undertaking tasks which would not previously have expected of themselves. They imagine how it is that they are supposed to act, and their willingness to help the hypnotist means that they make themselves do these things, even though they might not have done them in other circumstances.

Cooperation

The willingness to cooperate can in itself be a powerful force. Orne (1962) set up an investigation which began as an attempt to distinguish between people who were hypnotised, and people who were not, and ended up as a comment on the social psychology of the psychological experiment. In one experiment, people were asked to add up a whole series of numbers on a sheet of paper, and then to tear up the sheet of paper and throw it in the bin. They then were to start on a new sheet, and do the same to that when it was finished. Orne found that if people were asked to do this in a routine, everyday context, they would quickly refuse to continue – after the first or second sheets. But if they thought that they were taking part in a psychological experiment, they would carry on doing it indefinitely.

Orne expected that non-hypnotised participants would be like the people who didn't think they were taking part in an experiment and refuse to continue, while hypnotised ones would carry on. To his surprise, non-hypnotised people also continued, showing no signs of stopping. The process was eventually terminated by a bored experimenter. This showed, Orne argued, that special situations such as psychology experiments – or stage hypnosis – have demand characteristics which operate as a social force on the person concerned, an idea which we will come back to in the next chapter.

These demand characteristics are the total combination of psychological processes operating on the person. Role expectations, social contracts, cooperative tendencies and so on all come into play to influence how we behave, and they create a powerful social force acting on the "hypnotised" person. As a result, people continue to do what is expected of them, because they don't want to be uncooperative or confrontational.

Box 9.2   Hypnosis and reality

The experience of hypnosis can be quite surprising, and people often find it quite challenging to become aware of what they are capable of when they are hypnotised. But the reality of hypnosis is very different from the accounts presented in films and other forms of fiction. The image of the "Demon Headmaster" controlling all the children in a school, or the evil villain coercing his victims to commit murders through hypnosis, are familiar in fictional entertainment. But the reality is that nobody can be hypnotised to do something which is really against their principles. Even if they firmly believe in hypnosis, they will resist. Being asked to do something which they find morally offensive will almost always bring the person out of the hypnotic state altogether.

The really positive social uses of hypnosis are in the ways that it can be helpful in therapy. There is evidence that hypnosis can help people to control pain and to deal with illnesses. This is not disputed, but non-state theorists argue that it comes about because of the relaxation produced by the hypnotic process, and the expectations generated by it. The body has its own healing and regenerative processes, and these appear to work better in situations where the person is relaxed than under tension. The belief in the hypnosis may also help people to draw on inner reserves which they did not know they had – as in the many instances where it has helped people to give up smoking. But this too can be seen as resulting from social and personal expectations rather than as the results of a special state of consciousness.

By giving people that extra sense of belief in their own abilities, hypnosis has been shown to help in weight loss programmes, stopping smoking and dealing with addictions. It isn't enough in itself, of course; the person has to be strongly motivated to be successful as well (no hypnosis can make you do something you really don't want to do, remember?) But if the person really wants to succeed, hypnosis or self-hypnosis can provide them with additional psychological support, which can often help them through the most difficult times.

It may be that there really is a special mental state of hypnosis – nobody can tell for sure. But as we have seen throughout this book, our legacy as social animals has given us a social psychology which means that we prefer to cooperate rather than confront, which makes us highly sensitive to the non-verbal and unspoken cues from others as to the behaviour expected of us, and which means that we apply our social knowledge of situations, roles and social identity mechanisms even when we are unaware of doing so. What non-state theorists argue is that these mechanisms, together with the trusting relationship which the person has with the hypnotist, are in themselves enough to explain the phenomena which we think of as hypnosis. We don't need to invoke more complicated "states" to explain what is going on.

SOCIAL FACTORS IN MEMORY

Many, if not most of our memories are social in nature. We remember social episodes, such as special events or unusual incidents, and those memories are often associated with other people. We have other types of memory too, of course. We remember factual information and places, and even things which haven't actually happened, but which we intend to do sometime in the future. But some of our strongest memories have to do with other people; we recognise familiar faces, remember pleasant, unpleasant or embarrassing experiences with other people, and even (sometimes) people's names. In fact, recognising faces is so important to us that we even have a special area of the brain which is devoted to it (Bruce and Young, 1986; Haxby et al, 2000). It is a special form of memory, which shows us yet again how profoundly social the human animal is.

Meaning and motivation

Often, it is our social experiences which create the strongest memories. This is partly because we pay more attention to them – we often forget the everyday details of inanimate objects, but we generally remember what people have said to us, or how they have behaved. Or, at least, we remember the important details of what they have said or done. In one fascinating real-world study, Neisser (1981) found himself in a unique position to compare what someone remembered with what had actually happened. The context was the Watergate hearings in the US, which eventually resulted in the impeachment of American President Richard Nixon. One of the people who gave evidence at the trial was John Dean, a White House aide who was known to have an exceptionally accurate memory. Dean recalled in detail several meetings which had taken place between the president and his associates. His testimony was very precise, stating who had spoken with and what they had said.

Later in the proceedings (the trial took several weeks), a set of tapes was discovered which recorded the same meetings. What was interesting was that the people concerned didn't actually say the words that Dean had recalled; they were slightly different in almost every respect. But Dean had accurately recalled the gist of the conversations, the social meaning of what had taken place. His social memory was very precise, even though the actual details were often inaccurate.

In our own lives, too, we tend to remember the gist of what happened rather than the exact details. But our memories are malleable, they change over time, and with different contexts. If we are in a bad mood, we remember unpleasant things; if we are in a good mood, we remember happy times. The same applies in relationships – if our relationship is going well, we will recall pleasant or enjoyable incidents with that other person; if it is going badly, we recall unpleasant or hurtful events. This is one of the reasons why divorce cases can become so bitter, even when a couple has been close and loving for a significant part of their time together.

There are other ways in which our social lives affect our memories. For example, Morris et al (1981) showed how our social motivations influence how much we remember. He asked groups of people to remember pairs of words and numbers, in lists. When those lists were just made up by the researchers, there was no apparent social effect; but when the lists consisted of that day's football results, and were presented to real football fans, there was a definite difference. The football fans remembered far more of the lists than groups of non-football supporters did. The information meant far more to them, and they were working out the implications for each of the results as they came in, so they remembered more because of the cognitive "work" they had put in. But without the social motivation in the first place, they wouldn't have put in all that mental work.

Retrieving our memories can be strongly influenced by other people as well. We saw in Chapters 3 and 4 how influential our choice of words can be in communicating ideas or impressions. Loftus and Palmer (1974) performed a classic study which showed how words also influence what people remember. They showed participants a film of a traffic accident, in which two cars collided. They were asked to estimate how fast the cars had been going when they contacted one another – but they didn't use the word "contacted". Instead, they used "hit", "bumped into", "collided with" or "smashed into", and found that their participants estimated higher speeds with the more dramatic words.

A week later, they asked them about the film that they had seen, with a series of questions which included whether there had been any broken glass at the scene (there hadn't been). The participants who had been asked about the cars "smashing" into each other were much more likely to report broken glass than those who had heard milder words in the original questions. Furthermore, they remembered seeing this broken glass clearly, and insisted that it had been there in the film.

In a similar vein, Bjorkland et al (2000) showed both children and adults a
video of a theft, and then asked them first to recall what they had seen freely, and then to answer a series of questions. For some, the questions were unbiased, but for others they were deliberately misleading. When they interviewed a couple of days later, the researchers found a high level of incorrect recognition of the event – more so for the children than the adults, but still apparent with the adults. Interestingly, their recall was more likely to be inaccurate when they were interviewed by someone new; if it was the same person who had asked the questions originally, they tended to give answers which were closer to what they had originally said. So it isn't just the content of the questions, but also who is asking them which influences what we remember.

Autobiographical memories

What other people are doing also affects how much or what we remember. Peterson et al (2009) asked people to describe their early memories, and found that this was strongly influenced by what they had just experienced. They had two groups of participants: one group was just asked to think about their very earliest memories for two minutes, while the others listened to someone else describing their own very early memories, like taking their first steps or their second birthday party. Then they were asked to write down the very earliest memories they had of their own. The researchers found that the participants who had heard the other person reminiscing produced accounts which were roughly a year earlier than those who just been asked to think and recall – suggesting that social experiences can influence our own **autobiographical memories** as well as later ones.

A great deal of our autobiographical memory is surprisingly inaccurate. We misremember details of public events, and also the attributes of our past selves. We learn as we go through life, and it is often difficult to realise just how much we have changed, or to recall a time when we were ignorant of certain knowledge or information. But people also sometimes misremember childhood episodes, which either didn't take place at all, or are changed in both location and meaning from the actual event. Newman and Lindsay (2009) asked why false memories should be so common, and what purpose they serve for the individual. They concluded that being able to revise the past in this way might actually be a useful preparation for dealing with future events; and also, that having false memories helps us to preserve our self-image and meet our immediate or future social needs.

Forensic aspects of memory

The fact that memory can be so strongly influenced by social factors has profound implications for the legal system, as well as for our everyday understanding of personal relationships. A great deal of legal evidence relies on eyewitness testimony and memorised accounts, and forensic psychologists have developed a number of techniques to try to ensure that these are as accurate as possible. But as we have seen, social factors can seriously damage the accuracy of those memories, and once they have been changed, there is no way of telling the "real" memory from the "false" one.

> ### Talking point 9.3   Hypnosis as a special state
>
> As we've seen, it is very difficult to tell whether hypnosis actually exists as a separate mental state. But does it really matter whether hypnosis is a special state or not? It only really matters if either (a) a belief that hypnosis exists as a special state when it doesn't, or (b) a belief that hypnosis doesn't exist as a special state would have significant consequences.
>
> Look at it objectively. Draw up a table with two columns: one for option (a) as described above, and one for option (b). Then list all of the possible social, economic or personal consequences which might arise as a result of adopting one belief rather than another that you can think of. Is your table reasonably balanced, or have you found arguments for one side rather than another? Try getting a friend to do the same thing, and then compare your tables. Were they the same?

This, of course, means that the hypnosis debate is also relevant in the forensic context. Many people believe that it is possible to use hypnosis to retrieve hidden memories, and this can be a factor when it comes to witness reports. The problem, though, is that although people may be sure that their memories are accurate, that may not be the case. Krass et al (1989) explored how confident people felt about the accuracy of memories which they had produced under hypnosis. They found that the experience of hypnosis tended to make people feel extremely confident about their memories, even when those memories could be clearly demonstrated to be false.

The problem, of course, is the way that memory itself is affected by social factors. As we saw in Chapter 4, shared memories are often constructed through discourse and social agreement, and memories can also be affected simply by the words chosen to ask about them. One of the consistent findings of cognitive psychologists is that once our memories have been changed or adjusted in this way, it is simply not possible to go back to any "correct" version. Our memory system evolved for living in a real and social world, where re-playing events depends on their usefulness in their environmental or social context. It is so closely linked with our human capacity for learning that our memories, too, can be learned as we reinterpret our experience in the light of subsequent events or knowledge.

Compliance of the kind demonstrated by Loftus and Loftus is also active in situations where hypnotists are attempting to retrieve hidden memories. The hypnotised individual is attempting to cooperate, and to comply with the perceived demands of their situation. As a result, they make a real attempt to imagine the memories which the hypnotist is asking, and unconsciously construct the memories if they do not have the factual information. In a suggestible condition, people can respond to very subtle clues from the person asking the question and generate the answers they believe the person wants to hear. But it is impossible to distinguish between a constructed memory and a "real" one.

While this doesn't particularly matter if a stage hypnotist is asking someone to remember a "past life" as Alexander the Great or Cleopatra, it does matter in criminal investigations, where remembering what happened is important. For this reason, Gibson (1982) argued that the use of hypnosis to "assist" memory in criminal investigations was equivalent to tampering with evidence because the social cues offered by the hypnotist could permanently affect the witness's memory of the events concerned.

Other research suggested that hypnosis does not contribute anything special to the recovery of memory. Green and Lynn (2005) showed that there was no difference in accuracy of memory or confidence in memories for hypnotised and non-hypnotised participants, although those who had acquired their memories under hypnosis were more resistant to changing them when told they were inaccurate. And Kebbell and Wagstaff (1998) carried out a series of studies in which they showed that the actual interview technique itself was more effective in helping people to remember things than being hypnotised. They argued that the reason why hypnotists appeared to have more success in interviewing than police officers was simply because they had better interviewing skills. They proposed that the **cognitive interview** – a systematic approach to witness interviewing – would be more successful, and this technique has now been widely adopted.

Wagstaff (2009) suggested that there were some aspects of hypnotic interviewing which might be separated out and used with some benefits. Techniques such as focused breathing and eye closure have in themselves been shown to enhance memory, without being part of any hypnotic procedure. In reviewing the use of hypnosis in legal contexts, Wagstaff came to the conclusion that

Key Terms

cognitive interview
A specific form of interviewing designed to encourage accurate recall of events.

there may be some use for it, not in retrieving memories, but perhaps in helping to reverse the effects of misinformation. But such procedures would have to be used with considerable caution, to avoid accidentally "contaminating" the person's memories and therefore their evidence.

SOCIAL FACTORS IN PERCEPTION

The study of perception is concerned with how we interpret the information we receive about what is around us. We perceive things in many different ways: we use the five external senses of vision, hearing, touch, smell and taste, but we also use a number of inner senses, such as **proprioception**, which tells us about the positions of the body, and **kinaesthesia** which tells us about our bodily movements. Other internal senses tell us about hormonal states, emotions and other aspects of being alive, and the general estimate is that we have about fourteen senses in all.

Making sense of all of that information means that we have to develop shortcuts, otherwise we would simply be overwhelmed by the amount of information we receive. That's what perception is all about. Psychologists have studied numerous aspects of perception over the years, and much of it has focused on information processing – how we actually convert "bits" of information into meaningful units.

Perception is a core area of cognitive psychology, and on the surface, doesn't have much to do with social psychology at all. But the reality is very different. Social factors can even influence what we perceive. For example, in 1954, Allport showed how perception could be affected by attitudes. He used a stereoscope, which is a device which presents two different pictures to a person at the same time, one to each eye, and showed people pairs of people of different ethnic origins. They were asked to categorise the people that they saw.

People who weren't particularly prejudiced tended to be generally unsure about their categorisations, although fairly confident when it came to members of their own race. But highly prejudiced people, like the Afrikaners of the time who were noted for their racial prejudices, showed no uncertainties and didn't use any subcategories; they perceived the racial categories as very rigid. Also, if they were looking at ordinary scenes of people interacting, they tended to pick out ethnicity as the most important aspect of the scenes they saw.

In the first part of the 20th century, there was a great deal of research into the limits of capacity of our perceptual system, such as the faintest noises that we could hear, or the faintest light that we could see. Researchers were interested in establishing perceptual thresholds – that is, the changeover points where stimuli went from being undetectable to being perceptible. In 1948, Postman et al demonstrated that this isn't just a physical thing, social factors have their impact, too. They showed how "taboo" words, like obscene or offensive words, had a higher recognition threshold than ordinary words. People took more microseconds to identify the taboo words than they did to identify neutral ones. The researchers described this finding as evidence for perceptual defence – our cognitive system defending us against unwelcome stimuli.

This caused quite a stir, and some researchers argued that it wasn't actually an effect on perception, but rather a response bias, in that people were unwilling to say these words out loud. Bitterman and Kniffin (1953) performed a similar study, but this time asking their respondents to write down the words they saw rather than saying them out loud, and they found that the time difference disappeared, which they saw as evidence for a response bias. Others, though, argued that the time taken to write things down as opposed to say them was enough to obscure the perceptual defence effect – after all, it was microseconds that they were measuring.

Finally, a study by Worthington in 1969 appeared to resolve the issue. Worthington used the phenomenon known as **subliminal perception**, which happens when stimuli are presented so faintly that we are not consciously aware of them, but we perceive them nonetheless. In this study, the rude words were presented embedded in the centre of a dot of light shown on a screen, but so faintly that the observers were not aware of them. Worthington presented the dots in pairs, and asked the research participants to say which one of the two dots was the brightest. The dots containing rude words were systematically rated as being dimmer than dots with neutral words, even though the participants in the study were not aware of having seen any words at all, and they weren't called on to say any of them out loud.

Box 9.3   Subliminal perception

The idea that people may be able to perceive information without realising that they have done so has a long history in psychology, dating back to the very beginning of the 20th century. In the early studies, words, letters or numbers were presented either very rapidly or very faintly to people, and they were asked what they had detected. Even when they said they hadn't seen anything, if they were asked to guess, they would tend to guess the word or digit that had been presented to them. Later research also showed that people could respond to pictures, faces or spoken words which had been presented in ways which were too faint to be perceived consciously.

This idea captured the imagination of science fiction writers such as J. G. Ballard, and also advertisers. In 1957, a market researcher named James Vicary claimed that audiences at a film theatre had been presented subliminally with the messages "eat popcorn" and "drink Coca-Cola" while they watched the film, and that this had resulted in significant rises in sales of both items. However, he never presented any evidence for this and in 1962 he told the journal *Advertising Age* that he had invented it. That didn't stop the story from passing into modern folklore, though, and laws to restrict subliminal advertising were enacted in many modern countries.

Although there is no evidence for this, or other similar claims, there is nonetheless a considerable industry marketing tapes which can supposedly produce lifestyle changes from the subliminal messages embedded in them. The problem for the consumer, of course, is that by definition, it is not possible to know for certain whether these messages are actually there, or what they actually say. Repeated studies have shown little evidence that they are efficacious, but the use of such material is a consumer choice, and it may be that belief in itself can produce therapeutic or other positive effects.

Subliminal perception has been shown to be real in some ways, though. Merikle and Daneman (1998) discussed a number of examples, including the way that people under anaesthetic seem to be able to respond to stimuli they are given, and the phenomenon of blindsight, whereby people whose

Key Terms

subliminal perception
A form of unconscious perception which occurs below the threshold of awareness.

experience is of complete blindness are nonetheless able to avoid obstacles or guess the size or shape of stimuli they are presented with. So there does seem to be a real phenomenon underneath the marketing hype, but it isn't quite the controlling threat feared by science fiction writers and others.

 Some social aspects of perception may be wired into the brain itself. Phillips et al (1997) showed how certain neurones in the brain are activated when we perceive emotional expressions in other people – in particular, expressions of disgust. Interestingly, the same neurones are also activated when we experience disgust ourselves. Phillips et al referred to them as mirror neurones, and similar systems have been found in the brain relating to empathy.

There are several other types of studies which show how social factors influence our perception. Social perception is a major part of social psychology, because it determines how we respond to other people. But it is when we look at how our social beliefs and cultural ideas influence the physical aspects of our perception that we realise how deeply social human beings are. This observation holds true for other aspects of human cognitive functioning as well, as we will see if we look briefly at human learning, and at how human memory works.

LEARNING AND EDUCATION

As human beings, we learn all the time, and social processes are an important part of that learning. While early psychologists believed that human learning could be broken down into simple connections between stimuli and responses, it rapidly became apparent that other, more social forms of learning also played an important part in the human experience. We learn a great deal, for example, from imitating what other people do, and how they act. It is apparent when small children imitate the other people around them, but we also do it quite a bit as adults. If we are in a new situation, for example, we will almost unconsciously act in much the same way as the other people around us, while we work out what we are supposed to do.

Other types of learning are possible because of the human facility with language. We saw in Chapters 3 and 4 how complex human communication can be. By means of language and our imaginations, we learn about situations that we do not directly experience, which makes it possible for us to survive in the very complex modern societies that we have created. And our stored knowledge means that we are able to learn new things all of the time, not just about the physical world but also about other people and how they, individually, might act.

Some of our strongest learning comes from other people. We saw in Chapter 1 how infants are predisposed to learn from other people from the time they are born, and how we form attachments as infants with those people who are most sensitive to our own responses to them. This predisposition to react most strongly to social stimuli even applies to how we learn factual information. Socially based revision exercises for exams, like learning groups or quizzes, often help less motivated students to remember information better than more individual, paper and pencil techniques.

Psychologists investigating how students in higher education learn most effectively have found that emotions and language are inseparable from learning – and both language and our emotional reactions to others are social in nature. In school, too, it has been shown that children learn more from teachers that they like than from those they don't – possibly because they are more highly motivated and try harder (Hutchings et al 2008). Although several experiments have been made to develop educational systems which don't require a human being, such as B. F. Skinner's teaching machines, based on operant conditioning, (Skinner, 1961), they have generally been unsuccessful. Few people seem to be able to retain motivation without some kind of human contact.

This, of course, has implications for the increasing numbers of online and distance learning courses. But it is rare to find even an online course which has no human contact at all. Institutions which administer their course through the internet, such as the University of the Highlands and Islands, whose geographical area is too large to allow for the personal attendance of all students at classes, ensure that although the courses may be online, they are delivered through a specific, human tutor. Teaching is delivered through online video as well as through textual resources, and the tutor also holds live online contact sessions so that students can retain the human context. Holmes (2013) discussed how online communities are becoming increasingly recognised as an important part of online learning, and how their social dimensions as well as their cognitive content contribute to the positive impact they can make.

Social psychology tells us a great deal about the importance of social interaction in groups. In exam revision, too, this type of social contact is valuable. Advice from many educational institutions, including the Open University, encourages students to work in study groups when preparing for exams, since doing so accesses the social schemas in our memory as well as the academic schemas. For most of us, our storage of social events is more immediate and more powerful than our memory for abstract information; it has been, after all, much more important in human evolutionary history. Tapping into those processes when attempting to commit exam-relevant information to memory therefore provides a useful addition to individual cognitive strategies for learning.

The idea of community and social connectedness applies even in the massive open online courses (MOOCs) which have developed as a result of the increased emphasis on lifelong learning and worldwide skills development. While the sheer number of participants in these courses makes one-to-one contact impractical, the creation of an online learning community is a stated aim of just about all of these courses, which is usually achieved through the provision of student chatrooms and bulletin boards. The first of these courses began in 2012, and proved instantly popular. By mid 2014 there were over 1000 of these courses being offered (Steffens, 2015). However, Ho (2016) discussed how even the MOOCs offered by high-status learning providers such as Ivy League universities have high drop-out rates, and questioned how effective they are at generating a true online community for participants.

On the learning front, there have been many claims made for different ways of enhancing human performance. In a 12-year study of various factors which claimed to achieve this, (Druckman, 2004) found that the techniques which really helped people to enhance their performance – in everyday living as well as in sport or music – were those which were concerned with direct learning – training, mental and physical practice, cooperative learning and expert modelling. The study explored several different aspects of performance – individual, small group and organisational – and found that the more esoteric approaches such as hypnosis, sleep learning, meditation or total quality management were all ineffectual methods of improvement.

So we learn all the time, and we learn most effectively from other people. This means that, as with so many other aspects of human experience, social psychology is inextricably linked with learning; and to enhance learning, we need to look at its social aspects as well as its cognitive demands.

In this chapter, then, we've seen how social psychology can contribute to our understanding of many different aspects of both psychology and everyday life. We have looked at groups at work, at leadership, team-working and communication in work, sporting and medical contexts, and at the importance of social factors in dealing with addiction and in other forms of therapy. We have also seen how hypnosis may be the outcome of social psychological mechanisms working together, and how social factors can influence our memories and even our perception. In the next chapter, we will look at some of the general issues concerned in social psychological research, at different approaches in social psychology, at how we gather data and above all how we make sure that our research is ethically and socially acceptable in the modern world.

Summary: Chapter 9

1. Social psychological ideas have relevance in many areas of organisational psychology. The study of groups at work has included how group processes, norms, roles and organisational cultures influence organisational behaviour.

2. Studies of leadership include personal characteristics, leadership styles and the importance of expectations and values in the leader's interaction with their workforce.

3. Social identity processes and effective communication are important in our understanding of team working and the development of team pride.

4. Medical communication is not always clear, but health psychologists draw on our understanding of communication processes to improve and develop effective interaction between health professionals and the public.

5. Social factors such as attribution and social support have been shown to be important in the maintenance of well-being and in dealing with both drug-related and internet addiction.

6. Aspects of social psychology which have relevance to counselling psychology include the relevance of attributional styles in cognitive restructuring and the development of group therapy approaches. Family and relationship therapies also involve a range of social processes.

7. Hypnotherapy is the application of hypnosis to clinical problems. Although some see hypnosis as a special state of consciousness, others see it as the result of a combination of social psychological mechanisms in specific social contexts.

8. Social factors can exert a strong influence on memory, in terms of social meanings and social motivations. Forensic psychologists are aware of the importance of social factors in eyewitness memory for significant events.

9. Social psychological processes can even exert their influence on perception. This may have its origins in humans' evolution as social animals, and the way that the brain is structured to assist social perception.

10. Social factors are deeply important in human learning, ranging from modelling, the use of language, to aspects of social motivation. It has been suggested that online courses need to provide opportunities for social contacts between students in order to keep them motivated to continue studying.

Contents

Conducting social psychological research

10

As you have read through this book, you will probably have noticed that different social psychologists have very different ideas about what is important about how human beings act with one another. Partly, these different ideas come about because anyone doing psychological research needs to focus on a particular topic or area – human beings are just too complicated to be able to look at everything at once. Partly, they come about because the psychologists concerned are working within different traditions of social psychology. And partly, too, it happens because people are working at different **levels of explanation** – they are analysing one level of behaviour, and possibly incorporating one or two others, but not the whole spectrum.

Levels of explanation

Social psychology works at many different levels, eight of which are listed in Table 10.1. That table shows you how the range spanned by social psychology is huge – no one person could undertake research into all of these levels. So researchers specialise, working at one or two specific levels but always bearing in mind that they are only looking at one part of the jigsaw, and that really understanding people means taking all of these levels into account. In the early days of psychology, some psychologists believed that unlocking just one basic level would be enough to explain everything – an approach known as reductionism. Today we realise that each level of explanation has properties which are more than just the sum of their parts.

To clarify: we might describe a particular conversation between two people at the interpersonal and somatic levels, looking at their verbal communication through conversation analysis, and at their non-verbal communication, such as their body language through observation. But while that might tell us quite

Table 10.1 Levels of explanation in social psychology

Cultural: Our models of what constitutes appropriate forms and contexts for social interaction.

Societal: Our acceptance of widespread social representations and social norms.

Group: Our sense of belonging and identification with social groupings.

Interpersonal: How we are influenced by other people's physical behaviour towards us.

Cognitive: The way that we attribute meaning to other people's actions and discourse.

Somatic: How bodily movements and postures can communicate meaning to other people.

Physiological: The way in which emotions and moods can affect social judgements.

Neuropsychological: The way in which we have areas of the brain dedicated to face recognition or the production of language.

a lot about what they were discussing and their emotional reactions to one another, it wouldn't actually tell us very much about the social, societal or cultural meanings of what was going on.

Suppose, for instance, that the conversation was taking place in the run-up to an important election, and that the two people were affiliated with different parties. That would incorporate the group level of analysis, in terms of their social identifications, the societal level in terms of the accepted social meaning of the election, and the cultural level in terms of the accepted process of deciding who governs the country. If we really wanted to understand what was going on between those two people, we would need to look at it at all of these different levels.

That doesn't mean, though, that it is wrong to study the specifics of social behaviour – as we've seen in earlier chapters, we can learn a great deal from them. Studying the non-verbal signals involved in the conversation, for example, might help us to understand when it suddenly became very heated, or why what seemed to be a powerful disagreement eventually ended in an "agreement to disagree". Each level of analysis is valuable, but no single level is sufficient as a total explanation.

Talking point 10.1　Levels of analysis in psychological research

As we have seen, psychological research is extremely varied in its scope, and it also encompasses many levels of explanation. Here are four things a social psychologist might want to investigate:

1. Experiences of a music festival.

2. Training a telephone receptionist to communicate clearly.

3. Evaluating social revision methods (i.e., revision methods which involve two or more people working together).

4. Assessing someone's popularity with their peers.

Key Terms

levels of explanation
Perspectives for explaining a given phenomenon with lower levels including physiological (e.g., microbiological) and higher levels including cultural or socioeconomic explanations.

Identify an appropriate level of analysis for each of these topics and an appropriate research method.

Hypothetico-deductive and inductive approaches

There are two major approaches to scientific research. One of these is known as the **hypothetico-deductive method**, and it is often identified as the main approach required in psychology. But the other is the **inductive method**, and this too is a recognised approach to scientific study. The two methods often involve very different research techniques, and they certainly involve different perspectives, so it is worth looking at them more closely.

Hypothetico-deductive research is when a research project is set up to test a specific **hypothesis**, or several hypotheses. A hypothesis is a specific prediction made from a theory, and the idea is that it will allow researchers to test whether that theory seems to be valid by making one of the implications of the theory into a statement which can be tested objectively. So the researcher sets up conditions in their study where the findings will either seem to support the hypothesis, or to refute it. (In reality, of course, human beings are so varied and chance occurrences are so possible, that we can never really support the hypothesis. But we can say that the findings are unlikely to have happened by chance, and we can be quite specific about how definite we are in saying it.)

Hypothetico-deductive research, then, begins with a theory, and uses that theory to derive testable hypotheses. Popper (1959) argued that this was really the only truly scientific way of going about research, because only theories which could be disproved were really scientific. But Popper was taking a very narrow view of science – it isn't always possible to manipulate variables to test hypotheses. Think of astronomy, for example. We can't manipulate our observations of stars and galaxies, we can only draw conclusions from what we can observe. But nobody would dispute that astronomy is a science.

There are many other examples of scientific research and theories which have not adopted hypothetico-deductive methods, but have taken a different approach. That different approach is known as inductive research, and it involves gathering observations and drawing them together to make sense of what is going on. Our knowledge of the working human brain, for example, has been almost entirely developed using inductive methods. Until recently, opportunities to manipulate a working human brain have been extremely rare, apart from the occasional surgical opportunity. But that didn't stop neuroscientists building up models of how the brain works. And by and large, those models have been justified as better observational technology, such as **MRI scanning**, has some into play. That new technology does allow hypothetico-deductive research to some extent, and it has clarified and added additional detail to our knowledge of the brain, but, as with astronomy, nobody would dispute that the earlier studies were valid science.

Social psychology involves both inductive and hypothetico-deductive approaches. Sometimes we are able to investigate variables and test specific hypotheses by setting up controlled situations and measuring the outcome. At other times, we have developed our knowledge by observing closely what is going on, and pulling a range of observations together to develop theories. Both types of approach are valid, and both are reflected in social psychological research and the methods of analysis which it involves.

Key Terms

hypothetico-deductive method
An approach to research based on evaluating theories by testing hypotheses.

inductive method
Research in which investigation and observation are conducted first, and theory is developed on the basis of the outcome.

hypothesis
A prediction which states the outcome which is likely to take place if a particular theory is true and particular conditions are set up.

MRI scanning
A system of scanning the physical body using magnetic resonance imaging.

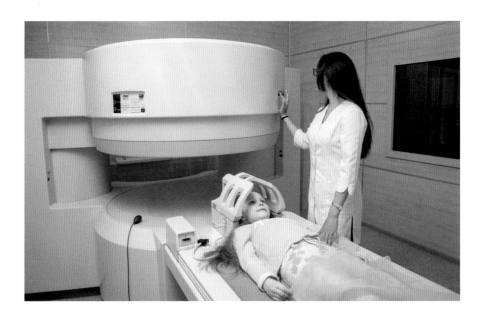

PERSPECTIVES IN SOCIAL PSYCHOLOGY

In the first chapter, we saw how modern social psychologists go about their research in many different ways, using a number of different perspectives. While most social psychologists are fairly eclectic in their approach, using whatever social research methods seem to be appropriate for their own area of study, we can nonetheless distinguish between at least six schools of thought in social psychology. Each of these has contributed to our understanding of the discipline in its own way. If you look back through the social psychology covered in this book you will find examples of each of these approaches.

Experimental social psychology

Experimental social psychology is primarily concerned with causes – that is, identifying the reasons why social behaviour has happened (Griffin, 1997). That means that it generally uses experiments as the approach to research which is best able to distinguish causality; and those experiments will mainly adopt quantitative forms of analysis rather than qualitative methods, which are more descriptive in nature. The emphasis in experimental social psychology, then is with collecting objective, measurable data, which means that they usually focus on the behavioural or physiological aspects of social experience – that is, those aspects of social experience which can be measured objectively. Experimental social psychologists almost always adopt a hypothetico-deductive approach in conducting their research.

Discursive social psychology

Discursive social psychology is just about the opposite of experimental social psychology in its focus. It is primarily concerned with the way that people construct their social worlds through conversation and other forms of social discourse, and it generally adopts an inductive approach to do this. We looked at discourse analysis in Chapter 4. Discourse analysis has always been an important part of discursive psychology. Potter (1997) discussed how discourse analysts are not particularly concerned about investigating objective reality. Instead, they are interested in how people use discourse and descriptions to construct and reconstruct their experiences. Because everyone sees the world differently, discursive psychology is inevitably relativistic; it doesn't look for a single "correct" viewpoint, but instead explores how the multiple forms of discourse and rhetorical frames act to shape human understanding.

European social psychology

European social psychology, as we saw in Chapter 1, developed as a reaction to the extreme individualism which appeared to have developed in American social psychology after World War II. It places particular emphasis on group membership and the impact of culture and cultural beliefs upon social understanding. European social psychology has two core theories: social representation theory and social identity theory. Social representations, as we saw in Chapter 4, are the shared beliefs of society in general and smaller groups as well. They form explanations for why things are like they are. Social identifications are about the way in which our thinking naturally falls into "us-and-them" categories, which, as we saw in Chapter 1, shapes our reactions to other people, often very significantly. Researchers in European social psychology generally work within this theoretical framework, using both qualitative and quantitative research methods in the process, and adopting either hypothetico-deductive or inductive methods as they seem appropriate.

Evolutionary social psychology

Evolutionary social psychology is all about how our biological evolution has come to affect our social and behavioural actions. As we have seen in several chapters of this book, our evolution as social animals has shaped our reactions – babies respond primarily to other people; we have a profound tendency to see other people in terms of familiar (in-groups) and unfamiliar (out-groups), and we are distressed by overt hostility and relieved by conciliation. All of these have evolved as a result of our being social animals, dependent upon the group for our survival. Evolutionary social psychology, then, takes the view that the complexity of our minds and bodies is an outcome of genetically inherited adaptations, which have built up through cumulative natural selection, over many generations.

Adaptations which have developed through evolutionary processes in this way are likely to be common to all human beings. They form human universals, which occur across all cultures and societies, rather than simply being examples of the preferences of certain societies, or of modern living. As we saw in Chapter 7, for example, perceptions of attractiveness vary so widely from one human culture to another that it would be meaningless to claim an evolutionary basis for them; whereas our predisposition to sociability and group identification is common across all cultures. Evolutionary social psychology is multidisciplinary, in that it brings together biological, psychological, geological and cultural knowledge to help us understand the human being, and it generally adopts an inductive approach to research.

Critical social psychology

Critical social psychology is another approach to social psychology. It is part of the general school of critical psychology, which is all about "deconstruction" –

that is, critiquing and challenging orthodox scientific psychology. Parker (1977) described how critical social psychology has two parallel tracks. One of them is concerned with examining social psychology's theoretical framework, and demonstrating how much of it is actually a social construction rather than a scientific truth – for example, showing how the individualistic representations of the self which are typical of Western societies are simply not valid for many other cultures. The second is all about developing what Parker referred to as "unscientific psychology" – in other words, putting together a theoretical framework which draws on philosophical perspectives such as postmodernism or the work of Wittgenstein. These perspectives, critical social psychologists argue, can provide us with challenges and alternatives to the existing conventional but culture-bound theories and perspectives.

Looking at all these approaches, we can see how varied the work of social psychologists can be. The assumptions about knowledge and science made by each approach are very different, and often directly contradictory. But that doesn't make the discipline itself fragmented. Social psychology has always encompassed many different approaches, and each of these perspectives can contribute to our understanding of social experience. If anything, having a multiplicity of approaches just enriches the discipline; it makes it wider in scope and more flexible in its orientation.

ETHICAL ISSUES IN SOCIAL PSYCHOLOGY

Social psychology isn't just a matter of common sense. Often its findings are surprising, and give us insights into what is going on that we might not otherwise have had. Sometimes the information which social psychologists have identified is challenging, making us re-evaluate important experiences or assumptions. So it is important that social psychological knowledge is based on a firm foundation. That foundation is research. But research also carries with it a level of responsibility, and that is the reason for the concern with ethical issues which we identified in Chapter 1.

Throughout this book, you will have noticed ethical "flags" at various points. These indicate studies which raise ethical questions in some way – either because they did or didn't take appropriate precautions, or because the topic of the study had the potential to be ethically challenging. In this section, we will look more closely at the ethical expectations on modern researchers. When you have read through it, you may find it helpful to go back and look at some of these ethical flags again.

Ethical issues are a fundamental aspect of all modern research, but that wasn't always the case. Our modern concern with ethical issues came about mainly because of the wanton disregard for ethical concerns which were shown by scientists in the first half of the 20th century. That wasn't just psychologists; the prevailing **modernist** ethos of the first half of the 20th century held that progress towards building a better world was all-important, and that science was the way that progress happened. So whatever scientists did in their quest for knowledge was outweighed by the greater good of the ultimate benefits to society.

The result was some seriously unethical studies, in which the participants – or "subjects", as they were called – were subjected to all kinds of disturbing and potentially damaging situations just so that the scientists concerned could

Key Terms

modernism
An approach to living, design and the arts popular in the first few decades of the 20th century, which emphasised scientific progress and consciously rejected traditional ways of doing things.

see the effects. From dosing people with radiation, to starving people to see what changes in the body and mind resulted, to secretly administering LSD, there was a whole catalogue of studies which were carried out right up to the 1960s, which today we would regard as completely unacceptable and certainly unethical.

Oddly enough, though, the research which brought ethical issues to the forefront in psychology was not one of these. It was a set of studies in which the researcher concerned had actually shown concern about the well-being of his subjects – the obedience studies conducted by Milgram (1963), which we looked at in chapter 6. Following the publication of Milgram's work, Baumrind (1964) published a paper which challenged the ethics of what he had done, arguing that the level of deception involved, and the potential distress produced in the participants at the knowledge of what they were capable of, meant that this study, and others of its type, were unacceptable practice.

Milgram himself pointed out that great care had been taken to make sure that his participants had not suffered from the experience, even including following them up some time after their experience of the experiment. Most of them, he argued, had actually expressed satisfaction at having participated, and both he and they felt (as many other people did) that the insights into human behaviour had made the study well worthwhile. But Baumrind's argument was less about the actuality of what had happened, than about the potential for harm which was caused by the experimental approach.

Researchers still argue about the ethics of Milgram's work. In 2014, Haslam et al examined the detailed archive of Milgram's studies, which were carefully documented, including records of the follow-ups. They found that there was little evidence of people being distressed, but that on the contrary, participants tended to express happiness at having been involved. Haslam et al, argued that the research was still unethical, because the participants' beliefs were a product of the experimenter's ability to convince them that they were contributing to the advancement of knowledge, and to progress. Haslam et al argued that the promotion of those ideologies was unethical in itself. But their argument largely ignores the **zeitgeist**, or spirit of the time, in which such beliefs were the dominant social representations in society, and were widely shared by lay people as well as scientists.

The important outcome of Baumrind's article wasn't the way in which it kicked off the Milgram debate, but that it stimulated discussions about ethical issues in psychological research. These eventually resulted in the development of **ethical guidelines** for researchers, for students, and for practitioners in psychology. These guidelines are regularly revised by the psychological organisations in various countries. In the UK they take the form of a Code of Conduct for researchers. All psychological researchers are expected to conform to the Code, and proposals for research have to be submitted to an ethics committee, who will review the proposed study in the light of the Code of Conduct to decide whether or not it is ethically acceptable.

| Key Terms |

zeitgeist
The "spirit of the time", including the established assumptions and general knowledge of that period.

ethical guidelines
Documents developed by professional bodies which provide guidance and principles concerning ethical aspects of research.

So what does the Code of Conduct contain? There are different guidelines for research with animals, of course, but the BPS Code of Human Research Ethics covers a number of issues. The fundamental principles underlying the code are outlined in Table 10.2, as well as the types of ethical issues which need to be explicitly considered.

Table 10.2 Ethical principles in psychological research

1. Respect for the autonomy, privacy and dignity of individuals and communities.

2. Scientific integrity.

3. Social responsibility.

4. Maximising benefit and minimising harm.

Source: BPS Code of Human Research Ethics (2014)

Risk

One of these is the risk, or potential risk, to the participants in the study. This doesn't have to be physical risk; it may take the form, for example, of risks to the participant's social status or privacy, or the potential for psychological harm as a result of distressing or disturbing experiences. Effectively, all proposed studies should include some kind of risk analysis, so that both participants and researchers are aware of the potential. But the reason why we have ethical committees rather than rigid laws is because there is always a matter of judgement involved. Sometimes, a degree of risk is regarded as acceptable if the appropriate precautions are in place to make sure it doesn't become excessive.

The code gives ten different examples of the kinds of risks which might be involved in psychological research (see Table 10.3). They include risks such as research involving potentially sensitive topics, such as people's sexual or legal behaviour; research that could induce psychological stress, anxiety or humiliation or cause more than minimal pain; and research that could lead to "labelling" of the participant, either by others or by themselves (e.g. "I am stupid" or "You're not normal").

Baumrind's objections to the Milgram study, of course, were based on the potential emotional and self-identity risk to the participants. In that sense, regardless of the care which Milgram took to ensure that his participants felt comfortable having been part of the research, some risk still existed. But the challenge presented by Milgram's work doesn't go away. We did learn important things about human nature from what he found out, and the fact is that even the professional psychologists and psychiatrists he interviewed beforehand had no idea that so many people would respond in the way that they did. So whether the level of risk was acceptable, given the precautions that he took, is still a matter of judgement.

Valid consent

It is not enough for people just to agree to take part in an experiment – they have to do so on the basis of adequate information. The key word here is "adequate"; the information needs to be appropriate to the research being undertaken, and provided in a way that maintains respect for their personal decisions and choices. If the person is not considered able to consider the

Table 10.3 Types of potential risk

1. Research involving vulnerable groups (e.g., children or dependent individuals).

2. Research involving potentially sensitive topics (e.g., sexual behaviour, experience of violence, gender or ethnic status).

3. Research involving a significant and necessary element of deception.

4. Research involving access to records of personal or confidential information.

5. Research involving access to potentially sensitive data through third parties (e.g., employee data).

6. Research that could induce psychological stress, anxiety or humiliation or cause more than minimal pain (e.g., repetitive or prolonged testing).

7. Research involving invasive interventions (e.g., drug administration, vigorous physical exercise, techniques such as hypnosis which would not usually be encountered during everyday life).

8. Research that may have an adverse impact on employment or social standing (e.g., discussion of commercially sensitive information).

9. Research that may lead to "labelling" either by the researcher or by the participant.

10. Research that involves the collection of human tissue, blood or other biological samples.

Source: BPS Code of Human Research Ethics (2014)

full implications of their own decisions – for example, in the case of children or those with impaired mental functioning – the researcher needs to obtain consent from two sources: from the participants themselves, but also from the parents or those with legal responsibility for children, and from family in the case of adults.

Informed consent is concerned with the act of participation, not just with what happens before the study begins. So it is important, for example, that the person can withdraw or modify their consent freely during the data gathering phase of the study. They can also ask for some or all of the data they have provided to be destroyed. If the data is to form part of a dataset for future researchers, for example for web-based research projects, as long as appropriate consent (e.g. including permission for future use) was obtained from the participants during the data-gathering process, it can be accessed without the need to contact the participants again. But sometimes, it is necessary to obtain two forms of consent: one for the data collection itself, and one for the ultimate use of the data.

Prior consent is therefore important, and the BPS Code of Ethics lists a series of headings which should be considered when drawing up a consent form, and which are summarised in Table 10.4. The list is lengthy, and is not meant to be used in full. Specific research studies are only likely to need some of the items, and the researcher should choose which are relevant. But it is useful to researchers by listing the items that a valid consent form might contain.

There are times, though, when some level of deception is absolutely necessary in order for the research to take place. One of the classic examples of this was the study of rebellion carried out by Gamson et al in 1982 which we looked at it in Chapter 6. Their experimental set-up inevitably involved a certain amount of deception, but they got round this by selecting participants

| Key Terms

prior consent
Agreement to accept research conditions which is given before the study takes place.

Table 10.4 Headings for consent forms

(Note: not all of these will apply to every research project.)

1. The aim(s) of the project.

2. The type(s) of data to be collected.

3. The method(s) of collecting data.

4. Confidentiality and anonymity conditions for the data including exceptions (e.g. regarding potential disclosures).

5. Compliance with the Data Protection Act and Freedom of Information Act.

6. The time commitment expected from participants.

7. The right to decline to offer any particular information requested by the researcher.

8. The opportunity to withdraw from the study at any time with no adverse consequences.

9. The opportunity to have any supplied data destroyed on request (up to a specified date).

10. Details of any risks associated with participation.

11. (If appropriate) a statement that recompense for time and inconvenience associated with participation will be given (no need to give specific details other than, e.g. reimbursement of travel costs).

12. The name and contact details of the principal investigator.

13. The name and contact details of another person who can receive enquiries about any matters which cannot be satisfactorily resolved with the principal investigator.

14. If appropriate, details of any insurance indemnity for the research.

15. Any debriefing that is planned.

16. How the data will be used and planned outcomes.

17. Potential benefits of the research.

18. How the results of the research will be made available to participants.

Source: BPS Code of Human Research Ethics (2014)

from a pool of people who had previously responded to a telephone survey. The questions in that survey included one which asked whether they would be prepared to participate in a study in which they were misled about the purpose until it had been completed. Only those who had answered "yes" to that question were selected for the study, and all of the participants were fully debriefed afterwards. For this reason, that level of deception was considered permissible by the ethics board who reviewed their research proposal.

Confidentiality

It ought to go without saying that confidential information must always be respected. This is particularly important today, when the internet allows such ready access to information, and even other people's research data. The code of ethics states that participants in a psychological study have the right to expect that the information they provide will be treated confidentially, and if it is published, that its source will not be identifiable.

One common way in which researchers deal with this requirement is by the use of code numbers or aliases to identify specific participants in a research project. It is important to be vigilant, though, as the data itself, particularly interview data, might reveal personal details which would indicate the identity of the person being interviewed, or of someone they were talking about. The usual convention is to replace the key words with blanks or asterisks in the transcriptions, so that the basic data is still available for scrutiny, but personal details are not revealed.

Giving advice

During the course of psychological research, there are times when it becomes evident that someone is seriously in need of advice of one kind or another. It may be that this is part of the research project itself, in which case there is no real problem as long as the person giving the advice has appropriate expertise. But sometimes a researcher may become aware that the person concerned has serious psychological or personal problems, even though they are unaware of them. In such cases, and if the researcher feels that the person's future well-being might be endangered by this lack of awareness, it is the researcher's responsibility to discuss the matter with the participant.

If the research is such that there is a good chance of such issues emerging – for example, in a role play situation which might bring up issues of bereavement or child abuse – then the research proposal should include a protocol for the steps which should be taken in such situations, and an appropriate referral route so that the person can obtain suitable guidance, and if necessary, treatment. All psychologists are bound by a Code of Conduct, which states that they may not act outside of their area of competence, so in the case of serious psychological disturbance, it is important to make sure that a fully qualified clinical or counselling psychologist is available for consultation.

Deception

The ethical assumption is that people taking part in psychological research have the right not to be deliberately deceived. Few people would disagree with this principle, but it has raised a number of problems in practice. Knowing what a study is about can influence the outcomes of that study. Precautions such as single and double-blind controls try to control the influence of participants' and experimenters' expectations, and are considered absolutely necessary in some situations, such as researching the effects of drugs. Yet they inevitably involve deception. So the BPS code differentiates between some of the details of the hypothesis being tested, and deliberately giving false information about the purpose of the study.

It's a tricky issue, and one where the judgements of **ethics committees** are really important. The baseline really is, as the Code states, that if people are likely to react with discomfort, anger or objections when the true purpose of the research is revealed, then deception is inappropriate. If the research would be compromised by full disclosure, then the ethics committee needs to have full information about what information will be withheld, and at what point participants will be informed about it. In other words, deception is only acceptable if it is absolutely necessary in order for the research to take place.

The principle about deception is really about the fact that participants are entitled to respect. So it also applies to studies taking place in public or natural

Key Terms
ethics committees Groups set up by professional and educational institutions which appraise research proposals and judge whether they conform to acceptable ethical practice or not.

settings. Studies which show a lack of respect for participants, or a disregard for other things which might be happening in their lives are nowadays not considered to be acceptable. For example, in the classic library study by Felipe and Sommer (1966), which we discuss in Box 10.1, we have no way of knowing whether their work was important, or whether the interruption led to negative personal consequences (see also Chapter 3).

This complete disregard of other people's personal concerns would not be considered acceptable nowadays. The BPS Code of Human Research Ethics states that only observational studies are acceptable in natural settings, unless the people concerned give their consent. Such studies also have to respect the privacy and psychological well-being of those people being studied, and take into account local cultural values and people's assumptions that they will be unobserved, even in an ostensibly public location.

Box 10.1   Case study: Investigating personal space

A well-known study in social psychology involved checking out people's reactions to invasions of their personal space. Felipe and Sommer (1966) did this by asking their researchers to go and sit much too close to people who were working in a university library. People's reactions were observed, so the researchers could see how people reacted to the invasion. Another of their measures was how long the person would continue to work in the library under those conditions before they packed their things up and left. (They also timed how long people worked in ordinary uninterrupted conditions.)

Some 55 per cent of their "victims" packed up and left within ten minutes, which nobody working without interruption had done. After half an hour, only 30 per cent of the people were still working in the same place, compared with 87 per cent of the controls. Those who remained had generally set up a barrier of books and papers between themselves and the intruder.

The researchers performed a similar study in a mental hospital, sitting next to people who were otherwise alone, and timing how long they stayed, with very similar results. They announced their findings as significant examples of the importance of personal space.

But what about the ethics of these studies? Personal space was a relatively new topic of investigation at the time, so the researchers felt that they were breaking new ground and opening up new areas for investigation. But was the way they went about it acceptable? If you were studying in a library, would you consider yourself "fair game" for such research, or would you see it as an invasion of your privacy? Which of the modern code of ethics for research would these studies contravene?

Debriefing

Whether participants have been actively deceived or not, they are entitled to a full debriefing at the end of their participation. This should inform them about the outcomes and nature of the research and check to make sure that they have not suffered any unforeseen harm, discomfort or misconceptions. At such times, psychologists need to be careful in expressing the outcomes of the research, bearing in mind that even apparently innocuous evaluations may be taken personally by participants, and lead to distressing misapprehensions.

Debriefing may also include undoing any changes which have taken place as part of the research, particularly if those changes are of a negative nature. For example, if the research has involved procedures designed to induce a negative mood, it would be appropriate for the researchers to take steps to induce a happier mood in the participants before they end their participation. But conversely, if the research was designed to introduce a happy mood in participants, it would not be considered appropriate to try to remove that happiness from them before the end! The overall idea is that participating in research should be a positive, not a negative, experience.

The challenges of ethical research

We can see, then, that the ethical principles applied by psychologists in modern research represent their own set of challenges. But in many ways, having to take account of these principles has led to more imaginative, and often more ecologically valid, forms of research. For example, Rhys Evans and Steptoe-Warren (2014) reported a case study regarding the teaching of emotions to psychology students. Obviously, it would be unethical to attempt to induce positive or negative emotions directly, but the way they approached it was to invite the students to design a fairground attraction aimed to induce emotional experiences. The students produced a range of designs, and in the process were able to explore and analyse a range of emotions.

While it is useful to find alternative ways of understanding experience, there are some times when it is also useful to conduct simulations of real social experiences. Reicher et al (2014) argued that we must avoid becoming so overwhelmed by legalistic requirements that we see ourselves as unable to manipulate social worlds for social psychological research. As we saw in Chapter 6, this team of researchers replicated the Zimbardo Stanford Prison Experiment, and managed to highlight a number of different aspects of the study which had been overlooked by Zimbardo and his team at the time. While such manipulations inevitably involve some deception, and some degree of risk, Reicher et al argue that they give us insights which we would otherwise be unable to achieve.

More to the point, without that, social psychology would fail in its aim of understanding our social lives. Their fundamental argument is that we need to be able to manipulate social worlds so that we can witness at first hand, how social and cultural factors shape social behaviour. If we were not able to vary the social environment, then we would only be able to identify individual variations, which would push social psychology into looking for individualistic explanations and becoming oblivious to other levels of experience. As we have seen throughout this book, social psychology integrates the individual levels of explanation with social, societal and cultural levels. So it is important that social psychological research, too, can deal with these levels in our quest to understand what it is to be human – and social.

CONDUCTING SOCIAL PSYCHOLOGICAL RESEARCH

Research in social psychology poses a number of unique problems, mainly because our subject matter is not inert material but living, breathing, thinking and enquiring human beings. In the first part of the 20th century, these aspects of social psychology's subject matter tended to be overlooked. The people who participated in experiments were known as "subjects", and generally regarded as inert material, doing only what the experimenter told them. We will see in the next section how misleading that assumption was. More recently, however, social psychological researchers have taken into account the way that their participants own ideas, motivations and perspectives also have a considerable influence on research outcomes. But what is research, and what forms does it take?

Modern social psychologists have a variety of research methods upon which they can draw. As with the levels of analysis that we looked at in Table 10.1, any given social psychologist may choose to adopt just one or two types of research method. Generally speaking, modern research tends to include more than one type of measure. But the variety of research methods on offer to the modern psychologists makes it easier to select those methods which are most appropriate for the particular aspect of social experience or behaviour which is being studied.

Talking point 10.2   Ethics of past research

One of the main ethical debates in psychology as a whole, including social psychology, is the question of how we deal with past research. There are many studies which would be considered to be completely unethical now, but which we continue to report and discuss, because sometimes they give us insights which we would not have had in other ways. Milgram's obedience studies are a classic example of this.

Some people argue that including such studies in the psychology curriculum is giving them implicit approval – after all, we wouldn't dream of including the barbaric twin studies or any other research conducted by the Nazi concentration camp doctors, so where should we draw the line? Others argue both that the studies have value in their own right, and also that learning about them serves to highlight and clarify ethical concerns in ways which would be meaningless, or at least very difficult, if we only learned about modern studies.

What do you think?

Experiments

Experiments involve manipulating situations or stimuli (known as variables) in order to bring about a particular result. Sometimes they are laboratory-based, which means that the experimenter is able to control many of the different environmental factors which might influence the outcomes. Milgram's study of obedience, which we looked at in Chapter 6, is a classic example of this type of experiment. Often, though, social psychological research involves field experiments, located in the everyday world. The Hawthorne studies which we looked at in Chapter 9 are typical field experiments. Field experiments are more realistic, but it is of course much more difficult to control all of the many aspects of the situation which might have an influence on the results.

Observational studies

It isn't always possible to conduct experiments, even field ones; so social psychologists often gather data from observing how people act in particular situations. Much of the information on personal space and proxemics which we examined in Chapter 3, for example, has come from observational studies investigating how people interact in public place, such as the distances they maintain during conversations with close friends or with strangers. In a classic observational study, the observer will be entirely separate from and not influencing those who are being observed; but this is not always possible in reality. People often know when they are being observed, and this can change how they behave – although with studies drawn from CCTV records that may be less of a factor, since they have become such a familiar aspect of everyday urban life.

Sometimes, though, the most practical way of gathering observations is by actually participating in what is going on. Festinger's study of the failure of religious prediction which we looked at in Chapter 5 is a classic example. If the researchers had not joined in as part of the group, they would have been unable to gather the views and opinions of the other group members. This method is known as **participant observation**, and it is another method by which social psychologists gather the data for their research.

Case studies

A case study is an in-depth investigation of a particular individual or group of individuals. Usually, a case study will involve a mixture of approaches: some observations, some account analysis, some document analysis, and so on. By bringing them all together in a detailed investigation, we can build up a picture of how different factors and social influences interact. Much of what we know about face recognition, for example, derives from case studies of particular individuals with **prosopagnosia**. Those people often experience profound social consequences from their inability to recognise people who ought to be familiar to them, and case studies are useful to identify different aspects of their experiences. Case studies can also be useful to explore detailed changes over time, as we saw in Chapter 8 with Smith's qualitative investigations of how pregnant mothers reconstruct their personal sense of identity as their pregnancy progresses. Because they focus explicitly on smaller samples, case studies are able to include a range of different forms of data, collected through observations, individual experimentation, conversations and often psychometric tests.

Interviews

Interviews involve the collecting of information from particular people in order to investigate their experiences or opinions about the topic under investigation. That information is collected in the form of verbal statements, gathered in conversation between the person and the researcher. Some interviews are extremely formal, being little more than questionnaires administered in a face-to-face form; some are semi-structured, with the conversation dealing explicitly with particular topics but allowing the person to express themselves freely in that context; and some are entirely open, enabling the person to give their ideas or opinions freely, in whatever way they like. Interviews are often combined with other approaches to clarify aspects of the participant's experience – for example, in Asch's famous conformity experiment which we looked at in

Key Terms

participant observation
Observational studies in which the researcher becomes one of the participants, and joins in the action which is being observed.

prosopagnosia
A brain disorder in which the person is unable to recognise faces.

Chapter 6. The interviews allowed Asch to gain insights into the social processes involved, and to recognise the tension experienced even by those who
refused to conform to the majority verdict.

Conversational, discourse and attributional analysis

Interviewing can also provide the material for more in-depth types of research.
Many modern social psychologists use in-depth interviewing or the recording
of occurring conversations to investigate social experiences and how they are
constructed. We looked at several of these approaches in Chapter 4, such as
how discourse analysis investigates the way that social meanings and shared
memories are constructed through discourse, and also how important shared
social representations are to making sense of our lives. Both discourse and
social representation research generally draw on the analysis of conversational
data, sometimes obtained from observation, but often from interviews.

Analysing conversational data may involve detailed conversational analysis, in which specific aspects of the conversation such as timings, vocabulary,
hesitations and control are all identified and collated, or it may be a more
general analysis of the forms of the discourse, such as the family discussions
recorded by Middleton and Edwards which we looked at in Chapter 4. A third
approach has been to use attributional analysis to identify underlying social
identifications or the dominant or recurrent social representations in the conversation, such as the study of delusional psychiatric patients conducted by
Beese and Stratton.

Document analysis

Social psychologists can also gather data through the careful examination of
documents – either historical ones, such as the close records of the Watergate
trials used by Neisser in his study of John Dean's memory (Chapter 9), or more
current ones, such as modern accounts posted on the internet. Many social psychological investigations of the uses of social media, for example, have drawn
strongly on document analysis in one way or another. One example might

be looking at the open content of Facebook to identify significant issues; or conducting numerical studies on Twitter or Reddit responses to particular submissions.

Another form of document analysis which is particularly important in psychology in general, including social psychology, is **meta-analysis**. This involves combining the findings of different research papers on a particular topic, in order to find out if there really is an identifiable general trend. For example, the meta-analysis on implicit personality theory which we looked at in Chapter 7 was able to identify some significant themes with consistent positive or negative connotations. These emerged strongly when the research was looked at as a whole, but were not so apparent in the data of the individual studies (Rosenberg et al, 1968).

Surveys and questionnaires

Surveys and questionnaires are a common way of finding out information, and they are much used by social scientists in general, although perhaps less often by social psychologists. The reason for this is that although they appear on the surface to be clear and valid sources of information, in practice they suffer from a number of problems. One of these is so common that it is known as the **questionnaire fallacy**, and that is the idea that a questionnaire will tell you what people will actually do. In reality, what they will tell you is how people have responded to your questionnaire – and that depends very much upon the way in which the questions have been phrased, and the options for responses which are available. Nonetheless, a well-constructed questionnaire can sometimes give useful information about a general topic, and can highlight areas which can be investigated in more detail by other forms of research. That is generally the way that they are used by social psychologists.

Many questionnaires involve the use of **rating scales**. These often adopt the Likert format of a range of values from "strongly agree" to "strongly disagree". The advantage of rating scales like this is that they provide a sort of quantifiable data, allowing researchers to compare different responses, not in an arithmetically accurate form, but in terms of the main trends of the responses. The disadvantage, of course, is that they only provide a simplistic range of options; there is no way for someone to communicate opinions which are more complex than the single dimension offered by the rating scale.

A great deal of attitude research involves measuring attitudes by using surveys and questionnaires. Box 10.2 outlines some of the major techniques which have been used to do this. The problem, though, is that we can never be sure how close people's stated attitudes are to their behaviour; as we saw in Chapter 5, the two can often be very different. That raises problems of ecological validity, which we will be looking at more closely later in this chapter.

Key Terms

meta-analysis
A research technique which involves examining effects found in a series of studies and calculating the overall probability, as evidence for whether there is an underlying effect or not.

questionnaire fallacy
The way in which people respond to the questions asked at the expense of providing valid information.

rating scales
Measuring scales used to assess or evaluate objects or ideas.

Box 10.2 Measuring attitudes

Measures of attitudes have taken many forms. The most popular and well-known type of measure is the Likert scale, which is typically a five-point scale allowing people to express how much they agree or disagree with a particular statement. A typical example might be:

The most important issue facing human beings today is the matter of the ecology.

strongly agree — agree — don't know — disagree — strongly disagree

A Likert scale has a midpoint, and gives ordinal data, which can be ranked and expresses degrees of opinion. So it is preferable to a simple yes/no question, but it does have some problems – for example, it is difficult to know exactly what a mid-point score means. In this example, a mid-score could mean one of at least five different things: that the person recognises the importance of the issue but doesn't know whether it would really be more important than other things; that they have no opinion either way; that they are aware of arguments for both sides and haven't made up their minds; that they really don't know anything about it; or that they just don't care.

Attitudes are emotional as well as factual, and the semantic differential was developed by Osgood (1966) to try to assess the emotional and associative nuances of an attitude. A semantic differential offers several different dimensions, and asks the person rate the relevance of each of them to the target. A semantic differential comparing attitudes towards schoolteachers might look like this:

Schoolteacher

angular ---------------------- rounded
weak ---------------------- strong
rough ---------------------- smooth
active ---------------------- passive
small ---------------------- large
cold ---------------------- hot
good ---------------------- bad
tense ---------------------- relaxed
wet ---------------------- dry
fresh ---------------------- stale

Although some of these dimensions may seem irrelevant, they help to tease out subtleties by encouraging the person to use their imagination.

A third approach to attitude measurement is the Bogardus Social Distance Scale (1947), which looks at the degree of ethnic or racial prejudice felt by an individual by asking the person to state whether they agree or disagree with a number of statements about possible relationships. For example:

Bulgarians

• would admit to close kinship by marriage;
• would admit to citizenship in my country;
• would exclude from my country;
• would admit to my street as neighbours.

This way of measuring attitudes is a bit transparent, in that it is very obvious what it is measuring. That makes it vulnerable to response bias, so it tends to be used in a disguised form – buried in with other questions or exercises – rather than explicitly on its own.

Some researchers have used polygraphs, or lie detectors, which measure the arousal associated with stimuli which the person finds emotionally stressful or distasteful. Pupil dilation is another physiological measure which can indicate attitude – in this case, how attractive someone finds something. But these are laboratory-based, or at least equipment-based methods, and only really useful for in-depth studies of single people: they can't really be used to tell us about more generally held attitudes.

So we are a long way yet from being able to measure attitudes, and still further from being able to assert that any one measure gives the definitive view. People vary in themselves, as well as from each other, and we may hold one attitude in one context and a different one in another.

Psychometrics

Psychometrics involve the use of professionally constructed psychological tests, designed to measure specific psychological characteristics. Sometimes these characteristics are social in nature – for instance, the psychometric measure of loneliness developed by Zimbardo and his colleagues which we looked at in Chapter 2. Some psychometric tests involve paper and pencil or computer-generated responses, some explore people's reactions to simulations or work-relate tasks, and some even take the form of computer games (Riley, 2015).

Whatever their form, though, psychometric tests are very far from being simple questionnaires. In order to become recognised as a valid psychometric test, each item in the test needs to have been evaluated and **norm-referenced**, so that the typical responses and their expected variations in the population at large are known (or at least the particular population that the test is designed for). They also need to have been assessed for reliability, to make sure that their results are consistent, and for validity, to ensure that they are really measuring what they purport to measure. A psychometric test is only considered acceptable when these rigorous criteria have been met – and often, they can only be administered by those who have had specialised training. So they are not necessarily available to everyone, but they can be a valuable research tool when used in an appropriate way.

Action research

Action research may involve several different approaches to gathering data, but it is different from classic experimentation or observation in that it is a much more involved process. Action researchers acknowledge that their investigations are part of a total social situation, and as such they will affect how the subjects of the research understand what is going on, and how they are likely to respond. Action researchers believe that trying to investigate social experiences without influencing them is both impractical and unrealistic. People will always wonder about the presence of the researchers and develop theories about what they are doing. So they accept that their investigation will have an influence, and take that fully into account, examining how that influence has worked as well as what else is going on. The study of a small company by Hayes and Lemon which we looked at in Chapter 9 is an example of this type of approach.

The increasing demand for understanding real-world experience means that action research has become increasingly popular as an approach to social investigation. It is not new. In 1947, Lewin published a paper outlining the

Key Terms
norm-referenced Measured up to criteria developed from the normative scores of a particular target group.

problems of feedback in social systems brought about by the presence of the researchers, and in 1948 he articulated action research clearly as a methodological approach. His ideas influenced many social researchers of the time, and many of the insights obtained in organisational research have adopted this approach. Although action research was under-recognised during the 1960s and 1970s, it became popular again in later years owing to its inclusion in an influential text by Reason and Rowan (1981) which outlined a "new paradigm" for social research.

New paradigm research

New paradigm research reflected the influence of Rom Harré, a social philosopher and psychologist who proposed that the study of human beings should focus on how people actually lived and understood their experiences, rather than on analysing small units of behaviour. It rejected the straightjacket imposed by behaviourist ideas of rigid experimentation, and maintained that those taking part in psychological research should be seen as participants in the whole social process, rather than as "subjects" to be manipulated by the researcher.

Harré (1979) argued that there were two fundamental aspects to new paradigm research, which made it very different from the conventional approach to research in social psychology. One of these was the idea that the basic unit of research should be the episode, rather than the act. Our social life is lived in meaningful episodes, and to take single acts or actions out of context means that much of their significance is lost. Harré's suggestion was that social episodes could meaningfully be studied using a **dramaturgical metaphor**, as if they were episodes in a play. So the study of an episode would include looking at the characters involved, their roles, scripts, the contexts and settings and so on. We can see how this approach could bring together several different aspects of social psychology, combining different insights to produce meaningful understanding of what is going on in a particular situation.

The other significant aspect of new paradigm research has now become much more commonplace, and that is **account analysis**. It seems fairly obvious now, but when Harré first proposed that gathering people's accounts of their experience was valid social data it was a distinctly radical idea. Until then, many psychologists had felt obliged to use the "hard science" model of scientific investigation, regarding their "subjects" as uninvolved and taking considerable precautions in their investigations to protect their findings against unwanted influence from those subjects. At the time, verbal accounts were considered to be woolly and unreliable data – only numbers were important.

That was unrealistic and led to a distortion of reality, Harré argued. The accounts which people give of their experience are important in understanding what is going on, because people's own beliefs influence how they act, and that in turn influences how other people act. By interviewing people, and collecting their versions of events, we can get a very different picture of what is going on than we might get from an "impartial" observation, even if such a thing was really possible. In an example of this, Marsh et al (1978) demonstrated how accounts from football "hooligans" showed that what was going on involved structured and ritualised sequences of action which looked frightening to outsiders, but rarely came to violence. Account analysis revealed a very different picture of what was happening between rival gangs on the terraces than the mindless aggression portrayed by the media.

As we saw in Chapter 4, account analysis has now become an accepted part of social psychology. But it still needs to be carried out carefully – it is too easy for a researcher to jump to conclusions, since people tend to notice only what they are interested in, and to apply their own schemas and scripts to what they hear. So modern account analysis involves a variety of qualitative approaches to analysis, designed to identify common or particular themes and issues in the context of the study. And the ways that the accounts are obtained also need to be careful and systematic, to avoid being affected by the interviewer's unconscious cues or bias.

Grounded theory

Grounded theory (Pidgeon and Henwood, 1997) is a form of qualitative research which allows researchers to explore entirely new areas. It begins with the collection of qualitative data, often recordings of people's accounts. These are then subjected to a detailed form of analysis in which concepts are derived from the data and subjected to an iterative process of refinement, until the researcher is able to develop a useful taxonomy or a fully-fledged grounded theory. The important aspect of this is that the analysis is reflexive, returning to the data frequently to ensure that any conclusions are fully grounded and not speculative, but that it is also sensitive to the realities experienced by the original participants in the study.

Grounded theory, then, is an inductive research method, using qualitative data, which can be extremely valuable in providing insights into people's experience in a rigorous and systematic way. It could be viewed as a form of account analysis, in that it certainly involves analysing accounts; but it goes deeper than many other forms of account analysis. Its rigour and reflexivity ensures that its outcomes can be regarded as valid theoretical contributions in social psychology, and will be appropriate as the basis for further research into the area concerned.

Internet-based research

The existence of the internet has added a new dimension to social psychological research. By offering the potential for huge samples, drawn from diverse backgrounds, it has expanded the range of possibilities for questionnaire studies, which can now reach participants who would be difficult to reach in any other way. It is now common to find studies which include thousands of respondents, where before these would have been very expensive and extremely difficult to carry out, and even studies exploring quite personal aspects of internet use, such as McKenna's study of self-disclosure (Chapter 8), have been able to draw on much larger samples than would otherwise have been possible.

Buchanan and Smith (1999) compared two samples of respondents to a personality questionnaire, one obtained in the conventional way from university undergraduates, and the other through the internet. They found that the results obtained from the questionnaires were directly comparable, but pointed out that the respondents obtained through the internet were true volunteers, whereas the undergraduates were motivated to cooperate either through coercion – being obliged to do it to complete their course – or through incentives (i.e., gaining additional course credits). They concluded that the internet was an extremely useful way of gathering data for research, often preferable to the more traditional approaches.

The internet has also offered researchers the opportunity to study how new forms of social behaviour have emerged. By opening up a new area of social interaction, the internet itself provides rich opportunities for social research. Sometimes these are new forms of behaviour which have emerged as a result. The study of unwritten Facebook rules by Bryant and Malmo which we looked at in Chapter 3, or Weisbuch et al's study of first impressions and internet attraction (Chapter 7) are examples of this. Sometimes, too, the internet offers new opportunities for behaviours which are already in existence – as Griffiths (2000) found in the study of addictions and internet which we looked at in Chapter 9.

We can see, then, that modern social psychology draws on a variety of investigative approaches. A social psychologist proposing to investigate a topic will select the research method which, to their mind, is most appropriate for what they are studying. The fact that analytical techniques now include qualitative methods as well as quantitative ones also extends the range of topics which can be investigated, and how conclusions can be drawn. For more detail on how to undertake any of these forms of research, and how to carry out quantitative or qualitative analysis, see my book on conducting psychological research (Hayes, 2005).

Evaluating research methods

Each of the methods we have looked at above has both strengths and weaknesses. But there is no arbitrary criterion by which we can say "this approach is the best, and this is worst". There have been a few attempts to rank research methods, to enable people to see which ones are more effective, but these have only applied in specific contexts. For example, Evans (2003) challenged the prevailing idea in medical circles that the only valid research involves randomised, controlled trials – that is, experimental studies which are tightly limited and controlled. By taking three different criteria into account, effectiveness, appropriateness and feasibility, Evans developed a framework for ranking the evidence supplied in health care interventions which is summarised in Table 10.5.

Evans' research gives us an idea of how some research methods might be compared for specific purposes – in this case health care – but it wouldn't really be useful to try to do this for the whole of social psychology. Many of the areas studied by social psychologists are concerned with social and personal experience and meaning. Although those can sometimes be relevant for health care, much of health care's primary concerns are to do with physical care and treatments, so empirical methods such as experimentation are much more relevant.

The different research methods used by social psychologists explore very different aspects of human social behaviour. Discourse analysis, for example, is particularly useful if we want to look at how people construct meanings for their experiences, and the way that these can be tied in with cultural or social expectations and explanations. Laboratory experiments, at the other extreme, have been useful in showing us detail, such as how physiological reactions such as pupil dilation connect with social experiences such as liking or attraction. Observational studies may show us general aspects of social behaviour such as

Key Terms

randomised, controlled trials
The "ideal" procedure for medical research, where everything is tightly controlled and measured.

Table 10.5 Evaluating medical research

Rating	Effectiveness	Appropriateness	Feasibility
Excellent	Systematic reviews Multi-centre studies	Systematic reviews Multi-centre studies	Systematic reviews Multi-centre studies
Good	Randomised controlled trials Observational studies	Randomised controlled trials Observational studies Interpretive studies	Randomised controlled trials Observational studies Interpretive studies
Fair	Before and after studies Uncontrolled studies with striking results Un-randomised controlled trials	Descriptive studies Focus groups	Before and after studies Descriptive studies Focus groups Action research
Poor	Descriptive studies Case studies Expert opinion Badly designed studies	Case studies Expert opinion Badly designed studies	Case studies Expert opinion Badly designed studies

Source: Evans (2003)

how people manage their personal territories, interviews may give us ways of understanding what social experiences mean to people, and grounded theory can open up new aspects of human experience for further investigation.

Each of the methods used in social psychology has its strengths, and, if applied inappropriately, its weaknesses. What we really need to do is to make sure that the research method we are using is appropriate for whatever it is that we are studying. In the modern world, we have the freedom to do just that; we can use qualitative approaches if we want, or quantitative ones if they are more useful. But this was not always the case.

CRITERIA FOR RESEARCH

Through the middle years of the 20th century, the dominant ethos in psychology was that it should be "scientific". Psychology, it was argued, should model itself on the natural sciences, emphasising experimental control and rigorous measurement. Psychological research should follow the hypothetico-deductive approach and produce quantitative data which could be subject to mathematical analysis.

There were, of course, a number of problems with this idea, including the way it ignored the actual range of different approaches used in the natural sciences – it adopted an idealised view of "science" which wasn't typical of the real work of practising scientists. Another problem was its rigorous insistence that only numerical data was valid, which made things very difficult for researchers dealing with real-world situations, where qualitative data was the main source of information. Box 10.3 describes one of the social consequences of this requirement, but there were many other examples.

Box 10.3   Quantification versus social responsibility

The rigorous insistence on "scientific" criteria and objective measurement was more than just a minor quirk of the psychological establishment. The rigorous insistence that only numerical data was valid caused significant problems for researchers studying complex real-life matters, and in some cases, it produced real harm. For example, in the Genie project, a study of language acquisition in a child who had been severely deprived until her teens, it meant that the whole project had to be abandoned after a couple of years, because research funding was stopped (Curtiss, 1977). There were no further funds for supporting Genie, or for continuing the emotional support and personal relationships she had built up with the researchers.

The outcome for Genie was devastating. She was placed in foster care, where she was again abused, and the linguistic gains she had made were lost. However, this narrow view of objective science was the dominant approach of the day, and research funding depended on meeting its criteria. The researchers actually had a wealth of qualitative data, in the form of audio and film recordings, which in modern times would be regarded as rich outcomes, entirely justifying funding for the project. But they were refused that funding because their findings were not quantified, presented as numbers and statistics, and were therefore deemed to be unscientific.

The emphasis on the natural sciences may have been a bit idealised, but it is nonetheless important to establish some level of quality control for psychological research. In that context, there are three criteria to which psychological research is expected to conform: validity, reliability and generalisability. Different research methods may emphasise one or two of these criteria more than others; in research with human beings, it is not easy to apply strict rules which will apply in all situations. But any approach to psychological research, if it is to be considered "real" research rather than just a demonstration or anecdotal evidence, will address these three criteria in some way.

The simple definition of **validity** is that it is all about whether something – a test or a measure of some kind – actually measures what it is supposed to measure. But clarifying what we really mean by that is not as simple as it sounds. In a psychological experiment, validity may refer to how accurately the experimental situation reflects the real-life issues which are being investigated, or it may refer to the relationship between the measure being taken and the theoretical construct which it reflects. In psychometric tests, a test's validity is considered to be how far the interpretation of the test scores is supported by evidence and/or theory. So there can be several different kinds of validity, each of which reflects a various different way of assessing or measuring it. Table 10.6 lists some of the more common forms of validity.

Reliability is all to do with consistency. In the classic experimental situation, reliability is the question of whether the measures used in a study will give consistent results in similar situations. In more complex social situations, however, such as in action research or qualitative case studies, strict measures of reliability are less important, because of the way that the study includes concepts of change and development. In research with human beings, situations vary and so do the ways in which people respond to things, so unless we are

Key Terms

validity
Whether a psychometric test or psychological measure really measures what it is supposed to.

reliability
Whether a test or measure is consistent over time in the outcomes that it gives.

Table 10.6 Forms of validity

Construct validity, or how closely the measure assesses the psychological construct which it has been designed to measure. This form of validity is generally regarded as the most important form of validity, and a number of the other forms of validity represent attempts to operationalise it.

Criterion validity, which is how far it measures up to some other standard or yardstick (e.g., comparing an employee selection test with employee performance records).

Concurrent validity, which is how well the results compare with other measures of the same thing (e.g., other intelligence tests), given at the same time.

Predictive validity, which is whether the results show a reasonable correlation with some future measurement of the same construct (e.g., intelligence tests taken at a later date).

Incremental validity, which is whether a particular test will increase our predictive ability about a particular variable – for example, whether using a new type of personality test will significantly enhance our awareness of or knowledge about, someone's personality.

Ecological validity, which is how far the measure being assessed actually relates to its real-world equivalent – for example, whether a psychometric measure of empathy actually reflects how empathic or socially sensitive people are in their everyday lives.

Face validity, aka surface validity, which is whether it (i.e., the set of results typically given by the test) looks as though it is probably valid.

looking at very specific forms of social behaviour, in controlled conditions, ensuring reliability may be less important, or in some cases entirely inappropriate. It all depends upon the question being investigated and the research method being used to investigate it.

There is one situation, though, where reliability is particularly important, and that is in psychometric testing. Test developers, and other psychologists who are developing measuring scales for their research, need to adopt specific strategies to ensure that a test dimension or scale will give consistent results. There are three of these. The test-retest method is when the same test is administered on two separate occasions to the same people. This is fine for simple tests such as measures of reaction time, but less appropriate if there is a danger of practice or familiarity affecting the results. An alternative strategy, particularly useful in the development of a measuring scale with multiple items, is to split it into two equal halves, and compare the results given by the two sets of items when they are administered to the same people. And the third option is to develop two alternate forms of the same measuring scale, again so that their results can be compared to see if they will give consistent results over time with the same people.

The third important criterion for psychological research is **generalisability**. This is the question of whether the findings of the research can be applied more widely – whether we can make generalisations about human behaviour in general – or whether they are limited to just the case we are studying. But generalisability doesn't mean that all of our findings have to apply to all of the human species. Our research could be applied just to a small population or set of people, such as those with a specific disability or challenge. Or it might relate to people in very special circumstances. But it does need to go a bit further than just the individual cases we are looking at.

Key Terms

generalisability
Whether a research procedure or measure would apply to general populations or situations, rather than just the immediate ones.

Again, the way in which we look at generalisability depends upon the nature of the research, and different research methods will adopt very different ways of addressing it. Traditional research methods, for example, place a strong emphasis on the way that the research sample is obtained, and there are many different ways of sampling which attempt to ensure that the sample is representative of the population concerned. Other research methods may involve a different approach, studying the unique and individual experiences of just one individual. But what is important is that we should be able to learn something from the research, that our conclusions should reflect more than just what that particular person has felt or experienced. Our generalisations might be wide, or narrow. A study could tell us something about psychological processes in general, about social or psychological mechanisms in typical contexts, or about mental strategies of coping in very special situations.

These three criteria – validity, reliability and generalisability – can each be interpreted in different ways, and the different research methods used by social psychologists take very different approaches to them. But even the most anti-experimental of approaches aims to have more academic rigour than just everyday chatter. If a study is to be counted as real research, and not just as anecdotal "ooh-look-ain't-it-interesting" journalism, its approach to research and analysis will address these three criteria in some form or another. But in some cases, the more rigorously we try to apply them, the more problems we create for ourselves, as the next section will show.

PROBLEMS AND ISSUES IN SOCIAL PSYCHOLOGICAL RESEARCH

Having a range of approaches means that we can avoid some of the more common problems in social psychological research – but only if we are aware of them. For many years, investigations into psychology, including social psychology, typically involved laboratory studies, in which subjects were asked to perform relatively distinct tasks under highly controlled conditions. However, this method raises problems of ecological validity. A study can only be described as ecologically valid if it really corresponds to real-life conditions and real-life behaviour. But people often act quite differently when they are taking part in a laboratory experiment than they would do in real life.

This problem came to light as a result of two important studies which showed how some very basic social mechanisms operate in psychological experiments. The first of these is known as the self-fulfilling prophecy, and one of the first investigations which highlighted the matter was Rosenthal and Fode (1963), who showed how the beliefs and ideas of the experimenter could influence the results of a psychological study – even if the subjects were animals!

The self-fulfilling prophecy

Rosenthal and Fode asked two groups of psychology students to undertake a maze-learning experiment using laboratory rats, a fairly typical task for the time. One group was told that their rats had been specially bred to be "maze-bright", but the other group were told that they hadn't had enough "maze-bright" rats for everyone, so theirs were "maze-dull". In fact, there were no differences between the animals. The students were expected to "teach" the rat to get through the maze using food rewards.

Key Terms
ecological validity
A way of assessing the validity of a measure or test which is concerned with whether it is really like its counterpart in the real, everyday world.
self-fulfilling prophecy
The observation that expectations about a person or group can become true simply because they have been stated.

When they tested the rats' performance a few days later, they found that the predictions had come true – the supposedly "maze-bright" rats had learned more quickly than the others. The students who believed their rats would learn quickly had encouraged them more, given them more learning sessions and handled them more. It had been a self-fulfilling prophecy; the fact that the experimenters – that is, the students – knew what was expected had influenced the outcome. How much more powerful, some psychologists argued, would that influence be when the "subjects" were real human beings, who could pick up on very subtle non-verbal cues?

Rosenthal and Jacobsen (1968) went on to perform the educational study of the self-fulfilling prophecy in the classroom, which we looked at in Chapter 7, and which is still discussed and debated today. But for psychologists, it was the Rosenthal and Fode study which gave the most serious warnings. It led, for example, to the increasing use of the **double-blind** technique – a version of experimental control in which neither the "subjects" nor the experimenter is aware of what the experiment is really all about. But that produced problems of its own, such as the extreme degree of deception which was involved, and the ethical challenges which it raised.

Demand characteristics

The same problems were faced in looking for ways of controlling the second issue, which was that of **demand characteristics**. As we saw in the last chapter, Orne (1962) was trying to find a way of distinguishing between people who were "truly" hypnotised and people who were "shamming", and only pretending to be hypnotised; but eventually he had to give up, unable to find any reliable way to tell them apart. In the process, though, he discovered that people would act quite differently if they thought that they were taking part in a psychological experiment than they would do in real life. The experimental situation, Orne showed, generated particular demand characteristics which influenced how people would act – meaning that they would do what they believed they were expected to do. And this can result in behaviour which is quite different from what people would do in an everyday situation.

Orne's conclusion was supported by Silverman (1977), who showed how many of the classic results obtained in psychological studies (such as people apparently being "conditioned" to use more plural nouns by being reinforced with a nod or a smile when they did so) would only happen if they actually realised what was expected of them. When the people who had just participated in these studies were interviewed informally afterwards, it was quite clear that they had tried to be "good", cooperative subjects so that the experiment would work out all right. In other words, they had responded to the demand characteristics of the experiment.

All social situations have demand characteristics of one form or another, but it is in the psychological experiment that they become particularly problematic. Orne and Whitehouse (2000) described demand characteristics as

Key Terms

double-blind
A research method in which neither the participants nor the experimenter is aware of what is being investigated.

demand characteristics
Features of an experimental situation which influence the participants to act in expected ways.

being the total set of cues and mutual expectations which are operating on an individual in a given social context, influencing either the behaviour or the self-reported experience (or both) of that person.

These findings, of course, relate to the whole of psychology (and to any formal investigation of people's behaviour), and not simply to social psychology. As with the discovery of the self-fulfilling prophecy, Orne's research increased the emphasis on the need for double-blind controls, which are still an essential component of medical and drug research. But the later emphasis on ethical issues and the need to avoid deceiving participants made it less suitable for social psychologists, since social psychology is directly concerned with studying how people interact, and the overuse of deception can interfere with that significantly.

As a result of these concerns, and the new research possibilities opened up by Harré's *Social Being* and Reason and Rowan's *New Paradigm Research*, which we discussed above, social psychology began to adopt a number of new approaches. As a general rule, social psychology has tried to move away from the formal laboratory experiment, and into more ecologically valid explorations of how people act. Formal experiments are still performed, of course, and there is a growing interest in the interaction between social experience and neuropsychology (see Chapter 7); but increasingly social psychologists have turned their interests towards social cognition (how people perceive what is going on around them) and investigations set more in the outside world and less towards the psychological laboratory.

Response bias

Response bias presents another challenge in social psychological research. People don't just try to cooperate with others; we also like to present ourselves as being socially acceptable, or having positive characteristics. Which can prove difficult when we are trying to investigate the less positive aspects of human interaction or experience. Nowadays, for example, people are aware that it is socially unacceptable to express racist attitudes, and that means that simply asking people about their attitudes is unlikely to uncover whether people are racist or not, except in unusually extreme cases. It has also been shown that asking questions about race tends to produce different responses depending upon the ethnic group of the person asking the question.

This tendency to give answers which are socially acceptable, or which the person believes to be the responses desired by the researcher, is known as response bias, and it is one of the perpetual challenges for psychologists designing attitude scales or other types of social investigation. It doesn't just relate to social acceptability, either. For example, there is a demonstrable tendency for people to give positive answers in other ways: to respond "yes" rather than "no", or "agree" rather than "disagree". It doesn't always happen, but it is more common than not. So survey design often includes reverse forms of questions to balance response bias, or lie scales designed to highlight responses which are exaggerating social desirability. But even then, response bias is not an easy matter to control.

Ecological validity

Another challenge faced by social researchers is the question of ecological validity. Often, the attempt to ensure that all of the influencing factors in a

Key Terms

response bias
The tendency which people have to respond in ways which will make them appear more socially acceptable than they are.

situation have been controlled means that the situation becomes so artificial that it no longer corresponds to its equivalent in the real world. So the study has lost its ecological validity. This can also happen when things have been taken out of context. Asch's findings of conformity, for example, appear very different when we look at their social context, and the way that the people who conformed either (a) did so because they believed in the authority of science and didn't want to "spoil" the experiment by being deviant; or (b) perceived the social issue (i.e., conformity) which was the focus of the study, and went along with it. What this shows us is that research takes place within a cultural and social context, and research participants bring that context with them. To assume that they abandon all their prior experience and social knowledge when they take part in a psychological experiment is simply naïve.

The studies of minority influence which we looked at in Chapter 5 also show us how some effects can take time; conversion to minority viewpoints doesn't happen instantly, but it does happen. So studies which take "snap-shots" and use that data to make generalisations about social processes can be seriously unrealistic (Hayes, 2003). New paradigm research, as we saw in the last section, is all about ways of addressing the problem of ecological validity, as are longitudinal studies of how things change over time. But it remains a challenge for any social researcher.

Simplistic measures

The use of overly simplistic measures is another aspect of the problem of ecological validity. It is very tempting when conducting social research to assume that something can be measured in an easy, straightforward way, when it is really much more complex. For example, studies of physical attraction have often been carried out by asking people to rate photographs for attractiveness. Even when their ratings have been statistically evaluated and shown to be reliable, they can still be influenced by very small details. Garwood et al (1980) showed, for example, that just giving each photograph a name, either a "desirable" or an "undesirable" one, would affect the ratings which people gave.

In real life, our judgements of whether people are attractive or not are based on far more data, including movements, facial expressions and the context in which we encounter that person. Ratings of photographs may appear to be useful, but really they are far too simplistic to tell us much about attraction in the real world. The same applies to many other measures apparent in social psychological research. For example, the minimal group studies which we looked at in Chapter 1 actually gave us different information about social identification processes than more realistic studies of group identification which allowed respondents more options of how to respond. Using overly simplistic measures can distort research findings significantly.

Reductionism

Reductionism in some ways is more of a theoretical problem than a methodological one, but it can have a serious effect on research methodology as well. As we saw earlier, reductionism is when an approach to understanding an issue focuses only on one level of explanation to the exclusion of others. If we believe, for example, that only individual factors such as personality or emotions are what determines social action, then the research we design will tend to ignore cultural or societal influences – and that can be another source of distortion.

Latané's Law of Social Impact (Chapter 6), for example, explains bystander behaviour purely in terms of the interaction of individuals – the presence of other people. But people's actions are also influenced by other factors, like social representations and social scripts (Chapter 4). If their social scripts include situations in which helping other people results in personal attack or other disastrous consequences, they are less likely to help regardless of how many other people are around. If their repertoire of social scripts facilitates helping and sees it as likely to bring personal or social reward, they are more likely to help. (This is, of course, why so many social psychologists are concerned about TV aggression – not for its content as such, but because of the way it shapes social scripts.)

Talking point 10.3   The questionnaire fallacy

The questionnaire fallacy is a very real problem in social research, although it is often overlooked by people using questionnaires to find out information. Some of the most common examples of the questionnaire fallacy can be seen in market research questionnaires – the sort you might fill in online, or be asked to respond to when you are shopping. The problem arises because people are faced with a set range of choices, which, given how very diverse people's beliefs and actions are, doesn't always include what they really do. When answering, they choose the option which is either (a) closest to what they really do, or (b) what they think they ought to do. Although such questions often provide a box for "other – please describe", it is quite unusual for people to use it. And the person or computer administering the research doesn't have the option of recording how certain people are about their answers.

This means that those analysing the research believe that they have got a snapshot of people's behaviour or opinions, whereas the reality is quite different. The differences would probably become more apparent if they did open-ended research, where people were just asked about things and able to respond freely, but those studies are complicated to analyse and expensive to carry out.

In a study of, say, dating behaviour, what consequences might arise from an investigative problem of this kind?

These factors all highlight the challenges of research with human beings. Real people are complex, active, thinking individuals who don't respond to situations passively, even if they seem to be doing so on the surface. They work things out, develop their own ideas about what is going on, and act accordingly. They may do things for more than one reason, or simply because they are in a particular mood. And the more we try to control their behaviour – to rule out these variable factors – the more artificial our studies can become.

We can see this clearly if we look at a classic study of attraction. In 1965, Aronson and Linder asked research participants to participate in what they were told was an experiment in verbal conditioning. The study was actually about the relationship between self-esteem and attraction. People were asked to have a conversation with a stooge who they believed was a genuine research participant like themselves, while at the same time counting the number of plural nouns which the person used – they were told that it was part of a "conditioning" study. After this, the research participants "overheard" the stooge giving an evaluation of them to the experimenter, which was either positive or negative.

This continued for seven sessions altogether. The research participants were then asked to say how much they had liked the stooge. In order to disguise what was really happening, the researchers used a kind of "double-bluff". They told the research participants that they were being asked questions about how much they liked the stooge in order to deceive the others into thinking that the study was about interpersonal attraction. So although the study really was about attraction, the research participant was misled into the idea that attraction was only the disguise, and it was really about verbal conditioning.

The levels of deception in this study are quite remarkable, and the study itself was extremely convoluted and complex. In the ethical code of conduct, we saw that there are some occasions when deception is considered to be acceptable as long as the participant is fully debriefed afterwards, but most ethics committees would consider that a study like this oversteps the line, and wouldn't be considered acceptable in the modern research climate. Perhaps one of the most telling comments on this whole approach to people and research was made by George Kelly, the founder of personal construct theory, who is reported as having said: "If you really want to know what the problem with the patient is, ask him. He might tell you" (Bannister and Fransella, 1980).

Today, we have better tools at our disposal to investigate different aspects of human experience, and this broadens the possibility of our understanding. We can adopt different methods of investigation to look at things in more than one way – a technique known as **triangulation**. By looking at a given topic using different methods, we approach it from different angles and gain a much richer picture of what is going on. For example, say you wanted to explore the question of whether computer gaming was harmful. You could accumulate evidence in many different ways. You might find it a useful exercise to work out a plan for a set of studies, each of which adopts a different approach (e.g., experimental, observational, qualitative, longitudinal, cross-sectional, highly controlled or naturalistic methods).

What such an exercise would show you is the many different ways we can approach a topic, but also how modern social psychology is able to address so many different aspects of social living. We don't have all the answers – nobody does, and I suspect that nobody ever will, if only because human beings are forever generating new questions! But as I hope this book has shown you, the insights from social psychology can go a long way in helping us to understand our social experiences.

Summary: Chapter 10

1. Social psychology covers many levels of analysis, but individual researchers tend to work only within one or two. Psychological research may adopt either a hypothetical-deductive approach of testing hypotheses, or an inductive approach of analysing openly received data.

Key Terms

triangulation
An approach to research which uses several different methods to "home in" on the target.

2. Common perspectives in social psychology include experimental social psychology, discursive psychology, European social psychology, evolutionary social psychology and critical social psychology.

3. The Code of Conduct for Research with Human Participants outlines ethical issues such as valid consent, risk, confidentiality, giving advice, deception and debriefing which psychologists must take account of when designing research projects.

4. Ethical demands have presented challenges to social psychology as they have made many of the older practices unacceptable. Modern psychologists aim to retain the ability to conduct valid research while still ensuring that their work is conducted in an ethical manner.

5. Experiments and observational studies used to be common research methods in social psychology, although the requirements of control and systematisation have sometimes presented challenges to researchers.

6. Many modern psychologists use case studies, interviews, conversation analysis or discourse analysis to explore aspects of social psychology such as personal experience or collective memory. Document analysis, including meta-analysis, is also becoming an increasingly important area of modern research.

7. Surveys and questionnaires are sometimes used to gain general information from large numbers of people. Psychometric tests are carefully standardised ways of gathering personal data, and so are different from questionnaires in their construction and application.

8. Action research and new paradigm research are ways of gathering data which are firmly rooted in real-world experiences. Examples of new paradigm research includes episode analysis, account analysis and grounded theory. The internet has also offered new opportunities for researchers.

9. The usual criteria for evaluating research include reliability, validity and generalisability. Although all of these may not apply to all types of modern psychological research, usually at least two of the three are important.

10. Social psychological research has to deal with a number of problems, including demand characteristics, the self-fulfilling prophecy, response bias, ecological validity and the need to avoid simplistic measures and reductionist explanations.

Glossary

absorption: The degree to which an activity demands concentrated attention.

accent: A shared distinctive speech pattern of emphasis and tone.

accentuation theory: A theory which stresses the importance of evaluative language.

account analysis: A method of gathering research data through the descriptions people give of their experiences.

affect: A general term for feelings and emotions.

affective domain: The part of the mind which is concerned with feelings and emotions.

agency: The ability to act in a self-determined way, and to make one's own choices.

agentic state: A condition of mind in which the person sees themselves as the agent of others and not able to act independently.

altruism: Acting in the interests of others and not oneself.

ambivalent sexism: A form of sexism in which the attitudes expressed may be either positive or negative.

anchoring: Setting ideas in a familiar context.

androgynous: Having both masculine and feminine characteristics.

arousal level: The extent to which the person is in a vigilant, physiologically excited state.

attachment styles: Distinctive patterns in the ways that attachments are formed and maintained.

attachments: Very close personal relationships, generally with some degree of dependency.

attraction: The experience of feeling drawn towards another person as a positive aspect of interpersonal experience.

attributions: The reasons people give for why things happen.

audience anxiety: Feelings of nervousness brought about by one's behaviour being observed by other people.

audience effects: The differences in people's actions when they know they are being observed, to when they are alone and unobserved.

authoritarian: A style of leadership which is commanding, directive and unconcerned with the views of subordinates.

autobiographical memories: Personal memories of events in one's own life.

autokinetic effect: A visual illusion in which a stationary dot of light in a dark room seems to move around.

autonomous state: A personal condition of independence and self-control.

avatar: A fictional image of a character, used in computer gaming to represent the player.

balance theory: The idea that incongruent or unbalanced cognitions cause tension which we try to reduce.

behavioural domain: The part of the mind which is concerned with acts and actions.

benevolent sexism: A form of sexism in which apparently supportive statements contain an implicit message of helplessness or inferiority.

benign violation theory: A theory of humour which emphasises challenging assumptions about the world in a non-threatening way.

BIAS map: A model of person perception emphasising Behaviour from Intergroup Affect and Stereotypes.

biological imperative: A behaviour which occurs as a result of inherited biological demands, and is therefore unavoidable.

boomerang effect: When an attempt at persuasion is so extreme that it produces the opposite effect in the recipient.

bystander apathy: The refusal of bystanders to intervene in an event where a person apparently is in need of help.

bystander intervention: The question of when bystanders will or will not intervene in an event where a person apparently is in need of help.

catharsis: The "draining off" of negative emotions or energies through other activities (e.g., sport).

central route processing: The direct approach to attitude change (e.g., directly instructing someone to buy something or change their attitude towards something).

chronic loneliness: An ongoing subjective experience of loneliness which may be experienced despite high levels of social interaction.

coaction: Doing things in the presence of others doing the same things.

coercive controlling violence: Violence which combines emotional with physical abuse.

cognitive algebra: A mental calculation, weighing up costs, benefits and other aspects of an experience.

cognitive behaviour therapy: A form of therapy which encourages adjustments in cognitions as well as the learning of new habits.

cognitive dissonance: The state of cognitive tension produced by holding contradictory beliefs.

cognitive domain: The part of the mind which is concerned with mental processes such as reasoning and memory.

cognitive interview: A specific form of interviewing designed to encourage accurate recall of events.

cognitive similarity: Having the same sort of thinking patterns or personal constructs as other people or another person.

collective action: Action which is take by a large number of people together towards a common goal.

collectivist: A type of culture which emphasises membership of the community over individualism.

compensatory strategy: A cognitive or behavioural approach designed to adjust for an imbalance or inequality of some sort.

complementarity: The idea that some relationships work because each member of a couple provides the other with the opposite qualities.

compliance: The process of going along with other people without really accepting their views.

conation: Intentionality: having intentions, plans or strategies.

conative domain: The part of the mind which is concerned with intentions and plans.

conditional positive regard: Love, affection or other positive emotion which is dependent on the person acting in certain ways.

conditions of worth: Internalised ideas about the personal qualities or achievements which will make someone a worthwhile person.

conformity: The process of going along with other people and acting in the same way that they do.

consensual beliefs: Beliefs which are shared by a group or community.

consensus: A factor in the covariance approach to attribution, which is to do with whether other people also act in the same sort of way.

consistency: A factor in the covariance approach to attribution, which is to do with whether the person always, or usually, acts in that way.

contingencies: Outcomes which result from specific circumstances or actions.

conversation analysis: A method of exploring the structures and implications of how people go about talking to one another.

conversion: Being persuaded that a different point of view is correct, and coming to believe it yourself.

correspondent inference theory: An attribution theory which uses stability and intentionality to attribute causes.

covariance: A variant of attribution theory which looks at three aspects of the situation: consensus, consistency and distinctiveness.

credibility: Having an air of authoritativeness or expertise, such that their opinion is readily believed.

cyberstalking: Pathological following of individuals through the internet, involving tracking their communications and intervening in their activities, often unpleasantly.

debriefing: Explaining all the aspects of an experiment or situation after it has taken place.

decentration: The process of gradually learning that the world is not centred entirely upon oneself.

deconstructionist: An approach to social research which involves examining the underlying social assumptions and beliefs of existing theories.

defence mechanisms: Protective strategies that the mind uses to defend itself against unwelcome or disturbing information.

de-individuation: A condition in which the anonymity produced by the lack of individual identifiers causes people to abandon such aspects of individuality as conscience, consideration, etc.

demand characteristics: Features of an experimental situation which influence the participants to act in expected ways.

dialect: A distinctive pattern of language use shared by a regional or socio-economic group, which has its own vocabulary and grammatical forms.

diffusion of responsibility: The idea that people are less likely to intervene to help someone who seems to need it if there are others present because they perceive responsibility as being shared between all present, and therefore see themselves as being less responsible personally.

discourse analysis: A method of studying human experience by analysing the things people say to one another, and how they express them, both symbolically and behaviourally.

dispositional: To do with the person's character or personality.

dispositional attributions: When a particular behaviour is believed to have resulted from the person's own personality or characteristics.

distinctiveness: Whether the person acts in the same way in similar situations to the one being considered, or not.

double-blind: A research method in which neither the participants nor the experimenter is aware of what is being investigated.

dramaturgical metaphor: A metaphor which treats the aspect of everyday life being investigated as if it were a stage drama, looking at roles, costumes, scripts, etc.

ecological validity: A way of assessing the validity of a measure or test which is concerned with whether it is really like its counterpart in the real, everyday world.

ego-defence: Protecting the mind against information which would form negative challenges or unwelcome truths.

elder abuse: Abuse directed at old people.

emojis: (aka emogees) Small icons shared in text messages and other internet contexts, illustrating emotions.

emoticons: Small icons representing faces, often shared in text messages, indicating emotions. Emoticons may be images of faces, or sets of punctuation marks resembling faces if viewed from the side, as in :-).

emotional intelligence: The degree to which an individual is sensitive to other people's reactions or expressions of emotion.

equal environments assumption: The assumption that twins in the same or similar families experience identical environmental influences as they are growing up.

equity theory: The idea that social conventions and norms are based around a principle of fair, though not necessarily strictly equal, exchange.

ethical guidelines: Documents developed by professional bodies which provide guidance and principles concerning ethical aspects of research.

ethics committees: Groups set up by professional and educational institutions which appraise research proposals and judge whether they conform to acceptable ethical practice or not.

ethnic prejudice: Prejudice against a particular social group based on ethnicity, usually translated as skin colour or nation of origin.

evaluation: How other people are weighing up or judging us.

evaluation anxiety: Nervousness concerning how other people are judging the person's behaviour or appearance.

event schema: The implicit social script which we use to guide our actions in response to specific circumstances or events.

evolutionary psychology: An approach to psychology which looks at how certain types of behaviour may have evolved for survival reasons in the primaeval past.

expressivity: How clearly a person demonstrates their feelings and thoughts.

externalisation: The extent to which a person openly channels innermost motives and emotions into their actions.

F test: A measuring scale for authoritarian attitudes (F for fascism).

facial feedback hypothesis: The idea that we infer our emotions from the expressions on our faces.

feedback: Knowledge about the effectiveness of one's performance, or how one is coming across to others.

feral children: Children who have apparently grown from infancy to childhood with no contact with human beings.

figuration: The use of images and metaphors to represent ideas.

figurative nucleus: The central, unchanging core of a social representation.

fixed mindset: An approach to one's own learning which sees ability as fixed, and effort therefore as of limited value.

flashpoints: Actions or events which generate spontaneous changes in crowd behaviour.

flourishing: Living life to the full, utilising one's potential and enjoying it.

forced compliance: An experimental procedure obliging participants to go through extremely boring tasks, and then lie about them.

fundamental attribution error: The way in which people tend to see other people's actions as dispositional, but their own as situational.

gaming: The playing of computer or video games.

generalisability: Whether a research procedure or measure would apply to general populations or situations, rather than just the immediate ones.

genetic trait: A personality characteristic or ability which is considered to have resulted from the influence of inherited genes.

gestures: Actions signalling meaning, usually made with the hands or arms.

group norms: Standards of expected behaviour which are applied to group members.

group polarisation: The observation that people will often make more extreme decisions when they are working in a group than the members of the group would make as individuals.

group therapy: A form of psychotherapy in which several patients interact with one another and the therapist, as opposed to the one-to-one situation of individual therapy.

groupthink: The way in which a group of people may become divorced from reality as a result of their own social consensus and make decisions which are dangerous or stupid.

growth mindset: An approach to one's own cognitive abilities which see them as able to develop with practice and experience.

halo effect: The attribution of a range of positive qualities to someone on the basis that they already have one liked characteristic.

hedonic relevance: Something which has either pleasant or unpleasant consequences or implications for the person making the attribution.

heritability: A statistical concept designed to indicate how much of a given trait can be deemed to have come about as a result of genetic influences.

hermeneutic: To do with meanings and interpretations.

homophobia: An irrational negative emotional response to homosexuality.

hostile sexism: A form of sexism which involves active denigration of the other sex.

hypnotherapy: Using hypnosis to help people to deal with psychological problems, usually through autohypnosis.

hypothesis: A prediction which states the outcome which is likely to take place if a particular theory is true and particular conditions are set up.

hypothetico-deductive method: An approach to research based on evaluating theories by testing hypotheses.

ideal self: An internal impression of the perfect person one would like to be.

identification: Feeling oneself to be the same as, or very similar to, another person and basing one's interactions on that comparison.

idiolect: The personal or idiosyncratic form of language used by a single individual or family.

immediacy: Exerting influence as a result of being physically in the same place.

implicit personality theory: The intuitive ideas about which character traits normally fit together, which form the basis of everyday predictions about other people and what they are likely to be like.

impression-relevant involvement: When an attitude is concerned with how someone likes to present themselves to other people.

incongruity theory: A theory of humour which states that we are amused by things we find distinctively unusual or disconnected.

indirect social aggression: Aggression which takes the form of indirect action, such as gossip or exclusion.

individualistic: A cultural approach which emphasises the individual over the group.

inductive method: Research in which investigation and observation are conducted first, and theory is developed on the basis of the outcome.

insecure attachment: A style of attachment in which the individual is anticipating rejection, and as a result may show excessive dependency.

instrumentality: How useful an attitude is to an individual in terms of achieving goals or ambitions.

intentions: Ideas or plans for ways of achieving outcomes in the future.

intergroup conflict: Competition between different social groups, which can often lead to powerful hostility.

internalisation: Absorbing ideas, beliefs or attitudes as one's own.

internet addiction: Excessive use of the internet, to the extent that it interferes with normal living.

kinaesthesia: Use of the bodily senses which inform us about the movement of the muscles and skeletal system.

laissez-faire: Uninvolved leadership in which subordinates are left to themselves and can act as they like.

language registers: Patterns of language use which are relevant for different types of social interaction.

Law of Social Impact: An explanation for bystander intervention which emphasises number, immediacy and relevance as the significant factors.

levels of explanation: Perspectives for explaining a given phenomenon with lower levels including physiological (e.g., microbiological) and higher levels including cultural or socioeconomic explanations.

Likert scale: A five- or seven-point ordinal measuring scale, commonly used to assess attitude strength.

looking-glass self: The idea that self-concept depends on feedback from others.

meta-analysis: A research technique which involves examining effects found in a series of studies and calculating the overall probability as evidence for whether there is an underlying effect or not.

minimal group studies: Research which involved creating artificial groups on the basis of minimal characteristics (e.g., tossing a coin), and then studying the in-group/out-group effects which resulted.

minimal group tasks: Activities or tasks required of groups constructed on the basis of minimal characteristics (e.g., coin-tossing or art preferences).

minority influence: When small groups of people sway the judgement or opinions of the majority.

MMORPG: Acronym for massive multiplayer online role-playing game.

mob psychology: The idea that a crowd is likely to behave in an irrational and unpredictable, even violent manner, because its members have descended into a conscience-less and impulsive state.

modernism: An approach to living, design and the arts popular in the first few decades of the 20th century, which emphasised scientific progress and consciously rejected traditional ways of doing things.

MRI scanning: A system of scanning the physical body using magnetic resonance imaging.

narcissists: People who are significantly absorbed in their own selves and the image they project.

need for achievement (nAch): An internal motivation to succeed in life, or in attaining particular goals.

need-fulfilment theories: Theories which propose that a given process occurs because it satisfies an internal need or drive.

negative buffering: Over-sensitising someone to a negative experience.

neglect: A form of child abuse which involves failing to supply the child's physical and social needs.

neonate: A new-born infant.

netiquette: "Rules" of acceptable internet behaviour.

networking: Developing groups of acquaintances or colleagues to achieve personal goals.

non-common effects: Effects which only apply in particular situations and not most of the time.

non-verbal communication: Communication which takes place without words.

non-verbal cues: Personal signs or actions which signify meaning without words.

normative conflict: Disagreement or conflict concerning what represents the norm or is acceptable.

norm-referenced: Measured up to criteria developed from the normative scores of a particular target group.

object appraisal: Weighing up or evaluating things to judge their worth or usefulness.

objectification: Expressing an idea or belief by representing it as an object of some kind.

online therapy: Psychotherapy which is conducted or delivered by means of the internet.

operant conditioning: The process of learning in which learning occurs as a result of positive or negative reinforcement of an animal or human being's action.

organisational cultures: The distinctive patterns of beliefs, traditions and practices of an established organisation.

"ought" self: The part of the sense of self which describes how the person should be if they conformed fully to expectations.

outcome-relevant involvement: An attitude which helps a person achieve a personal goal or ambition.

paralanguage: Non-verbal cues contained in how people say things, such as in tones of voice, pauses, or "um" and "er" noises.

paralinguistic cues: Aspects of paralanguage which convey information or help to guide conversation.

participant observation: Observational studies in which the researcher becomes one of the participants, and joins in the action which is being observed.

peripheral elements: Those aspects of a social representation which can change easily with circumstances or over time.

peripheral norms: Expectations and assumptions which are felt as less important than others.

peripheral route processing: The indirect approach to attitude change, in which attention is not focused directly on the information being transmitted, but is elsewhere.

person perception: The way in which we come to acknowledge other people as characters or individuals.

person schema: The set of memories, knowledge and intentions which someone holds about a particular person.

personal constructs: Individual ways of making sense of the world, which have been developed on the basis of experience.

personalism: The tendency that people have to be more likely to make a dispositional attribution if the target affects them personally.

personification: Expressing a social representation in terms of a specific person who might be considered to embody it.

pictograms: Signs expressing meaning through pictures or images.

pivotal norms: Expectations and assumptions which are considered fundamental and unchangeable.

pluralistic ignorance: When a group of people defines a situation as a non-emergency to justify lack of action.

positive emotions: Emotions which enhance personal feelings of well-being or promote social harmony.

positive regard: Liking, affection, love or respect for someone else.

positivity bias: Our tendency to prefer positive cognitive connections or interactions.

postural echo: The way in which people who are in intense conversation or rapport will often unconsciously mimic one another's stance or posture.

potency: The strength, or powerfulness of a positive emotion.

prejudice: A fixed, pre-set attitude, usually negative and hostile, and usually applied to members of a particular social category.

prejudice reduction: Approaches to challenging prejudice which aim to reduce or eliminate prejudice from the individual.

primacy effect: Experimental outcomes which have occurred because this is the first time that the participant has encountered the phenomenon. Or: the way that the first things you encounter make more of an impression than later ones do.

prior consent: Agreement to accept research conditions which is given before the study takes place.

private self: Those aspects of the self-concept which are kept hidden from other people.

private self-awareness: The individual sense of self which we retain, even when participating in crowds.

projective test: Psychometric tests which involve providing the person with ambiguous stimuli, and seeing what meanings they read into them. The idea is that this will illustrate the concerns of the unconscious mind.

proprioception: The sensory information provided by nerve cells which receive information from the muscles, skeleton and internal organs.

prosopagnosia: A brain disorder in which the person is unable to recognise faces.

Proteus Effect: The idea that remodelling images of the self can also change the personal self.

proxemics: The study of personal space.

psychometric scale: One of (usually) several factors measured by a psychometric test, which will have been carefully constructed and standardised.

psychometric test: A measuring instrument, often resembling a questionnaire but more systematically constructed, designed to measure psychological characteristics.

public self: Those parts of the self-concept which are apparent to other people.

public self-awareness: The open, participating sense of self involved in events with others.

Pygmalion Effect: The way in which we may come to live up to an image of our own creation.

qualitative: An approach to collecting and analysing research data which looks at meanings rather than numbers.

quantifiability: Being able to be measured in terms of numbers and quantities.

questionnaire fallacy: The way in which people respond to the questions asked at the expense of providing valid information.

randomised, controlled trials: The "ideal" procedure for medical research, where everything is tightly controlled and measured.

rating scales: Measuring scales used to assess or evaluate objects or ideas.

reaction-formation: A defence mechanism in which a repressed impulse turns into its opposite (e.g., repressed homosexuality turning into aggressive homophobia).

realistic conflict theory: The idea that if two groups are in competition, the "haves" will be in conflict with the "have nots".

reciprocity: The idea that some relationships work because each member of a couple provides the other with the same qualities.

redefinition of the situation: A process used to justify bystander apathy by deciding that the situation is not as serious as it appears.

reductionist: Focusing on one single level of explanation and ignoring others. The opposite of interactionist.

reinforcement: The strengthening of learning in some way, usually through reward.

relational aggression: A form of aggressive behaviour involving indirect actions, such as malicious gossip or exclusion.

relational self: The idea that our self-concept includes our significant relationships as well as personal ideas and experience.

reliability: Whether a test or measure is consistent over time in the outcomes that it gives

repertoires: Patterns of speech or behaviour which, taken together, constitute a fully meaningful action.

repertory grid: A technique for identifying and representing data about personal constructs

replication: Repeating a study or research project in such a way as to make sure that all of the important elements are identical, or at least very similar.

resilience: The ability to "bounce back" and take positive action again after negative life-experiences.

response bias: The tendency which people have to respond in ways which will make them appear more socially acceptable than they are.

risky-shift phenomenon: A form of group polarisation which involves the observation that some people will tend to make riskier decisions when acting as members of a group or committee than they would as individuals.

role expectations: The behaviour which is expected as a result of a social part that one plays in society.

role schema: The total set of memories, actions and intentions associated with a particular social role: the understanding of that role.

sanctions: Social forms of punishment or disapproval.

schema: A mental framework or structure which encompasses memories, ideas, concepts and programmes for action which are pertinent to a particular topic.

script: A well-known pattern of social action and interaction which has been socially established and accepted, and is implicitly and automatically followed by people in the relevant situation.

search for coherence: The way in which we seek to make our cognitions make sense.

secure attachment: An attachment style marked by confidence in the lasting nature of the relationship, allowing exploratory and similar behaviours.

self-actualisation: The making real of one's abilities and talents: using them to the full

self-awareness theory: The idea that we are aware of our shortcomings as well as achievements, which motivates self-improvement activities.

self-categorisation: The idea that we perceive ourselves as belonging to various social categories.

self-disclosure: Revealing aspects of the private self which would normally not be disclosed.

self-efficacy belief: The belief that one is capable of acting effectively.

self-esteem: The evaluative dimension of the self-concept, which is to do with how worthwhile and/or confident people feel about themselves.

self-evaluation maintenance: Strategies used to maintain self-esteem.

self-fulfilling prophecy: The observation that expectations about a person or group can become true simply because they have been stated.

self-image: The factual or descriptive picture which people hold of themselves, without the evaluative component implicit in the concept of self-esteem.

self-perception theory: The idea that we develop an impression of our own personality by inferring what we are like from the way that we act.

self-presentation: The image or impression of self that we like to show to others.

self-reconstruction: Adjusting memories of the self at earlier times so that they fit the current self-image.

self-regulation: Balancing the self-concept and minimising any sense of failure through promotion of successes and trying to avoid negative outcomes.

self-schema: The total set of memories, representations, ideas and intentions which one holds about oneself.

self-serving bias: The idea that we judge our own behaviour more favourably than we judge other people's.

semiology: The study of symbolism in everyday life.

semiotics: The use of symbols to express meaning in everyday life.

sexting: Internet messaging which involves transmitting intimate or sexy images of the self to another person.

situational: To do with the circumstances and environmental pressures active at the time.

situational attribution: A reason for an act or behaviour which implies that it occurred as a result of the situation or circumstances that the person was in at the time.

situational couple violence: Violent interactions in domestic disputes resulting from stressful circumstances.

situational loneliness: Loneliness which happens as a result of the circumstances in which the person finds themselves.

sleeper effect: An effect or result which does not show up immediately, but takes some time to manifest itself.

social adjustment: An attitude function concerned with getting on with other people.

social attraction: Attraction because someone acts in a positive or prosocial way (e.g., is kind to others).

social comparison: The process of comparing one's own social group with others, in terms of their relative social status and prestige.

social desirability: The tendency to adjust one's image or self-report to seem more socially acceptable (e.g., concealing racist attitudes).

social exchange theory: An approach to the understanding of social behaviour that sees social interaction as a "trade", in which the person acts in certain ways in return for some social reward or approval.

social facilitation: The observation that the presence of other people can influence how well they perform on a task, often improving their performance.

social identification: A theory which emphasises membership of social groups as part of the self-concept, determining some social responses.

social loafing: The observed tendency in some situations for individuals to devote less effort to a group task than they would give to the same task if they were doing it on their own.

social representations: The shared beliefs which develop and are transmitted in social groups and in society as a whole, and explain why things are as they are.

social roles: The parts people play in society.

social schema: The collection of cognitions which we use to guide social action.

social script: A pattern of accepted social action, followed automatically in everyday situations.

speech act: An utterance or set of utterances which serves a single social purpose.

spiritual: A dimension of positive emotion which includes uplifting sensations, and sometimes religious ones.

stereotyping: Classifying members of a social group as if they were all the same, and treating individuals belonging to that group as if no other characteristics were salient.

subjective norm: Our individual perception of what is acceptable in a given situation.

subliminal perception: A form of unconscious perception which occurs below the threshold of awareness.

symbolic interactionism: The approach to social understanding which looks at how people perceive and respond to one another as social symbols, such as roles, rather than as individuals.

systemic level analysis: Analysing social phenomena in terms of the social systems and structures which have made them possible.

team-working: Organising working practices so that they are carried out by teams, with collective responsibility for the outcomes.

technological addiction: A form of obsessive behaviour in which the person engages in some form of technology-related activity to the extent that it disrupts their ability to live normal lives.

theory of mind (TOM): The development of the idea that other people have minds of their own, and may hold different beliefs or ideas.

theory of planned behaviour: The idea that attitude change depends on the person's perception that they are in control of their ideas and actions.

theory of reasoned action: The idea that people normally behave in a reasonable manner, and will change their attitudes if it seems appropriate in their circumstances.

trait aggression: Aggression which is considered to be a characteristic of the person's personality, rather than the result of circumstances.

transactional leaders: Leaders who are primarily focused on work and the tasks at hand.

transactions: A form of behavioural exchange or interchange between two individuals.

transformational leaders: Leaders whose main aim is to inspire confidence and promote optimism in their workforce.

triad: A set of three.

triangulation: An approach to research which uses several different methods to "home in" on the target.

trolling: A form of internet aggression in which the person directs anonymous spiteful or aggressive hate messages towards another person.

unconditional positive regard: Love, affection or respect which does not depend on the person's having to act in particular ways.

utilitarian: Having a useful value, emphasising functional purpose.

validity: Whether a psychometric test or psychological measure really measures what it is supposed to.

value-relevant involvement: The role of an attitude in protecting or defending someone's personal values.

values: Personal beliefs of worth or importance.

violent resistance: Domestic violence which happens as one person resists the controlling coercion of the other.

zeitgeist: The "spirit of the time", including the established assumptions and general knowledge of that period.

References

Abramson, L. Y., Seligman, M. E. P. and Teasdale, J. D. (1978) Learned helplessness in humans: Critique and reformulation. *Journal of Abnormal Psychology*, 87: 49–74.

Adams, R. E., Santo, J. B. and Bukowski, W. M. (2011) The presence of a best friend buffers the effects of negative experience. *Developmental Psychology*, 47: 1786–1792.

Adorno, T. W., Frenkel-Brunswik, G., Levinson, D. J. and Sanford, R. N. (1950) *The Authoritarian Personality*. New York: Harper.

Ahern, N. and Mechling, B. (2013) Sexting: Serious problems for youth. *Journal of Psychosocial Nursing and Mental Health Services*, 51(7): 22–30.

Ahmetoglu, G., Swami, V. and Chamorro-Premuzic, T. (2010) The relationship between dimensions of love, personality, and relationship length. *Archives of Sexual Behavior*, 39: 1181–1190.

Ahrens, S. R. (1954) Beitrage zur Entwicklung des Physiognomie und Mimikerkennes [Contributions on the development of physiognomy and mimicry recognition]. *Zeischrift für Experimentelle und Angewandte Psychologie*, 2: 412–454.

Aiello, J. R., Nicosia, G. and Thompson, D. E. (1979) Physiological, social and behavioural consequences of crowding on children and adolescents. *Child Development*, 50: 195–202.

Ajzen, I. (1988) *Attitudes, Personality and Behaviour*. Milton Keynes: Open University Press.

Ajzen, I. (1991) The theory of planned behavior. *Organizational Behavior and Human Decision Processes*, 50: 179–211.

Ajzen, I. and Fishbein, M. (1977) Attitude-behaviour relationships: A theoretical analysis and review of empirical research. *Psychological Bulletin*, 84: 888–918.

Ajzen, I. and Fishbein, M. (1980) *Understanding Attitudes and Predicting Social Behaviour*. Englewood Cliffs, NJ: Prentice-Hall.

Alberici, A. and Milesi, P. (2013) The influence of the internet on the psychosocial predictors of collective action. *Journal of Community & Applied Social Psychology*, 23: 373–388.

Alford, J. R., Funk, C. L. and Hibbing, J. R. (2008) Beyond liberals and conservatives to political genotypes and phenotypes. *Perspectives on Politics* 6(2): 321–328.

Alicke, M. D. and Zell, E. (2009) Social attractiveness and blame. *Journal of Applied Social Psychology*, 39(9): 2089–2105.

Allen, V. L. and Levine, J. M. (1968) Social support, dissent and conformity. *Sociometry*, 31: 138–149.

Allen, V. L. and Levine, J. M. (1971) Social pressures and personal influence. *Journal of Experimental Social Psychology*, 7: 122–124.

Allport, F. H. (1920) The influences of the group upon association and thought. *Journal of Experimental Psychology*, 3: 159.

Allport, G. W. (1935) Attitudes. In: C. M. Murchison (ed), *Handbook of Social Psychology*. Worcester, MA: Clark University Press.

Allport, G. W. (1954) *The Nature of Prejudice*. Wokingham: Addison-Wesley.

Amodio, D. M. (2008) The social neuroscience of intergroup relations. *European Review of Social Psychology*, 19: 1–54.

Amodio, D. M. and Devine, P. G. (2006) Stereotyping and evaluation in implicit race bias: Evidence for independent constructs and unique effects on behaviour. *Journal of Personality and Social Psychology*, 91: 652–661.

Andersen, N. M. and Chen, S. (2002) The relational self: An interpersonal social-cognitive theory. *Psychological Review*, 109(4): 619–645.

Anderson, C. A. (2004) An update on the effects of playing violent video games. *Journal of Adolescence*, 27(1): 113–122.

Anderson, C. A., Shibuya, A., Ihori, N., Swing, E. L., Bushman, B. J., Sakamoto, A., Rothstein, H. R. and Saleem, M. (2010) Violent video game effects on aggression, empathy, and prosocial behavior in Eastern and Western countries: A meta-analytic review. *Psychological Bulletin*, 136(2): 151–173.

Anderson, N. (1981) *Foundations of Information Integration Theory*. Boston, MA: Academic Press.

Antaki, C. (2004) Conversation Analysis. In: S. Becker and A. Bryman (eds), *Understanding Research Methods for Social Policy and Practice*. London: Policy Press, pp. 313–317.

Antaki, C. (2011) Six kinds of Applied Conversation Analysis. In C. Antaki (ed),

Applied Conversation Analysis. Basingstoke: Palgrave-Macmillan.

Antaki, C. and Fielding, G. (1981) Research on ordinary explanations. In: C. Antaki (ed), *The Psychology of Ordinary Explanations of Social Behaviour*. London: Academic Press.

Antaki, C. and Naji, S. (1987) Events explained in conversational "because" statements. *British Journal of Social Psychology*, 26: 119–126.

Antaki, C., Finlay, W. M. L. and Walton, C. (2007) Conversational shaping: Staff-members' solicitation of talk from people with an intellectual impairment. *Qualitative Heath Research*, 17: 1403–1414.

Antaki, C., Billig, M., Edwards, D. and Potter, J. (2003) Discourse analysis means doing analysis: A critique of six analytic shortcomings. *Discourse Analysis Online*, 1(1), http://www.shu.ac.uk/daol/previous/v1/n1/index.htm.

Apple, W., Streeter, L. A. and Krauss, R. M. (1979) Effects of pitch and speech rate on personal attributions. *Journal of Personality and Social Psychology*, 37: 715–727.

Archer, J. and Coyne, S. M. (2005) An integrated review of indirect, relational and social aggression. *Personality and Social Psychology Review*, 9(3): 212–230.

Arendt, H. (1963) *Eichmann in Jerusalem: A Report on Banality of Evil*. New York: Viking Press.

Argyle, M. (1975, 2nd ed. 1984) *Bodily Communication*. London: Methuen.

Argyle, M. (1990) *Relationships* Lecture Delivered at Psychology Teachers' Updating Workshop, Oxford, 1990.

Argyle, M., Alkema, F. and Gilmour, R. (1971) The communication of friendly and hostile attitudes by verbal and non-verbal signals. *European Journal of Social Psychology*, 1: 385–402.

Argyle, M. and Crossland, J. (1987) The dimensions of positive emotions. *British Journal of Social Psychology*, 26: 127–137.

Argyle, M. and Dean J. (1965) Eye-contact, distance and affiliation. *Semiotica*, 6: 32–49.

Argyle, M. and Henderson, M. (1984) The rules of friendship. *Journal of Social and Personal Relationships*, 1: 211–237.

Argyle, M., Lalljee, M. and Cook, M. (1968) The effects of visibility on interaction in a dyad. *Human Relations*, 21: 3–17.

Aron, A. and Westbay, L. (1996) Dimensions of the prototype of love. *Journal of Personality and Social Psychology*, 70: 535–551.

Aronson, E. (1976) *The Social Animal*. San Francisco: W. H. Freeman & Co.

Aronson, E. and Linder, D. (1965) Gain and loss of esteem as determinants of interpersonal attractiveness. *Journal of Experimental Social Psychology*, 1(2): 156–171.

Aronson, E., Willerman, B. and Floyd, J. (1966) The effect of a pratfall on increasing interpersonal attractiveness. *Psychonomic Science*, 4: 227–228.

Asch, S. E. (1946) Forming impressions of personality. *Journal of Abnormal & Social Psychology*, 41: 258–290.

Asch, S. E. (1951) Effects of group pressure on the modification and distortion of judgements. In: H. Guetzkow (ed), *Groups, Leadership and Men*. Pittsburgh: Carnegie Press.

Attridge, M. and Berscheid, E. (1994) Entitlement in romantic relationships in the United States: A social exchange perspective. In: M. J. Lerner and G. Mikula (eds), *Entitlement and the Affectional Bond: Justice in Close Relationships*. New York: Plenum, pp. 117–148.

Austin, J. L. (1962) *How To Do Things with Words*. Oxford: Oxford University Press.

Ayar, A. (2006) Road rage: A psychological disorder. *Journal of Psychiatry and the Law*, 34: 123–150.

Azuma, H., Hess, R. D. and Kashiwagi, K. (1981) *Mother's Attitudes and Actions and the Intellectual (Mental) Development of Children*. Tokyo: Tokyo University Press.

Bagozzi R. P. (1998) The role of arousal in the creation and control of the halo effect in attitude models. *Psychology and Marketing*, 13(3): 235–264.

Baker, L. and Oswald, D. (2010) Shyness and online social networking services. *Journal of Social and Personal Relationships*, 27(7): 873–889.

Bales, R. F. (1950) *Interaction Process Analysis*. Cambridge, MA: Addison-Wesley.

Bandura, A. (1977) *Social Learning Theory*. Englewood Cliffs, NJ: Prentice-Hall.

Bandura, A. (1989) Perceived self-efficacy in the exercise of personal agency. *The Psychologist*, 2: 411–424.

Bandura, A., Ross, D. and Ross, S. (1963) Imitation of film mediated aggressive models. *Journal of Abnormal and Social Psychology*, 66: 3–11.

Banikiotes, P. B. and Neimeyer, G. J. (1981) Construct importance and rating similarity as determinants of interpersonal attraction. *British Journal of Social Psychology*, 20: 259–263.

Bannister, D. and Fransella, F. (1980) *Inquiring Man: The Psychology of Personal Constructs* (2nd ed.). Harmondsworth: Penguin.

Banyard, P. (1989) Hillsborough. *Psychology News*, 2(7): 4–9.

Banyard, P., and Hunt, N. (2000) Reporting research: Something missing? *The Psychologist*, 13(2): 68–71.

Barak, A. (2007) Phantom emotions: Psychological determinants of emotional experiences on the internet. In: A. N. Joinson, K. Y. A. McKenna, T. Postmes, and U.-D. Perips, (eds), *The Oxford Handbook of Internet Psychology*. Oxford: Oxford University Press.

Bargh, J. and Shalev, I. (2011) The substitutability of physical and social warmth in daily life. *Emotion*, 12(1): 154–162.

Bargh, J. A., McKenna, K. Y. A. and Fitzsimons, G. M. (2002) Can you see the real me? Activation and expression of the true self on the internet. *Journal of Social Issues*, 58: 33–48.

Baron, R. A. and Bell, P. A. (1975) Aggression and heat: Mediating effects of prior provocation and exposure to an aggressive model. *Journal of Personality and Social Psychology*, 31: 825–832.

Baron, R. S. (1986) Distraction – conflict theory: Progress and problems. In: L. Berkowitz (ed), *Advances in Experimental Social Psychology*, 19. New York: Academic Press.

Baron, R. S. (2005) So right it's wrong: Groupthink and the ubiquitous nature of polarized group decision making. *Advances in Experimental Social Psychology*, 37: 219–253.

Baron, R. S., Moore, D. M. and Sanders, G. S. (1978) Distraction as a source of drive in social facilitation research. *Journal of Personality and Social Psychology*, 36(8): 816–824.

Baron-Cohen, S., Leslie, A. M. and Frith, U. (1986) Mechanical, behavioural and intentional understanding of picture stories in autistic children. *British Journal of Developmental Psychology*, 4: 113–125.

Bartholow, B. D. and Anderson, C. A. (2002) Effects of violent video games on aggressive behaviour: Potential sex differences. *Journal of Experimental Social Psychology*, 38(3): 283–290.

Bartlett, F. C. (1932) *Remembering*. London: Cambridge University Press.

Bass, B. M. (1985) *Leadership and Performance Beyond Expectations*. New York, NY: Free Press.

Baumrind, D. (1964) Some thoughts on the ethics of research: After reading Milgram's "Behavioural study of obedience". *American Psychologist*, 19: 421–423.

Baxter, J. S., Manstead, A. S. R., Stradling, S. G., Campbell, K. A., Reason, J. T. and Parker, D. (1990) Social facilitation and driver behaviour. *British Journal of Psychology*, 81: 351–360.

Baxter, L. A. (1986) Gender differences in the heterosexual relationships rules embedded in break-up accounts. *Journal of Social and Personal Relationships*, 3: 289–306.

BBC (2011) "The Doctor's Wife" by Neil Gaiman, *Doctor Who*, Series 6, Episode 4, First broadcast 14 May 2011, BBC UK.

Beaulieu, C. (2004) Intercultural study of personal space: A case study. *Journal of Applied Social Psychology*, 34(4): 665–886.

Becker, J. C. V., Zawadski, M. J. and Shields, S. A. (2014) Confronting and reducing sexism: A call for research on intervention. *Journal of Social Issues*, 70(4): 603–614.

Bee, C. and Madrigal, R. (2012) Outcomes are in the eye of the beholder: The influence of affective dispositions on disconfirmation emotions, outcome satisfaction, and enjoyment. *Journal of Media Psychology*, 24(4): 143–153.

Beese, A. G. and Stratton, P. (2004) Causal attributions in delusional thinking: An investigation using qualitative methods. *British Journal of Clinical Psychology*, 43: 267–283.

Belbin, R. M. (1981) *Management Teams*. London: Heinemann.

Belbin, R. M. (1993) *Team Roles at Work*. Oxford: Butterworth Heinemann.

Bell, N. J., McGhee, P. E. and Duffy, N. S. (1986) Interpersonal competence, social assertiveness and the development of humour. *British Journal of Developmental Psychology*, 4: 51–55.

Bem, D. J. (1967) Self-perception: An alternative interpretation of cognitive dissonance phenomena. *Psychological Review*, 74: 183–200.

Bem, D. J. (1972) Self-Perception Theory. In: L. Berkowitz (ed), *Advances in Experimental Social Psychology*, Vol. 6, pp. 1–62. New York: Academic Press.

Bem, S. L. (1976) Sex typing and androgyny: Further explorations of the expressive domain. *Journal of Personality and Social Psychology*, 34: 1016.

Benewick, R. and Holton, R. (1987) The peaceful crowd: Crowd solidarity and the pope's visit to Britain. In: G. Gaskell and R. Benewick (eds), *The Crowd in Contemporary Britain*. London: SAGE.

Bentler, P. M. and Newcomb, M. D. (1978) Longitudinal study of marital success and failure. *Journal of Consulting and Clinical Psychology*, 46: 1053–1070.

Berkowitz, L. (1978) Whatever happened to the aggression frustration hypothesis? *American Behavioral Scientist*, 32: 691–708.

Berne, E. (1973) *Games People Play*. Harmondsworth: Penguin.

Berscheid, E. (1985) Interpersonal attraction. In: G. Lindzey and E. Aronson (eds), *The Handbook of Social Psychology* (3rd ed.). New York: Random House.

Bethlehem, D. W. (1985) *A Social Psychology of Prejudice*. London: Croom Helm.

Bharati, A. (1985) The self in Hindu thought and action. In: A. J. Marsell et al (eds), *Culture and Self: Asian and Western Perspectives*. London: Tavistock Publications.

Bierhoff, H. W. (2002) *Prosocial Behaviour*. East Sussex: Psychology Press.

Biko, S. (1978) *I Write What I Like*. New York: Random House.

Bilewicz, M. and Kogan, A. (2014) Embodying imagined contact: Facial feedback moderates the intergroup consequences of mental simulation. *British Journal of Social Psychology*, 53: 387–395.

Billig, M. (1990) Collective memory, ideology and the British Royal Family. In D. Middleton and D. Edwards (eds), *Collective Remembering*. London: SAGE.

Billig, M. and Tajfel, H. (1973) Social categorisation and similarity in intergroup behaviour. *European Journal of Social Psychology*, 3: 27–52.

Biro, M. (1995) Psychological characteristics of the "Homo Communisticus". British and Eastern European Psychology Group Conference: "Psychology in a Changing Europe", Matej Bel University, Banska Bystrica, Slovakia, 27–31 August 1995.

Biro, M., Ajdukovic, D., Corkalo, D., Djipa, D., Milin, P. and Weinstein, H. M. (2004) Attitudes towards justice and social reconstruction in Bosnia Herzegovina and Croatia. In: E. Stover and H. M. Weinstein (eds), *My Neighbor, My Enemy: Justice and Community in the Aftermath of Mass Atrocity*. Cambridge: Cambridge University Press.

Biro, M. and Milin, P. (2005) Traumatic experience and the process of reconciliation. *Psihologija*, 38(2): 133–148.

Bitterman, M. E. and Kniffin, C. W. (1953) Manifest anxiety and perceptual defense. *Journal of Abnormal & Social Psychology*, 48: 248.

Bjorkland, D. F., Cassell, W. S., Bjorkland, B. R., Brown, R., Park, C. L., Ernst, K. and Owen, F. A. (2000) Social demand characteristics in children's and adults' eyewitness memory and suggestibility: The effect of different interviewers on free recall and recognition. *Applied Cognitive Psychology*, 14(5): 421–433.

Bochner, S., Buker, E. A. and McLeod, B. M. (1976) Communication patterns in an international student dormitory: A modification of the "small world" method. *Journal of Applied Social Psychology*, 6(3): 275–290.

Bogardus, E. S. (1947) Measurement of personal–group relations. *Sociometry*, 10(4): 306–311.

Bogdonoff, M. D., Klein, E. J., Shaw, D. M. and Beck, K. W. (1961) The modifying effect of conforming behaviour upon lipid responses accompanying CNS arousal. *Clinical Research*, 9: 135.

Bond, C. F. (1982) Social facilitation: A self-presentational view. *Journal of Personality & Social Psychology*, (42): 1042–1050.

Bond, M. H. and Hewstone, M. (1988) Social identity theory and the perception of intergroup relations in Hong Kong. *International Journal of Intercultural Relations*, 12: 153–170.

Bond, M. H., Hewstone, M., Wan, K.-C. and Chiu, C.-K. (1985) Group-serving attributions across intergroup contexts: Cultural differences in the explanation of sex-typed behaviours. *European Journal of Social Psychology*, 15: 435–451.

Bond, M. H. and Venus, C. K. (1991) Resistance to group or personal insults in an ingroup or outgroup context. *International Journal of Psychology*, 26: 83–94.

Bower, P. (1998) Understanding patients: Implicit personality theory and the general practitioner. *Psychology and Psychotherapy: Theory Research and Practice*, 71(2): 153–163.

Boyd, B. (2004) Laughter and literature: A play. *Theory of Humor Philosophy and Literature*, 28(1), April: 1–22.

British Crime Survey (2010/2011) https://www.gov.uk/government/statistics/crime-in-england-and-wales-2010-to-2011.

British Psychological Society. (2014) *Code of Human Research Ethics*. Leicester: British Psychological Society.

Brown, G. W. and Harris, T. (1978) *Social Origins of Depression: A Study in Psychiatric Disorder in Women*. London: Tavistock.

Brown, K., Ryan, R. and Creswell, J. (2007) Mindfulness: Theoretical foundations and evidence for its salutary effects. *Psychological Inquiry*, 18(4): 211–237.

Bruce, V. and Young, A. W. (1986) Understanding face recognition. *British Journal of Psychology*, 77: 305–327.

Bryant, E. M. and Marmo, J. (2012) The rules of Facebook friendship: A two-stage examination of interaction rules in close, casual, and acquaintance friendships. *Journal of Social and Personal Relationships*, 29(8): 1013–1035.

Buchanan, T. and Smith, J. L. (1999) Using the Internet for psychological research: Personality testing on the World Wide Web. *British Journal of Psychology*, 90: 125–144.

Buijzen, M. and Valkenburg, P. M. (2004) Developing a typology of humor in audiovisual media. *Media Psychology*, 6: 147–167.

Burger, J. (2009) Replicating Milgram: Would people still obey today? *American Psychologist*, 64: 1–11.

Burger, J. M., Girgis, Z. M. and Manning, C. C. (2011) In their own words: Explaining obedience to authority through an examination of participants' comments. *Social Psychological and Personality Science*, 2(5): 460–466.

Buss, A. R. (1966) Instrumentality of aggression, feedback and frustration as determinants of physical aggression. *Journal of Personality and Social Psychology*, 3: 153–162.

Buss, D. M. (1995) Evolutionary psychology: A new paradigm for psychological science. *Psychological Inquiry*, 6: 1–30.

Buss, A. H. (1986) A theory of shyness. In: W. H. Jones, J. M. Cheek and S. R. Briggs (eds), *Shyness: Perspectives on Research and Treatment*, pp. 39–46. New York: Plenum.

Butler, J. M. and Haigh, G. V. (1954) Changes in the relation between self-concept and ideal concepts consequent on client centred counselling. In: C. R. Rogers and R. F. Dymond (eds), *Psychotherapy and Personality Change*. Chicago, IL: University of Chicago Press.

Butterfield, L. (1989) Paul Masson California Carafes: 'They're really jolly good!' In: C. Channon (ed), *Twenty Advertising Case Histories* (2nd series). London: Cassell.

Byrne, D. (1971) *The Attraction Paradigm*. New York: Academic Press.

Cacioppo, J. T., Bush, L. K. and Tassinary, L. G. (1992) Microexpressive facial actions as a function of affective stimuli: Replication and extension. *Personality and Social Psychology Bulletin*, 18: 515–526.

Cacioppo, J. T., Cacioppo, C., Gonzaga, G. C., Ogburn, E. L. and VanderWeele, T. J. (2013) Marital satisfaction and break-ups differ across on-line and off-line meeting venues. *Proceedings of the National Academy of Sciences of the United States of America*, 110(25): 10135–10140.

Caillaud, S., Kalampalikis, N. and Flick, U. (2012) The social representations of the Bali Climate Conference in the French and German media. *Journal of Community & Applied Social Psychology*, 22(4): 363–378.

Calvert, R., Kellett, S. and Hagan, T. (2015) Group cognitive analytic therapy for female survivors of childhood sexual abuse. *British Journal of Clinical Psychology*, 54(4): 391–413.

Calvert, S. L. and Tan, S.-L. (1994) Impact of virtual reality on young adults' physiological arousal and aggressive thoughts: Interaction versus observation. *Journal of Applied Developmental Psychology*, 15(1): 125–139.

Campbell, W. K., Sedikides, C., Reeder, G. D. and Elliot, A. J. (2000) Among friends? An examination of friendship and the self-serving bias. *British Journal of Social Psychology*, 39(2): 229–239.

Cannon, W. B. (1929) *Bodily Changes in Pain, Hunger, Fear and Rage*. New York: Appleton.

Carducci, B. J. (2000) Shyness: A bold new approach. *Contemporary Psychology*, 45: 99–101.

Carducci, B. J. and Zimbardo, P. G. (1995) Are you shy? *Psychology Today*, 28: 34.

Carlbring, P. and Andersson, G. (2006) Internet and psychological treatment: How well can they be combined? *Computers in Human Behaviour*, 22(3): 545–553.

Carlson, M., Marcus-Newhall, A. and Miller, N. (1989) Evidence for a general construct of aggression. *Personality and Social Psychology Bulletin*, 15: 377–389.

Carnahan, T. and McFarland, S. (2007) Revisiting the Stanford Prison Experiment: Could participant self–selection have led to the cruelty? *Personality and Social Psychology Bulletin*, 33(5): 603–614.

Carr, C., d'Ardenne, P., Sloboda, A., Scott, C., Wang, D. and Priebe, S. (2012) Group music therapy for patients with persistent post-traumatic stress disorder – an exploratory randomized controlled trial with mixed methods evaluation. *Psychology and Psychotherapy: Theory, Research and Practice*, 85(2): 179–202.

Carrell, M. R. and Dittrich, J. E. (1978) Equity theory: The recent literature, methodological considerations, and new directions. *Academy of Management Review*, 3(2): 202–210.

Carugati, F. F. (1990) Everyday ideas, theoretical models and social representations: The case of intelligence and its development. In: G. R. Semin and K. J. Gergen (eds), *Everyday Understanding: Social and Scientific Implications*. London: SAGE.

Carver, C. S. and Scheier, M. P. (1981) *Attention and Self-regulation: A Control-theory Approach to Human Behavior*. New York: Springer-Verlag.

Chaiken, S. (1980) Heuristic versus systematic information processing and the use of source versus message cues in persuasion. *Journal of Personality and Social Psychology*, 39: 752–766.

Cheng, H. and Furnham, A. (2001) Attributional style and personality as predictors of happiness and mental health. *Journal of Happiness Studies*, 2(3): 307–327.

Chesney, T. (2005) Online self-disclosure in diaries and its implications for knowledge managers. *UK Academy for Information Systems Conference Proceedings*, pp. 22–24. Cited in: Joinson and Payne, 2007.

Chidambaram, L., and Tung, L. L. (2005) Is out of sight, out of mind? An empirical study of social loafing in technology-supported groups. *Information Systems Research*, 16(2): 149–168.

Choi, I., Nisbett, R. E., and Norenzayan, A. (1999) Causal attribution across cultures: Variation and universality. *Psychological Bulletin*, 125: 47–63.

Christou, C. and Michael, D. (2014) Aliens versus humans: Do avatars make a difference in how we play the game? Paper delivered at the 6th International Conference on Games and Virtual Worlds for Serious Applications, Vs–Games, 2014.

Clark, M. S. and Grote, N. K. (1998) Why aren't indices of relationship costs always negatively related to indices of relationship quality? *Personality and Social Psychology Review*, 2: 2–17.

Clarke, K. and Preece, D. (2005) Constructing and using a company Intranet: 'It's a very cultural thing'. *New Technology, Work and Employment*, 20(2): 150–165.

Clarke, S. (2013) Safety leadership: A meta-analytic review of transformational and transactional leadership styles as antecedents of safety behaviours. *Journal of Occupational and Organisational Psychology*, 86: 22–49.

Clegg, J. (2012) Stranger situations: Examining a self-regulatory model of socially awkward encounters. *Group Processes and Intergroup Relations*, 15(6): 693–712.

Coghlan, E. and Kirwan, G. (2013) Gender-bending in virtual worlds: Investigating "need for achievement" between goal-oriented and non-goal-oriented environments. In: A. Power and G. Kirwan (eds), *Cyberpsychology and New Media*. New York: Psychology Press.

Collins, B. E. and Hoyt, M. F. (1972) Personal responsibility for consequences: An integration and extension of the "forced compliance" literature. *Journal of Experimental Social Psychology*, 8: 558–593.

Collins, J. L. (1982) Self-efficacy and ability in achievement behavior. In: A. Bandura. Perceived self-agency in the exercise of personal agency. *The Psychologist*, 2(10): 411–424.

Commisso, M. and Finkelstein, L. (2012) Physical attractiveness bias in employee termination. *Journal of Applied Social Psychology*, 42(12): 2968–2987.

Cook, M. (1978) *Perceiving Others*. London: Routledge.

Cooley, C. H. (1902) *Human Nature and the Social Order*. New York: Scribners.

Coopersmith, S. (1968) Studies in self-esteem. *Scientific American*, 218: 96–106.

Costa, P. T., McCrae, R. R. and Zonderman, A. B. (1987) Environmental and dispositional influences on well-being: Longitudinal follow-up of an American national sample. *British Journal of Psychology*, 78(3): 287–423.

Cotterell, N. B. (1972) Social facilitation. In: C. G. McClintock (ed), *Experimental Social Psychology*, pp. 185–236. New York: Holt, Reinhart & Winston.

Cotterell, N. B., Wack, D. L., Sekerak, G. J. and Rittle, R. H. (1968) Social facilitation of dominant responses by the presence of an audience and the mere presence of others. *Journal of Personality & Social Psychology*, 9: 245–250.

Cowan, M. and Little, A. (2013) The effects of relationship context and modality on ratings of funniness. *Personality and Individual Differences*, 54(4): 496–500.

Cowpe, C. (1989) Chip pan fire prevention 1976–1984. In: C. Channon (ed), *Twenty Advertising Case Histories* (2nd series). London: Cassell.

Crane, M. F. and Platow, M. J. (2010) Deviance as adherence to group norms: The overlooked role of social identification in deviance. *British Journal of Social Psychology*, 49: 827–847.

Crozier, W. R. (2001) Shyness, self-perception, and reticence. In: R. J. Riding and S. G. Rayner (eds), *International Perspectives on Individual Differences: Vol. 2. Self-Perception*, pp. 53–76. Westport, CT: Ablex.

Crutchfield, R. S. (1955) Conformity and character. *American Psychologist*, 10: 191–198.

Cuddy, A. J. C., Fiske, S. T. and Glick, P. (2008) Warmth and competence as universal dimensions of social perception: The stereotype content model and the BIAS map. In: J. M. Olson and M. P. Zanna (eds), *Advances in Experimental Social Psychology*, p. 40. London: Elsevier.

Culbertson, K. A. and Dehle, C. (2001) Psychological sequela of sexual assault as a function of relationship to perpetrator. *Journal of Interpersonal Violence*, 16: 992–1007.

Curtiss, S. (1977) *Genie*. New York: Academic Press.

Cutrona, C. E. (1982) Transition to college: Loneliness and the process of social adjustment. In: L. A. Peplau and D. Perlman (eds), *Loneliness: A Sourcebook of Current Theory, Research and Therapy*. New York: Wiley.

Darley, J. M. and Latané, B. (1968) Bystander intervention in emergencies: Diffusion of responsibility. *Journal of Personality and Social Psychology*, 8: 377–383.

Darley, J. M. and Latané, B. (1970) Norms and normative behaviour: Field studies of social interdependence. In: J. Macauley and L. Berkowitz (eds), *Altruism and Helping Behaviour*. New York: Academic Press.

Darwin, C. (1872) *The Expression of the Emotions in Man and the Animals*. London: John Murray.

Dashiell, J. F. (1930) An experimental analysis of some group effects. *Journal of Abnormal & Social Psychology*, 25: 190–199.

Davis, D., Shaver, P. R. and Vernon, M. L. (2003) Physical, emotional, and behavioral reactions to breaking up: The roles of gender, age, emotional involvement, and attachment style. *Personality and Social Psychology Bulletin*, 29(7): 871–884.

Davis, R. A. (2001) A cognitive-behavioral model of pathological Internet use. *Computers in Human Behavior*, 17: 187–195.

Dawkins, R. (1976) *The Selfish Gene*. Oxford: Oxford University Press.

Derrida, J. (1989) *Of Spirit: Heidegger and the Question*, trans. G. Bennington and R. Bowlby. Chicago, IL: University of Chicago Press.

de Saussure, F. (1993) Third Course of Lectures in General Linguistics (1910–1911): Emile Constantin ders notlarından, In: E. Komatsu and R. Harris (eds and trans), *Language and Communication series*, Vol. 12.

Devine-Wright, H. and Devine-Wright, P. (2009) Social representations of electricity network technologies: Exploring processes of anchoring and objectification through the use of visual research methods. *British Journal of Social Psychology*, 48(2): 357–373.

DeVos, G. (1985) Dimensions of the self in Japanese culture. In: A. J. Marsell et al (eds), *Culture and Self: Asian and Western Perspectives*. London: Tavistock Publications.

de Waal, F. B. M. (1989) *Peacemaking among Primates*. Cambridge, MA: Harvard University Press.

DeWall, C. N. and Bushman, B. J. (2011) Social acceptance and rejection: The sweet and the bitter. *Current Directions in Psychological Science*, 20(4): 256–260.

Diamond, L. M. (2003) What does sexual orientation orient? A biobehavioural model distinguishing romantic love and sexual desire. *Psychological Review*, 110: 173–192.

Diener, E. (1979) Deindividuation, self-awareness and disinhibition. *Journal of Personality & Social Psychology*, 37: 1160–1171.

Di Giacomo, J. P. (1980) Intergroup alliances and rejections within a protest movement (analysis of the social representations). *European Journal of Social Psychology*, 10: 329–344.

Dixon, J. and Levine, M. (2012) *Beyond Prejudice: Extending the Social Psychology of Conflict, Inequality, and Social Change*. Cambridge: Cambridge University Press.

Dixon, J., Levine, M., Reicher, S. and Durrheim, K. (2012) Beyond prejudice: Are negative evaluations the problem and is getting us to like one another more the solution? *Behavioral and Brain Sciences*, 35(6): 1–15.

Dollard, J., Doob, L. W., Miller, N. E., Mowrer, O. H. and Sears, R. R. (1939) *Frustration and Aggression*. New Haven, CT: Yale University Press.

Doms, M. and van Avermaet, E. (1981) The conformity effect: A timeless phenomenon? *Bulletin of the British Psychological Society*, 34: 383–385.

Donnerstein, E. and Wilson, D. W. (1979) Effects of noise and perceived control on ongoing and subsequent aggressive behaviour. *Journal of Personality and Social Psychology*, 36: 180–188.

Döring, N. (2014) Consensual sexting among adolescents: Risk prevention through abstinence education or safer sexting? *Cyberpsychology: Journal of Psychosocial Research on Cyberspace*, 8(1): article 9.

Douglas, K. M. and McGarty, C. (2001) Identifiability and self-presentation: Computer-mediated communication and intergroup interaction. *British Journal of Social Psychology*, 40(3): 399–416.

Dovidio, J. F. and Ellyson, S. L. (1982) Decoding visual dominance: Attributions of power based on relative percentages of looking while speaking and looking while listening. *Social Psychology Quarterly*, 45: 106–113.

Drouin, M. and Landgraff, C. (2012) Texting, sexting and attachment in college students' romantic relationships. *Computers in Human Behavior*, 28(2): 444–449.

Druckman, D. (2004) Be all that you can be: Enhancing human performance. *Journal of Applied Social Psychology*, 34(11): 2234–2260.

Drury, J., Novelli, D. and Stott, C. (2013) Psychological disaster myths in the perception and management of mass emergencies. *Journal of Applied Social Psychology*, 43(11): 2259–2270.

Duck, S. W. (1977) *The Study of Acquaintance*. Farnborough: Gower.

Duck, S. (2007) *Human Relationships* (4th ed.). Thousand Oaks, CA: SAGE.

Duck, S. (2011) Similarity and perceived similarity of personal constructs and influences on friendship choice. *British Journal of Social and Clinical Psychology*, 12(1): 1–6.

Dunn, J. (1988) *The Beginnings of Social Understanding*. Oxford: Blackwell.

Durkin, K. and Barber, B. (2002) Not so doomed: Computer game play and positive adolescent development. *Journal of Applied Developmental Psychology*, 23(4): 373–392.

Dutton, D. G. and Aron, A. P. (1974) Some evidence for heightened sexual attraction under conditions of high anxiety. *Journal of Personality and Social Psychology*, 30: 510–517.

Dweck, C. S. (1975) The role of expectations and attributions in the alleviation of learned helplessness. *Journal of Personality and Social Psychology*, 9: 17–31.

Dweck, C. S. (2006) *Mindset: The New Psychology of Success*. New York: Random House.

Eagly, A. and Chaiken, S. (1998) Attitude structure and function. In: D. T. Gilbert, S. T. Fiske and G. Lindzey (eds), *The Handbook of Social Psychology* (4th ed.), Vol. 1. Boston, MA: McGraw Hill.

Ebbinghaus, H. (1885) *Memory: A Contribution to Experimental Psychology*, Refurbished 1964. New York: Dover.

Edwards, A. (2003) Communicating risks through analogies. *British Medical Journal*, 327: 749.

Edwards, A., Thomas, R., Williams, R., Ellner, A. L., Brown, P. and Elwyn, G. (2006) Presenting risk information to people with diabetes: Evaluating effects and preferences for different formats by a web-based randomised controlled trial. *Patient Education and Counselling*, 63: 336–349.

Edwards, D. (1997) *Discourse and Cognition*. London: SAGE.

Eibl-Eiblesfeldt, I. (1972) Similarities and differences between cultures in expressive movements. In: R. A. Hinde (ed), *Nonverbal communication*. Cambridge: Cambridge University Press.

Eiser, J. R. (1971) Enhancement of contrast in the absolute judgement of attitude statements. *Journal of Personality & Social Psychology*, 17: 1–10.

Eiser, J. R. (1975) Attitudes and the use of evaluative language: A two-way process. *Journal for the Theory of Social Behaviour*, 5: 235–248.

Eiser, J. R. (1979) Attitudes. In: K. Connolly (ed), *Psychology Survey No 2*. London: Allen & Unwin.

Eiser, J. R. (1983) From attributions to behaviour. In: M. Hewstone (ed), *Attribution Theory: Social and Functional Extensions*. Oxford: Basil Blackwell.

Eiser, J. R. and Mower-White, C. J. (1974) The persuasiveness of labels: Attitude change produced through definition of the attitude continuum. *European Journal of Social Psychology*, 4: 89–92.

Eiser, J. R. and Ross, M. (1977) Partisan language, immediacy and attitude change. *European Journal of Social Psychology*, 7: 477–489.

Ekman, P. and Friesen, W. V. (1969) The repertoire of non-verbal behaviour: Categories, origins, usage and coding. *Semiotica*, 1: 49–98.

Ellison-Potter, P. A., Bell, P. A. and Deffenbacher, J. L. (2001) The effects of trait driving anger, anonymity, and aggressive stimuli on aggressive driving behaviour. *Journal of Applied Social Psychology*, 31: 431–443.

Ellsworth, P. C. and Langer, E. J. (1976) Staring and approach: An interpretation of the stare as a nonspecific activator. *Journal of Personality and Social Psychology*, 33: 117–122.

Emerson, J. (1969) Negotiating the serious import of humour. *Sociometry*, 32: 169–181.

Emmanuel Ogbonna, E. and Harris, L. C. (2006) Organisational culture in the age of the Internet: An exploratory study. *New Technology, Work and Employment*, 21(2): 162–175.

Engel, A. D., Haxby, J. V. and Todorov, A. (2007) Implicit trustworthiness decisions: Automatic coding of face properties in the human amygdala. *Cognitive Neuroscience*, 19(9): 1508–1519.

Erikson, B. E., Lind, A., Jonson, B. C. and O'Barr, W. M. (1978) Speech style and impression formation in a court setting: The effects of "powerful" and "powerless" speech. *Journal of Experimental Social Psychology*, 14: 266–279.

Erikson, E. (1968) *Identity: Youth and Crisis*. New York: Norton & Co.

Eron, L. D., Huesmann, L. R., Lefkowitz, M. M. and Walder, L. O. (1972) Does television violence cause aggression? *American Psychologist*, 27: 253–262.

Evans, A. and Lee, K. (2013) Emergence of lying in very young children. *Developmental Psychology*, 49(10): 1958–1963.

Evans, D. (2003) Hierarchy of evidence: A framework for ranking evidence evaluating healthcare interventions. *Journal of Clinical Nursing*, 12(1): 77–84.

Fanon, F. (1965) *The Wretched of the Earth*. New York: Grove Press.

Fanon, F. (1966) *Black Skin, White Mask*. New York: Grove Press.

Fazio, R. H. (2000) Accessible attitudes as tools for object appraisal: Their costs and benefits. In: G. R. Maio and J. M. Olson (eds), *Why We Evaluate: Functions of Attitudes*. New Jersey: Lawrence Erlbaum Associates.

Federico, C. M. (2004) Predicting attitude extremity: The interactive effects of schema development and the need to evaluate and their mediation by evaluative integration. *Personality and Social Psychology Bulletin*, 30(10): 1281–1294.

Feinberg, J. M. and Aiello, J. R. (2006) Social facilitation: A test of competing theories. *Journal of Applied Social Psychology*, 36(5): 1087–1109.

Feldman, D. C. (1984) The development and enforcement of group norms. *Academy of Management Review*, January: 47–53.

Felipe, N. J. and Sommer, R. (1966) Invasion of personal space. *Social Problems*, 14: 206–214.

Festinger, L. (1954) A theory of social comparison processes. *Human Relations*, 7: 117–140.

Festinger, L. (1957) *A Theory of Cognitive Dissonance*. Evanston, IL: Row, Peterson.

Festinger, L. and Carlsmith, L. M. (1959) Cognitive consequences of forced compliance. *Journal of Abnormal & Social Psychology*, 58: 203–210.

Festinger, L., Riecken, H. W. and Schachter, S. (1956) *When Prophecy Fails*. Minneapolis, MN: University of Minneapolis Press.

Fincham, R. (2002) Narratives of success and failure in systems development. *British Journal of Management*, 13: 1–14.

Finlay, W. M. L. (2014) Denunciation and the construction of norms in group conflict: Examples from an Al Qaeda-supporting group. *British Journal of Social Psychology*, 53: 691–710.

Finn, J. and Banach, M. (2000) Victimisation online: The downside of seeking human services for women on the internet. *Cyberpsychology and Behaviour*, 3(2): 243–254.

Firestone, I. J., Lichtman, C. M. and Colamosca, J. V. (1975) Leader effectiveness and leadership conferral as determinants of helping in a medical emergency. *Journal of Personality & Social Psychology*, 31: 343–348.

Fischler, C. (1980) Food habits, social change and the nature/culture dilemma. *Social Science Information*, 19: 937–953.

Fishbein, M. (1977) Consumer beliefs and behaviour with respect to cigarette smoking: A critical analysis of the public literature. In: J. Murphy et al (eds), *Dialogues and Debates in Social Psychology*. London: Erlbaum.

Fiske, S. T. and Taylor, S. E. (1983) *Social Cognition*. Reading, MA: Addison-Wesley.

Fitzsimons, G. M. and Bargh, J. A. (2003) Thinking of you: Nonconscious pursuit of interpersonal goals associated with relationship partners. *Journal of Personality & Social Psychology*, 84: 148–164.

Flament, C. (1989) Structure et dynamique des représentations sociales. In: D. Jodelet (ed), *Les Représentations sociales Partis*. Paris: Presses Universitaires de France.

Folomeeva A. V. (2014) Social representations of terrorism and terrorists in youth. *Psikhologicheskie Issledovaniya*, 7(33): 8 (in Russian, abstract in English), http://psystudy.ru/index.php/eng/2014v7n33e/944-folomeeva33e.html.

Foxx, R. M., McMorrow, M. J., Hernandez, M., Kyle, M. and Bittle, R. G. (1987) Teaching social skills to emotionally disturbed adolescent inpatients. *Behavioural Interventions*, 2(2): 77–88.

Fredrickson, B. L. and Losada, M. F. (2005) Positive affect and the complex dynamics of human flourishing. *American Psychologist*, 60 (7): 678–686.

Freeman, H. R. (1977) Reward vs. reciprocity as related to attraction. *Journal of Applied Social Psychology*, 7(1): 57–66.

Freeman, L. C. (1992) Filling in the blanks: A theory of cognitive categories and the structure of social affiliation. *Social Psychology Quarterly*, 55: 118–127.

Freud, S. (1901) The psychopathology of everyday life. Republished 1953 in: J. Strachey (ed.), *The Standard Edition of the Complete Psychological Works of Sigmund Freud*, Volume 6. London: Hogarth.

Friedman, H. and Friedman, L (1979) Endorser effectiveness by product type. *Journal of Advertising Research*, 19(5): 63–71.

Friedman, H. S., DiMatteo, M. R. and Mertz, T. I. (1980) Nonverbal communication on television news: The facial expression of broadcasters during coverage of a presidential election campaign. *Personality and Social Psychology Bulletin*, 6: 427–435.

Frost, D. M. and Forrester, C. (2013) Closeness discrepancies in romantic relationships: Implications for relational well-being, stability, and mental health. *Personality and Social Psychology Bulletin*, 39(4): 456–469.

Frostling-Henningsson, M. (2009) First-person shooter games as a way of connecting to people: "Brothers in Blood". *CyberPsychology & Behavior*, 12(5): 557–562.

Gaggiolo, A., Mantovani, F., Castelnuovo, G., Wiederhold, B. and Riva, G. (2003) Avatars in clinical psychology: A framework for the clinical use of virtual humans. *Cyberpsychology and Behaviour*, 6: 117–125.

Gahagan, J. (1984) *Social Interaction and Its Management*. London: Methuen.

Galesic, M. and Garcia-Retamero, R. (2013) Using analogies to communicate information about health risks. *Applied Cognitive Psychology*, 27: 33–42.

Gallagher, S., Meaney, S. and Muldoon, O. T. (2013) Social identity influences stress appraisals and cardiovascular reactions to acute stress exposure. *British Journal of Health Psychology*, 19(3): 566–579.

Galli, I. and Nigro, G. (1987) The social representation of radioactivity among Italian children. *Social Science Information*, 26: 535–549.

Gamson, W. B., Fireman, B. and Rytina, S. (1982) *Encounters with Unjust Authority*. Homewood, IL: Dorsey Press.

Garwood, S. G., Cox, L., Kaplan, V., Wasserman, N. and Sulzer, J. L. (1980) Beauty is only "name" deep: The effect of first name in ratings of physical attraction. *Journal of Applied Social Psychology*, 10: 431–435.

Gazzaniga, M. S. (2004) *The Cognitive Neurosciences III*. Cambridge, MA: MIT Press.

Gee, J. P. (2003) What video games have to teach us about learning and literacy. *Computers in Entertainment (CIE) – Theoretical and Practical Computer Applications in Entertainment*, 1(1): 10–20.

Geen, R. G. (1978) Some effects of observing violence on the behaviour of the observer. In: B. A. Maher (ed.), *Progress in Experimental Personality Research*, Volume 8. New York: Academic Press, pp. 49–93.

Gerbner, G. and Gross, L. (1976) The scary world of TV's heavy viewer. *Psychology Today*, 9: 41–45.

Gervais, M.-C. and Jovchelovitch, S. (1998) Health and identity: The case of the Chinese community in England. *Social Science Information*, 37(4): 709–729.

Gibson, D. E. (2005) Taking turns and talking ties: Networks and conversational interaction. *American Journal of Sociology*, 111: 1561–1597.

Gibson, H. B. (1982) The use of hypnosis in police investigations. *Bulletin of the British Psychological Society*, 35: 138–142.

Gilbert, D. T. and Malone, P. S. (1995) The correspondence bias. *Psychological Bulletin*, 117(1): 21–38.

Gilbert, G. and Barton, H. (2014) The motivations and personality traits that influence Facebook usage. In: A. Power and G. Kirwan (eds), *Cyberpsychology and the New Media: A Thematic Reader*. Hove: Psychology Press.

Gilbert, G. N. and Mulkay, M. (1984) *Opening Pandora's Box: A Sociological Analysis of Scientists' Discourse*. Cambridge: Cambridge University Press.

Glick, P. and Fiske, S. T. (2001) An ambivalent alliance: Hostile and benevolent sexism as complementary justifications for gender inequality. *American Psychologist*, 56: 109–118.

Goffman, E. (1959) *The Presentation of Self in Everyday Life*. New York: Anchor.

Goleman, D. (1996) *Emotional Intelligence: why it can matter more than IQ*. London: Bloomsbury.

Goodall, J. van Lawick (1974) *In the Shadow of Man*. London: Collins.

Gorn, G. J. (1982) The effects of music in advertising on choice behaviour: A classical conditioning approach. *Journal of Marketing*, 46: 94–101.

Gosling, S. D., Rentfrow, P. J. and Swann, W. B. (2003) A very brief measure of the Big–Five personality domains. *Journal of Research in Personality*, 37: 504–528.

Green, J. P. and Lynn, S. J. (2005) Hypnosis versus relaxation: Accuracy and confidence in dating international news events. *Applied Cognitive Psychology*, 19(6): 679–691.

Griffin, E. (1997) *A First Look at Communication Theory*. New York: McGraw-Hill Companies.

Griffiths, M. D. (1995) Technological addictions. *Clinical Psychology Forum*, 76: 14–19.

Griffiths, M. D. (2000) Does internet and computer "addiction" exist? Some case study evidence. *CyberPsychology & Behavior*, 3: 211–218.

Griffiths, M. (2001) Sex on the internet: Observations and implications for internet sex addiction. *Journal of Sex Research*, 38(4): 333–342.

Guadagno, R. E., Okdie, B. M. and Muscanell, N. L. (2013) Have we all just become "Robo-Sapiens"? Reflections on social influence processes in the Internet age. *Psychological Inquiry: An International Journal for the Advancement of Psychological Theory*, 24(4): 301–309.

Guimond, S., Bégin, G. and Palmer, D. L. (1989) Education and causal attributions: The development of "person-blame" and "system-blame" ideology. *Social Psychology Quarterly*, 52: 126–140.

Gunderson, E. A., Gripshover, S. J., Romero, C., Dweck, C. S., Goldin-Meadow, S. and Levine, S. C. (2013) Parent praise to 1–3 year-olds predicts children's motivational frameworks 5 years later. *Child Development*, 84(5): 1529–1541.

Guthrie, E. R. (1938) *The Psychology of Human Conflict: The Clash of Motives within the Individual*. New York: Harper Brothers.

Haberstroh, S., Duffey, T., Evans, M., Gee, R. and Trepal, H. (2007) The experience of online counseling. *Journal of Mental Health Counseling*, 29: 269–282.

Hald, G. M., Malamuth, N. M. and Yuen, C. (2010) Pornography and attitudes supporting violence against women: Revisiting the relationship in nonexperimental studies. *Aggressive Behavior*, 36: 14–20.

Hall, E. T. (1968) *Proxemics Current Anthropology*, 9: 83–108.

Hall, G. C. N. and Hirschmann, R. (1991) Towards a theory of sexual aggression: A quadripartite model. *Journal of Consulting and Clinical Psychology*, 59: 662–669.

Hallingberg, B., Moore, S., Morgan, J., Bowen, K. and Van Goozen, S. H. M. (2015) Adolescent male hazardous drinking and participation in organised activities: Involvement in team sports is associated with less hazardous drinking in young offenders. *Criminal Behaviour and Mental Health*, 25: 28–41.

Hamilton, D. L. (1981) *Cognitive Processes in Stereotyping and Intergroup Behaviour*. Hillsdale, NJ: Erlbaum.

Haney, C., Banks, W. C. and Zimbardo, P. G. (1973) Interpersonal dynamics in a simulated prison. *International Journal of Criminology and Penology*, 1: 69–97.

Hansel, T. C., Nakonezny, P. A. and Rodgers, J. L. (2011) Did divorces decline after the attacks on the World Trade Center? *Journal of Applied Social Psychology*, 41(7): 1680–1700.

Harari, H. and McDavid, J. W. (1973) Name stereotypes and teacher's expectations. *Journal of Educational Psychology*, 65: 222–225.

Harold, C. M. and Holtz, B. C. (2015) The effects of passive leadership on workplace incivility. *Journal of Organisational Behaviour*, 36: 16–38.

Harré, R. (1979) *Social Being*. Oxford: Basil Blackwell.

Harris, P. L. (1988) *Children and Emotion: The Development of Psychological Understanding*. Oxford: Blackwell.

Harrison, R. (1972) Understanding your organisation's culture. *Harvard Business Review*, May–June 1972.

Haslam, S. A., Reicher, S. D. and Birney, M. E. (2014) Nothing by mere authority: Evidence that in an experimental analogue of the Milgram paradigm participants are motivated not by orders but by appeals to science. *Journal of Social Issues*, 70: 473–488.

Haslam, A., Reicher, S. D., Millard, K. and McDonald, R. (2014) "Happy to have been of service": The Yale archive as a window into the engaged followership of participants in Milgram's "obedience" experiments. *British Journal of Social Psychology*, 54(1): 55–83.

Hastie, R. (1984) Causes and effects of causal attribution. *Journal of Personality and Social Psychology*, 46: 44–56.

Haugen, E. (1966) Dialect, language, nation. *American Anthropologist*, 68: 922–935.

Haxby, J. V., Hoffman, E. A. and Gobbini, M. I. (2000) The distributed human neural system for face perception. *Trends in Cognitive Sciences* 4(6): 223–233.

Hayes, N. J. (1983) *African Religion and Western Science: Some Barriers to Effective Science Teaching*. M. Ed. thesis, University of Leeds.

Hayes, N. (1991) *Social Identity, Social Representations and Organisational Culture*. PhD thesis, CNAA/Huddersfield.

Hayes, N. J. (1992) *Social Identity, Social Representations and Organisational Culture*. PhD thesis, CNAA/Huddersfield.

Hayes, N. (1998a) Psychological processes in organisational cultures I: Social representations and organisational semiotics. *Human Systems*, 9(1): 59–65.

Hayes, N. (1998b) Psychological processes in organisational cultures II: Social identity and organisational groups, *Human Systems*, 9(3/4): 231–237.

Hayes, N. J. (1998c) Organisational cultures as social representations I: Myths and metaphors. *Human Systems*, 9(1): 59–65.

Hayes, N. (2002) *Managing Teams: A Strategy for Success*. Harlow: Thomson Learning.

Hayes, N. (2003) Description, prescription and ideal forms: The nature of modelling in organisational theory. *Human System: The Journal of Systemic Consultation and Management*, 14(1): 3–9.

Hayes, N. (2005) *Doing Psychological Research*. Milton Keynes: Open University Press.

Hayes, N. and Lemon, N. (1990) Stimulating positive cultures: The Concorde Informatics Case. *Leadership and Organisation Development Journal*, 11(7): 17–21.

Haythornthwaite, C. (2007) Social networks and online community. In: A. Joinson, K. Y. A. McKenna, T. Postmes and U. D. Reips (eds), *The Oxford Handbook of Internet Psychology*. Oxford: Oxford University Press.

Headey, B. (2008) Life goals matter to happiness: A revision of set-point theory. *Social Indicators Research*, 86(2): 213–231.

Heider, F. (1958) *The Psychology of Interpersonal Relations*. New York: Wiley.

Heim, A. (1936) An experiment on humour. *Journal of Psychology*, 27(2): 148–161.

Heller, N. (1956) An application of psychological theory to advertising. *Journal of Marketing*, 20: 248–254.

Helmreich, R., Aronson, E. and Lefan, J. (1970) To err is humanising – sometimes! Effects of self-esteem, competence and a pratfall on interpersonal attraction. *Journal of Personality and Social Psychology*, 16: 259–264.

Henderson, L. and Zimbardo, P. G. (1998). *Shyness: Encyclopedia of Mental Health*. San Diego, CA: Academic Press.

Henderson, L. M., Zimbardo, P. G. and Carducci, B. J. (2001) Shyness. In: W. E. Craighead and C. B. Nemeroff (eds), *The Corsini Encyclopedia of Psychology and Behavioral Science*, 4, pp. 1522–1523. New York: John Wiley & Sons.

Hendrick, C. and Hendrick, S. S. (1988) Lovers wear rose-coloured glasses. *Journal of Social and Personal Relationships*, 5: 161–183.

Henley, N. (1977) *Body Politics: Power, Sex and Nonverbal Communication*. Englewood Cliffs, NJ: Prentice Hall.

Hennenlotter, A., Dresel, C., Castrop, F., Baumann, A. O. C., Wohlschläger, A. M. and Haslinger, B. (2009) The link between facial feedback and neural activity within central circuitries of emotion – new insights from botulinum toxin–induced denervation of frown muscles. *Cerebral Cortex*, 19: 537–542.

Hershcovis, S. M. and Barling, J. (2010) Towards a multi-foci approach to workplace aggression: A meta-analytic review of outcomes from different perpetrators. *Journal of Organisational Behaviour*, 31: 24–44.

Hess, E. (1965) Attitude and pupil size. *Scientific American*, 212(4): 46–54.

Hewstone, M. (1989) *Causal Attribution: From Cognitive Processes to Collective Beliefs*. Oxford: Blackwell.

Higgins, E. T. (1987) Self-discrepancy: A theory relating self and affect. *Psychological Review*, 94(3): 319–340.

Hilgard, E. R. (1977) *Divided Consciousness: Multiple Controls in Human Thought and Action*. New York: Wiley.

Himmelfarb, S. and Eagley, A. (eds) (1974) *Readings in Attitude Change*. New York: Wiley.

Hinde, R. A. (1987) *Individuals, Relationships and Culture: Links between Ethology and the Social Sciences*. Cambridge: Cambridge University Press.

Ho, A. D. (2016) *The Mismeasurement of MOOCs: Lessons from Massive Open Online Courses about Metrics for Online Learning*. Paper delivered at the 10th Conference of the International Test Commission, Vancouver, Canada 2016.

Hodges, B. (1974) Effects of volume on relative weight in impression formation. *Journal of Personality and Social Psychology*, 30: 378–381.

Hofling, K. C., Brotzman, E., Dalrymple, S., Graves, N. and Pierce, C. M. (1966) An experimental study in the nurse–physician relationship. *Journal of Nervous and Mental Disorders*, 143: 171–180.

Hogg, M. A. (2001) Social categorization, depersonalization and group behaviour. In: M. A. Hogg and R. S. Tindale (eds), *Blackwell Handbook of Social Psychology: Group Processes*. Oxford: Blackwell.

Hogg, M. A. and Abrams, D. (1988) *Social Identifications: A Social Psychology of Intergroup Relations and Group Processes*. London: Routledge.

Hogg, M. A. and Vaughan, G. M. (1995) *Social Psychology: An Introduction*. London: Prentice Hall / Harvester Wheatsheaf.

Hogg, M. A. and Vaughan, G. M. (2011) *Social Psychology: An Introduction*, 6th ed. Harlow: Pearson.

Hollander, E. P. and Julian, J. W. (1969) Contemporary trends in the analysis of leadership processes. *Psychological Bulletin*, 71(5): 387–397.

Holmes, B. (2013) School teachers' continuous professional development in an online learning community: Lessons from a case study of an e-twinning learning event. *European Journal of Education*, 48(1): 97–112.

Homans, G. (1974) *Social Behaviour: Its Elementary Forms*, 2nd ed. New York: Harcourt Brace Jovanovitch.

Horowitz, L. M., French, R. de S. and Anderson, C. A. (1982) The prototype of a lonely person. In: L. A. Peplan and D. Polman (eds), *Loneliness: A Sourcebook of Current Theory, Research and Therapy*. New York: Wiley.

Hovland, C. I., Lumsdaine, A. A. and Sheffield, R. D. (1949) *Experiments in Mass Communication*. Princeton, NJ: Princeton University Press.

Hovland, C. I. and Sears, R. (1940) Minor studies in aggression IV: Correlation of lynchings with economic indices. *Journal of Psychology*, 9: 301–310.

Hovland, C. I. and Weiss, W. (1951) The influence of source credibility on communication effectiveness. *Public Opinion Quarterly*, 151: 635–650.

Howarth, C. (2002) Identity in whose eyes? The role of representations in identity construction. *Journal for the Theory of Social Behaviour*, 32(2): 145–162.

Howarth, C., Wagner, W., Kessi, S. and Sen, R. (2012) The politics of moving beyond prejudice: Peer commentary on Dixon et al. *Behavioral and Brain Sciences*, 35(6): 27–28.

Hsu, F. L. K (1985) The self in cross-cultural perspective. In: A. J. Marsell et al (eds), *Culture and Self: Asian and Western Perspectives*. London: Tavistock Publications.

Hunt, S. M. (1979) Hypnosis as obedience behaviour. *British Journal of Social and Clinical Psychology*, 18(1): 21–27.

Hurley, Matthew M., Dennet, Daniel C. and Adams, Reginald B. Jr. (2011) *Inside Jokes: Using Humor to Reverse-Engineer the Mind*. Boston, MA: MIT Press.

Hussain, Z. and Griffiths, M. D. (2008) Gender swapping and socialising in cyberspace: An exploratory study. *CyberPsychology & Behavior*, 11(1): 47–53.

Hutchings, M., Carrington, B., Francis, B., Skelton, C., Read, B. and Hall, I. (2008) Nice, kind, smart and funny: What children like and want to emulate in their teachers. *Oxford Review of Education*, 34(2): 135–157.

Inkpen, A. C. (1998), Learning and knowledge acquisition through international strategic alliances. *Academy of Management Executive*, 12(4): 69–80.

Insko, C. A. (1965) Verbal reinforcement of attitude. *Journal of Personality and Social Psychology*, 2(4): 621–623.

Jackman, M. (1994) *The Velvet Glove: Paternalism and Conflict in Gender, Class, and Race Relations*. Berkeley: University of California Press.

Jackson, J. M. and Latané, B. (1981) All alone in front of all those people: Stage fright as a function of number and type of co-performers and audience. *Journal of Personality & Social Psychology*, 40: 73–85.

Jacobs, P. A., Brunton, M. and Melville, M. M. (1965) Aggressive behaviour, mental subnormality and the XYY male. *Nature*, 208: 1351–1352.

Jaffe, D. T. and Kanter, R. M. (1979) Couple strains in communal households: A four-factor model of the separation process. In: G. Levinger and O. Moles (eds), *Divorce and Separation*. New York: Basic Books.

Jaffe, J., Stern, D. and Peery, C. (1973) "Conversational" coupling of gaze behavior in prelinguistic human development. *Journal of Psycholinguistic Research*, 2: 321–329.

James, W. (1890) *Principles of Psychology*. New York: Holt.

Janis, I. L. (1972) *Victims of Groupthink*. Boston, MA: Houghton Mifflin.

Janis, I. L. (1983) *Groupthink* (2nd ed. revised). Boston, MA: Houghton Mifflin.

Janis, I. L. and Feshbach, S. (1963) Effects of fear arousing communications. *Journal of Abnormal & Social Psychology*, 48: 78–92.

Jarvis, W. B. G. and Petty, R. E. (1996) The need to evaluate. *Journal of Personality and Social Psychology*, 70(1): 172–194.

Jellison, J. M. and Davis, D. (1973) Relationships between perceived ability and attitude similarity. *Journal of Personality and Social Psychology*, 27: 430–436.

Jodelet, D. (1984) The representation of the body and its transformations. In: R. M. Farr and S. Moscovici (eds), *Social Representations*. Cambridge: Cambridge University Press.

Jodelet, D. (1991) *Madness and Social Representations*. London: Harvester Wheatsheaf.

Johnson, B. T. and Eagly, A. H. (1989) Effects of involvement on persuasion: A meta-analysis. *Psychological Bulletin*, 106: 290–314.

Johnson, R. D. and Downing, L. E. (1979) Deindividuation and valence of cues: Effects on prosocial and antisocial behaviour. *Journal of Personality & Social Psychology*, 37: 1532–1538.

Joinson, A. N. (2001) Self-disclosure in computer mediated communication: The role of self-awareness and visual anonymity. *European Journal of Social Psychology*, 31: 177–192.

Joinson, A. N. and Payne, C. B. (2007) Self-disclosure, privacy and the internet. In: *Oxford Handbook of Internet Psychology*, Chapter 16. Oxford: Oxford University Press.

Joinson, A. N., Woodley, A. and Reips, U.-R. (2007) Personalisation, authentication and self-disclosure in self-administered Internet surveys. *Computers in Human Behaviour*, 23(1): 275–285.

Jones, E. E. and Berglas, S. (1978) Control of attributions about the self through self-handicapping strategies: The appeal of alcohol and the role of under-achievement. *Personality and Social Psychological Bulletin*, 4: 200–206.

Jones, E. E. and Davis, K. E. (1965) From acts to dispositions: The attribution process in person perception. In: L. Berkowitz (ed), *Advances in Experimental Social Psychology 2*. New York: Academic Press.

Jones, E. E. and Harris, V. A. (1967) The attribution of attitudes. *Journal of Experimental Social Psychology*, 3: 1–24.

Jones, E. E. and McGillis, D. (1976) Correspondent inferences and the attribution cube: A comparative reappraisal. In: J. H. Harvey et al (eds), *New Directions in Attribution Research* (vol. 1). Hillsdale, NJ: Erlbaum.

Jones, W. H. (1981) Loneliness and social contact. *Journal of Social Psychology*, 113: 295–296.

Jones, W. H., Hobbs, S. A. and Hockenbury, D. (1982) Loneliness and social skills deficits. *Journal of Personality and Social Psychology*, 49: 27–48.

Jourard, S. M. (1966) An exploratory study of body accessibility. *British Journal of Social and Clinical Psychology*, 5: 221–231.

Kaës, R. (1984) Representation and mentalisation: From the represented group to the group process. In: R. M. Farr and S. Moscovici (eds), *Social Representations*. Cambridge: Cambridge University Press.

Kafai, Y. B., Heeter, C., Denner, J. and Sun, J. (eds) (2008) *Beyond Barbie and Mortal Kombat: New Perspectives on Gender and Gaming*. Cambridge, MA: MIT Press.

Kahlbaugh, P., Sperandio, A., Carlson, A. and Hauselt, J. (2011) Effects of playing Wii on well-being in the elderly: Physical activity, loneliness, and mood. *Activities, Adaptation and Aging*, 35(4): 331–344.

Kahn, W. A. (1989) Towards a sense of organisational humor: Implications for organisational diagnosis and change. *Journal of Applied Behavioural Science*, 25: 45–63.

Kalick, S. M., Zebrowitz, L. A., Langlois, J. H. and Johnson, R. M. (1998) Does human facial attractiveness honestly advertise health? Longitudinal data on an evolutionary question. *Psychological Science*, 9: 8–13.

Kanter, R. M. (1983) *The Change Masters: Corporate Entrepreneurs at Work*. London: George Allen & Unwin.

Karney, B. R. and Bradbury, T. N. (1995) Assessing longitudinal change in marriage: An introduction to the analysis of growth curves. *Journal of Marriage and the Family*, 57: 1091–1108.

Katz, D. (1960) The functional approach to the study of attitudes. *Public Opinion Quarterly*, 24: 163–204.

Kebbell, M. R. and Wagstaff, G. F. (1998) Hypnotic interviewing: The best way to interview eyewitnesses? *Behavioural Sciences and the Law*, 16(1): 115–129.

Kebritchi, M., Hirumi, A. and Bai, H. (2010) The effects of modern mathematics computer games on mathematics achievement and class motivation. *Computers & Education*, 55(2): 427–443.

Kellaris, J. J. and Cox, A. D. (1989) The effects of background music in advertising: A reassessment. *Journal of Consumer Research*, 16: 113–118.

Kelley, H. H. (1973) The process of causal attribution. *American Psychologist*, 28: 107–128.

Kelly, G. (1955) *The Theory of Personal Constructs*. New York: Norton.

Kelly, J. B. and Johnson, M. P. (2008) Differentiation among types of intimate partner violence: Research update and implications for interventions. *Family Court Review*, 46: 476–499.

Kelman, H. C. (1958) Compliance, identification and internalisation: Three processes of attitude change. *Journal of Conflict Resolution*, 2(1): 51–60.

Kelman, H. C. and Hovland, C. I. (1953) Reinstatement of the communicator in delayed measurement of opinion change. *Journal of Abnormal & Social Psychology*, 31: 245–253.

Kendon, A. (1967) Some functions of gaze direction in social interaction. *Acta Psychologica*, 26: 22–63.

Kenny, D. A. and DePaulo, B. M. (1993) Do people know how others view them? An empirical and theoretical account. *Psychological Bulletin*, 114(1): 145–161.

Kenny, K. and Euchler, G. (2012) "Some good clean fun": Humour, control and subversion in an advertising agency. *Gender, Work and Organisation*, 19(3): 306–323.

Keys, A., Brožek, J., Henschel, A., Mickelsen, O. and Taylor, H. L. (1950) *The Biology of Human Starvation (2 volumes)*. Minneapolis: University of Minnesota Press.

Kidd, D. C. and Castano, E. (2013) Reading literary fiction improves theory of mind. *Science*, 342 (6156), 18 October: 377–380.

Kierein, N. M. and Gold, M. A. (2000) Pygmalion in work organisations: A meta-analysis. *Journal of Organisational Behaviour*, 21(8): 913–928.

Kilham, W. and Mann, L. (1974) Level of destructive obedience as a function of transmitter and executant roles in the Milgram obedience paradigm. *Journal of Personality & Social Psychology*, 29: 696–702.

Klotz, A. C. and Bolino, M. C. (2016) Saying goodbye: The nature, causes and consequences of employee resignation. *Journal of Applied Psychology*, 101(10): 1386–1404.

Knapp, M. L., Hart, R. P. and Dennis, H. S. (1974) An exploration of deception as a communication construct. *Human Communication Research*, 1: 15–29.

Kogan, N. and Wallach, M. A. (1967) Risk-taking as a function of the situation, the person and the group. In: G. Mandler et al (eds), *New Directions in Psychology II*. New York: Holt, Rinehart & Winston.

Koluchova, J. (1976) Severe deprivation in twins: A case study. In: A. M. Clarke and A. D. B. Clarke (eds), *Early Experience: Myth and Evidence*. London: Open Books.

Korsch, B. M. and Negrete, V. F. (1972) Doctor–patient communication. *Scientific American*, 227: 66–75.

Kowert, R. and Oldmeadow, J. (2015) Playing for social comfort. *Online Video Game Play as a Social Accommodator for the Insecurely Attached Computers in Human Behavior*, 53: 556–566.

Krahé, B. (2013) *The Social Psychology of Aggression* 2nd ed. Hove: Psychology Press.

Krahé, B. and Fenske, I. (2002) Predicting aggressive driving behaviour: The role of macho personality, age, and power of car. *Aggressive Behaviour*, 28: 21–29.

Krass, J., Kinoshita, S. and McConkey, K. M. (1989) Hypnotic memory and confident reporting. *Applied Cognitive Psychology*, 3(1): 1–94.

Kroon, M. B. R., Van Kreveld, D. and Rabbie, J. M. (1991) Police intervention in riots: The role of accountability and group norms. A field experiment. *Journal of Community & Applied Social Psychology*, 1(4): 249–267.

Kruglanski, A. W. (1980) Lay epistemo–logic, process and contents: Another look at attribution theory. *Psychological Review*, 87: 70–87.

Kruglanski, A. W., Baldwin, M. W. and Towson, M. J. (1983) The lay epistemic process in attribution making. In: M. Hewstone (ed), *Attribution Theory: Social and Functional Extensions*. Oxford: Blackwell.

Kulik, J. A. (1983) Confirmatory attribution and the perpetuation of social beliefs. *Journal of Personality and Social Psychology*, 44: 1171–1181.

Kurth, S. B. (1970) Friendship and friendly relations. In: G. J. McCall et al (eds), *Social Relationships*. Chicago, IL: Aldine.

Kuss, D. J., Griffiths, M. D., Karila, L. and Billieux, J. (2014) Internet addiction: A systematic review of epidemiological research for the last decade. *Current Pharmaceutical Design*, 20: 4026–4052.

Lalljee, M. (1981) Attribution theory and the analysis of explanations. In: C. Antaki (ed), *The Psychology of*

Ordinary Explanations of Social Behaviour. London: Academic Press.

Lalljee, M. and Widdicombe, S. (1989) Discourse analysis. In: A. M. Colman and G. Beaumont (eds), *Psychology Survey 7*. Leicester: BPS Books.

Lalljee, M., Laham, S. M. and Tam, T. (2007) Unconditional respect for persons: A social psychological analysis. *Gruppendynamik und Organisationsbereitung*, 38(4): 451–464.

Lalljee, M., Tam, T., Hewstone, M., Laham, S. and Lee, J. (2009) Unconditional respect for persons and the prediction of intergroup action tendencies. *European Journal of Social Psychology*, 39(5): 666–683.

Lamm, H. and Myers, D. G. (1978) Group-induced polarisation of attitudes and behaviour. In: L. Berkowitz (ed), *Advances in Experimental Social Psychology, 11*, pp. 145–195. New York: Academic Press.

Langer, E. J., Blank, A. and Chanowitz, B. (1978) The mindlessness of ostensibly thoughtful action. *Journal of Personality and Social Psychology*, 36: 635–642.

Langlois, J. H., Kalakanis, L., Rubernstein, A. J. Larson A., Hallan, M. and Smoot, M. (2000) Maxims or myths of beauty? A meta-analytic and theoretical review. *Psychological Bulletin*, 126: 390–423.

LaPiére, R. T. (1934) Attitudes vs. actions. *Social Forces*, 13: 230–237.

Larsen, S. F. and Laszlo, J. (1990) Cultural-historical knowledge and personal experience in appreciation of literature. *European Journal of Social Psychology*, 20(5): 425–440.

Latané, B. (1981) The psychology of social impact. *American Psychologist*, 36: 343–356.

Latané, B. and Darley, J. M. (1968) Group inhibition of bystander intervention in emergencies. *Journal of Personality and Social Psychology*, 10: 215–221.

Latané, B. and Harkins, S. G. (1976) Cross-modality matches suggest anticipated stage fright, a multiplicature power function of audience size and status. *Perception and Psychophysics*, 20: 482–488.

Latané, B., Williams, K. and Harkins, S. (1979) Many hands make light work: The causes and consequences of social loafing. *Journal of Personality and Social Psychology*, 37: 822–832.

Latané, B. and Rodin, J. (1969) A lady in distress: Inhibiting effects of friends and strangers on bystander intervention. *Journal of Experimental Social Psychology*, 5: 189–202.

Le, K. M. and Peng, W. (2006) What do we know about the social and psychological effects of computer games? A comprehensive review of the current literature. In: Vorderer, P. and Bryant, J. (eds), *Playing Video Games: Motives, Responses,* *and Consequences*. New Jersey: Lawrence Erlbaum Associates, pp. 327–345.

Leavitt, H. J. (1951) Some effects of certain communication patterns on group performance. *Journal of Abnormal and Social Psychology*, 46(1): 38–50.

Le Bon, G. (1895) *The Crowd: A Study of the Popular Mind*. New York: Viking Press.

Lee, J. A. (1976) *The Colours of Love*. New York: Bantam.

Lerner, M. J. and Lichtman, R. R. (1968) Effects of perceived norms on attitudes and altruistic behaviour towards a dependent other. *Journal of Personality and Social Psychology*, 9: 226–232.

Leventhal, H. R., Singer, P. and Jones, S. (1965) Effects of fear and specificity of recommendations upon attitudes and behaviour. *Journal of Personality and Social Psychology*, 2: 20–29.

Levin, K. D., Nichols, D. R. and Johnson, B. T. (2000) Involvement and persuasion: Attitude functions for the motivated processor. In: G. R. Maio and J. M. Olson (eds), *Why We Evaluate: Functions of Attitudes*. New Jersey: Lawrence Erlbaum Associates.

Lewin, K. (1947) Feedback problems of social diagnosis and action. *Human Relations*, 1: 147–153.

Lewin, K. (1948) Action research and minority problems. In: G. W. Lewin (ed), *Resolving Social Conflicts*. New York: Harper.

Lewin, K., Lippitt, R. and White R. K. (1939) Patterns of aggressive behaviour in artificially created social climates. *Journal of Social Psychology*, 10: 271–299.

Leyens, J.-P., Camino, L., Parke, R. D. and Berkowitz, L. (1975) Effects of movie violence on aggression in a field setting as a function of group dominance and cohesion. *Journal of Personality and Social Psychology*, 32: 346–360.

Li, S., Hietajärvi, L., Palonen, T., Salmela-Aro, K. and Hakkarainen, K. (2016) Adolescents' social networks: Exploring different patterns of socio-digital participation. *Scandinavian Journal of Educational Research*, 1–20.

Likert, R. (1967) *The Human Organisation: Its Management and Value*. Tokyo: McGraw Hill.

Littleton, H., Horsley, S., John, S. and Nelson, D. V. (2007) Trauma coping strategies and psychological distress: A meta-analysis. *Journal of Traumatic Stress*, 20(6): 977–988.

Loew, C. A. (1967) Acquisition of a hostile attitude and its relationship to aggressive behaviour. *Journal of Personality and Social Psychology*, 5: 335–341.

Loftus, E. F. and Palmer, J. C. (1974) Reconstruction of automobile destruction: An example of the interaction between language and memory. *Journal of Verbal Learning and Verbal Behavior*, 13: 585–589.

Lopez, S. J. and Snyder, C. R. (2009) *The Oxford Handbook of Positive Psychology*. Oxford: Oxford University Press.

Lorenz, K. (1950) The comparative method in studying innate behaviour patterns. *Symposium of the Society of Experimental Biology*, 4: 221–226.

Lorenz, K. (1966) *On Aggression*. New York: Harcourt, Brace & World.

Lott, A. and Lott, B. (1968) A learning theory approach to interpersonal attitudes. In: A. Greenwold, T. Brock and T. Ostrom (eds), *Psychological Foundations of Attitudes*. New York: Academic Press.

Lowenthal, M. F., Thurner, M. and Chiriboga, D. A. et al (1975) *Four Stages of Life*. San Francisco, CA: Jossey-Bass.

Lutz, C. A. (1990) Morality, domination and understandings of "justifiable anger" among the Ifaluk. In: G. R. Semin and K. J. Gergen (eds), *Everyday Understanding: Social and Scientific Implications*. London: SAGE.

Lyons, J. (1981) *Language and Linguistics: An Introduction*. Cambridge: Cambridge University Press.

Maass, A. and Clark, R. D., III (1983) Internalisation versus compliance: Differential processes underlying minority influence and conformity. *European Journal of Social Psychology*, 13: 197–215.

Mach, M., Dolan, S. and Tzafrir, S. (2010) The differential effect of team members' trust on team performance: The mediation role of team cohesion. *Journal of Occupational and Organizational Psychology*, 83: 771–794.

Machiavelli, N. (1977 [1513]) *The Prince*. Trans. R. M. Adams. New York: Norton.

Maier, N. R. F. (1955) *Psychology in Industry*. New York: McGraw Hill.

Maio, G. R and Olson, J. M. (2000) Emergent themes and potential approaches to attitude function: The Function–Structure model of attitudes. In: G. R. Maio and J. M. Olson (eds), *Why We Evaluate: Functions of Attitudes*. New Jersey: Lawrence Erlbaum Associates.

Major, B., Quentin, W. and McCoy, S. (2002) Antecedents and consequences of attributions to discrimination: Theoretical and empirical advances. In: M. P. Zanna (ed), *Advances in Experimental Social Psychology*, 34: 251–330.

Manis, M. (1977) Cognitive social psychology. *Personality and Social Psychology Bulletin*, 3: 550–556.

Maragoni, C. and Ickes, W. (1989) Loneliness: A theoretical review with implications for measurement. *Journal of Social and Personal Relationships*, 6: 93–128.

Marks, H. and Nurius, P. (1986) Possible selves. *American Psychologist*, 41(9): 954–969.

Marler, P. R. (1982) Avian and primate communication: The problem of natural categories. *Neuroscience & Biobehavioural Reviews*, 6: 87–94.

Marques, J. M. and Yzerbyt, V. Y. (1988) The black sheep effect: Judgemental extremity towards ingroup members in inter and intra group situations. *European Journal of Social Psychology*, 18: 287–292.

Marsella, A. J. DeVos, G. and Hsu, F. L. K. (1985) *Culture and Self: Asian and Western Perspectives*. London: Tavistock.

Marsh, P., Rosser, E. and Harré, R. (1978) *The Rules of Disorder*. London: Routledge.

Marteinson, P. (2006) *On the Problem of the Comic*. Ottawa: Legas Press.

Marten, K. and Psarakos, S. (1995) Evidence of self-awareness in the bottlenose dolphin (*Tursiops truncatu*s). In: Parker, S. T., Mitchell, R. and Boccia, M. (eds), *Self-awareness in Animals and Humans: Developmental Perspectives*, pp. 361–379. Cambridge: Cambridge University Press.

Martin, A. and Olson, K. (2013) When kids know better: Paternalistic helping in 3-year-old children. *Developmental Psychology*, 49(11): 2071–2081.

Martin, J. (2015) Organizational culture. *Wiley Encyclopedia of Management*, 11: 1–7.

Martin, J., Knopoff, K. and Beckman, C. (1998) An alternative to bureaucratic impersonality and emotional labor: Bounded emotionality at the Body Shop. *Administrative Science Quarterly*, 43(2): 429–469.

Maslow, A. H. (1954) *Motivation and Personality*. New York: Harper & Row.

Mayo, E. (1933) *The Human Problems of an Industrial Civilisation*. London: Macmillan.

Mbiti, J. S. (1970) *African Religions and Philosophy*. New York: Doubleday.

McFarland, C. and Ross, M. (1982) The impact of causal attributions on affective reactions to success and failure. *Journal of Personality and Social Psychology*, 43: 937–946.

McGinley, H., LeFevre, R. and McGinley, P. (1975) The influence of a communicator's body position on opinion change in others. *Journal of Personality and Social Psychology*, 31: 686–690.

McGraw, A. P. and Warren, C. (2010) Benign violations: Making immoral behavior funny. *Psychological Science*, 21: 1141–1149.

McGregor, D. (1960) *The Human Side of Enterprise*. New York: McGraw Hill.

McKenna, K. Y. A. (2008) Through the internet looking glass: Expressing and validating the true self. In: A. Joinson, K. McKenna, T. Postmes and U. Reips (eds), *Oxford Handbook of Internet Psychology*. Oxford: Oxford University Press.

McKenna, K. Y. A. and Bargh, J. A. (2000) Plan 9 from cyberspace: The implications of the internet for personality and social psychology. *Personality and Social Psychology Review*, 4(1): 57–75.

McKenna, K. Y. A., Green, A. S. and Gleason, M. E. J. (2002) Relationship formation on the Internet: What's the big attraction? *Journal of Social Issues*, 58: 9–31.

Mead, G. H. (1934) *Mind, Self and Society*. Chicago, IL: University of Chicago Press.

Merikle, P. M. and Daneman, M. (1998) Psychological investigations of unconscious perception. *Journal of Consciousness Studies*, 5: 5–18.

Middleton, D. and Edwards, D. (eds) (1990) *Collective Remembering*. London: SAGE.

Middleton, R. (1976) Regional differences in prejudice. *American Sociological Review*, 41: 94–117.

Mikulincer, M. (1986) Motivational involvement and learned helplessness: The behavioral effects of the importance of uncontrollable events. *Journal of Social and Clinical Psychology*, 4: 402–422.

Milberg, S. and Clark, M. S. (2011) Moods and compliance. *British Journal of Social Psychology*, 27(1): 79–90.

Milgram, S. (1963) Behavioural study of obedience. *Journal of Abnormal Psychology*, 67: 371–378.

Milgram, S. (1970) The experience of living in cities. *Science*, 167: 1461–1468.

Milgram, S. (1973) *Obedience to Authority*. London: Tavistock.

Miller, D. T. and Ross, M. (1975) Self-serving biases in the attribution of causality: Fact or fiction? *Psychological Bulletin*, 82: 213–225.

Miller, G. R., Mogeau, P. A. and Sleight, C. (1986) Fudging with friends and lying to lovers: Deceptive communication in interpersonal relationships. *Journal of Social and Personal Relationships*, 3: 495–512.

Miller, J. D. (2013) Social capital: Networking in Generation X. *The Generation X Report: A Quarterly Research Report from the Longitudinal Study of American Youth*, 2(2).

Miller, J. G. (1984) Culture and the development of everyday social explanation. *Journal of Personality and Social Psychology*, 46: 961–978.

Mishna, F., McLuckie, A. and Saini, M. (2009) Real-world dangers in an online reality: A qualitative study examining online relationships and cyber abuse. *The Oxford Journal*, 33(2): 107–118.

Montefiori, L. (2016) Game-based assessment: Face validity, fairness perception and impact on employer's brand image. *Assessment & Development Review*, 8(2): 19–22.

Montoya, R. M. and Horton, R. S. (2004) On the importance of cognitive evaluation as a determinant of interpersonal attraction. *Journal of Personality and Social Psychology*, 86: 696–712.

Moorhead, G. Ference, R. and Neck, C. P. (1991) Group decision fiascos continue: Space shuttle *Challenger* and a revised groupthink framework. *Human Relations*, 44(6): 539–550.

Moreno, J. L. (1953) Who shall survive? *Foundations of Sociometry, Group Psychotherapy and Sociodrama Sociometry*. New York: Beacon House.

Morojele, N. K. and Stephenson, G. M. (1992) The Minnesota model in the treatment of addictions: A social psychological assessment of changes in beliefs and attributions. *Journal of Community & Applied Social Psychology*, 2(1): 25–41.

Morris, P. E., Gruneberg, M. M., Sykes, R. N. and Merrick, A (1981) Football knowledge and the acquisition of new results. *British Journal of Psychology*, 72: 479–483.

Morris, W. N. and Miller, R. S. (1975) The effects of consensus – breaking and consensus – preempting partners on reduction of conformity. *Journal of Experimental Social Psychology*, 11: 215–223.

Morrison, L., Moss-Morris, R., Michie, S. and Yardley, L. (2014) Optimizing engagement with Internet-based health behaviour change interventions: Comparison of self-assessment with and without tailored feedback using a mixed methods approach. *British Journal of Health Psychology*, 19: 839–855.

Moscovici, S. (1976) *Social Influence and Social Change*. London: Academic Press.

Moscovici, S. (1980) Towards a theory of conversion behaviour. In: L. Berkowitz (ed), *Advances in Experimental Social Psychology* (Vol. 13), pp. 209–239. New York: Academic Press.

Moscovici, S. (1984) The phenomenon of social representations. In: R. M. Farr and S. Moscovici (eds), *Social Representations*. Cambridge: Cambridge University Press.

Moscovici, S. and Faucheux, C. (1972) Social influence, conformity bias and the study of active minorities. In: L. Berkowitz (ed), *Advances in Experimental Social Psychology (Vol. 6)*, pp. 149–202. New York: Academic Press.

Moscovici, S., Lage, E. and Naffrechoux, M. (1969) Influence of a consistent minority on the responses of a majority in a colour perception task. *Sociometry*, 32: 365–380.

Moscovici, S. and Personnaz, B. (1980) Studies in social influence V: Minority influence and conversion behaviour in a perceptual task. *Journal of Experimental Social Psychology*, 16: 270–282.

Moscovici, S. and Zavalloni, M. (1969) The group as a polariser of attitude. *Journal of Personality & Social Psychology*, 12: 125–135.

Mugny, G. (1982) *The Power of Minorities*. London: Academic Press.

Mullin, C. R. and Linz, D. (1995) Desensitization and resensitization to violence against women: Effects of exposure to sexually violent films on judgments of domestic violence victims. *Journal of Personality and Social Psychology*, 69: 449–459.

Mummendey, A. and Schreiber, H. J. (1984) Social comparison, similarity and ingroup favouritism: A replication. *European Journal of Social Psychology*, 14: 231–233.

Munton, A. G. and Antaki, C. (1988) Causal beliefs among families in therapy: Attributions at the group level. *British Journal of Clinical Psychology*, 27(1): 91–97.

Murphy, J. H., Cunningham, I. and Wilcox, G. (1979) The impact of program environment on recall of humorous TV commercials. *Journal of Advertising*, 8: Spring: 17–21.

Neff, K. and Germer, C. K. (2012) A pilot study and randomized controlled trial of the mindful self-compassion program. *Journal of Clinical Psychology*, 69(11): 28–44.

Neisser, U. (1976) *Cognition and Reality: Principles and Implications of Cognitive Psychology*. San Francisco, CA: W. H. Freeman & Co.

Neisser, U. (1981) John Dean's memory: A case study. *Cognition*, 9: 1–22.

Nelissen, R. and Mulder, L. (2013) What makes a sanction "stick"? The effects of financial and social sanctions on norm compliance. *Social Influence*, 8(1): 70–80.

Nemeth, C. and Brilmayer, A. G. (1987) Negotiation versus influence. *European Journal of Social Psychology*, 17: 45–56.

Nesdale, D., Durkin, K., Maass, A., Kiesner, J. and Griffiths, J. A. (2008) Effects of group norms on children's intentions to bully. *Social Development*, 17(4): 889–907.

Newcomb, T. M. (1961) *The Acquaintanceship Process*. New York: Holt, Rinehart & Winston.

Newcomb, T. M. (1968) Interpersonal balance. In: R. P. Abelson et al (eds), *Theories of Cognitive Consistency: A Source Book*. Chicago, IL: Rand McNally.

Newell, S., Scarbrough, H., Swan, J. and Hislop, D. (2000) Intranets and knowledge management: De-centred technologies and the limits of technological discourse. *Managing Knowledge*, 88–106.

Newman, E. J. and Lindsay, D. S. (2009) False memories: What the hell are they for? *Applied Cognitive Psychology*, 23(8): 1105–1121.

Nicolson, N., Cole, S. G. and Rocklon, T. (1985) Conformity in the Asch situation: A comparison between contemporary British and American university students. *British Journal of Social Psychology*, 24: 91–98.

Nisbett, R. E., Caputo, C., Legant, P. and Marcek, J. (1973) Behaviour as seen by the actor and as seen by the observer. *Journal of Personality and Social Psychology*, 27: 157–164.

Niven, K. and Totterdell, P. (2012) How to win friendship and trust by influencing people's feelings: An investigation of interpersonal affect regulation and the quality of relationships. *Human Relations*, 65(6): 777–805.

Noller, P. (1985) Negative communications in marriage. *Journal of Social and Personal Relationships*, 2: 289–301.

Norton, M. I. and Gino, F. (2014) Rituals alleviate grieving for loved ones, lovers and lotteries. *Journal of Experimental Psychology*, 143(1): 366–372.

Ogbonna, E. and Harris, L. C. (2006) The dynamics of employee relationships in an ethnically diverse workforce. *Human Relations*, 59: 379–407.

Okado, B. M., Lachs, L. and Boone, B. (2012) Interpreting tone of voice: Musical pitch relationships convey agreement in dyadic conversation. *The Journal of the Acoustical Society of America*, 132(3): 208–214.

Olk, P. M. and Gibbons, D. E. (2010) Dynamics of friendship reciprocity among professional adults. *Journal of Applied Social Psychology*, 40(5): 1146–1171.

Olson, J. M., Vernon, P. A., Harris, J. A. and Jang, K. L. (2001) The heritability of attitudes: A study of twins. *Journal of Personality and Social Psychology*, 80(6): 845–860.

Olweus, D. (1993) *Bullying at School: What We Know and What We Can Do*. Oxford: Blackwell.

Oosterhof, N. N. and Todorov, A. (2009) Shared perceptual basis of emotional expressions and trustworthiness impressions from faces. *Emotion*, 9(1): 128–133.

Orne, M. T. (1962) On the social psychology of the psychological experiment, with particular reference to demand characteristics and their implications. *American Psychologist*, 17: 276–783.

Orne, M. T. and Whitehouse, W. G. (2000) Demand characteristics. In: A. E. Kazdin (ed), *Encyclopedia of Psychology*, pp. 469–470. Washington, DC: American Psychological Association and Oxford University Press.

Osborn, A. and Flood, C. (2014) Establishing an online counselling service for substance use: An exploratory study. In: A. Power and G. Kirwan (eds),

Cyberpsychology and the New Media: A Thematic Reader. Hove: Psychology Press.

Osgood, C. E. (1966) Dimensionality of the semantic space for communication via facial expression. *Scandinavian Journal of Psychology*, 7: 1–30.

Overall, N. C., Fletcher, G. J. and Simpson, J. A. (2006) Regulation processes in intimate relationships: The role of ideal standards. *Journal of Personality and Social Psychology*, 91(4): 662–685.

Packer, D. J. (2008) Identifying systematic disobedience in Milgram's obedience experiments: A meta-analytic review. *Perspectives on Psychological Science*, 3: 301–304.

Packer, D. J. (2009) Avoiding groupthink: Whereas weakly identified members remain silent, strongly identified members dissent about collective problems. *Psychological Science*, 20: 546–548.

Pagano, V. and Debono, K. (2011) The effects of mood on moral judgement: The role of self-monitoring. *Journal of Applied Social Psychology*, 41(12): 2785–3048.

Parker, I. (1997) *Social Psychology: A Critical Approach*. Paper delivered at the British Psychological Society Social Psychology Conference, Sussex, September 1997.

Parker, T., Blackburn, K., Perry, M. and Hawks, J. (2013) Sexting as an intervention: Relationship satisfaction and motivation considerations. *American Journal of Family Therapy*, 41: 1–12.

Parkes, C. M. (1972) *Bereavement: Studies of Grief in Adult Life*. Harmondsworth: Penguin.

Parkes, C. M. and Weiss, R. (1983) *Recovery from Bereavement*. New York: Basic Books.

Parkinson, B. (2011) How social is the social psychology of emotion? *British Journal of Social Psychology*, 50: 405–413

Parzuchowski M. and Wojciszke, B. (2014) Hand over heart primes moral judgments and behavior. *Journal of Nonverbal Behavior*, 38: 145–165.

Pasahow, R. J. (1980) The relationship between an attributional dimension and learned helplessness. *Journal of Abnormal Psychology*, 89: 358–367

Paton, J. J., Belova, M. A., Morrison, S. E. and Salzman, C. D. (2006) The primate amygdala represents the positive and negative value of visual stimuli during learning. *Nature*, 439: 865–870.

Patterson, F. and Gordon, W. (1993) The case for the personhood of gorillas. In: P. Cavalieri and P. Singer (eds), *The Great Ape Project*. London: The Fourth Estate.

Paulus, P. B. and Murdock, P. (1971) Anticipated evaluation and audience presence in the enhancement of dominant responses. *Journal of Experimental Social Psychology*, 7: 280–291.

Pavlov, I. P. (1927) *Conditioned Reflexes: An Investigation of the Physiological Activity of the Cerebral Cortex*. New York: Dover.

Pennebaker, J. W. and Evans, J. (2014) *Expressive Writing: Words that Heal*. New York: Idyll Arbor Books.

Pennebaker, J. W. and King, L. A. (1999) Linguistic styles: Language use as an individual difference. *Journal of Personality and Social Psychology*, 77: 1296–1312.

Pennington, D.C. (1982) Witnesses and their testimony: The effects of ordering on juror verdicts. *Journal of Applied Social Psychology*, 12: 318–333.

Peräkylä, A. (2004) Two traditions of interaction research. *British Journal of Social Psychology*, 43: 1–20.

Perlman, D. (2007) The best of times, the worst of times: The place of close relationships in psychology and our daily lives. *Canadian Psychology*, 48(1): 7–18.

Perrin, S. and Spencer, C. (1981) Independence or conformity in the Asch experiment as a reflection of cultural and situational factors. *British Journal of Social Psychology*, 20: 205–209.

Peters, T. L. and Waterman, R. H. (1982) *In Search of Excellence: Lessons from America's Best-run Companies*. New York: Harper & Row.

Peters, W. (1987) *A Class Divided: Then and Now*. New Haven, CT: Yale University Press.

Peterson, T., Kaasa, S. O. and Loftus, E. F. (2009) Me too! Social modelling influences on early autobiographical memories. *Applied Cognitive Psychology*, 23(2): 267–277.

Petty, R. E. and Cacioppo, J. T. (1979) Effects of forewarning of persuasive interest and involvement on cognitive responses and persuasion. *Personality and Social Psychology Bulletin*, 5: 173–176.

Petty, R. E., DeSteno, D. and Rucker, D. D. (2001) The role of affect in attitude change. In: J. P. Forgas (ed), *Handbook of Affect and Social Cognition*, pp. 212–233. Mahwah, NJ: Erlbaum.

Phillips, M. J., Young, A. W., Senior, C., Brammer, M., Andrews, C., Calder, A. J., Bulmer, E. T., Perrett, D. I., Rowland, D., Williams, S. C. R., Gray, J. A. and David, A. S. (1997) A specific neural substrate for perceiving facial expressions of disgust. *Nature*, 389: 495–498.

Piaget, J. (1952) *The Origins of Intelligence in Children*. New York: International Universities Press.

Pickard, H. (2016) Denial in addiction. *Mind & Language*, 31(3): 277–299.

Pidgeon, N. and Henwood, K. (1997) Using grounded theory in psychological research. In: N. Hayes (ed), *Doing Qualitative Analysis in Psychology*. Hove: Psychology Press.

Piliavin, I. M., Rodin, J. and Piliavin, J. A. (1969) Good Samaritanism: An underground phenomenon? *Journal of Personality and Social Psychology*, 13: 289–299.

Pillai, D., Sheppard, E. and Mitchell, P. (2012) Can people guess what happened to others from their reactions? *PLoS ONE*, 7 (11). doi.

Pinto, D. C., Reale, G., Segabinazzi, R. and Rossi, C. A. V. (2015) Online identity construction: How gamers redefine their identity in experiential communities. *Journal of Consumer Behaviour*, 14: 399–409.

Platow, M. J., McClintock, C. G. and Liebrand, W. B. (1990) Predicting intergroup fairness and ingroup bias in the minimal group paradigm. *European Journal of Social Psychology*, 20: 221–239.

Plester, B., Wood, C. and Joshi, P. (2009) Exploring the relationship between children's knowledge of text message abbreviations and school literacy outcomes. *British Journal of Developmental Psychology*, 27(1): 145–161.

Plotnik, J. M., de Waal, F. B. D. M. and Reiss, D. (2006) Self-recognition in an Asian elephant. *Proceedings of the National Academy of Science*, 103(45): 17053–17057.

Plous, S. and Zimbardo, P. G. (2004) How social science can reduce terrorism. *The Chronicle of Higher Education*, September 10: pp. 9–10.

Pondy, L. R., Frost, P. J., Morgan, G. and Dandridge, T. C. (eds) (1983) *Organizational Symbolism*. Greenwich, CT: JAI.

Popper, K. (1959) *The Logic of Scientific Discoveries*. London: Hutchinson.

Porter, H. (1939) Studies in the psychology of stuttering: Part 14 – Stuttering phenomena in relation to size and personnel of audience. *Journal of Speech Disorders*, 4: 323–333.

Postman, L., Bruner, J. S. and McGinnies, E. (1948) Personal values as selective factors in perception. *Journal of Abnormal & Social Psychology*, 43: 142–154.

Postmes, T., Haslam, S. A. and Swaab, R. I. (2005) Social identity and social influence in small groups: Communication, consensualization and socially shared cognition. *European Review of Social Psychology*, 16: 1–42.

Postmes, T., Spears, R. and Lea, M. (2000) The formation of group norms in computer-mediated communication. *Human Communication Research*, 26(3): 341–371.

Potter, J. (1997) *Social Psychology: A Discursive Approach*. Paper delivered at the British Psychological Society Social Psychology Conference, Sussex, September 1997.

Potter, J. (2012) Re-reading Discourse and Social Psychology: Transforming social psychology. *British Journal of Social Psychology*, 51: 436–455.

Potter, J. and Reicher, S. (1987) Discourses of community and conflict: The organisation of social categories in accounts of a "riot". *British Journal of Social Psychology*, 26: 353–371.

Prentice-Dunn, S. and Rogers, R. W. (1982) Effects of public and private self-awareness on deindividuation and aggression. *Journal of Personality and Social Psychology*, 43: 503–513.

Prestwich, A. and Lalljee, M. (2009) The determinants and consequences of intragroup respect: An examination within a sporting context. *Journal of Applied Social Psychology*, 39(5): 1229–1253.

Prochaska, J. O., DiClemente, C. C. and Norcross, J. C. (1992) In search of how people change: Applications to addictive behaviors. *American Psychologist*, 47(9): 1102–1104.

Pundt, A. and Herrmann, F. (2014) Affiliative and aggressive humour in leadership and their relationship to leader–member exchange. *Journal of Occupational and Organisational Psychology*, 88(1): 108–125.

Quinn, S. and Oldmeadow, J. A. (2012) Is the *i* generation a "we" generation? Social networking use among 9- to 13-year-olds and belonging. *British Journal of Developmental Psychology*, 32(1): 136–142.

Rabbie, J. M. and Horwitz, M. (1988) Categories versus groups as explanatory concepts in intergroup relations. *European Journal of Social Psychology*, 18: 117–123.

Ramsay, R. W. (1977) Behavioural approaches to bereavement. *Behavioural Research and Therapy*, 15: 131–135.

Rasmussen, H. N., Scheier, M. F. and Greenhouse, J. B. (2009) Optimism and physical health: A meta-analytic review. *Annals of Behavioural Medicine*, 37: 239–356.

Reason, P. and Rowan, J. (1981) *Human Inquiry: A Sourcebook of New Paradigm Research*. Chichester: Wiley.

Reicher, S. D. (1984) The St. Pauls' riot: An explanation of the limits of crowd action in terms of a social identity model. *European Journal of Social Psychology*, 14: 1–21.

Reicher, S. and Haslam, S. A. (2006) Rethinking the psychology of tyranny: The BBC prison study. *British Journal of Social Psychology*, 45: 1–40.

Reicher, S. D., Haslam, S. A. and Miller, A. G. (2014) What makes a person a perpetrator? The intellectual, moral and methodological arguments for revisiting Milgram's research on the influence of authority. *Journal of Social Issues*, 703: 393–408.

Reis, H. T. and Patrick, B. C. (1996) Attachment and intimacy: Component processes. In: E. T. Higgins and A. W. Kruglanski (eds), *Social Psychology: Handbook of Basic Principles*. London: Guilford Press, pp. 523–563.

Rhys Evans, T. and Steptoe-Warren, G. (2014) Teaching emotions in higher education: An emotional rollercoaster. *Psychology Teaching Review*, 21(1): 39–43.

Richardson, K. and Norgate, S. (2005) The equal environments assumption of classical twin studies may not hold. *British Journal of Educational Psychology*, 75(3): 339–350.

Riley, P. (2015) Should we play? *Gamification in Assessment and Selection Assessment & Development Matters*, 7(2): 13–16.

Rochat, P. (2003) Five levels of self–awareness as they unfold early in life. *Consciousness and Cognition*, 12 (4): 717–731.

Roethlisberger, J. W. and Dickson, W. J. (1939) *Management and the Worker*. Cambridge, MA: Harvard University Press.

Rogelberg, S., Scott, C., Agypt, B., Williams, J., Kello, J., McCausland, T. and Olien, J. (2013) Lateness to meetings: Examination of an unexplored temporal phenomenon. *European Journal of Work and Organizational Psychology*, 1–19.

Rogers, C. R. (1951) *Client-Centred Therapy*. London: Constable.

Rogers, C. R. (1957) The necessary and sufficient conditions of therapeutic personality change. *Journal of Consulting Psychology*, 21: 95.

Rogers, C. R. (1961) *On Becoming a Person: A Therapist's View of Psychotherapy*. London: Constable.

Rogers, C. R. (1970) *Carl Rogers on Encounter Groups*. New York: Harper & Row.

Rogoff, B. (2003) *The Cultural Nature of Human Development*. Oxford: Oxford University Press.

Rokeach, M. (1948) Generalised mental rigidity as a factor in ethnocentrism. *Journal of Abnormal and Social Psychology*, 43: 254–278.

Rokeach, M. (1960) *The Open and Closed Mind*. New York: Basic Books.

Rokeach, M. (1973) *The Nature of Human Values*. New York: Free Press.

Rosanna, E., Guadagnoa, D. M., Rempalab, S., Murphy, C. and Okdied, B. M. (2013) What makes a video go viral? An analysis of emotional contagion and Internet memes. *Computers in Human Behavior*, 29(6): 2312–2319.

Rose, S. (1983) Biology, ideology and human nature. Address delivered to the Annual General Meeting of the Association of the Teaching of Psychology, London.

Rose, S., Kamin, L. J. and Lewontin, R. C. (1984) *Not in Our Genes: Biology, Ideology and Human Nature*. Harmondsworth: Penguin.

Rose, S. and Serafica, F. C. (1986) Keeping and ending casual, close and best friendships. *Journal of Social and Personal Relationships*, 3: 275–288.

Rosenbaum, M. E. (1986) The repulsion hypothesis: On the nondevelopment of a relationship. *Journal of Personality and Social Psychology*, 91: 87–95.

Rosenberg, M. J. and Hovland, C. I. (1960) Cognitive, affective and behavioural components of attitudes. In: C. I. Hovland and M. J. Rosenberg (eds), *Attitude Organisation and Change*. New Haven, CT: Yale University Press.

Rosenberg, M. J., Nelson, C. and Vivekanathan, P. S. (1968) A multidimensional approach to the structure of personality impression. *Journal of Personality & Social Psychology*, 9: 283–294.

Rosenfield, D., Stephan, W. G. and Lucker, G. W. (1981) Attraction to competent and incompetent members of co-operative and competitive groups. *Journal of Applied Social Psychology*, 11(5): 416–433.

Rosenthal, R. and Fode, K. L. (1963) The effect of experimenter bias on the performance of the albino rat. *Behavioural Science*, 8: 183–189.

Rosenthal, R. and Jacobsen, L. (1968) *Pygmalion in the Classroom: Teacher Expectations and Pupil Intellectual Development*. New York: Holt, Rinehart & Winston.

Ross, L., Amabile, T. and Steinmetz, J. (1977) Social rules, social control, and biases in social perception processes. *Journal of Personality & Social Psychology*, 35: 485–494.

Ross, L., Lepper, M. and Hubbard, M. (1975) Perseverance in self-perception and social perception: Biased attributional processes in the debriefing paradigm. *Journal of Personality & Social Psychology*, 32: 880–892

Roter, D. L. and Hall, J. A. (1991) Health education theory: An application to the process of patient–provider communication. *Health Education Research*, 6: 185–193.

Rotter, J. B. (1966) Generalised expectancies for internal vs. external control of reinforcement. *Psychological Monographs*, 80(1).

Rubin, Z. (1973) *Liking and Loving: An Invitation to Social Psychology*. New York: Holt, Rinehart & Winston.

Rubin, Z. (1975) Disclosing oneself to a stranger: Reciprocity and its limits. *Journal of Experimental Social Psychology*, 11: 233–260.

Rusbult, C. E. (1983) A longitudinal test of the investment model: The development (and deterioration) of satisfaction and commitment in heterosexual involvements. *Journal of Personality and Social Psychology*, 45: 101–117.

Rusbult, C. E. and Buunk, A. P. (1993) Commitment processes in close relationships: An interdependence analysis. *Journal of Personality and Social Psychology*, 10: 175–204.

Sack, D. (2014) Limerence and the Biochemical Roots of Love Addiction. http://www.huffingtonpost.com/david-sack-md/limerence_b_1627089.html, 1–28.

Sacks, H. (1974) On the analysability of stories by children. In: R. Turner (ed), *Ethnomethodology*. Harmondsworth: Penguin.

Sammut, G. and Howarth, C. (2014) Social representations. In: T. Tea (ed), *Encyclopaedia of Critical Psychology*. New York: Springer.

Sarbin, T. R. and Slagle, R. W. (1972) Hypnosis and psychophysiological outcomes. In: E. Fromm and R. E. Shor (eds), *Hypnosis: Research, Developments and Perspectives*. Chicago, IL: Aldine-Atherton.

Sargant, W. (1957) *Battle for the Mind*. London: Heinemann.

Savage-Rumbaugh, E. S., Rumbaugh, D. M. and Boysen, S. L. (1978) Symbolic communication between two chimpanzees (*Pan troglodytes*). *Science*, 201: 641–644.

Schachter, S. and Singer, J. E. (1962) Cognitive, social and physiological determinants of emotional states. *Psychological Review*, 69: 379–399.

Schaffer, H. R. and Emerson, P. E. (1964) The development of social attachments in infancy. *Monographs of Social Research in Child Development*, 29(94).

Schank, R. and Abelson, R. (1977) *Scripts, Plans, Goals and Understanding: An Enquiry into Human Knowledge*. Hillsdale, NJ: Erlbaum.

Scheier, M. F. and Carver, C. S. (1981) Private and public aspects of self. *Review of Personality and Social Psychology*, 2: 189–216.

Schein, E. H. (1988) *Process Consultation: Its Role in Organisational Development Vol 1*. Reading, MA: Addison-Wesley.

Schein, E. H. (1990) Organizational culture. *American Psychologist*, 45: 109–119.

Schein, E. H. (1996) Culture: The missing concept in organizational studies. *Administrative Science Quarterly*, 41: 229–240.

Schirmer, A., Reece, C., Zhao, C., Ng, E., Wu, E. and Yen, S.-C. (2015) Reach out to one and you reach out to many: Social touch affects third-party observers. *British Journal of Psychology*, 106(1): 107–132.

Schmitt, B. D., Gilovich, T., Goore, N. and Joseph, L. (1986) Mere presence and social facilitation: One more time. *Journal of Experimental Social Psychology*, 22: 242–248.

Schmitt, D. P. (2002) Personality, attachment and sexuality related to dating relationship outcomes: Contrasting three perspectives on personal attribute interaction. *British Journal of Social Psychology*, 41(4): 589–610.

Schnall, S. and Laird, J. D. (2003) Keep smiling: Enduring effects of facial expressions and postures on emotional experience and memory. *Cognition and Emotion*, 17: 787–797.

Scott, M. B. and Lyman, S. (1968) Accounts. *American Sociological Review*, 33: 46–62.

Seavey, C. A., Katz, P. A. and Zalk, P. R. (1975) Baby X: The effect of gender labels on adult responses to infants. *Sex Roles*, 1(2): 103–109.

Segal, M. W. (1974) Alphabet and attraction: An unobtrusive measure of the effect of propinquity in a field setting. *Journal of Personality and Social Psychology*, 33: 517–520.

Seger, C. R., Smith, E. R., Percy, E. J. and Conrey, F. R. (2014) Reach out and reduce prejudice: The impact of interpersonal touch on Intergroup Liking. *Basic and Applied Social Psychology*, 36(1): 51–58.

Seguin-Levesque, C., Lyne, M., Lalibertea, N., Pelletier, L. G., Blanchard, C. and Vallerand, R. J. (2003) Harmonious and obsessive passion for the internet: Their associations with the couple's relationship. *Journal of Applied Social Psychology*, 33(1): 197–221.

Seligman, M. E. P. (1975) *Helplessness: On Depression, Development and Death*. San Francisco, CA: Freeman.

Seligman, M. (1998) *Learned Optimism*. New York: Pocket Books.

Seligman, M. and Csikszentmihalyi, M. (2000) Positive psychology: An introduction. *American Psychologist*, 55(1): 5–14.

Shanab, M. E. and Yahya, K. A. (1977) A behavioural study of obedience in children. *Journal of Personality and Social Psychology*, 35: 530–536.

Sharp, S. and Smith, P. K. (1995) *Tackling Bullying in Your School: A Practical Guide for Teachers*. London: Routledge.

Sheridan, C. L. and King, K. G. (1972) Obedience to authority with an authentic victim. *Proceedings of the 80th Annual Convention of the American Psychological Association*, 7: 165–166.

Sherif, M. (1935) A study of some social factors in perception. *Archives of Psychology*, 27(187).

Sherif, M. (1936) *The Psychology of Social Norms*. New York: Harper & Row.

Sherif, M., Harvey, O. J., White, B. J., Hood, W. R. and Sherif, C. W. (1961) *Intergroup Conflict and Co-operation: The Robbers Cave Experiment*. Norman: University of Oklahoma Press.

Sherif, M. and Hovland, C. I. (1961) *Social Judgement: Assimilation and Contrast in Communication and Attitude Change*. New Haven, CT: Yale University Press.

Sherrard, C. (1997) Repertoires in discourse: Social identification and aesthetic taste. In: N. J. Hayes (ed), *Doing Qualitative Analysis in Psychology*. Hove: Psychology Press.

Sibley, C. G., Overall, N. C. and Duckitt, J. (2007) When women become more hostilely sexist toward their gender: The system-justifying effect of benevolent sexism. *Sex Roles*, 57: 743–754.

Siddiquee, A. and Kagan, C. (2006) The internet, empowerment, and identity: An exploration of participation by refugee women in a Community Internet Project (CIP) in the United Kingdom (UK). *Journal of Community & Applied Social Psychology*, 16: 189–206.

Sidorowicz, L. and Lunney, G. (1980) Baby X revisited. *Sex Roles*, 6(1): 67–73.

Sigall, H. and Ostrove, N. (1975) Beautiful but dangerous: Effects of offender attractiveness and nature of the crime on juridic judgement. *Journal of Personality and Social Psychology*, 31: 410–414.

Silverman, I. (1977) *The Human Subject in the Psychological Laboratory*. New York: Pergamon.

Silvern, S. B. and Williamson, P. A. (1987) The effects of video game play on young children's aggression, fantasy and prosocial behaviour. *Journal of Applied Developmental Psychology*, 8(4): 453–462.

Simon, B. and Brown, R. (1987) Perceived intragroup homogeneity in minority majority contexts. *Journal of Personality & Social Psychology*, 53: 703–711.

Sinclair, A. (2009) Seducing leadership: Stories of leadership. *Development Gender, Work and Organization*, 16(2): 266–284.

Singh, R. and Tan, L. S. C. (1992) Attitudes and attraction: A test of the similarity-attraction and dissimilarity-repulsion hypotheses. *British Journal of Social Psychology*, 31: 227–238.

Skinner, B. F. (1961) Why we need teaching machines. *Harvard Educational Review*, 31: 377–398.

Slater, M., Antley, A., Davison, A., Swapp, D., Guger, C., Barker, C. et al (2006) A virtual reprise of the Stanley Milgram obedience experiments. *PLoS ONE*, 1: e39.

Smith, J. A. (1997) Developing theory from case studies: Self-reconstruction and the transition to motherhood. In: N. J. Hayes (ed), *Doing Qualitative Analysis in Psychology*. Hove: Psychology Press.

Smith, K. K. (1983) A role for community psychologists: As participant-conceptualizers. *Australian Psychologist*, 18(2): 143–160.

Smith, M. B., Bruner, J. S. and White, R. W. (1956) *Opinions and Personality*. New York: Wiley.

Smith, P. B. and Peterson, M. F. (1988) *Leadership, Organisations and Culture*. London: SAGE.

Snyder, M. and Miene, P. K. (1994) Stereotyping of the elderly: A functional approach. *British Journal of Social Psychology*, 33(1): 63–82.

Spapé, M. M., Kivikangas, J. M., Järvelä, S., Kosunen, I., Jacucci, G. and Ravaja, N. (2013) Keep your opponents close: Social context affects EEG and fEMG linkage in a turn-based computer game. *Public Library of Science* 8(11): e78795.

Spears, R. and Lea, M. (1992) Social influence and the influence of the 'social' in computer-mediated communication. In: M. Lea (ed), *Contexts of Computer-Mediated Communication*, pp. 30–65. Hemel Hempstead, UK: Harvester Wheatsheaf.

Spears, R., Lea, M., Corneliussen, R. A., Postmes, T. and Ter Haar, W. (2002) Computer-mediated communication as a channel for social resistance: The strategic side of SIDE. *Small Group Research*, 33: 55–574.

Spears, R., Lea, M. and Postmes, T. (2007) Computer-mediated communication and social identity. In: A. Joinson, K. McKenna, T. Postmes and U. Reips (eds), *Oxford Handbook of Internet Psychology*. Oxford: Oxford University Press.

Spielberger, C. D., Krasner, S. S. and Solomon, E. P. (1988) The experience, expression and control of anger. In: M. P. Janisse (ed), *Health Psychology: Individual Differences and Stress*, pp. 89–108. New York: Springer-Verlag.

Stang, D. J. (1973) Effects of interaction rate on ratings of leadership and liking. *Journal of Personality and Social Psychology*, 27: 405–408.

Stanley, B. and Standen, P. J. (2000) Carers' attributions for challenging behaviour. *British Journal of Clinical Psychology*, 39: 157–168.

Steffens, K. (2015) Competences, learning theories and MOOCs: Recent developments in lifelong learning. *European Journal of Education*, 50(1): 41–59.

Stepanikova, I., Nie, N. and He, X. (2010) Time on the Internet at home, loneliness, and life satisfaction: Evidence from panel time-diary data. *Computers in Human Behavior*, 26 (3): 329–338.

Stern, D. (1977) *The First Relationship: Infant and Mother*. London: Fontana.

Sternberg, R. J. (1987) *The Triangle of Love*. New York: Basic Books.

Stevenson, C. and Abell, J. (2011) Enacting national concerns: Anglo-British accounts of the 2002 Royal Golden Jubilee. *Journal of Community & Applied Social Psychology*, 21: 124–137.

Stokoe, E. and Edwards, D. (2008) Did you have permission to smash your neighbour's door? Silly questions and their answers in police–

suspect interrogations. *Discourse Studies*, 10(1): 89–111.

Stoner, J. A. F. (1961) A *Comparison of Individual and Group Decisions Involving Risk*, MA thesis. Cambridge, MA: MIT School of Industrial Management.

Storms, M. D. (1973) Videotape and the attribution process: Reversing actors' and observers' points of view. *Journal of Personality & Social Psychology*, 27: 165–175.

Stoughton, J. W., Thompson, L. F. and Meade, A. W. (2013) Big Five personality traits reflected in job applicants' social media postings. *Cyberpsychology, Behaviour and Social Networking*, 16(11): 800–805.

Strack, F., Martin, L. and Stepper, S. (1988) Inhibiting and facilitating conditions of the human smile: A nonobtrusive test of the facial feedback hypothesis. *Journal of Personality & Social Psychology*, 54: 768–777.

Stratton, P. M. (1983) Biological preprogramming of infant behaviour. *Journal of Child Psychology and Psychiatry*, 24(2): 301–309.

Stratton, P. M., Heard, D., Hanks, H., Munton, A., Brewin, C. R. and Davidson, C. R. (1986) Coding causal beliefs in natural discourse. *British Journal of Social Psychology*, 25: 299–313.

Stratton, P. M., Munton, A. G., Hanks, H., Heard, D., Brewin, C. and Davidson, C. (1988) *The Leeds Attributional Coding System*. Manual Leeds: LFTRC.

Stratton, P. M. and Swaffer, R. (1988) Maternal causal beliefs for abused and handicapped children. *Journal of Reproductive and Infant Psychology*, 6: 201–216.

Streater, S. A. and McBurney, D. H. (2003) Waist–hip ratio and attractiveness: New evidence and a critique of a "critical" test. *Evolution and Human Behaviour*, 24: 88–98.

Strid, C., Andersson, C., Forsell, Y., Öjehagen, A. and Lundh, L.-G. (2016) Internet-based cognitive behaviour therapy and physical exercise: Effects studied by automated telephone assessments in mental ill-health patients; a randomized controlled trial. *British Journal of Clinical Psychology*, 55(4): 414–428.

Sublette, V. A. and Mullan, B. (2012) Consequences of play: A systematic review of the effects of online gaming. *International Journal of Mental Health and Addiction*, 10(1): 3–23.

Suler, J. (2004) The online disinhibition effect. *CyberPsychology & Behavior*, 7(3): 321–326.

Sullivan, P. and Feltz, D. L. (2003) The preliminary development of the Scale for Effective Communication in Team Sports (SECTS). *Journal of Applied Social Psychology*, 33(8): 1693–1715.

Sullivan, P. and Short, S. (2011) Further operationalisation of intra-team communication in sports: An updated version of the Scale of Effective Communication in Team Sports (SECTS–2). *Journal of Applied Psychology*, 41(2): 471–487.

Tajfel, H. (1969) Cognitive aspects of prejudice. *Journal of Social Issues*, 25: 79–97.

Tajfel, H. (1970) Experiments in intergroup discrimination. *Scientific American*, 223: 96–102.

Tajfel, H. (1982) Social psychology of intergroup relations. *Annual Review of Psychology*, 33: 1–39.

Tajfel, H., Billig, M. G., Bundy, R. P. and Flament, C. (1971) Social categorisation and intergroup behaviour. *European Journal of Social Psychology*, 1: 148–178.

Tajfel, H. and Turner, J. (1979) An integrative theory of intergroup conflict. In: W. G. Austin and S. Worchel (eds), *The Social Psychology of Intergroup Relations*, pp. 33–47. Pacific Grove, CA: Brooks/Cole.

Tanis, M. (2007) Online social support groups. In: A. Joinson, K. Y. A. McKenna, T. Postmes and U. D. Reips (eds), *The Oxford Handbook of Internet Psychology*. Oxford: Oxford University Press.

Tantinger, D. and Braun, A. (2011) Virtual coach reaches out to me: The V2me-project. *ERCIM News*, 87: 34–35.

Taylor, F. K. (1955) On some principles of group therapy. *Psychology and Psychotherapy: Theory Research and Practice*, 25(2/3): 128–134.

Taylor, F. W. (1911) *The Principles of Scientific Management*. New York: Harper & Brothers.

Te Molder, H. F. M. (1999) Discourse of dilemmas: An analysis of communication planners' accounts. *British Journal of Social Psychology*, 38(3): 245–263.

Temkin, J. and Krahé, B. (2008) *Sexual Assault and the Justice Gap: A Question of Attitude*. Oxford: Hart Publishing.

Tennov, D. (1979) *Love and Limerence: The Experience of Being in Love*. Lanham, MD: Madison Books.

Tennov, D. (1998) Love madness. In: V. C. De Munck (ed), *Romantic Love and Sexual Behavior: Perspectives from the Social Sciences*. Greenwood Publishing Group.

Terry, D. J., Gallois, C. and McCamish, M. (1993) *The Theory of Reasoned Action: Its Application to AIDS-Preventive Behaviour*. Oxford: Pergamon Press.

Tesser, A. (1988) Toward a self-evaluation maintenance model of social behavior. In: L. Berkowitz (ed), *Advances in Experimental Social Psychology*, 21: 181–227.

Tesser, A. (1993) On the importance of heritability in psychological research: The case of attitudes. *Psychological Review*, 100: 129–142.

Thomas, A. G. and Johansen, M. K. (2012) Inside out: Avatars as an indirect measure of ideal body self-presentation in females. *Cyberpsychology: Journal of Psychological Research on Cyberspace*, 6(3): article 1.

Thurstone, L. L. (1928) Attitudes can be measured. *American Journal of Sociology*, 33: 529–554.

Tierney, R. and Palmer, M. (2014) Participation, interaction and learner satisfaction in a professional practice wiki for teachers. In: A. Power and G. Kirwan (eds), *Cyberpsychology and the New Media: A Thematic Reader*. Hove: Psychology Press.

Totterdell, P., Hershcovis, M. S., Niven, K., Reich, T. C. and Stride, C. (2012) Can employees be emotionally drained by witnessing unpleasant interactions between co-workers? A diary study of induced emotion regulation. *Work & Stress*, 26: 112–129.

Totterdell, P., Niven, K. and Holman, D. (2010) Our emotional neighbourhoods: How social networks can regulate what we feel. *The Psychologist*, 23: 474–477.

Triplett, N. (1898) Dynamogenic factors in pacemaking and competition. *American Journal of Psychology*, 9: 507–533.

Turner, J. C. (1991) *Social Influence*. Milton Keynes: Open University Press.

Twenge, J. M. and Campbell, W. K. (2003) Isn't it fun to get the respect that we're going to deserve? Narcissism, social rejection, and aggression. *Personality and Social Psychology Bulletin*, 29(2): 261–272.

Umadevi, L., Venkataramaiah, P. and Srinivasulu, R. (1992) A comparative study on the concept of marriage by professional and non-professional degree students. *Indian Journal of Behaviour*, 16: 143–173.

Utz, S. (2000) Social information processing in MUDs: The development of friendships in virtual worlds. *Journal of Online Behaviour*, 1(1).

Utz S. (2008) (Selbst)marketing auf Hyves [(Self) marketing on Hyves]. In: P. Alpar and S. Blaschke (eds), *Web2.0. Eine empirische Bestandsaufnahme [Web2.0 – An Empirical Inventory]*, pp. 233–258. Wiesbaden, Germany: Vieweg & Teubner.

Utz, S. and Kramer, N. C. (2009) The privacy paradox on social network sites revisited: The role of individual characteristics and group norms. *Cyberpsychology: Journal of Psychosocial Research on Cyberspace*, 3(2): article 1.

Valins, S. and Ray, A. A. (1967) Effects of cognitive desensitisation on avoidance behaviour. *Journal of Personality and Social Psychology*, 7: 345–350.

Van den Tol, A. J. M. and Edwards, J. (2015) Listening to sad music in adverse situations: How music selection strategies relate to self-regulatory goals, listening effects, and mood enhancement. *Psychology of Music*, 43(4): 473–494.

Van Dijk, T. A. (1987) *Communicating Racism: Ethnic Prejudice in Thought and Action*. Newbury Park, CA: SAGE.

Van Gyn, G. H., Wenger, H. A. and Gaul, C. A. (1990) Imagery as a method of enhancing transfer from training to performance. *Journal of Sport and Exercise Science*, 12: 366–375.

Van Zomeren, M., Postmes, T. and Spears, R. (2008) Toward an integrative social identity model of collective action: A quantitative research synthesis of three socio–psychological perspectives. *Psychological Bulletin*, 134: 504–535.

Verma, G. and Bagley, C. (1979) *Race, Education and Identity*. Basingstoke: Macmillan.

Waddington, D., Jones, K. and Critcher, C. (1987) Flashpoints of public disorder. In: G. Gaskell, and R. Benewick (eds), *The Crowd in Contemporary Britain*. London: SAGE.

Wadell, T. F. and Ivory, J. D. (2015) It's not easy trying to be one of the guys: The effect of avatar attractiveness, avatar sex, and user sex on the success of help-seeking requests in an online game. *Journal of Broadcasting & Electronic Media*, 59(1): 112–129.

Wagner, W. and Hayes, N. (2005) *Everyday Discourse and Common Sense: The Theory of Social Representations*. Basingstoke: Palgrave Macmillan.

Wagner, W. and Kronberger, N. (2001) Killer tomatoes! Collective symbolic coping with biotechnology. In: K. Deaux and G. Philogene (eds), *Representations of the Social: Bridging Theoretical Traditions*. pp. 147–164. Oxford: Blackwell Publishers.

Wagstaff, G. F. (2009) Is there a future for investigative hypnosis? *Journal of Investigative Psychology and Offender Profiling*, 6(1): 43–57.

Wallach, M. A., Kogan, N. and Bem, D. J. (1962) Group influence on individual risk-taking. *Journal of Abnormal and Social Psychology*, 65: 75–86.

Walster, E., Aronson, V. and Abrahams, D. (1966) On increasing the persuasiveness of a low prestige communicator. *Journal of Experimental Social Psychology*, 2: 325–342.

Walster, E. and Festinger, L. (1962) The effectiveness of "overheard" persuasive communications. *Journal of Abnormal and Social Psychology*, 65: 395–402.

Walther, J. B., Celeste, L. S. and Tidwell, L. C. (2001) Is a picture worth a thousand words? Photographic images in long-term and short-term computer-mediated communication. *Communications Research*, 28(1): 105–134.

Warner, S., Dixon, M. A. and Chalip, L. (2012) The impact of formal versus informal sport: Mapping the differences in sense of community. *Journal of Community Psychology*, 40(8): 983–1003.

Watson, J. B. (1913) Psychology from the standpoint of a behaviourist. *Psychological Review*, 20: 158–177.

Weinberg, R. S. Gould, D. and Jackson, A. (1979) Expectations and performance: An empirical test of Bandura's self-efficacy theory. *Journal of Sport Psychology*, 1: 320–331.

Weiner, B., Nierenberg, R. and Goldstein, M. (1976) Social learning (locus of control) versus attributional (causal stability) interpretations of expectancy of success. *Journal of Personality*, 44: 52–68.

Weisbuch, M., Ivcevic, Z. and Ambady, N. (2009) On being liked on the web and in the "real world": Consistency in first impressions across personal webpages and spontaneous behavior. *Journal of Experimental Social Psychology*, 45(3): 573–576.

Weiss, R. F. and Miller, F. G. (1971) The drive theory of social facilitation. *Psychological Review*, 78(1): 44–57.

Wellman, B. (1985) Domestic work, paid work and network. In: S. W. Duck and D. Perlman (eds), *Understanding Personal Relationships Research: An Interdisciplinary Approach*. London: SAGE.

Wellman, B. and Haythornthwaite, C. (2002) *The Internet in Everyday Life*. Oxford: Blackwell Publishers.

Westphal, J. D. and Shani, G. (2016) Psyched to suck-up: Self-regulated cognition, interpersonal influence, and recommendations for board appointments in the corporate elite. *Academy of Management Journal*, 59(2): 479–509.

Wetherell, M. and Potter, J. (1988) Discourse analysis and the identification of interpretative repertoires. In: C. Antaki (ed), *Analysing Everyday Explanation: A Casebook of Methods*. London: SAGE.

Whitty, M. (2005) The realness of cybercheating: Men's and women's representations of unfaithful internet relationships. *Social Science Computer Review*, 23(1): 57–67.

Whitty, M. T. and Carr, A. N. (2006) *Cyberspace Romance: The Psychology of Online Relationships*. Basingstoke: Palgrave Macmillan.

Whitty, M. T. and Joinson, A. N. (2008) *Truth, Lies and Trust on the Internet*. London: Routledge.

Wiesenthal, D. L., Endler, N. S., Coward, T. R. and Edwards, J. (1976) Reversibility of relative competence as a determinant of conformity across different perceptual tasks. *Representative Research in Social Psychology*, 7: 35–43.

Wilder, D. A. (1984) Intergroup contact: The typical member and the exception to the role. *Journal of Experimental Social Psychology*, 20: 177–194.

Williams, K., Harkins, S. and Latané, B. (1981) Identifiability as a deterrent to social loafing: Two cheering experiments. *Journal of Personality & Social Psychology*, 40: 303–311.

Wills, T. A. (1981) Downward comparison principles in social psychology. *Psychological Bulletin*, 90(2): 245–271.

Wilson, T., Ellis, D., Ford, N. and Foster, A. (2000) Uncertainty in information seeking. *Library and Information Commission Research Report 2000*.

Winch, R. F. (1958) *Mate-selection: A Study of Complementary Needs*. New York: Harper & Row.

Witkin, H. A., Mednick, S. A., Schulsinger, F. Bakkestrom, E., Christansen, K. O., Goodenough, D. R., Hirschhorn, K., Lundsteen, C., Owen, D. R., Philips, J., Rubin, D. B. and Stocking, M. (1976) Criminality in XYY and XXY men: The elevated crime rate of XYY males is not related to aggression. *Science*, 193: 547–555.

Witt, S. D. (1997) Parental influence on children's socialisation to gender roles. *Adolescence*, 32(126): 253–259.

Wollstonecraft, M. (1792) *A Vindication of the Rights of Women*, reprinted 1990. Harmondsworth: Penguin.

Woollett, K. and Maguire, E. A. (2011) Acquiring "the knowledge" of London's layout drives structural brain changes. *Current Biology*, 21(24): 2109–2114.

World Health Organisation (2006) *Preventing Child Maltreatment Report*, http://apps.who.int/iris/bitstream/10665/43499/1/9241594365_eng.pdf.

Worthington, A. G. (1969) Paired comparison scaling of brightness judgements: A method for the measurement of perceptual defence. *British Journal of Psychology*, 60(3): 363–368.

Wright, D. B., London, K. and Waechter, M. (2010) Social anxiety moderates memory conformity in adolescents. *Applied Cognitive Psychology*, 24(7): 1034–1045.

Wright, K. B. (2004) On-line relational maintenance strategies and perceptions of partners within exclusively internet based and primarily internet-based relationships. *Communication Studies*, 55(2): 239–253.

Wrzus, C., Hänel, M., Wagner, J. and Neyer, F. J. (2013) Social network changes and life events across the life span: A meta-analysis. *Psychological Bulletin*, 139(1): 53–80.

Wundt, W. (1900–1920) *Völkerpsychologie: eine Untersuchung der Entwicklungsgesetze von Sprache, Mythus und Sitte 10 vols*. Leipzig: Engelmann.

Yee, N. and Bailenson, J. N. (2007) The Proteus Effect: The effect of transformed self-representation on behavior. *Human Communication Research*, 33: 271–290.

Yee, N., Bailenson, J. N., Urbanek, M., Chang, F. and Merget, D. (2007) The unbearable likeness of being digital: The persistence of nonverbal social norms in online virtual environments. *Cyberpsychology and Behaviour*, 10(1): 115–121.

Young, K. (1996) Psychology of computer use: XL. Addictive use of the Internet: A case that breaks the stereotype. *Psychological Reports*, 79: 899–902.

Young, K. (1999) Internet addiction: Evaluation and treatment. *Student British Medical Journal*, 7: 351–352.

Yuki, M., Maddux, W. W. and Masuda, T. (2007) Are the windows to the soul the same in the East and West? Cultural differences in using the eyes and mouth as cues to recognize emotions in Japan and the United States. *Journal of Experimental Social Psychology*, 43(2): 303–311.

Zaadstra, B. M., Seidell, J. C., Van Noord, P. A., Te Velde, E. R., Habbema, J. D., Vrieswijk, B. and Karbaat, J. (1993) Fat and female fecundity: Prospective study of effect of body fat distribution on conception rates. *British Medical Journal*, 306: 484–487.

Zadny, J. and Gerard, H. B. (1974) Attributed intentions and informational selectivity. *Journal of Experimental Social Psychology*, 10: 34–52.

Zajonc, R. B. (1965) Social facilitation. *Science*, 149: 269–274.

Zajonc, R. B. (1968) Attitudinal effects of mere exposure. *Journal of Personality and Social Psychology*, 9: 1–27.

Zajonc, R. B. (1994) Evidence for nonconscious emotions. In: P. Ekman and R. J. Davidson (eds), *The Nature of Emotion: Fundamental Questions*, pp. 293–297. New York: Oxford University Press.

Zajonc, R. B. and Burnstein, E. (1965) The learning of balanced and unbalanced social structures. *Journal of Personality*, 33: 153–163.

Zanna, M. P., Kiesler, C. A. and Pilkonis, P. A. (1970) Positive and negative attitudinal affect established by classical conditioning. *Journal of Personality & Social Psychology*, 14(4): 321–328.

Zillman, D. (1979) *Hostility and Aggression*. Hillside, NJ: Erlbaum Associates.

Zimbardo, P. G. (1960) Involvement and communication discrepancy as determinants of opinion conformity. *Journal of Abnormal and Social Psychology*, 60: 86–94.

Zimbardo, P. G. (1969) The human choice: Individuation, reason and order versus deindividuation, impulse and chaos. In: W. J. Arnold and D. Levine (eds), *Nebraska Symposium on Motivation 17*. Lincoln: University of Nebraska Press.

Zimbardo, P. G. (1986) The Stanford shyness project. In: W. H. Jones, J. M. Cheek and S. R. Briggs (eds), *Shyness: Perspectives on Research and Treatment*, pp. 17–25. New York: Plenum.

Zimbardo, P. G. (2005) Mind control in Orwell's 1984: Fictional concepts become operational realities in Jim Jones' jungle experiment. In: M. Nussbaum, J. Goldsmith and A. Gleason (eds), *1984: Orwell and Our Future*, pp. 127–154. Princeton, NJ: Princeton University Press.

Zimbardo, P. G. (2007) *The Lucifer Effect: How Good People Turn Evil*. New York: Random House.

Index